Acclaim for *A Matter of Principle*

"Authoritative and highly readable. . . ."
— Andrew Roberts, *The Daily Beast*

"[A] gripping memoir of [Black's] nightmarish trek through America's justice system and business governancc culture. . . . Black is a writer of great force and panache." — *New Criterion*

"The former international media baron's observations from prison are funny, poignant, touching, sympathetic (except for prison authorities) and beautifully chronicled." — *Ottawa Citizen*

"A remarkable work – unlike any of its kind that I've ever read. . . . Conrad seems to have total recall of everything, and he lays it out coherently and colourfully. . . . Precise, blunt, succinct. A fascinating book about the trial."
— *Huffington Post*

"[*A Matter of Principle*] is a brutally honest memoir of [Black's] turbulent run-in with American injustice." — *Irish Independent*

"A big book by a big man. . . . A hard-eyed and detailed indictment of that legal system, from U.S. attorneys to our federal prisons."
— *The American Spectator*

"*A Matter of Principle* is Conrad Black's most personal and gripping book."
— Troy Media

"[Conrad Black's] candor on just about every conceivable topic is not only surprising but practically unprecedented." — *Vanity Fair*

"A riveting memoir and a scathing account of a flawed justice system."
— IndieBound

"A *Matter of Principle* is a laudable achievement."
— *Winnipeg Free Press*

"When a great writer is falsely imprisoned for a crime he didn't commit and decides to write a tell-all non-defensive account, the result is likely to be riveting. Conrad Black's memoir does not disappoint."
— Alan M. Dershowitz

"Conrad Black's A *Matter of Principle* is a fascinating, erudite, and defiant prison memoir – must-read for lawyers, politicos, and gossips alike!"
— Margaret Atwood, on Twitter

A MATTER OF PRINCIPLE

CONRAD BLACK

A MATTER OF
PRINCIPLE

ENCOUNTER BOOKS

NEW YORK · LONDON

First edition published in 2011 by McClelland & Steward Ltd.
First American edition published in 2012 by Encounter Books,
an activity of Encounter for Culture and Education, Inc.,
a nonprofit, tax exempt corporation.
Encounter Books website address: www.encounterbooks.com

Manufactured in the United States and printed on
acid-free paper. The paper used in this publication meets
the minimum requirements of ANSI/NISO Z39.48 1992
(R 1997) (*Permanence of Paper*).

FIRST AMERICA EDITION

LIBRARY OF CONGRESS CATALOGING IN PUBLICATION DATA

Black, Conrad.
A matter of principle / Conrad Black.
pages cm ISBN 978-1-59403-659-0 (pbk.) – ISBN 978-1-59403-660-6 (ebook) (print)
1. Black, Conrad. 2. Black, Conrad–Trials, litigation, etc.
3. Publishers and publishing–Canada–Biography.
4. Newspaper publishing–Canada History–20th century.
5. Newspapers–Ownership 6. Capitalists and financiers–Canada–Biography.
7. Journalists–Canada–Biography. I. Title.
Z483.B53B58 2012
070.5092–dc23
[B]
2012012385

To Barbara, my indomitable, unofficial co-defendant, and my daughter Alana and sons Jonathan and James; to my dear friends June Black, Dan Colson, Midge Decter, David and Murray Frum and Nancy Lockhart, Roger and Susan Hertog, Laura Ingraham, George Jonas, Roger Kimball, Seth Lipsky, Joanna MacDonald, Joan Maida, Brian Mulroney, Norman Podhoretz, Andrew Roberts, William Shawcross, Brian Stewart, Bob Tyrrell, and Ken Whyte; and to Rob Jennings, and other friends in the prison to which I and many of them were unjustly sent; and to all others who have sustained and encouraged me in this difficult time, including thousands of strangers in many lands. All in their different ways have been magnificent. I will never forget their encouragement and will try to repay, or at least justify, their kindness.

Ravelston, Argus, and Hollinger

Conrad Black (65%)
David Radler (14%)
Peter White (13.5%)
Daniel Colson (3%)

Dixon Chant estate (1.5%)
Peter Atkinson, Jack Boultbee, and Charles Cowan, each 1%

The Ravelston Corporation Limited 100%

(Except for about $8 million worth of permanent, fixed dividend, Argus Corporation preferred shares that did not participate in capital appreciation or loss)

Argus Corporation Limited

There were specialized, wholly owned operating divisions that owned some real estate from the old Dominion Stores (Domgroup Ltd.), corporate aircraft, and 40% of the Cayman Island newspaper, *Caymanian Compass*

78%

Hollinger Incorporated Ltd. (Hollinger Inc.) (Canada)

30% of equity, 72% of voting shares through a two-tier share structure

---

Hollinger International Inc. (Hollinger International) (U.S.A.)

(This company became Sun-Times Media Group in 2005)

100%

The Telegraph Group Ltd. (U.K.), *London Daily* and *Sunday Telegraph*, *The Spectator*, half interest in London and Manchester printing plants, prior to 1998, 25% of Fairfax Newspapers (Australia), *Sydney Morning Herald*, *Melbourne Age*, *Australian Finacial Review*, *Sunday Sun-Herald*

American Publishing Company, at one time, more than 100 community daily and several hundred community weekly newspapers in 30 states of the U.S.

The Jerusalem Post (Israel)

Sun-Times Publishing Company, *The Chicago Sun-Times* and six other daily newspapers and more than 100 weekly and bi-weekly in the Chicago Metropolitan Area

Prior to 1999, The Southam Company (*National Post*, *Victoria Times-Colonist*, *Vancouver Sun* and *Province*, *Calgary Herald*, *Edmonton Journal*, *Windsor Star*, *Ottawa Citizen*, *Montreal Gazette*, *Halifax Daily News*, and many smaller newspapers)

Unimedia Inc (Quebec City *Le Soleil*, Ottawa *Le Droit*, Chicoutimi *Le Quotidien*, and some weekly newspapers)

Sterling Newspapers Ltd. (approximately 45 daily newspapers across Canada, giving the company 59 of Canada's 105 daily newspapers, including Regina *Leader-Post*, Saskatoon *Star-Phoenix*, Kingston *Whig-Standard*, Sherbrooke *Record*, St. John's *Telegraph*)

[CONTENTS]

A Matter of Principle   1

Postlude: Reflections on the American Justice System   515
Appendices   542
Index   557

All photographs are courtesy of the author.

[Chapter One]

I sleep in a cubicle that shares a ceiling with sixty other identical spaces, rather like partitions in an office, except that these are painted cinder block and there are no potted plants. At 10:30 p.m., the ceiling lights placed every twenty feet or so go out. The residents turn out their cubicle lights, leaving only an overhead row of red, dimly lit panels, pierced here and there by the beam of portable reading lamps, which enable the readers among us to escape into books, letters, newspapers, snapshots, and tokens and reminders of the world beyond the gates. In the morning, daylight creeps past the condensation generated by the confrontation between the Florida heat and the fierce air conditioning of the Federal Bureau of Prisons into the outside cubicles through narrow rectangular windows grudgingly set in the concrete walls.

Here, we concern ourselves with how many postage stamps (the local currency) are needed to buy an extra notepad. We see and hear the talking heads on television in the activities room or, in my case, read in the newspapers of the steady failures or crises of great institutions: AIG, General Motors, Citigroup, the State of California, the New York Times, the Harvard

University Endowment. How could this country have become so incompetent, so stupid, and why was this debacle so unforeseen? The pundits have the usual uninformed answers, not greatly more well thought out, and less entertaining, than those of some of my fellow residents. Lying in my bunk after the lights have gone out, I reflect on the ludicrous demise of my great love affair with America.

Bemused by the economic and political shambles, created largely by people I have known, I fight on from this absurdly shrunken perimeter for recovery of my liberty, reputation, and fortune. I still expect to win.

My prison number, 18330-424, is stamped on my clothes and mandatory on all correspondence. I am sixty-five years old. I entered these walls a baron of the United Kingdom, Knight of the Holy See, Privy Councillor, and Officer of the Order of Canada, former publisher of some of the world's greatest newspapers, and author of some well-received non-fiction books. In December 2007, a courteous federal district judge in Chicago sentenced me to seventy-eight months in a federal prison and imposed a financial penalty of $6.2 million. This is all winding its way through final appeals and is completely unjust, but so are many things. I was convicted of three counts of fraud and one of obstruction of justice, of all of which I am innocent. Three charges were dropped and nine led to acquittals. I have gone through but survived straitened financial circumstances, have sold two of my homes, and am responding to and initiating endless civil litigation. For the last six and a half years I have been fighting for my financial life, physical freedom, and what remains of my reputation against the most powerful organization in the world, the U.S. government.

My shrunken newspaper company, once owner of distinguished titles in Britain, Canada, Australia, and America, as well as the *Jerusalem Post*, was now bankrupt under the dead weight of the incompetence and corruption of my enemies, who have hugely enriched themselves under the patronage of American and Canadian courts of law and equity. I am estranged from some of my formerly professed friends, including a number of famous people, though in greater solidarity than ever with some others. Much of the press of the Western world was long agog with jubilant stories about the collapse of my standing and influence. For years I was widely reviled, defamed, and routinely referred to as "disgraced" or "shamed" and "convicted fraudster." (This was the preferred formulation of the London *Daily Telegraph*, of which I was chairman for fifteen years.) In light of my lately improving fortunes most of my less rabid critics are now hedging their bets. Whatever happens, this will not be the end of my modest story. But it seems an appropriate moment to update it.

OCTOBER 2003: MY HOME, KENSINGTON, WEST LONDON
London's yellow afternoon light filtered in from windows overlooking gardens on three sides of my room. All about me was the reassuring evidence of an active career and an eclectic range of interests. Shelves of leatherbound first editions giving every side of the French Revolution and Napoleonic Wars. Depictions of the great English cardinals Henry Manning and John Henry Newman. Jules Mazarin and the esteemed diplomat Ercole Cardinal Consalvi, strikingly rendered, looked down impassively upon, among other things, a small bust of Palmerston, a fine crystal model of the *Titanic* given to me by my tragically deceased driver, Tommy Buckley, and an iron copy of the death mask and hands of Stalin that I had bought from the estate of the great British maverick politician Enoch Powell. Gifts: a shield from Chief Buthelezi of the Zulus, a naval painting from our directors in Australia, the extravagantly inscribed latest memoirs of Henry Kissinger and Margaret Thatcher, each evoking interesting times and powerful friends, historic figures who had helped me and whom I had helped.

My lengthy biography of Franklin D. Roosevelt lay in galleys on my desk. This was a room that had weathered all efforts of interior decorators and remained comfortable and practical for my work. Good chairs and reading lamps, a large and deep sofa on which I sometimes napped, its antique decorative pillows turned backward to hide the scorching received when one of my younger son's friends fell asleep on it and knocked over a lamp. Though large, the room exuded a sense of safety, a barricade at the far end of the house away from prying eyes and noise. All the same, increasingly I felt an indefinable foreboding. Mazarin, the protegé and successor of Cardinal Richelieu, could have warned me. He knew the signs of insurrection well. All was silent; I was uneasy, but my vision was impaired.

I knew well enough where the trouble lay. Some of our large institutional shareholders were attempting to break up the newspaper company I had created, Hollinger International, in order to sell it off for a good short-term price while newspaper stocks were sluggish but newspaper enterprise values – the sale of newspapers as going concerns – were still buoyant. Now, firmly riding the hobby horse of shareholder activism, a backdoor attempt to overthrow me and achieve the sale was in progress – though I didn't entirely grasp it at the time. All I knew was that allegations of overly generous payments to myself and other executives were keeping business writers, especially those of competing newspapers, phoning around for colourful anecdotes to illustrate our supposed extravagance with company funds. In response, I had agreed to establish a special committee to examine these matters, confident of our complete vindication. Now these committee members were beavering noisily away, with the concentration and attitudes of antagonists. I did not know then how easily a special committee could decapitate even a controlling shareholder. But I knew enough to be uneasy. If I could be rattled severely enough, the company could be sold and all the shareholders instantly gratified. I thought more could be achieved by gradualism, selling assets when they were ripe, and separately to targeted buyers, as few companies would be attracted at top prices to such geographically disparate newspaper properties. I also considered, and the directors and shareholders professed agreement, that these were decisions for the managing and controlling shareholders who had built the business. This was the core of what became a huge controversy.

FROM MY EARLY YEARS, I thought that publishing large and high-quality newspapers was the most desirable occupation of all: this was a business that could offer commercial success, political influence, cultural and literary potential, and access to everything and everyone newsworthy in every field. As a young person I read about famous newspaper owners such as W.R. Hearst, Lord Beaverbrook, Lord Northcliffe, Lord Rothermere, Colonel Robert McCormick, and Canadians that my father knew: J.W. McConnell, Joseph Atkinson, George McCullough, John Bassett, the Siftons.

During a break in my university years, I took over an uneconomic weekly newspaper in Knowlton, Quebec, about fifty miles east of Montreal, from my friend Peter White, who had become a special assistant to the premier of Quebec, Daniel Johnson. I paid Peter $500 for half of the

Eastern Townships Advertiser, approximately $499 more than it was worth. I wrote, edited, and laid out the eight-page half-tabloid and sold whatever advertising could be had in the elderly English-language minority of that area, who lived chiefly from the avails of maintaining and milking the country houses of wealthy Montrealers. I even dealt with some of the circulation distribution. In winter, the wind whistled across frozen Brome Lake, and I often needed snowshoes to get to and from my car. I read a great deal and found the life of a *coureur de bois* exhilarating, especially when the first signs of spring began to appear.

When I was in my third year at the Laval University law school, Peter White and I, together with David Radler, a new acquaintance Peter introduced me to, bought the insolvent *Sherbrooke Daily Record,* another twenty miles east of Knowlton. This newspaper had a circulation of seven thousand. Its press had been repossessed by the manufacturer and it was in dire straits. We paid only Can$18,000 for it. I became the first university student, at least in Canadian history, to be a publisher of a general-interest daily newspaper. David Radler, who was almost a caricature of a penny-pinching businessman, focused entirely on costs and revenues. He was alert, suspicious, and often entertaining.

I had moved from Toronto to Quebec in 1966, suffused with enthusiasm for Canada as a country that had the advantage of having the two greatest cultures of the West within itself. I became fluent in French, studied the civil law, and wrote a book about Quebec's longest serving and most controversial premier, Maurice L. Duplessis, which has stood as a serious work on the subject.

I moved back to Toronto in 1974, just before my thirtieth birthday, exasperated with Quebec's endless threats to secede from Canada – while retaining all the economic benefits of Confederation, including huge transfers of money from English Canada in institutionalized annual Danegeld. I became a fairly vocal and widely publicized advocate of a strong line against Quebec separatists, suspecting, correctly, that they could never get near half the votes without an umbilical association with Canada that in effect combined official independence in the world with continued provincial dependence, both eating and retaining the cake. The whole concept was a fraud. I was also an advocate of transforming Canada into a greater enterprise state than the United States, one that could, by its low crime rate and tax reductions, attract industry and people that would otherwise go to the United States or had already moved there. My views were widely mistaken as annexationist – that is, advocating federal union with the United States. I made the point that Canada would be better off making a deal with the U.S., including instant parity for our 65-cent dollar, than continuing endless fruitless tractations with Quebec separatists who wanted concessions but would never make a durable agreement.

However I was seen, I couldn't regard myself as a pillar of the Canadian establishment, which at that time, it seemed to me, operated a back-scratching, log-rolling operation that took care of its own but underperformed the vast potential for the country. As much as I was out of favour with the comfortable Canadian centre-right, I could never make common cause with the Canadian left because of their anti-Americanism and their addiction to high taxes and excessive unionization and wealth redistribution and their imitative mediocrity. They received almost no international attention. I often felt like a party of one.

MY ENTRY INTO THE CORPORATE WORLD was a splash. In 1978, following the death of its incumbent chairman,* one of Canada's famous holding companies, Argus Corporation, of which my father had been a sizable shareholder, became the subject of a sharp takeover struggle. My parents had died only ten days apart in June 1976, and my brother and I now had our father's 20 per cent of the shares of the company, the Ravelston Corporation, that owned 60 per cent of the voting shares of Argus Corporation. Factional disagreements ensued. My brother and I were one of the factions, and we were successful. What we took over in Argus was a mixed bag of assets in an obsolete structure.† There were influential but

---

* John A. (Bud) McDougald, who had succeeded his brother-in-law, W. Eric Phillips, and the company founder, renowned industrialist and sportsman E.P. Taylor.
† Ravelston and Argus were private companies that I owned/controlled. All my voting shares in Hollinger Inc. (Canada) were held in Ravelston. So ultimately, Ravelston was the source of my control of Hollinger. Ravelston provided the management team for our newspapers, and the management fees for services provided to it. When I wanted to access American capital, we went public in America by creating Hollinger International (U.S.) into which we

not really controlling shareholdings in Massey Ferguson (tractors and farm equipment), Dominion Stores (supermarkets), Domtar (forest products), Hollinger (through a subsidiary, iron ore royalties), and a genuine controlling interest in a radio station and television company. The reputation of the founders had made Argus Corporation famous, but the reality was a moth-eaten hodgepodge of positions of questionable value.

Through the Byzantine financial structure the former owners had created, Argus itself owned 14 per cent to 24 per cent of the first four of these companies. Four-fifths of Argus's shares did not vote. My brother and I now had 57 per cent of a company that had 51 per cent of the company that owned 60 per cent of the shares that voted (i.e., we had 12 per cent of the Argus voting shares and 8.4 per cent of its total equity, as we owned some of the non-voting shares separately). And beneath that were the 14 per cent shareholdings, apart from the radio and television business. Our interest had an apparent economic value of about Can$18 million, and there were significant loans against that. This was my baptism in close-quarters financial manoeuvrings, and I saw both their possibilities and their hazards.

I set about trying to refashion the company toward something the owners would really own and would have some aptitude to manage. In my 1992 book detailing some of the complicated manoeuvres, I cited Napoleon's dictum that "mass times speed equals force." In those early business years, I had had little mass but great speed. My corporate performance was far from Napoleonic, but I got on. Deals now occurred with such profusion and rapidity that the *Toronto Star* referred to me as "Canada's answer to [the American television program] *Let's Make a Deal*." I gave the Massey Ferguson shares away to the company pension plans to assist in a refinancing, which did then occur and helped to save the company. Over several years, the Domtar shares were sold, the supermarket and radio and television assets were sold, and energy assets were bought

put all the newspapers, leaving Hollinger Inc. as the holding company managing Hollinger International. To eliminate some confusion, Hollinger Inc. will be referred to as Inc. (Canada) and Hollinger International as International (U.S.). There was one more change. After my ejection from the companies, Hollinger International had a name change to Sun-Times Media Group (STMG).

and sold. The group was consolidated, with something close to a real owner, and refocused in the newspaper business. All this activity, which was more financial engineering than operational progress, attracted the interest of regulators, who actually rewrote the Canadian "complex transaction" rules in my honour. The convoluted progress through these various businesses stirred up some controversy in Canada at times, but all was resolved without much difficulty.

I was a financier, and a fairly agile one, but still only an industrialist in the newspaper business. I did not seek out controversy, but as someone who expressed controversial views trenchantly and hovered about several different vocations, I was bound to attract a fair bit of comment, especially in such an understated country as Canada. I enjoyed debate and political argument but had an imperfect sense of public relations and never saw the need to concern myself with it. As a result, I became a catchment for many traits and opinions I did not hold, dwarfed by a caricature public image that has lurched about like a clumsy monster for decades. Though wounded at times by this portrayal, I never grasped the real danger in it and simply made a virtue of necessity: I boxed on, still am.

The transition to being truly involved in the newspaper business again came when, on behalf of our company, I acquired control of the *Daily Telegraph* in London for Can$30 million in 1986. From this, all else follows. The newspaper was suffering from an aging readership, antiquated equipment, all the usual British labour problems, and elderly but conscientious management. We installed an almost entirely new management team and ethos and expanded the *Daily Telegraph* to be a full-service newspaper. Two-thirds of the aged employees were negotiated into voluntary retirement, which they sought but had been unable to consider under the company's frugal pension scheme, and the *Telegraph* titles recovered admirably. Robert Maxwell, the egregious proprietor of the *Daily Mirror*, whom I did not yet know, said, "Mr. Black has landed Britain's biggest fish with history's smallest hook."

AT A MEETING OF THE DIRECTORS of The Telegraph plc in December 1986, the owner, Lord Hartwell, fainted. His loss of consciousness was prompted by the realization he had lost control of the newspaper that his family, the Berrys, had acquired in late-Victorian times. The boardroom sounded to me like something out of a Mitford novel. "Daddy, Daddy," called his son Adrian from one end of the boardroom table. His other son, Nicholas, was hissing at his father for what he thought was a rotten deal and at the Canadian "predators" for taking up the deal. Rank and decorum were firmly maintained throughout by Hartwell's admirable secretary, who stood over him as the paramedics arrived, pronouncing, "I will not allow just anyone to lay hands on Lord Hartwell."*

Hartwell had done his best to maintain the editorial excellence of The Telegraph plc but had dragged it almost to bankruptcy largely through an ambitious attempt to install modern presses in two vast plants in Manchester and London. But he had made no effort to arrange demanning from the unionized workforces, nor to arrange long-term financing with banks, and just kept writing large and extraordinary construction payments against a current account.

Hartwell, who fortunately suffered nothing more than a fainting spell, remained chairman for another two years as we sorted things out. I would not consider treating him abruptly. The fissiparous Nicholas Berry vowed eternal vengeance and did everything in his power to poison the waters with concocted stories about my associates and me. Adrian Berry, an exceedingly amiable British eccentric liked by all, with esoteric scientific interests that entirely possessed him, remained at the *Telegraph* as its science writer and a director. Mercifully, the pestilential Nicholas peevishly resigned.

Gaining control of The Telegraph plc in the U.K. changed my life. As its proprietor, I finally had a meaningful political voice (which I did not at that point have in Canada) and access to echelons of international decision-making I had not previously enjoyed, because of the influence of one newspaper and the British custom of deference to national news-paper owners.

For seventeen years the fortunes of the *Telegraph* and its staff were pre-eminent in my thoughts. Running a leading British quality newspaper

---

* I have always found that in distressed companies such as The Telegraph plc and Massey Ferguson, the secretaries and executive assistants are as impressive and unflappable as the principal executives are demoralized and exhausted.

requires some agility. The waters are shark-infested, with seventeen national newspapers, including the Sundays, which are considered separate and often have different titles, competing in London.

The Telegraph plc had been a way of life for more than a century. A writer might mention the *Telegraph* in a novel or essay, as George Orwell did in *The Lion and the Unicorn,* and that reference would be shorthand for an entire set of values, idiosyncracies, and even colour of shoes. The *Daily Telegraph* was generally thought to be the greatest bastion of the British Conservative Party. The men who built it up, Lord Burnham and Lord Camrose, were influential Conservative peers. The *Daily Telegraph* had engaged Winston Churchill at various times in his career, including after the Munich Agreement (which the *Telegraph* commendably opposed). The editor at the time our company invested in it was Bill Deedes, a former minister of the Harold Macmillan Conservative government and said to be the model for Evelyn Waugh's accidental hero in his famous newspaper novel, *Scoop.* It was the pre-eminent newspaper of middle England, the gin-and-tonic, cricket-watching backbone of the nation. To be proprietor of the *Telegraph* was instantly to enter to the core of Britain, with all the benefits that implies. Once installed in Britain, I got a free pass on the many tests of accent, lineage, school, and other yardsticks by which the British subtly calibrate one another. I was Canadian, apparently literate, but it was assumed, in the unerringly apt words of my magnificent and distinguished friend Lord Carrington, that "he doesn't quite get it." Which I sometimes did not.

The British had long been accustomed, since their days of empire, to assimilating foreigners into prominent places in their society, especially from their former empire. This was an adjustment to geopolitical realities, not a relaxation of English xenophobia.

They are contemptuous of those who are abrasively foreign and of those who seem ingratiatingly imitative. It is a subtle and invidious game, and the British are difficult to please. I understood that the natives found me somewhat irrepressible and overbearing, in the manner that fits their caricature of North Americans, though. I was generally credited with literacy and a fair knowledge of British history.

—

IN 1986, THE BRITISH SOUL was still absorbing Thatcherism. Margaret Thatcher's long-standing chief adviser, Charles Powell, said that her first meeting with me was "love at first sight, politically speaking."

Outwardly, the Conservative Party was united behind Thatcher. But from fairly early on in my time in the United Kingdom, I was impressed at the size of the pockets of resentment in her own ranks. She was too pro-American. She was too "uncaring," had pulled the rug out from under former prime minister and Conservative Party leader Edward Heath when she defeated him for the leadership in 1975. (Except for Stanley Baldwin and Sir Alec-Douglas Home, all British Conservative leaders since Bonar Law in 1923 have been undercut by their own ostensible supporters, even the octogenarian Churchill in 1955.) But most of all, in stylistic terms, she was the champion of "bourgeois triumphalism" (a slightly sniffy phrase coined by our *Sunday* editor, Peregrine Worsthorne), and she was "that woman" and thought to be a bossy woman (not entirely without reason). My position kept me in touch with all the Conservative factions, although my personal loyalty to Thatcher was well known. It must be said that she was rather insouciant; she could have warded off the problems that came down after the damning resignation speech of her deputy prime minister, Geoffrey Howe, in 1990 and would almost certainly have been re-elected in 1992. But her many victories had dulled her sense of self-preservation. I warned her and her chief loyalists several times of the conspiratorial fermentation among the MPs, obviously without naming anyone, but was treated as a well-meaning alarmist. I had been around politics, albeit in less storied places and with less distinguished leaders, a long time, and I knew unsafe levels of restiveness when I found them. Her enemies were not her peers, her successors were relatively undistinguished, yet "great (Thatcher) fell."

Three candidates for the succession emerged from the scrum, and the usual editorial infighting began as to whom the *Telegraph* would support. Michael Heseltine was a tall, handsome man with thick, wavy blond hair and superbly cut Savile Row suits, an accomplished businessman and former defence minister, and a formidable public speaker. He was the closest in policy terms to Thatcher, with the important exception of the issue that still burns in the United Kingdom while barely being noticed in

North America – namely, the degree to which Britain should be assimilated into a unified Europe. Heseltine was an ardent Euro-joiner.

Douglas Hurd was to the left of the party, a Tory "wet." His shock of spiralling white hair and his efforts to play down his Eton and Oxford background by wearing buttoned cardigans while talking about his work as a "tenant" farmer (on his family's land) made him a natural target for such diabolical mimics as Britain's Rory Bremner, who would play Hurd in a red cardigan sitting surrounded by little children serenading him with a song: "Douglas, you're useless and so is all that you do. Douglas, you're clueless and that's what we think of you." (The tune was from a popular British sitcom.)

The *Sunday Telegraph* endorsed John Major, the son of a trapeze artist from Pittsburgh. He had no university education, let alone an Oxbridge background, and his contribution to the campaign was to talk about Britain's new "classless society" in flat, unadorned prose that some saw as altogether too representative of his vision.

I erred on the side of liberality and left the editors to make their own choices. Douglas Hurd exercised an intellectual domination over Max Hastings, the otherwise formidable editor of the *Daily Telegraph*, as thorough as that which Douglas would soon assert over John Major. We should have gone for Heseltine as the strongest leader, or Major as Thatcher's choice, but as Worsthorne on the *Sunday* was supporting Major, and I was happy to have a foot in two camps, and Heseltine was Thatcher's nemesis, and I felt that I owed it to her inspired leadership that I was in Britain at all, I didn't overrule Max. I liked all three candidates personally.

One of our leading editorial commentators, Sarah Hogg, wife, daughter, and daughter-in-law of Conservative cabinet ministers, was a Euro-joiner and urged upon me, at Max Hastings's prompting, the view that John Major was not intellectually qualified to be prime minister. I was slightly surprised when she called me a few days after Major's victory to ask that I say nothing of her opinion of the new leader, as she was about to become head of his Downing Street policy unit. Her appreciation of him rose.

The *Daily Telegraph* did its best, along with most of the major national newspapers, to help Major win the general election of 1992. This was the first time a British party had won four full-term consecutive elections since the First Reform Act had expanded the electorate beyond a small and comparatively wealthy group in 1832. But it was not long before we began to have some reservations. An amiable man and a talented former whip, Major was better at organizing and conciliating than he was at leading in a way that rallied the fractious elements of the Conservative Party. Max Hastings parted company with Major more on the basis of this evaluation of his leadership abilities than of his policies. Hastings started the rumour that John Major tucked his shirt inside his underpants, a uniquely British, snobbish (and out-rageous) reflection. Major weakly told me that at least where he had gone to school, he did not have to fear for his safety when he picked the soap off the floor of the shower stall, referring to alleged homosexuality in Britain's famous private-sector schools. There was an unseemly disregard for the prime minister and a pattern of unconfident responses from him.

The deputy editor of the *Daily Telegraph* was Charles Moore, former editor of the *Spectator*. Moore was a particular type of Englishman: reserved, well mannered, difficult to read, a man who had been accepted to Eton and Cambridge because of his considerable intellectual prowess rather than family connections. He and Hastings had a very abrasive rela-tionship. Where Hastings was a closet Euro-joiner and more or less a Red Tory in all matters except taxes and unions, Moore was a Euro-skeptic and High Tory of Edwardian leanings. For Moore, the defining moment in the evolution of his opinions and in his career development was when Hong Kong under British rule (until the 1997 handover to the Chinese) admit-ted and then forcibly expelled the Vietnamese boat people.

Moore, who before this had had the standard High Tory doubts about the basic reliability, civility, and good taste of America, suddenly decided that the United States was the only country that had the integrity, courage, and bearing of a great power. Max jubilantly told me that Charles had put in for the position of Washington correspondent.

I determined that if Moore had come to this realization, it was time for him to move up and not down, and appointed him editor of the *Sunday Telegraph*. Under Charles Moore, the Major government got a very rough ride, which brought out the proprietary instincts of the Conservative Party. They believed they had the right to the unwavering adherence of what was often called the Torygraph and that anything less than that was a betrayal. To the credit of the editors and the political desk, even Neil Kinnock, the leader of the Labour Party in the 1987 and 1992 elections, told me that though he did not agree with the *Telegraph*'s editorial positions, he regarded it as a newspaper of scrupulously fair reporting.

The wheels started to come off the Major government. Chancellor Norman Lamont was dumped in 1992 after the Exchange Rates Mechanism fiasco (fixing the pound opposite European currencies in a narrow band that the pound fell out of), though he had been one of Major's leading backers for the party leadership. He then became an intractable opponent of the prime minister, accusing him of being "in office but not in power." At the Bilderberg meeting in Bürgenstock, Switzerland, in 1995, I probed this subject with him over some local wine. He exclaimed, "I am prepared to discuss treason, but not while drinking this ghastly Swiss weasel-piss." We moved to a more potable French wine.

John Major decided to clear the air by resigning as party leader and calling an instant vote of his caucus in a new leadership election, where he would stand to replace himself. I learned this while I was a guest of Lord Woodrow Wyatt at the horse races at Ascot. Cellphones were not yet popular in Britain, so I went out to my car, which was equipped with a phone, and called Rupert Murdoch to ask whether he would join in a solid front for Michael Portillo, a possible candidate for the leadership – a rather exotic and unlikely member of the Tory caucus due to his Spanish ancestry and interest in opera. He said he would, so I called Portillo, who said he had just announced he would not run but explained he had rented space and ordered the installation of a large number of telephones because he thought someone else would stand and force Major out, and he could take advantage without the opprobrium. Trying to be a loyalist while really being an opportunist is risky. Portillo's balancing act undid him, and his promising career as a politician went into decline. Major easily retained the leadership.

A number of rather odd initiatives were launched to rally the *Telegraph* to the Tory government's aid. At one point John Major intervened with the Canadian High Commissioner, Fred Eaton, to ask me to impose moderation on the paper's reflections on the government. Lord Wyatt, a bibulous, gossip-addicted, and almost incomprehensible salonnier who had lived for years off the Thatcher government's patronage as head of the horse race betting authority, hatched a scheme to offer me a peerage in exchange for extinguishing the criticism of the Major government in the *Daily Telegraph*. Wyatt was by now so ineffectual that he never made this plan clear to me, though I would have paid no attention if he had. I discovered the scheme only when reading John Major's memoirs and Wyatt's incoherently acidulous, posthumously published diaries. Major demanded to know of Wyatt why I wasn't responding. Did I not have control of the *Daily Telegraph?*

Technically, of course I did have control of the newspaper, but I was always wary, there as in the *National Post* and elsewhere, of imposing my will too strongly on valued editors, other than for the most overwhelmingly important issues. I asserted my views forcefully but have met the full range of editorial resistance tactics. Raising children is a good formation for dealing with editors and journalists. They are all fiendishly clever at promising compliance with the wishes of the owner, appearing to give superficial adherence while in fact continuing in their exceptionable practices. A cat-and-mouse game ensues, in which my refusal to be made a mockery of struggles for mastery with my desire not to have to micro-nanny every detail of the production of the newspaper and my concern not to be ground down by arguing endlessly with the editor and his entourage.

In Moore's case, the entourage was what is known as the leader conference, the editorial page writers. They were a medieval collection of learned eccentrics. Where Max Hastings had been impatient with comment and published banal editorials, except for those on military matters, Moore was preoccupied with comment. Both Max and Charles are elegant writers: Max a vigorous journalist and Charles a fine commentator. But where Max was impatient, Charles tended to adopt, or at least propose, positions that were, to say the least, impractical, which aggravated our problems of seeming to be an esoteric, or even reactionary, newspaper. I found myself fighting hard to prevent the newspaper from dedicating a section to the five hundredth anniversary of Archbishop Cranmer's death at the stake.

The lot of the proprietor, especially if he has an international business to run, is not easy if he aspires to uphold a line against the guerrilla activities of his editors. There may be more instances of proprietorial abuse than of irresponsible editorial positions, but finding the right balance depends on the relationship between the publisher and the editor.

—

WE GREW QUICKLY INTO A far-flung newspaper company. We rolled in the newspapers we had bought between 1969 and 1974 (Prince Rupert, B.C., *Daily News*; Summerside, Prince Edward Island, *Journal Pioneer*; and others) and those that David Radler had added since. We had a group of French-Canadian newspapers, including the slightly historic *Le Soleil* of Quebec City and *Le Droit* of Ottawa, and began acquiring small American community newspapers, ultimately owning such newspapers in thirty-one states. The *Telegraph* flourished, and we were able, in 1991, to borrow against its earnings to buy the largest stake in the leading Australian newspaper company, Fairfax, which had gone into receivership when a leveraged buyout put twice as much debt on the company as it could afford to carry.

The *Sydney Morning Herald*, *Melbourne Age*, and *Australian Financial Review* were fine titles, but the Australians were paranoid about foreigners. Australian prime minister Paul Keating allowed us to raise our percentage of shares in these papers from the initial 15 per cent to 25 per cent but, frustratingly, did not allow us to go further, to 35 per cent as he had indicated a willingness to do. Keating was an extremely entertaining and in some ways brilliant man, a likeable scoundrel – a larrikin, in Australian parlance. But by this time, the legendary Kerry Packer, Australia's most formidable resident businessman, owner of a television, magazine, and casino company, who had initially organized our bid and then been forced out by a combination of cross-media ownership rules and political pressure, had become resentful of our position. He was also hostile to Keating. Keating claimed that with the physically imposing Packer and me, he was choosing between "a 900-pound gorilla and a fucking Thesaurus." He was not a solomonic judge. As political and business skirmishing accelerated, my talented friend and associate Dan Colson, with whom I had gone to the law school at Laval, visited the opposition leader and next prime minister, John Howard, arriving concealed – to avoid the press – under a blanket in the back seat of an automobile as it entered the garage of Howard's office building. Finally, we concluded that owning 25 per cent of Fairfax but having entire responsibility for it was not a long-term strategy we wished to pursue. We sold out at a $300-million tax-favoured gain.

In 1992, we bought a 23 per cent block of shares in Canada's largest newspaper company, Southam. Torstar (publisher of the *Toronto Star*) had sold out to us because it had been ring-fenced and confounded by the independent directors and the remnants of Upper Canada's old families who had controlled the company for most of its history. Southam owned the only, or the leading, newspapers in Montreal (English language), Vancouver, Ottawa, Edmonton, Calgary, Hamilton, Windsor, and several smaller cities. Southam was a serious contributor to the Canadian malaise, as I conceived it. Meekly publishing derivative, dull, and complacent newspapers, and without owning one in Toronto – Canada's principal city – the country's national newspaper company deprived itself of any influence. I was confident that Southam could be turned around quickly, in product quality and financial performance.

As our newspaper company grew, I attempted to combine aspects of the traditional newspaper owner with contemporary requirements of corporate conduct. I did believe in trying to do things with a little style and to use the access accorded the press to become acquainted with leading figures in different fields while never forgetting the obligations of heading a public company.

When I entered the newspaper business in Quebec in the late 1960s, it was a commercially good business, not particularly labour or capital intensive, generally yielding an operating profit margin of 20 per cent or more; that is, a fifth of its total revenues was profit, before allowing for depreciation and taxes. Managerial talent in the industry was spotty. There were some inspired cost-control managers, of whom the most famous was Roy Thomson.

There were very few newspaper companies that were seriously concerned with both quality and profitability. The *Washington Post* was one of the few.

In general, the chains deadened newspapers, made them bland, cookie-cutter purveyors of wire service copy and uniform soft-left reporting and comment. Few managers had any newspaper editorial experience, and most assumed that if more money were allocated to the editors, this would improve the content of the newspaper in the hands of the reader. More often, it merely compounded the existing shortcomings.

The key is to engage the best personnel, control the numbers of staff, and insist on – and reward – high professional standards. The old Southam was a prime example of the Faustian bargain in which non-interfering owners are praised as ideal as long as they are extravagantly indulgent of the editorial workforce. In the last great boom of the newspaper industry, profits were such that the editorial department could be given a blank cheque for cost and quality – profits would still roll in, enabling management to look good while basking in the praise of the working press. It was a commercially fragile and intellectually corrupt arrangement.

The most important function of the editor or publisher is to assure a just tenor to the newspaper while encouraging lively writing and an imaginative variety of perspectives, and enforcing as strict as possible a separation between reporting and comment. We rarely asked the editors for more than equal time for our views, which were an economically conservative and, in foreign affairs, generally pro-American alliance position. We didn't try to banish contrary opinion or slant reporting. Our record was not perfect, but it was pretty good.

Gradually, I bought out my brother and the other partners at substantial profit to them. We privatized Argus Corporation, all of these share acquisitions financed by the sales of the old Argus constituent assets. In 1992, Argus Corporation and its affiliates owned about 40 per cent of Hollinger, which owned about 65 per cent of the *Telegraph*, 23 per cent of Southam, and one hundred of the smaller Canadian and American newspapers. The *Telegraph* owned 15 (and then 25) per cent of Fairfax (Australia). There was a fair amount of debt, but the group was solid enough, and the promise lay in the possibility of gaining absolute control of Southam and Fairfax.

This was the scene shortly after I married Barbara Amiel in 1992. Hollinger was a good but modest company, with many bits and pieces and quite a lot of debt but possibilities for dramatic growth. The central engine was the income generation of the *Telegraph*. If that continued and was amplified, if our Australian and Canadian positions could be transformed to ownership of the flows of cash those assets could produce under serious management, and if the newspaper industry did not give way under technological pressures or the deliteration of society, great prospects beckoned.

I ALREADY REGARDED RUPERT MURDOCH as the greatest media proprietor of all time. He had come from a faraway place, had conquered the

London tabloid field, buying the derelict *Sun* from the *Mirror* and swiftly outpacing the *Mirror*. He had cracked the Fleet Street unions that had reduced the industry to a financial shambles for decades, and I was the only Fleet Street chairman publicly to acknowledge the debt we owed to Murdoch for this. We all were able to pension off most of our workforces, automate the typesetting and printing processes, and see the whole industry move from the financial margin to solid profitability. Murdoch was a modern pioneer of media integration, buying a film studio and television stations, and he was about to crack the triopoly of television network domination in the United States and break new ground in satellite television.

We had a joint printing venture in Manchester and several other direct arrangements with him. I had always found his word to be fairly reliable, and he was a straightforward negotiator. He developed astonishing enthusiasms at times. Once, he telephoned to urge me to buy the satellite transmission air space allocated to Canada by treaty with the United States in order to fill it with his American-directed signals. I replied that there would be an international dispute over which country would have the honour of prosecuting us: the Canadians for piracy or the Americans for trespass.

Personally, Murdoch is an enigma. My best guess is that culturally he is an Archie Bunker who enjoys locker room scatalogical humour and detests effete liberalism. I have long thought that his hugely successful animated cartoon television program, *The Simpsons*, is the expression of his societal views: the people are idiots and their leaders are crooks.

His airtight ruthlessness does have amusing intermissions. From time to time, he conducts a campaign to humanize himself in the media of others: appearing recumbent on a bed in one of the glossies; dressed in black, with dyed orange hair, pushing a baby carriage in Greenwich Village; explaining to the *Financial Times* that he was on guard against errors and arrogant misjudgment in his company; claiming to be a churchgoer and mentioning his possible conversion to Catholicism.

Murdoch has no friendships, only interests; no nationality emotionally – the company he has built is his nation. Except Ronald Reagan, and perhaps Tony Blair, he has deserted almost every politician he ever supported, including Paul Keating, Margaret Thatcher, John Major, Jimmy Carter, and Hillary Clinton, to several of whom he owed much.

In the summer of 1993, my wife Barbara and I chartered a boat with some friends in the Aegean. While loitering around the Greek islands, I read of Murdoch's plan to restore *The Times*'s strategic position by lowering its cover price. He would start with a regional discount only. But, knowing Rupert as I did, knowing his compulsive belligerence as a competitor – and his daring – I was sure that if there was any encouragement in the response, he would cut prices very aggressively. Across the gleaming waters of the Aegean, with its splendid yachts and frolicking porpoises, I saw a disquieting vision of the economics of the British national newspaper industry being torn apart by my formidable competitor.

It was not an idle concern. The preliminary results were encouraging enough, and the Furor Murdochus that I had feared ensued. *The Times* cut its cover price from fifty pence to thirty pence. The *Telegraph* was at forty-eight pence. We remained there for six months, gamely doing our best with contests, promotions, discount coupons, and so forth, and generally held the *Daily Telegraph*'s circulation at just above a million, almost as great as the combination of its three broadsheet rivals: *The Times*, *Guardian*, and *Independent*.

The tabloid market was largely dominated by Robert Maxwell's *Mirror* and Rupert Murdoch's *Sun* and *News of the World*. Maxwell was a notorious figure, obscure, immense (more than three hundred pounds), bombastic, a vintage charlatan. A British government inquiry declared him unfit to be a director of a public company. His dealings with Iron Curtain dictatorships were particularly contemptible. "Tell me, President Ceaușescu, why do your people love you so?" he asked the Romanian president a few weeks before Ceaușescu was overthrown and executed amid popular rejoicing. Following Maxwell's death in 1991 and the collapse of his company into receivership, Murdoch had cut the cover price of his own tabloid *Sun*, which had been running about even in circulation with Maxwell's *Mirror*. The court-appointed administrators could not respond to Murdoch's price cuts, and the largely working-class readership of the *Mirror* was very price-sensitive. The *Sun* opened up a circulation lead of almost six hundred thousand over the *Mirror*; Murdoch clearly thought he was on to something. He accompanied his price reduction at *The Times* with an intensified effort to clone the *Telegraph*, including our daily separate sports section and to hire our personnel (at which he was not very successful), and conducted a massive promotional blitz.

A couple of years before, when Murdoch faced a dangerous financial crisis, I had given an address at the Media Society at the Café Royal, convened by Charles Wintour (former editor of the *Evening Standard* and father of *Vogue* editor Anna Wintour), and expressed confidence that Murdoch would come through his problems and that most of his critics were motivated by spite and envy. Murdoch wrote to thank me for my support. (He swiftly recovered from his financial crisis, as I had predicted.) I sought and expected no competitive quarter, but did not foresee the frenzied and relentless abuse I received from his organization when I passed through the valley of humiliation.

As the price war developed, the *Independent* in particular squealed in pain and with the *Guardian* and others made several pilgrimages to the Office of Fair Trading, to complain about predatory pricing, which is defined in the U.K. as selling at below the cost of production and distribution. Of course Murdoch was doing just that, but so were many other people in various industries. I refused to join these protests and publicly stated that as a capitalist myself, I believed in a man's right to lower his prices if he wished to. My supportive noises were reciprocated but led to no early de-escalation of the price war. Murdoch made it clear, including to a couple of our *Sunday Telegraph* reporters, that in a few years there would be only three newspapers in London: *The Times*, the *Sun* (both owned by his company), and the *Mail*. The *Financial Times* and the *Guardian*, he generously allowed, might survive as niche products for the financial community and the academic and clerical left, respectively.

In London and Australia, Murdoch's newspapers routinely referred to News Corporation's ability to control Hollinger International's profit by tuning the London broadsheet price war up and down. There was, unfortunately, some truth to this. Hollinger's only revenue was dividends from the *Telegraph* only because the ineptitude of the Southam management had forced the cancellation of their dividend. Hollinger was short of cash and still had some debt to service. All this was known to Murdoch, and he put on all the pressure he could. In the early spring of 1994, we sold some *Telegraph* shares because of Hollinger's cash needs.

IN SUCH A SITUATION there was no alternative but to play it aggressively, as Murdoch himself would. Barbara and I returned to London from New York on June 9, 1994, and I was greeted the next day by a phalanx of determined editors and senior executives advising that we cut the cover price immediately or lose our position as market leader. The only dissenters were a couple of men approaching retirement who were very concerned with the options given them to reinforce the comradely esprit of the company and spread the profit around. I wanted all the employees to think of themselves also as owners. But it didn't happen. As we were not a listed stock, every day the company secretary would calculate a reference price from the price/earnings ratios of listed U.K. newspaper companies, and descend to the lobby of our building to post the price prominently before everyone entering. The company would buy the options at this price, once they had vested, though I hoped the employees would continue on as shareholders. With almost no exceptions, the employees sold as the rights vested.

To Murdoch's considerable astonishment, as was severally reported to me, we abruptly cut our cover price from forty-eight to thirty pence. He had assumed that I would react like other publishers he had fought: husband the profit, economize, protect short-term gain even at the expense of the franchise, and hope for a merciful relaxation of the competitive pressure. I knew better than to anticipate any mercy from Murdoch. He at once implemented a further cut, to twenty pence. The balance between circulation and advertising revenue in the United States and Canada is about one to four, but in Britain it is between one to two and one to one. Cutting our cover price from forty-eight pence to thirty pence could cost the *Telegraph* more than $50 million annually. Only a controlling shareholder, prepared to eat such a heavy loss and face the abuse of the minority shareholders, could afford to take such a step and jeopardize short-term profits so seriously. But nothing less was necessary if we were to preserve the leading position of the *Telegraph*.

After our cover-price reduction, I tasted the temper of the city of London. Financial analysts stirred up the media with allegations that our sale of the block of *Telegraph* shares was fortuitously just ahead of our cover-price reduction. Cazenoves, who had been our broker for the sale and assured us that they would do nothing precipitate, abruptly resigned their association with us, telling the *Financial Times* that this was an unprecedented step for them. We had loyally stayed with the firm when one of their senior executives, David Mayhew, was facing criminal charges (of which he was acquitted). The London Stock Exchange investigated the sale and quickly discovered that there was no thought of cutting the price at the time the block of shares was sold and that this decision was made only after I returned from overseas to face an almost unanimous recommendation from the executive team, led by the editor. Two years later, we privatized the *Telegraph* at approximately the share price it had enjoyed before the cover-price cut, and all the shareholders departed happily. But the performance of Cazenoves was scandalous, a harbinger of some of what was to come when a much greater crisis developed nearly ten years later.

I received twice-daily bulletins on circulation and followed our sales in every corner of the United Kingdom. We imported circulation-building techniques we had developed in Australia, of the sale of discounted, pre-paid subscriptions. By the end of 1994, it was fairly clear that we were holding our own in the battle to retain our status as market leader. Our research also revealed that Rupert Murdoch, in his fierce quest for our circulation, had followed his natural instincts and brought *The Times* editorially down market, which again tended to make it a second read for the mid-market tabloid readers. It gave us the opportunity, which we took, to invest in product and take over much of the traditionally *Times*-reading top income and top education-level readers. The old Colonel Blimp *Telegraph* would emerge from its ordeal almost the newspaper of record of the British establishment and national institutions, and the greatest and most respected daily newspaper in Europe.

The pressure of the price war was relentless. Murdoch was wooing our staff with salaries we couldn't possibly meet, but we lost few people as the *Telegraph* was a relatively happy ship, without News Corp.'s constant Australian back-biting and chippiness, which Murdoch likes and promotes. Barbara's job at Murdoch's *Sunday Times* gave her independence from charges of spousal favouritism but at the cost of justifying moves to Murdoch by our own editorial people. I had to tell Barbara she could not continue working for Murdoch. She left, but not happily.* Most of our management cracked under the pressure. The managing director, Joe Cooke, had a minor stroke and retired. The finance director, promotions director, and several other senior people retired or otherwise departed. Dan Colson, my old friend from the Laval University law school and the very capable vice chairman of the *Telegraph*, became the co-chief executive, and he and I took direct control of the management. Our editor, the redoubtable Max Hastings – dashing and irrepressible but with a short concentration span and even shorter temper, at times an almost Monty Python–like awkwardness, and a hodgepodge of dissonant, half-formed opinions – also left abruptly.

He developed an elaborate catalogue of concerns including dislike of the Docklands as a place of work and concern about money being invested in our Sunday newspaper. All the same, Max told me that with a stylized option and bonus package, he would stay. I worked like a beaver for three days and prepared a plan for him, designing around his current divorce proceedings, in consultation with tax and benefit specialists, and assuring him a tax-designer sourced income of over $400,000, but when Max arrived for our meeting, he said, "I'm leaving. I've signed with the *Evening Standard*." He subsequently wrote a memoir of his time at the *Telegraph* that was perfectly amiable but represented me as an overbearing proprietor. There was little truth to this, and it is the usual beetle-browed self-dramatization of the frazzled editor, which journalists always absorb with gape-mouthed credulity. I intervened forcefully once, to reverse his original opposition to the American air raid on Libya in 1986. I defended him from all comers, from

---

* At David Radler's enthusiastic suggestion, Barbara shortly became the company's editorial vice president, and as it grew, her wholly benign influence on editorial quality grew also. She was an authentic expert on how to produce a good and lively newspaper, as a successful former editor of the *Toronto Sun* and an award-winning columnist in the uniquely competitive London newspaper market. There would be inevitable criticisms, but her impact on the *Chicago Sun-Times*, and some of the larger Canadian newspapers especially, was very positive. Because she was an executive, she was underpaid as a columnist and not paid as a director, and her compensation level was beneath what she could have commanded in the free market. Max was already calling her, more or less humorously, but very unjustly, "Lady MacBeth," but she never intervened at the Telegraphs, though she didn't hesitate to critique the paper to me. Sometimes I agreed with her, and sometimes not.

the widow of one of his former schoolmasters, offended by Max's vitupera-tive obituary, to Lauren Bacall, who claimed to have been misquoted, to Margaret Thatcher, over her daughter Carol's disembarkation from the *Daily Telegraph*. And although our working hours were quite different, I telephoned him after midnight only once, when I read in our principal op-ed piece that the best cure for clinical depression was a cup of tea. His stub-bornness and the philistinism of some of his opinions were exasperating. But he was a great newspaperman and a strong leader. Furthermore, I liked him. At the least, he was non-stop entertainment.

Dan Colson and I had a stab at hiring Paul Dacre, editor of the *Daily Mail*, as Max's replacement. In a cloak-and-dagger meeting one evening, Dacre came to our house in Chester Square and enthusiastically accepted in principle, saying that it had always been his dream to be the "editor of the U.K.'s leading broadsheet newspaper." A few details remained. The next day, Dacre ensured that our conversation was leaked, and the group's editor-in-chief, David English, offered Dacre a large raise and his own posi-tion, with English himself moving up to chairman of the *Daily Mail*. Dan and I did not especially mind Dacre using us to better his own lot. But we found his self-righteous public claims that he had dismissed our overture – and asked English for an increase in the editorial departmental budget only after English inexplicably got wind of our discussions – tiresome. Dacre and I had a rather acerbic exchange in the *Guardian*, of all places. I have not seen him again.

A couple of nights later, I had dinner with Vere, Lord Rothermere, chairman and principal shareholder of Associated Newspapers, which owned the *Mail* and *Evening Standard*, where Max Hastings was now going, and told him I did not highly appreciate his poaching our editor. (It was only after his raid that we approached Dacre.) Vere admonished me with all the authority of the head of the Harmsworths and the heir to Northcliffe, saying that we are just theatre owners and that the journalists and editors are actors. They play in our theatres but have no interest in or loyalty to us. It was an apt metaphor.

The *Sunday* editor, Charles Moore, became editor of the *Daily Telegraph*. Dominic Lawson moved from the clever and stylish 175-year-old *Spectator* magazine, which Andrew Knight and I had bought in 1988, to the *Sunday Telegraph*. Both proved to be successful appointments. One of the group's most brilliant writers, Frank Johnson, became editor of the *Spectator*. After a few years, Frank reverted to writing and Boris Johnson (no relation) became the *Spectator*'s editor. Boris, with his shock of unkempt blond hair, Wodehousian pratfalls, and endearing teddy-bear appearance and personality, was already something of a folk figure in Britain. His columns were hilarious, and so was almost any conversation with him. When he was doorstopping in his 1997 parliamentary campaign, a housewife informed him that she was going to vote for him. "But why, madam?" Boris famously replied. We managed to get a solemn promise from him that in exchange for the editorship he would not run for election again. A few weeks later, he threw his hat in the ring in two constituencies and was eventually elected as successor to Michael Heseltine in Henley in 2001. In 2007, he deposed the two-term hard-line Marxist Ken Livingstone, generally known as Red Ken, in the election for mayor of London.

ONE OF THE MANY INITIATIVES we examined was the possibility of buying the competing daily newspaper the *Independent*. The main shareholders were my left-of-centre friends Carlo Caracciolo (Fiat owner Gianni Agnelli's brother-in-law and the ultimate limousine liberal) and Juan Luis Cebrián of *El Pais* in Madrid. In the end, they chose to sell to the *Mirror*, then headed by Rupert Murdoch's former editor of the *News of the World* and *Today*, David Montgomery. (Murdoch claimed to have fired Montgomery because he "stared at me." I was incredulous, but Rupert told me to note carefully how he stared the next time I met Montgomery, a serious and intense Ulsterman. I did and found that Rupert had a point.)

In January 1995, Barbara and I attended the World Economic Forum at Davos. The days were crisp, with perfectly blue skies and icy, snow-covered pavements. I appeared on a panel in a plenary session with Rupert Murdoch. In the questions we answered jointly after the panel discussion and during the private lunch that followed, with Barbara, Murdoch, and his wife, Anna, Murdoch said he foresaw an early rise in the London newspaper cover prices, to allow for newsprint price increases. Anna, whom I had first encountered when we were receiving communion at the Brompton Oratory, left us early to stop in at church. I thought it inappropriate to accompany her in prayerful thanks at her husband's signal of de-escalation in the price war, though I felt the urge to set to work on yet another corporate reorganization. The price war continued, but less intensely. The mortal threat dwindled to a serious nuisance.

THROUGHOUT THE PRICE WAR, I had been toughing it out with our Southam investment in Canada. Here, I was struggling with a suffocating group of grey and greedy minds. We were getting nowhere, ring-fenced by the old management teams and directors. I came up with a plan to merge Southam and Hollinger by exchanging our newspaper assets for their shares. That would give us effective control of the company. But the notion of me in charge of Southam was too much for the independent directors, who began feverish attempts to find a counterbalance.

The familiar and formidable figure of Paul Desmarais, chairman of Power Corporation and probably Canada's most distinguished businessman, loomed. Driving out to the airport in London to fly to Toronto for a Southam directors meeting the next day, I responded to a message from Desmarais, and he told me that, by invitation, he was taking up an equal shareholding to Hollinger's with shares issued by Southam's treasury. I knew this "invitation" was going to be a difficult battle.

On the airplane, I considered how to deflect the dangers of this move while Barbara, already fatigued with the price war and having some sense of what lay ahead, toyed with the possibility of ejecting herself from the plane mid-flight. I had great respect for Paul, but this was essentially a project for his son André, an amiable young man. Paul is a multi-billionaire, and neither he nor his son really intended to run Southam and maximize profits and transform its newspapers into agents for change in Canada. Their holdings were diverse and included some newspapers, but they were not newspaper publishers the way we were.

Power Corporation could sideline us to a marginal position, where we would depend on the talents of the incumbent Southam management to raise the value of our investment. This was an unpromising state of affairs. It is difficult for those not familiar with the company to grasp how incompetently managed Southam was and how dreary and disliked most of its newspapers were. The management had come from other industries. The publishers and unit heads tried to manage their divisions second-guessed by head office. Head office specialized in endlessly summoning unit management to Toronto for lengthy question-and-answer sessions.

The result was an immense infestation, a teeming anthill, of superfluous people and the dedication of much corporate energy to backbiting and internecine struggles. The newspapers were ruled by soft leftist editors who were themselves captives of soft leftist cadres of journalists. They were under instructions to keep coverage local, and this led to endless antagonisms between the newspapers and the principal figures in the communities where they were supposedly building goodwill.

It took a night of international calls to independent Southam directors from Japan to Hungary, but we managed, by the narrowest of margins, to defeat the original Power Corporation acquisition of treasury shares at the Southam board. André Desmarais and his father telephoned, and we met in Palm Beach a few days later. They were still eager buyers and the other Southam factions couldn't be held indefinitely, so our best course was to let them in on terms we could live with. I had won this round but did not want to push it. At least Paul was dealing with me now, and not trying to come in the back door. As I recorded in my earlier book, published in 1993 about my career up to that time, we agreed that we would have equal rights, so that there was at least some incentive for the Desmaraises not to collude altogether with the old families and banish us to the corner to be tormented with sharp sticks and hot irons, as Torstar had been. As long as we and Power Corporation acted in unison, we would have determining influence on the company.

At the next annual meeting, Paul Desmarais sat right behind me. The company president, Bill Ardell, a pleasant and attractive man who had done well in other businesses but had no background in newspapers, gave a very defensive and gloomy report on the newspaper business. Desmarais leaned forward and whispered to me, in French: "When are we selling our shares?"

The official Southam line, as in so much of the newspaper industry, was that new technologies were a grave threat to newspapers and that the challenge for the industry was "managing decline," as if our task were the dismemberment of the British Empire. In this way, no insufficiency of performance could be blamed on management. Their comments would be legitimized ten years later but were no excuse for the results they were producing then. I carried the flag for the business, and from time to time the *Wall Street Journal* and other publications asked me to take up the fight on behalf of newspapers. At Davos and the Museum of Television and Radio meetings, I was a virtual anachronism, like a member of the Flat Earth Society, and I became the most frequent advocate of the viable future of the newspaper industry.

My contention was that with the new technology we could deliver our newspaper content in any format – online, via telephones, or on flexible screens unrolled from pockets. People would pay for newspapers they liked, with individual writers who engaged them and news and features carefully edited and imaginatively presented. This could not be done with the Southam formula of bland, soft-left criticism of anyone who was actually trying to accomplish anything in the communities where the newspapers circulated. But lively, well-written, provocative, informative, and balanced newspapers could keep their readers, I ritualistically repeated, at Davos, in the *Wall Street Journal*, at Southam board meetings. I almost said it to passersby on Fifth Avenue or in Knightsbridge. I claimed, despite my lack of background in any form of technology and a desperate lack of rapport with new gadgetry, that in a few years everything would be broadband. We would use the same screen, with the same picture definition, for television (satellite or terrestrial), the Internet, video games; anything anyone wishes to put up. In these circumstances, there would be no television franchises left. The fragmentation of the market might overwhelm the networks, and the strong newspaper franchises would have an incomparable ability to build market share for those contesting for mastery of the screen.

To some degree, I believed this. But these were times of sheer drudgery for us, and there was little excitement or pleasure in the constant fight for business survival. Our social life was lively and interesting, but the corporate life on which it largely reposed was in constant turmoil. I became progressively more disgruntled with the failure of our Southam investment to achieve anything, and with the squandered opportunity, and with the lassitude of Power Corporation. We were simultaneously fighting the price war in London and being flimflammed by the politicians in Australia. There was a squeeze throughout our company, and the inert, unremitting investment in Southam was a large part of the problem.

Paul Desmarais was not at all antagonistic, but neither was he an active supporter. For us to get anywhere, I knew this had to change. I invited him to buy our position. Desmarais was unenthused. Eventually, the lack of any progress at Southam became so irritating that I lobbied Paul on the theory of exchanging our shareholdings for a number of Southam's non-metropolitan assets. Ultimately, the situation was resolved by its cause: the astonishing vanity and complacency of the Southam directors. The unaffiliated directors, "the independents," as they styled themselves, had engaged an obnoxious lawyer. The independents instructed their counsel to compose a lengthy and dismissive letter to Paul and me jointly. The letter – from the chairman, Ron Cliff of Vancouver, but clearly inspired by the independents' egregious lawyer – informed us that we had no standing to waste management's time devising such schemes as an exchange of a block of stock for a carve-out of assets, and that henceforth we could deal with the management only through the independents. By now I was fairly accustomed to being cuffed around by these people, but given that Power Corporation and Hollinger between us had more than 40 per cent of the stock, this was a fairly nervy stance.

Paul telephoned me in Prague, where I was attending a New Atlantic Initiative Conference (one of the many forums I attended for a while, and one of the better ones). He was so disgusted by the letter, he said, that he was prepared to sell us his stock at his cost. We quickly agreed, and Paul promised that the Power Corporation votes at the next directors meeting would be cast in favour of a special shareholders meeting to remove what I soon publicly described as "the obdurate rump" of our antagonists. We still had a couple of supporters on the board, and the motion passed. The intended targets of the special meeting abstained, a little like East German Communist leader Erich Honecker voting for his own removal in order to preserve party solidarity.

The shareholders meeting took place when Barbara and I were in Biarritz in the spring of 1996, as we were trying to find a holiday destination with a level of light that would not inflame her dermatomyositis. (Biarritz and the Pyrenees were not the place, but good Jew Barbara found Lourdes astonishing. The birthplace of Marshal Foch in Tarbes she found quaint, but she was distinctly less riveted by it than I was.) The Southam shareholders threw out the five designated retirees by a margin of well over 80 per cent. We could have won without casting any of the Power and Hollinger votes. Even the long-suffering regular shareholders had had enough.

We went through the head office like a scythe. The millions of dollars that fell off the payroll were imperceptible to the functioning of the company and freed up time for the publishers to operate their newspapers. The editor in Montreal, a distinguished woman who would not represent the interests of 1.5-million primarily English-speaking Quebec readers by being anti-French (an attitude she and we would not tolerate), but was, I felt, quite inadequate in the leadership she was prepared to give the community, graciously retired.

The *Ottawa Citizen* was such a shockingly inadequate newspaper for the capital of a G7 country that I suggested Russell Mills, its publisher, retire. He asked to see me. I told him that the editor would have to be changed, and he said that he had been about to propose the same move, and he accepted my suggestion for a replacement, Neil Reynolds, then an editor for the Irving family in New Brunswick.

Mills and Reynolds produced an almost unrecognizably improved *Ottawa Citizen* within a few months, and after a grand relaunch, the newspaper's circulation began to rise slightly following a decade of decline in one of Canada's faster growing metropolitan areas.

I suggested to the publisher in Calgary that the oil and ranching capital of the country, the closest Canada has to the ethos of Dallas or Houston, could do without a friendly socialist as editor, who daily debunked the wellsprings of Calgary's prosperity and the very raison d'être of the city. This was done.

Beyond that, we laid down only a few general guidelines, disabused the advertising team of the notion that we were managing decline, culled fat, and worked with the publishers and editors to improve their products. In less than three years, the straight profit from operations increased from barely $100 million to $300 million, confirming the sense of our gamble on what newspaper franchises in such rich cities as Vancouver, Calgary, Edmonton, Ottawa, and Montreal could do if operated seriously, and the stock price rose quickly by 50 per cent. There were not many further personnel changes, only steady pressure for integrity, balance, good writing, and lively presentation. Canada's national newspaper company was no longer something to be ashamed of, and almost all of our critics in the Canadian media accepted this fact, however reluctantly. When we consolidated our control over Southam in 1996, Hollinger owned 59 of the 105 daily newspapers in Canada.

Once we were in charge of the company, all those shareholders who had conspired to prevent us from taking control of it joined forces to jack up the price for us. This was fair business, but unctuous cries of shareholder rights were a little hard to take from those people, as they often are.

Our initial effort at a takeover bid brought us up to only a little more than 50 per cent, so we allowed the offer to die rather than raise the price. We wanted Southam's operating income for our company in order to liberate its dependence on dividends, the ancient curse of Argus Corporation. This required ownership of all the shares: intercorporate dividends are tax-free, while debt interest is tax-deductible, so we needed operating income from which to deduct, for tax purposes, the cost of interest on our debt, thus effectively laying off much of it on the tax collector. We were the victims of our own improvements to Southam's operating performance. The method we adopted to take out the public was to declare a six-dollar special dividend and then bid at a slightly lower price for the ex-dividend stock. This was thought by some to be devious and by others to be clever, but it accomplished our objective to privatize Southam.

American stock analysts were not as pleased as we had hoped. Concerns were rising over the future of newspapers. We were winding toward the climax of the dot-com bubble. Hucksters and dreamers in the initial Internet-related business could foist almost anything on the stock market and achieve an immediate success, with no attention to business plans. Nor were American investors particularly impressed with Canada. They thought of it as a socialist country and were so America-centric that even a country that to most is largely indistinguishable from neighbouring American states was regarded with skepticism.

PERSONAL DREAMS NOW COINCIDED with business ambitions. So long as Southam had no Toronto newspaper, I was facing the worst of both worlds: denounced as a monopolist while shut out of any real influence in the country. National opinion in English-speaking Canada was largely controlled by the *Globe and Mail*, the *Toronto Star*, and the CBC, with a slight assist from the principal Canadian magazine, *Maclean's*.

A striking illustration of our powerlessness occurred in 1997. I had Southam commission extensive polling throughout English Canada and in Quebec to gauge support for the official position of appeasing the Quebec nationalists with pre-emptive concessions while ignoring the endless provocations of Quebec's separatist government. Our polls showed that this response enjoyed only lukewarm support in Quebec and was despised in the rest of the country. There was heavy support, even in Quebec, for the proposal I repeatedly made to successive prime ministers that if any province voted to secede from Canada, any county within that province that voted against secession would secede from the province and remain in Canada. This would have buried separatism once and for all. The publication of these poll results, based on an unusually comprehensive survey, received no attention whatever from the *Globe and Mail*, the *Toronto Star*, the CBC, and *Maclean's*. It completely undercut the excessively appeasing line they had all been preaching for decades.

For Southam to breach the fortress of the Toronto media would require a new newspaper, an unpromising idea on its face in a city that already had three general daily newspapers. But with local Southam papers in virtually every city in Canada, we had the advantage of being able to print and distribute a newspaper all around the country a good deal more economically than the *Globe and Mail*. Carving out circulation in the metropolitan area of Toronto, however, would be a challenge.

The existing Toronto newspapers had divided up the Toronto market quite thoroughly. The *Sun* (of which Barbara had once been the editor) was the low-brow, populist tabloid newspaper, though it had largely forgotten where its natural readership was. The *Star*, Canada's largest circulation newspaper for many decades, was a middle-brow, oppressively Toronto-centric, anti-American, soft-left product, with acres of flabbily written pap sniping at capitalism, traditionalism, Christianity, and anything remotely American. The newspaper's bylaws pledge allegiance to the Liberal Party of Canada. The *Globe and Mail* passed for a high-brow newspaper. In fact, it was ashen, with little personality, and only five degrees to the right of the *Star*. It had lost much of the tradition it had had as a writers' paper and had been largely run out of Toronto by the *Star* and the *Sun*. But it had ingeniously hired a few correspondents around the country, printed fifty thousand or so copies in outlying cities, and proclaimed itself "a national newspaper." This was essentially a scam, but it was carried off almost with the panache of W.C. Fields (a considerable achievement for such an oppressively sober newspaper).

The founding of a new national newspaper headquartered in Toronto was, I thought, a commercial necessity. It would increase Southam's value by inserting it into the country's metropolis, giving it national influence, and liberating it from the investors' perception of Southam as a provincial newspaper company. A new national newspaper would also be a public service and my final try at testing the limits of the Canadian settlement: government always to the left of the United States – higher taxes, more generous social programs, more moral relativism in all things than in the United States.

After considering a few alternatives, I settled on Ken Whyte as editor of what would become the *National Post*. Ken, a quiet but determined and thoughtful Albertan, had been a good editor of *Saturday Night* magazine, which we had owned since 1987. He is an astonishingly persuasive recruiter of people, and his ability to find writing talent in the most unlikely places gave us writers and editors with more minority group hybrids than any progressive publication.

He was not supposed to raid elsewhere in our group but could approach British and American employees with a Canadian connection. This produced what Barbara called "the Ken Whyte broadjump," as he would unearth the fact that someone's great-aunt or second cousin had vacationed at Qualicum or gone to a Filles d'Isabelle summer camp at Baie-Saint-Paul in Edwardian times.

We devised a novel layout and launched the *National Post* with great fanfare in October 1998. Its editorial stance, including the placement of stories, headlines, cartoons, and most but not all comment, was intelligent conservative. The paper advocated lower taxes; a more rigorous examination of welfare claims, of the status of the supposedly homeless, and of government transfer payments; and a cessation of any appeasement of provincial separatism. We conducted extensive polling on taxes and published analyses of the sources of tax revenues and of comparative taxing jurisdictions and their economic performances, all original to the national media of Canada.

Apart from the *Telegraph*, this was the happiest of my newspaper associations. Whyte is very intelligent and has an excellent sense of humour and devious persistence in his views. His cadre of writers was a breath of fresh air. The *National Post* was not only an informative and provocative newspaper, it was well written and strong through all departments. Arts were innovative; sports were especially well written. The editorial and op-ed editor was the distinguished commentator and former policy adviser to Margaret Thatcher, John O'Sullivan. He had been editorial page editor or deputy editor of the *Daily Telegraph*, *The Times*, and the *New York Post*, and had succeeded Bill Buckley as editor of the *National Review*. O'Sullivan was an old friend of Barbara's and mine and moved into our house in Toronto and lived there for almost two years.

After an early bout of curiosity, the circulation was around 250,000 solid. Promotions pushed it over 300,000. The *Globe and Mail* had been at around 325,000 and promoted to about 350,000. It held the edge in Toronto, but we crowded or surpassed it in the rest of the country, where we took advantage of our promotional abilities through ownership of local newspapers. Meanwhile, the *Globe and Mail* also upped its game and became a much snappier product. Coverage was beefed up in many areas, layout improved, and editorial became less drearily predictable. The owners – the Thomson organization – changed publishers early, then changed editors, poured in money, and, after a complacent start and a panicky second reaction, settled into grim trench warfare with no quarter with the new rival.

Almost everyone praised the *National Post* as a first-class product and a vital addition to the country's media. Even my old opponents among the Canadian working press acknowledged its contribution and gratefully agreed that Ken Whyte's hiring practices and my fairly broad notion of what constituted start-up costs had raised salaries among daily newspaper journalists, increased competition, sharpened and reinvigorated the industry, and put a stop, at least for a time, to the notion of the decline of the Canadian newspaper. Still, many of the people who praised the paper read it in waiting rooms or at the office and were reluctant to trade in their old newspaper or buy a new subscription. They didn't come in adequate numbers.

Though our cost-per-thousand argument was good, and we were pitching a political position to which almost the entire business community was more amenable than they were to the waffling of the *Globe and Mail*, there was a real reluctance to give the new newspaper advertising. But the reticence went beyond that. The newspaper culture in Canada did not have the roots it had in Europe, and the *National Post* struck too non-conformist a note for many Canadians. What many took to be adoration of America was simply irritation with Canadian smugness, and with the national media's addiction always to claim superiority to the United States in all intangible and human qualities. We never advocated absorption into the U.S.; we advocated an overthrow of the Toronto-centric, narcissistic Canadian fantasyland of moral exaltedness, and successful friendly Canadian competition with the U.S., which I never doubted Canada could conduct if it had the courage to try. This was largely why I supported free trade, as a confidence-building measure for Canada, not because I thought it an economic panacea.

Legends arose that Whyte was monstrously extravagant and that the operating costs of the *National Post* went vastly over budget. It became an accepted fable that Whyte sent correspondents all over the world for two-day assignments, that the *National Post's* anniversary parties were bacchanalian celebrations of crushing expense. In truth, the annual parties were spartan affairs and far from extravagant, offering only drinks and rudimentary food. The dancing was more than the usual spectacle given the pulchritude and panache of many of the female staff. There was only slight incidence of Whyte spending too much on correspondents, though it must be said that if he had been a little less of a perfectionist, the paper would have been 2 per cent less interesting and perhaps 5 per cent less expensive to own.

The cost of launching the *National Post* and sustaining it through the first two years did not greatly exceed expectations. After the first year, I was fairly confident that the *National Post* was losing less than the *Globe and Mail*. After a couple of years, the Thomson Corporation sold 70 per cent of the *Globe and Mail* to Bell Canada, which bought the CTV television network at a price so exaggerated that the head of the company, Jean Monty, was let go for his extravagance. Southam was now a more valuable property because, finally, it had a serious voice in the Toronto market. *The Economist* rightly called the *National Post* "the most successful launch of a new newspaper since World War II." Launching a paper was a risky project, but I had combined two ambitions: to create additional value for our Canadian newspaper group and to create an intelligent voice for the Canadian moderate right. This meant a different approach to Canadian public affairs than the old and tired consensus, which like all such inflexible stitch-ups had long since become a joint venture between those addicted to exploiting its obsolescence (the separatists and provincial decentralizers) and those addicted to masquerading as benefactors, with decennial levitations to the status of self-acclaimed saviours of, in this case, Canadian Confederation.

AS OUR COMPANY GREW, we had to reduce debt. This could be done only by issuing stock, which would have been punitive at the current unrepresentative price, or by selling assets. The strain of constantly conducting a two-front war – one in quest of adequate operating results and frequent acquisitions and the other to ensure that the chain of control was not threatened by the debt burden at any point – was very wearing and often preoccupied me. As long as the Canadian banking system relied on client relationships and bet on the client, companies such as ours would be fine, as we never overpaid for assets and never financially mismanaged them. None of the many banks we had dealt with in many countries had done anything but make money with us.

We took advantage of the low stock price as best we could by steadily buying in and cancelling shares, but there were limits to how much money was available for such a purpose given the various loan conditions (covenants) we had. Our relations with note and bond holders were excellent. We issued paper at higher interest rates than premium issuers like the federal government, because we were considered an aggressive company, but didn't have to pay a large premium for risk as junk bond issuers did. With assets of our quality, there was no chance of their losing money with us, and our instruments always traded at well above par. But the conditions normally stipulated by buyers of our long-term debt would be tighter than we would find comfortable if there were a downturn.

Later on, we sometimes needed to sell assets to meet obligations. This didn't endanger our control of the company as long as we held all the super-voting shares, but it was in some respects self-sacrificing. A smaller company meant reducing the size of our management fee, which was largely used to pay interest in the holding companies and secure our stock position in Hollinger International, the operating company. Our aim was to buy in shares in order to be real proprietors, not just "owners" through gerrymandered super-voting shares. Super-voting shares are common in the newspaper industry (The New York Times Company, Dow Jones, Associated Newspapers, the *Washington Post*, and News Corporation all had them), but given attitudes to newspapers, the unenthusiastic response of some shareholders to investment in the product for long-term gain, as well as our dependence on increasingly fickle lenders, I thought it prudent to have as much of the company as possible in our hands. This approach – buying back shares and holding a large block of single-voting shares against substantial borrowings – has been represented by some as retrograde. In fact, this approach was like stock options, except that we accepted the entire downside risk; we elected to allocate more than half of our salaries to pay interest on loans secured by single-voting Hollinger International shares that were necessary to be large-equity participants but not to sustain ourselves in control of the business. This was a vote of confidence in the company and in our ability to operate it to the benefit of all shareholders.

However this was also the root of much of my trouble: my determination not to mimic the sort of sham ownership I had seen in the original Argus Corporation led to a vulnerable financial situation that attracted predators. My instincts of financial survival and industry trends were well developed and informed by strenuous vigilance, but I didn't have a cushion against a thunderbolt from an unexpected quarter. In commercial as in other matters, rapid movement is a good defence as long as the enemy's fire is not too accurate, in which case, the fate of H.M.S. Hood opposite K.M. Bismarck awaits. I smelled danger, but couldn't see any unmanageable vulnerability.

As the Internet evolved, it had become impossible to generate any enthusiasm for newspapers in the investment community. Newspapers could be sold at twelve times operating income, but newspaper stocks were discounted and were often traded at seven or eight times net profit, a much smaller base figure than operating income because depreciation and taxes were deducted. This made it possible to buy in and cancel shares for much less than the underlying values of the assets if they were sold as going concerns. Value would steadily accrue to the continuing shareholders as the company shrank itself, cancelled shares, reduced debt, and retrenched to its best assets. This was my strategy for dealing with improvident times, and it worked very well, almost to the end. There were also increasing frictions with some institutional shareholders who viewed the tangled structure we had accumulated to minimize taxes as impenetrable and even sinister.

I never lost sight, even if most observers did, of the fact that all that the controlling shareholders had put in a business that was now the third largest newspaper publisher in the Western world (after Gannett and Murdoch's News Corporation) was $2 million worth of my father's Argus stock, net of minority interests. And there was some debt against that. All I had invested personally in the business was the $500 I paid Peter White for a half-interest in the *Eastern Townships Advertiser* in 1966. What I inherited in what became Hollinger from my father had had a value, net of debt, and provincial succession duties (which required more than twenty years to settle), of about $1 million.

We had certainly operated our business at a profit in the intervening years, but there was almost US$2 billion of debt after we took the public out of Southam. We could easily manage it with our current annual operating income of more than $400 million, but with any economic downturn, we might scrape some of the covenants (borrowing conditions). In the holding company, Hollinger Inc., the cost of ending the old Argus Corporation imposture as owners was that there was a substantial accumulation of debt there too.

Our company had acquired scale, our operating results were commendable and improving, and our products were almost universally admired, other than by diehard political opponents. The distinction of many of our board members (we had individual boards for many publications, like the *Spectator* and the *Jerusalem Post*), and our association with many successful political leaders, led by Ronald Reagan, Margaret

Thatcher, the Bushes, Tony Blair (in Irish and Alliance matters), and the leading provincial premiers in Canada, as well as prime ministers Brian Mulroney, Paul Martin, and Stephen Harper (as opposition leader), and the association with swashbuckling capitalists such as Jimmy Goldsmith, Gianni Agnelli, Dwayne Andreas, James (Lord) Hanson, Jacob (Lord) Rothschild and Sir Evelyn de Rothschild, the Reichmanns, and, with some toing and froing, Kerry Packer, Hal Jackman, Peter Munk, and Paul Desmarais – not only brought our companies a great deal of business experience and access but their stature gave our company some instant recognition. But beneath a glittering and proud facade, dangers lurked that gnawed at me constantly. The capital structure was rickety, and some of the institutional shareholders, disapproving what they regarded as the proprietary style in which my associates and I ran the company, detected that some shares would have to be sold out of the control bloc. They began holding hands to depress the stock price, trying to starve us out, as a couple of them admitted to me, while agitating against the scale of management fees we were receiving. These fees were not abnormal and were independently approved by the Audit Committee. The stock was not heavily traded, as the big blocs, ours and those of several institutions, accounted for 60 per cent of it, and the stock had been moving slowly or treading water, as there was nothing to prompt heavy activity. In these circumstances, it is not difficult to move or freeze the price if the market operators don't have to file insider reports. The institutional world can always use friendly-hands buyers and sellers. I well knew how it was done and that it was being done, but there wasn't much I could do about it, except raise the underlying per-share value by buying and cancelling whatever shares our means could afford to take up without straining the loan covenants. The assets and the profits were real, but if recession struck and the deglamorization of newspapers accelerated, it could become problematical. Then I might find I was building an airplane in the sky; the aerodynamics were sound but perhaps not if the financial weather became extremely turbulent.

Despite my endless expressions of confidence in the future of the newspaper, it was obvious that wringing a value from newspaper franchises was going to be a good deal more complicated than it had been.

—

FOLLOWING MY ENCOUNTER with Rupert (and Anna) Murdoch at Davos, where Rupert hinted at the likelihood of a de-escalating price war in London, I concluded that it was time for another corporate reorganization. Unfortunately for non-commercial readers, these are complicated. The plan was to concentrate operations in the U.S. company, American Publishing, which had a dual-tier share structure (multiple votes for one class), and to move the Canadian company toward privatization by offering American Publishing shares to the Canadian shareholders (American Publishing was renamed Hollinger International). This would give us access to U.S. capital markets, a more flexible capital structure, and have the effect of a merger between companies. Both the sale of the Canadian assets and their eventual resale would each generate a profit of nearly US$100 million. Like all the related-party transactions we produced (where some parties are on both sides of the deal), this one enured greatly to the benefit of the public shareholders of both companies, the Canadian Hollinger Inc. and the U.S. Hollinger International.

BACK IN LONDON, the newspaper price war, though de-escalated, continued with erratic initiatives by Rupert Murdoch, which we countered. *The Times* went to ten pence on Monday for the "Summer of Sport," including the 1996 Olympics and World Cup. The "Summer" lasted almost two years. *The Times* cut its Saturday paper to thirty pence for a time. Only when he virtually wrapped *The Times* in five-pound notes, as in his insane inclusion of Eurostar tickets (the tunnel train between London and Paris), could he narrow the gap between us from 400,000 to about 250,000. A few of these pyrrhic episodes disabused him of this expedient. In the early stages of the war, I had not been able to set foot out of doors without encountering someone who would tell me that the *Telegraph* was doomed. As transatlantic television personality David Frost foretold: "You will know you're winning when people you knew thought that you would lose tell you they knew you could do it. You will know you have won when the same people tell you that not only did they know you could do it, but if you recall, you have won by following their advice."

The end of the price war produced an awkward silence. Almost everyone in Britain except the officers of the *Daily Telegraph* was so terrified of

Murdoch, and smart opinion was so convinced of the inexorable decline of the *Telegraph*, that the failure of *The Times* to catch the *Telegraph* was simply not mentioned.

The conventional reaction of the British chattering classes was unimpressive. Almost to the last man and woman they expressed their dislike of Murdoch as down-market, treacherous, anti-British, and anti-monarchist in particular. Yet it was obvious when the price war broke out that the majority of opinion hoped for and expected a Murdoch victory. No one attacked the Royal Family as violently and effectively as News Corporation, and especially the Prince of Wales as his marriage faltered. Yet the Prince had his official biography excerpted in Murdoch's *Sunday Times*. It was as if Murdoch were head boy of the British school: unpopular but terrifying and inevitable and the devil they knew. The Duke of Edinburgh, whom I have always found an impressive man in all respects and in a very difficult role, was so outraged at this truckling to Murdoch that his office called, unsolicited, and offered us a wide-ranging interview. It was a thoughtful gesture and a very good interview.

Yet there was obviously a perception that I had had it too easy in Britain, that I had gained control of the *Telegraph* rather effortlessly, and while the newspaper had improved and I had continued the *Telegraph* policy of strong support for traditional British institutions, there was a reticence about me. In fact, as a friend who knew the British well said, "There was always a target on your back in England." Because of British understatement, British envy and xenophobia, at least toward foreigners exercising an influence in their midst, may be disguised at times, but they are never out of mind, as I discovered.

This mortal struggle in London, coupled with the refusal of the Australian political leaders of both parties to honour their promises to allow us to take real control of Fairfax, and the dilatory tactics of our factional opponents at Southam, denied us the opportunity to become one of the world's largest media companies.

By the time these problems had been resolved, the commercial hour of the newspaper was passing. Newspaper company shares were not good currency for acquisitions; cash flows were no longer bountiful enough to facilitate growth into other media. British national newspaper revenues never fully recovered and eventually became an albatross to News Corporation. Shareholders were already becoming restive about the sluggish market in newspaper share prices.

The price war was a sideshow to Murdoch but a life-or-death struggle to us. However under-recognized our achievement, and whatever new worlds Rupert might conquer, as I said to Barbara, we could stand in our broom closet in the dead of night and sip champagne together because we had, in fact, won a great victory – but the sun was setting on the industry.

[CHAPTER TWO]

WHAT WAS MOST ENJOYABLE about the *Telegraph* was not the stiff cardboard invitations to almost every important social, cultural, and political event in London and certainly not the grand state dinners. It was being at least a presence in the great debates over the foreign policy issues of our time. According to U.K. political correctness, I often brought the *Telegraph* out on the wrong side of those debates. I didn't think so, but we played a part in them. I had access to Cabinet ministers and historians, academics from the best British universities, and thinkers from that extraordinary seam of British intellectual life. The *Telegraph's* magic opened doors in Europe and even some in North America.

It wasn't all pleasant, and occasionally there were conflicts and rows, such as the fracas mentioned earlier over Max Hastings's firing of Carol Thatcher (whose mother was a great and friendly prime minister with a parliamentary majority of over 100), but also involving many other writers. The *Sunday Telegraph* managed to libel Muammar Gadhafi's son as a terrorist, and the uncommonly difficult and gigantic Scots writer Bruce Anderson, a sidekick of Perry Worsthorne and Frank Johnson, referred to the Attorney General of Ireland, Mr. Murray, as "a shifty unshaven fellow, who would try to sell a gypsy a three-legged horse." Perry Worsthorne, editor of the *Sunday*

Telegraph, had found a charming lawyer who did not believe in the tort of libel, and some of these liberties were unfortunately expensive. I never penalized the offending reporters.

I was always attracted by the traditional newspaper publisher's influence on public affairs, when cautiously exercised, but I was always peering over my shoulder at the electronic media, looking at the corporate mirror for any potential financial vulnerabilities, and staring furtively about at the more redoubtable of our competitors, Rupert Murdoch and Vere Rothermere. Most political influence, like supposed influence on one's journalists or even children, and like, I later discovered, instructions to counsel, was illusory or fleeting. But even the false sensation of importance was bracing.

A good part of my determination to keep the *Daily Telegraph* upmarket was not only because I was certain this was the best way to ensure its viability, but because I believed in its power to influence positively to some extent the serious political arguments of the time. This was a dangerous addiction, as I kept telling Barbara when contemplating whether we had reached the right time from a shareholder's point of view to sell the newspaper.

There were many issues that ignited firestorms at the paper. The most heated moments at editorial conferences were over the Irish Question. Northern Ireland was the United Kingdom's longest-festering domestic problem – an issue of great matter to a swathe of the British and almost no matter to anyone else, except some Irish Americans, such as the Kennedys, whose take on the issues was very tribal. Much blood had been shed over whether Northern Ireland could secede from the U.K. On this matter as on the question of integrating into Europe, Max Hastings and Charles Moore were in direct opposition to each other. The *Sunday Telegraph*'s Moore was against any compromise. Although he is himself a Roman Catholic convert, Charles strongly identifies with the Ulster Protestants, to the point where he almost ran as an independent Unionist MP in a Northern Ireland by-election. I have always found it difficult to understand the appeal of a political movement whose raison d'être is to stage provocative and insulting marches through the residential neighbourhoods of other religious groups. This is perverse even by Irish standards. The *Daily*'s Hastings wanted to pull British troops out, oblivious of the requirements of British sovereignty and the fate of the abandoned Ulster Unionists' majority.

Bombs planted by the Irish Republican Army had gone off in London streets and shops and then finally in 1996 at Canary Wharf, where our newspaper offices were housed. The bomb, intended primarily for our paper though other papers and large financial firms were also housed there, took the roof off the *Guardian's* printing plant, and so we printed their next day's edition. Several people died, including my newsagent, a pleasant East Indian who was stationed directly in front of our offices. As the *Telegraph* had substantial influence in Northern Ireland, Prime Minister Tony Blair intervened with me when he structured the Good Friday Agreement in 1998 to prevent Moore from endorsing a no-vote. Our editorial of support, a bland and tepid one at that, was wrung from the leader conference only by my threat to write the editorial myself – always a means of setting a fire under the editor's chair. I didn't mention the prime minister but said that we were not going to ally ourselves with the Sinn Fein terrorists and the Paisleyite anti-papist bigots in opposing an arrangement that, whatever its limitations, was supported by all respectable elements involved, including the British and Irish governments and parliaments. The *Telegraph* was not decisive in the referendum and chiefly spared itself needless embarrassment.

IF THE IRISH QUESTION – rather like the Quebec Question in Canada – was of little interest and matter to anyone but the British and some Irish Americans, the European Question was of tremendous importance to America but never to America's public, press, or political elites. The European Union (EU), headquartered in massive splendour in Brussels, is a huge, overbearing, and petulant organization. From 1996 to 2009, the EU commissioners have struggled to get their equally massive constitution (forty times longer than the American Constitution) ratified by member countries. Joining up to the EU is in effect resigning one's own national sovereignty. For America, it would be equivalent to Congress turning over most of its serious powers to some multinational institution of the Organization of American States who would in the name of unity "harmonize" its members' domestic, monetary, and foreign policies. Initially, it was thought all EU members would hold a referendum on the new constitution. When the French and Dutch referendums resulted in a "no" vote, Germany and the United Kingdom put their referendums on hold. The EU approach is that of an admirer turned stalker: Brussels never takes "no" for an answer. Should a referendum go against its constitution, the EU arranges either for a second vote (Ireland) or for the parliaments of the various countries to vote "yes" without the direct consent of the electorate. People cherish their national institutions, and while, to differing degrees, they may want to be part of this union – and its grants, trade policies, subsidies, and transfer payments – electorates tend to dislike giving away their sovereignty. The parlous financial situation is gradually weakening the EU, a situation not helped by the inclusion of countries from Central and Eastern Europe with tottering economies, nor by the propensity of the EU to leap on every costly passing bandwagon, such as the unachievable 20 per cent reduction in carbon emissions, despite unconvincing evidence connecting them to global warming, which it is not clear is actually occurring.

As it is now, the EU is an attempt to set up a challenge to American power by a continent that still wants America to solve its problems. For some reason, no U.S. administration has really grasped this, though Nixon and Reagan and Bush Jr. all expressed reservations (to me) about the motives of the Euro-integrationists. Domestically, it is an attempt to establish permanently a body of regulators (in Brussels) composed of the most enthusiastic Euro-joiners among the politicians and civil servants of the member countries and turn absolutely everyone else, including the political classes of each European country, into the regulated, following the rules of some polite version of syndicalism. The *Daily Telegraph* had been, with *The Times*, the *Mail*, and the *Sun*, the leading bulwark against Britain being subsumed into a federal Europe, in spite of the enthusiasm of Max Hastings for signing up.

Western Europe is a tired, socialistic continent, without the energy even to reproduce biologically, almost incapable of private-sector job creation, and reduced in strategic terms to forming a European Union rapid deployment force that was, in fact, for some years nothing more than parade ground units ready to march down the main boulevards of the European capitals on their national days and often even relying on American air transport to get them there. Nine of the ten most aged populations in the world are in Western Europe. In Italy, only three people in ten work, at least officially. In fact, many retirees work in the grey market. In the 1990s, in the United States, 44 million jobs were eliminated as superfluous or inefficient and 75 million private-sector jobs were created, for 31 million net new jobs. In the European Union, outside the United Kingdom, a net 5 million jobs were created in the same decade, all in the public sector. The paradox of this has been that the Europeans do not see that American power, which they resent, maintains their ability to be weak, to have shrunken defence budgets, a relatively stagnant economy, and a general attitude of righteous lassitude.

Cardinal Carter had me to dinner with the visiting Joseph Cardinal Ratzinger, later Pope Benedict XVI, in 1990 at his home. Only the three of us and Cardinal Carter's chancellor were present. Cardinal Ratzinger lamented "the slow suicide of Europe:" its population was aging and shrinking, and the unborn were being partly replaced with unassimilable immigrants. He thought that Europe would awaken from its torpor, but that there were difficult days ahead. Like other cardinals of my acquaintance (including our host), he was a far-sighted judge of important secular matters.

IT WASN'T EASY TO MAKE these strategic points in serious circles in the United States. Senator Phil Gramm of Texas, former chairman of the Senate Banking Committee, was my great ally in Washington, urging that the U.S. compete with Europe for intimacy with Britain, invite the U.K. into the North American Free Trade Area, and not just wave Britain into the arms of the Franco-Germans. We testified together at the U.S. International Commerce Commission in 2002 that the United Kingdom should be invited to join the renamed and generally expanded North American Free Trade Area.

The United States, through much of the Cold War and for a time after, tried to propel Britain by the scruff of the neck and the small of the back into Europe, understandably, to make better Cold Warriors of the Europeans. By sheer momentum, the U.S. continued to advocate this policy after the collapse of the Soviet Union and the Soviet bloc, oblivious of the fact that this was not in the U.S. national interest. The well-regarded

U.S. ambassador in London, Raymond Seitz (who became a Telegraph plc director when he retired and will, unfortunately, re-enter this narrative), told me Britain should join Europe "to keep German troops out of Paris." I suggested he was over-reacting.

As with Ireland, I found myself refereeing internecine disputes between our editors. Max thought Europe essentially a good thing to be furthered, so long as it didn't lead to higher taxes or more belligerent trade unions. Max was not very contemplative, enjoyed holidays in Italy, and was generally able to rely on his editorial entourage and his friendship with Douglas Hurd to reassure himself that the concerns of the skeptics were ill-founded. Charles feared the worst of the Brussels Euro-government and was frequently encouraged in this by Euro-spokespeople, who spewed out the thousands of insane directives purporting to regulate everything from lavatory manners in European boarding houses to the size of bananas and condoms.

The head of the European Commission, Jacques Delors, formerly France's socialist finance minister, poured gasoline on the fire by telling British labour audiences that whatever Margaret Thatcher had taken from them, Europe would restore. Improving relations between the European nationalities is a great and admirable development, but the official agents of it are often hard to take seriously. This was well before Europe's current problems began to hemorrhage.

THE *TELEGRAPH* AND ITS READERS were naturally very much involved with European politics. Germany remained the most formidable power, and through my friend George (Lord) Weidenfeld, German chancellor Helmut Kohl invited me several times to dinner with him in the Kanzlerbungalow, the quaint Bauhaus glass house on the east bank of the Rhine where the chancellor lived in Bonn.

Kohl was very preoccupied with the Battle of Verdun, where several family members died in both World Wars. From my days as a teenaged summer tour guide in and around Paris, I was able to go verbally over the ground with him, from the Douaumont Fort, then the largest in the world, where Charles de Gaulle was taken prisoner when wounded, on March 1, 1915, to the monument to André Maginot, to the Ossuary, where there are the remains of 180,000 French combat dead.

Kohl allowed that it had been one of the great frustrations of his career that he had made so little headway with Thatcher in alleviating her anti-German attitudes. (I have often thought that one of the major strategic errors of the German air war was bombing Grantham, Lincolnshire, where Margaret Thatcher was growing up. She has spoken of it angrily for more than sixty years since.)

A stroll around the forest of building cranes of Berlin induced the feelings that disquiet Helmut Kohl. There is something of the national teenager in the unfocused muscularity of great and proximate monuments of the official architecture of successive failed regimes in Germany's tortured history, in layers like those of a tree from Prussian times to the fall of the Wall. There is great strength and attractiveness, and even occasionally charm, but also the uneasy feeling of awkwardness and lack of discernment and judgment. Frederick the Great's Brandenburg Gate, Bismarck's Reichstag, soon the Hohenzollerns' restored *schloss*, remnants of the Third Reich including Hitler's sealed bunker, and Stalin's gigantic East German embassy are all within a few hundred yards of each other. Kohl feared these lacunae and developed a policy of Euro-federalism as an antidote. I am convinced he sincerely meant "a European Germany, not a German Europe."

Charles Moore, our foreign editor, and our Berlin correspondent and I visited Kohl's successor, Chancellor Gerhard Schröder. The government had moved from Bonn to Berlin. The Brobdingnagian new chancellery was not ready, so we visited Schröder in his temporary office, formerly occupied by Ulbricht and Honecker, in a Stalinist Socialist Realist building in East Berlin. With wooden floors and stained-glass windows and Spartan furniture, it looked more like the refectory of an underfunded religious order than the office of the leader of one of the world's greatest nations. Where Kohl felt passionately the dangerous currents of German history, Schröder seemed to me a modified Bill Clinton; none of the policy wonk but all of the good-time Charlie with a twinkle in his eye.

The two issues that caused me the greatest controversy were my views on Israel and America. These issues were never a formal part of my later troubles, but the intensity of antagonism among much of the British media and chattering classes levelled against Israel and America was notable –

and noted by American commentators in the *Wall Street Journal* and elsewhere. I was not on the acceptable side of the street as far as these two matters were perceived in London society, politics, or the media. When my troubles began, it was payback time, reflected in the heightened hostility of much of the U.K. press. This hostility was eagerly picked up by both the Canadian press and Murdoch's *New York Post,* though neither shared the anti-Israeli sentiment. But the repetition of these damaging stories made dampening Hollinger's corporate strife that much harder. This steady stream of stories in New York, London, and Toronto, accompanied by the most irritating photos or cartoons, contributed to a confected atmosphere of received contempt for us that grew like Topsy and held that we were crooks, and nasty self-important crooks at that. This had to be grappled with sometimes, to prevent it from becoming accepted conventional wisdom.

IT WAS ALLEGED THAT UNDER the saturnine Hebraic influence of Barbara, I was a Zionist propagandist. There is no truth to any of this. Barbara is unwaveringly proud of her Jewish heritage but not a particularly peppy Zionist, and finds the State of Israel difficult and often unreasonable. She believes that, having been established, it should not fail, and particularly not at the hands of those who would cheerfully kill all the Jews. Nor does she understand why Israel should be held accountable for a level of behaviour that no other country in the world – least of all its neighbours – must meet. I share her view and did long before we were together.

The antagonism toward Israel in the U.K. and much of Europe was and remains intense. In December 2002, we held a dinner at our home in London for then *Spectator* editor Boris Johnson, after his election to parliament as Michael Heseltine's successor in Henley. The guest list came from Boris, and among those he invited was the French ambassador, Daniel Bernard, whom I knew quite cordially. He was a protegé of Chirac's and a fairly integral Gaullist in his foreign policy view – one that included championing Quebec's independence, which he now privately acknowledged was a lost cause, and truckling to the Arabs while disparaging Israel.

Bernard maintained the customary Gaullist facade for his position by claiming to be opposed to anti-Semitism and not to be poorly disposed to the United States, except when that country was manifestly in error, which is at practically all times when it is not engaged in assisting France. He spent most of his energies, as the Quai d'Orsay has since de Gaulle's return to office in 1958, harassing and obstructing the elaboration of American foreign policy. Bernard was rather accessible to the Arab interpretation of Middle East peace issues.

He and I were seated at the same table, and at one point he volunteered that most of the problems of the world were now the fault of "that shitty little country Israel." I expressed some incredulity and asked in French if I had heard him correctly. He assured me that I had and repeated the same words in French, adopting "shitty" as an anglophone might adopt *coup d'état* or *savoir faire*. I mentioned the episode to Barbara, who was writing a column on the acceptability of anti-Semitism in polite society. Barbara referred to this incident and to some other social utterances of the same general tenor in her column but carefully wrote only of "the ambassador of a prominent EU country." Other newspapers began phoning around, and Bernard's staff unwisely put their hand up and admitted that their man was the author of the remark. The French embassy then began the casuistical process of redefining the phrase, claiming that the ambassador meant only to say that "Israel was a small but not undistinguished country." This was enough for someone to put a sign on one of the editorial lavatory doors at the *Telegraph*: "A place for the Performance of Small but not Undistinguished Activities."

A considerable furor ensued throughout Europe. Some suggested that Barbara had breached etiquette by printing remarks made at a private dinner at her home. Many were outraged at the ambassador's inelegant and undiplomatic remarks, and many were also amazed that a prominent French ambassador would be so stupid as to confess to such comments. Bernard wrote the *Telegraph* a letter for publication claiming that he had said nothing of the kind. I told the editor that he should advise the ambassador that we would run the letter but would put beside it a refutation by the other people at the table, and that he might prefer something that would improve appearances somewhat. He did, and wrote a tasteful and not evidently mendacious letter that we printed without comment. I called upon him and we agreed that the incident was now closed. He was soon transferred to Algiers, far from a promotion, and unfortunately died prematurely a couple of years later.

I don't find that anti-Semitism in Britain goes much beyond people looking down their noses at "Jew" matters and the occasional act of vandalism by Muslim thugs or non-sectarian skinheads. But there is room for a less quiescent interpretation, and those moments sometimes occurred in the pages of the *Spectator*. My friend Taki Theodoracopulos, one of my staunchest supporters in my recent problems, wrote a piece in early 2001 that effectively stated that the United States Air Force was commanded by the Mossad in the Israeli interest and that the Israeli Defence Forces, as a matter of blood sport, impaled and otherwise killed Palestinian youth. I came home to find Barbara in tears over the piece. She found the level of Jew-baiting in London perfectly tolerable, but to see it in one of our own publications written by a man she both liked and admired hurt her deeply.

Tears or not, the piece was too much for me. I took recourse to the standard practice in rebutting anti-Semitism since the time of Dreyfus and Zola, with a *J'accuse* response. I advised Boris Johnson that it was on its way, catching him on a Saturday evening on his cellphone, as he explained, at the top of the "hardest, steepest piste in Gstaad, staring into the face of death." Shortly after the fracas with Taki, Piers Paul Read, A.N. Wilson, and William Dalrymple, three competent writers of high position and reputation in British journalism, and Charlie Glass, a former correspondent and hostage in Beirut who fell in love with his guards and captors, wrote a letter to the *Spectator* decrying my ownership of the *Jerusalem Post* and comparing the newspaper unfavourably to the *Jerusalem Report*, which in fact we also owned. Through leaks from their chums at the *Spectator* they learned of their error and tried to withdraw their letter. But I would not allow it to be withdrawn. (I had banned Dalrymple for a time from the *Telegraph* after he published a fictitious account of Israeli desecration of Christian religious sites.) The fierce firefight that bubbled on in the pages of the *Spectator* was a moderately entertaining read.

THE OSLO ACCORDS IN 1994 opened up the fissures within our newspapers, especially the *Jerusalem Post*, over the Mid-East peace process. The accords committed Israel to handing over Gaza and, in sequence, most of the West Bank, and committed the Palestinians to ending terrorism, assisting the Israelis in rounding up designated terrorists, expunging the anti-Israel clauses from the Palestine National Charter, and maintaining a police force of twenty-eight thousand lightly armed officers. Yasser Arafat never honoured any of this. Instead, he developed a heavily armed, quasi-military police force of forty thousand, provided no co-operation at all in combating terrorism, and unctuously blamed other Palestinian elements for the continuation of terrorism. The National Charter remains un-amended more than fifteen years after the Oslo Accords.

Editor David Bar-Illan attacked the Oslo settlement in the *Jerusalem Post*. I wrote a piece for the *Jerusalem Post*, the *Daily Telegraph* (which endorsed Oslo), and some of our other newspapers, offering the most tepid endorsement of Oslo but urging ratification by the Knesset (parliament). I thought it would be disastrous for Israel's credibility if the Knesset repudiated Rabin and Peres. Bar-Illan took civilized issue with me in the *Post*, while the publisher, the militant Colonel Yehuda Levy, who on occasion attended the office in his battle fatigues (though claims that he brought his Uzi machine gun with him are untrue), and the former acting editor, David Gross, wrote fulminations against me, in the usual contentious Israeli manner. This was a dust-up of rare proportions as the general public made their views known on our letter pages and in competing media. I was attacked in Israel, Britain, and Canada by the Arabists and the general ranks of pacificators of all ethnicities as being insufficiently enthusiastic about this Nobel Prize–winning breakthrough for peace. And in Israel and in some circles in the United States, I was rounded upon with equal fervour for approving the sale of Israel down the river to its enemies.

I have always understood the Arab view that the terrible things that were done to the Jews in Europe in the 1930s and 1940s were not done by the Arabs and that the great powers had sought to expiate their own indifference to the plight of the Jews by giving them Arab land. But it was not Arab land. There has been a continuous Jewish presence in what is now Israel for thousands of years, and the land that is Israel has never been governed by Arabs; the Romans were replaced by the Byzantines, then the Turks, then the Crusaders, the Turks again, the British, and finally the Jews.

The existence of Israel is symbolic of the Arab decline in general over many centuries, and Israel is not the cause of that decline. The answer to the decline is for the Arabs to govern themselves more intelligently, to become a factor in the world for reasons other than the exportation of oil and terror, and to add the cubit to their own stature necessary to end the unnatural obsession with Israel. They are surely capable of it. Much of the preoccupation with a return to 1967 borders with Israel is also humbug. Most of the militant Arabs, when questioned closely, do not accept those borders; they are merely a waystation on the trek to the total occupation of Israel by an Arab majority. The demand for a return to the 1967 borders presumes that those borders had an unbreakable legitimacy, and it assumes that the initiation of aggressive war and response to it, and victory and defeat in that war, are interchangeable positions. The Arabs unleashed the 1967 war, and Israel won it, though Israel made serious strategic errors after that war.

The Arabs were never going to be pushed out, and they were never going to become contented citizens who would prefer a good Jew to a bad Arab as a leader. This had effectively been the contention of Jerusalem's splendid fourteen-term mayor, Teddy Kollek. But the 1967 borders had severely divided Israel, leaving the West Wall in Muslim hands and reducing Israel to nine miles in width as its narrowest point. The outline of a durable peace emerged in the discussions that Ehud Barak had with Yasser Arafat at Camp David in 2000. The Palestinians would have a state. Whatever the doubtfulness of their claim, being an indistinct nationality with an ancient and inexact name, they had been dispossessed, and the Israeli argument that they had departed voluntarily in 1948 is sophistry.

At the *Telegraph*, the divisions between those who tended to note perceived Jewish particularities and those who didn't were easy to notice. We had a group of well-connected Englishmen, for whom "Jew" matters caused them to look as if their fish were off a bit.

Princess Margaret, who took a drink and was frequently a rather entertaining woman, used to exclaim: "Oh, that is Jew!" On one occasion, she distinguished between two lyrical variations of Frank Sinatra and Barbra Streisand, saying "Sinatra is Sicilian; Streisand is Jew." (The fact that they were both Americans was deemed superfluous.) This practice reminded me of some rabidly partisan U.S. Republicans (starting with Senator

Joseph R. McCarthy) who always refer venomously to "the Democrat Party."

Max's subsequent marriage to a Jewish woman complicated things. Max told me he became so accustomed to leaving dinner parties at his wife's insistence, because of what she regarded as anti-Semitic slights, that he had to remind her on one occasion that they were in their own home and she could throw out whomever she wished, but he wasn't going anywhere. For them, any peace agreement would be progress and any absence of peace was Israeli unreasonableness. Charles Moore was better than that but lapsed easily into tired British relativism. It seemed to me, though I know of no one who agrees with me, that the otherwise inexplicable British dislike of the Jews comes in part from the unpleasant fact that the British effectively sold the same real estate (Palestine) twice in the darkest days of World War I. They feel the Israelis are ingrates, caused unnecessary agitation in the twilight of their empire, and since there has never really been any solution except to divide the territory between the two claimants, that the Israelis should have been more conciliatory, as the stronger faction.

WHEN THE LATE AUGUSTO PINOCHET, the former Chilean president, came to Britain in 1998 on a military purchase mission, with a special passport and a Ministry of Defence escort, he was briefly hospitalized in Britain and subsequently detained on a technically defective warrant taken out in Spain by a headline-seeking Spanish far-left judge and prosecutor, under pan-EU rules. The warrant alleged atrocities by Pinochet against Spaniards in Chile at the time of the overthrow of the Communist Allende government in 1973.

The history of the Spanish left would suggest they were not a natural source for complaints about civil rights. Clearly, this was an internal Chilean matter, which was the subject of a delicate balance of political power within that country. Eventually, the British judicial process established that the only period for which complaints against Pinochet could be heard was after he had reconstituted a democratically elected congress and a popularly approved constitution. The clear and unhelpful lesson of this ill-considered intervention to the world's dictators was that they should never step down but hang on to power, like Franco, the Castros, or Robert Mugabe. To retire voluntarily as Pinochet had done, relinquishing absolute power, would render any dictator's life hazardous.

The day after Pinochet's detention, Henry Kissinger telephoned me and urged editorial opposition to what had happened. He'd also phoned Rupert Murdoch. We had already adopted that line, as had Murdoch. Barbara and I went to lunch with Pinochet in the modest house where he was detained near Windsor. A family member stayed with him at all times, and he had become Internet-adept, keeping in close touch with Chile by this means.

Though in his mid-eighties, Pinochet struck us as alert, cheerful, relatively uncomplaining, and somewhat mystified by the inhospitable reception accorded him. His movements were restricted to about twenty feet out to the front or back of the house where he lived. The five or six soldiers on guard in the house watched television all evening. He was at pains to say that he had spent much of his life in barracks and that his custodians were "nice fellows." But the noisiness and bright lights that illuminated the house all night made sleep difficult. Pinochet, a fervent Roman Catholic, was not allowed to go to church. For alleged security reasons, he was not even allowed to go out for a drive.

I spoke about Pinochet's detention with both the prime minister and the lord chancellor (Derry Irvine, who called it "a cock-up"), without effect as far as I know, though he was released eventually and lived on to a prodigious age. I don't whitewash Pinochet or the horrors of the Allende-Pinochet struggle, but this was neither the place nor the way to resolve these deep grievances.

WHEN BARBARA AND I MARRIED, I was living in a roomy cottage-style house with a specially built library and solarium in Highgate, north London, on a double lot adjoining a park. My children had returned to Toronto, and their attic playroom had become Barbara's workroom, where she became accustomed to "friendly little spiders marching solemnly across my word processor." She did not want a large house, just a more centrally located one. London, where she was born and had spent part of her childhood, had been her home for the last eighteen years, and she had worked fiercely to develop close friendships. We compromised, moving to a larger home than Barbara had wanted but in a more central location.

Later, fantastic stories circulated of the opulence of our homes. Our London home had five bedrooms, a dining room, and a very generous but awkwardly U-shaped drawing room. Much of the remainder was used as book and work space. There was a very small exercise room and a rather showy indoor swimming pool and Jacuzzi decorated with faux-Greco mosaics installed by the former owner. The house was large, certainly, but far from grandiose or overpowering.

My house in Toronto was the single place that could always bring me peace. I had rebuilt and extended my parents' house and expanded the property to almost eleven acres, unusually generous for a Toronto home. The contents are not particularly noteworthy, but it is a correct and pleasing Georgian house improved since 1976. Now it has two double-height, connected libraries entirely panelled in oak as well as a spacious workroom for Barbara with large windows and French doors overlooking the gardens. The house probably contains more than twenty thousand books, as well as the hundreds of still unpacked boxes of books that were moved there from London. The rebuilding of the house was the first serious residential project of Thierry Despont, a French architect and Harvard alumnus who has gone on to great architectural eminence, so it is a milestone in a noteworthy career. Despont subsequently designed a handsome indoor swimming pool, a walled garden, and a chapel, which was consecrated by Cardinal Gerald Emmett Carter and Cardinal Aloysius M. Ambrozic of Toronto. We have had a number of events there, including my installation as a Knight of the Order of St. Gregory the Great, and I use the chapel every day when I am in that house.

I am always happy there. I was brought up on the property and know most of the trees individually. (No, I do not converse with them.) I could almost walk around its acres of lawns and glades blindfolded. It has been my address for sixty years. Whatever the fluctuations of my relations with Canada, I have always felt that that house is home. I still do.

Barbara did not want anything in Palm Beach; I did. My house there was a family home on a quiet street. It had no ocean or water views, and to her it was just another house in one of the most boring cities in North America. She had accepted Toronto out of spousal respect for the ties of family and sentiment. We compromised by moving to a larger house at the far south end of Palm Beach spanning ocean to lake with fine views of both.

We eventually bought an apartment in New York. It had two bedrooms, and two workrooms. On the fashionable side of town, on an unfashionable second floor, the apartment was perfectly commodious for our purposes. I could work there and make business telephone calls feeling confident that they would not be the subject of office discussion. The legend created by my opponents in the media that features Barbara and me as latter dissolute Caesars, lolling and social climbing in palaces bought from my pilferage of public companies, is unfounded in all respects, as was eventually made clear in court. It is particularly unjust to lay any of this on Barbara. When I married her, she sat happily most evenings at her desk in a comfy but small flat with a galley kitchen, wearing a telephone headset as she gathered research for her newspaper and magazine columns. Her social list seemed to consist of six close friends whose time zones coincided with her nocturnal working hours.

Unfortunately, the media has represented her as a Marie Antoinette, bullying or inducing me into the pathways of extravagance and even ostentation. Barbara dislikes dinner parties, especially her own, and one of the few aspects of our current difficulties she enjoys is the decline of social pressures. I like large houses, and I like interesting people and stimulating dinner conversation. The now infamous photograph of us going to an eighteenth-century *fête de campagne* costume party at Kensington Palace dressed supposedly as Marie Antoinette and Cardinal Richelieu showed, in fact, Barbara as an ersatz bourgeoise and me as a generic cardinal, both of unknowable nationality. We couldn't make up our minds about whether to attend, and by the time we did, we had only a day before the party to find our costumes. Her blue Viyella dress and my red religious garb were the two last available outfits at Angels Fancy Dress. Unlike my cardinal, Richelieu had a moustache and goatee, and always wore the insignia of some of his many offices (from court chaplain to grand admiral), and while Marie Antoinette may well have sported the elaborate hairdo that Barbara's Lebanese hairdresser so brilliantly designed, I doubt if paniered Viyella would have been the late Queen's choice even for shepherdess days.

Regrettably, we seem to have reached the point in the United States, Britain, and Canada where if a man enjoys himself, knows some famous people, expresses opinions in public, and has a glamorous and autonomously successful wife, he mounts the guillotine of public and media opprobrium. Perhaps it has always been so. Anyway, I don't doubt I could have played my cards more diplomatically (and will when I return).

THERE IS A PASSAGE AT THE beginning of Thackeray's *Book of Snobs* that Barbara was particularly fond of reading to me when urging me to come to sleep. I thoroughly enjoyed a varied social life and at the same time I was committed to our business and wanted to write books. I normally got up between ten and eleven, reached the office at eleven to eleven-thirty, left at seven, returned from dinner, if out, or turned to work if in, at about eleven, and worked until around 4 a.m. She would enter my study at some point, usually around two-thirty when I was still writing or exchanging transatlantic faxes in a difficult deal, William Makepeace in hand, and intone: "'I have long gone about with a conviction on my mind that I had work to do – a Work, if you like, with a great W; a Purpose to fulfil; a chasm to leap into, like Curtius, horse and foot; a great Social Evil to Discover and to Remedy. That conviction has pursued me for years. It has dogged me in the Busy Street; Seated itself by me in The Lonely Study; Jogged my elbow as it lifted the Wine-cup at the Festive Board . . .'" and so on. The passage continues in that vein, and is highly amusing. I thought I was more focused than that, but it was a cautionary tale, and somewhat germane. Neither Barbara nor I knew quite how apt it would become.

OUR COMPANY'S ADVISORY BOARD annual dinner grew out of the old Hollinger Mines dinner, and in the reflections of critics, the advisory board was transmogrified into a snobs' ladder for "social climbing." That I enjoyed contact with the extraordinary mix of people we had on the board was undeniable. They enjoyed each other. Otherwise, they would not have come, because I didn't pay them much.

Allan Gotlieb had served with distinction as Canada's ambassador to the United States. I invited him to become the publisher of Canada's *Saturday Night* magazine and a director of Hollinger Inc. He suggested to me in 1992 that we might want to follow the example of a number of companies and set up an advisory board. These were essentially groups of exceptional people, often retired, who would gather once a year to give their views of the world for a modest fee and would generally be available throughout the year in the event of a specialized need. They had no legal liability, unlike an orthodox director, and so it was a convenient arrangement and not overly costly to the company. I thought it would be a resource for the management and help broaden the views of editors and journalists. Allan was well placed to recruit interesting Americans, and I thought I could round up some interesting British and Europeans.

I was accused first of hobnobbing and then of orchestrating and bankrolling an international right-wing conspiracy. We recruited Gianni Agnelli (controlling shareholder of Fiat and legendarily stylish Italian senator and former playboy); Dwayne Andreas (builder and head of Archer Daniels Midland, the world's greatest agribusiness, and one of America's most politically influential businessmen); Moshe Arens (former Israeli defence minister and ambassador to the United States); David Brinkley (renowned newscaster and commentator for NBC and ABC); Zbigniew Brzezinski (national security advisor under President Jimmy Carter); William F. Buckley (famed conservative publisher, author, and debater); Peter (Lord) Carrington (former U.K. foreign and defence secretary and secretary-general of NATO); Martin Feldstein (chairman of President Ronald Reagan's Council of Economic Advisers); Valéry Giscard d'Estaing (former president of France); Sir James Goldsmith (flamboyant anglo-French financier and political activist); Chaim Herzog (former president of Israel); Joseph Joffe (German magazine editor and commentator); Henry Kissinger (former U.S. secretary of state and national security advisor); Richard Perle (President Reagan's assistant secretary of defense for national security policy); Jacob (Lord) Rothschild (financier and patron of the arts); Margaret Thatcher (former U.K. prime minister); Paul Volcker (former chairman of the U.S. Federal Reserve); George Will (U.S. columnist and commentator); and, later, former U.S. House Speaker Newt Gingrich. Apart from Kissinger, Perle, Gotlieb, and me, some directors also entered in fully, including Richard Burt, Marie-Josée Kravis, Robert Strauss, George (Lord) Weidenfeld, and, on one occasion, Cardinal Carter.

It was a remarkably talented group and no hallelujah chorus for the American right. Jimmy Goldsmith was at this point quite critical of the Americans, as was Valéry Giscard d'Estaing much of the time. (Goldsmith created a rather awkward atmosphere at a small dinner I gave in Paris for Pamela Harriman, the U.S. ambassador to France, by his aggressive remarks about President Clinton, to which she responded by placing her handbag on the table and refusing to either eat or speak. It was not my most rousing success as a host.)

My original point in agreeing with Allan Gotlieb's suggestion for an advisory board was that it would be an interesting association and might help to de-Southam-ize some of our journalists by introducing Canadian journalists and editors to the world and possibly even liberating British journalists from some of their stereotypes about the United States.

Our Advisory Board embodied a wealth of experience. Gianni Agnelli, next to the Pope probably the most admired man in Western Europe since the death of Charles de Gaulle, died in 2003, after Fiat, the greatest of all his passions, encountered severe difficulties, from which it has largely recovered. He served with Rommel in Africa – "a star," he called him – and then with the Italian contingent in Russia. He concluded the war in the Italian army, fighting on the Allied side to liberate Italy from the Germans, and pointed out to me from his yacht on Lake Como the approximate place where Mussolini was shot by partisans after being apprehended trying to escape Italy dressed as a German soldier.

When asked how he had arranged for the Fiat shareholders to receive the company's profits and the Italian government to defray much of the losses when they occurred, he stared into the distance and said, "You must remember, we are the country of Machiavelli." But not even Machiavelli would have had the imagination to devise some of Gianni's initiatives. When he lost control of the shoproom floor and the Communist unions brought Fiat to the verge of bankruptcy, he brought in Libyan Colonel Muammar Gadhafi as a sizable shareholder.

When the crisis had passed, he prevailed upon his sister Sunni, then Italy's deputy foreign minister, to advise the American ambassador in Rome that Fiat might not be eligible for defence contracts in the United States because of having a designated terrorist government as a large shareholder. Fiat was duly advised that this was the case, and the Italian parliament obligingly assisted in removing Gadhafi as a shareholder, albeit at a substantial profit.

Dwayne Andreas (who built up Archer Daniels Midland from a few grain elevators to an immense company) was friendly with all American politicians. He could mobilize the farm state senators and on any important matter colluded with Lane Kirkland of the American Federation of Labor and Congress of Industrial Organizations to round up an insuperably large number of senators. The irony was especially cruel when this intimate of Thomas E. Dewey (who died in Dwayne's Sea View Hotel in Miami Beach), Richard Nixon, Hubert Humphrey, Howard Baker, and Bob Dole, among many other prominent politicians he had befriended and supported, came to grief in family legal problems. His declining years were shadowed by the imprisonment of his son.

Chaim Herzog had been nicknamed Vivian when he had served in the British army in the Second World War, because people couldn't pronounce his first name. His father had been the chief rabbi of Northern Ireland. After the war, Herzog joined the Israeli independence movement and subsequently became one of the leading lawyers in Israel, a member of the Knesset, an ambassador, the military governor of Jerusalem, a chairman of one of the country's largest companies, and ultimately the president of the State of Israel. While a slightly ponderous man, he was fascinating to me because of his recollections of the kaleidoscope of life he had witnessed.

It was a fierce passion for history that interested me in this group. Herzog had fought with Ben Gurion. Giscard d'Estaing had worked closely with de Gaulle. Peter Carrington commanded the defence of a reach of the south shore of Britain in 1940 "with fifty World War I rifles, one antiquated field piece, and my revolver, but it never occurred to me that we would not win." A few weeks before, he had stood for seven hours in chest-deep water at Dunkirk, waiting to be evacuated. When he recounted being strafed by German aircraft, almost run over by Allied ships, and almost incinerated by gas flaming on the waters, he drily repeated what his brother-in-law, a banker, had then said: "I cannot believe that this operation has come off as planned." Lord Carrington is an inexhaustible storehouse of amusing recollections and spontaneous quips. There are few people still active who can authoritatively express, naturally and even soulfully, rather than surmise, the unconquerable will of Britain in a time when the whole future of civilization depended on so few warriors, very young and very brave. He held the small dinner on his eightieth birthday party at the German embassy in London: he wished to emphasize his desire for good relations with Germany, having seen at first-hand the devastation of that country in 1945. He is the ultimate Whig nobleman.

I remember reading of Giscard d'Estaing's prowess as de Gaulle's finance minister when I was sixteen years old and he, aged thirty-four, delivered lengthy and detailed budget speeches to the National Assembly from memory. I also remember when he deserted the general in 1969 "with sadness but with certitude," providing the margin of victory for de Gaulle's enemies. I had not, until fairly shortly before, dreamt of having the opportunity to sit in Giscard d'Estaing's house, brandy in hand, and gently ask the former president of the republic about these times and events.

Many books have been written about Sir James Goldsmith. His obituaries described him as "one of the most buccaneering and charismatic figures" of our time. On his father's side, he was descended from a prominent Frankfurt Jewish banking family. His mother was a French Catholic. His own business skills were superb and made him an early billionaire. I met him through Andrew Knight, then editor of *The Economist* (later for three years the chief executive of The Telegraph plc) at a *diner à trois*. Afterwards, Goldsmith invited me to lunch at his office and introduced me to his circle, the first of a number of occasions staged in order to try to recruit the *Telegraph* to one or another of his mad causes.

When I first arrived in Britain in 1986, Goldsmith was a great legend. I remember seeing his performance at the U.S. senatorial committee over his hostile takeover attempt of one of the country's leading rubber companies. The utility of a "white knight" was raised. He responded, referring literally to pigmentation and honours: "I'm white, I'm a knight." His most famous aphorism was "When one marries one's mistress, it creates a vacancy." Jimmy had several wives and concurrent bearers of children, and assaulted bourgeois sensibilities. He was a remarkably vital, formidable, powerful presence. Exquisitely mannered, perfectly tailored, physically imposing, graceful like a great cat, very courteous yet evidently capable of savage verbal outbursts, he was the most compelling outsider I have known.

With his comrades and acolytes, Goldsmith operated a Darwinian parallel establishment that used to be known in its heyday as the Clermont set.

It mocked and shocked the British establishment. John Aspinall (Aspers), who founded the Clermont Club in London's Mayfair in 1962 and used his casino profits to sustain wildlife sanctuaries in Britain for gorillas and tigers, was perhaps his closest friend.

After Aspinall lost a third keeper in the tiger cages of his splendid private zoo, the local municipality banned people from entering tiger cages. Aspers set up a great controversy, denouncing this as an infringement of the Magna Carta and of the birthright of the British people for a thousand years, hiring aircraft to tow banners proclaiming the right to enter tiger cages above the south shore sea resorts of Britain during the summer, and so forth. He formed a grand coalition from left to right, and when he overpowered the mystified and unoffending local council, he held a party at his casino, where Barbara sat next to the former (and future) far-left mayor of London, Ken Livingstone. (It was he whom Boris Johnson defeated in 2007, calling him "Ken Leavingsoon.") Other contemporaries included Jonathan Aitken (a member of parliament and Lord Beaverbrook's grand-nephew), the outrageous but likeable and often brave columnist Taki Theodoracopulos, of a Greek shipping family, and a number of others.

Aspers campaigned for Jonathan Aitken in his constituency and bellowed at the astonished voters to tear down their schools and hospitals, renounce their state benefits, refuse to pay their taxes, and return to the independent notion of citizenship of olden time. His colourful harangues were immensely popular.

From my earliest days as a resident in London, I became something of a habitué of these people. They wished to entice me, and the *Daily Telegraph*, into their counter-establishment. At this they were unsuccessful. I am no upholder of the establishment in Britain or elsewhere, but nor am I an anti-establishment iconoclast. Though I was not prepared to join them in their unholy apostasy, I loved them in a way. They were more loyal to me than was much of London's orthodox society. They were not going to succeed in establishing a new society, but they were faithful to themselves to the end. Jimmy fought an election campaign at the head of his preposterous Referendum Party, keeping the pancreatic cancer and chemotherapy treatments he was having a complete secret from the press. Although he achieved only about 1 per cent of the vote, he did help ensure that Britain would not join the European Monetary System without a referendum. He died less than eight weeks after the election.

He had previously been a member of the European parliament. He asked me how I thought he would get on as a legislator, and I replied that he would be a splendid success: he would ravish those women whose appearance warranted it, bribe the men, and reduce the already disorderly parliament in Strasbourg to chaos. He bellowed appreciatively and said that this was his intention exactly.

Goldsmith's parental skills were as novel as his marital notions. One day in about 1980, Jimmy discovered that his son from his second marriage, Manos, had sold the silver from Jimmy's London house to pay gambling debts at Aspinall's casino. He asked the *Daily Telegraph* information service to locate the closest community to the exact opposite side of the world from London. The answer was a small town on the south island of New Zealand. Jimmy telephoned the directory information of that town and arranged a menial job, at his own expense, for Manos in a restaurant there. Off the young man went.

Aspers also succumbed to cancer. I had always thought that when the end was near, John would go among his tigers and not return alive. He had lost half his face to cancer and then was mugged on the streets of Belgravia with his wife. Naturally he fought back. Henry Kissinger and I went out to Kent to see him two weeks before he died. He was as brave as one of his great beasts, though terribly withered by then. There was no self-pity, morbidity, or even apparent sadness. We took our leave with firm handshakes and reciprocal thanks. Henry wept discreetly.

Had they lived, both Goldsmith and Aspinall would have avoided the squalid and demeaning spectacle I am now undergoing. Their instincts would have told them to get clear of the corporate governance zealots before they could become homicidal Lilliputians.* They would have been

---

* A clarifying word about corporate governance: I personally took the telephone calls and replied to the letters and questions of doughty individuals, no matter how small their shareholdings and no matter how obscure or eccentric their concerns. I considered that anyone who had invested in our company was entitled to access to me. I was happy to do this and usually enjoyed the contact, especially in Britain and Australia, where such activist shareholders tended to be rather colourful. My objections were to corporate guerrilla war waged

invaluable through this difficult time and magnificent allies uncontami-
nated by the bourgeois notions of hypocritical seemliness that affected
many of my acquaintances. Jimmy's flamboyant and splendid widow,
Annabel, and her family, have been fiercely supportive. When the controversy arose over the cover-price cut at the *Telegraph* and Cazenoves scurried for cover in the almost unbroken City tradition, both men
congratulated me on not being intimidated by the false rules of a rigged
game. I miss them.

I sat beside Gianni Agnelli at the secular memorial service for Jimmy
Goldsmith in Smith Square. A succession of eulogists, from Margaret
Thatcher to Chief Buthelezi, remembered Jimmy, almost all with great eloquence. Toward the end, Gianni said to me, in his exquisite English accent
with slightly de-emphasized *r*'s: "It's so splendid it almost makes dying
worthwhile." Gianni's own funeral five years later required special trains to
bring mourners to Turin. His family shook hands with more than two
hundred and fifty thousand members of the public. All the leadership of
the Italian state and church were present; it was an occasion for almost
medieval popular grandiosity for the greatest Italian; not the pagan tribute
to the Western world's great outsider that Jimmy had earned.

In the egalitarian levelling that has made glamour repulsive and social
fraternization at any more intellectual a level than the bowling alley into
an orgy of toadyism or vulgar exhibitionism, going out to a sit-down dinner
is a sign of Ludovican self-importance. But as a general rule, hospitality is
done with *sprezzatura* – the effort concealed and all done with the appearance of ease, as Anthony Blunt defined it – and brings together good conversation and interesting people, then the palate, eye, and brain can be
pleased simultaneously.

I believe the Advisory Board served its purposes well, including that of
facilitating business opportunities for the company and sharing know-how.

by well-oiled institutional bully-boys, holding hands with their fellow raptors in violation of
the spirit of the securities rules, though their antics were generally and deliberately overlooked by the SEC, and using other peoples' money to masquerade as champions of the odd-
lot shareholders. Almost equally nauseating were those piously hypocritical executives who
appeased them and substituted richly compensated self-abasement for industrialism and
serious management.

By 2002, I had decided it would be wound up. The costs had spiralled up and it was also becoming too time-consuming. Our journalists had benefited as much as I thought they could, and besides, many of its members were getting on in years and beginning to lose touch. With the multiplication of advisory boards, general meetings, and symposiums, it was also becoming more difficult each year to get a good outside speaker. Allan Gotlieb argued strongly in support of retaining the Advisory Board on the grounds that it was the principal source of my standing and influence in the world, which to me was a convincing display that the time was more than ripe for its cessation.

A favourite insult of the prosecution at my trial in 2007 was to speak contemptuously of my wanting to go to tea with the Queen, as if such an outing were a vain frivolity. Had the Queen asked me to tea, I would have considered it a remarkable invitation. The Queen is a woman who has been at the forefront of much of contemporary history, has met almost all the people that our times have honoured. In a purely ex officio role as chairman of the *Telegraph*, I did meet the Royal Family, including the Queen, and more often the Queen Mother, who was a neverending source of anecdotal history and gave me several remembrances of Franklin Roosevelt.

In London, the Royal Family is a distinct social entity. They are naturally the ultimate leaders of society and continue to be the subject of a good deal of obsequious deference. They are, to the very limited degree that I know them, courteous and conscientious people. It would be an exaggeration to say that the hereditary principle has endowed the United Kingdom and the Commonwealth with a super-abundantly gifted first family. Their intelligences vary, but they work hard. The Queen Mother and Princess Diana were the great stars, as is now Prince William. Princess Alexandra is the most charming. The Duke of Edinburgh and the Princess Royal are both very intelligent. So, though not overly imaginative, is the Queen. Princess Diana came to dinner with us a couple of times and was very witty as well as very beautiful. She was scheming and was possessed by the fury of a scorned woman. The only brake on her republicanism was her desire to be mother of the King. Though uneducated, and with an office of giggly, jolly-hockey-sticks Sloane-rangers, Princess Diana was running a parallel monarchy in her last few years and was skating rings around the real Royals.

Royals are different. Polite though they are, they are almost never close to non-royals and have mastered the secret of aloofness. And they have a rural bourgeois perspective, even the wealthy European royals of the Bourbon tradition. I saw this most plainly at a birthday party, I believe it was his sixtieth, for the exiled king of Greece, Constantine, a very amiable man of monarchic mien. The party was held at Highgrove, the home of the Prince of Wales. Guests were primarily from the royal families of Europe. The few of us who were not members of a royal family included some of King Constantine's wealthy, Greek ship-owning backers and a few others. (Barbara, trapped in her social unease, which was especially acute when it came to royal families, had pleaded illness. This was not unfamiliar to me. When the Duke of Edinburgh came to Toronto and visited our house with newspaper mogul Ken Thomson to see my ship model and naval book collection, I had to plead her absence due to a New York commitment. She was in fact upstairs in her workroom behind a locked door.) Constantine's birthday party was an insight to royalty at play. Guests were entertained by a slapstick comedian wearing a dinner jacket and carrying a giant cello out of which he produced some dirty laundry, as if from a washing machine. This led to some slapstick of the British lavatory variety. All the royalty were shaking with laughter, tears streaming down their faces, from Princess Caroline of Monaco to the centenarian dowager Queen of Denmark, including both Queens Elizabeth. A delightful and intelligent Greek lady friend of mine was sitting next to me, and we stared at each other in straight-faced disbelief as the crowned and coroneted contents of the current Almanach de Gotha split their sides watching the buffoonery.

IT WAS INTERESTING TO CIRCULATE simultaneously in relatively exalted circles in London and New York. Where London mixed all manner of people, occupations, and nationalities together, reflecting the capital of an important country and the diverse nature of the crossroads city of the world, New York society was topped out by a few continuators of the Astor-Belmont-Vanderbilt 400 aristocracy of a century before. Beside and around it surged the teeming plutocracy and meritocracy of New York's mighty competition of achievers and hustlers in every field.

The different groups would come together at the expensive galas each championed in support of their preferred causes, especially the Metropolitan Museum and Metropolitan Opera, the Museum of Modern Art, and Carnegie Hall. In the great apartments of Park and Fifth Avenues, and along the East River north from 59th Street, apart from the permutated and adoptive aristocracy, only the odd museum director, orchestra conductor, diva, or writer would appear, and only the more culturally involved of the business community.

It was largely because of Brooke Astor, the crafty and timeless widow of Vincent Astor (who spent her first forty years – socially – climbing slowly, hand over hand, and literally knew the ropes), that the notion of a WASP aristocracy had a golden, fifty-year, Indian summer (WASP in style and foibles, as there were many Roman Catholics and Jews, some African-Americans, and even a few Muslims among them). It was always an unstable and not very legitimate patriciate, afflicted by philistinism, English-imitative, but stylish and brilliantly opulent, and most of its tenured regulars were pleasant and interesting. Their hospitality was always sumptuous.

As Johnson & Johnson heir David Netto said after being rushed by the Met (Museum), referring to Brooke Astor's comrades and social heirs, Jayne Wrightsman and Annette de la Renta, "They're irresistible, if that's your thing; living treasures, and you don't meet people like that every day. If you care about the 'top people,' you'll want to hang on. There's something about them that's pure magic." (*Rogues' Gallery*, Michael Gross, p. 476.)

That could include a little youthful hyperbole, but it is a convivial and sometimes swashbuckling group. It was in many ways all an imposture, as most of the doyennes had closets as full of skeletons as of couture, but this is the unwitting source of much of their interest. Although the noblesse oblige tradition of Roosevelts, Harriman, Sumner Welles, Douglas Dillon, David Bruce, the Dukes, and others has died out, Henry Kissinger has filled the public service and intellectual voids and has been bound to their souls with hoops of steel.

Brooke Astor kindled public curiosity by courting the press, and admitting some of them, such as Barbara Walters and Charlie Rose, to her inner circle, and by gaining publicity for her charitable works and by stepping out in splendid livery and with great panache. She was scrambling much of the way, and was conversationally pretty erratic at times. (She was a practising Episcopalian but gave a country home to Francis J. Cardinal Spellman, and later told me that Spellman had disappointed her because he was a sexual exhibitionist.) Spellman had disappointed her with private indiscretions, which, though not completely implausible, are not easily believable either and do not merit repetition here, but were a diverting conversational gambit.

Her last seven or eight years she was not really competent, and vulgar litigation has revealed a sad story of her later life. No one has taken up the torch to continue the same notion of a New York aristocracy, and the whole concept is probably long past its sell-by date. I must add one word of special thanks to Jayne Wrightsman, who has been a generous friend through thick and thin for thirty years. She is a voluntary owner of a "Conrad Will Win" T-shirt.

EARLIER IN THIS CHAPTER I mentioned how my pro-American sentiments were a source of enmity in the U.K. and to a lesser degree in Canada. When the tragedy of September 11, 2001, took place, Barbara and I were in Toronto preparing to leave the next day for New York. There was a tremendous outpouring of sympathy in the world. At a human level, it was hard not to identify with the thousands of innocent victims, the brave firefighters, and the unconquerable spirit of New York. Many were doubtless influenced by the unfamiliar spectacle of the United States as a victim. But it was clear from President George W. Bush's remarks before the day was over that it would not remain a victim for long.

In all our newspapers, as well as in the House of Lords, of which I was by then a member, and in a number of speeches and articles, I defended the post–September 11 Bush-Blair position, which attracted a rare congeries of opposition. The United States was accused of being trigger-happy. The mantra "They can't go it alone" was endlessly repeated, but its real meaning, of course, was that the United States could do just that, much to the consternation of those who found their own marginalization grating, but not sufficiently so to galvanize them into doing anything about it.

I have never understood where the idea arose that the armed forces of the United States could be deployed in response to successive acts of war against the United States only with the permission of the other permanent members of the United Nations Security Council – particularly France, Russia, and China. It was advocated, in effect, that the United States, having built and sustained an immense military capacity, had to put it at the behest of countries that did not wish the United States well, do not necessarily share its values, and affect a neutrality between, on the one hand, a wronged America and affronted international law and, on the other, the evil of Saddam Hussein. Obviously, no sane person in the United States would subscribe to any such concept.

In the Iraq debate in the House of Lords at the end of 2002 (where the Conservatives' votes were necessary to pass approval of the government's war policy), I said that this interpretation of the relationship between the United States and the United Nations Security Council was an attempt to treat the United States as a great St. Bernard dog, which would take the risks and do the work while others, and not necessarily genuine allies, would hold the leash and give the instructions. One of my noble colleagues leapt excitedly at the metaphor and asked if I had ever tried to restrain a St. Bernard bitch in heat. Another said that the U.S. was not a St. Bernard but a Rottweiler.

I was interested in ending the double stalemate with the two major Persian Gulf powers, Iran and Iraq, whose combined animosity to the West (just about all they could agree on) made it almost impossible to exercise any influence in the area. I also thought it would be useful to give the masses of an important Arab country a taste of power-sharing, if not perfect democracy. Saddam Hussein was an enthusiastic terrorist supporter in Israel and Palestine, and I was not especially concerned with weapons of mass destruction, as they could be eliminated without the drastic step of occupying the entire country.

At the time of the invasion of Iraq, I never imagined that the United States would disband the Iraqi armed forces and police, hurling four hundred thousand people into unemployment while leaving them their weapons and munitions, hoping they would all become quail hunters or target-shooting enthusiasts; this was arguably, along with failing to cut the Ho Chi Minh Trail in the Vietnam War, the greatest military blunder in U.S. history. Nor did I imagine that the United States would for a long time prove so inept at the manipulation of local factions. Nor that there would be such inadequate attention paid to protecting, among other sites, Iraq's electric generators, oil pipelines, and museums. (Of course, I also didn't imagine, and could not have conceived, that the United States would persecute me half to death either.)

By expanding its annual current account deficit to $800 billion and by stranding almost its entire conventional ground forces capability in Iraq and Afghanistan, the United States has reduced its influence in the world. If weakening the country was the aim of the French and Russians, instead of obstructing the United States in Iraq, they should have urged it forward vigorously.

For urging Canada to compete with the United States and take an imaginative role in reorienting the Western alliance, I was widely portrayed as an unpatriotic Canadian. For urging upon Britain a course that would preserve British identity and maximize Britain's advantages as vital to both Europe and America, I was reviled – by ultra-skeptic Enoch Powell and Euro-joiner Edward Heath, with both of whom I was reasonably cordial – as an American Trojan horse and by European commentators as a CIA parrot screeching at Europe from an ill-gotten gilded cage on Fleet Street. And in Israel, where we eventually moved the *Post* back from the Jabotinskyan inflexibility of David Bar-Illan to the pragmatic realism of Bret Stephens (now one of the *Wall Street Journal*'s writers), I was, like so many sober voices indigenous to the country, caught in the crossfire between the hardened factions pursuing peace or security, the one virtually to the exclusion of the other, when they are in fact ultimately inseparable.

My only serious political objective in the United Kingdom was to resist Euro-integration until Britain would not be trading the institutions that have served it well for centuries for inferior ones, would not be going back to pre-Thatcher tax levels and industrial relations, and would not be subsuming its relations with the United States into the relations of France and Germany with that country. Chancellor Kohl professed to find those criteria reasonable during our conversations. My brief period of modest influence in British public policy did not end as I would have wished, but my only serious public policy objective was embraced by a majority of Britons. I no longer have any standing, but I did what I could.

I have referred to my contacts with a number of leaders of several countries. The only request I have ever made of any government, apart from supplementing our requests for zoning changes in Chicago when we were building a new printing facility and redeveloping our office site there, was when I asked the incoming Harris government in Ontario not to impose compulsory helmets on adult bicyclers in the parks system. The new premier made an exemption in his order-in-council that has enabled me to continue my leisurely rides through the parks near my house in Toronto without putting on the airs of a Tour de France contestant. This is not much to show for millions of dollars of contributions and a great deal of editorial support and advocacy, but it is all I ever actually asked or specifically wanted.

[CHAPTER THREE]

IN 2000, NATIONAL POST EDITOR Ken Whyte was having a grand time badgering Prime Minister Jean Chrétien. Chrétien was formerly a 25 per cent owner of a golf club with an adjoining hotel that had received federal government assistance. As scandals go, this never seemed to me like a particularly promising one; however, Chrétien and his entourage added to their woes by allowing suspicious aspects of the problem to fester while trying to deter any official or journalistic research into the controversy. This was catnip to Whyte, an honest and straightforward man of the Prairies, apparently unaware of the traditional dangers of affronting a Quebec prime minister. (Premier Duplessis had tried to shut off newsprint supply to opposition newspapers, among other unsportsmanlike actions.)

Chrétien telephoned me about this matter several times and wrote an extensive letter, which we published prominently and without comment, although it contained a number of obvious inaccuracies. Whyte's badgering was excessive, but then Chrétien's shabby one-party rule was depressing. In the last hundred years, Canada's Liberals had won twenty-five elections plus one draw, out of thirty-four. The Opposition Progressive Conservatives were crumbling into oblivion, their party already riven into ideological and geographical factions.

I was one of many people before whom Chrétien dangled the possibility of being Governor General when Roméo Leblanc was retiring from that position in 2000. I did not think Chrétien was serious – and I had no interest in the position, for which I had little aptitude – but that was the high water mark of our long but desultory relationship. Of late, all I had heard were Chrétien's rather bitter complaints about the *National Post* and what he regarded as unflattering photographs of him in other Southam newspapers. There was a tinge of a threat in his comments. He reminded me, and not very obliquely, that federally Canada was effectively a one-party state.

By then, I had been based in the U.K. for fourteen years. As a peerage would normally go at some point to whoever was proprietor of the *Telegraph* ex officio, it was fairly clear that the British House of Lords was my opportunity to take part in public life. I had no illusions that I could achieve elected office. Principle and pride prohibited me from seeking a peerage, but when William Hague, John Major's successor as opposition leader, called me to ask if I would accept one in 1998, I was delighted. The House of Lords is a junior legislative chamber, but the quality of its membership is high and that of its debates often very high. It was not so much the title that interested me, but the window, however modest, on a fascinating time in British history. Whether Britain entered Europe entirely or remained close to both Europe and the United States was one of the great strategic questions in the world, and I wanted to have a say in that debate.

I asked the Toronto law firm Tory & Tory if a Canadian citizen could accept the peerage. They felt there was no need to consult Canada, since what was being proposed was an honour of the United Kingdom, for which a Canadian citizen is eligible, for services rendered in the United Kingdom. I gave their opinion to Tony Blair when he called me about Hague's proposal. Blair, being aware that after the retirement of Brian Mulroney as Canadian Conservative leader, the number of federal Tories in the Canadian parliament declined to two, thought the Tory & Tory letterhead was a send-up.

As I was a Canadian citizen at that point, existing protocol between the United Kingdom and Canada required that the matter be referred to the Canadian government, which was done through the British High Commissioner in Ottawa and the Canadian chief of protocol. The response eventually came back that Canada had no objections to a peerage provided I did not use my title in Canada and became a dual citizen. Tony Blair called to tell me this and said that he would send me a citizenship application. If I filled it out and sent it back to him, he would take care of it. I did so, and a day later I was accepted. The prime minister and the home secretary, Jack Straw, were my sponsors.

All seemed in order until the Toronto *Globe and Mail*, hearing rumours of my elevation at its London bureau, publicized the story in a tendentious manner that I was attempting to sneak into a peerage, an antiquated and contemptibly inegalitarian honour, through the back door, and indicating I was not receiving an adequate number of invitations to foxhunts and so forth. It was assumedly intended to rouse the hostility of Chrétien, whose disenchantment with the *National Post* was well known. Chrétien swiftly descended on the issue. His chief of staff, Jean Pelletier, called the Queen's assistant. The Chrétien position, as Tony Blair told it to me, which Pelletier had now conveyed to the Palace, was that the Nickle Resolution of 1919 required him to oppose my elevation to the peerage.

The Nickle Resolution was a non-binding request to King George V not to give British honours to Canadian residents. As I was not a Canadian resident and was now a dual citizen, it had no application to me. I telephoned Chrétien and presented the facts in a very conciliatory way. He did not dispute the facts but said I should aspire to the Canadian Senate. I said I would be happy to do both and might even be a Liberal senator while a Conservative peer. My attempt at levity was not successful. He received the call coolly and promised to call back. He did not. In his place was Pelletier, whose tone to me was one of heavy condescension. I was treated like an unsuccessful mendicant, which I must admit was a new experience for me, though likely not unfamiliar to many others with whom Pelletier dealt.

The British were horrified. They knew Chrétien's position was nonsense, but they couldn't put the Queen in the invidious position of resolving conflicting opinions on a constitutional point between two prime ministers of countries of which she was the monarch – and over so trivial a matter. Blair was asked to defer the recommendation of me, and I couldn't blame him for doing so.

But it was infuriating. Chrétien was in effect taking the entirely false position that he had the legal obligation to stop me from becoming a member of the House of Lords. He was making me the first and only member in a new class of citizens in a foreign country. I was to be the one solvent, unincarcerated, and sane adult in the United Kingdom ineligible for a U.K. honour given by the United Kingdom in recognition of services deemed to have been rendered in and to the United Kingdom. In view of our exchanges over the *National Post*'s coverage of him, I didn't think it much of a stretch to deduce that the reason for this unsought singling out was that Chrétien objected to the editorial position of some newspapers I influenced. I sued Chrétien in the Canadian courts for my rights as a dual citizen. It was not justiciable in Britain, and in any case I could hardly attack the British authorities who were trying to confer an honour on me.

The predictable articles appeared in the Canadian press describing the House of Lords as a geriatric assembly of masters of fox hounds and chinless descendants of once great men. In fact, the hereditary component was down to ninety-two people, who emerged from a fiercely contested election to retain their places. Almost 85 per cent of the peers are life peers, who were named because of some distinction they had achieved. Not much of an aristocracy, but compared with any other legislative chamber in the world, they are a formidable meritocracy.

I trusted the courts to be sensible, even though the respondent was the federal government – and despite the fact that, as Chrétien laboured to a number of mutual acquaintances who visited him, he himself appointed the judges.

My balloon quickly deflated. The Ontario Superior Court and then the Ontario Court of Appeal denied that they had jurisdiction. The non-deciding judge first seized of the case, who took many months to decide that he had no jurisdiction, soon retired to the private sector, where his new law firm cited his abdication on my case as evidence of his distinguished judicial career. Hostile Canadian media referred to this as my being "thrown out of court." In fact, tiers of judges abdicated.

All my concerns about Canada were cresting. I love Canada. I believed fervently in its potential and was therefore constantly irritated by what I saw as public policy holding Canada back from exploiting its God-given resources – human and natural. I had uprooted myself from Quebec, a province to which I felt closely attached and one that was the base of my newspaper business, as a protest against separatist and anti-English senti-ment. There was room for legitimate argument about whether the course I championed – less regulation, greater competition, more pro-American policies such as NAFTA – was the right or wrong way to exploit Canada's greatness, but I don't know how anyone could question the depths of my patriotism, though many did.

Canada had obviously been good to me in many ways, but I was fatigued with fighting the good fight pretty much alone and being pum-melled and caricatured for both my views and just about every aspect of my personal being, as well as many views and traits I did not, in fact, hold or possess. Now I discovered that there was no worthwhile recourse to the courts in cases where the federal government was a party. And almost two-thirds of the population, 63 per cent of English-speaking Canadians, thought Jean Chrétien, a cunning and determined philistine and place-man, was a good leader of the country, according to a poll we published in the *National Post* in 2000. I had failed to make any visible inroads in Canada in policy terms.

Chrétien was inviting me to choose between Britain and Canada. When the deliberations of the Court of Appeal had gone on for an absurdly protracted time, I commenced action to renounce my citizen-ship. I published a statement in the *National Post* that I was taking this step "with regret but without rancor" and made it clear I hoped to be allowed to take back my citizenship when conditions changed. Had I known that the Liberal Party would eject Chrétien in a couple of years, or that my action would be resented as much as it apparently was, I would have been more patient. I said I would leave and thereafter would have no further comment on Canadian public affairs. I have adhered to that. I have never uttered one disparaging word about Canada since and publicly did not mention the country at all until I resumed my residency. Naturally, I have often wondered if this whole episode has been a terrible mistake. It arose suddenly. If I had had informed advice from Torys, I would have applied for British citizenship before the issue started simmering. If I had known how much ill will would be aroused in Canada (I didn't think many Canadians cared what my citizenship was), I would probably not have proceeded. If the House of Lords is completely emasculated in the next couple of years, or I don't go back to Britain, or my legal travails are too durably compromising to enable me to return to Their Lordships' House, then it will certainly have been a mistake. If not, then perhaps it may yet work out.

One frequently imputed indication of error is the uninformed claim that if I were only still a Canadian, I would be evacuated out to Canada and escape the worst aspects of the U.S. legal system, which at time of writing still bedevils me. In fact, I have an equally advantageous arrangement with the United Kingdom, whose government is traditionally more influential in Washington, and nothing can be done with any foreign government without a degree of cooperation from American prosecutors that I was never going to abase myself adequately to obtain. I may have made a mistake in renouncing my Canadian citizenship, which I have never ceased to promise to try to regain, but we don't know yet.

The fact is, I found the whole episode heartbreaking. When I threw in the towel after decades of involvement in the Canadian public debate, having achieved almost nothing that I could detect, the *Toronto Star* ran a cartoon of me that I found deeply affecting. They portrayed me not as a flabby plutocrat, as was the custom of most Canadian caricaturists at the time, but as a rather intrepid canoeist in a Royal Navy uniform, setting out from Canadian shores, with a cheerful beaver holding a Canadian flag in one hand and a life preserver in the other waving kindly after me. It reminded me poignantly of our family's many years at our summer cottage at Lake of the Woods, where I learned the essence of geographical Canada. ("The cry of the loon and the dip of the paddle.") Perhaps there was a less benign interpretation of the cartoon, but this is how I chose to see it.

Leaving the country I had loved all my conscient life – and love still – but where I felt like a punching bag for a permanent complacent majority, was a painful step. Being sandbagged by the judiciary of my own country in what should have been a routine exercise of indisputable rights was jarring. If only I had become a dual citizen earlier, which I could easily have done, there would have been no consultation with Canada. My peerage would have been uncontroversial. As it was, I had become an exemplar of the phenomenon I was trying to stop: the departure of people who could make a visible contribution to Canada's future. Millions had left silently; my lot was to leave with unpleasant fanfare, having for decades advocated measures that would incentivize resistance to the temptation to emigrate.

WHEN DAVID RADLER TOLD ME that to buy American community newspapers would now cost twelve times the operating income, I told him that we should sell, that there was no possible justification for paying such multiples for small, minimum-growth operations in towns whose name even the head of the American Geographical Society would not recognize. Radler did a very capable job of disposing of these units, frequently achieving multiples to operating income exceeding twelve – after jacking up the income by his relentless pressure on costs and with novel but well-tried ideas of how to generate revenues in unconventional ways. He and I had been at this, he continuously, since the Eastern Townships more than thirty years before; we did not have much left to learn about how to raise the profit margins in small-town newspapers.

I had been loudly proclaiming for years, in my single-combat defence of the newspaper, that we had the content and the franchise and the ability to attract the proverbial eyeballs. But I was getting well into middle age and I wanted to do something else as an occupation than be a tout for a declining industry and sit up night after night soothing banks, reassuring noteholders, and generally being like the little Dutch boy who put his finger in the dyke. Rather, it was time for Hans Brinker's *Silver Skates*. If this environment continued, I worried, newspapers could very rapidly become a vanity occupation, even though we were still making excellent profits.

I also wanted to bury my ancient nightmare of *Almayer's Folly* once and for all. Joseph Conrad's novella about a Dutch merchant in Indonesia who gradually lost all the proceeds of forty years of work had haunted me since I read it. The fear that all my efforts in the newspaper business, from the Knowlton *Eastern Townships Advertiser* in 1966 on, could come to nothing financially if the lenders were spooked or the industry imploded oppressed me.

Unlike the United Kingdom or the United States, Canada has ante-diluvian media ownership rules that restrict foreign ownership of the nation's newspapers to 25 per cent. I could circumvent this, if necessary, by putting some of my stock in trust for my children, or my wife (who was an uncontested dual U.K.–Canadian citizen). This was the time to sell out in Canada.

With a market restricted by nationality, the pool of buyers for our Canadian assets was just about empty. Power Corporation had sold its Southam interest to us. Ted Rogers had exited, selling the *Sun* newspapers to a leveraged buyout group led by former Metropolitan Toronto chairman Paul Godfrey, who then sold to Quebecor. The financially strapped Quebecor was scrambling and not a buyer. Thomson had all but vacated the business except for a minority interest in the *Globe and Mail*, the *Winnipeg Free Press*, and a few smaller assets that they were trying to sell. In fact, the final catalyst to announce our sale was a conversation with the president of Woodbridge, the Thomson holding company, the distinguished and affable John Tory (one of Tory & Tory). He telephoned me at home on a Sunday evening and asked if I was interested in buying their remaining papers, apart from the G&M minority interest. I put down the phone, poured myself a glass of wine, and reassured myself that I could move faster than the slightly ponderous, though very well managed, Thomson Corporation.

With no visible buyers for our main properties, Canada was closing in like a financial vise. I wished to reduce our company's financial dependence on the newspaper industry, and on debt generally.

The big sale began in the spring of 2000. In April, our stock price languished, despite huge increases in profit. We announced that we would be prepared to seek "strategic alliances" for most of our assets and would possibly sell some of our non-metropolitan Canadian newspapers. We also made clear that the *Telegraph* was not for sale.

David's sale of American community newspapers yielded capital gains to the company of US$562 million on an initial acquisition price totalling US$466 million. Since most of the acquisitions had been financed entirely on borrowing and repaid from operating profits, the real gain on these sales was almost all of the $1.03 billion sale proceeds. These sales rolled in from 1998 through 2000. We sold the papers and on request promised the buyers not to compete in their markets in return for non-compete payments. This was standard in the industry, and we had paid out non-compete fees ourselves, sometimes to companies, sometimes to individuals, depending on the situation. We were known as fierce competitors and any buyer wanted to be sure there was no way for us to get back in. As both Hollinger Inc. (the Canadian parent company) and Hollinger International (the U.S. company) had been owners and operators of newspapers, buyers of our newspapers usually wanted both those companies in the agreements. And since David and I were employed by Ravelston, which contracted our management services to International, there were also payments to us individually. In the event we ever separated from the public company, most vendors wanted to be sure we would be durably prevented from re-entering the market as competitors.

Acquisitions of community newspapers could often be self-financed. Indeed, that's how we initially built our company with very little cash of our own. We would borrow half the cost of new properties, dealing with the other half of the sale price as a promissory note to the vendors. In the days of reasonable interest rates and buoyant newspaper advertising markets, these deals could be paid off from operating profits within four or five years. That was how we had founded Sterling Newspapers in the early 1970s. Then we ran the operations efficiently enough to ensure that we paid down both balances and gradually assumed the equity in the business. As our track record became better, we could borrow more. But obviously, when others were acquiring newspapers from us, the same sort of self-financed deal was vulnerable to competitive pressures, and the buyers and their lenders had to be assured of non-competition from those who knew the market best – the vendors.

There were no outside lawyers arranging the formalities on these dispositions in the United States. Company secretary Mark Kipnis, an affable, Chicago-based lawyer and normally rather thorough practitioner, under the general supervision of Peter Atkinson, one of Canada's outstanding barristers before he joined us as legal vice-president in the Toronto office, was relied upon to make sure all was handled to the best standards of documentation and independent approval where appropriate.

Years went by, and the auditors, KPMG, and the Audit Committee repeatedly assured us that all documentation and disclosures of non-competition payments and all other matters were completely satisfactory. The U.S. community newspaper division, with head offices in Chicago, at the *Chicago Sun-Times*, was run autonomously by David Radler. I had no reason to imagine anything had been done improperly. Where there were leftover individual community newspapers without buyers, David Radler grouped them together and sold them to non-arm's-length groups assembled and headed by himself, at formula prices based on audited figures. This was the beginning of what are called in this narrative the private newspaper companies, which included Horizon Operations (Canada), Horizon Publications, and Bradford Publishing (both in the U.S.). I invested in those three as a silent partner, as well as some arm's-length acquisitions, passed on others, and had no hand in the management whatever.

These transactions were approved by the independent directors, but would lead to substantial controversy eventually. The allegation would be made that Radler had arranged a low-ball price in most cases. And in the particular case of Horizon Operations (Canadian community newspapers), Radler represented his understudy, Todd Vogt, as a 25 per cent shareholder, as were David and I. It would come to light that Vogt had no equity in the business, and was fronting for Radler, with no knowledge of the deception Radler had conducted opposite the directors, especially me. When I learned this, several years after the transaction, it was the first warning that Radler's conduct was ethically deficient, and that we were no longer compatible as associates. This will be referred to hereafter as the Vogt affair.

A couple of weeks after our announcement of possible sales, the founder and chief builder of CanWest, Canada's second private-sector television network, Israel Asper, telephoned me and asked if we would be prepared to sell some of our larger Canadian newspapers. This was the call I had been waiting for. We had no other strong and plausible expressions of interest. I had known Izzy Asper for many years and had always liked him. I had sold him the Crown Trust Company in 1979. In 1975, I had negotiated with the owners of the eastern portion of the Global television network, of which Izzy then controlled the western part, to sell them our Sterling newspaper interests. That deal did not go through, but Izzy and I had kept in touch.

Negotiating with the Aspers over the sale of the Canadian newspapers was not like falling off a log. Bargaining continued non-stop through the spring and summer of 2000. Our discussions knew no day or night, frequently entailing long, hand-written letters faxed by Izzy at 4 a.m. revoking what had been agreed at 3 a.m. only to be reinstated with small modifications at 5 a.m. His style was very different to mine, but his constant sense of humour made the difficult possible. As we approached an agreement, they were prepared to buy all our Canadian newspapers except some of the smaller ones in British Columbia. The *National Post* was a special negotiation, since its survival depended on printing and delivery by the Southam chain, which we were selling to CanWest. I didn't want to part with the *National Post*, but for Izzy too it was the big trophy, so we divided ownership evenly, with me continuing as its publisher. I was happy to share the loss and Izzy was content for the time being to share the prize. The last stages of this complicated sale were carried out on my cellphone from Bayreuth, Germany, home of Richard Wagner, where Barbara and I were attending a series of operas at Wagner's Festspielhaus. In the intermissions I would try to sort out the final details with Izzy and his son Leonard. Wagner's operas are of sufficient length and the Germans so dedicated to eating that the intermissions were just long enough to make an agreement that could then be reinterpreted and renegotiated when we arrived back at our hotel.

This semi-madness was fitting, as we were staying at Pflaums Posthotel in Pegnitz, a wonderfully eccentric hotel run by a family dedicated to Wagner. I would talk to Izzy in its corridors in the shadow of six monitors all playing Wagner and fit my negotiations to the background music: a night's ride with the Valkyries followed by Valhalla crumbling. On the penultimate night of the negotiations, the bathtub in our room, which was curiously placed at the foot of our bed where one might normally find a bench or sofa, self-started as we were sleeping. Neither Barbara nor I could decide what precise meaning this had, but in the normal way of things, I saw it as a hopeful sign, verging on a self-revealing spring, as at Lourdes, while Barbara muttered about the deluge, as in the last hours of Louis xv.

When the deal was announced in July, the Canadian media responded with joyous stupefaction. I was actually getting out of their faces. They were generally convinced of my desire to retain a majority of Canada's newspapers and to conduct a long-term campaign against the soft Canadian left. The tenor of media comment was that Asper had "wrested control of Black's newspapers," as reported in *Maclean's*. The *Globe and Mail* portrayed me as a stuffed turkey, with Asper setting out to carve me up. It was assumed that because Asper was a Manitoba Liberal, though a rather conservative one, he would be more ideologically amenable to official Liberal views than I had been. In fact, there wasn't much difference between us in ideological or policy terms.

As the negotiations to conclude our deal continued through the summer and autumn, elements of the media saw what a remarkable deal this was for Hollinger and did a 180-degree turn, trying to sandbag the sale. Having celebrated my departure, they now tried to warn Izzy off by claiming that I had taken him over the barrel. Consideration in the transaction was ten times operating income, plus Can$100 million for half of the *National Post*, plus Can$30 million for the money-losing website www.canada.com. On its face, this was the definitive deliverance of Hollinger from the jaws of debt, allowing us to retain the *Telegraph* titles and the strong group of assets we had in the Chicago area, half the *National Post*, our Quebec properties, and a scattering of smaller newspapers. The total consideration was Can$3.6 billion, a gain in a little over four years of about Can$1.4 billion, and set up in a tax-favoured deal structure. One-fifth of the consideration was in shares and one-fifth in high-yield notes.

By October, the Canadian Imperial Bank of Commerce (CIBC), which was financing Asper, had a partial case of cold feet. They indicated that they wanted the scope of the deal reduced slightly, and we managed to accommodate that. By Christmas 2000 the deal had been closed. Finally, I had largely extricated myself from debt, from Canada, and from the newspaper business, of all of which I had become wary. Largely extricated, yet not quite sufficiently to assure a peaceful transition to the new life I had started to plan.

FOR ALMOST A YEAR following the closing of the sale of most of the Canadian assets to CanWest and others, corporate life was less worrisome than it had been. It quickly became clear that we had moved at the most advantageous time. A couple of months after the completion of the main transaction, the economy started to falter. Advertising revenues, especially in the newspaper business, went into a steep decline, and income at the main continuing units, the *Daily Telegraph* and the *Sun-Times*, eroded very seriously. I looked upon this with a slightly cavalier indifference at first, as the elimination of bank debt left us much less vulnerable to such fluctuations and I was confident revenues could rebound.

However, there remained an excess of debt in the Canadian holding company, Hollinger Inc. Getting money from Hollinger International to Hollinger Inc. could be done but had to be navigated with care. The remaining debt terms from bond-holders and lending banks were a patchwork of complicated cross-warranties and ratios governing asset values and cash generation. The CanWest deal and those that followed on smaller asset packages dramatically reduced debt and removed concerns about any business downturn or unforeseen developments. They did not, however, make matters objectively simple.

The initial relief in the Canadian media that these newspapers would now be in the hands of Liberals swiftly gave way to howls of rage at alleged ownership interference, the perceived bumptiousness of the new owners, and very faint groans of nostalgia for our era. My longstanding critics on the left of the Canadian media now turned on the Aspers, ridiculing them unjustly as ignorant meddlers and inept businessmen who had swallowed the then fashionable "convergence" dream and couldn't digest the newspapers they had bought so dearly. The price of CanWest's shares declined by 90 per cent, from $25 to $2.50, because of the unkind perceptions that Izzy Asper had overpaid and was an unsuitable owner of such franchises. We bailed out of the stock about halfway down, but our capital gain on the entire transaction was reduced by about Can$100 million.

CanWest needed a refinancing to cope with the acquisition of these properties and had the assets for one. Their predicament was not the failure of "convergence" but rather the failure of their banker, CIBC, to grasp the basic structure and psychology of the U.S. financial market. The big New York merchant banks in those pre-crisis days operated a tight cartel. CIBC thought they could raise money in the United States without using one of its members as co-lead in the issue. This did not go over well with Morgan Stanley, Lehman Brothers, Salomon Smith Barney, Merrill Lynch, Credit Suisse First Boston, Goldman Sachs, and one or two of the others. All that was necessary to sabotage the entire underwriting was for representatives from these firms to advise their main institutional investors that if they just sat on their wallets, the deal would come back to them on more advantageous terms and the favour in swatting down this Canadian interloper would be remembered. CIBC looked like innocents in Babylon.

I groaned resignedly at the stupidity of the CIBC as they smugly shot themselves in the foot, knowing that the next shot would come at us and to a far more vulnerable spot. It did. The Canadian banking system then determined that, since CanWest was having difficulty refinancing itself out of its bank debt, the CanWest paper that we held was not acceptable collateral for our loans. This was a significant inconvenience of a kind that we had hoped we had outgrown.

We continued to sell secondary assets. A group of Canadian community newspapers, mainly in Ontario, were sold to a management buyout group led by Michael Sifton, scion of a celebrated Canadian newspapering family, from whom we had purchased the main newspapers in Saskatchewan in 1996. We gained a further profit for Hollinger International of Can$120 million. But we certainly followed financier and presidential adviser Bernard Baruch's advice to "leave something on the table for the next guy" and were pleased when, three years later, Sifton floated the newspaper company at a profit. His family and mine have been friendly for generations, and still are.

Dan Colson and I sold Hollinger International's French-Canadian newspaper company to Paul Desmarais's Power Corporation. One of our great strengths was knowing when to sell. I had bought this company, Unimédia, from Jacques Francoeur in 1986 for Can$50 million. We had taken more than $50 million out of it and sold it from Hollinger Inc. to Hollinger International in 1995 for about Can$75 million. This had been another related-party transaction in which the shareholders of both related companies made a very large score. We sold it to Power Corporation for $145 million.

(Jacques Francoeur was a colourful Québécois of the old Duplessis school. He maintained his office where it had always been, in the unfashionable east end of Montreal, with a police radio transmitting behind his desk. He would tear out of his office like a cub reporter if something interesting came over the radio, including twice when I was visiting him. I accompanied him, once to a fire and once to a bank that had been robbed. This was not as distracting as the habit of his and Paul Desmarais' great rival Pierre Péladeau, the controlling shareholder of Quebecor and *Le Journal*, of interrupting himself in mid-sentence to utter a prayer or receive a purported revelation. I went through this a couple of times too and at first thought that Péladeau was having an attack of epilepsy.)

With these and other smaller sales, we eliminated all but our long-term debt and reduced the number of outstanding shares at what would prove very advantageous prices. As we shrank the company, we cancelled shares for less than the per-share value of assets we sold, adding to underlying per-share value. As we had expanded our company, we had had recourse to some exotic instruments to maintain our control of the company while obtaining the funds necessary for expansion. The method was to find debt instruments that were technically equity or at least had characteristics that would not affront ratios and covenants on existing debt. In shorthand, for readers not conversant with financial jargon, we had to find a way to raise money and we did it through such methods as Liquid Yield Option Notes (LYONs) and a Total Return Equity Swap (TRES), to buy and cancel shares and increase our interest in the company, as well as reduce debt.

This arrangement worked well, until the banks started to become skittish. The first sign of this occurred in 2001, when Bank of America began to agitate. The banking system was approaching another one of its cyclical crises of unwise lending. Middle-echelon bank executives were insisting on shorter-term loans and higher fees for renewing them. The best accounts were made to suffer equally with the underperforming accounts. We were on a treadmill that was being swiftly accelerated, but whenever I called the senior bankers with whom I dealt, I was assured that everything was satisfactory. It wasn't.

THIS WAS A CLOUD ON THE HORIZON when Barbara and I embarked on one of the most misconceived holidays I have had, in August 2001. We were thinking of returning to Australia, where we had had a happy commercial and personal experience, to see whether the endless reports of a changing political attitude to foreign media ownership were accurate. I had always had a romantic notion of Bora Bora and Tahiti as tropical paradises that had a brave Gaullist political history, rejecting the cowardice and defeatism of Vichy as soon as de Gaulle founded the Free French movement in 1940. I had mentioned Bora Bora to Barbara as a place we might visit en route to Australia the previous year. She had vetoed it on mistaken grounds. Barbara, as she herself would agree, has a very weak grasp of geography but sensed that Bora was somewhere in the Pacific. She assumed, since I was interested in it, that it must be a U.S. naval camp on some atoll. When confronted about her assumption, she confessed that, actually, she had connected the name with an old film she didn't like called *Bora! Bora!* (she was thinking of "Tora, Tora, Tora," an excellent dramatization of the attack on Pearl Harbor) that she thought had servicemen in it. All the same, I gave in and we went on our usual continental holiday in France instead. But this year she had given me the role of vacation director. I decided that since Australia loomed once more, now was the moment to resurrect Bora Bora as a way station. I went ahead and made the arrangements as a "surprise."

So it was. Bora Bora proved to be a completely aptly named and boring island. A drive around it took fifteen minutes and revealed nothing of interest. There was no town, no colonial buildings, no churches of note, no bars or restaurants. There were only the hotels, and these were infestations of honeymooners: large, loutish young men in droopy shorts and their perky brides or girlfriends. Apart from the slightly bibulous manager of our hotel, who had formerly worked at the King Edward Hotel in Toronto and claimed to remember my brother and me, the only social connection we made was the Indo-Madagascarian doctor, an alumnus of the University of Strasbourg, whom we called because of the acute bronchitis I swiftly contracted and to recover a contact lens lost somewhere in Barbara's eye. We conversed in French inside our thatched bungalow while Barbara worked on her laptop. Her French is fairly primitive, but she did hear the word "dengue" as we chatted and swivelled around like a cobra raising its head. "Dengue," she said, fixing the doctor with her injured eye. This elicited the hitherto unknown information that the island was in the grip of an epidemic of dengue fever, something the authorities and travel agents had omitted to mention. Should we decide to venture outside the hotel's beach area, which he strongly advised against, we should be sure to wear thick socks and cover up. Barbara's single contribution to the vacation itinerary, a suggestion that we might try to escape the honeymooners by a good walk in the less developed part of the island that still had some wild vegetation, was clearly off limits. The doctor came back a third time to minister to a severe laceration on my leg, the result of an unplanned encounter with coral. We had been taken to an area where snorkelling would permit us to swim with sharks – sand sharks only, I assumed (mistakenly). Snorkelling while suffering bronchitis is at best a doubtful exercise, and the blood from my wound caused the guide to round us all up into the boat and return to the hotel lest I become shark bait. This did not endear me to the other divers, especially the two young, attractive Japanese honeymooners kitted out in the most sophisticated diving apparatus and useful accessories of all kinds.

Tahiti was no better. There was more on the island, but the ever-popular over-the-water bungalow in which we were billeted was at the bottom of the package tour spectrum as well as what appeared to be runway number one of the Tahiti airport. The food was inedible. The bed linens were as raspy as a lion's tongue, and Barbara, a light sleeper, could not sleep at all on them. I found her wrapped up in my raincoat on top of the covers. When she went to plug in her laptop to file her *Telegraph* and *Maclean's* columns, nothing happened. The "technician" who eventually turned up like a fugitive from an Ionesco play fiddled about with a screwdriver for a while and then acknowledged to me in his rich Polynesian French that he knew nothing about technology or even electricity. With a bright, dentally challenged smile, he said that his instructions were to put on a show so that we would not realize the hotel had no facilities for Internet connections. I gave him twenty dollars as a reward for straight talk. We took a forty-five-minute taxi tour of Papeete the next morning, gave up on the whole voyage to the South Pacific, and returned to Seattle, where we had tickets to attend the *Ring Cycle*.

There were problems even here. Fierce heat made days too hot to do anything that involved walking. My bronchitis was still so tenacious, even after all the ministrations of the Indo-Madagascarian doctor, that I was afraid I might not be able to sit through the opera without disrupting the house by compulsive coughing. Barbara developed a terrible migraine as well as skin and muscle discomfort related to her dermatomyositis, so, after the Four Seasons Hotel doctor abdicated any prescribing responsibility, I took her to a local hospital to get some medicine. The emergency ward was crowded with overweight marathoners under observation for heat prostration, having run in favour of some local charity. Hours passed until finally Barbara whispered in a pathetic little voice: "I want to go home." We both limped back to the hotel, where she found some old pills in her medicine bag. I know nothing about such things, but she told me they were Demerol and Percocet and would help. She took several in case they had lost their potency and appeared to go happily into some trance, rather fitting for the *Ring*.

I set out on foot to take communion in the Roman Catholic cathedral and tripped over an uneven paving stone and badly skinned an elbow, the first time I had fallen on a street sidewalk since I was a toddler. With torn shirt and dirty trousers, blood still oozing from my forearm, I returned to our hotel only to encounter a number of opera lovers, including the impeccably dressed former British Conservative cabinet members David (Lord) Young and Michael Portillo and their wives. The "holiday" was assuming the farcical proportions of the travel fiascos described by Evelyn Waugh or John Mortimer (such as where Mortimer confused the king of Libya for the head bellhop of the Mammounia Hotel in Marakesh).

As the *Ring* Cycle proceeded, the next instalment of our recurrent financial problems came to the fore due to the steady tightening of credit and the indiscriminate nervosity and pettifogging of bankers. The Hollinger Inc. banking group was agitating for a paydown of the company's loans for no particular reason, while noisily protesting their faith in the company and the value of the connection with us. This would require the sale of some remaining Canadian assets by Hollinger International, including CanWest notes. For any sale of the CanWest commercial paper, which would now be at a discount because of the accumulated clumsiness of the CIBC as CanWest's financial adviser and the unconvincing launch of the Aspers as newspaper operators, the agreement of the Aspers was necessary. I found myself, in scorching Seattle with lingering bronchitis and a tender elbow, between *Siegfried* and *Götterdämmerung* in the familiar position of trying to negotiate out of a tight financial corner. My frequent similar past experiences didn't make the activity any less tiresome.

Our discussions quickly revealed that Izzy felt that co-ownership of the *National Post* with me as publisher was not working. I felt the same way. But the cards were in Izzy's hands. He had the newspaper chain across the country that printed and distributed the *Post* in all the places where it surpassed the *Globe and Mail,* and an unenthusiastic co-owner would be a real danger to it. In addition, constant vigilance was needed to make sure the individual editors of local newspapers didn't try to sabotage the national paper they saw as a competitor. The *Post* was losing about $1 million a week, not greatly exceeding my expectations for a start-up cost of a national franchise, and though we were now only responsible for half that, it was a strain on the downsized Hollinger Inc. Izzy believed that the losses at the *Post* were largely due to my indulgence of Ken Whyte's spending propensities, which was a canard, but he felt confident that under his control this would be solved. Painfully, to solve the latest financial jam, I had to buy Izzy's consent to sell his notes with the *National Post*. We dodged a large annual loss in this, but selling out our entire position in the *National Post* was a wrenching decision for me.

The only honourable course was to go to the *National Post* and address the staff, which I did with Leonard Asper shortly after my return from Seattle, two days after working out an arrangement with Izzy Asper. I still, and will always, recall the faces arrayed in front of me as I explained what had happened and why. As always, I was impressed with the appearance of the *National Post* personnel: attractive and alert people of all ages and descriptions, motivated, bright, interesting, a workforce to be proud to be associated with in any capacity. Christie Blatchford, an excellent writer and refreshingly straightforward and raunchy woman, who had worked with Barbara when she was editor of the *Toronto Sun,* embraced me. Some people wept. I shared the impulse, though I didn't act on it. I never cry, other than in laughter.

There was some feeling that I had created the *Post* and abandoned it. I did create it, and I dedicated Can$200 million to launch it (including the acquisition of the *Financial Post*), but I left it in secure hands. Jean Chrétien could no longer dismiss the *National Post* as my bully pulpit. Now he would have to deal with a perspective that was ideologically unchanged but impossible to isolate as being hostile to the federal Liberal Party (which I wasn't). This was an important step forward in the possible influence the *National Post* could exercise, provided the Aspers played their cards well.

The participations in the CanWest notes were promptly sold and the looming Hollinger Inc. financial crisis subsided. Once again, our timing was exemplary, as a few days later terrorists seized civil airliners and smashed them into the World Trade Center towers and the Pentagon, plunging financial markets into chaos and further depressing the U.S. economy. We had had a narrow escape from a possible financial scramble.

I WAS INDUCTED INTO the House of Lords at the end of October 2001, sponsored by Margaret (Lady) Thatcher and Peter (Lord) Carrington. Henry and Nancy Kissinger, who happened to be in London, sat with Barbara in the gallery. I took the oath by the dispatch box where Benjamin Disraeli (once he became the Earl of Beaconsfield) and Salisbury had stood. On this first day, the House was well attended and by a much less geriatric group than the usual caricature. The Lord Chancellor, Derry Irvine, greeted me warmly. This was as close as I would get to having any status as a legislator. It was, and is, an honour.

After the second transaction with the Aspers in September 2001, financial concerns again receded from the Hollinger companies for a time. But I was never to get clear of them. Keeping editorial franchises healthy without damaging their editorial quality was rewarding but difficult. Fighting the growing rapacity and cowardice of banks, rating services, aggressive institutional investors, and changing regulations was simply a survival scenario with debilitating effects. Barbara would come down to the library in London at 3 a.m. as I was struggling with new plans and sending out lengthy emails to Toronto and New York and see what she called my "fist-face" of concentration. Any pleasure in my work had been far outstripped by the financial worries that had begun with Murdoch's price war and had multiplied as the economic and financial climate changed and the electronic media hypnotized investors. As the post–September 11 advertising recession and banking liquidity problems deepened, our stock price declined and prudence required a reduction in the Hollinger International dividend. The banking consortium in the "swap" (the financial instrument containing Hollinger debt and backed by a group of banks) became very neurotic.

By early 2002, Bank One and the Bank of Nova Scotia (BNS) were both agitating. Once the BNS began to express concern, the remaining constituent bank in the swap, the Toronto-Dominion Bank (TD), was moved to do the same. As always happens in bank club deals, when one bank demands concessions and professes alarm, the others claim to be much more resolutely confident of the account but are forced by the protocol of the banking industry to require an equivalent level of security, regardless of whether this translates itself into a rockslide that crushes the equity of the borrower. At the best of times, lending banks show neither cunning nor agility. When the times are difficult and unpredictable, as they were after September 11, 2001, the banks resemble nothing so much as large, stupid, frightened animals, charging mindlessly in a shared direction, oblivious of the consequences.

In the case of Hollinger International's swap, this was particularly complicated and potentially dangerous, because BNS and TD were swap participants and, with CIBC, lenders to Hollinger Inc. The recourse open to the swap participants, should they become concerned with that arrangement, was to liquidate their Hollinger International shares.

But Hollinger International shares underpinned, and were the collateral for, the loans to Hollinger Inc. At no time did either BNS or TD show the slightest recognition that in dumping millions of Hollinger International shares into the market, they could trigger a default of Hollinger Inc., entitling them (if litigation by us did not prevent it) to seize the collateral and liquidate it without regard to the impact on the equity values of the borrower. We had only the good sense and goodwill of the banks to rely on to prevent this. This counted for something with CIBC and to some extent TD and BNS, but was a negative factor with Bank One.

After we had bought out Bank of America, Bank One was the first of the remaining swap banks to bug out. They made threatening noises about liquidating their positions. David Radler was the logical person to see them, as they are a Chicago bank, and to point out the underlying values, the impossibility of them or any lender losing money lending to us, and the irresponsibility of an overhasty liquidation of their shareholding.

The banks were contractually committed to the avoidance of precipitate action, but their undertakings in this as in many other respects proved to be unreliable. David arrived in Chicago ready to persuade only to be informed that Bank One had sold their position. Fortunately for us, an institutional investor, Southeastern Asset Management (SEAM) of Memphis, bought virtually all their shares, so the divestiture did not shake the share price, as would have happened if our trading volumes had remained at their normal levels.

Bank One's departure further aroused the Bank of Nova Scotia. By late spring 2002, I was advised that the derivatives desk of BNS in New York was threatening our controller with default and demanding that dividends be maintained regardless of what the covenants on the high-yield debt imposed through ratios and the so-called basket of eligible funds. They wanted the revenue to protect the SWAP value. At the same time, BNS personnel in Toronto were demanding that the dividend be lowered. They wanted to stay away from any debt covenant problem. It proved useless advising them that their own people were demanding, in the most belligerent terms, exactly opposed dividend policies in New York and Toronto. This problem was becoming more worrisome as we approached the annual meeting in New York in May 2002.

As has been mentioned, the main CanWest transaction generated sizable non-competition payments, demanded by Izzy Asper in respect of David Radler and me. These totalled Can$80 million (divided unevenly between Ravelston, our ultimate parent company, and David, Peter Atkinson, Jack Boultbee, and me) and did not reduce the promised return to Hollinger International of ten times pre-tax cash flow of Hollinger International. Our Canadian lawyers, Tory & Tory, whose New York office also acted for us, assured us that these non-competition payments did not have to be disclosed. In the context of arranging a debt issue, we were advised by Cravath, Swaine & Moore that they did have to be disclosed, and we were able to publish them adequately and promptly in the financial results for 2000.

Our third-largest shareholder after Hollinger Inc. and Southeastern,

Tweedy Browne, was already grumpy about our management fees and became quite demonstrative about non-competition payments. It was obvious from correspondence from them and from some of their public comments that they were going to raise these issues quite vocally at the annual meeting. I did not find this prospect at all disconcerting. The non-competition payments are standard in the newspaper industry; we had paid them ourselves dozens of times, sometimes to companies and sometimes to individuals. Without them, the Aspers would have had no assurance that we would not have bought the competing *Sun* newspapers.

The management fees were also not hard to justify. The total of what we received had been sharply reduced when we shrank the company. It would have been possible to retain the fee pretty much where it had been and still reduce debt by pouring out cheap stock had we not perceived ourselves to be pre-eminently shareholders rather than paid placemen. The Audit Committee had approved all the original management fees and non-compete payments, and the shareholders were the clear beneficiaries of the $1.5 billion of capital gains we added to the value of the company and its shares by the American Publishing and Southam transactions.

Unhappily, the spirit of the times was changing to one of increasing deference to institutional investors, an insistence on directors being complete strangers and preferably antagonists to the management, and the de-emphasis, if not ostracism, of controlling shareholders. I was from twin traditions that I never thought needed to be contradictory: the tradition of the proprietor-publisher with the authority and financial independence to defend his newspapers from economic and political interests and the tradition of the fair controlling shareholder who never engaged in unequal treatment of shareholding minorities.

But I had a tin ear for the *Zeitgeist*. The trend to shareholder activism and rigorous imposition of ever more exacting corporate governance standards was not one whose force I correctly foresaw. "Corporate governance," after all, by definition simply refers to the necessary rules, disclosures, and processes that a corporation follows. (Our corporate governance was carefully monitored at Hollinger Inc. by committees headed by corporate governance expert and director of many leading Canadian and U.S. companies

Ralph M. Barford.) Like many words and phrases that newly enter the language, it has become a euphemism for a more ominous interpretation: today it is a blunt weapon with which to attack CEOs, especially those who are also controlling shareholders, and a useful mask for those who have more exceptionable designs on a company than improving its "corporate governance." The proclaimers and enforcers of contemporary corporate governance are most often people who have never faced the complexities of actually running a company but want to make up more and more rules on how to do it. I had never imagined that a controlling shareholder could be vulnerable to recalcitrant minority shareholders – particularly greenmailers out for short-term gain. I never had much difficulty dealing with the complaints or questions of the advocates of corporate governance, even the most militant ones, and have never had much difficulty justifying our own behaviour or levels of compensation. Certainly, in the light of subsequent corporate controversies, we and the directors who approved payments to us look very conscientiously compliant and quite restrained and frugal. As the cultural problem arose between the corporate governance zealots and my associates and me, the stock price suffered. What I called a "capital strike" ensued, in which large shareholders (who would normally have wanted the stock price to go up) devoted themselves to keeping it down, recognizing that Hollinger Inc. would need to sell shares to reduce its debt and they could pick them up at a bargain price. What occurred was a chicken game in which we used disposable cash to buy in and cancel Hollinger International shares cheaply, and in which several of our leading shareholders were delighted if others were prepared to sell at undervalued levels. They added to their own holdings and did the necessary to keep the share price down, hoping that Hollinger Inc. would be forced to put the whole company up for sale, taking out everyone at a handsome profit.

I never doubted that the triumph of the institutional investors would not only deglamorize but emasculate American corporate life. Management would turn into the equivalent of highly paid civil servants, concerned only with their pensions and pay packets and maintaining the status quo through safe choices. Not owning any significant part of the company they were running, they would be unwilling or unable to make difficult choices in the company's long-term interest and would always have to put the short-term first to satisfy their masters – the analysts, the ratings agencies, the ever noisier and greedier activist shareholders, and the financial media.

The icons of American business, instead of suggesting moderation or resisting the trend, rolled over like poodles. Warren Buffett and Bill Gates, two brilliant and ruthless businessmen, toured around university campuses in corduroy trousers, open-necked shirts, and tweed jackets decrying traditional corporate prerogatives in their dovish role as non-commercial philanthropists. Buffett eventually demanded that his taxes be raised to help the disadvantaged. He could have written the cheque himself, without waiting for the government to take his money (and waste most of it). After he lost more money than any individual in the world in the 2008–09 financial crisis, he became less vocal about the need for higher taxes.

As I had been a lonely defender of the newspaper against the depredations of television and the Internet, so I became a lonely defender of the prerogatives of corporate management, and especially the controlling shareholders. It was a role in which I was to become a good deal lonelier. The huge scandals that were about to break, at Enron, WorldCom, Adelphi, Tyco, and elsewhere, where there were insolvencies or serious reductions of shareholder value and allegations of felonies, with some convictions, poisoned the atmosphere and put the advocates of traditional, capitalist, individualist chief executives such as me out in the cold in open and deadly season. The most trying time of my life was about to begin.

THE 2002 ANNUAL MEETING of Hollinger International was a lively affair. There was little warning that shareholders were agitated; the opening atmosphere certainly was not tense. The chief activists, Christopher Browne and the aggressive and ineffable Laura Jereski, from Tweedy Browne, which held about 8 per cent of the stock, were much in evidence. Ms. Jereski left the *Wall Street Journal*. She was an abrasive and controversial figure. The visual effect created by Ms. Jereski, with her facial flinch, thick glasses, anti-glamorous tastes, and a child's schoolbag strapped to her back, was bizarre, especially as a complement to the effete and often rather bitchy Browne. Their questions, though irritatingly formulated at times, were civilized and not particularly difficult. Lee Cooperman, another institutional investor incapable of resisting a trend to abuse a meeting chairman, had his rather ineffectual turn at bat.

And then there arose a Mr. Ruffo, who claimed that Browne and Cooperman had accused the management of "theft." I said that they had done nothing of the kind and that if that was what Ruffo thought, he should get out – by which it was clear I meant both from the room and out of any shares of ours he had. Christopher Browne graciously chimed in that he had not accused us of theft, and Ruffo hastily left the room. It did not enhance the credibility of the independent directors that none of them bothered to turn up for the meeting.

I WAS UNDOUBTEDLY INSOUCIANT about the shareholder-relations issues, and not just because we controlled the company and were the largest public shareholders or because most of the rest of the shareholders supported us, and because our results, as acquirers, managers, and vendors, were consistently good. I was bemused by the fact that such shareholder-relations problems as there were were not caused by normal market forces, but by synchronized poor-mouthing by Jereski and kindred spirits, and by what amounted to (barely) licit but shabby wash-trading by investors trying to force a sale of the company, on a basis that I did not believe was possible, much less desirable, or within the rightful province of agitating minorities to effect. I had great difficulty taking seriously the complaints of people who were the causes of the problems they decried.

I have never seen a corporate governance militant who was not by nature either a tedious and distracting fidget, like an annoying insect, to no good purpose, or a charlatan, attempting pretextual agitation for disguised and usually self-aggrandizing purposes. (This is what makes the "activism" of amiable and cunning buccaneers like Carl Icahn and Nelson Peltz so entertaining, and even gratifying.)

I don't doubt the sincerity of moderately engaged corporate governance advocates, but businessmen should obey the law and produce results, not elect hostile directors and collegialize and equivocate as the governance enthusiasts urge. This would require an extensive essay to treat in any depth, but I saw this focus on governance as an aspect of the mania for the superficiality of appearances and the evasion of responsibility. No manner of governance can long disguise the inexorable arithmetic of poor management, and no absence of the most zealous, cutting-edge pandering to the fad will, in itself, produce commercially relevant consequences. It always seemed to me to be part of the general trend to duck responsibility and substitute appearances for performance.

I was right and wrong, as the balance of this volume tells. I underestimated the strength of the movement, and was decisively defeated, and as a capitalist Darwinian, conceptually I have no great problem with that. And philosophically and as an historian, I believe such defeats, even being beaten as badly as I would (temporarily) be, if accepted constructively, can be quickly forged into the stuff of future success. Nothing is quite as educational, for the mind, the spirit, and the intuition, as being ground to powder, provided the chastisee survives it with redoubled determination (as I have).

This was where my enemies went awry: by attacking my ethics and honesty, which had never been deficient, they attempted more than a coup, and escalated their assault to non-physical homicide (though the pressures they generated and applied have often led to mortal consequences with others in similar positions). There was no colour of right to this, and it incited a fierce and ultimately successful resistance. Honest error, if abetted by the pride that goeth before disaster, successfully eroded my position. I deserved to be punished, for a tactical, rather than substantive, mistake, but not to be morally exterminated.

Recourse to the corporate assassins' trade by my enemies produced counter-guerrilla war that finally ramified through the whole commercial culture of America and up the entire regulatory and legal systems to the highest courts in the United States and (at time of writing, probably) Canada. The roles of those who seemed to win and those who seemed to lose had not yet been determined, and many surprises were to come.

THE CONCERNS OF THE corporate governance militants about Hollinger's management fees and non-competition payments further perplexed the company's bankers. Never courageous, busily cutting their loan portfolios in the contracting conditions that followed the terrorist attacks in the

United States, the banks became further concerned that if flows of cash were cut to the group's controlling shareholder, this would further imperil their loans (which were not, in fact, in the slightest danger).

As soon as Barbara and I returned to Toronto from Europe in late July 2002, our legal vice president, Peter Atkinson, and I called on my old friends Peter Godsoe and David Wilson, chairman and vice chairman of BNS, respectively. They could not have been more pleasant and understanding. Peter Atkinson and I left satisfied that BNS would be easier to deal with henceforth. They were – for about three days.

The Toronto-Dominion Bank maintained a more plausible pretense than the others of being a willing lender while they were pitching us a debt reorganization. As time went by, it became clear that the proposed refinancing would become an exercise in usury that could damage the entire group. The TD's "flex" rates provided immense elasticity upward as the negotiations reached their climax; the terms would be a garrotte.

I broke off these discussions in August and arranged a US$40 million bridge facility with Jack Cockwell, head of the Brascan group and one of Canada's most talented businessmen. When TD learned of this development, they described it not as a bridge but an "exploding pier," although it was at two points below what they were cranking up to offer and with much less restrictive terms. Our plan was to reduce the bank loans and, as this was done, transfer proportionate amounts of the collateral pledged to them to collateralize the Brascan bridge loan. In order to make our lives more difficult, the banks were very sluggish in cooperating with this plan and professed to believe that the collateral was being double pledged, which was not the case. BNS and TD spent most of the rest of 2002 grimly muttering "default," like James Joyce penitents semi-audibly reciting their rosaries, moved from time to time by spikes of zeal to escalate their incantations to include "loan call." It was very tiresome.

We had had a few minor encounters with the Wachovia Bank, an oddly named result of a series of successful amalgamations headquartered in Charlotte, North Carolina, and using the name of a Moravian-American bank that had been one of the original units in the merger. We negotiated hopefully with them through the autumn, struggling every fortnight or so to prevent a loan call or official declaration of default whenever one of the ulcerous personalities at the derivative desk of the Bank of Nova Scotia in New York had a particularly difficult day (or night).

At the beginning of December 2002, we were ready to start a punishing double road show with Wachovia to sell the complete refinancing. David Radler led one team in the western states, and Dan Colson and I toured institutions in New York, Boston, Philadelphia, Connecticut, and New Jersey.

(Just before the tour began I went to the memorial service for my distinguished friend and publishing mentor Walter Annenberg, who had died aged ninety-four. He was another supporter in my life who could not be replicated: patiently and with wisdom and business experience that were invaluable, he had encouraged and boosted me. He was eulogized by the incoming governor of Pennsylvania, Ed Rendell, as "the greatest Philadelphian since Benjamin Franklin" and by the senior U.S. senator from the state, Arlen Spector, who said that in addition to his other attainments, "Walter was a good man to have a martini with." Julie Nixon Eisenhower represented the Nixons and the Eisenhowers, Nancy Reagan represented the Reagans, Barbara Bush represented the Bushes. Gerald Ford, George Shultz, and Colin Powell all spoke with great eloquence, humour, and taste. It was a moving tribute to a generous and admirable man.)

Our road show unfolded with the usual grind of going over the same prospectus with groups of underwriters for hours on end. The issue was hugely oversold, and ten days before Christmas, the money flooded in and we paid out all the banks and high-yield holders of Hollinger International. The problems of Hollinger Inc., though smaller in quantum, were more pressing and awaited resolution. However, the end of the swap,* with the

---

* Again, the swap was a borrowing from four banks (Bank of America, Bank One, Bank of Nova Scotia [BNS], and Toronto Dominion Bank [TD]), into whose hands we had consigned shares that resulted from the exercise of warrants we had bought for nothing just as they expired, applying the proceeds of the exercise price to cancellation of other shares at lower prices. The stock dividend largely covered the interest on the borrowing that constituted the other side of the swap (it was a swap between a holding of shares and a cash borrowing, unwindable by either party with the carrying imbalance to the account of our company). A decline in the market price, produced in this instance by the antics of Jereski and the other

cancellation of a total of 11 million shares at prices that would soon appear very advantageous, and the end of the high-yield debt in the face of the guerrilla warfare conducted by one of our lenders, gave us a brief respite.

After we dismissed Toronto-Dominion, the *London Daily Express* published the story that we had been dumped by TD as a borrower because we had falsified our figures to that bank. This was too much, so I sued the rumbustious owner of the *Express*, Richard Desmond, for libel, adding in our financial pages what I called a Christmas greeting when the Wachovia deal closed. In it I referred to his company as a defamation and pornography operation directed by a group of reprobates and in free fall. He countersued me. A rather amusing lawsuit was eventually settled two-thirds in our favour: Desmond's company contributed twice what we did to designated charities.

Immediately after completing the Wachovia deal, in scrutinizing the new figures that reflected the refinancing, I realized that while technically the inter-company account between Hollinger International and Hollinger Inc. was fairly balanced, there was an imbalance in International's favour of around $40 million in terms of what would be repayable in cash during the next year or so. There was nothing improper in this, but it created another obstacle that had to be addressed. The Wachovia deal had brought to my attention a fact that had been skillfully disguised from everyone by Jack Boultbee's invocation of accounting technicalities – namely, that Hollinger Inc. owed Hollinger International Can$70 million (and much of this was quite correctly offset by historical accounts, most of which were notional, like transferred depreciation, and would not, in fact, have to be paid). Accounting rules allow for a good many of these things, and they can gradually distort accrued sums. To a company of Hollinger International's size, this did not much matter, but to Hollinger Inc., it could be material. I cobbled together a repayment system based partially on cancellation of 2 million Hollinger International shares owned by Hollinger Inc. What complicated the usual competitive commercial pressures and

choristers agitating for the break-up and sale of the company, could produce a disorderly sale of shares and heavy cash-calls on the company if the shares were sold at a large discount to their original collateral value. We did well to eliminate the shares at a good price, paying off the four-bank group with some of the Wachovia loan proceeds. We had again outwitted Browne, Cooperman, et al.

the ambitions of some institutional shareholders was the very public zeal with which other media companies magnified or invented our problems. Had we manufactured widgets or rubber bands rather than non-left-wing newspapers, we would not have been so mercilessly put under the media spotlight, a spotlight that could inflame and affect the perception of our company by susceptible shareholders and lenders. I apologize to non-commercial readers for these complexities, but they occur in business and this narrative would have large holes in it if the more important ones were not dealt with here.

Perceptions are crucial in financial markets, where psychology is at least 50 per cent of the story. The perceptions of our company could be and were manipulated sometimes with no reference to truth or reality by ruthless competitors in the media or bandwagons of lazy journalists unwilling to do real research. This was the business I was in by choice and I couldn't complain; I could only fight back as best I could. There were three distinct constituencies: the readers and advertisers wanted high-quality products that are expensive to produce; the shareholders wanted instant financial gratification and didn't care what damage we did to the franchises producing it; and our long-term creditors wanted solid conservative financing. Spurred by another on-rushing bank deadline (at Hollinger Inc.), I worked through the holidays on a debt consolidation and refinancing for Hollinger Inc. The last thing I did before going with Barbara to a New Year's Eve dinner with our flamboyant Palm Beach neighbour Donald Trump at his Mar-A-Lago resort was to discuss terms of a parent company deal with Wachovia.

Our Wachovia refinancing of Hollinger International had been so successful that we were able to return to the same sources to complete the financing of Hollinger Inc., with a somewhat higher but still manageable rate of interest, provided Ravelston backed up Hollinger Inc. The independent directors of Hollinger Inc., concerned that Hollinger Inc. be assured a cash flow from Ravelston, insisted on a support agreement from Ravelston, the ultimate controlling shareholder and recipient of the Hollinger International management fees. The directors were being conscientious, and we had no reason or alternative but to agree. But the revelation in the bond indenture that Ravelston would transmit US$14 million per year to Hollinger Inc. proved a dangerous signal of vulnerability to the massing forces of corporate governance activism.

The investment firm Tweedy Browne now represented to all who would listen that the Hollinger International shareholders had been paying for the Ravelston owners to service the loan on the basis of which their control of the company was maintained. This was presented to skeptical shareholders and the cynics in the financial press as a self-serving round trip that caused us to inflate the management fee. As has been mentioned, the loans in Ravelston had been subscribed to buy large numbers of single-voting shares that were not necessary for the exercise of control and inflicted inconvenience on the controlling shareholder while demonstrating our confidence in the company.

This incorrect thesis was taken up and magnified by competing media companies. We now had a steady problem debriefing many of our own personnel. The fact was, we chose to redirect a large part of our income to pay interest on loans subscribed to buy and hold the largest possible shareholding in our company, instead of simply stuffing ourselves with cost-free options like Alsatian geese (and like most non-owner managements).

Only three days were required to sell out this issue, and we had the undoubted pleasure of paying the banks completely out. We had ended the nightmarish banking liquidity problem but enjoyed only a one-month escape from the endless drumfire of financial harassments before new problems arose to torment us.

At the request of the chairman, Barbara and I invited the CIBC's present and former directors to the annual dinner (which occurs on the evening of the annual shareholders' meeting) at our home in Toronto. This was the first time this dinner had not been hosted by the bank itself. We dined in the boarded-over swimming pool; Barbara suggested that we might want to arrange it so that we could dunk selected board members by pressing a button. The evening felt convivial to me, though Barbara, as usual when she was the hostess, felt it was a complete disaster. Still, it seemed to mark the end of a difficult period in our banking arrangements. Of course, appearances can be deceiving.

As the second Wachovia transaction closed, we settled in to a month of spontaneous relaxation in our new home in Palm Beach. The only cloud on the horizon was the issue of Can$100 million of Hollinger Inc. Series III preferred shares that was due for redemption in April 2004. Thirteen months would normally be quite enough time to take care of redeeming them. But Torys now told us we had to issue a liquidity warning on our Series III preferred shares, although they had given no hint of this as the second Wachovia transaction was being negotiated and marketed.

Hollinger Inc. was technically, for tax reasons, a mutual fund. That meant all shares had to be retractable – that is, shareholders had the right to cash out at any time. The announcement that Torys told us we had to make would guarantee that shareholders would exercise this right with the Series III preferred shares; a precautionary warning could be reasonably assumed to cause a stampede of shareholders demanding redemption of their shares, rather like a run on the bank. This was a tedious re-enactment of a familiar story line. Our own advisers expected to be well paid to enlighten us about the negligence of their previous failure to advise us of dangers that they now triumphantly unveiled and demanded be disclosed. If we had had some warning of this problem, we would have tried to secure a larger bond issue from Wachovia or to make a less explicit arrangement with the independent directors, to ensure the cash flow to the company.

The announcement that Torys had pushed us into making precipitated a supreme financial crisis. Though we worded it as innocuously as possible, it could not fly under the radar. After Reuters prominently ran the initial story, our enemies immediately recognized the potential and pounced on us like leopards. An especially mouthy Bloomberg correspondent was close behind them. I was not surprised at the sadistic delight of the *Guardian*, but the immediate, venomous, and relentless malice of the Murdoch newspapers was more damaging and also unexpected. The chief assassin in the financial pages of the *New York Post* told our vice president of investor relations that Hollinger was his principal assignment.

This particular vice president, Paul Healy, had been a large part of the problem. He emerged unsuspected as a key player in a dangerous role. After a head hunter identified him for us, Radler and I had hired Healy away from the mergers and acquisitions department of the Chase Manhattan

Bank. He had been given about three hundred thousand options (his salary and bonus combined were at or above $500,000 a year for his last years). Healy believed that our method of paying management fees and non-competition payments had reduced the share price and deprived him of his rightful rewards as an option holder. He had helped build a Trojan horse by recruiting investors and analysts who were "value investors," which in practice meant greenmailers who would rely on the mantle of corporate governance to cause as much commotion as possible and try to force a sale of the company. I was aware of his views but tolerated his antics. In truth, my reluctance to fire Healy was based on my calculation that firing him would cause even more problems than keeping him. This was a delicate time, and the last thing I needed was him calling up all our large and institutional shareholders to say he had been sacked because he had discovered bad things. He was so deferential in my presence, and so easily converted to flashes of supportiveness, that retaining him with suitable pep talks from time to time seemed the best course tactically until the problems had been resolved. I was looking at methods of privatization. Had that been accomplished, all our problems would have been solved. Meanwhile, I was being assaulted by a Jurassic predator in the form of Rupert Murdoch, with whom I had thought I was conducting a civilized competition.

Soon the London *Sunday Times* managed to make a malignant connection that would prove very intractable. It located the inimitable Laura Jereski of Tweedy Browne, who jubilantly told the reporter that I did not "run Hollinger in the shareholder's interest." I wrote Christopher Browne that this was an outrageous assertion and an idiosyncratic way for the company's third largest shareholder to promote the company's stock. Of course it was obvious that what Browne was saying would not likely raise the stock price. Especially because Murdoch trumpeted the financial pressures on Hollinger Inc., Browne would have sensed the possibility of forcing the sale of our company at going-concern prices, enabling him to reap a full profit at enterprise values (twelve times operating profit rather than the seven or eight multiple in the stock market). He could flex his muscles before the whole financial community.

Browne believed that now was the time to sell the whole company and take the best profit on his stock. I thought he was wrong and told him there would be no buyers for the whole company, the time was not right, and we were better to continue with piecemeal sales such as we had successfully made. The *Telegraph* could easily command a good price on its own (and did two years later), but we knew it would hold that value if managed properly while we polished up the rest of the company. No one could be more sensitive to where the *Telegraph's* value was going than Dan Colson and I. We sniffed the air and analyzed the water around it every morning – as we had to in shark-infested London. We felt we needed to find buyers so keen to get it that they would buy up everything Hollinger International owned at a top price and sell off the less sought after assets themselves. This view would soon be justified by events.

Despite our disagreements, I tried to develop some common ground with Browne, but his terms were impossible. His guru was shareholder activist Herbert Denton, who once famously declared that assaulting corporate management was "the most fun you could have while keeping your clothes on." (When I eventually met him, Denton seemed to me slight and bookish and unlikely to be overly riotous and hedonistic when liberated from his clothes, but so, I suppose, did Groucho Marx and Woody Allen, from whom he stole the line.) Essentially, Browne wanted to pack our board and begin investigating the company in order to unearth anything useful as ammunition to oust me. We were to conduct a corporate self-torturing exercise directed by Browne against us at our expense. Unable to do that immediately, he resorted to scattergun allegations: a Hollinger International bond issue promised to transfuse money in stipulated amounts to Inc. – this was fiction. I had put a poison pill in the bond issue so that a change of ownership would be a default. I explained that provision was there at the insistence of the buyers, who regarded our control as essential to the company's future (which proved to be accurate). Without any acknowledgement of error, Browne would simply move on to other huffs and puffs. An enemy axis under the informal direction of Healy and Browne materialized. A Baltimore media analyst for Jeffries & Company produced a buy recommendation on our stock, on grounds that if management fees were to be reduced, the whole structure would collapse and we would have to sell the company.

By the beginning of 2003 the atmosphere around Hollinger was confused and ominous. I opened discussions with Bruce Wasserstein, chairman of Lazard, to talk over a range of proposals for our future, including, for the first time seriously, a possible sale of it all.

Southeastern Asset Management, the second-largest shareholder after Hollinger Inc., and who were still supportive, popped up as the atmosphere became heavier and said they would be prepared to work out an arrangement with us if we were prepared to give up the super-voting shares, even gradually. These shares were a bugbear to Southeastern, although Browne was not at all concerned about them. Browne was scandalized by the management fees and the non-competition payments, but the Southeastern managers, Mason Hawkins and Staley Cates, thought we had earned every cent of these payments. Pressed financially and by the corporate militants, I began negotiating with Southeastern as I prepared to depart London for the Bilderberg meetings at Versailles. Bilderberg had brought me good fortune in the past – it was there I made the contacts that led to the purchase of the *Telegraph*.

In between the sessions at Versailles, I was on the telephone with Cates in Memphis trying to work out a deal that would resolve the Hollinger Inc. liquidity issue, reinforce us against the emerging assault on the management fees and non-competition payments, and not require us to surrender control of the company. The conversations were cordial and we made progress. These conversations were still underway when Barbara and I departed London for New York on the evening before the 2003 annual meeting.

On the day before the meeting, Tweedy Browne had filed a 13D (a Securities and Exchange Commission public filing of material interest to the shareholders) as a hostile shareholder and were demanding a special committee of the directors to investigate all the complaints they put in their 13D filing and the accompanying letter, specifically about the management fees and non-competition payments, which they represented as "misappropriations of funds." At that point I had no idea what such a filing from a Special Committee really meant and I certainly had no idea that there was any legal vulnerability. I reached a tentative arrangement with Cates and Hawkins that we would sell them between 5 million and 10 million Hollinger International shares at $11.60, a 15 per cent premium to current market (which had risen from $7.50 since March). There would be a five-year phaseout of the super-voting rights, in which time we would hope to have bought in and cancelled enough shares and exercised enough options to restore a substantial portion of voting control. (I owned 65 per cent of Ravelston, which through its 100 per cent subsidiary, Argus Corporation, owned 78 per cent of Hollinger Inc., which owned 30 per cent of Hollinger International but had 70 per cent of the votes because it owned all the Class B shares, which had ten votes per share.)

There would also be a payment, to be negotiated and independently approved, from Hollinger International to Hollinger Inc. for surrendering the super-voting rights, and a voting agreement with Southeastern that would assure our control beyond five years. Southeastern were free to sell their shares at any time, though they had a brief first refusal arrangement with us. Southeastern would support a management fee of $20 million and a limit of $6 million to me personally (which was twice what I have ever received) because I had contributed so much of my part of the fee to paying interest on loans that sustained our shareholding in single-voting shares. This was a good agreement to be pulled out of the hat at this late stage, hours before the annual meeting – a meeting for which our corporate governance enemies were clearly well prepared and which would likely see open hostilities.

There was a big press contingent in front of the Metropolitan Club as we arrived. The (London) *Sunday Times* reporter mouthily asked whether I was overpaid. I suggested that he probably was but that I was not. All the independent directors were present except Henry Kissinger, who had a meeting of the Eisenhower Foundation. Jim Thompson, the former governor of Illinois, even missed a meeting of the committee to investigate the events of September 11, 2001, to attend.

I gave an upbeat summary of events in my remarks. I mentioned that we had made an *ex gratia* cut of $2 million in our management fee in 2003. I also acknowledged that some matters could be handled less controversially. Because our office in London was in the Docklands and my home was in Kensington, which was a much more convenient place for many people to meet me, one-third of the salary of a butler and one-half of the salary of a chef (who also worked intermittently at the *Telegraph*) were on the company's account. I announced that the practice would cease, as would the practice of the company paying a share of the maintenance costs for my apartment in New York, even though my main reason to be in New York was a corporate one.

I allowed Jim Thompson to take the podium briefly to say that he would be setting up a special committee. It became clear that he had even less idea than I did about what a special committee in the corporate relations culture of the time consisted of because he thought that he and the rest of his Audit Committee would transmogrify into the Special Committee. I assured the shareholders that I was happy with the Special Committee and would welcome any fair analysis of our corporate practices. I said then, and still believe now, that we had been exemplars of full disclosure, even to our own public relations disadvantage, as in the revelation of the payment of one-third of the salary of my butler in my home, even though it could lead to accusations of self-indulgence.

I outlined the arrangements with Southeastern, and then Southeastern's Mason Hawkins took the microphone and credited my associates and me with creating $2 billion of value and running an excellent company. He defended the non-competition payments and said that a $20 million man-agement fee was earned and defensible. Christopher Browne, Laura Jereski, Herbert Denton, Lee Cooperman, and others intervened in a fairly direct but perfectly courteous manner. I had no problem responding to them and took a particularly strong line with Cooperman.

Cooperman said that Hollinger was underperforming its peers, an argument he and I had gone over before. I pointed out that the companies he had in mind – the *New York Times, Washington Post*, Dow Jones, *Chicago Tribune*, Gannett Company, and Knight Ridder (most of whom were also managed by super-voting shares, and most of which would soon be in des-perate straits) – were not our peers. The assets we had taken over, principally in London and Chicago, had been basket cases when we got control of them. We were building them into powerhouses, like the monopolies owned by all the companies Cooperman purported were our peers. It was precisely because we aspired to become, and believed Hollinger could become, a peer of such companies that we had all invested in it. I pointed out to him that he had piled into Tyco, which was then in a state of collapse with the senior management under indictment, and I could more justly criticize his judgment for squandering his clients' money in Tyco than he could object that we did not yet own a *New York Times*.

The meeting had been held up for a few minutes while Southeastern's Hawkins and Cates tried to persuade Browne to withdraw his 13D in light of the arrangements we were making. Browne declined. There was skepticism from the start on the part of Tweedy Browne, especially from Laura Jereski, that anything would come of the Southeastern agreement. On the immediately succeeding days there was a beleaguering variety of calls about implementation, given that the stock we would be selling them was entirely pledged in the second Wachovia bond issue. I explained different methods to implement the arrangement – in particular exercising our right to pay down the notes substantially and doing so with the proceeds of the share sales to Southeastern, or bringing a new investor into Ravelston and applying the proceeds of that investment to purchase for cancellation of some of the notes, freeing some of the shares for Southeastern, and repeating the process with the proceeds of those sales.

The meeting ended agreeably enough, even though Christopher Browne had nominated himself as a non-director member of the Special Committee, a suggestion so presumptuous I ignored it. Gordon Paris, a debt market adviser who had travelled from firm to firm with no great distinction but had been useful to us in some of our transactions and in the first Wachovia underwriting, had been elected a director to comply with the Sarbanes-Oxley Act requirement of including a designated financial expert.

The directors meeting after the board meeting was upbeat, and everyone thought we had come through a difficult challenge quite well. Unfortunately the manager of the Metropolitan Club had ruled that the working press was not welcome inside. We advised the journalists to walk around the block and come in claiming to be shareholders and said we would vouch for them. This was less attractive to journalists than pretending to have been barred at our instruction and then making up out of whole cloth their description of the meeting. Such a technique was employed by Murdoch's newspapers as well as by the *Financial Times*. Nevertheless, analysts' coverage and press comment on the meeting was extensive and rather positive.

There would be some difficulty completing the Southeastern deal, because the stock price started to rise. Not the least irony in these matters was that I had cracked the capital strike. The stock moved up to about $13 over the next couple of months, and it became steadily more difficult to consider asking the Hollinger International independent directors to approve a $40 million payoff to Hollinger Inc. for dispensing with the super-voting rights of the B Shares. Our argument was that by giving up the super-voting shares (over the next five years as the agreement was to stipulate), we would increase the value of the single-vote shares. With the price of single shares going up in anticipation that there would be a bid for the company, this argument was harder to sell to the independent directors. Southeastern would vote for it, but a majority was not assured, and we were chasing a moving target on the price.

As had been predicted by everyone except the Audit Committee members themselves, the notion that they could sustain themselves as the Special Committee soon had to give way to legal advice that this was out of the question. Because everyone else was somehow conflicted out, we were left with a Special Committee of one, Gordon Paris. We recruited two new members for him, Graham Savage, an experienced Canadian financial officer, and Raymond Seitz, former U.S. ambassador in London and chairman of Lehman Brothers International, who I mistakenly thought would be a sensible and fair occupant of that position.

The day after the shareholders meeting, I called upon Christopher Browne to see whether anything could be done to accelerate the good momentum of the previous day. He was in leisure attire, about to go to the Hamptons for the weekend. Our exchange was cordial. He joked that if Donald Trump and Lee Cooperman were the people I saw in Palm Beach, he didn't know why I went there. (Donald and Melania had attended the meeting, and Donald graciously commended management. He would remain a faithful friend through all that was to come.) I replied that I had seen some lounge lizards in the Hamptons who made even Cooperman seem couth, suave, and self-effacing. He conceded the point. It would be downhill after this. We would never speak again.

For the briefest period, all seemed to be calm. The Audit Committee was now composed, apart from Jim Thompson and Richard Burt, of company director Marie-Josée Kravis, the glamorous and clever wife of leveraged buyout king Henry Kravis, and Gordon Paris.

While their forlorn efforts to reconstitute themselves as the Special Committee were under discussion, Burt prevailed upon the others to agree to the appointment of Richard Breeden, former chairman of the U.S. Securities and Exchange Commission and the special monitor in the spectacular WorldCom-MCI reorganization, as counsel to the Special Committee. Breeden was emerging as America's Mr. Corporate Governance. The enabling by-laws of the Special Committee gave it practically unlimited powers of inquiry and insistence on process and procedure, and the committee counsel had an almost unlimited ability and mandate to direct the committee, advise, and require best practice, and bring anything he wished to the attention of the Securities and Exchange Commission (which, again, Breeden had chaired, and clearly could influence, no matter how unaffectionately almost everyone at the SEC volunteered their recollection of him to be). This was enough to drive Marie-Josée off the board. She had already told Barbara, on the day of the annual meeting, that the "appointment of a special committee is the end." She warned me that Breeden "will stay forever, tear the company apart, and cost a fortune."

She told me in late September 2003 that she was retiring because she might find herself in a conflict due to her husband's far-flung activities (Kohlberg Kravis Roberts). It was obvious that this was not the real reason. It was a grievous loss; she was the most commercially intelligent of the outside directors. Her departure incited in me a profound unease about the impending course of events.

Marie-Josée had a reputation for being among the first off the ship when corporate waters became rough. I was not so much interested in dissuading her as I was in finding out what was afoot. She had warned me about Breeden, but she must have been hearing murmurs of substantial problems to make such a hasty exit on such a slim pretext. She could not have been more agreeable on the telephone, combining her withdrawal with an invitation to dinner. But my attempt to probe her real motives was unsettlingly unsuccessful. She told Henry Kissinger, I subsequently learned, that Breeden was "out to destroy" me. I would have enjoyed a little advance notice of this myself. Instead, there was an ominous silence as the undeclared enemy approached. But for the fact that Marie-Josée was such an elegant woman, images of rodents descending the hawser would have commended themselves.

In June, Breeden had attended a directors meeting conducted by telephone. He had said that we should be prepared to hand over our emails and that he hoped to finish by Christmas. As early as August, it was clear that my authority as chairman was shrinking. Prior to the filing of the quarterly statement, there was a demand that my proposed wording of a paragraph describing the state of discussions with Southeastern Asset Management be checked with executives of that company. I offered the Audit Committee's lawyer my emails with Mason Hawkins of Southeastern that confirmed the contents of the paragraph. This wasn't adequate, however, and he insisted on calling Hawkins himself, who confirmed the accuracy of my summary.

Breeden's agents arrived unannounced in our office in Toronto, demanding the right to take everything off my computer's hard drive. They were sent packing, and it was eventually agreed that a lawyer from each side would go through all ten thousand of my emails and if there was any disagreement over what was relevant this would be referred to Ray Seitz and me to settle.

AS THIS CRISIS RUSHED TOWARD ME, I was just finishing the most ambitious intellectual undertaking of my life, a comprehensive biography of Franklin Delano Roosevelt. My friend George (Lord) Weidenfeld, the remarkable and inexhaustible Viennese-British publisher, had invited me to contribute a brief biography of Roosevelt to the series he conceived on a great range of famous people. It was not to exceed forty thousand words. Roosevelt had fascinated me since I was very young and looking at picturebooks of the Second World War a few years after its end. Like his contemporaries, I was struck by the panache and natural charm and flamboyance of his appearance and demeanour, the aristocratic timbre of his voice and inflection, his unequalled political success, and his triumph over a merciless infirmity. This triumph was not only over polio's physical consequences, but also over any public awareness of the extent of its effect on him and, posthumously, over polio itself, as Roosevelt's

March of Dimes and Warm Springs Institute financed the discovery of the Salk vaccine.

By the end of 2000, the project welled up within, and I knew that writing must begin. Words surged out of my thoughts and fingertips, and I began to pour forth on my computer a mighty torrent of what topped out as a draft of 650,000 words in fifty-three weeks. I wrote the first three paragraphs of the book on New Year's Eve 2000, before the arrival of our New Year's celebrants. I had promised my brother, Monte, when he found out he was terminally ill that I would dedicate the book to him. I was able to tell him that I had finished all but the editing a few days before he died, January 10, 2002. They were among the last intelligible words we exchanged.

MY BROTHER, MONTE, WAS SIXTY-ONE when he died. This was really slamming the nursery door. Our parents had died only ten days apart in 1976 and were buried from the same church as my brother and, in my father's case, with the same clergyman presiding. His first wife had predeceased him by two days, two doors down in the same hospital. Their funerals were on consecutive days. Standing next to the family graveyard on a wretched day of bone-chilling wind and rain, I watched my brother's coffin lowered, leaving me the sole member of our original family alive. I concluded my eulogy at his very heavily attended funeral with a citation from Housman's "To an Athlete Dying Young" and with the heartfelt comment: "It was, and will always remain, an honour to be his brother."

Cardinal Carter's passing in 2003 was another terrible loss, though at the age of ninety-one, he could not be described as dying prematurely. He was an irreplaceable source of wise counsel. At my last meeting with him in hospital a couple of weeks before he died, he greeted me with the words "You lost your brother and you are about to lose another brother." We conversed easily for half an hour, as we had more than a thousand times before over the last twenty-five years. He was, as always, well-informed, and we ranged over many subjects, from Iraq to our company. (He had become a director of Argus Corporation when he retired as archbishop of Toronto and remained so to the end of his life.)

Finally, there came the moment I had dreaded for years, but which I could not dodge or defer, to say goodbye. I managed the hope that I could call on him again when next in Toronto, as I always did. I asked him the state of his morale. "Excellent," he said. He felt no fear and had no significant regrets, was thankful for the great life he had had, but was already somewhat detached from it. I asked if he was curious about what lay before him. "Yes, I am very curious. Given my occupation, it would be astonishing if it were otherwise."

Emmett, Cardinal Carter was my friend and guide, the one man I could turn to in the darkest hour and who lightened my burdens through his friendship and our shared faith. He must have had faults, but I never detected any. He was a great man, yet the salt of the earth. He said so much to me that was so sensible and intelligent, a good deal of it personal and uniquely insightful about himself and about me, that the benefit of our friendship is imperishable. Even in the gloomy times in which I now write, he is a guide and an inspiration.

THOUGH I HAD SOMETIMES suffered business disappointments and personal setbacks, including the premature death of my immediate family, I felt that my life until now had been on an upward trajectory. I had no experience of real misfortune. In almost every way, I was completely unprepared for the impending challenge. What sustained me were my faith and my marriage.

My faith had been arrived at after a journey of extensive consideration and reading over many years, and comprehensive discussions with my friends Cardinal Léger and Cardinal Carter. I have described this process at some length elsewhere. For my purposes here, it is enough to say that I concluded that spiritual forces do exist, that Christ was spiritually inspired, a divine, that he had told St. Peter to found a church, that as miracles do sometimes occur, any miracle could occur, and that for all its failings, the continuation of what Christ told St. Peter to build is the Roman Catholic Church. Therefore, if one wished to communicate with the spiritual forces of the cosmos, the most legitimate, the surest way, though not a sure way and not the only way, was within the Roman Catholic Church. I gradually lost my former faith in the non-existence of God, and it became, both intellectually and psychologically, less difficult to believe than not.

I am not a pious or fervent person. My faith inspires me when I most need inspiration and consoles me when I am most in need of reassurance that my life has a value and a meaning, especially when public comment and even harsh introspection lead me to consider the opposite conclusion.

But the strongest fortification I have, one that has been helpful beyond estimation in the recent crisis, is my marriage. No man could ask for a braver and more supportive spouse than Barbara. The crisis in my career culminated in her unimaginably unjust firing as a *Telegraph* columnist and widespread denigration in the competing British media, and in some places in Canada. But her loyalty did not waver. I have seen a few relationships in which the partners are romantically faithful, best friends, intellectual soulmates, co-workers, and virtually therapists to each other, but none so completely successful as my present marriage. When I was temporarily defeated by my enemies, Barbara was widely assumed to be looking for her fifth husband. I would not have blamed her if she had, and I told her so. This was never a prospect.

To be oppressed by the militant charlatans of corporate governance and to be victimized by the misguided justice systems of two of the world's most advanced countries is something of an honour. But to have this fate shared voluntarily and philosophically, even proudly, by an inspiring wife, is as great an honour as a man can have in the adversity of his personal life.

[Chapter Four]

I SPENT MUCH OF THE SUMMER of 2003, the last that would have any semblance of normalcy for a long time, visiting private equity firms and seeking financing to buy out the public shareholders of our companies. Almost everyone (Madison Dearborn, Quadrangle, Warburg Pincus, and four or five others) expressed enthusiasm at first but flaked off later. There was an eerie similarity to the sequence: first, confident assurances that the hostile climate was no obstacle to a private firm, followed by apparently successful due diligence procedures and negotiations. Then silence. I would telephone, once, twice, only to be put off and finally to have someone tell me – regretfully or distantly – that unfortunately it couldn't be done. Steve Schwartzman of Blackstone told me that he would like to buy, but he had to await the Special Committee process. Finally, Bain & Company of Boston were positive, and we negotiated an acceptable term sheet that would privatize both Hollinger companies and leave us as equal shareholders and managing partners.

As summer gave way to autumn I was still hopeful, despite the storm signals, that if the Special Committee did not find any technical problems with the company's accounts – and Peter Atkinson, Jack Boultbee, Mark Kipnis, the Audit Committee, and the auditors repeatedly assured me that all was in order – then we could see off the corporate governance zealots. The only complaint of Browne and the others was that we had been too generously compensated. They glossed over the accretion in the company's value, claiming that the self-indulgent mores of the management, with the supine acquiescence of the directors, had disguised underlying value. This was nonsense, as subsequent events were to prove.

If the independent directors held firm and the Special Committee found nothing to stampede the independent directors away from the management, we could weather the tempest Jereski, Browne, and a few others had created.

The insistence of the Audit Committee in August on checking my wording of the 10Q quarterly statement about the status of our negotiations with Southeastern illustrated the extent to which my authority as chairman had diminished. Next the Audit Committee simply refused to honour a demand note due to Hollinger Inc. when payment was demanded. The note was connected to a lingering obligation to CanWest that Hollinger Inc. would assume. Normally, there would be no balkiness at any of this, but normalcy was already fleeing.

I toiled in the footnotes and corrections to my Roosevelt book and then went to London for a couple of weeks. Shortly after I returned to New York in late October, Bain & Company abruptly pulled out right at the point of closing. I was informed by several sources that the Special Committee staff were warning off potential investors. The hostile press, especially News Corporation, and the officious Special Committee investigators were all closing in on our point of maximum vulnerability. We needed to re-finance the Canadian company, and they were making any recapitalization impossible.

With the defection of Bain, it was time to bring Bruce Wasserstein and Lazard (the investment bank of which he was chairman) forward. I intensified discussions with possible investors: Teddy Forstman, with whom I had had a connection at Gulfstream, and even Wasserstein himself, in his own private company Wasserco, while he was leading a discussion on behalf of Lazard on the same general subject. I found Wasserstein's conflict startling, but he was so brazen about it, I assumed that this was how the ethics of the New York financial community had evolved. All my instincts were that we were tumbling toward a very difficult climax, carefully authored by invisible, but not unidentifiable, enemies. I braced myself as best I could for unbidden events.

These began to reveal themselves on the morning of October 30. I was about to leave the office in New York to promote my book on a local authors television program when a call came in from Jack Boultbee, Fred Creasey (the controller of both Hollingers), and Peter Atkinson. It seemed that two lots of non-competition payments totalling a little more than US$30 million, from the sale of American community newspapers in 2000, had not been formally approved by the Hollinger International Audit Committee. My heart sank. Our enemies not only had a smoking gun, but all but one of its chambers were still loaded, and we had conveniently handed it to them pre-targeted to our foreheads. How could this have happened? As usual when disaster due to human error occurs, the humans who committed the error had no recollection of it.

David Radler had bought, managed, and sold these newspapers. He had performed every one of these phases very capably and generated a huge capital gain for the company. He knew nothing of any of it and immediately began the kind of fingerpointing that is the joy and staple of the life of prosecutors looking for cooperating witnesses. He said Mark Kipnis had told him he had Audit Committee approval. Then he said that Jack Boultbee must have made the arrangements, because only Boultbee knew the tax and other complexities involved. Kipnis acknowledged that Radler must have thought that he had Audit Committee approval but said that he had never been asked to obtain it and apparently, therefore, had not. (It wasn't up to the company secretary to request approval from the Audit Committee for $30 million of payments.) Boultbee said he had never had anything to do with any part of these transactions. They were entirely Radler's doing; he knew nothing. Peter Atkinson was paid the formidable sum of $1.2 million per year to ensure that all legal matters were handled properly. He had been told, as I had, back in 2000 by Radler, that these were non-competition payments that had been approved by the Audit Committee. Kipnis had assured Atkinson that they were in order.

Beyond this, no one knew anything. Somewhere in this group, a serious oversight had occurred, but I encountered a pandemic of amnesia. It was like interviewing a group of children after some frightful accident had befallen a piece of furniture or precious ornament when no adult was present. No one knew anything – except that it had nothing to do with him. None of these highly compensated and generally competent executives could remember anything except their own complete, mystifying, oblivious non-involvement. They had failed, but the full force of the joyful malice of our enemies was about to fall like a pack of famished wolves on me.

As has been recorded, non-competition agreements, in the case of small local newspapers in North America, are almost always part of any agreement of sale, not only because of the presumed expertise of the vendor but because of the competitive ease with which anyone, especially someone familiar with the market, can establish what are called "shoppers." They are the free papers full of ads you see often at the supermarket cashiers or on the street corner. A vendor who knows the market can quickly come up with a "shopper" and undercut the economics of the business that has been sold. The reason the Thomson Corporation lost so much ground in local markets was that it put such cost-cutting pressures on its publishers that they squeezed the product to produce the required margins, making them vulnerable to shoppers published or supported by disgruntled local merchants. Thomson ignored these shoppers, and their franchises suffered.

Whether the non-competition payments were made to individuals or corporations depended on whether the feared competition was corporate or personal. If the vendor was a large public company such as Gannett, without a controlling shareholder, the payment would be made to the selling corporation. Where the vendor was a personal or private corporation, or as in the case of Hollinger International, a public corporation with controlling shareholders who had built up the company and closely operated it, the payment was generally made either to the individuals or to the combination of corporation and individuals.

As we unloaded newspapers in our build-down to a solid and relatively debt-free platform anchored in London and Chicago, the Audit Committee had routinely approved non-competition payments and had frequently expressed their satisfaction, echoed by the directors as a whole and many shareholders, with the immense capital gains that the company was racking up. The company's debt was reduced by 80 per cent, and the normalized cash flow by only about 40 per cent. And by far the most promising growth assets were retained. These two lots of non-compete payments had gone through the usual chain of approvals several years earlier: they were discussed in SEC filings and company reports; the auditors and outside counsel were aware of them; the Audit Committee had signed off on documentation of them but had not, apparently, explicitly approved them by resolution.

Dreadful as this was, I felt that while the process was incomplete, it was sufficiently open that human error was the most likely explanation. In my worst imagination, I could not foresee that five years on, these two incompletely authorized groups of payments and nothing else would have led to the bankruptcy of the two companies I had built that now had nearly $2 billion of shareholder equity and underlying value. Nor could I imagine that this was the spark for years of criminal and civil litigation with covens of lawyers, auditors, inspectors, monitors, regulators, judges all drawing fees and funds into the hundreds of millions in order to provide kindling for my career's funeral pyre. What I did imagine was afoot was grim enough.

At this point, the only American lawyer I had was a Delaware corporate law specialist, Jesse Finkelstein. I had often spoken to him on the telephone but had never laid eyes on him. He lived near Wilmington, travelled much of the time, and had no background in the sort of situation that now loomed. I was put onto him when Paul Saunders, a distinguished corporate litigator who had acted for me in the M.A. *Hanna* case in 1982,* recommended him. Paul himself could not act for me, because in the two hours between our July directors meeting, which included telephone attendance by Breeden, and when I called to retain him, Henry Kissinger had called Paul's firm, Cravath, Swaine & Moore, and engaged him, claiming that I had urged all the directors to retain individual counsel. (I had not, but it didn't much matter. In due course, we found out that Radler had hired criminal counsel the moment the Special Committee had been formed.)

---

* M.A. Hanna Company, named after President McKinley's chief backer, had been Hollinger Inc.'s associate in iron ore mining ventures in Labrador and Quebec, which supplied many of America's largest steel companies. We made a takeover bid for Hanna in 1982, which was resisted, and there was some lively litigation in Cleveland, and an amicable settlement that left us with 28 per cent of the stock, and a strong board position.

When I finally did meet Jesse Finkelstein, my assessment of him tilted in his favour on the slight grounds that he reminded me, in appearance and manner, of the late Igor Kaplan, who had been an invaluable counsel at the time I had taken over Argus Corporation in 1978. He proved to have all of Kaplan's decency and elegance but not his worldliness. I had asked Finkelstein to recommend a tough, experienced corporate litigator whose knowledge would go up to the edge of criminal law matters, as our enemies would likely not downplay the felonious possibilities of the story that was about to break. He arranged for the famous barrister David Boies (most recently known for his unsuccessful championship of Vice President Al Gore's claim to victory in the 2000 presidential election) to call on me. But this could not be done before November 14. This was two weeks on but it seemed manageable. While I had grave intuitive forebodings, they were somewhat cabined by an unworldly attachment to logical limits to possible damage. My historical observations told me this could quickly become a revolutionary climate, proceeding to upheavals and figurative executions. At this moment and for some days to come a delay in securing a heavy-duty legal team seemed less disturbing than it should have been.

Much would now depend on the directors. I assumed I would receive a reasonable degree of benevolence from them, as some were close personal friends and would know that I could not conceivably have done anything unethical. I thought that if I started to advise and lobby them now, especially before I was in a position to shed much light on these developments, it could be misunderstood. I pieced together what I could from endlessly repeating the same questions to my amnesiac colleagues. It did not require a clairvoyant to deduce that the shadowy Richard Breeden was about to show his hand, and that the fairness and judgment of the directors, a distin-guished group, was about to be tested, in very improvident circumstances.

Social life in New York continued at its usual hectic autumn pace. In the first weeks of November, the usual brittleness in the endless gatherings of more or less the same people in the apartments of Fifth Avenue and Park Avenue possessed a greater air of unreality than ever. I had seen the light-ning. I would not have long to wait for the thunder.

The directors were a varied group of apparently competent and independent-minded but thoroughly well-disposed people. Two of the most capable directors apart from Marie-Josée Kravis had retired in the last year. The talented investor Ray Chambers, former partner of, but a less mercurial and abrasive personality than, the Nixon-era treasury secretary Bill Simon, had retired at the end of 2002 in order to pursue a life of travel and philanthropy. Leslie Wexner, one of the world's greatest and wealthiest retailers and founder and controlling shareholder of The Limited, had retired before the 2003 annual meeting because he disliked the risks inherent in public companies and found no countervailing interest here to retain his adherence. In 2002, I had retired the directors aged eighty or older: Dwayne Andreas, Bob Strauss, and George (Lord) Weidenfeld. Robert Strauss, former Democratic Party chairman, U.S. trade representative, Middle East peace negotiator, and ambassador to the Soviet Union and the Russian Federation, a delightful man of immense astuteness, felt uncomfortable serving on a board beyond his eightieth birthday. George Weidenfeld, though not particularly well versed in commercial matters, was a remarkably well-connected and imperishably energetic man whose loyalty would have been entirely reliable through the crisis that was about to break. I did not feel that I could retire some octogenarians but not all, and I parted with him with reluctance. A social and political force of surpassing acuity, he would have been invaluable. He came to London from Vienna in 1938, just after the *Anschluss*, was in the German monitoring service of the BBC during the war, and became one of the world's best-known and most successful book publishers with Weidenfeld & Nicolson.

Alfred Taubman also retired. I had re-elected him in 2002 after he had been convicted of a felony, a restraint of trade in his capacity as controlling shareholder of Sotheby's, of which I was a director. I did not believe that his conduct had been unethical, and felt he had been convicted on the denunciation of the company president as part of the plea bargain system and after what he believed was an inept legal defence. He had been a conscientious, diligent, and useful director of ours and gave us invaluable assistance in negotiating arrangements with Donald Trump for the redevelopment of the *Sun-Times* building in Chicago. He, too, would be missed.

Apart from Barbara and my associates Dan Colson, David Radler, and Peter Atkinson, there were the members of the Audit Committee, the Special Committee, and Henry Kissinger, Richard Perle, and our Israeli director, Shmuel Meitar. Meitar had been our partner in the publication of the Israel *Yellow Pages*, known locally as *Golden Pages*. The contract to print these pages had been given to the *Jerusalem Post* and then unexpectedly withdrawn from our company in favour of a firm with which Meitar was closely associated. He did not inform us of this connection. When I found out, Radler, who had effectively concealed the fact, said that Meitar claimed he was powerless to restrain his own associates. It was a mystery to me why Radler wanted him to continue as a director, other than to avoid embarrassment, to which he was always pathetically sensitive. As events unfolded, Meitar became progressively more difficult to reach, vanishing on frequent and prolonged alleged holidays in the bowels of the Orient.

In Gordon Paris's first week as a director, he joined the Audit Committee and the Special Committee when it was set up. From the beginning he made references to upcoming lunches and meetings with Laura Jereski and others. I couldn't blame him for informing himself, but when he made it clear that he did not necessarily believe the version of our discussions with Southeastern Asset Management that I had written for the quarterly report in the summer of 2003, he arrayed himself as an antagonist. This was a role to which he quickly warmed and for which he was handsomely paid.

Because Chicago is such an impressive city, I had always assumed that someone who held the governorship of Illinois for fourteen years as Audit Committee chairman Jim Thompson had would be as impressive as a comparably successful officeholder in New York. I was disappointed. His Audit Committee colleague Richard Burt was a man who was, and certainly held himself out as, a friend. He had been often to our home, had confided some of his marital difficulties, and had latterly spent a good deal of effort trying to entice me into investing in a sequence of hare-brained ideas prompted by his Saudi employers.

The other member of the Audit Committee had been economist Marie-Josée Kravis. Because I had known her longer and more favourably than the others and she had departed the company, as I described earlier, discreetly and without having to take a stance in the early skirmishing that ensued, I did my best to leave her out of the controversy. I had known her fairly casually for twenty-five years. She parlayed the Hudson Institute's two-person office in Canada into a position of some apparent importance and capitalized on her connections to the Trudeau government to enhance her social status and money-earning capacities as a royal commission member and recipient of other official preferments. She lived for some years with Jean-Pierre Goyer, one of Trudeau's cabinet ministers. I admired her candid and contemporary approach to her private life, her staunch federalism, which was not popular in the Quebec intellectual milieu that she often frequented, and her cool, alluring manner.

Ms. Kravis has never, in my observation of her, misspoken, embarrassed herself, said too much or too little, or been anything other than elegant and detachedly self-possessed. After her marriage to the conductor of the Montreal Symphony Orchestra, Charles Dutoit, failed, I invited her to Bilderberg. Thus I could claim a slight role in bringing her together with the prominent financier Henry Kravis. From all outward appearances, it has been a splendid marriage and she handled her entry into New York society with consummate skill. Never too eager for acceptance nor too standoffish, she quickly overcame the barrage of skepticism and envy that greeted her originally, and after a few months, even a few of the more sulphurous doyennes were comparing her to Jackie Kennedy Onassis for her French graciousness and worldliness and good taste. Her coolness can be chilling and haughty at times, but she had always been pleasant to me and has greeted the ups and downs of her life with outward reserve and imperturbable dignity. She is an able and attractive woman, but will re-enter this narrative less benignly after an absence of several years.

After Rick Burt had brought in his government and post-government acquaintance Richard Breeden as Special Committee counsel, we needed additional members for the Special Committee. Graham Savage was Peter Atkinson's suggestion. Savage had served many years as the chief financial officer of Ted Rogers's formidable Canadian cable and media group. This furnished him invaluable experience in many areas that could be of use to the Special Committee. Savage is the allegorization of the colourless Canadian accountant: soft-spoken, slight, earnest, and to me instantly forgettable. A cipher.

I had recruited Ray Seitz, former assistant secretary of state for Europe and Canada (a successor of Burt's), well-regarded ambassador to the United Kingdom, and chairman of Lehman Brothers International. He seemed urbane, intelligent, and gracious, a fine diplomat who seduced the British as elegant, understated foreigners sometimes can, and who, like David Bruce (ambassador in the Kennedy and Johnson years), received the supreme accolade of the London salon: "He is one of us."

I importuned him to take this position, confident that he would be a judicious counterweight to Breeden, about whose character and intentions warnings flooded in after the initial concern from Marie-Josée, and also to Gordon Paris, who I doubted possessed the gravitas or intellect to lead or even make a very useful contribution, although he was a competent salesman. I expected Savage to be plodding but sensible and counted on Seitz to steer the whole effort justly, applying diplomatic talents where necessary to prevent Breeden from transmuting his supposedly impartial inquiry into a lynch mob. I sized up Breeden (sight unseen), and even Savage fairly accurately, though I underestimated Paris. I misjudged Seitz.

The board's two most eminent participants, Richard Perle and Henry Kissinger, were men I counted as close personal friends, as they frequently proclaimed themselves to be even as the coming nightmare unfolded. Their extremely high intelligence, affective personalities, and remarkable careers are well known. I admired them from a distance long before I met them. I largely owed my relations with them to the Bilderberg conferences, where, as at some other meetings, we often spoke on the same platform and almost always on the same side, against the appeasers in the latter days of the Cold War, against the hydra-headed forces of anti-Americanism, and against those in the world who wished to collegialize American strength through the assumption of moral exaltation for themselves without any practical effort.

This was enjoyable work in agreeable surroundings for all of us. And although I make no claim to speak from the same background of public service as these statesmen, I was no less vehement for that. The high-level international conference circuit breeds a fine spirit of camaraderie, and with Henry Kissinger it was greatly elevated by our frequent encounters in New York when Barbara and I became part-time residents there.

Richard Perle is unpretentious, unaffected, gregarious, rather disorganized, and thoroughly endearing. He is relatively undiscriminating in his thoughts about matters outside the strategic world and in people. He is a constant source of dubious commercial ideas from his "smart newspaper box" to all manner of dot-com and bio-novelty ventures. His genius does not translate well into fields other than official national security policy, an area of which he tired before the Reagan administration ended. His subsequent career has been an anticlimax.

I recruited him to our American board soon after I got to know him, and he became the chairman of the independent directors, in which capacity he performed exemplary work. With the help of his astute if gratuitously bombastic lawyer, Dennis Block, Perle put through the transfer of the *Telegraph* and the Canadian assets to American Publishing, which then became Hollinger International, with great skill and complete fairness.

When new technologies became so influential they overshadowed the traditional media, and any company wishing to retain any currency in the securities markets had to make some gesture to it, Perle, with his absorbing interest and contacts in the new media, seemed the natural person to head this effort on our behalf. My brother's stepson, Matthew Doull, an authentic techie who had worked for us at the *Telegraph*, became the president of Hollinger Digital, as this new division was called, and Perle became the chairman.

Matthew's restlessness with what he saw as Perle's inefficiency was such that we eventually divided Digital in two; each took his own section. Of course there were many losers among the investments and both Richard and Matthew proved distinctly fallible, but we had our share of successes. The last I saw, the company had a fighting chance to come out of it more or less at break-even, a respectable performance compared with the billions squandered in the dot-coms by larger companies with more apparently qualified experts and more orthodox business methods.

In geostrategic matters, Richard Perle was a refreshing Californian, unburdened by the chronic world-weariness, pessimism, and respect for the status quo of centuries that afflicted Henry Kissinger. The night of the Iraqi invasion of Kuwait, I telephoned Perle at his home in France to recruit him for the Advisory Board we were setting up. He was engaged until after 4 a.m. his time, raising bellicose spirits among his former colleagues now in the first Bush administration, before he called me back to accept. When we next met in London, he got into my car and handed me a manifesto of an organization he co-chaired with two well-known American leftists and bearing a pacifistic, if not bucolic, name. He said, "This is my latest initiative, supposedly to find a peaceful resolution of the Kuwait invasion, but really to get the war started."

Always witty, patient, and philosophical, never intimidated by adversity, Perle was a delight as a dinner companion, as a houseguest, or on a Mediterranean cruise (where he and his wife and son twice joined us, once in a particularly uproariously amusing cruise along the Côte d'Azur with Bill and Pat Buckley in 1996). In the crisis, Perle was the last ally to break and run, though break and run he did, but at least he expressed regret.

This is not the place for a comprehensive biographical sketch of Henry Kissinger. It need hardly be emphasized that he is a world historic figure and one of the great personalities of the last third of the twentieth century. He has a remarkable and unflagging intellect and a brilliant sense of humour; he is a political operator of impressive dexterity within any sphere; and he has a wife, son, and daughter (from his earlier marriage) who do him honour. Allegations that he has no patriotic or sectarian loyalty, no deep attachment to people, and that he lacks respect for institutions of which he is not a natural adherent are untrue (he even has a sophisticated respect for the Roman Catholic Church). Of all twentieth-century statesmen, only Winston Churchill and Charles de Gaulle surpass him as a stylistic memoirist, and they were, after all, symbols and executants of the regeneration of great nations. Kissinger's best works are a contribution to literature as well as history.

He also possesses great physical courage. When we were together in Belgium at another Bilderberg meeting, he called me at 3 a.m. to tell me that he had lost the sight of one eye. I accompanied him to the hospital and sat up with him all night. He had suffered a thrombosis and lost the sight of his right eye permanently, but he insisted on chairing his scheduled session a few minutes after we returned to the conference centre at 8 a.m.

He was like the Earl of Uxbridge at Waterloo, calmly informing the Duke of Wellington that he had just lost his leg (to a French cannonball). His sang-froid, taking down the names and addresses of the doctors and nurses at the Louvain hospital so that he could write to them, and mentioning the incident to no one, was an inspiration.

He is not at all without sentiment. I have discussed how, two weeks after this incident with his eye he returned to England so that we could go together to make our farewells to John Aspinall, the flamboyant casino and zoo owner, who died of cancer a few days later. Kissinger wept without embarrassment as we left. When my own brother, whom he scarcely knew, was dying of cancer, he telephoned him and spoke words of great encouragement. He is a punctilious and eloquent correspondent.

His self-importance, irritability, and roughshod treatment of subordinates are considerable, but he recognizes his own foibles. When we returned from Amman to Berlin for yet another conference, after he had changed hotels because of the inadequacy of the suite accorded him, we went, together with Nancy Kissinger, to Frederick the Great's palace at Sans Souci. A motorcade was provided that sped to our destination, the docile Germans pulling to the sides of the roads more respectfully than Parisians, Londoners, or New Yorkers would have done. After a few miles of screaming sirens and steady acceleration, Kissinger said, "You know, this isn't bad for someone who has been out of office for twenty years."

When he was secretary of state, he was asked by a journalist as he arrived at the bar mitzvah of the son of a friend whether this reminded him of his own bar mitzvah in Germany. He instantly responded. "Actually, von Ribbentrop wasn't able to come to mine." He knows to mock his own egotism: when Lord Peter Carrington met him and apologized at the end of their conversation for having arrived a few minutes late, Kissinger demurred and said, "You are feeding my megalomania."

He is almost always implacably gloomy about the ability of successive American administrations to achieve anything and about international affairs generally – unless asked what would be possible if he were in charge of the State Department. Yet he is morbidly preoccupied with criticism and easily destabilized by negative press comment. He peremptorily withdrew as chairman of the 9/11 Committee when there was the slightest hint of criticism and then blamed his failing to intimates such as Barbara and me on faulty legal advice. He has contempt for almost everyone and so sees no inconsistency in trying to make friends of his enemies.

By background, experience, study, and taste, he is a Metternichian manoeuvrer, always aware of weaknesses, with an un-American sense of vulnerability and cautious belief in what is possible, conferring the accolade of friendship on multitudes, of intimate friendship on a more select group, but in fact respecting few and confiding in no one except his wife. His transitory interest prevails over everything, effortlessly, but in the aftermath, genuine sentiment, a historical regard for those who lose, and a desire not to leave enemies behind him causes him to doff his cap to the fallen. Withal, he is, in many ways, a great man, and most of his critics do not deserve to be taken seriously.

He is a grateful American, a loyal son of Germany, a serious though not especially proud and not religious Jew, an exemplary husband, and, up to a point, a good friend. I have a vast correspondence of warm letters of imperishable friendship from him, and he said under oath in the Hollinger proceedings that I had been one of his closest friends in the world for decades. Our houses contain many books inscribed by him to Barbara and me as "indispensable pillars of my life." Unfortunately, none of this prevented him from dispensing with us for seven years without a warning or even a pretext when his association with me became even a slight inconvenience.

It was on these people that I largely depended as I was swept down into the deepest crisis of my life.

On November 6, 2003, I received a peremptory letter from Paris and Thompson in their capacities as chairmen of the Special and Audit Committees to "instruct" me to answer many questions about the two lots of supposedly unauthorized non-competition payments. They gave me five days. I did another telephone canvass. Based on what I learned, mostly from Mark Kipnis, as Jack Boultbee and David Radler were unable to recall anything and Peter Atkinson simply threw up his hands and concluded that one of the others had become recklessly addicted to non-competition fees, I cobbled together a reply as best I could. I sent it to Jesse Finkelstein, who was still the only American lawyer I had at the time. My reply was essentially suppositions in respect of the $15.5 million paid to executives, including rather more than $5 million to me. I knew nothing about the origins of the $16.5 million paid to Hollinger Inc., although I naturally recalled when the money came in and had been assured that it had been properly approved (as a court eventually determined to be true). The payments to executives had been declared by the auditors and the Audit Committee to have been approved and fully disclosed many times. I made these points and suggested that the two committees defer taking a position until the Special Committee had finished its work. While I was skeptical about Breeden's Christmas timeline, it did not seem to me unreasonable to propose trying to put the whole matter in the context of the full report.

Jesse Finkelstein was in Los Angeles at the time. He made some modest changes only, put the essence of my letter onto his letterhead to preserve lawyer-client privilege, and sent it to Paris and Thompson. He seemed satisfied with what I had written. I thus received very little legal advice, and that from a lawyer whom I hadn't yet met. Though I realized this was a deadly struggle, I had no real understanding of what corporate warfare in America involved: I was no innocent, but I was an entrepreneur with mainly Canadian and U.K. experience.

Jimmy Goldsmith had said he would never attempt business again in America, that it was a corrupt system and one had to fight the U.S. government and its agencies as well as the normal business battles. And Jimmy was as fierce a businessman as I have met. James (Lord) Hanson had similar accounts of his run-ins. But much as I respected them both, I had assumed there was some element of exaggeration. I had read accounts of corporate battles in American business, but such accounts didn't illuminate the way regulatory agencies were used: not as umpires or "truth-seekers" but as legions to be deployed against the fashionable target of the day, making up new rules as they went along under the flag of "exceptional circumstances." I had no idea of who or how to find battle-hardened American corporate lawyers and anyway there was no time.

Finkelstein's arrangement for David Boies to call on me was made for November 14. On November 11, Thompson and Paris telephoned and suggested they meet me at our New York office the following day in the late morning. There was no mention of their being accompanied by anyone, and I assumed that we would have a fairly informal discussion of the allegedly unauthorized payments. The fact that the two had written to me jointly and claimed to be co-chairs of a joint committee confirmed my fears that a Faustian bargain had been struck to shelter the Audit Committee in exchange for its full assistance to Breeden against the management. Subsequent events would only confirm that impression.

Because I was chiefly preoccupied with trying to refinance Hollinger Inc. and get out from under the liquidity problem, which had already kicked up Can$27 million of unhonoured preferred-share retractions, I started the day with a meeting with Jonathan Rothermere of Associated Newspapers at the Carlyle Hotel, to explore the possibility of uniting the two British newspaper groups for business purposes, while retaining editorial control of the *Telegraph*. Rothermere was accompanied by British Merrill Lynch officials, and it was quite a satisfactory opening discussion. I revisited them at the end of the afternoon, but by then my world had changed forever.

Proceeding down Fifth Avenue to meet Paris and Thompson, I was eventually informed that they and two other men awaited me in the boardroom. I joined them and took the head of the table. The others were Jim McDonough, independent counsel to the Audit Committee, with whose sluggish approach to many matters I was already familiar by telephone, and Richard Breeden. Finally, the person I felt instinctively and by tidbits of corporate intelligence would be my nemesis, and possibly a mortal threat to my position, showed himself.

Breeden's appearance was not reassuring: round, flabby face; dull, lifeless eyes behind thick spectacles; a brusque, humourless, and unanimated demeanour. He reminded me of nothing so much as a regional commissar of Beria's, with the bloodless, piscine coldness of someone whose power vastly exceeded his intelligence. I was not optimistic that appearances were deceiving.

He said little. When he spoke, it was to restore the prosecutorial tone of the proceedings. As the meeting wore on and its direction was firmly established – my head on a stake – Breeden brought to mind Kafka's description of Mr. Pollunder in *America*: "the words rolled furiously over his sagging lower lip, which like all loose heavy flesh was easily agitated."

In the brief period of our civilized exchanges, the only sparks of life I was able to fan from the phlegmatic hulk of Breeden's personality were his pride in his sons and his love of sailing. I could identify with these, at least, but it was gruel too thin to vary his hostile purposes.

In a pattern that was to become familiar, it was Paris who delivered Breeden's message. The payments were rigorously unauthorized and improper. The many retroactive statements of approval of the payments to executives, on SEC forms all filled out long before there was any mention or even thought of a Special Committee, did not alter that fact. They had canvassed the buyers of the newspapers and there was no possibility that they had requested the non-competition agreements from Hollinger Inc. (Eventually, almost the entire Paris–Breeden position would be rejected at trial, and the rest vacated on appeal.) All of the independent directors (Richard Perle was not considered independent) had been consulted, and they were unanimous that I had to go as chief executive officer, leaving me as non-executive chairman in charge of meetings, and that Radler had to go completely. Kipnis and Boultbee had to go as officers, and Atkinson had to go as a director but could remain for a time as an officer. The sums would be repaid in full, with interest, 10 per cent at New Year's and the balance by June 1, 2004. The management services agreement with Ravelston would end.

It was agreed that Lazard – with whom I had been dickering since May and whom I proposed to engage to assist in smashing the capital strike and getting our stock price up – would be engaged for what Breeden portentously called a Strategic Process. This would be defined as an exploration of a whole range of alternatives, from doing nothing to selling the entire company. Hollinger Inc. should avoid any refinancing that would constitute a dilution of the control of the existing principal share-holder, Ravelston. The controlling shareholder was to be transformed at once into a eunuch, bound hand and foot to Breeden's war chariot, and I was to acknowledge, in effect, that my control had been merely a mas-querade, an imposture. The jig was up, and I was to drop any pretense to directing the company's affairs or having any real equity in it and humbly retire, like a schoolboy resuming his place after receiving a severe thrash-ing in front of his classmates. Paris said any balkiness on my part would lead to the whole board going to court to remove us all. These measures would be written up in what would be referred to from now on as the Restructuring Agreement.

It was a thorough putsch. My dear colleagues on the board, whom I had not lobbied because I thought it would be unseemly, gave me no notice of the stroke Breeden had prepared, though it subsequently emerged in a deposition of Kissinger's that Breeden had been bandying about for several weeks the likelihood of crimes having been committed. Kissinger later told me, during the weeks while he was still pledging never to desert me, that Seitz had instantly called for far more extreme measures – namely the summary dismissal of all of us, and that he, Kissinger, had defended my status as chairman of the *Telegraph*.

I had to choose between resistance and collaboration, and decided to see whether the carapace of my visitors could be probed. I said that of course if money had been paid improperly, it should be returned. I could not speak for anyone else, but I had done nothing wrong. No allegation of wrongdoing against me had been made, and it was impossible that there was evidence of any. Obviously, if it were otherwise, I would not have been invited to remain as chairman. I could accept having a co-chief executive officer. I emphasized, and they agreed, that perceived financial instability at the top of the group was a bad thing for the whole group and that they should not hobble Hollinger Inc. It was a public company in another country with its own shareholders, and they should not try to control it.

It was a perfectly civilized and courteous exchange, and they gave some ground. It was agreed to reconvene at dinnertime at Le Cirque. I returned to meet with Rothermere at the Carlyle, went home and telephoned Atkinson and Radler, and then went to dinner. My guests straggled in half an hour to an hour late, without a hint of an apology, and negotiation recommenced. Again it was quite cordial, and I did what I could to loosen things up without seeming to take our purposes lightly. It was clear that they had again canvassed the directors, as they acknowledged, and steadied the ranks in a somewhat more forward position than where we had left off in the afternoon. Again I had to defend the prerogatives of Hollinger Inc. and again I protested that I could not commit that company which was in a different jurisdiction with a separate board of directors or commit any other person to terms I might negotiate. I would do what I could to persuade Inc.'s board to accept its part of any Restructuring Agreement I agreed to, if the allegations proved accurate and provided International would keep up its cash-flow obligations to Inc. for six months. We fenced through dinner. When Thompson proposed to retain the level of cash flow to Ravelston and therefore Hollinger Inc., even if that meant at its current level through to June 2004, and even if that meant front-loading the payment, I promised a best effort at agreement from Hollinger Inc., provided the version of events they gave me was confirmed.

I got Thompson to reminisce about his political career, and elicited the fact that Paris was an opera enthusiast, which gave us some common ground. Breeden's conversational forte was noisily dropping the name of George Bush Sr. and talking about his time as SEC chairman, but he did lighten up a little. He volunteered that I had been terribly let down by subordinates and acknowledged that, in his brief and modest time as an executive (before he discovered his true métier as the snarling, righteous face of corporate governance), he, too, had counted on others to do what I had counted on others to do in this case. Breeden was severely critical of KPMG and the Torys law firm – one of the few subjects in which we were in complete agreement. McDonough, apparently at the outer limits of his amoeboidic social capacities, sat mercifully mute and inert. A few weeks later, when they were challenging every conceivable expense, it was suggested that I, and not the company, should pay for this dinner at Le Cirque. When I pointed out that this quartet was not my idea of a social occasion, they had, for the only time, the decency not to challenge me.

I spoke to Atkinson, Radler, and Kipnis. Again, Kipnis and Atkinson could give me no legal support at all. They had simply dropped the ball. Radler remembered nothing and blamed the whole situation on everyone else. He made no effort to remain in his position in the company and only regretted leaving "with my tail between my legs." I suggested that, should he want to refuse, that would be fine with me, as long as he could defend his conduct. I was trying to find some resistance I could embrace and a line of defence we could hold.

Paris had mentioned that, in his response to the Paris-Thompson letter, Radler's lawyer had said that the payments to executives had been "initiated" by me. I asked Radler what he meant by this, and he said that this was based on my statement that, since he had done such a fine job selling the community newspapers in question, he should be rewarded for it. He confirmed that I certainly never mentioned anything about non-competition agreements and had a payment from Ravelston in mind (again, our private company). I taped this conversation, but trial counsel later said it would be of no evidentiary use to us. I didn't really believe that, but I wasn't able to argue the point. The wording raised a storm signal, however, that Radler's counsel, a former U.S. attorney in Chicago and a protegé of Thompson, was putting down a marker from which Radler could rat out a plea bargain. For a long time, I considered it unlikely that Radler would plead himself to jail, but I was not under any illusions about his ethics.

Atkinson had simply capitulated. He meekly accepted any concessions demanded of him. He did not inform me that he had already undercut my bargaining position by replying to Paris and Thompson that he agreed entirely with the tenor of their letter, nor that he had already started to repay his share of the contested non-competition payments. He had been temperamental for some time, and it was obvious that he was not going to have the psychological or moral stamina to be of much use to me in the very difficult times now upon us.

I finally reached Boultbee. He was made of sterner stuff than the others. He was not prepared to agree to any of it without talking to lawyers. He would be unable to do so, as it turned out, for several days.

We met again the next morning. McDonough had rendered our agreement to paper, in a bowdlerized deformation. We started again. No, I repeated, they could not dictate to Hollinger Inc. This time Seitz and Burt were on the phone and Savage was present in person. I was now negotiating with seven of them. By the end of the day, we had got pretty well back to where we had been the evening before, and we adjourned. I consulted with my ill-assured colleagues. Atkinson was in favour of total capitulation; Radler was of the same view and was trying to negotiate his share options; Boultbee was almost unreachable but indicated he would not agree to anything. Kipnis threw in the towel. I was still without a lawyer in New York. The only legal counsel I had was Finkelstein telling me from Los Angeles that if I were satisfied that this was a sincere settlement on the part of the other side and not just a sighting shot on an endless demand for concessions, "it could be justified." On looking back, I think that my naïveté in attending these meetings without aid of thoroughly qualified counsel was a serious mistake. What I negotiated was defensible, but I allowed too many ambiguities to survive in the signed agreement, which a competent counsel would have flagged; it was not until criminal counsel was brought on board a month later that I started to get adequately aggressive advice. By then, some of America's leading barristers had counselled and seconded moderation. My intuition was to go to war at once, but I would have forfeited all goodwill from the directors from whom I still expected some support, would have been plunged into completely unknown waters, and would have been prosecuted, and probably removed, by the SEC, and I had absolutely no one to help pilot me through this instantly dangerous crisis. Sinister though it all was from the start, it took everyone some time to realize the proportions of Breeden's assault, since he was now strenuously uttering placatory noises. Even three months later, eminent counsel thought my construction of the Restructuring Agreement was legally unassailable. That being the case, it is not clear that absence of counsel in November made much difference. Why would they have thought otherwise in November, when such counsel as I had did not?

I believe I could have shaken loose some support from the directors, and weakened Breeden's hold on them, but he had complete control of the Special Committee, dominated them professionally and suborned them financially, and had thoroughly intimidated the Audit Committee with his threats to accuse them of negligence or involvement with unauthorized payments. Both committees would be taken seriously by the SEC and the courts, as they were until we got to a relatively serious trial.

The collapse of Radler, Atkinson, and Kipnis meant that at the board table only Barbara, Dan Colson, and up to a point Perle could be counted on. Breeden had what he needed and I don't think I could have shaken that. Even Boultbee, though a doughty resister, was not interested in collective security. He had a Canadian hedgehog strategy, based on wrongful dismissal by Canadian standards, which he had a right to have applied, and on brokering his unique knowledge of the many tax issues. Going to war, given the cash-flow difficulties I experienced on a more leisurely timetable, would have created intolerable financial strain on my defence strategy, which, by necessity, had to be one of attrition, until the correlation of forces moved into closer balance, a long way back from my opening front lines.

The facts, only dimly recognizable at first, were that a coup d'etat had been skilfully executed. I had been decisively beaten before it started. (It reminded me of hockey fights I had in primary school. I lost more than I won, but most were determined by a flurry of punches at the beginning. In this case, Breeden had despatched me face down to the ice before I had even gotten my gloves off.) I made the best deal I could with Breeden and his minions. If they had honoured it, I could have stayed as non-executive chairman until it was clear that I had done nothing wrong and that they had no idea how to run the company, and could have reasserted myself. If they didn't honour it, I would have three options: I could join Radler in his already contemplated course of acknowledging crimes, though I had committed none; I could collapse on all points except admission of crimes, like Atkinson; or I could fight, and never stop fighting, until I won or died.

Morally, there was only one choice. It would be terribly difficult and would require endurance of many more humiliating defeats until I could start to disassemble the pre-cooked Special Committee case against me, echoed by the media. Perle and Kissinger would waffle for a while until recognition of the balance of power would require, with finite regret, that I be abandoned and betrayed. Breeden had the hammer over Perle of claiming he had been over-compensated and had made self-serving investment recommendations, and indeed, investments (as he had, though I don't think the company lost thereby, because we only acted on the ones that worked for us). Kissinger just followed the correlation of forces, as he did in all things, great and small. The life I had worked thirty years to build had been taken from me in an irresistible stroke, so swift and overwhelming it was hard to grasp at first.

All this is to say that if Breeden double-crossed me on the Restructuring Agreement, I would fight to the end, until success or a collapse of my ability to fight on; I have never considered giving up for a second. Nor will I.

The directors meeting scheduled for the appointment of Lazard occurred Friday morning, November 14. The meeting took place in our Manhattan offices on Fifth Avenue. I took the chair at the head of the boardroom table as if nothing had changed, surrounded by the directors I had appointed, with Breeden halfway down the table, his chair set slightly away from the table as if in a semi-observer position, rather than the man pulling the string. He spent most of the meeting sending and receiving messages, with his chubby thumbs and fingers on a childish-looking yellow plastic messaging device. I had no idea how much the independent directors really knew of the negotiations going on between Breeden's group and me, but there was no reference to them. We were there to discuss the "Strategic Process," as it was now known, which was essentially how we were going to sell the company – in part or in whole. Bruce Wasserstein and Louis Zachary (whom I had known in the same media mergers and acquisitions role at several previous employers) arrived and gave their statement of what might be attainable, including their preliminary estimate of $18 to $24 for the Hollinger International stock, if the decision was to seek a buyer for the whole company. I correctly judged that this would finally gelignite the stock price upward, though I also (correctly, as it turns out) saw no chance of achieving such a price and said so. Nor did I want to sell the company at all unless a tremendous price could be had. Breeden was throwing in with the Browne faction, but at this point claimed only to be addressing discontent and taking advantage of Wasserstein's wonder price. At $24, the stock would go at three times its value at the start of the year. At that price, I would have been delighted, and a huge beneficiary of a sale. No one except me was telling the truth, but it wasn't clear who was lying and who was merely mistaken.

In response to a question of Barbara's, Wasserstein acknowledged that Hollinger Inc. had its own requirements and could be seeking recapitalization at the same time that Hollinger International was examining its alternatives. This strengthened my hand in the continuing tug-of-war as Breeden and his fig leaves, Paris and Thompson, tried to ensure that Hollinger Inc. would be paralyzed while Breeden pursued his leisurely and well-paid course. Lazard was engaged. Discussions with the other side had reached the point by this time where Paris and I were envisioned as being the co-directors of the Strategic Process.

The lawyer David Boies and two of his associates from Boies, Schiller & Flexner arrived for the now almost stale-dated 2 p.m. meeting with me.

Breeden and his cohorts, in person and by telephone, continued their sit-in occupation of the boardroom. Boies and Breeden met in the corridor as Breeden was on his way to the washroom. They had known each other at Cravath, Swaine & Moore, a firm Breeden had quit because he was not going to be offered a partnership and Boies had eventually left, as a partner, to found his own firm.

In a later court judgment, the fact that I had been bushwhacked by events and had no opportunity to get proper counsel in time for these meetings was dismissed in the judgment of Vice Chancellor Leo Strine of the Delaware Chancery Court. He even claimed that I had choreographed Boies's visit to the washroom so he could encounter Breeden there. I never quite understood why I would do this, but in the event, I had no ambition to control nor, as far as I knew, any influence on the bladders of opposing counsel. Boies told me, as Finkelstein had, that the concessions I was making were generous, but that if this was a comprehensive settlement, it could be justified. I had a feeling that more safeguards should be built into the agreement, but if Boies saw no need, I was satisfied. Barbara, who thought that Boies was not going to be the answer to anything, later said I was in shell-shock. I was stunned, but I was doing the best I could after being ambushed in very unfamiliar territory.

Atkinson was an excellent lawyer and colleague in relatively serene times, a cheerful workhorse with a good sense of humour. He covered himself in benefits he had earned by his diligence but, as chief legal officer, he was not blameless in leaving us all vulnerable to the inferno that followed. In those dreadful times, many people from whom I had expected better snapped. And some from whom I expected little held. It was constantly erupting human drama, its full implications visible to no one except Breeden and myself, both of us working for radically different endings.

On Saturday, I telephoned Paul Saunders. As Paul was an old friend who was advising Kissinger, I asked him about Henry's attitude, which he assured me was very positive and reliable. I asked him about Breeden, as Paul, too, had been at Cravaths when Breeden and Boies were there. He did not have a high opinion of Breeden's talents or personality, but he did feel that Breeden's word could be relied upon when given.

This was the key to the present question. Boies, Saunders, and Finkelstein (and later lawyers from Sullivan & Cromwell) all had told me Breeden's word was reliable. Breeden was pledging to do what he could to assuage the concerns of the SEC and assure it that the company was curing itself. These were experienced and sophisticated lawyers who knew the man and had no reason to mislead me as far as I knew. This was also Kissinger's advice. Their assurances carried the day. Breeden, Burt, Paris, and Seitz all said that they admired the forthrightness with which I had accepted the principle that if money had been improperly paid and received, it should be repaid – instead of taking refuge in technical defences. They pledged to put the best possible public relations face on developments, although this was obviously going to be difficult.

They offered to show me the press release before it went out. All accepted the principle of assisting Hollinger Inc. in a phased transition away from its income that flowed through the management fee to Ravelston and on into Hollinger Inc. If their word was good, something manageable might just be possible. I had grave reservations, but peace was worth a try; if it did not work, war would be upon us soon enough.

On the information I had, I made the correct decision. Unfortunately, as would recurringly be the case in this horrible sequence of events, I was misinformed. The directors meeting resumed on Saturday evening, to rubber-stamp the Restructuring Agreement terms. I was to resign as CEO and remain on as a non-executive chairman. The allegedly unauthorized payments would be repaid according to a specified timetable commencing in December. Gordon Paris and I would be co-chairmen of the Strategic Process, which was to be conducted by Lazard and would explore the most profitable way to sell the whole company. There were a clutch of other provisions, including an insulting one restricting my use of the company plane to "business purposes." I had rarely used it otherwise and had on such occasions repaid the company fully – and more than fully, as later events showed. Richard Perle was brought into the deliberations for the first time and strenuously objected to the whole line of reasoning leading to the Restructuring Agreement. He said that people were being judged on insufficient evidence and that reputations would be damaged unjustly. Barbara and I agreed with him.

It was the most difficult meeting I have ever chaired, and it was conducted entirely by telephone. Unfortunately, Dan Colson was unable to call in. Atkinson voted for the entire agreement. Radler was so inarticulate in his own defence that I had to improvise a defence for him, emphasizing all the profit he had earned the company in his acquisition, management, and disposition of the community newspapers; the part he had played in creating the huge gain in the Canadian assets; and the great improvement he had effected in the fortunes of the Chicago group.

I expressed, and felt, remorse that any ambiguity could arise over the payment of fees to the management where I had been the chief executive and expressed reservations about aspects of the proposal. But I said I could live with it if it was the directors' wish and provided it was understood in all its elements, including the freedom of Hollinger Inc. to refinance, the need to maintain a steady upward flow of income to June 2004, and a shared effort to present a positive public face to the way these events had been addressed. My mistake was not to have insisted that all these matters be in the agreement, since I had now lost control of the writing of board minutes, which, when McDonough finally produced them, were severely spliced. Boies' partner was on the call and took minutes reflecting what was actually said, but the opportunity to cite them never arose.

Henry Kissinger, after I acquainted him for the first time with something other than Breeden's party line, wobbled until Breeden and Thompson spoke sharply about what the directors had agreed in their caucuses without management participation. Henry meekly retreated, and said no more. Richard Perle and Barbara continued to disagree and voted against the Restructuring Agreement, after Barbara had elicited from Breeden an admission that there was no evidence of wrongdoing by me. I and the other interested parties withdrew from the meeting, but not before I made it clear that my signing was provisional on confirmation of the facts as they alleged them. I could have refused to sign the agreement, but it seemed irresponsible. Breeden was promising to keep the SEC from turning this into a public relations fiasco for the company (as well as for me), and I thought that Breeden's acknowledgement at the meeting that there was no evidence of wrongdoing by me and my retention as non-executive chairman were reassurance that they were living up to their word. Had I refused, it was clear that Breeden would go to his former employers, the SEC, and have them bring charges against me immediately and probably remove the management. I knew enough about the litigious climate in America to know that civil charges could be commenced at the drop of a hint and criminal proceedings could be quickly launched also. At least locking into the Special Committee process would drag things out while Breeden cranked out his invoices, before the U.S. government became a plaintiff, if it was going to, through the SEC or the Justice Department.

On the following day, Sunday, November 16, there was an executive committee meeting by teleconference. I was no longer the chairman of this committee (Seitz was), but I was still a member. The issue was whether to fire Jack Boultbee as an officer since he had refused to resign. Jack, it turned out, had some fears about what Radler might have done, but true to his characteristic terseness and reserve, he didn't share them with me. Boultbee's refusal was the correct move and he would successfully sue Hollinger International for wrongful dismissal (in an Ontario court). I warned the other people on the call, Burt, Paris, Savage, and Thompson, that dispensing with Jack would make the company unnecessarily vulnerable to a tax hit on a capital gains assessment by the Canada Revenue Agency of several hundred million dollars, which only Boultbee, as the chief tax strategist, had a clear idea of how legally to avoid. They paid no attention at all and fired him. I said I could not possibly support the dismissal of a valued officer without hearing his side of the case. I was the only dissenting voice, but they were soon asking for his advice and made a side deal with him to pay all his legal fees in all these proceedings. In the end, their cavalier treatment of Boultbee was a major factor in the bankruptcies of both Inc. and International. Without Boultbee's know-how, hundreds of millions of tax liabilities would remain unnecessarily.

Later that night I flew to Toronto, having sent out a few warning emails of what was about to happen, particularly to the Southeastern people (the last communication I am ever likely to have with them), and my dear and faithful assistant in London, Rosemary Millar, who was already suffering from a cold, which shortly escalated to pneumonia, and then, six weeks later, was diagnosed as inoperable lung cancer. We had worked together closely for fourteen years. I would never see her again.

When I got to Toronto, I sent my final suggestions for the press release announcing my resignation, the Restructuring Agreement, and the Strategic Process, which Breeden most graciously accepted, and I emailed Breeden back, thanking him for his consideration. He responded the next day in the same spirit. This was the absolute high-water mark of our relations. There was an email from my dear Barbara, addressed to "Fat Fingers," a brave attempt at simulation that life would go on as it had (replete with her endearing reflections on comparative svelteness). But all was changed utterly.

[CHAPTER FIVE]

THE PRESS RELEASE WAS ON the wires the following Monday morning. In the next twenty-four hours, the full force of the media hostility to anyone suspected of abusing an executive position – and to me personally – came pouring forth in Britain and Canada and a few sections of the United States. Murdoch's newspapers had been stoking up all through the run-up and went straight into joyous orbit. The London *Sun* began a widely emulated trend by announcing in a headline that I was likely to be sent to prison. Murdoch's *New York Post* did the same. Most of the newspapers that reprinted and even embellished the extraordinary vitriol of the British press had no idea that part of the anger with me was an ideological divide. Instead, like children wallowing in a mudbath, North American press and television picked up without any pretense of investigation every last vicious canard written in the U.K. newspapers about Hollinger, Barbara, and me.

MURDOCH HAD HIS OWN MOTIVES, of course. His *New York Post* became the outlet for every fictional tale of my enemies and then some enthusiastically invented by the *Post* itself. One day it would report that I had terrorized a table at the New York restaurant La Goulou after overhearing their table chat. Another time it recounted a negative incident involving

Barbara that took place, according to the *Post*, at a London party when she was, in fact, in New York. The inventions were tabloid gutter, which, after all, has never ceased to be Murdoch's chief stock in trade, in print, and on television. In the post-Enron frenzy, the climate was so hostile to well-paid executives it was hard to rule out anything. I had recently seen Martha Stewart, a casual acquaintance, at a social engagement, and was impressed at her tough Polish Catholic imperviousness to the criminal charges that would lead to her brief imprisonment. I had experienced some of the fury of the corporate governance movement, but rabidly pro-American as I was, I assumed that justice could be had for those who were, in fact, innocent. Whatever might happen, I was going to bear up with as much dignity as I could muster.

I had been a disdainful resister to corporate governance poseurs such as Tweedy Browne and now, denuded of defences and presumed by an eager international press to be an embezzler, came the public relations lynching. My reputation, which I had been building assiduously since my tumultuous secondary-school days, almost vanished in two days. The Toronto *Globe and Mail*, which had run a very generous review of my Roosevelt book by the distinguished historian Roger Morris on November 15 (including a photograph of my face super-imposed on a picture of FDR, complete with cigarette holder), gave me the entire front page on November 18, under the massive headline "BLACK'S DARKEST DAY." As I was almost instantly without a reputation I was practically unable to sue anyone. Even in countries that, unlike the United States, maintained the civil tort of defamation, damages would be impossible to prove. The initial *New York Times* front-page story implied that I had been revealed as an embezzler. The ending of Camus's *The Stranger* came to mind: I was going to my execution as mobs howled their execration. And it was deafening.

It was one thing to convict executives of Enron and WorldCom, companies in which there had been colossal bankruptcies, a large accounting fraud, billions lost in the stock market, tens of thousands unemployed, and destruction of evidence. Executives at Adelphi appeared to have been involved in the misappropriation of billions of dollars, disguised from the auditors. Could the corporate governance movement reach such a level of ferocity that an innocent man could be prosecuted in the absence of evidence and effectively convicted and sentenced by a hostile press? I thought not, but I was in free-fall now, so swift had been the collapse of the life I had known. Watching my name crawl across the bottom of the television screen linked to accusations of fraud and "looting" on American news stations was unearthly.

I received generous notes and telephone calls from many individuals, including Marie-Josée and Henry Kravis separately. Attacks came from totally unexpected quarters. In Canada, the initial announcement of the perceived instability of my financial condition came from a man who was generally assumed (including up to a point by me) to be a friend of mine, the Honourable Henry (Hal) N.R. Jackman. He was a prominent financier, chancellor of the University of Toronto, former Lieutenant Governor of Ontario, and former associate of mine. In late October he gave a press interview to proclaim that my career was now ending in a shambles and my company was on the verge of financial collapse as he had, he happily announced, long predicted. He restated his oft-repeated theory about my having both a death wish and a Napoleon complex. For good measure, he threw in that Barbara's life had been "absurd."

He and I had many amusing moments over the years, and some sharpish exchanges too, but I was shocked by the tenor of his attack, though he avoided casting any aspersions on my business ethics and gave me generous credit as a writer and historian. (After the lapse of several years, my relations with this intelligent and amusing man would be patched together once again.)

In Canada old comrades from Southam and the *National Post*, such as Ken Whyte and Terence Corcoran, and political allies, such as David Frum, spoke up on my behalf. The reviews of my FDR book continued to pour in almost universally positive, including Ray Seitz's generous review in *The Times*. It was a strange leitmotif to the business and public relations debacle. I will never know how much better the book would have sold if I had been able to market it effectively, nor how much more depressing the time would have been without it. But the publication at least made it more difficult to claim I was just another sticky-fingered, grubby businessman.

In Britain, apart from book reviewers, the media assassination squads ruled the coverage. The Murdoch newspapers played the prison card for

Looking out at Crossharbour and Greenwich from the fifteenth-floor office of the chairman of the *Daily Telegraph* in the Canary Wharf tower in 1993. I commissioned the bust of Cardinal Newman (from Marcelle Quinton). The watercolour on the wall is of World War II Japanese battleships, all of which were sunk shortly after the date they were sketched.

Barbara, at our wedding dinner at Annabel's, July 21, 1992, holding up a hilarious mock front page written by Max Hastings. It was as happy an occasion as it appears, and so have been the married years that have followed. We are looking forward to our twentieth anniversary, finally free of the travails of the last eight years, through all of which Barbara has been magnificent. She was then a prominent columnist of the *Sunday Times*, which explains the headline.

Left to right, reading Max's special wedding edition: Margaret Thatcher, CB, the Duchess of York, distinguished publisher George (Lord) Weidenfeld, Tessa Keswick, former U.S. assistant secretary of Defense Richard Perle, and Barbara. It was a very jolly evening and most of those who attended, though not all, have remained friends through all the years and events since.

Nancy and Henry Kissinger and Lady Thatcher and Lord Carrington, with Barbara and me after my installation as a member of the House of Lords, November 2001. It was a great honour to have as my sponsor and co-sponsor Peter Carrington, Britain's greatest nobleman and ultimate contemporary Whig, and the greatest prime minister since Mr. Churchill, without whose revitalization of the United Kingdom, I never would have lived or seriously done business in that country.

With Henry Kissinger and then Prime Minister Margaret Thatcher, at the Hollinger annual dinner in Toronto, June 1988, at the end of the G-7 Summit meeting. At the height of her powers and prestige, Margaret Thatcher was a tremendous personality, and always, including in more recent difficulties, very considerate of Barbara and me.

With the always delightful Nancy Kissinger at the Hollinger annual dinner, Spencer House, London, in May 1995. Elegant, statuesque, and indomitable, she too could have written the playbook for the supportive spouse. Henry often claimed that Nancy and Barbara were a great deal fiercer than we were. He was probably correct.

With Barbara and Princess Diana, also at the Hollinger dinner in 1995. Though temperamental and not formally well educated, the Princess was extremely witty and vivacious, as well as startlingly beautiful and stylish. After her marriage came unstuck, she ran a parallel monarchy beside the real royals, with considerable public relations success. She was as great a star up close, at least on casual acquaintance, as to her vast, admiring public.

Our home in Palm Beach, which became a contentious issue with U.S. prosecutors, who tried unsuccessfully to force its sale for three years. This house easily covered over $15 million of invoices from avaricious American lawyers. I sold it in April 2011 at a satisfactory price. After the economic debacle of 2008, I lost most of the respect for American capitalism that had attracted me to Palm Beach thirty years ago.

The Conrad Black "Industry": I tried to reduce the number of books and articles about me by writing a book about myself in 1992, which was quite well-reviewed and sold well, to which this is a sequel. But it didn't achieve its purposes. Several books and a TV movie came out as my legal problems burst. This threshold was not recrossed until years later.

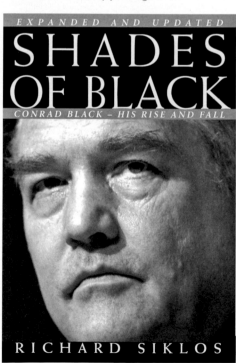

U.S. and U.K. press coverage, in 2004.

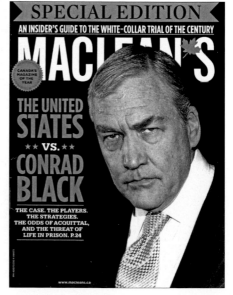

The front covers of Canada's weekly
newsmagazine, *Maclean's*, over the years.

all it was worth. The *Guardian* and *Independent* joined them. I knew there was no point appealing to my friend Tony O'Reilly at the *Independent*; he would never try to influence a newspaper he controlled. One edition of the *Financial Times*, generally a fairly responsible newspaper, bannered the front-page headline that I had taken a £94 million dividend (about $200 million at the exchange rates of the time) from the *Telegraph*, a complete invention. (We did at least extract a "clarification" on this story.)

During the discussions of a possible business merger with Associated Newspapers, the *Mail* and the *Evening Standard*, which they owned, were quite reasonable, and even Richard Desmond showed comparative restraint at the *Express*. The *Daily Telegraph* was factual but gradually gave way to showing it was no gentler than the competition. Dominic Lawson and the former editor of the *Catholic Herald*, William Oddie, and of the *The Times*, William (Lord) Rees-Mogg, wrote in support of me. The distinguished *Daily Mail* columnist Melanie Phillips deplored the *schadenfreude* at my travails. Novelist Freddie Forsyth wrote in the same spirit, adding that the word should be used sparingly now that housemaids were frequently uttering it. Taki, writing in the *Spectator*, despite our previous disputes, was magnificent from start to finish.

Max Hastings and Charles Moore were guarded. Boris Johnson said a few nice things about me on television and, later, also to his biographer. Charles Moore telephoned me, ostensibly to offer encouragement but really to ask about the future of the *Telegraph* and to insist that I understand how upsetting the *Telegraph* journalists and editors found the uncertainty. I suggested that I found it disagreeable to be the subject of hate from people for whom, as Charles knew, I had worked and risked to provide secure, respected, and generous employment. He dismissed this as merely the "five minutes of hate" Orwell had described in reference to Emmanuel Goldstein in *Nineteen Eighty-Four*. It was more durable than that, but he was probably right insofar as it was faddish and orchestrated. Understandably, he had no concept of what the corporate governance hurricane could do to normal corporate organization. I had no purchase on the fury of events.

The general attitude of the *Telegraph* journalists from the start was that they had suffered through a pay freeze while my associates and I had stuffed our pockets with non-competition fees – which, to the anti-capitalist,

Gladstonian, or non-conformist conscience, or even socialist reflexive habits, of Britain, was a moral outrage. That we had rescued the *Telegraph* from insolvency; turned it into a full-service newspaper; downsized the workforce generously and without upheaval; got it onto new presses and into new premises; brought it through the price war successfully; improved salaries, working conditions, and product quality; and defended our editors and journalists against all comers seemed, for a time, to have been forgotten. I was deemed to be a crook and compared to Robert Maxwell, who had apparently committed suicide at sea in 1991 after looting the company pension plans before his company went bankrupt.

The unseemly joy that so many seemed to take in the thought of me incarcerated in America was slightly unnerving. I reread de Gaulle's description of the fall of France, and excerpts of *The Bonfire of the Vanities*, to try to gain both a historian's and a novelist's insight into how to cope with a sudden, overwhelming rout and collapse, when, in de Gaulle's words, a slope becomes a fall.

Most of the people who knew me at all well in the United Kingdom remained solicitous and supportive through all the travails that followed. But the press, whose members I had always treated with consideration, continued to attack in the vilest and most relentless assault I have seen on anyone entitled to the benefit of any doubt about his conduct. Such reflexive, resonating, widespread antagonism was unnerving and contagious.

Because Barbara was a journalist and I was steeped in the North American tradition of limited or no social stratification, we often had journalists in our home and treated them hospitably. I also did many personal favours for journalists who were having marital, health, or financial problems, sometimes structuring their incomes to help them with divorce settlements and extending health and pay benefits far beyond what was legally required. Some remembered such consideration; some did not.

A special case among British journalists was Elinor Mills, a *Telegraph* journalist who had recently been raided by the *Sunday Times*. She was the stepdaughter of the psychiatrist I had seen in the late 90s, at Barbara's request when she had urged me to get confirmation that my proposal of marriage to her in 1991 was rational. We needed to round up the numbers for a dinner following a Sotheby's board meeting, and Mills was one of those recruited by Charles Moore. I had not met her before. When it was related to one of the principals of Sotheby's that there would be someone present who was about to start at the *Sunday Times*, I was urged to disinvite Mills. Mrs. Taubman didn't want any press people other than those I could vouch for from the *Telegraph* and judged that a departing employee didn't make that cut. After some unsuccessful remonstration, I did so – with lengthy apologies, because disinviting an innocent guest was a horrid thing to do. The whole matter quickly got into the press and I apologized again. We sent a gift and a note, and I corresponded with Mills's stepfather. I confessed what I considered to be the inappropriateness of my action at the Brompton Oratory.

When the problems of late 2003 arose, Elinor Mills came forth to the press and again retailed the entire episode to a very receptive world media audience, this time blaming Barbara, who was completely unaware of the disinvitation of Elinor. My conduct was universally condemned. I agreed with the criticism but was less delighted that such behaviour was represented as not untypical of me. I even replied, unusually, to one Toronto reporter who telephoned about it, and I said that Elinor Mills was correct, that I had behaved disgracefully, that it was aberrant, and that it relieved my conscience to be saying so. Nonplussed, he asked if this was on the record. I assured him that it was and asked him to print it verbatim. He didn't; apparently, a statement of conscientiousness was not what his editor had had in mind.*

I do not believe in false, extorted, or unspontaneous allocutions such as Radler's, which demean the spirit of confession and repentance and reduce justice to corruptly procured self-humiliation.

Throughout my conscient life, I have been, within reason, a person of law and order, as long as justice is tempered by mercy when advisable. I have been accustomed to punishment for misdeeds since my earliest years, and while fear of retribution has rarely been a deterrent to me, I have never resented its application when I have misbehaved, including in these dolorous events.

---

* I eventually had a very congenial correspondence with Elinor, and she accepted my invitation to dinner when I return to London. I look forward to it.

I had not behaved dishonestly and had relied on well-paid executives and professional advisers to do their jobs properly. But I should have been more suspicious of Radler and more thorough in following up after Atkinson and Kipnis, both overworked and neither a commercial specialist. I certainly had a right to expect better from them, but the buck stopped with me. More important, I had publicly scorned the corporate governance zealots, without any idea what inroads they had made legally and how easily they could undermine my position as controlling shareholder and director.

My moral and practical objections to the zealots were well founded, as subsequent events, especially their ruination of our companies, demonstrated, but my pride and haughty spirit were of the nature that often leads to a fall. As years went by, more and more companies substituted obsequious grovelling to the fund managers, corporate governance zealots, and shareholder activists for commercial performance. The focus was on a smokescreen of executive humility while executive authority was abdicated, delegated, or collegialized.

From the start, I feared that I had hit a buzz saw and that any compromise with Breeden would make matters worse – and that in the end, I would have to endure the risk of judicial conviction and even imprisonment before I could live in peace again, so powerful and mindless were the forces against me.

The fight would be not just to maintain morale through the prolonged and desperate struggle, but to retain faith that the evil afflicting me was not omnipotent. Through the terrible darkness that has followed, though there were many troubled nights and anxious days, I always returned to my belief that whatever my failings, my honesty would ultimately prevail over malice. However excruciatingly it unfolded, there was no moral or practical choice but to fight it out to the last inch. It was terribly difficult to discern any pattern in events. Providence intervened again and again to prevent my complete annihilation, but never in year after year sufficiently to set me free from the awful persecution.

Mine was the fate many people enjoy seeing inflicted on apparently overconfident, powerful, even glamorous people who seem to be too much enjoying themselves. Much of it was envy and the aesthetic pleasure of a sudden exposure of the weakness behind an imposing facade; pride quickly crumbles into dust. It is an amusing, gratifying, even reassuring spectacle. I couldn't proclaim to the world my merits as a person; I had to seize this frightful challenge as an opportunity to try to demonstrate them.

In the rugged world I had inhabited, I received much of what I deserved, and took my lumps as I always had, but not when the attack was against my honesty, which was, in fact, unimpeachable. That was unjust. It was in rebellion against that injustice that the resistance within me arose and guided me through the very difficult years ahead, saying in self-reassurance, as the French Maquis in the Second World War had done, "The night will end."

My book launch in Toronto began with two very civilized interviews, one at the CBC with Michael Enright and another with the very cultured Robert Fulford. The next morning, at the flagship Indigo bookstore, I moved in a unit surrounded by scores of journalists. My old friend Heather Reisman, owner of the bookstore chain, handled it magnificently. Once I got to the front of the store, questions were on Roosevelt only. I signed three hundred books. We had a quiet lunch, after making our way through the pack complete with reporters asking if I did not, as a practice, "suck the blood out of companies" as one of them said, and asking whether I had committed fraud and would, inevitably, go to prison.

Just for a moment, I rose to the bait and unwisely pointed out that the stock was rising. My actual words were that I had made "$50 million yesterday. This is a flame-out I could get used to." The journalists were there to get precisely that sort of ill-advised remark and I made their day. What they could not know was that I had been trying for a long time to put some upward pressure under the stock price and that although this was never going to have been my idea of how to do it, at least the stock price was rising. And we could all be happy for that. Needless to say, from the moment after I said it, I regretted it. The rise in the stock price was attributed to my ejection as chief executive, said my questioners, debating with me. I replied that I thought the prospect of sale was more of a ratchet than any skepticism about the outgoing management. I also pointed out that the underlying value had been created by the exiting management, not by Tweedy Browne and the directors who had approved what was now the subject of controversy.

That evening, I flew back to New York. It was the last time I would see our corporate airplane. I did not even have the opportunity to say, as

General Gordon did to his camel at Khartoum, that we would "ride no more under desert stars." One of the provisions of the Restructuring Agreement was that that plane would function as it had until the end of the year, by which time Gordon Paris and I would work out a new regime for it through to June 1. It later emerged from a deposition of Jim Thompson's, uttered with the eloquence one would expect of the continuer of the Illinois political tradition of Abraham Lincoln and Adlai Stevenson, that there was concern that I would use the plane for a book tour. Thompson became "pissed off" and grounded the aircraft, in complete contravention of the agreement.

They need not have feared. A full book tour was impossible, and I would not have put that expense on the company anyway. I gamely went to a fine reception at Hunter College, near my home in New York, where I was to be given a tour of the Roosevelt home on 65th Street. But we were inundated with aggressive reporters; a book tour was out of the question. Very few interviewers could promise to keep to the subject, and the advice of my lawyer, rudimentary as it was, was that I should not talk about my ouster as CEO and the so-called unauthorized payments, to avoid the fate of Martha Stewart.

I was not about to go to the mat with Breeden and Paris on the issue of the plane. Commercial aviation had been the means of travel for most of my life and I could quickly get used to it again. I merely recorded with Paris the fact that the agreement had been violated. Evidence started flooding in that the other side had already made our agreement into a Swiss cheese. Outrageous stories of improper financial conduct were floated with the approval of the Special Committee counsel's staff and shareholder-relations vice president, Paul Healy. Radler and I had tolerated him because he did have moments of effectiveness. His friendship with Christopher Browne in particular was disquieting and we should have got rid of him long before.

It was leaked and reported in the press that I had spent $14 million of the company's money on my house in Palm Beach and that I had spent an additional undisclosed and unauthorized $4 million from the same source on Roosevelt papers. Barbara had supposedly spent $3 million decorating the aircraft. David Radler was said to have been taking kickbacks on newsprint purchases, and importing drugs on our plane from Mexico. Another such story was the *Financial Times* story that I had taken £94 million of dividends directly from the *Telegraph*, bypassing the private and public companies between the *Telegraph* and me. These and other fantastic stories popped into the press and remained there until we stamped them out, which took considerable time. There was never a retraction, merely an end to the retailing of the story and a movement onward to the next falsehood planted or amplified by our co-contractants, who had promised to put the best possible public relations face on events.

On November 21, the Kravises, de la Rentas, and Jayne Wrightsman held a book launch party for me at the New York Four Seasons Restaurant. I had given them plenty of opportunity to dodge it, but they insisted. The former Treasury secretary, Robert Rubin, was holding a reception in the neighbouring room that naturally pulled a great many more people – and many of the same ones.

The presence of Candice Bergen, Joan Collins, Barbara Walters, the Kissingers, former and current mayors Ed Koch and Michael Bloomberg, World Bank president Jim Wolfensohn, Bill Buckley, long-serving district attorney Robert Morgenthau, Mrs. Nelson Rockefeller, the Ahmet Erteguns, the George Livanoses, Barry Diller and Diane von Fürstenberg, Bob Silvers of the *New York Review of Books*, the Podhoretzes and others from *Commentary* magazine, and a considerable swath of New York finance and society convinced even the *New York Post* that "the New York power structure rallied in support of Conrad Black." A more widely held view was that of Tina Brown, an undoubted expert on the subject of career reversals from her own and her husband's experiences, that it was more like a wake for the life we had had. Both descriptions were partly true, but I nevertheless had enjoyed myself. Barbara described herself as "in rigor mortis" throughout the evening.

The dinner afterwards at Jayne Wrightsman's was a touching and exquisite occasion. Henry Kissinger, the Weidenfelds, and the Sid Basses were especially generous in their comments, about both the book and its author. But this agreeable interlude could not long distract me from the fact that I was now in a truly horrible crisis.

No time is ideal for a crisis of such proportion, but this one came at the most inopportune possible point. Though I had tried to give up my citizenship gently, I had incurred great and understandable resentment in Canada for renouncing the country. The British were not generally impressed with someone who appeared as eager as I was mistakenly portrayed to be to become a peer. There was apparently much resentment in that country of what was widely considered my use of the *Daily Telegraph* and *Sunday Telegraph* to promote somewhat un-British notions of solidarity with the United States. In the United States, it was a straight rise-and-fall story, leavened by the current hostility to perceived corporate excess. But there was also broad and touching dissent among many who knew me personally and expressed their views privately, with an elegance that often only the British can achieve.

A blizzard of SEC subpoenas indicated that Breeden had done his best to bring that organization heavily down on our backs. I surmised that they would shortly assault the sources of our revenue as well.

The extent of the opprobrium I attracted had only one partial precedent in my life: the more jagged moments of my school career. I had been twice expelled from high school, the first time amid great unpopularity because my theft and resale of examination papers had caused hundreds of students to be required to write their examinations over again. I was not a naturally dishonest person, but, in full revolt against a school I disliked, I set out to reduce it to chaos. I was more successful than I wished or expected. The second unscheduled departure from a boarding school was for general insubordination.

The lesson of these far-off and not overly creditable events was that adversity endured does pass. My world had collapsed and many of my social acquaintances together with the press were rejoicing in this. I believed intuitively that if I could stay afloat financially rather than drown in personal bankruptcy, I could eventually rebuild some position and work to regain much of what I had lost in the dramatic suddenness of my setback.

I accepted the Gaullist formula that I had lost a battle, but not the war of my life. I became a Gaullist in 1955, from reading the general's memoirs and identifying with what he called his "rejection of the dictates of a false discipline." My francophilia and realization of the impermanence of triumph and disaster, the value of endurance, and the manipulability and forgetfulness of general opinion dated from these days. I had learned and admired how a civilized country like France could move so quickly between the glories of 1918, of Foch and Clemenceau, and the shame of 1940 to de Gaulle's proposal of a revival of French grandeur. Of course these were a ten-year-old schoolboy's narrow perceptions, as de Gaulle was writing of a false military strategy, a corrupted political structure, and national survival. I was complaining only about school teachers.

To readers who encounter just the normal amount of human frailty and unattractive qualities, the seemingly endless list of morally deformed people you are about to encounter may seem exaggerated and not credible. Please think of it as a sharks' feeding frenzy: when the possibility of tens (if not hundreds) of millions of dollars is dangled above the open mouths of people who have dreamed of or pursued such sums without significant success all their lives, hunger takes over. Greed, mendacity, viciousness, and even megalomania – which live in most people at a level they can more or less suppress and control – come to the fore in pathological surges. Hollinger International and Hollinger Inc., with their hundreds of millions of dollars and important newspapers, became magnets. Moral codes slipped; the centre could not hold. I was driven often to thinking about Yeats's poem through one ugly catastrophe after another. In these matters, there was a sort of alchemy that transformed people of some distinction into self-seeking sharpers and the randomly venal into rabid fiends. We were in a psycho-horror film, scripted and produced with, for a time, an almost Hitchcockian gift for terror.

I AM GENERALLY SKEPTICAL of schoolyard parables, but my school days had familiarized me with the hypocrisy and cowardice and false morality of mob anger, artificially incited. Breeden would have been a good schoolmaster of the old type: authoritarian, and without humour. I knew early on what I was dealing with, not only in him, but in insipid goody-goodies such as Seitz – polishing an apple for teacher and snitching on tardy students. When Breeden threw down the mask and called me a looter and a crook, as he soon did, I was fighting not for my place in school, but for my life.

THE FIRST DESERTION OF long-standing Canadian allies was the demand of Hollinger Inc.'s independent directors in Toronto that what had happened at Hollinger International be replicated at Hollinger Inc. I would have to go as chief executive, David Radler as president and director, Peter Atkinson as director, Jack Boultbee as director and officer. They had no reason, only that the same had been demanded and accepted in the United States. Even Barbara would have to go, which Breeden had not requested for the American board. We told them in vain that we had only accepted Breeden's demands for resignations and signed the Restructuring Agreement in New York in order to spare Hollinger Inc. a financial squeeze. Such circumstances had no application in Toronto. Whatever irregularities there were alleged to have been in Hollinger International did not apply to this company. We explained carefully that there was a difference between Ravelston's debt-free ownership of 78 per cent of Hollinger Inc. and Hollinger Inc.'s debt-encumbered ownership of 30 per cent of Hollinger International. And even so, there was no evidence that all the comparatively distinguished Hollinger International directors would have quit had we not negotiated the arrangements that we did, though the Special Committee would have litigated. We made no headway.

The four independent directors were Maureen Sabia, Fred Eaton, Douglas Bassett, and Allan Gotlieb. Sabia had become a champion of corporate governance, addicted to preparatory full-day meetings prior to full-day Audit Committee meetings. Peter Atkinson and Fred Creasey, the controller, told me well before the debacle of November that they could not function with her demands on them. Sabia was a lawyer without a real practice, who worked from home. She is an authority on corporate governance and eventually became the non-executive chairman of the large and successful retailer, Canadian Tire. She rightly declined to agree to the return of the allegedly unauthorized non-compete payments Inc. received from International just on Breeden's say-so. She suggested we turn the matter over for investigation to Joseph Groia, a former director of enforcement for the Ontario Securities Commission. His extensive report, which concluded that the payments were sufficiently authorized, was later proved correct in court.

Fred Eaton I had known almost all my life. Eaton was the most famous corporate family name in Canada, a household word like Rockefeller, or Guinness in the U.K. I joined the Eaton board in 1976, when it was in serious financial difficulties, and stayed with it through a revival for which Fred was largely responsible. After I went to Britain, he came there as High Commissioner. He performed well, and had more style than most of his recent predecessors, but he was not a born diplomat. There were lapses, such as when he had a party for Ray Seitz, the U.S. ambassador at the time, and asked another guest, who happened to be the husband of the famous and beloved singer Vera Lynn, to fetch him a drink on the assumption that an unfamiliar face in a dinner jacket was hired help. Then there was his dinner for the Queen, when he assured Her Majesty that Canada would remain loyal to the Crown even if she felt obliged to abdicate and the throne thus passed to the Prince of Wales.

I had sponsored Douglas Bassett as a member of the Toronto Club and as a director of the Canadian Imperial Bank of Commerce. I had been a friend of his father and a pallbearer at his funeral. His defection was a disappointment, but he keeps solicitously in touch with my elder son.

Allan Gotlieb had been, without question, an extremely distinguished Canadian ambassador to the United States. When he left government service, I gave him the sinecure of being publisher of *Saturday Night* and persuaded Sotheby's to engage him as their well-paid Canadian chairman. I had supported his charitable causes and publicly spoken in his support when he was suing several publications for libel. One would have expected better from this relationship.

After the presentation of the directors' ultimatum that if we did not do as they demanded they would all resign, the meeting ended and those physically present left, except for the four independent directors. Unknown to the four putative authors of the coup, Barbara remained on the conference line (as did Douglas Bassett, who was at a holiday location) and she recorded their reflections. They could not explain what they were doing, even to themselves.

They chatted on for a long time about how they did not believe a word I uttered about the impending refinancing deals I had been working so hard on since last summer. "I'm finished with Conrad's con, con, cons. I never want to hear another one," said Sabia to general agreement. They were contemptuous of several of my colleagues, including Peter Atkinson, who had worked hard and earnestly to accommodate them and deserved better. Barbara listened to Eaton and Sabia's description of her as a person whose only concern was for herself and whose expression of concern for my reputation was an act. Gotlieb commended himself for his "Oscar"-worthy performance of concern and his ability to refrain from laughing at both Barbara and me. Bassett was admirably discreet.

But I had fought hard, and would continue to do so, for Hollinger Inc., which, as the proportions of Breeden's efforts emerged, would be in a desperate condition. The Hollinger Inc. cabalists would have managed the company into receivership and caused the shareholders' interest to evaporate in quick time – a few weeks at most. Their resignations would be only a minor embarrassment in the dreadful agony that was unfolding and would make it possible for the board to function again.

We rejected their demands unanimously, even the conciliatory Peter Atkinson. They resigned and departed the room. Since there was no rational explanation for their leaving, it had to indicate the extent of peer pressure and the influence of the advice of their counsel from Davies Ward Phillips & Vineberg – the firm that the independent directors had retained and whose fees Inc. paid. It was the beginning of a long sequence of bellicose and overpaid advice, ultimately netting that law firm more than $10 million while the company descended into bankruptcy.

All I had to do now, I believed, was exceed the expectations of complete self-annihilation. This would not be easy. But if we survived, we would win. Should we not survive corporately, it would not be through banishment by this puny quartet. In New York, there were tactical and conscientious arguments for retreat and return. In Canada, the battlements had to be defended.

My worst fears were soon realized. Hollinger International reneged on its debts to Ravelston under existing management agreements. And the front-loading that Thompson had proposed, and that had been accepted to ensure a flow of funds to Ravelston and Hollinger Inc. until June, was shortly defined by Breeden to one of my counsel as a 95 per cent reduction and the complete denial of the contractual payout sum of six months at the end of the management agreement. Hollinger Inc. would be put quickly to a severe test, as it had to make $14.4 million of annual payments to its bondholders. Ravelston had now lost 80 per cent of its income; if it failed to make the annual support payments of $14 million to Hollinger Inc., a default could quickly lead to a seizure of most of our Hollinger International shares and a complete evaporation of Hollinger Inc. shareholders' equity.

Jack Boultbee and I redoubled our efforts to devise short-term patch-through methods. Under Hollinger Inc.'s debt covenants, the super-voting shares were pledged to shareholders, who could seize them in a default. Any change of hands outside Hollinger Inc. would rob these shares of their super-voting rights and we would lose control of both companies. Inc. itself no longer had a line of credit.

The intention of the usurpatory regime at Hollinger International was clearly to set this chain of events in motion, bankrupt Hollinger Inc., and seize the super-voting shares with which Hollinger Inc. controlled Hollinger International. It was not immediately obvious how we could deal with this, so I began an intensified canvass of refinancing alternatives. I made it clear to Breeden, Paris, and Thompson verbally and in emails with McDonough that under the Restructuring Agreement of November 15, Hollinger Inc. would do what was necessary and prudent to its commercial interest to avoid default. When we next met in New York in January, Breeden professed regret that anyone had behaved improperly, i.e., by telling the press that we were all crooks, which he did not dispute regularly occurred. It was clear that he had shredded the Restructuring Agreement the day after it was signed, but he continued to represent me as the aggressor.

Though the Restructuring Agreement established Paris and me as co-directors of the Strategic Process, I was never consulted about it, apart from one contact. I was pledged, under that agreement, not to have transactions with any party that would impair the possible success of the Strategic Process, unless threatened with default. As Hollinger Inc. now clearly was threatened with default, I considered, with supportive legal advice, that the Strategic Process would best be served by whatever avoided a default.

As the public relations debacle unfolded in the second half of November, I engaged Linda Robinson, whom I had known socially, as my public relations adviser. She recommended Sullivan & Cromwell as counsel because she had worked closely with them before. Three of their senior lawyers, John Warden, Ben Stapleton, and David Braff, visited me on November 20, and I engaged them. Warden and Stapleton had excellent reputations, and as the firm had been led by John Foster Dulles and had negotiated the initial acquisition of the Panama Canal zone, I was biased in their favour to the considerable exasperation of Barbara, who felt that my affection for historical antecedents occasionally marred my vision. They recommended that I retire two days early as chief executive of International and leave it to Paris to sign the 10Q if he chose to do so. I followed their advice.

I finally had serious lawyers, supplemented by David Boies's firm in specific matters (Boies himself was too busy to act for me, but was available for advice at times) and by Jesse Finkelstein in specialist Delaware questions. I relied heavily on my friend Eddie Greenspan, Canada's most famous defence lawyer, to advise me on criminal matters, which were so universally touted as being of imminent importance. At this time, Greenspan was invaluable. He early expressed reservations that whatever Sullivan & Cromwell's talents in commercial and civil matters, they had little sensitivity to the potential implications of dealing with so dangerous an enemy as Breeden. For a long time, Sullivan & Cromwell showed no recognition of the seriousness of Breeden's intent. When they eventually did recognize it, they were not the best-suited firm to reply to so sinister an opponent. Even had he been well intentioned, the powers available to Breeden as counsel to the Special Committee and as the man who had given Paris his job as nominal chairman of that committee were practically unlimited. He was in charge of any aspect of the investigation that had legal implications and he determined its entire scope. He had the power to identify derelictions and to critique directors' and officers' performances, not just in cozy office sessions but in published reports. He was responsible for the Special Committee report and had a power of moral suasion, if not intimidation, before which everyone buckled except Barbara, Dan Colson, Jack Boultbee, and me. No substantive move could take place at Hollinger International without his prior approval.

Evidence of Breeden's real intentions continued to accumulate. In late November, I had received a gratingly obnoxious letter from Gordon Paris, cutting off credit cards, expense accounts, car leases, and telephone arrangements and relegating the continuing chairman of the board and chief stockholder to the status of a junior employee. Back in early December in our New York City apartment I had shown Greenspan a letter from Paris. He read it and looked at me quizzically: "You think you can make a deal with these people? This is war."

As important elements of the agreement were in the ambiance of the settlement, and the ambiance had been poisoned, all sense of goodwill and cooperation was vaporized. It is hard to give a sense of the relentless psychological pressure Breeden and his new lackeys asserted. They specialized in a sort of quiet terror – one never knew what new charge would be made or what old perquisite or aspect of your job would be taken away. Our apartment doorbell would ring. The private entrance outside it would be empty but for an envelope lying on the floor. Inside, on Hollinger International letterhead embossed with the name of my successor, would be a new list of personal divestments by fiat. I could no longer do this. I no longer had that. My car had been taken. Access to the company email server had been severed, although I was still the chairman of the company. Each item could be replaced or done without (though the email server presented rather more difficulties not eased by the irritation that International had managed to pre-empt virtually every combination of my name and Barbara's that would make a recognizable domain), but as a campaign it was successful. I was living every moment with that terrible feeling of missing a step in your sleep, or losing a heartbeat. The psychological treatment almost instantly cracks weak people – of whom, unfortunately, we had no shortage. Many, with the right sticks and carrots, were prepared falsely to denounce others to spare themselves even slight inconvenience. (The best recent illustration of this was the Grasso affair, where many of Wall Street's lions, most of whom have since hit the wall, deserted Dick Grasso, former head of the New York Stock Exchange – except for the magnificent Ken Langone, who then made a bid to buy the NYSE. Of course, Grasso and Langone were vindicated.)

After the resignation of the Hollinger Inc. directors, the next element of the Canadian establishment to desert with a minimum of decorum was the Canadian Imperial Bank of Commerce, of which I had been a director for twenty-seven years. As soon as the November events were announced, I heard from the non-executive chairman, Bill Etherington, that the bank would require my retirement as a director at the next annual meeting, a few months later. I replied that this was premature and that I would have expected a little more benefit of the doubt.

As weeks went by and the enemy succeeded in steadily poisoning the wells in the press, it became obvious that all the public companies I was associated with were going to come under great pressure not to re-elect me. In the circumstances, I phoned John Hunkin, the chief executive of CIBC, and said that I did not want to embarrass the bank. I suggested that I might need a well-secured loan from CIBC. He didn't commit himself but was encouraging.

What happened then was predictable but disappointing. I was informed that the bank's nominating committee had met and that while no vote or resolution was taken, it was their view that I should not stand for re-election, and that this view had been informally approved by the directors. I had had no notice that this was being discussed, and no ability to arrange a more dignified exit for myself from a bank for which I had generated many millions of dollars of profits over more than thirty years.

Practically all other departing directors were thanked in resolutions and at the annual meeting and in the annual report. I received one parting email of good wishes from a fellow director, a person whom I did not know well, as well as a gracious word from my friend of nearly forty years, Galen Weston. My loan request was denied by Hunkin in an email beginning: "We would not normally make a loan to someone in your condition." Perhaps because I was already becoming punch-drunk, I couldn't help thinking of the cartoon from *Punch* more than a century ago, of the cardinal and the admiral on the railway platform, where the cardinal mistakes the admiral for a baggageman and the admiral replies: "I wouldn't be travelling in your condition, Madame." I was a director also of Brascan, CanWest, and Sotheby's, though my association had been briefer than with CIBC. These three public companies also concluded that they did not want to brave the barrage of hostility from institutional investors. Even though all of them were more or less controlled companies, they were concerned about their stock price. They put their views very courteously and they profusely thanked me, in both the annual meetings and in the annual report, for my services to them.

At a practical level, I had no credit facilities of any kind, although I had an apparent personal net worth of hundreds of millions of dollars. Tony Fell, Canada's leading merchant banker and a friend and neighbour in Toronto of fifty years, had kindly visited me in New York in December. I asked him whether the Royal Bank might consider a loan, heavily secured. He phoned back promptly and in his opening sentence included the phrase "fraudulent preference."* I interrupted and said he need not continue and that I would not be bothering the Royal Bank (of which I had been invited to become a director in 1976) again.

It is hard for someone who has not been through it, as I had not, to grasp how inaccessible assets become. (I had several times lent money to financially distressed friends and asked no security, though the amounts were not negligible, and told them to pay me back when they could, if they could; sometimes they did, sometimes not.) I found that credit cards were all right, as long as there were no deferrals of settlement dates, which I never engaged in anyway. But apart from that, only cash could be used. No loans or overdrafts were available, as no collateral was thought to be invulnerable. Prosecutors were apt to claim that anything was ill-gotten gains. These wells were poisoned immediately by Breeden's allegations, as he had driven off the private equity firms in the summer of 2003, before he had a hint of any problems, as he isolated and started to starve his quarry.

Now most lawyers would be more concerned to assure collectibility of their invoices to me than about doing what my burgeoning legal problems required. I was then overbilled for counsel's unjustified belligerencies to collect their invoices – I was billed for superfluous extra-collection measures on myself. My income stopped almost at once, and all that could be used to replace it was cash on hand and asset sales. These were fine for a time (I was particularly pleased to sell my CIBC shares at a fine gain), but not the nature of most of my assets. American and Canadian lawyers

---

* This was the fear that if my finances collapsed, the Royal Bank could be accused of advancing the interests of one creditor over others by monopolizing, for security purposes, a principal asset, to the exclusion of other creditors. Five years later, Canadians would be grateful for such caution in their bankers, but it wasn't really caution here; it was an infelicitous fusion of terror and animosity, and was absurd in practical terms.

lectured me on the need to sell my homes and other assets to have a pool of cash to pay them with, and presumed to lecture me on the limits of my means (about which none of them knew anything). I was to ensure that they, and not other claimants, took every cent I had. Fortunately, I had laid in enough over the years, and could rely on reserves with adequate agility, to avoid that fate, but there would be many tight corners and narrow passages. Brendan Sullivan said, "Money is the ammunition of this war." It was, I suppose, but it often seemed to be all that the well-paid and not overly successful warriors were interested in.

What ensued was a prolonged, intricate, and ultimately very successful series of asset sales, often through interposed vendors so as not to rouse the bottom feeders, who were more numerous, devious, and passionately convinced of whatever they wanted to believe about the prostration of the vendor, than I had ever imagined. In these respects, I had spent all my career in the cozy cocoon of the establishment, a bank director since I was thirty-two, and able, fairly effortlessly, to get whatever money I needed, when I needed it. I had an absolutely perfect credit record (and still do), and over forty-five years as an autonomous businessman, sometimes including corporate loans of billions of dollars. It was no use to me now.

I don't think personal bankruptcy was ever in prospect, but a disorderly retreat, a rout in which I peddled fine assets at knockdown prices, was. And ghoulish publicity, alleging or implying extreme financial discomfort, was a hardy journalistic favourite for a long time, even up to the *Globe and Mail*'s fanciful account of the virtual forced sale at a knock-down price of my Palm Beach house in early 2010. The story was republished all over the world, having been lifted without verification from the *Palm Beach Daily News*, a seasonal photo paper that is probably the most inane newspaper in the English-(more-or-less)-speaking world. In fact, the sale was conditionally revocable and at a price still to be finalized.

By 2010, I had no trouble returning fire with stinging accuracy, where it was worth doing so, in this case, at the end of a *National Post* column. But for several years I was pasted by the press at almost every opportunity. It was very unpleasant, but, I suppose, character-broadening.

—

THE REAL PROBLEMS, now about to unfold, were harrowing enough.

The screws were tightening everywhere. David Boies's law partner told me that David's son had a high-risk, high-yield, money-lending operation. He had read that I might sell my Palm Beach house and suggested a mortgage could be arranged (at double the normal rates). When we got to Palm Beach, our housekeeper was informed that we had to pay cash for the newspapers at the local newsagent despite my having been a customer for more than twenty-five years. Apparently there was concern about whether I was good for the cost of newspapers. There were also irritating stories of arrears on charitable pledges, and the charities in question, especially those headed up by the more exalted figures of New York society, showed indecently little discretion. Every pledge was fulfilled to the last cent, and would have been even if I had had to sell my own possessions and wash dishes for a living to accomplish it. It was very discouraging, or would have been, had I permitted it to become so.

Although it was never acknowledged that this was his intention, the Breeden strategy to bankrupt Hollinger Inc. was now being pressed relentlessly. The only solution I could see was to begin serious negotiations to generate money at the Hollinger Inc. level, while remaining well within the terms of the Restructuring Agreement and the requirement not to impair the Strategic Process with Lazard. I felt this could be done so long as I made sure that any agreement I reached contained the express proviso that the contracting party work with Lazard in the future disposition of the company. But I was equally sure that I could not, in advance, inform Breeden via Gordon Paris of whom I was dealing with while they were busy trying to bankrupt Inc.

Sir David and Sir Frederick Barclay, wealthy and somewhat reclusive, almost identical twin brothers in the United Kingdom, had periodically expressed an interest in buying the *Telegraph* whenever our competitors managed to generate a negative story about our financial condition. David Barclay was back, so I initiated discussion with him, in parallel to talks with Jonathan Rothermere at Associated Newspapers and Mathias Döpfner of Axel Springer, a most charming and intelligent man whom I had known for some years. I would have been happy to deal with any one of them, and pursued discussion with each.

Also in the frame was the inimitable chairman of Triarc, Nelson Peltz, a swashbuckling buccaneer of colourful phrase and manner, a financially well-travelled sidekick of Michael Milken, Carl Icahn, and even Kerry Packer. (At one point in December, my financial condition was so strapped I had to borrow $100,000 from Nelson to pay our public relations firm, a fact that shortly made its way into the press. I repaid the loan after one month at the agreed, very fair, interest.)

Peltz is in most respects a delightful man. He is a brilliant raconteur and has had a rich business and, in a general sense, social history. Since he spends his time scrutinizing the business press and attempting to take advantage of distressed situations, he has encountered an astonishing range of people and businesses. If it is possible to align one's interests with his, a powerful and ingenious champion is acquired. But Peltz could never resist the temptation to believe what he wanted to believe: that I had no practical choice but to accept his offer, no matter how one-sided.

Because our personal relations were (and remain) so congenial, we generally reached a provisional agreement on whatever we were talking about, which moved trapezoidally into a cave-in to Peltz when committed to paper by his amanuenses. As a result, we never agreed on anything material, except that loan to pay my public relations agency.

The great advantage of associating with Nelson Peltz, apart from the fact that he was a rewarding dinner companion and a pure capitalist who was not overly preoccupied with the excesses of corporate governance, was that he frightened the living Jehovah out of my enemies. The report that he and I had dinner together (in a restaurant that Peltz owned) was enough to set my enemies thinking that they should adopt a poison pill. This is a restriction on acquisition of control of a company. In this case, the restriction would be imposed by a subsidiary, the acting management of Hollinger International, on its parent, Hollinger Inc., an unheard-of concept.

Despite a reasonably active business and social life in New York in December, I found my days very lonely and difficult. For the first time in my life, I had night sweats. I was awakened by my racing heart, stirred to acute fear by unremembered dreams. People were taking their distance as the press virtually throughout the world pounded me daily as a "disgraced" and greedy executive quite possibly on my way to prison. My faith and determination were assaulted but not seriously shaken. But it was horribly nerve-wracking and hard on Barbara, who was losing weight and colour. Her remedy was to work even more frantically. She continued and even increased the frequency of her writing, and the quality of it was better than ever.

As money evaporated, Breeden closed in on his objective of breaking Hollinger Inc. and dictating terms of eliminating the tangible fruit of my more than thirty-five years in the newspaper business. Of the groups that had already surfaced, the Barclays, as owners of a private company little disposed to excessive dalliance with financial advisers, were the most promising. Peltz was unshakably convinced that no one would bid for Hollinger Inc. because it would not be able to complete its year-end audit due to non-cooperation from Hollinger International. He was skeptical that any of my future deals to extract myself from the problems would be successful. He never offered more than to take an option to buy our shares. He would then pad around to meet Breeden and Christopher Browne. The film rights to such meetings would have been valuable, but his offers were not.

The auditors, KPMG, turned in one of the most shameful performances of all in these awful days. Having endlessly attested to the full approval of the non-competition payments to individual executives, they now claimed to have been misinformed. Breeden and I had agreed that their turn as litigation respondents would come and that it would be painful. (Sadly this was not to be. Breeden became Special Monitor of KPMG, which had its own legal problems, and was conflicted. Even before he became Special Monitor for Hollinger International he had determined not to sue them. My informed intuition is that he believed this would make it easier to prove the case against us.)

Throughout December I continued to narrow my differences with David Barclay, with the capable technical assistance of Ben Stapleton, an experienced high-level corporate negotiator, who met with the Barclays' emissaries in New York. I sat in my cluttered little library in New York and sent my own faxes to the Barclays, who live in a castle they built in the Channel Islands. I once asked David Barclay how far he was from one of the main islands if he wished to go out to dinner. He replied that there was no need for that because he had built a replica of the main dining room of London's famous restaurant Mark's Club in their castle.

We had to use faxes because employees of Richard C. Breeden and company (known to us as Breeden's thought police) were scanning all our emails and I did not want to arouse suspicions at this point by changing to another email channel. I occasionally took advantage of this by planting completely false messages in them.

One of the many depressing episodes in the steady erosion of my position was my visit to the SEC in Chicago in response to a subpoena, on December 22, 2003. I assumed that Breeden had generated the subpoena, which, at least for a long time, was not accompanied by any parallel action to gain testimony from other Hollinger officials, past or present. I also thought it likely the Special Committee staff were acting in Breeden's name and with the benefit of his connections, to generate the concurrent rumour of a Department of Justice criminal investigation, which was eagerly taken up and publicized by the *New York Post*, though Murdoch's flunkies were certainly capable of hatching this brain-child themselves, with no more encouragement than a wink from their boss.

Since we could achieve no confirmation of the existence of a criminal investigation and the SEC refused a brief deferral or informal questioning, there was no possibility that I could testify. The prosecutor's greatest specialty in current U.S. practice is to put anyone under investigation into a position where he or she gives sworn or even unsworn testimony to several authorities. The slightest discrepancy can then be seized on to allege obstruction of justice and perjury. John Warden and David Braff of Sullivan & Cromwell as well as Eddie Greenspan (out of solidarity and at great inconvenience to himself) accompanied me to Chicago. It was a tedious but civil process as I endlessly invoked the Fifth Amendment formula against self-incrimination, which, like most people, I had long unjustly associated with gangsters.

I correctly judged that invoking the constitutional right not to testify would be used to undermine what was left of my position in Hollinger International. We were completely responsive to SEC subpoenas for documents and handed over more than one hundred thousand pages of material, withholding nothing except what benefited from a clear lawyer-client privilege, just as I had handed over all of my more than ten thousand emails to Breeden's committee.

CHRISTMAS WAS EXTREMELY GLOOMY. My children were with their mother. Barbara's former husband, George Jonas, a delightful and very cultured man, and his wife, Maya, came to lunch. It was the only day in the period from November 15, 2003, through to the end of 2004 that my press service reported no references to me at all. This was a Christmas present of sorts, as most days there were never less than a dozen and often more than fifty negative stories. Barbara and I vowed that we would emerge from under this horrible cloud in the ensuing year. I spent New Year's Eve reading the Barclays' latest proposal for the acquisition of Hollinger Inc. and, with it, control of Hollinger International and the *Telegraph*, apparently the long-standing citadel of their heart's desire.

By the end of December, rumours of my social and financial activities had created such alarm among my enemies that they circulated a proposal for a poison pill. That would impose an inability for anyone to acquire a control block. In essence Hollinger Inc. would not be able either to vote or sell its shares in Hollinger International. Virtually all monies to me and my company had now been blocked and this would render our shares useless. When I received the twenty-four-hour directors' notice of the suggestion that Hollinger Inc. would be handcuffed in this way, I concluded that it might be time to go to war.

I called Henry Kissinger and told him that I found this so outrageous that I was considering sacking some of the directors. He urged me to be cautious, and I suggested that if he could intervene with Breeden and arrange "substantive discussions toward a comprehensive settlement," I would enter whole-heartedly into them. Henry had persevered in a state of friendliness through December. He and Nancy had most kindly invited me to Thanksgiving dinner at their home in Connecticut, which is always a warm occasion, with family, neighbours, and old friends, including in 2003 the recently widowed wives of Lane Kirkland and Isaac Stern. Barbara pleaded illness, preferring to stay home.

I had a conference call with Henry and his lawyer, Paul Saunders, and John Warden on Sunday, January 4. From it, discussion arose between

Warden and Breeden that led to a two-week standstill and the promise of "substantive negotiations." It was specifically understood that Hollinger Inc. could negotiate in that period if it chose to, but could not conclude an arrangement. Henry subsequently put it about that he had laboured mightily to bring these talks about and to persuade me not to have "another Saturday night massacre," an invocation of Richard Nixon's firing of Watergate special prosecutor Archibald Cox, which led to the resignations of Attorney General Elliot Richardson and the dismissal of his deputy, William Ruckelshaus. The comparison was completely spurious. I was being threatened with something I was advised and convinced was an illegality and breach of contract. And I wasn't threatening to fire everybody, unless it was the only way to preserve the interests of the parent company, to which Breeden, Paris, and Thompson had paid ample lip service. Henry's efforts consisted of one telephone call with Breeden, admittedly a taxing undertaking, but hardly a prodigy of diplomacy by his historic standards.

Our first meeting with Breeden and Paris in the Kissinger Substantive Round was on January 7, 2004, at the Sullivan & Cromwell conference centre in midtown Manhattan. The session, which now included Warden, began cordially enough. I gave a summary from memory of about forty minutes, touching upon the principal evidence of approval of the non-competition payments to executives that they claimed had not been authorized. I pointed out that the former director of enforcement of the Ontario Securities Commission, after his extensive investigation, had concluded that the buyers of the newspapers in question had requested that the non-competition agreements include Hollinger Inc. I also contended then, and again in a letter to the Hollinger International Board of Directors two weeks later, that Thompson had misled the directors about discussions he had had with the auditor about the non-competition payments. (Thompson's versions of these events were rebutted at the eventual trial.)

I went over the threats Paris had made to me on November 15, when he had asserted that any hesitation on my part or of our management to resign would lead to litigation. I reminded them of their pledge to put the best possible public relations face on my departure as chief executive and the Restructuring Agreement and their assurance that the flow of cash to

Hollinger Inc. would be front-loaded to continue as closely as possible the former rate of cash flow until June 2004. Six clauses out of eight, including my status as joint director of the Strategic Process with Lazard and the arrangements for the aircraft, had been violated. This, I pointed out, was a worse record of breach of agreement than Stalin's violations of the Yalta Accords. I had been grossly defamed, and Savage and Seitz especially, since they had property in Canada and the United Kingdom, could be vulnerable to libel action when the legality of my conduct was no longer in question. I said that I had been wrongfully deprived of my position and my reputation and that I intended to regain both.

There was a break in proceedings, and when we reconvened they gave us a very lame reply. We agreed to meet again in a few days. The next meeting was January 13, in the same place. I said I would not pay back the so-called unauthorized payments because they had been authorized, but that I was happy to defer that discussion until the end of their proceedings and try to negotiate a final settlement. I told them candidly that there were a number of negotiations underway at Hollinger Inc. and offered to sell them Hollinger Inc. for preferred shares, and to give them a first refusal on any bona fide offer we received for Hollinger Inc. Paris gave me a sanctimonious lecture on how they did not value the stock at above $15, which was well below what Lazard professed to be seeking and was even a couple of dollars below the current market price and below the imputable value of the impending Barclay offer. This was the first control block discount I have ever heard of. He said that they would have to canvass our noteholders, and that it would require months for them to consider this. (I had never had any difficulty getting consents from the same noteholders within a couple of weeks.) They had no proposals except that Hollinger Inc. should pledge to do nothing for at least four months, in which time it would, they obviously hoped, go into default. We agreed to meet again by telephone on Thursday, January 15.

By this time, most of the personnel were showing great wear and tear. Poor Rosemary Millar, my brilliant and devoted London assistant, was in hospital. Although her lung cancer was inoperable, there were various chemotherapies for her, which she paid for by selling her options at the current higher prices. Peter Atkinson, who had been monosyllabic and almost catatonic for some time, had finally reached the breaking point and abruptly resigned on January 9. As the war for survival steadily intensified, he was not a fit combatant. He was opposed to any initiative that might keep the company functioning, had lost faith in what we were trying to do, was concerned for his own health and that of his wife, and presumably bore some burden of guilt for his own failure – as legal vice-president – to correct the documentary incompleteness of the now notorious payments.

He thanked me for what I had done for him; I returned the sentiment and wished him well. It was a sad end to what had at times been a distinguished association. Like so many other things in my life, a valued and trusted relationship had crumbled under the pressure of unforeseeable events and the frailties of formerly trusted comrades.

ON JANUARY 8, I HAD GONE to find Barbara for dinner, and she was not in the house. There was an agitated and ambiguous note from her on my desk. Her cellphone was not with her. Her car was in the garage. There were footprints in the snow to the chapel and then out onto the driveway, but it was impossible to follow them into the road. I called George Jonas, who came to our house. The night was bitterly cold. I called the police and drove around the neighbourhood looking for her. The police called for the canine unit, but because they were careful not to put it over the police radio, there was a delay in the arrival of the dogs. I was on the phone with Eddie Greenspan, when Barbara, almost frost-bitten, entered through the front door. She had walked three miles to the Don Mills shopping centre and back and bought me two combs, items that I did not need but have used fetishistically ever since. She appeared to have spent a number of hours outside in the snow, but I didn't want to badger her with questions. She was upset and had dealt with it her own way. It was a harrowing time and the police were magnificently efficient, solicitous, and discreet. This was the only time that Barbara allowed the strain of events to get the better of her briefly and she overcame that herself.

The controller of the Hollinger companies, Fred Creasey, was full of good intentions but was so nervous he started grinding his teeth at night. He ended up having to go to the dentist for it. He fainted when his lawyer told him that the SEC wanted to interview him, and eventually vanished for three months' rest, which stretched to several years. Peter White, unflappable and indefectibly loyal, rushed in to be a daily presence in the office.

We needed independent directors to represent the shareholders after the resignations of the previous year. Peter White recruited Gordon Walker, a former justice minister of Ontario (a resonant-sounding position that was in fact only the chairmanship of a committee of justice-related ministers in the Ontario cabinet) who had represented the city of London, Ontario, in the provincial legislature, and I persuaded Richard Rohmer, a much decorated general of the Canadian Reserves, a lawyer, author, and old friend, also to become an independent director.

I faxed David Barclay that I had offered Hollinger International a first refusal on any sale of Hollinger Inc., although the authors of what Barclay called the "vendetta" against me had not shown much interest. I wrote that if they took up the offer I would have to abide by that. Our telephone meeting with Breeden and Paris on January 15 was a failure. They showed no interest in my proposals. We agreed on a further telephone conference the following day, January 16. I pushed the Barclay deal forward to close immediately after the expiry of the agreed stand-still period, at midnight on Saturday, January 17.

All my legal advice from Sullivan & Cromwell and Jesse Finkelstein was that the Barclay deal, fortified by their promise to support the Strategic (Lazard) Process, was legally bullet-proof. I thought of papering our exchanges off with special-purpose faxes to reinforce the record but was assured that that was not necessary.

Breeden peremptorily cancelled the meeting on January 16, and we learned at the end of the day, after the opposition had leaked it to the press, that the ex-officers of Hollinger International and I had been sued by Hollinger International for $200 million, including a demand for the disgorgement of all dividends Hollinger Inc. had received from Hollinger International in the last six years. The news report said that Hollinger International had acknowledged to the SEC that it had filed some false statements and had alleged to the SEC that the Special Committee was under threat. This was completely false, but the company had "consented" to the imposition of Breeden as "special monitor" if we altered the composition of the board of directors. A special monitor has tremendous power made even greater by the fact that those powers are unspecified.

This was a disgraceful stitch-up; the SEC had simply taken Breeden's word for it (a terrible mistake I had already discovered), that his committee was under threat from me, which it wasn't – I had only asked for adherence to the Restructuring Agreement and threatened eventual defamation actions where appropriate, and in the first of several acts of ex parte pseudo-legal gangsterism, had installed Breeden in another impregnable sinecure riveted on the neck of our company on his own assurances of a non-existent threat by a party not invited or permitted to respond. Bernard Madoff went on pillaging his investors. Wall Street and its rating agencies went on shoveling out worthless mortgages and consolidated debt obligations, and the SEC cheerfully turned our company into a trussed-up partridge for Breeden.

It subsequently came to light that Louis Zachary had told Wasserstein that the effect of the SEC consent decree was to assure that "no one would invest in" Hollinger Inc. Breeden had now become the humanoid equivalent of a poison pill.

Saturday, January 17, 2004, was an eventful day. The Argus Corporation, Ravelston Corporation, and Hollinger Inc. directors met and approved the sale after ample but constructive discussion.

In the midst of this intense day, Nelson Peltz called to say that Packer had withdrawn their joint offer (which, in any event, was so stingy I had not replied to it) and to predict that the Barclays would not go ahead with a deal. Then my ex-wife phoned to say that she thought it timely for me to settle a large amount of cash on our two sons and daughter. With considerable patience, I explained that her request was quite impractical at the moment. I did not tell her that I was down to barely $100,000 in cash. My financial condition was critical.

I had called Alfred Taubman, a former director of Hollinger International and a former controlling shareholder of Sotheby's International, and asked whether, in an emergency, I could borrow something from him. I said that I could pledge one of my houses to him. He said that he would certainly lend me money, that he didn't need a pledge, that all he needed to know was the amount required and the place to which it should be sent. Alfred, at least, did not forget favours, at least not for a time, and his promise, though I never acted upon it, was a great comfort. (Unfortunately, when I later did seek his assistance, he was not forthcoming.)

The Hollinger International executive committee met at 7 p.m. As usual, they had given us just twenty-four hours' notice and no indication of the purpose of the meeting. I feared that they might be trying to institute a poison pill, so I made sure the Barclays' New York lawyer and one of ours were in an office in New York with all the sale documents in front of them. Barbara was on the phone to them from the other telephone in my library. That way I could signal to her if a poison pill was in contemplation and she could ensure the deal was consummated before the pill was installed.

This proved not to be necessary. There were three issues for the executive committee. First, the previous day's consent arrangement with the SEC was approved, with me in dissent. It had been approved by the Audit and Special Committees after five minutes of discussion. No one was able to tell me the justification for the claim that the Special Committee was under threat. I expressed shock that Burt and Thompson would have been a party to a bogus concession of guilt implicating themselves and that all of them would subscribe to such a false bogeyman as a threat to the Special Committee, and further to such a rape of the rights of shareholders as the special monitor provisions. I was speaking to myself, but I hoped it would be on record. Next was approval of their lawsuit of the previous day. Again I dissented and received no coherent response. There was no real defence of either measure. They were merely executing Breeden's instructions.

The third item was announced by Seitz as being a consideration of my position. I was assured that this was the last item, so I was able to signal digitally to Barbara to stand easy in her hookup with New York. Given the treachery of my interlocutors, it was not appropriate to end the telephone connection, so the lawyers at the other end of her call remained on standby. Seitz moved that I be fired as chairman, as casually as he might ask for some small capital expenditure. I asked for a reason. Answer came there none. Finally, poor, plodding Jim Thompson said that it was "in the power of the board to take this action." I replied that this committee was not the board and that that was not my question. I added that they would all have the opportunity to answer my question in due course, when silence would not be an option. (At time of writing, that moment impends.) A pristine silence continued. Eventually, after I was again outvoted four to one, termination of the meeting was proposed. I said that I would be delighted to make that motion unanimous.

Barbara and I had dinner and I enjoyed the better part of a good bottle of claret. The sale of Ravelston and Argus corporations' 78 per cent of Hollinger Inc. to the Barclays was concluded shortly after midnight. Reciprocating the plentiful courteous notice of important events that our enemies traditionally gave us, Sullivan & Cromwell sent a faxed notice of the impending sale to Breeden's office at about nine o'clock that evening.

While I was right to resist the corporate governance fanatics as I did, am proud to have done so, and am sure I will eventually be vindicated, and at the time of writing, I substantially have been, I had underestimated their strength and identified my own contempt for the movement too strongly with the corporate interest. If the motion to remove me had been presented for the correct reasons and in acceptable terms, I would have abstained. Of course, under any scenario, I intended to return, as Gordon Paris couldn't run a two-car funeral, and it shortly became clear that it was precisely toward just such a fate that Paris, with the help of Breeden and Seitz, was driving the company. But for me to cling on to an impotent position, fronting for the usurpatory acting (in each sense of the word) management, was an intolerable state of affairs.

Most important, I did not want to be associated in any way with the vandals now in control, with Paris acting in Breeden's name, as chairman, president, and chairman of the Special Committee. The events of the last few days made the distinction clear between those who built, largely owned, and would normally control the company and those complicit in their overthrow and in the subsequent destruction of the Hollinger companies. The Hollinger International shareholders would pay a terrible price for the fact that their fate was to be entrusted to Breeden.

Breeden and I had both crossed the Rubicon in opposite directions. I assume that he was accustomed to, and had achieved, in his corporate governance role, the complete submission of his targets, and was even addicted to it. Certainly, that was what he had effortlessly extracted from Radler, Atkinson, and the independent directors, except, up to a point, Perle. And that is how his operatives behaved, from his law firm down through the people who appeared at our offices to take our hard drives (with a peremptoriness usually reserved to bill collectors or minibar inspectors).

In making a Swiss cheese of our Restructuring Agreement, and a farce of our "substantive discussions," and then launching a legal onslaught while we were supposedly in constructive negotiation, he had escalated our disputes to a war which had to result in one of us being completely crushed. He had seized, and for a (long) time, would retain the high ground, and I was severely defeated at the outset and repeatedly. But my weakness was my strength. I had little left to lose, and I was, after all, innocent of wrongdoing, if not of misjudgment.

I had just demonstrated an ability to continue the fight that startled the other side. The more the war escalated, the greater the danger to Breeden would become. With each new overreaching act of belligerence, Breeden would risk more; we were locked in a death struggle on a runaway train. He had to finish me off as the crook he falsely claimed I was, or fail.

No matter how often and noisily I was pronounced dead, it wouldn't happen if Breeden, to borrow what has become an American political expression, couldn't close the deal, by destroying me. He took the task upon himself, and kept raising the stakes. He has sown, and he shall reap.

[CHAPTER SIX]

WE DREADED FRIDAYS. The pattern established by International early on was for a week of skirmishing ending with the minimally required twenty-four-hour notice given either Thursday or Friday of a board meeting – no agenda. The new management would convene to issue another Breeden Bull, guaranteeing us a weekend of gloom as we scrambled to devise some reply to his latest manoeuvre.

For once, we had roared back and left the enemy scrambling like asphyxiated cockroaches. With the sale to the Barclays, Breeden and his committee had the rug pulled out from under them. The media, now accustomed to me as a completely passive and deposed figure, were startled by this turn of events. Sunday headlines of "BLACK SUED FOR $200 MILLION AND SACKED" were followed by Monday's and Tuesday's headlines of "BLACK'S BUSY WEEKEND" and "BARCLAYS: HOLLINGER BID 'DONE DEAL.'" There was great excitement among worried Hollinger Inc. shareholders that they would now see money, as all classes of stock would be taken out at good prices by the Barclays. Once these counter-attacks were launched, Jesse Finkelstein and Sullivan & Cromwell reconfirmed that this sale was legally invulnerable. I allowed my infant but precociously growing wariness about the operation of the U.S. legal system to be overborne by their confident assurances. It would all be part of a most expensive and painful education.

This time International did not have the luxury of waiting for Friday. A Hollinger International board meeting was called for Monday, January 20. It was probably the most disagreeable directors meeting I have ever attended. (From then on, all Hollinger International board attendances by me, except one, were by telephone.) Gordon Paris was elected chairman. Barbara and I voted against; I pointed out that he was completely unqualified and in a clear conflict of interest as chairman of the Special Committee. Then a Corporate Review Committee (CRC) was established, comprising all the directors except Barbara, Dan Colson, and me, to review the Barclays' transaction and any other matters. All powers of that committee could be delegated to a subcommittee of two, to be called on minimal verbal notice.

It was designed to be the completion of our marginalization, prior to our completely unforeseen counter-stroke. Henry Kissinger, in his chivalrous confusion, objected (only) to Barbara's exclusion. Obviously, one had either to reject the concept of the committee entirely or agree to the proposed composition, which, as Barbara pointed out, excluded the only three people on the board who knew anything about the business the company was in. Dan Colson was ostensibly the chief operating officer but was being ceaselessly and ignorantly interfered with by Paris.

Then came approval of the $200-million lawsuit. (It would shortly be escalated to over $1 billion by adding new, even more fantastic counts, and the peculiarly American flourish of the civil version of the Racketeer Influenced and Corrupt Organizations Act, RICO; yes, civil racketeering. I asked myself if the crime of civility could be far behind.) Richard Breeden gave a rambling pastiche of accusations about the original problems of unauthorized payments, which I rebutted in a calm, low voice – so calm it was not entirely understood by some on the call. I reaffirmed the contents of a letter I had sent the directors over the weekend debunking the unauthorized payments theory and referred to the letter the Barclays also sent to the directors in which they objected to the "vendetta" against my associates and me and promised full support for the Strategic (Lazard) Process.

The lawsuit was approved. Dan Colson had to abstain; Richard Perle was not yet on the call. Barbara and I were the sole votes against. I asked

Henry Kissinger if he had voted for the suit, since I had not heard him. He replied that he had. I said, after a brief pause: "Et tu, Brute?" This hung heavily in the air for a few moments. Then Henry said that he wasn't approving the contents of the lawsuit, only upholding the right of the company to take it, and asserted his standard comment that I had "been one of [his] best friends in the world for decades."

The great Metternichian was befuddled by this sudden agitation in the balance of forces in a small matter, like a *coup d'état* in the Balkans or, in our times, even in Central Africa. He got it wrong as the passage of years would show.

The final motion of the telephone meeting called for adherence to the Restructuring Agreement. I detailed the company's violation of six of the eight provisions of that agreement and explained why I believed that the Barclay transaction, supported by the letter the Barclays had sent the directors and the letter I had sent, conformed to the agreement. Richard Perle had now joined the call and supported the position I was taking that the Restructuring Agreement had to be upheld by all parties. The motion passed and the meeting adjourned. Dan Colson, who attended by telephone from London, was so disgusted by the meeting that as soon as it ended, he went to his washroom and vomited.

In the U.S., a controlling corporation can adopt a consent motion that alters the board and the committees of a subsidiary. We used this at Hollinger Inc. and gutted all the Hollinger International committees, required unanimous approval of various categories of motions, and required one week's notice of any meeting rather than the twenty-four-hour specials International favoured. We were, after all, still the controlling shareholders of the companies we had built. Both Jesse Finkelstein and Sullivan & Cromwell again assured us this was a legally unassailable step.

Our right to sell to the Barclays would now be challenged by International in the chancery courts of Delaware – which was where International was incorporated. I continued my cheerful daily conversations and fax exchanges with the Barclays, a rather pleasant interlude with two intelligent and humorous businessmen, among the more agreeable people I have dealt with. They issued a 13D (a public SEC filing, which Tweedy Browne had used to call for the appointment of a special committee) in early February that indicated they were prepared to offer $18 a share for all Hollinger International shares but stated that Wasserstein had been instructed by Paris, who was supposed to consult with me about the Strategic Process (and who had told me in the "substantive discussions" two weeks before that the stock wasn't worth more than $15), to insist on a higher price. I urged the Barclays to stop the tease and make the offer.

They were confident based on advice from their lawyers, Skadden Arps (who had ignored any possible conflict in that they were also acting for both Tweedy Browne and Lazard), which was that we would win the case in Delaware and that they could buy the *Telegraph* from International via Hollinger Inc.'s controlling interest in that company without having to bid for all the International shares. My plan was to sell Hollinger Inc. and with it International at the best possible price. It didn't take a genius to see that Breeden and Co. would never be able to run a newspaper company profitably and their animus to me was so clear that co-existence was never an option, though I gave it a try. Nor, from his conduct, was it ever intended to be an option. Only Greenspan, our Canadian lawyer, had seen immediately what we were up against.

In ordinary times we should have been able to get the Ontario Securities Commission (OSC) to intervene to protect the rights of the Hollinger Inc. shareholders from being hog-tied by a putschist faction in the U.S. subsidiary. But a little research confirmed that the OSC saw Hollinger Inc. as me (as my associates and I owned 78 per cent of it), and didn't approve of multiple-voting shares (with which the parent controlled the subsidiary). Some of the OSC staff remembered being cuffed around by Breeden when he was at the SEC, and importantly, as it turned out, didn't want to go through it again.

Now came the first of many trials in this saga, in which Hollinger International sought to block the sale of Hollinger Inc. to the Barclays. We were quickly into depositions for the trial in Wilmington, Delaware. The first inkling that there might be greater problems than I had been warned about was Finkelstein's statement to me that the designated Chancery Court judge, Leo Strine, was flaky, controversial, and unpredictable. Barbara did some research and found him to be an intelligent judge with a creative view of his role, a shareholders' rights activist, and a left-liberal Democrat whose elevation to the bench had been closely contested in the Delaware State Senate. It wasn't clear in this case which side a shareholders' rights advocate ought to be on, but given the public relations debacle, I was unlikely to be the beneficiary of that current of opinion. Though a shareholder myself, I belonged to a category out of favour with the governance movement and one being hunted into extinction: the controlling shareholder with dual-class stockholdings.

We were told Breeden had gone judge-shopping in Wilmington, but I suspect that was quite unnecessary. Breeden and Strine were peas in a pod as far as views on corporate governance activism went, and this case would be one in which Strine would have special interest. Strine's involvement came from a genuine belief in the need for more radical measures to protect shareholders. He was critical of Sarbannes-Oxley on grounds that it put the regulation of business into the hands of government agencies rather than the courts.

Breeden appeared also to see corporate governance as a profit centre. He had a law firm to deal with miscreants, a governance consulting business to rake in preventative fees, and would soon start his own investment and hedge fund business that could provide financing to companies caught in, or potential targets of, governance demands – had they not been prudent enough to invest with him in the first place. I find it hard to believe that his funnelling such rich business to the New York law firms O'Melveny & Myers and Paul, Weiss went altogether unrewarded.

Businessmen may be familiar with it, but to the larger society, Chancery Court is pretty much unknown. Most states abolished Chancery Courts long ago (New York, for example, in 1847) and whatever cases fell under their auspices were delegated to regular courts of law. A Chancery Court is not tied to rules of law, though naturally the law is considered. Its decisions are based on "equity" and the maxims of equity. This gives the judge, known as chancellor, if chief judge, or vice chancellor, very broad latitude. He is the trier of facts (there is no jury) and is not bound by law or precedent. Delaware, whose Chancery Court was established in its 1792 constitution, has evolved into the most important player in

America's corporate disputes. Early on, the state had a conservative business environment. But no institution can immunize itself against the fashions and fads of the times. Leo Strine would rather lead and extend a fad than resist it.

The good, gentlemanly lawyers of Sullivan & Cromwell had, with the best and most honourable intentions, but seemingly no knowledge of the chancery bench, led me into an ambush. I was a bull in a china shop, a clumsy capitalist interloper in the regulatory minefield. Once Strine was the chosen judge, we were doomed.

The depositions came in well. Kissinger revealed that Breeden had been loudly proclaiming the commission of criminal acts when he phoned around in November, though Kissinger himself did not believe his claims. Had Kissinger called me then and questioned me about these so-called criminal acts or "unauthorized" payments, he would actually have fulfilled his fiduciary duty to the shareholders. He was the sole person on that board who had the personal weight and stature to halt Breeden. But he was too fearful. This extraordinarily intelligent refugee of Nazi Germany seemed not to understand that the contemporary version of "I was only following orders" is "My lawyer advised me not to." He kept quiet, followed his lawyer's directions to a T, and left me and every public shareholder to be fleeced. Thompson and Burt, both Audit Committee members, were hopeless. They knew nothing, read nothing that they had signed, and had no knowledge of the nature of the poison pill. When Burt was asked about my offer to Breeden and Paris to give Hollinger International a right of first refusal on any bona fide offer received for Hollinger Inc., he snorted derisively and said that that was like "the letter Hitler sent the Czechs at Munich." There was no such letter, but the comparison was scandalous.

My deposition seemed to go smoothly. The only emerging issues that I could see were the interpretation of the clause about not tampering with the strategic process with Lazard and the question of how close Hollinger Inc. was to a default, relieving it of most of the obligations under the Restructuring Agreement. Following my deposition on February 13, I went to Kennedy Airport to await Barbara, who was returning from our home in England.

She duly emerged, pushing one suitcase and pulling the other, flamboyant, indomitable, and glamorous as always, despite her long trip. I was inexpressibly pleased to see her; we hate being apart. She had found my studio in our London home, where for years I had directed our British operations and written much of my Roosevelt book, very sad, empty, and lifeless. There was, she said, a pathetic fallacy about the home: its limbs were in necrosis. Our brilliant and devoted driver, Tommy Buckley, a delightful Irishman, had just died of a brain tumour in his mid-thirties, leaving three small children, and my London assistant, Rosemary Millar, was fighting for her life in a battle she was about to lose. I was technically still the chairman of the *Telegraph* but with no practical ability to function. This phase of my life was ending, amid the ululations of triumph of my enemies and a conspicuous silence from many whom I had taken for friends.

I went to Wilmington on the evening of February 16 with John Warden, one of Sullivan & Cromwell's leading corporate litigators and a very congenial man. I was reading a newspaper in my hotel room the next morning when he telephoned after the judge's pre-trial lawyers' conference and told me that we stood no chance; Strine had bought Breeden's case like a salmon leaping out of the water for the bait. Warden said we should consider abandoning any defence of the lawsuit and moving immediately to dismiss the directors, which we had the authority to do.

I rejected Warden's advice. If we were about to be trashed in our attempted sale, we would certainly receive the same treatment for a general sacking of the directors – with the added joy of Breeden as special monitor. I wasn't even convinced, and still am not, that with such an 'activist' (i.e., unlimitedly aggressive and opinionatedly meddlesome) judge as Strine, turfing out the directors would have ended their case against us. I still think it would have just reinforced Strine in his prejudices, and that he would have reinstalled the directors in addition to any other severities it might please him to inflict on us. This was poor and late advice from Sullivan & Cromwell. There was nothing for it but to fight out the case, no matter how uphill. Still, we had something of an ace in the hole: Warden, our best lawyer, had been present at the "substantive discussions" with Breeden and was prepared to testify to the misleading and deceptive nature of Breeden's statements about them, no small step for a lawyer of Warden's stature. It meant he would not be able to lead me in direct examination or cross-examine, but we judged it worth that loss. In the end, Strine did not allow Warden to testify, so we had him as neither witness nor barrister. We had agreed to too constricted a timetable and did not use even that judiciously.

The night before I testified I had a drink with Paul Saunders, there representing Kissinger. Paul and I agreed that this matter should be settled, and he said he would see what he could do. Henry was upset at the deterioration in our relations and might be ready to have another try at getting some sort of agreement going. Henry, whose ability to resist flattery is not one of his most noteworthy characteristics, had apparently been duped by Breeden into co-authoring a "statement of principles" that, when it was eventually produced on a documentary subpoena, was one of the most platitudinous compositions I have read. Even Gordon Paris declined to endorse it.

I testified most of the day on February 20. Jesse Finkelstein touchingly gave me a piece of the rock of Masada, which I held throughout my time on the stand. The BBC credited me with a "magnificent performance." The *New York Post*, faithful to its master's orders, declared that my "well-known charisma was not evident." The truth probably lay somewhere in between. Warden and Paul Saunders both congratulated me on the strength of my testimony, and Skadden Arps advised the Barclays that we would win the case. I was too confident in the power and truth of my testimony, and elemental advice about the merit of brevity in responses to questions had not been emphasized to me. I had the passion of a man wronged. Much of my testimony, which could have been corroborated by witnesses and documents, went in unsupported. Strine was courteous. Though his sense of humour escaped me, there was no doubt of his intelligence and assiduity.

His reception of me and my counsel's satisfaction with my performance were such that there was some hope in some circles that we had retrieved the situation. Certainly that was the view of the Barclays, whose Skadden Arps lawyer in Wilmington assured them that we would win. David Barclay called to congratulate me on my testimony. We all thought that Strine's judgment, if adverse, would at least have to be polite. We were mistaken.

Strine's judgment came out by email on Thursday, February 26. The first two sentences pulled down the curtain. "As former Chancellor Allen has said, the most interesting corporate law cases," wrote Strine, "involve the color gray, with contending parties dueling over close questions of law, in circumstances when it is possible for each of the contestants to claim she was acting in good faith. Regrettably, this case is not one of that variety." I half noted the use of the pronoun "she" in the very first sentence, presumably one of Strine's little teases with novelty.

Strine resisted using my surname as a synonym for my actions that were in his mind satanic. That is all he resisted. I was "cunning" and "calculated" in my conduct, which "threatens grave injury to International and its stockholders by depriving them of the benefits that might flow from the Strategic Process's search for a value-maximizing transaction." My malfeasance rendered the normal corporate rights of a controlling shareholder and parent company inoperable due to these "extraordinary scenarios." He was issuing an injunction against the Barclay's deal to "rectify the irreparable harm Black's wrongdoing obviously threatens."

Not only had Strine found my character flawed and my behaviour improper; he also described the unauthorized payments as, at the very least, "constructive fraud." I had only signed the Restructuring Agreement to avoid being charged, he wrote. All this would be refuted by the jury at a proper trial and was outrageously biased and wrong-headed, but Strine had bought a line. He did, however, confirm the Breeden-Paris blackmail, mouthed at the November 12 meeting , that without an agreement, I would have been charged at once. (In fact, the SEC required another six months from this case to charge, and the Justice Department another fifteen months after that. So to some extent, Breeden's threat may have been hollow, though the government might have moved more quickly if Breeden were not already in control of the company.)

"I am in a good position," wrote Strine confidently, "to make certain credibility determinations and have done so. Generally, I found the key International witnesses – Paris, Seitz, and Breeden – entirely credible. I can discern no improper motive they may have had at any time to testify other than truthfully."

This would prove to be an unintended confession of monumental naïveté. He must have had some notion of the millions the three pharisees stood to gain from their putsch, and even of the fact that they could not so enrich themselves by any other method, unlesss they took to armed robbery, for which activity they might have had the ethics but probably not the energy. Strine, like Christopher Browne, would realize too late that Breeden was a false prophet. In neither case was there even the least recognition of the role they had played in fixing these insatiable bloodsuckers on the necks of the unconsulted shareholders, in whose name all iniquities were inflicted. On my side were, with one exception, decent, gentlemanly lawyers and businessmen, sitting ducks, all of us, for the delectation of our enemies. This was the equity of the jungle.

My sophistical answers, wrote Strine, were all of piece with my taking the Fifth Amendment at the SEC hearing, though he knew perfectly well why I had to take it and it had nothing to do with credibility or evasiveness. (Strine had small faith in the Barclays' credibility either, which so angered them that they issued a rebuttal press release.)[9] He had one cautionary footnote after his factual findings: "This is not to say that there is not evidence from which another reasonable mind might draw different conclusions on some of the factual points." Bingo; unfortunately, he wasn't reasonable. He was gullible and cocksure. A not particularly brilliant or fair-minded, but more exacting jury later eviscerated his findings, but too late to help the shareholders, victims on whose behalf he waxed so righteous.

The Strategic Process, which the judgment said "had great promise for the shareholders" so long as the court prevented my deal with the Barclays, with its anticipated stock values in the $20 to $24 range, did not materialize. Breeden and Paris quickly decided to sell only the *Telegraph* to the Barclays, without making them pay for the entire company, which they most certainly would have were it their only means of getting International's crown jewel (as they had asserted in their 13D). Shareholders saw a total of $6 per share in special dividends after the *Telegraph* sale, before the stock descended into bankruptcy. No other offers for the entire company materialized. The Special Committee that Strine wrote would wrap up its work in June 2004 would continue to pay itself through 2008, with Richard Breeden staying on as monitor (a well-paid, completely redundant post to which he prevailed upon the docile, terrorized directors to elevate him in 2006) until January 2009. Gordon Paris would lose $70 million of shareholders money investing in sub-prime mortgages – an unusual venture for a media company – but he would leave with $13 million for himself. Chairman Ray Seitz (annual salary $600,000, board earnings and perquisites as yet unknown) would only be separated from his office effective January 2009 by a vote of the bondholders.

These were governance buccaneers, and Thompson and Burt, and later Kravis, and even Perle, were press-ganged, with an inelegant lack of reluctance in some cases, into complicity. Seitz, Savage, and Paris may have begun their roles on the Special Committee with every intention of acting fairly on behalf of all shareholders. When Breeden arrived with a more murderous agenda, they seem to have fallen into line.

Thompson, Seitz, and Burt, like Perle and Kissinger were names known in the world beyond boardrooms. I had admired the accomplishments of each, yet here they were engaged in unworthy activities, now voting (except Kravis who had withdrawn), for motions that they should have known to be empty and fatuous, or at least requiring abstention.

Seitz counts as one of the most horrifying mistakes of my life in judging character. Behind the impeccable facade of the ambassador of a great nation lurks a bureaucrat, a process freak, the ancient curse of the foreign services, disguised by unusually fine packaging. Too intelligent to be a time-server, but too long separated from anything not requiring the instincts of a safe player to be effective outside the foreign service cocoon and lacking the cunning, daring, or cross-disciplinary background of a great foreign minister (like Kissinger), Seitz proved to be only a bloodless valise-carrier ambling gracefully among more formidable players. Seitz would not budge from our corporate trough until, finally, in November 2008 he was muscled out by impoverished debt-holders. The stock at that point was worth .08 cents per share, on a vertical descent to zero at the speed of gravity.

To become the four-term governor of as large a state as Illinois shows that Jim Thompson had a very sharp political intuition. Tall, loquacious, banal, simulating folksiness when not engaged in scowling righteousness, Thompson never in the ten years he was on our board showed any spark. He too disappointed me.

If Thompson's performance under fire was a disappointment, it was a mere sorbet compared with Richard Burt. Burt succeeded Perle as the informal chairman of the independent committee of directors when Perle became an employee. The related-party transactions, which were necessary as we consolidated assets in one company and then dismantled the secondary assets of the company when we delivered at the height of the economic boom, had been skilfully handled by Richard Perle and Dennis Block and never became a source of controversy; both Hollingers greatly profited. But they were relatively sloppily handled by Radler with only Burt and Thompson as overseers.

Gordon Paris has a perfectly nondescript and entirely forgettable personality, except for a penchant for self-righteous inflexibility, when he assumes a whiny, grating persistence, like a malfunctioning appliance. He hit the jackpot with our company.

Had Breeden not breeched the Restructuring Agreement, I would still have had to sell out. Once there was a Special Committee, my ability to act as a real CEO was gone, as Marie-Josée had foreseen. Breeden was in charge and I knew the newspaper business was in decline. All I could hope for was to get the highest price for the company and take my share of cash and move on to something else. The Barclays were the best bet, as events confirmed.

The Strine judgment was the official seal of approval on Breeden's demonization of me. From that moment on, his words, endlessly quoted, tainted every move I tried to make to rescue Inc. and International. The press, which we had brought around a long way to seeing the weakness of the initial Breeden-Paris-Thompson case about the so-called unauthorized payments, lapsed back into the mode of regarding me as an ethically flawed character.

I had already heard from Paul Saunders before the judgment came down that he could not deliver serious peace discussions. Breeden did not want peace. Strine's judgment gave as much impetus as a civil case could to a criminal prosecution. Though Strine would not have been moved from his pseudo-populist biases, I believe that if Sullivan & Cromwell had administered our evidence more effectively, he would not have been able to assassinate my credibility as severely as he did. As it was, Strine had to note my efforts to act within the rules of the Restructuring Agreement but could shunt these efforts aside with only a reference to them prefaced with an "admittedly" or an "although," something he could not have done if our evidence had gone in with adequate corroboration.

We publicly took the position that we were disappointed, we appealed the case, and we told Hollinger International to "put up or shut up." They were supposed to produce a third-party offer of $20 to $24 per share; we said, let them get on with it, knowing they neither could nor wished to do anything of the kind.

THE BENEFIT OF THE JUDGMENT was that International's stock now rose sharply on Strine's enthusiastic endorsement of the Lazard process and his belief that I had undervalued the company in my prospective sale to the Barclays. Jack Boultbee and I worked with Canadian counsel on a plan to capitalize on this. We would package up almost all of Hollinger Inc.'s Hollinger International single-voting shares and sell them as Series II exchangeable preferred shares of Hollinger Inc. This would fulfill certain indenture conditions and eliminate all the arrears and outstanding unhonoured retractions (which had started the rockslide on our company in April 2003), leaving us with a reasonable cash balance. It was the old trick of turning adversity to advantage: the Strine-created balloon in the stock price.

After taking some time to recover my balance from the Delaware disaster, I retreated to our house in Palm Beach, which I had not seen in eleven months. To the great delight of the international press, the house was for sale. But our rising stock price enabled me to sell my own Series II preferred shares, thus repaying Hollinger Inc.'s loans to me, which had been a bugbear to Maureen Sabia and to Strine (or "Swine," as Eddie Greenspan now generally called him). I withdrew the house from sale. I had one conversation with David Barclay, who was now so paranoid about the United States that he insisted that we both speak on cellphones (for all the good that would have done us, as mobile phones are even easier to intercept than land lines, as even royal victims of media intercepts in London would know). It was cordial, but they were the last words we would exchange.

The weeks in Palm Beach flowed agreeably past. I had a reasonably active social life, and rejuvenated my tattered strategic plan. First, I needed new counsel. I arranged a teleconference with Brendan Sullivan, who had been recommended by Brian Mulroney, Alan Dershowitz (who was very generous with his advice and time), and Eddie Greenspan. Sullivan was the chairman of Williams & Connolly and the successor to that firm's founder, the legendary Edward Bennett Williams. He came to Palm Beach on his way to visit his mother for her eighty-ninth birthday. Eddie Greenspan, who was in Miami, joined us, and Sullivan brought his partner, David Aufhauser, a former Treasury chief counsel and specialist in money-laundering cases. (Aufhauser was latterly general counsel of UBS Investment Bank when he was accused by the SEC in 2007 of insider trading. Aufhauser settled for $6.5 million. On my acquaintance with him, I don't believe he would have done anything unethical.)

Both Sullivan and Aufhauser knew Breeden slightly and despised him almost as much as I now did. Sullivan, whom I had seen in action in the Iran-Contra hearings, where he represented Colonel Oliver North, was very impressive. He has a slight trace of a New England blue-collar accent and speaks in a spare, efficient way. He makes no effort to impress with vol-ubility or his legendary legal experience. He is a nuclear-tipped missile of a man; wiry, not a pound overweight, no vices, very direct, fanatically par-tisan for his client. I had the sense that we were finally reaching for the best. He would be busy on a trial for several months, probably until the end of August, but we would not need him until then, if at all, and in the mean-time his firm would take over my legal position.

Williams & Connolly familiarized themselves with the complicated case but remained in the background as strategic and potential criminal counsel. We agreed on a search for "fresh eyes and fresh minds," as Eddie Greenspan put it, on both the securities and the civil side.

Strine had written that Breeden's fear that I "might transfer assets to jurisdictions from which recoupment is practically impossible is not irra-tional," and it soon became clear that Breeden had excited at least some of the SEC staff to believe that I might just seize the proceeds of my sale of Hollinger Inc. preferreds and flee. Hollinger Inc.'s Chicago counsel, Nate Eimer, was told by the Chicago SEC office chief that the Breeden demo-nization of me was taken seriously in Washington. John Warden called upon the SEC's director of enforcement and had a very civilized exchange. But the SEC was stirring up the Ontario Securities Commission (OSC), which kept layering in more and more onerous conditions for getting the

Hollinger Inc. sale of the preferred shares, a reasonably routine transaction, approved. In other circumstances, it would have gone through like an express train. Finally, after a long session with officials of both regulators at 11:57 p.m. on April 2 three minutes before the deadline (revealing more clearly than ever that the OSC is a branch-plant operation of the SEC), the deal was approved for offering.

The acting management of Hollinger International dropped the next shoe by firing Dan Colson, managing director and co-chief executive of The Telegraph plc, and chief operating officer of the company, thus depriving the company of the last executive who knew anything about the business. This was at another meeting of Seitz's lynch mob on the executive committee, and I was again in dissent. I asked what possible excuse there could be for this, and was told by Jim Thompson in his folksy, oafish voice, as if it were emanating from a prematurely enlarged teenager: "It's time." I said, "What do you mean, Jim, it's time? He's a brilliant manager. You have no one adequate to replace him. Dan has performed prodigies in terribly difficult circumstances. It's time for what, more wrongful dismissals of the people who built the business, for capricious reasons?" Thompson replied, "For Gordon to put in his own team." To which I retorted: "Jim, you've promised to sell the company for a lot more than the $18 per share we were going to get. Gordon has no team and has no capacity to assemble one." Then Thompson fell mercifully silent, like the rest of Breeden's spear-carriers. It was another disgrace, even though they all represented Dan Colson's departure as a retirement. Consistent with their usual ethical standards, Seitz and Paris reduced Colson's retirement package as much as they could, and then added him as a defendant in a civil suit a few weeks later, despite having given him an indemnity for his legal expenses as part of his "retirement."

BARBARA AND I LEFT PALM BEACH in mid-May. It had been a welcome stay after the horribly tempestuous late autumn and winter, right through to the mockery in Delaware. Liberated, after six years, from working on Roosevelt, I was able to return to traditional reading and rereading. There were two busy weeks in New York. Neal Kozodoy arranged for my Roosevelt book and me to receive a considerable ovation at the *Commentary* magazine annual dinner. There were reports in the press of my social ostracism, but in fact I was out most evenings. In New York, as in Palm Beach, Barbara was less inclined than I to mingle. I felt reasonably social anyway but was particularly determined to show that I was not afflicted by the slightest embarrassment.

My poor Barbara was blameless but nevertheless buffeted by these events, and more vulnerable to them. One of the heaviest blows of all fell when International reformulated their lawsuit, claimed that the Racketeer Influenced and Corrupt Organizations Act (RICO) applied, and trebled the damages claimed to $1.25 billion. They included Barbara and Dan Colson in the lawsuit, though not in the RICO part of it, and then dismissed Barbara as a *Telegraph* columnist. (They could not have done that without removing Dan Colson first.)

The disgraceful initiative of dismissing Barbara was taken by the editor that Dan Colson and I had installed, Martin Newland, previously deputy editor of the *National Post*. This brave act was made more odious by his endless prattling that he had agonized over it and that therefore it was somehow brave of him to have stabbed Barbara – an unoffending and much-appreciated columnist writing at the very top of her game – in the back. The saddest sight from this entire series of horrors was when I was walking up Fifth Avenue alone on the day of the outrage and saw Barbara ahead of me, ambling distractedly along, oblivious of the rain and, as I suspected, crying. It was a horribly humiliating injustice to inflict on someone against whom they had no possible grievance. Barbara had her own haters and they were out in force.

Where were the previously chivalrous now when they should have helped Barbara? My contempt for almost all of them is almost, but not quite, beyond my powers of expression.

I returned to Toronto on May 25 and chaired the Hollinger Inc. special shareholders meeting, which approved the refinancing of the company. There had been one very obstreperous objector, a Newton Glassman, who objected to everything, especially when he was excluded from the issue because he had failed to meet the deadline for filing the objection, a mistake a law articler would not make. The measure passed. Glassman then launched what amounted to an oppression action, which is, in theory, a claim by minority shareholders who believe their statutory or regulatory rights have been infringed. In practice, it is a fishing expedition for the complainants to go after anything they can find.

Later the same day, Hollinger International announced that it was rolling back the Strategic Process to just the British assets. Breeden either had had no real intention of seeking a bid for all the shares, contrary to everything he said as they attacked our transaction with the Barclays, or else had never taken on board my repeated advice to Wasserstein, Zachary, and the board that selling the *Telegraph* alone would make it very difficult to sell the remaining company. My own conclusion was that he wanted to continue billing International millions of dollars while using it as a platform from which to vanquish those who created the company he and his team were now dismantling.*

We had a class of Hollinger Inc. shares that were convertible into Hollinger International shares. We sold them all (plus a chunk out of treasury) at more than $17 per single voting share on the very morning of the day that International threw in the towel and announced there would be no bid for all the shares. Nelson Peltz generously phoned to tell me that he had never seen such timing. The stock closed that day between $14 and $15 and went steadily down from there, taking the Hollinger Inc. stock price with it.

In musings in teleconferences with lawyers, Strine rambled on, in his discursive, chipper manner, about subjects he was not called upon to adjudicate nor qualified to judge. Strine criticized Breeden for enjoying his position too much and staying too long. He warned them that eventually the company would revert to its shareholders and that Paris and the rest would not then be re-elected. Even he understood that we could not continue forever as a controlling shareholder that could neither exercise nor sell control, but he underestimated Breeden and Paris. It was only four months since, peering like Mr. Peepers from his provincial high chair, he had found "no improper motive" that Paris, Seitz, and Breeden may have had at any time to testify other than truthfully. It was still not too late to

---

* Needless to say, there was still not a peep from the little Grotius of Wilmington, who had claimed to be salvaging half a billion dollars of added value for the shareholders when he killed my deal with the Barclays.

change sides (or optometrists). But it again revealed Strine's naïve inability to grasp the nature of the war that he had aggressively declined to bring to a swift and happy end with his mad and unjust verdict. This was corporate Armageddon, Götterdämmerung, not another Delaware commercial law tiddly-winks match.

He then said that if the *Telegraph* were sold, he thought that that would require a shareholders vote as the *Telegraph* comprised most of the company's asset value. This was a small beam of light in the darkness: if a sale of the *Telegraph* required a vote of all the shareholders, we could defeat it.

Meanwhile, Strine, *in loco parentis* as self-inserted co-managing director of International with Breeden, urged that the independent directors of both companies meet to try to reduce the gap between the companies because of the bad feelings between Breeden and me. He recommended arbitration for the financial elements of disagreement. We accepted this and Breeden rejected it without bothering to refer his decision to International's board. His view of corporate governance did not extend so far as to allow anyone but himself to participate in such decisions.

Indeed, when I mentioned these overtures to the directors at one of our farcical telephone board meetings, Thompson and Burt expressed surprise and pleasure, while their lawyer, Martin Flumenbaum of Paul, Weiss, hissed his usual claptrap about violating the Strategic Process clause of the Restructuring Agreement. For once, a sharp rejoinder (from me) shut him down. Brian Mulroney, who knew Rick Burt from the Archer Daniels Midland board, helpfully tried to generate settlement talks. Burt was willing, but he was shortly slapped into silence by his former protegé, Breeden.

Next, I was informed that the *Telegraph* board of directors, now subjected to the crowning infamy of including Paul Healy, had removed me as chairman and accused me of bringing the newspaper into disrepute. That my career at the *Telegraph* would be ended in this tawdry manner was an appropriate bow to tie around this phase of the drama: a British national institution, which Dan Colson and I had made strong and influential, was now a football frolicked over by an American careerist and a self-inflating balloon of a Chancery judge in a state with fewer people than Nottingham. Sally Griffiths, the capable and very gracious *Telegraph* company secretary, followed this information with a most generous private note. (Shortly after, she left the *Telegraph* for another company.)

There was a cascade of these shabby events. Barbara was let go by *Maclean's* magazine after twenty-seven years as a columnist. Her dismissal was a particularly loathsome performance: not a word from the editor, only a simpering telephone call followed by an email from a senior section editor who had often asked me for a job but had never passed an interview.

My next disembarkation was signalled in a note from Martin Taylor, the general secretary of the Bilderberg Group, asking me to "quietly drop off the Steering Committee" and not attend the 2004 meetings, though I had been invited, had accepted, and had even aided in organizing and financing the Canadian delegation. This was a man whom I had helped install as Secretary General. He had been dismissed from the chair of Barclays Bank, then from W.H. Smith, and had recently had a nervous breakdown because of the complexities of his corporate and romantic life, none of which detracted from his intellectual merit but may have played a role in his emotional responses. It was also deeply wounding, almost more so for the fact that it was apparently unintentional. Taylor wrote back regretting the "infelicities" of his previous letter.

After twenty years, I was tired of Bilderberg, tired of raising polite opposition to the endless smug togetherness of Euro-federalists and American liberal Democrats exchanging timetables as they proceeded on their wrong-headed policies. And I was tired of patronizing tribalism, the bright Young boys, the Winston Lords, Andrew Knights, Jim Wolfensohns, were patted on the head by the David Rockefeller–Eric Roll elder sages. In later years, especially when I was in prison, I was amused by stories of Bilderberg's world influence, but the sense of entitlement that pervaded it, especially among the precocious, was often almost impenetrable. A few more or less amiable scoundrels like Vernon Jordan and Victor Halberstadt played the associations for all they were worth.

The group-think was almost always wrong; George Will, Richard Pipes (and they never returned), and I were a voice in the wilderness about Reagan. Bilderberg missed the rise and then the fall of Japan, the end of the Cold War (except for my Hollinger colleague Dwayne Andreas), the problems of Euro-federalism, almost anything to do with Islam, and the current economic debacle. They all but waved the incense pot before Bob Rubin and Alan Greenspan.

Yet the discussions and social conviviality were of high quality. And it was the closest I had had to a sort of fraternal association and it had been my initial window on the world, where I had made the contacts that had enabled me to buy the *Telegraph*. I would be happy to see many of the Bilderbergers again, including some of those just mentioned, but not, I think, at Bilderberg.

I had gone from being a person of prominence in some circles to a negative ex-presence, someone it was desired and enjoyable to humiliate, if not deliberately, by cavalier demonstration of my new insignificance. So many aspects of my life crashed simultaneously. It was discouraging, hateful in fact, but, in the abstract, paradoxically, as a historian and someone who once considered pursuing psychoanalysis as a career, I found it interesting.

There was no such problem at the Trilateral Commission. I was invited to remain by the European chairman, Peter Sutherland of Ireland, whom I had often debated on his Euro-federalist views. The *Telegraph* had often called him a "mellifluous Euro-fanatic," so it was generous of him to be so broadminded. As I had discovered in previous, lesser crises of my life, pretended friends are the most lethal dangers to a person's security.

It was eerie moving between our houses, which were now like mausoleums. Most of my telephone calls were with lawyers and merchant bankers, and I had learned not to believe much of what was said. I would not allow myself to become self-conscious about my shattered status, though obviously I was constantly aware of it. But I countered my rejections eventually with the knowledge that at least I knew how unjust all this was and that most of my critics could not have endured such a strain themselves for a month.

STRINE FLIPPANTLY DECIDED, without even being asked, to make me jointly responsible for Hollinger Inc.'s repayment to Hollinger International of the $21 million non-compete fees and accumulated interest Inc. had received, and also required me to pay back to Hollinger International for the contested non-compete payments I received, with interest, a total of $8 million. I paid personally $23 million as a result of this; Hollinger Inc.

paid the rest. This precipitated another financial crisis. Obviously a legal default would be a disastrous state of affairs. Eventually the U.S. government would claim in criminal charges that these non-compete payments were illegal. A jury would decide otherwise, and the trial judge would determine that they were not even improper by the civil law standard of proof of balance of probabilities. But by then Hollinger Inc. would be in receivership and unable to pay me back the millions that Strine extorted from me. This provides a piercing glimpse into Strine's grasp both of law and of equity.

In the meantime, Inc. needed money to meet its obligations. Inc.'s income had been severely reduced when International stopped the management payments to Ravelston in favour of "managing" the newspapers themselves. This made payment of the Wachovia notes Inc. had issued too onerous. Cerberus, a robust fund that ranged from the vulture level up to reasonable quality private equity, came forward to offer to refinance Hollinger Inc. They had been to see me before, on Richard Perle's and former vice-president Dan Quayle's invitation, in December. Their proposal then had consisted of such a dilution of our interest in Hollinger International (to about 7 per cent) that I did not respond and closed with the Barclays instead. (Barbara particularly disliked the Cerberus visitors. She had hopped out of her workroom at my request to make coffee for them and was wearing one of her writing outfits of a T-shirt and leggings when she brought the tray in and left. Within days of the meeting, a nasty squib appeared in the press about how she pranced in front of the prospective financiers in a tight leotard.)

Cerberus had come back several times after the massacre of innocents in Delaware, but their proposals were much less interesting than our own financing based on the inflated International stock price. Now they were back again, proclaiming, as they had on their previous forays, that they had a good relationship with Richard Breeden (whom they professed to find as nauseating a personality as I did) through their large shareholding and board position at WorldCom-MCI.

Breeden had been appointed special monitor of WorldCom after the Bernie Ebbers $11 billion accounting scandal. He represented "the eyes and ears of the court," according to his testimony in Delaware. (The thought of his piscine eyes and porcine ears representing the American judiciary would have been more horrifying to me if my chief encounter with that bench had not been the myopic and scrawny Leo Strine.) On WorldCom's board of directors with him was the president of Cerberus, Mark Neporent. Cerberus said that as a courtesy they would have to tell Breeden that they were thinking of lending to Hollinger Inc. but given their good relationship this shouldn't present any problem. I had the sinking feeling that Breeden was about to do another turn. My suspicions were heightened by the habit of my Cerberus contacts, Robert Warden and Bret Ingersoll, both solemn men, of regularly launching into obviously rehearsed recitations of the peerless virtue and high ethical standards of their company. (If this wasn't enough, I should have been warned off by their online home page: "Cerberus believes that strong corporate governance is the cornerstone of our business.") Dan Quayle, who is not quite the moron the liberal press portrayed him as, but is no financier either, kept assuring me of Cerberus's goodwill. I thought him honest, but as his role was to bring in business, I wasn't sure how conversant he was with what was really afoot.

Sensing an opportunity at least for disinformation, I described to the Cerberus emissaries a grander deal, which consisted of taking both Hollinger International and Hollinger Inc. private. They professed interest and requested the information package from Lazard. While this was in train, the regime at Hollinger International produced a new plan that they hoped would be a replication of the November defamation of us. They called a special directors meeting to report a circulation scandal at the *Chicago Sun-Times*. Dan Colson and I pointed out that virtually everything they cited was common practice in the industry and that if they were uncomfortable with any of it, they should just discontinue the practice. But they had already hopefully informed the SEC and the Department of Justice, on the thin reed of an excuse that the Justice Department was looking at circulation irregularities at *Newsday*, a *Chicago Tribune* newspaper on Long Island.

I dampened their fun somewhat by pointing out that if they contrived to get the *Sun-Times* suspended from the Audit Bureau of Circulation, there would be no more advertising of any kind except for incontinence garments, pornography, and artificial limbs and zimmer frames, as had happened to the *New York Post* in 1992 (when Peter Kalikow owned it).

This would not endear them to the shareholders. The real story was that, contrary to my advice, they had instituted a 60 per cent cover price increase at the *Sun-Times* and had lost fifty thousand circulation. This decline came at the very moment they were supposedly trying to maximize value for shareholders; they tried to mask their ineptitude by blaming (and magnifying) Radler's alleged fiddling with an overstated circulation. Ultimately, this "confessional" designed to smear us further would cost shareholders $20 million in repayments to advertisers by International after a court settlement. The antics of the Paris Keystone Kops took my breath away, even after many months of exposure to it.

The Cerberus discussions had been broadened to include some bridging financing for the repayment of the $30 million by Hollinger Inc. and me to Hollinger International, in accordance with Strine's order. This was putting a lot of freight on a wagon I expected to career out of control at any moment. By this time rumours were rife that the *Telegraph* was about to be sold by International. My old friends the Barclays were likely buyers, but Strine had effectively invited us to attack such a transaction as requiring a shareholder's vote. I was thus in a position that caused me acute discomfort on two counts. First, I would be relying on a company that was in close contact with Breeden to spare Hollinger Inc. and me, both personally and as a guarantor of Hollinger Inc., a default on a court-ordered payment. Second, I would be going back to the court of the pugnacious, flippant judge who had savaged me and ordered (wrongly, again as a jury determined years later) the $30 million payment I was negotiating to have Breeden's friends at Cerberus finance. Yet Strine professed apparent readiness to interrupt the sale of the *Telegraph*. Given my attachment to that newspaper, there would be no alternative but to try to do so when the deal came.

In their chronic inefficiency, the staff in our New York office had not changed the list of emailed recipients of the schedules of people working in that office, so Joan Maida in my Toronto office received regular reports of what they were all up to. It was like observing mischievous children who do not know they are being watched. Frequently the purpose of an upcoming meeting was stated frankly, for example, "to discuss CMB's finances." (Fortunately, I was the only person, then and subsequently, except perhaps for Jack Boultbee, who knew anything about my finances, a subject of which Healy, who was supposedly rendering the tutorial, was sublimely ignorant.) By this means, as well as the oppressive rumour-mongering of the ever-narcissistic British press, we had a good idea of when the *Telegraph* sale would come.

This was on June 22, shortly after we had delivered to Paris, as securities laws required, a notice that we believed Cerberus was interested in bidding for all the Hollinger International A (single-voting) shares. On June 24, we filed an SEC form 13D that revealed that there was a possibility of a bid for those shares. The *Telegraph* sale announcement caused the stock price to fall slightly, while our 13D raised it modestly. We filed for injunctive action against the *Telegraph* sale as Strine had effectively advised us to do, and International started public allegations that we were in violation of Strine's injunction and of the obligation not to tamper with the Lazard process. A few weeks before, they had accused me of violating the confidentiality agreement when a London *Times* reporter – the very pleasant and professional Madeleine Rainer – called me at my home in New York to ask about the possible sale and I said, "I really don't know anything, I doubt if it will be resolved today. We're chasing a bouncing football, goodbye." Even Strine, who fancies himself a sports fan, dismissed their claim and said that this was an accurate description.

There were a number of simultaneous deals being discussed, some real and some designed to hold me up so both Inc. and I would default on the payments. The Barclays were genuinely trying to buy the *Telegraph* for cash from Hollinger International. Lazard was spinning hard that they had achieved a miraculous price for the *Telegraph*, which was at first claimed to be $1.327 billion. This included $117 million of paid-for cash in the *Telegraph*'s bank account. Because they had taken no tax-avoidance precautions, they would pay $190 million of capital gains tax, so the net proceeds to Hollinger International were $1.03 billion, certainly no more than the imputable value I had negotiated from the Barclays in January, or than was implicit in their bruited offer of $18 per Hollinger International share.

I assumed Cerberus was in cahoots with Breeden, in trying to force a default and pick up the post-*Telegraph* assets of Hollinger International cheaply, and that Strine had kindly set up the ambush for them. They said Breeden was expressing concern that Strine would block the *Telegraph* sale. To return the disinformation, I told the Cerberus contacts I dealt with that I would collapse financially if this deal didn't go through. I assumed that Cerberus (a major private equity fund), Breeden (America's leading corporate governance advocate), Glassman (a Cerberus alumnus as well as a slavering public admirer of Tweedy Browne), and Strine (an aggressive and somewhat publicized corporate law vice chancellor) were all jubilating at this prospect.

Cerberus was at first delighted by the *Telegraph* sale, as they would much rather have the cash in Hollinger International than own the *Telegraph*. They indicated that Neporent was continuing his discussions about privatizing the company with Breeden. Paris, acting always in concert with Breeden, told Lazard (who were acting as the sales agent for Hollinger International) that Cerberus could have the Lazard deal material only if Cerberus signed a confidentiality agreement that precluded any financing arrangements with Hollinger Inc. It wasn't immediately clear whether Breeden intended this to discourage an offer for all the shares of Hollinger International, since clearly privatization would be the end of his sinecure, or whether it was understood between Cerberus and Breeden that the effect would be to spin me along and then toss out any Inc. refinancing.

Strine's judgment requiring payment of $30 million from Inc. and myself had a deadline of July 15. On July 7, Cerberus abruptly informed me that they were pulling out altogether, from everything. As a matter of principle, I accepted the unsurprising news without comment or even a change of intonation; I was having to dance like Muhammad Ali in order to respond to all the financial games and cross-deals designed in good part to bankrupt me and being carried on by the courts and regulators with the companies I had built. It was a mess of eels. Cerberus claimed great outrage at Breeden and acknowledged I had been right about him. It only confirmed my assumption that all of this was a setup, that the fix was probably in in Delaware again, and that Strine's placatory words had precipitated a form of judicial sting operation that enticed us into another of his pseudojudicious Venus flytrap ambushes.

It was with real delight that I saw, in 2009, Cerberus parted from nearly $2 billion that they had invested in buying Chrysler Corporation from

Daimler-Benz, especially as Gianni Agnelli's heirs at Fiat were the beneficiaries of it. In the newspaper columns I was then writing, I proclaimed this to be the new Obama administration's most morally uplifting act. This was followed by the implosion of their main fund, as the company founder claimed that he had bought Chrysler out of patriotism. (Perhaps Dr. Johnson was right about patriotic scoundrels.) The *New York Times* reported this unlikely freshet of muscular Americanism from one of Wall Street's weediest vultures, defoliated of feathers, credibility, and investors, with becoming and wry amusement.

In this fast-moving kaleidoscope of men and events, some secondary players stepped up to play strong roles. With the vital help of Lionel Conacher and his colleagues at Westwind Capital Partners, I scrambled to shore up an arrangement to pay Hollinger International $23 million of the contested money, directed by Strine's February judgment. Nelson Peltz made his usual usurious proposal.

Murray Sinclair, of Quest Capital Corp. in Vancouver, was a specialist in this form of financing and the son of a man who had frequently been an investor of ours, always successfully. I partially mortgaged my London and Toronto homes to Quest and brought in the money to meet the Hollinger International payment on deadline just before it was due. So eager and confident of a default were Paris and Breeden that they instituted seizure proceedings against the company's famous offices at 10 Toronto Street and my home in New York. Healy confessed in emails he inadvertently copied to us that he had been almost sure I would default. These premature sallies were abandoned. It was the beginning of a very satisfactory relationship with Quest.

IT WAS ON TO DELAWARE AGAIN, to argue the case of the *Telegraph* sale. The main point at issue, again, was whether selling the *Telegraph* was such a large sale of assets that it required a Hollinger International shareholder's vote. I gave a nine-hour deposition to Martin Flumenbaum in New York. This time I was well prepared, and he got nowhere. The case was heard by Leo Strine in Wilmington on July 23. Because Strine and shareholder Newton Glassman had placed such emphasis on independent directors Gordon Walker and Richard Rohmer, we had given them authority to constitute a litigation committee and hire their own lawyer.* Rohmer, Walker, and their new lawyer, Harvey Strosberg, along with Eddie Greenspan, John Warden, and a Williams & Connolly lawyer representing my interest, attended upon Strine on July 23. It was clear at the end of the day that we had lost the case. We seemed to have done well on a couple of minor matters. On the main point, of whether this sale crossed the threshold of "substantially all of the assets" of the company, Strine was clearly applying the conventional meaning of the words, which was a higher hurdle than the jurisprudential one. Our contention was that since the pre-tax proceeds of the *Telegraph* sale were $1.2 billion and the entire stock market value and net debt of the company was about $1.7 billion, a shareholders vote was required.

The transaction was to close July 30, and Strine promised to render judgment before then. The only real suspense was whether he would have another try at provoking a criminal prosecution of me. He did not. He had three concerns: Does "substantially all" mean anything at all that was more than "approximately half" (which is not what we alleged)? It did not. Does a controlling shareholder involved in "misconduct" have a right to veto the good faith business decisions of the independent board? He/she did not. Should mere rules prevent directors who have broken them from selling an asset "after a full and fair auction" and an "ardent" and "serious exploration of other strategic alternatives?" They should not. How he was able to judge "misconduct" that had not been proved or even charged or how he could establish that Breeden was acting "in good faith" when there had been no "ardent" exploration of other strategic alternatives, and he and Breeden had locked arms to prevent the only alternative that could be found (by me), and how three-quarters of the value of a company vested in one property did not meet the "substantially all" bar is in the non-existent cordon sanitaire between Strine's fragile ego and his powers of reasoning.

---

* It will be remembered that Strine urged that Thompson and Paris try to work something out with Rohmer and Walker (though he did not at that point know their names). He was still unaware of the nature of the Breeden Monster he had wrought and empowered, but was already expressing misgivings about Breeden's love of his well-paid position and ever-lengthening notion of the duration of his mandate. And Glassman had long been claiming that the independent directors were patsies of ours (a total misconception) and that he must replace them.

After accepting Breeden & Co.'s stock explanations of why the company was not sold (tax liabilities and the cratering of potential buyers for the whole company by my attempt to sell Hollinger Inc.), Strine confidently pointed out in his judgment that "it is clear that International will retain economic vitality even after the sale of the *Telegraph* because it is retaining other significant assets, one of which, the Chicago Group, has a strong record of past profitability and expectations of healthy profit growth." Past profitability under us, yes. Future expectations, zero. Within less than three years, the Breeden-Paris-Seitz commercial miracle would render the Chicago Group worthless. The judgment was so threadbare in its reasoning, it revealed, if such revelation was necessary, stark commercial ignorance. This time he refrained from calling me devious and cunning. Now I was described "as an accomplished man . . . justifiably proud" of building the company that was so eagerly being dismantled. Lest this be too effusive, he made a few sideshots about integrity and said that Dan Colson and I had not tried to maximize profit at the *Telegraph*.

He revealed a juvenile fixation on the Queen. References to "dinner" with Her Majesty appeared several times in the judgment as part of Strine's suggestion that being the *Telegraph*'s publisher is "cool." He even managed to drag Barbara in: "It may be," Strine speculated, "that there exists somewhere an International stockholder (other than Mrs. Black or perhaps some personal friends of the Blacks) who values the opportunities that Conrad Black had to dine with the Queen. . . ." If anything, Strine himself seemed more closely to match his description of the stockholder with "aberrational sentiments. . . . who invests money to help fulfill the social ambitions of inside managers and to thereby enjoy (through the ownership of commonstock) vicariously extraordinary lives themselves."

Thus, in a glib phrase, did this chirpy little Chancery judge recognize that the Barclays were paying thirty times the amount for the *Telegraph* that Hollinger had. The Telegraph Group, which was insolvent when we bought it, made from $50 million to $120 million annually, against Times Newspapers' losses of $40 million. We had turned it into the finest newspaper in Europe and won the greatest metropolitan circulation war in a hundred years against the most formidable media owner in history – but Strine felt we could have done better. As we expected, Strine held up his verdict until the night before the closing, July 30 at 5 p.m. Eastern Time, so that no appeal was possible.

It wasn't Strine's fault that he got the case and that Delaware is the premier U.S. corporate jurisdiction, but he should have risen to the occasion. Instead, he compounded the indignity of it all. Judge Lance Ito did better at the circus of the original O.J. Simpson trial, when one of the leading U.S. late-night television shows opened for a month with five diminutive, berobed, apparently Asian men called the Flying Itos cartwheeling across the stage.

The Canadian securities regulators should not have tolerated a foreign judge stopping the sale of Hollinger Inc. to the Barclays, nor Strine imposing an unelected regime on Hollinger International and empowering it to anaesthetize its Canadian parent, no matter what they thought of the controlling shareholder. Once Canada had abdicated, the U.K. should have intervened to be the determining official influence on the identity of the owners of the Telegraph Group. Strine should not have had any more influence on the destiny of Europe's geatest newspaper than an opinionated Yorkshire magistrate would on the ownership of the *New York Times*.

As I prayed in my chapel that night, I thought that this must be for the best. When current emotionalism subsided, no one would be able to dispute that I had been a positive and successful proprietor of the *Telegraph* and the *Spectator*. Because of the war conducted by News Corporation, our profit was effectively capped. No one knew how long the newspaper advertising revenue recession in the United Kingdom would last. (It proved to be permanent and the Barclays' investment was a disaster.) Newspapers were not a growth industry, there were the problems of tabloidization (Murdoch had even turned the *Times* into a tabloid), and the journalists had rejoined the National Union of Journalists. And dealing with Desmond as co-owner of the London printing facility was not something I envied the Barclays.

I had often said to Barbara that owning the *Telegraph* was an addiction that could be dangerous, though not for the fatuous social reasons Strine envisioned. The economics of the newspaper industry were deteriorating, and the pleasures of owning the *Telegraph* could interfere, if allowed to, with best business judgment. It brought me deference, preferments, and a peerage, but I had loathed almost every minute of my job during the five years before the disaster of November 2003. If the asset were not cashed in, we seemed doomed to an endless sequence of crises and would run some risk of being spent to the mat by Murdoch, even after we had repulsed him in the price war.

It was shabby, and would have been humiliating if I were not now almost beyond humiliation, but it was not the worst fate commercially. As with the February judgment, he who seemed to lose could still win. Perhaps I could now do a better deal than I did with the Barclays. Strine wanted all the shares of Hollinger International sold, parting company with Breeden, for whom he obviously had a low regard but whose animosity toward me he shared, though apparently for socio-ideological reasons.

I put my house in Britain up for sale at once. My life in that country as I had known it was over. I had hugely enjoyed it, but I no longer had an occupation there, and the avalanche of hatred against me in the media, contradicted by only four or five pieces from supporters, showed that although I had some good and reliable British friends, my eighteen-year effort in that country, other than professionally and financially, had not been successful. Even then, the first was widely contested and the second would have to be retrieved from Breeden's deviltry.

But if Jimmy Goldsmith could claim to have forced a referendum on the issue of Monetary Union, I had certainly played a role in keeping the Conservative Party out of the hands of Michael Heseltine in 1990 and of Kenneth Clarke in 1997 and 2001 – both of whom I liked and admired but who would have plunged headlong into Europe, mouthing anti-American shibboleths as they did – and delivering it to Michael Howard in 2003. (By now, I thought the anti-American shibboleths might have more merit than I had suspected, but Euro-immersion still wasn't the answer.)

Strine claimed not to seek an offer for all the Hollinger International shares, and not just the super-voting shares owned by Hollinger Inc. (although he did nothing to enable the putative Barclay offer for all the shares in February 2004, to go forward). Now the *Telegraph* sale would facilitate that, as Hollinger International now had the resources to buy in and cancel its own shares. This would be the best antidote to the endless legal battles. The litigation would depart with the sale of the shares. A sale would, I believed, please the SEC and the Department of Justice with the sight of shareholders happy and prosperous. A double privatization, with practically no debt and the Chicago assets to build on, would make me stronger than ever before. I could then end the legal stigma and work toward becoming at least a modest figure in American finance, and make my peace, quietly, eventually, and on my own terms, with Britain and Canada.

Britain, where Barbara had been born, where she had lived for the past twenty-two years, and where almost all her much-missed friends were, was now my country too. I was proud of the nationality, whatever my lack of rapport with the more vocal of my new countrymen's journalists. I would return to it some day quietly. Time would heal the wounds, and I would not miss Fleet Street. And so, with a sigh, at midnight on July 30, in my moonlit chapel at my parents' home in Canada, from which I had gone forth to make my way in Fleet Street eighteen years before, the *Telegraph* era of my life ended.

[CHAPTER SEVEN]

Now we faced autumn with the release of Breeden's Special Committee report. I was about to be drawn and quartered with any remains burned at the stake and ashes dumped into the sewage system. The report would be a murderous assault, that would destroy any little credibility left after the depredations of the last nine months. I braced myself.

After fourteen months of labour, the $60 million operation gave birth. Breeden's Special Committee report titled "A Corporate Kleptocracy" was released on August 30. It was more brazen than I had expected and created a firestorm. My associates and I were labelled as racketeers. We had fraudulently looted $400 million. The company had been used as a piggy bank for "our sole benefit and in a manner that violated every concept of fiduciary duty." We had taken 95.2 per cent of Hollinger's entire adjusted net income from 1997 to 2003 and lined our pockets "almost every day, in every way" we could devise. This was always what Breeden was going to do and the appeasers, like Atkinson and the Audit Committee, were shown no mercy.

My counsel and I were relieved, though not surprised, that there was nothing new in it: old, stale wine in a new Nebuchadnezzar bottle. It fetched up at 513 repetitive pages of bombast and polemics, but impressed the media as an unanswerable indictment of our "kleptocracy." I thought at once that Breeden had finally opened the kimono to reveal the modesty of what it had concealed.

My relief was genuine in the sense that by now confidence in some of my associates was challenged and I knew Breeden would not hold back. So no newly discovered or alleged skulduggery was something of a tonic. But I was under no illusions. I was having difficulty enough functioning in the poisoned climate already and the report would make my life even rougher. This was a bombshell of misinformation and error with the appearance of being fully researched and notated. What journalists or commentators, after all, would or could carefully analyze more than five hundred pages and meet their deadlines? And to be fair, how indeed were journalists to evaluate the report? How were they to establish that in fact the Audit Committee had been told of payments when the report said they hadn't? How were they to distinguish truth from error? Most of the media wanted to believe what was in the report, it was so damning and so colourful (the authors knew their market's tastes well). It was beyond belief that a report could be so sure of itself, so apparently detailed in its revelations of wrong-doing and yet untrue. Apart from the Murdoch media, which would have retailed a snow-white report as a nightmare of rapine and felony, or our old foes on the left like the *Guardian*, most journalists are not inclined to outright falsification.

In his assault, Breeden and his amanuenses improvised mightily. I had no right to have the company support charities sponsored by direc-tors. This was such an unheard of concept, it didn't resonate. Little more successful was the foray into Rooseveltiana. The fact that I wrote the book meant that I was not "a full-time chairman," and the fact that there were six footnotes out of over 2,000 total that mentioned Roosevelt memora-bilia I had had Hollinger buy, impugned my right to my royalties. But the pièce de résistance came with the allegation that I had had the company pay over $7 million for Roosevelt material Breeden claimed (the auction house) Christies had found was worth only $2.4 million. They squeezed what they could out of this absurd allegation, and did not correct the record when the U.S. government intervened to stop the sale, and by act of Congress the material was deeded to the National Archives for a tax receipt (not that the company had any taxable operating income after Breeden and his claque took it over), of undisclosed size, but vastly exceeding Christies' piffling stitched-up pseudo-valuation.

The day after the report was released, I was sent one hundred pages of negative newspaper stories about myself. This was only a partial selection of English-language reports and didn't take into account newspapers across the world, especially in Europe and Australia. This media lambasting continued apace for nearly eighteen months. I had not been featured in a *New York Times* editorial before and this was not my dream debut. Their September 2 editorial headlined "CORPORATE KLEPTOCRACY" began "White-collar crooks typically skim from the top, but Conrad Black stands accused of pocketing the whole top, the middle and much of the bottom of his company's assets." I could hear the squeals of delight this must have caused Jonathan Rosenberg, counsel at O'Melveny & Myers, who was apparently the co-author of the report with Richard Breeden, as he and Breeden saw their title so prominently featured. Though the editorial managed a qualified "stands accused" in the first line, it went on to equate us matter-of-factly with Enron and Tyco and "other tales of corporate thievery." This became the template for reporting.

The *Chicago Sun-Times*, our company's newspaper, took up quoting from the report with fervour. The *National Post* had one of my children living in a "caravan" on my luxurious Toronto property, implying either a callous father or wicked stepmother. In the early days a great deal of attention was focused on the allegations against "spendthrift" Barbara. She was accused of frivolous spending both of company money and my money (which by the report's definition was the company's money as well – apparently I was entitled to no pay for my work) and of manipulating me to spend so much money on our lifestyle that I was reduced to stealing from the company to meet her endless demands.* The assertions

---

*This became the official News Corporation version: The *Times* couldn't catch the *Telegraph*'s circulation but drove me to theft from my own company to maintain a cash flow adequate to sustain Barbara's profligate lifestyle. Not one additional cent was extracted from the *Telegraph*, and its profits were at all-time highs on the heels of its price war victory when the controversial payments, from huge North American asset sales, occurred.

were bunk but trotted out endlessly and most often by female writers. Mary Kenny in the *Guardian* derided, "Barbara Amiel, Lady Black, who was paid 600,000 pounds for her weekly dose of relentlessly pro-Israeli propaganda," an anger made worse, Kenny confessed, because she felt she had been underappreciated and underpaid herself at the *Telegraph*. Kenny was a writer Barbara had always championed and respected. At the London *Times*, deputy editor Mary Ann Sieghart, a cordial social acquaintance, felt well enough informed to ridicule Barbara for "claiming her jogging clothes on expenses, despite being paid $1.1 million for doing very little." This much-mentioned jogging suit listed at $140 has never been found by us and would never have been charged to the company in the first place even if it existed. Nor are we aware that the exemplary journalist Ms. Sieghart knew a fig about how much work Barbara did, what she was paid, or cared.

I was compared to Dr. Faustus in the *Globe and Mail*, Richelieu and Fagan in the *Independent* (which could not be expected to know that they were hardly compatible characters). The U.K. press was unequalled in its malice. The Peter Simple column in the *Daily Telegraph*, written by another favourite columnist of Barbara and formerly fawning *Telegraph* courtier, delighted in naming a toad Amiel. Later on, the *Mail on Sunday* even went so far as to track down and badger Barbara's eighty-eight-year-old stroke-ridden mother, in southwestern Ontario, feeding her lies about how her daughter had publicly blamed her for all her misfortunes and waving money in front of the mentally compromised old lady if she would "tell all." The double-spread story featured a photo of Barbara's mother in a wheelchair, and began with the quote "Barbara always blamed us." Barbara's stepfather wrote her an apology but she chose not to complain to the British Press Council because that would have exposed her mother's condition.

From this point on, I was described as "disgraced," compared unfavourably with every white-collar fraudster and crook, while countless people who had been my guests at a lunch or dinner put in their oar by feeding the appetite for nasty anecdotes to reveal how odious both Barbara and I were. Given the thousands of pages of nasty articles, it's pointless to select individual abominations. We faced this every day, month after month.

In terms of real damage, the report created a nuclear fallout from which I would not soon recover. The initial "improperly authorized payments," a concept that had been heavily compromised from its original presentation as more and more evidence that Breeden, Paris, and Thompson had withheld about them in November came to light, were nevertheless elevated to proof of criminal wrongdoing. They now had "the character of thefts." Breeden had publicly stated in January that he had no evidence of foreknowledge of these payments by me. Nothing had happened since, except for my refusal to be an accomplice in his destruction of our company. The related-party transactions were all mendaciously trotted out. The great gains that the company received from our efforts as buyers, managers, and vendors of assets were never mentioned. That we gained more than a billion dollars of added value for the shareholders, improved every newspaper we bought, defeated Murdoch in the London price war, shrank the company at great advantage to the shareholders even though it meant reduced income for us, and sustained ourselves as owners of a large number of single-voting shares though it was burdensome to do so and unnecessary for control of the company, was also never mentioned. The 95 per cent of profits claim was false and a red herring; the per cent taken by management should have been calculated against cash flow. The difference is that net profit was reduced by large non-cash items, especially depreciation and amortization, which reduced taxes and amplified cash, which could be applied to debt reduction, acquisitions, dividends, and so on. In such businesses, cash flow is a more important yardstick of performance than net profit. By this measure, as the Special Committee was perfectly well aware,* our compensation was standard for the industry and not controversial.

Furthermore, our compensation was deducted from taxable income, which was assessed at a rate of about 35 per cent. So, although the allegation was made to incite the inference that we scooped 95 per cent of operating profit, only the one per cent of the media-consuming public that is familiar with financial terminology would realize that the entire central

---

* Especially Paris, who had vouched for the presentability of our accounts when assisting in our corporate bond issues in the five preceding years.

management function cost the company, after tax, not 95 per cent of what would have been the net profit, as was implied, but about 27 per cent of what would have been the pre-tax profit, or 17 per cent of the net profit, or 13 per cent of the cash flow. (In each case as if there had been no cost of management at all. Cash flow is net cash after all cash expenses, including taxes. It effectively adds depreciation and amortization, non-cash charges, back to net profit, and in a business where there is extensive physical plant and assets like newspapers, depreciation tends to be high, though capital expenses are moderate, due to the relatively long life of presses.) These percentages were normal, were published every year in full detail, and were judged unremarkable by everyone except Christopher Browne and Laura Jereski.

The thrust was clear. I was never to return to Hollinger. I was to be made bankrupt (my net worth was less than what Hollinger must recoup from me, Breeden stated) and I was to go to prison. If Breeden could not generate indictments and convictions from this report, he would fail.

The directors had been whipped into line, espousing an account of events they ought to have known was wrong, by threats of Breeden siding with Christopher Browne, who from time to time demanded publicly that the directors be made complicit with us. Such threats were a significant cause of all that was to follow. Though empty, the notion was terrifying to timorous men used to a world in which their eminence and probity were celebrated. None of them wanted their time taken up with endless depositions and sessions with their lawyers. In the post-Enron climate, it was too dangerous as well as tedious. Their lawyers would have advised complete and immediate co-operation with Breeden, the SEC, the prosecutors, and, if necessary, the local witch doctor.

In return, Breeden (deservedly) gave the independent directors a clean bill of health in the report legally. It was only a few weeks before I received a conciliatory overture from Henry Kissinger, via Norman Podhoretz, a loyal friend who had been editor of *Commentary* magazine for thirty-five years. I picked up the olive branch (which was for a time used as firewood by Barbara) by assuring Norman, who told Henry, that I assumed we could resume relations when this contemptible farce had been concluded.

I had warned Rick Burt that his Faustian bargain in engaging Breeden would not work: Breeden used the Audit Committee in his vendetta against my associates and me and then threw the Audit Committee to the wolves also.

I had also cautioned Richard Perle, when his lawyer, the capable but monumentally abrasive Dennis Block, said that "Supporting Conrad is the kiss of death" and urged cuddling up to Breeden, that this would not work. Breeden attacked Richard in his report as a "faithless fiduciary" and demanded the return of every cent he had received from Hollinger. The Audit Committee and Richard Perle had been put on the spit and roasted like Saint Lawrence.

Richard Burt, Jim Thompson, and the hastily departed Marie-Josée Kravis were accused of being negligent and incompetent to the point of yielding their rights to the directors' and officers' liability insurance. Kravis had at least remained publicly silent and thus retained a little freedom to retreat from the Thompson-Burt position that they had been duped by David Radler year after year on a scale that somehow constituted racketeering by me. They and Richard Perle could have screwed up their courage from the beginning and said that the payments approved had been in recognition of an undoubtedly fine management performance, that the amounts were not out of order with comparable companies, and that they need not apologize for any of it. As it was, Burt and Thompson by approving the acceptance and publication of Breeden's report, engaged in wholesale self-defamation.

It was a classic revolutionary sequence, as the long-established gave way to moderates (in my brief interregnum as non-executive chairman) who evolved into or were replaced by radical reformers, then terrorists, until common sense asserted itself, Thermidor shone forth, and vengeance was visited on the extremists. It is a complete and deadly cycle, though in this case the end is visible but not yet achieved as I write.

It was also another mighty ratchet upwards of Breeden's war. In addition to being a cornucopia of lethal accusations, it was also a promise to recover a billion dollars from the deposed owners, and to lead the company forward to unprecedented profitability. Except for Perle, they all signed on to this, Thompson and Burt agreeing implicitly to their own life-threatening flagellation. After minor skirmishing over press leaks and perquisites, Breeden declared war when he sued and fired me. Hostilities commenced in earnest with the first *Telegraph* sale-case in Delaware. Now we had moved to total war. The nuclear phase awaited.

I began at once to organize a counter-attack. I had to refinance Hollinger Inc. sufficiently to get it clear through the crisis and the call date on the Wachovia notes in March 2007, and establish a double firewall between those involved in the principal litigation and the voting rights in Hollinger International, so that Breeden's lawyers would have much greater difficulty exploiting my tarnished reputation and claiming in every court they entered that anything was justified to protect the shareholders from me. This could be done by putting my Ravelston shares in the hands of respected trustees and having Hollinger Inc.'s control of Hollinger International also voted by an unimpeachable group of trustees.

I would engage Jefferies & Company and also Westwind Capital to proceed on the privatization of both companies and try to expose Breeden's interference with the Strategic Process. He was responsible for Lazard's denial of information to the bona fide prospective bidder I sent to them. Strine, the SEC, and the directors, especially now, after Breeden had put several of them over the side, all wanted a bid for Hollinger International. Certainly the shareholders did. I was under Strine's injunction not to tamper with the Strategic Process; I was trying to make it work, and Breeden was preventing it from doing so.

I would exploit the lack of any judicial immunity for the report in Canada and launch a colossal libel suit against Breeden, Seitz, Savage, Paris, and Healy. From the notification by automatic email circulation of the whole appointments schedule of the New York office, I could trace Healy's frequent lunches with the most venomous of our media enemies to bilious articles in the appropriate media outlet. Finally, there would be our try at SEC negotiations. These, I was assured, would have to begin in early October, after the staff of the commission had gone through the motions of reading and rejecting our Wells Notice reply.

Hollinger International had $800 million in cash and no debt except for a tax liability of $376 million that frightened everyone else, but Jack Boultbee and I were confident that little of it would actually have to be paid, given our tax planning. And the company had another $450 million of realizable assets without touching the core of the Chicago assets. We ought to be able to buy out all the shares except our own at a historically high and probably irresistible price. But we would have to make this offer to the shareholders in the teeth of Breeden's knockout victory in the court of public opinion with the Special Committee report and of his efforts to bankrupt Hollinger Inc., and to generate a criminal prosecution. It was going to be stormy weather for quite a while.

Meanwhile we had to fight Breeden surrogates in Toronto, where shareholder Newton Glassman, the excitable and antagonistic former Cerberus employee who managed a fund named Catalyst, fancied himself the Tweedy Browne of Canada and had been loudly proclaiming for some time that he was going to throw a wrench in the Hollinger works. I have never met him, but from all accounts he is an intelligent but almost terminally bumptious personality. From his conduct with us, this second quality was obvious, but not the first.

He launched an oppression action, demanding an inspector be named by the court to look through all related-party transactions involving Hollinger Inc., Ravelston, and the principal owners. In Toronto, he had the good fortune to have his motion heard by Justice Colin Campbell of the Ontario Superior Court, a former medical-malpractice lawyer who was now inflicting himself on commercial matters. What Campbell lacked in Strine's intelligence he replaced with obstinacy and similar weakness for the limelight. Together with the Ontario Securities Commission, he would be the prime factor in destroying Hollinger Inc. Within a week of the Special Committee report, Campbell had agreed to the retaining of an inspector. This would be a plum bit of patronage. In his ruling, Campbell wrote that he "recognized the legitimate concern of the company that it not be subjected to an interfering, overly intrusive, long and costly process." Campbell allowed the inspector and his team from Ernst & Young accountants to keep going for five years at a cost of $26 million to the shareholders in order to have them report not one cent or incidence of past wrongdoing. They were then appointed receiver of the bankruptcy to which they had so largely contributed and made a few more millions.

Our Hollinger Inc. directors were beginning to hyperventilate. Gordon Walker, timorous and repetitive but at this point not apparently lacking in goodwill, was concerned for his potential legal liability and was easily fussed on almost every subject. General Richard Rohmer is a more noteworthy character – author, lawyer, reserves general, and political roué. Unfortunately, it was Rohmer, whose conduct was in other respects honourable and constructive, who brought in Harvey Strosberg, a well-known former official of the Law Society of Ontario, as counsel to the independent directors, and chaos ensued. It soon became clear that we had the Breeden of the North in our midst. Strosberg saw himself as a ruthless and brilliant lawyer. He thought it an achievement to be known as something of a fixer and was always on the lookout for the next opportunity.

Strosberg careened quixotically about, blustering and bullying and then, as is his custom, falling silent when his plan collapsed around his ears and moving on to some new scheme like a pollinating bee. He agitated to have one of his protégés in the Law Society and a partner of his both named Hollinger Inc. directors. His duty was to represent and advise the independent directors effectively while maintaining as smooth a relationship as possible with the 78 per cent shareholder.

The status of the independent Hollinger Inc. directors (Walker and Rohmer) had evolved through the year. They had come on the board initially to approve the Barclay deal and had expected to leave again in a couple of months. Strine had emphasized the role of the independent directors and recommended discussions between the independent directors of both Hollingers. This played to the ambitions of Walker and Rohmer, who understandably didn't want to seem to be anyone's cat's-paw. Rohmer even resorted to the Gaullist – and Caesarean – formula of referring to himself in the third person, and went those two one better by invoking his rank: "The General will not be moved." It was often difficult to believe that any of it was happening.

More dangerous, Strine's emphasis on the independent directors enflamed the ambitions of Strosberg. At the second Delaware appearance in July 2004, Strosberg announced to our delegation that Hollinger Inc. should be put into creditor protection, for reasons I never understood, as the company's financial condition justified no such drastic step. Yet he was sworn to uphold the interests of the independent shareholders, as were his clients. The surest way to savage the equity interests of the shareholders was to enter any such arrangement.

Strosberg opened up another front in his war against me by claiming that Strine's decision that I was jointly responsible for the Hollinger Inc. repayment to Hollinger International legally transferred some of Hollinger Inc.'s debt to me permanently. The money I was lending to Hollinger to pay disputed amounts yet to be adjudicated was now to become a permanent *ex gratia* infusion of cash by me to the company. This was an outrageous concept. Right after losing the original Glassman action, and after submitting legal bills for $915,000 for three uniformly unsuccessful months, Strosberg left for Italy, where I had visions of him lolling, in all his amplitude, on beaches and in posh cafés, advising his clients by telephone, as they huddled around the speaker phone in our boardroom, passing time in their daily day-long, hideously over-compensated meetings. They were an infestation and should have been the subject of corporate pest control, rather than the fawning of an addled judge.

JUST BEFORE THE BREEDEN REPORT was published, we received the Wells Notice from the SEC, informing us of the staff recommendation that I be charged with civil infractions of the Securities and Exchange Act. The SEC was eager to show its independence of Breeden, their former chairman, though, of course, they were in close and intimate contact with him. I felt that a trial – a civil one – would put me on a more equal footing than I had been on in the many months of preceding character assassination, with the steady peeling away of former friends and the complete absence of any sense of due process, presumption of innocence, or benefit of doubt. I was psychologically ready to face my accusers if I must and more confident of the outcome of a trial than of my ability to sustain Barbara's and my own morale and credibility and possibly financial means, should the endless pounding of the Breeden persecution – with its echo chambers in the media and the lower courts of both countries – continue indefinitely.

I still doubted there would be a criminal charge, though that was obviously a possibility. Received wisdom was that my story, whose denouement had been joyously proclaimed in the media and at dinner tables for months now, was going to be satisfactorily resolved only by some horrible end, preferably in a prison cell, bankruptcy and divorce courts, and, if possible, a funeral home. (My possible suicide was a matter of public speculation.) I was too thoroughly defamed and thus too unsympathetic a figure to attract any underdog sentiment, or even, at this point, much credit for tenacity.

The whirlwind of abuse would subside eventually; Breeden's ambition would be exposed, and I comforted myself with my belief that ultimately people respect those who bear adversity with some dignity, and it is respect untainted by the envy that conventional success attracts. Public and media opinion would move in tandem, and the impressionable denizens on the bench would be dragged behind them like clumps of seaweed on a ship's propellers. Thus would justice unfold. It was a war of attrition. If I could survive, I would win, though I was aware that my hopes were based on frail armour and weapons protecting the fact that I was not guilty of any of the allegations. It was far from an idealized version of the rule of law, but I had to believe that I could still win.

Only when my dear Barbara, always prone to attacks of generic rabbinical pessimism, sadly whispered, "They're going to take you away from me," did I really fear a criminal trial. In general, despite the corruption of the American system, the pre-trial advantages to the prosecution, and a climate hostile to my version of capitalism which could portray any sense of individualism as licence and vanity and wanton self-indulgence, I still thought we would win because I knew, better than anyone, how unfounded Breeden's whole onslaught was.

Disposing of Strosberg would be made somewhat easier by the retirement of Rohmer, his original champion. The general retired graciously in early August 2004. He is a substantial man and remains a friend. Don Vale and Paul Carroll – the first a very positive English business troubleshooter, the second a lawyer-businessman, who had been, and remained, Argus directors – moved up to the Hollinger Inc. board, which now had three independent directors. Carroll had squandered tens of millions of dollars of other people's money in unwise ventures and had been branded by a Nova Scotia court as a "liar" in a famous financial case twenty-five years before. I did not know any of this when he was invited at the suggestion of a friend who could not accept himself but volunteered to get someone suitable. The proposer meant well but like many other well-intentioned people had no idea of the pressures and temptations that would soon engulf anyone who embarked on our financial group at this stage. Getting directors of any sort, let alone those of integrity and with proper qualifications for any company to which my name was linked, had become increasingly difficult. My attempts to recruit qualified directors were among the least rewarding chores of this very difficult time. This was a far and sorrowful cry from the days when Carrington and Kissinger had been directors of Hollinger International and Marie-Josée Kravis, when asked by me if she would like to be a director of the company, instantly replied, "I'd love to."

Barbara and I went to Washington in the third week of August and interviewed some competing law firms as new civil counsel. In the end, we went with William Jeffress, one of the most respected trial lawyers in the United States, of the firm Baker Botts LLP. Breeden had been a partner in this firm, so Jeffress had to do a check to ensure that attacking Breeden would not occasion any difficulties with his partners. Breeden was not pleasantly remembered, and Jeffress was encouraged to "blow Breeden's ass off" if that was what the client's interest required. It did. Brendan Sullivan of Williams & Connolly was now criminal counsel, as well as co-securities counsel with John Warden of Sullivan & Cromwell (who graciously agreed to discount their bill after the fiasco in Delaware*). Jeffress would take over as civil counsel for the U.S. cases, including the Delaware appeal and the $1.25 billion Breeden racketeering lawsuit in Chicago (as it had become).

I had turned sixty on August 25, 2004. For my fiftieth birthday, there had been no significant celebration because we were in the middle of the price war in London and it would have been inappropriate. Needless to say, we were hardly in a state for much celebration now. This time we had a

---

* I would be remiss not to emphasize that though their efforts were not overly successful, both John Warden and Ben Stapleton are excellent lawyers and delightful gentlemen.

small gathering: George Jonas and his wife, Maya Cho, a splendidly brave blind Korean; Brian Stewart* and his wife, Tina; Ken Whyte and his wife, also Tina; as well as my children, Jonathan, Alana, and James, who were living with us in the Toronto house. It was a pleasant evening.

James went off to university a few days later, eighteen years old and six feet, five inches in height. I remembered leaving from the same house, forty-two years earlier, to go to university in Ottawa, and suddenly felt very old, though physically I felt as I had in 1962. In mid-September, my executive assistant of sixteen years, Rosemary Millar, succumbed to her lung cancer at the age of sixty-two. She had always seemed indestructible, a Thatcherite force of exquisite courtesy, correct formality, high intelligence, and splendid British humour. Her passing was not, at this point, a great surprise, nor probably an unmerciful development, but it was terribly hard to accept. She was a wonderful woman and one of the aspects of Britain I most enjoyed and relied on. Rosemary and I had emailed almost to the end. She had been appalled at the horrible press inflicted on me in Britain, and we sent each other encouragements up to a few days before she died. It was a great sorrow to think now that I would not be seeing her again. A few months later, Morton Berg, the psychoanalyst I had frequented many years before and whom I occasionally still consulted, died in Toronto. Their deaths added to a leaden cumulative sadness.

—

---

* Brian Stewart, the senior network news commentator of CBC Television for many years, could have been mentioned on almost any page of this book, as we have been close friends since we fetched up together in the same high school in 1960, both at tangled academic moments. We often travelled together, in Canada, the U.S., and many parts of Europe and Africa, on university holidays and after. No one could ask a truer, more constant, more amiable, intelligent, and even-tempered friend. Apart from some different historical perspectives (and not many of those), especially over what I consider his unjust disparagement of the military command talents of General Douglas MacArthur, there has not been an impatient word between us since he considered me, with some reason, an unruly sub-tenant of his in Twickenham, England, in 1966. We have been much involved with each other's lives, including many of their most intense moments, from our teens to our officially designated "golden years," including those recorded here.

His friendship has been an inexpressible pleasure and consolation for many decades.

BACK AT THE WITCHES' COVEN now based at my 10 Toronto Street office, Gordon Walker, under the domination of the chief warlock, Harvey Strosberg, had decided that Jack Boultbee and David Radler, as well as Barbara and I, should be kicked out as Hollinger Inc. directors. Walker had already told the *Globe and Mail* that I should "move on." I met with the three independent directors and faced Walker down. I said that I was prepared to entertain retirement to the private companies when Hollinger Inc. had been refinanced, the Damoclean sword of default had been removed, and my other objectives in response to the Special Committee report had been accomplished. Then, a wild card intruded. At this point in my career, such unbidden events were never positive.

Dixon Chant, an elderly partner of ours from the very first days of the Argus takeover out of which I had created Hollinger, died, leaving his eighty-five-year-old widow. His estate had Ravelston shares that we had agreed to buy in the event of his death, and Peter White, who had performed admirably as a replacement for Peter Atkinson, had, for the best of motives, transferred $1.1 million from Hollinger Inc. to Ravelston to buy in and cancel them, feeling it was more honourable to owe the money to one of the companies than to leave his widow waiting for it. (With all the court orders demanding payments and restricting our ability to sell our own shares, raising a million dollars in cash required a bit of time.) Peter's action was ethically correct – but in the circumstances lethally inopportune. I had thought this money was coming from Ravelston itself. Jack Boultbee cautioned Peter in an email not to transfer the money without the approval of the Hollinger Inc. independent directors, but Peter didn't see the email until after the cheque had been issued in early July. Radler and Barbara did not hear of it until many weeks later.

When Strosberg heard of the transfer at the end of August 2004, he squealed with delight, described it from his Italian watering place as "theft," and urged a public statement and confidential confession to the Ontario Securities Commission of an "unauthorized payment." He well knew the explosive and excessive nature of what he was counselling and, by now, the suggestibility of the judge involved. On

September 24, Strosberg, now conveyed back from Italy, attended upon the inevitable Justice Colin Campbell in chambers together with Glassman's counsel and revealed the $1.1 million transfer in the most tendentious terms possible.

Our directors met on September 27. Unaware of Strosberg's and Walker's stab into what was now the crowded pincushion-dartboard between my shoulder blades, on the preceding business day, I put through my whole program: the election of two new independent directors; the terms of the refinancing; the proclamation of my firewall plan to re-empower Hollinger Inc. as a Hollinger International shareholder; the engagement of Jefferies & Company and Westwind Capital to explore privatization of both the U.S. and Canadian companies; the disbandment of the litigation committee because the independent directors were now half the directors; and the end of Strosberg's retainer. I felt that we had accomplished this fine surgical stroke in time. So we had, but on a tighter basis than I had any reason to believe. In the middle of the September 27 meeting, a message was delivered to the boardroom stating that Glassman had launched a new action seeking to remove all the Ravelston directors from the board. I mistakenly assumed that Glassman was not acting on the basis of any new facts and that he had overreached. We had agreed to repay the $1.1 million. The court intervention of the previous Friday was not mentioned.

The two new directors, Alan Wakefield and Robert Metcalfe, were recruited by Peter White. Alan was an unemployed technology executive with whom I had gone to boarding school forty-four years before. I told him it was "a long time between conversations." Robert Metcalfe was a non-practising lawyer and former head of the Sifton family's holding company, Armadale. Both men were well intentioned but not temperamentally well equipped for the rough-and-tumble world they were entering.

On the evening of Monday, September 27, I was walking in Central Park, closing in on the bench Mayor Bloomberg had donated in the name of Barbara and me, when Barbara called my cellphone and told me there was an urgent message. Thus did I learn of Strosberg's outrage. He was in open collaboration with Glassman to eject us from our company and had reported us to the judge. Don Vale called me back when he came in from dinner and assured me that Strosberg had no such mandate from the independent directors to go to court as Walker had claimed and Strosberg had done. The next day Vale wrote up a comprehensive affidavit, with fellow independent Paul Carroll's support, debunking the Strosberg-Walker version, which had been featured in the *Globe and Mail* after they had interviewed Walker speaking eagerly from France.

We proceeded satisfactorily through the week. We completed and announced the refinancing of Hollinger Inc. on Thursday, October 1, and my Can$1.1 billion libel suit, the largest in Canadian history, on Friday. With a knife at my throat, I worked urgently to turn the crisis to advantage. Over the ensuing weekend, I worked out a plan to sell some corporate real estate we had been discussing as a replacement for my Toronto home as the subject of a mortgage, and to privatize Hollinger Inc. This would slam the door on Breeden, Glassman, and Walker.

The enemy's battle now was to have Campbell pitch Boultbee, Barbara, Radler, and me off the board of Inc., based on our role as Ravelston directors in Peter White's payment to the Chant estate. (The fact that Barbara was never a Ravelston director nor shareholder was irrelevant. The Special Committee report had labelled her as one and that was The Word.) Walker and Strosberg, in their affidavits and depositions, alleged that the $1.1 million transfer through Ravelston to Dick Chant's estate had been a straight act of oppression of the shareholders and even theft. Strosberg prattled on for one hundred pages of transcript about how I had objected to his invoices, now totalling more than a million dollars for less than four months of advice.

The deposition was classic Strosberg. The US$15 million I had advanced the company pursuant to Strine's order in July was represented by Strosberg in his deposition as a manifestation of my blundering in signing the Restructuring Agreement in November 2003 (which did not commit Hollinger Inc. to repay anything). He claimed that the debt had effectively been transferred from the company to me by Strine's order. Strosberg's was a false opinion that was contradicted by an opinion I had obtained from Sullivan & Cromwell at Strosberg's request. This Strosberg version crept into Walker's affidavit and Kelly's comments, and constituted the attempted legitimization of outright theft from me by a company of which I was the ultimate majority shareholder.

Walker was now just as dangerous, as he appeared to be speaking as much in disarming sorrow as in anger. He gave some credit to Peter White and to me, but required that we be judicially dismissed from the board, White not so much for the $1.1 million mistake as for his association with me, notorious pickpocket of the defenceless shareholders. This version was being endlessly retailed in the press. And because judges tend to read the press with the attentiveness (and, in the case of some, the approximate intelligence) of bloodhounds on the trail, there was a general feeling among counsel that we were all at risk. All my opponents needed to do was bandy my name about, like Chamberlain flourishing his signed agreement with Hitler after Munich in 1938, to achieve their ends. My American counsel feared a "Strine-of-the-North" excoriation in Canada that would resonate very badly in the endless and countless American legal battles, and advised me to resign before it happened. It was at this point that George Jonas referred to American and Canadian judges as "the *Zeitgeist* in robes."

In his affidavit, Walker also gave the impression that the independent directors, under Strosberg's guidance, met constantly by telephone through September, consistently celebrating the fact that they were "steeled" and "irrevocable" in this view that I had to go as chairman and as a director, which I learned only from the newspapers, taking all the Ravelston representatives with me. Once they were in my presence, which was not infrequently, none of them, not even Walker, could find voice for their grievances, unfounded as they were. These prolonged daily meetings were the method by which they ran up their $100,000 individual monthly fees. (According to loyal sources within 10 Toronto Street, these directors' fees were helping the Canadian economy, if not the Hollinger Inc. shareholders: expensive new cars and even condominiums were now being acquired with them.) It was during this time that Glassman and Walker together were promiscuously soliciting new directors. For weeks at dinners around Toronto, people had regaled their dining companions that they were about to become Hollinger directors on the Glassman slate. It was, like so much else, very irritating.

OUR LEGAL FORTUNES WERE briefly uplifted by a Chicago Federal Court judge, who threw out the civil RICO charge on October 8, 2004, and dismissed the rest of the Hollinger International claim without prejudice. The opposition lawyer, the mouthy and cynical Jonathan Rosenberg, co-author of the Special Committee report, was, from all accounts, thunderstruck by the decision. In order to reject civil RICO charges, the judge must consider even if all the underlying allegations are true that other civil statutes adequately provided for them. This was a high hurdle, but under the excellent advocacy of Barbara's lawyer Greg Joseph, who was recruited by John Warden, the judge arrived at that conclusion. Thus vanished the uniquely American absurdity of the civil offense of habitual criminality.

On the heels of this RICO victory, the opposition went back to their faithful Strine, asking for an extension of the injunction against my tampering with the Lazard Strategic Process. This was a bit rich, as I was trying to make that process function and they were trying to shut it down. Breeden wanted to keep his million-dollar-a-week gravy train going (about 10 per cent of that to him personally) which would be impossible if Hollinger International were to stop action against us. He also knew that whatever hopes he had of producing criminal charges would shrink if there were a takeout of all the shareholders. What had begun as a routine corporate putsch had clearly become a fight to the financial and reputational finish involving billions of dollars in claimed damages.

The hypocrisy of seeking an extension of an injunction against my engaging in nefarious activities that he was in fact conducting and I was opposing was not completely undetected, even by Strine. He blasted Hollinger International counsel and suggested that the parties try to reach a compromise, apparently unmindful that he had done more than anyone except Breeden to ensure that this couldn't happen, by loading the dice for my enemies.

When Strosberg was dismissed, we arranged for the well-regarded but very cautious David Roebuck to replace him as counsel to the independent directors. This would have introduced a lawyer of unquestioned stature and integrity. Unfortunately, Roebuck fumbled around for five critical days before concluding that he had irremediable conflicts (which he later overcame). He proposed Toronto lawyer Tony Kelly as his replacement, and the directors hired him, practically sight unseen. He quickly fell in with the

Walker-Strosberg line of running out the clock on privatization. The bond-holders had given me an extension on the Inc. notes until March 31, 2005, to make the privatization offer, and the simplest way of killing my attempt would be to have me miss the deadline.

I called an emergency meeting of the Inc. directors to sort out our legal position opposite International in accordance with Strine's instructions for the two sides to negotiate. Our legal position was quickly revealed as schizophrenic. Kelly took the position that he had sole carriage of any legal issues involving Hollinger Inc., as if Inc.'s own legal firm of Fogler Rubinoff in Toronto did not exist. I asked Inc.'s Chicago counsel to prepare settlement terms for International in concert with John Warden. Chicago counsel replied that he had instructions from Walker and Kelly to require minimal concessions from International. Notwithstanding, I managed to construct a list of requirements from International that included getting the proceeds owed to Inc. from the *Telegraph* sale; the implementation of the co-operation and confidentiality agreement between International and Inc. and we asked for the reactivation of the Lazard restructuring process for bona fide prospective investors whom we sent to Lazard.

The Hollinger Inc. directors ignored Walker's snuffling and approved these terms. All were accepted by Hollinger International on October 21, 2004, except the reopening of the Lazard process, which Breeden was determined to keep closed, despite seeking an extension of the requirement that I not obstruct it.

This agreement was approved by the court. Strine was away for the weekend, so Warden had to deal with the juvenile farce of Hollinger International's counsel asking for assurance that I would not violate the injunction between midnight on October 31 and the opening of business hours the following day, when Strine would be back to endorse the agreement.

Unfortunately, Strine returned to his usual form over the reopening of the Lazard process and dismissed our request with a flippancy about how he would consider it if we had an offer for a billion dollars for the *Sun-Times* that Breeden's robots were not taking seriously. However, the international financial press did cartwheels of astonishment at what they portrayed as my triumph. Laura Jereski snapped that this was "Conrad's greatest victory." (I have been impressed throughout that these people refer to me with such familiarity, even Breeden, as if I were a likeable scoundrel.)

We presented the privatization package to the Hollinger Inc. directors on October 26, adjourned the meeting to October 28, and gave Catalyst the two days' notice our interim agreement required of any material related-party transaction. Catalyst predictably responded with injunctive action, describing privatization as a "stratagem."

If we could survive the Glassman imposture as a regular shareholder and investor (he was a holder of shares convertible into Hollinger International shares and so was not really a Hollinger Inc. shareholder at all), we should be able to force recognition of the right of the shareholders to an offer we wished to make and they wished to accept. It was preposterous that a court would take seriously the antics of Glassman, someone claiming to emancipate the shareholders whom he was himself disadvantaging. But so perverse was the climate that the Catalyst effort was a deadly threat. Having navigated through to the beginnings of a legal turn and being within sight of a safe financial port, I was in danger of being driven from my principal remaining redoubt by the manipulation of an unworldly and credulous judiciary, with the help of the extravagant pests to whom the court had delivered a great public company for safekeeping.

Because Breeden's entourage had some of his insouciant arrogance, Hollinger International passed a great deal of information along an Internet channel they shared with us, but which we, for obvious reasons, scarcely used. They also continued to send us, as in olden times, the weekly appointment schedule of everyone in the New York office.

Thus, from looking at the Internet site, we had all the accumulated costs of the Special Committee, including the nearly $7 million that Breeden had taken for himself in fees.

In the arguments before Campbell, the judge regularly became flushed, rude, and aggressive with my counsel, Alan Mark. We concluded that Campbell's rudeness was based on his having bought into the line that I was a corporate governance delinquent and he lacked the judicial temperament necessary to extend normal courtesies to the legal counsel for such an abominable client. Hollinger Inc. lawyer Avi Greenspoon participated importantly on the call that determined the fate of the Glassman injunction against privatization on the evening of October 27. He completely but courteously demolished the spurious arguments of Glassman's lawyer. The judge ruled that the process of privatization must be allowed to proceed.

Later that evening at a reception, Justice Campbell explained to Jack Boultbee's lawyer that he sought a "win-win" outcome, meaning that he wanted the shareholders to get the benefit of any privatization offer but that he also wanted to support proper corporate governance by installing and maintaining the inspector. In another pattern with which I would become distressingly familiar, the judge had not thought it through. He had not weighed the balance between the inspection process he had unleashed, on the one hand, and the requirements to complete the facility from the noteholders, which had to be acted upon by March 31, 2005, on the other.

In his "win-win" world, condensed into his Warholesque fifteen minutes of fame, as the international financial press watched and attended his courtroom, Campbell thought he could conduct a comprehensive inspection of the company, thus inciting the expectations of the enemies of the shareholders who wished to stop the privatization, while at the same time espousing the privatization.

Privatization of Hollinger Inc. was approved by the directors on October 28, 2004. The relatively solid Robert Metcalfe was made chairman of the privatization committee; Wakefield and Walker were the other members. The hearing on the composition of the board was on November 2 and 3. In order to run no risk of being thrown out, I retired that morning (November 2), as Alan Mark informed the court. I emphasized in my press release that I was doing so to facilitate the privatization of the company.

After an inexcusable three weeks of deliberation, on November 18, Campbell rendered his decision. Alan Mark was successful in his argument that Glassman had no standing and that his interests diverged from those of the common shareholders. Peter White was exonerated of anything but an innocent error and retained. However, incomprehensibly, Campbell ruled that although Barbara and Radler knew nothing of the $1.1 million transfer and Boultbee had warned White against it, an oppression remedy was justified. So, he removed all three from the board.

What ensued was the predictable attempted putsch by Walker. He arrived, very crisply turned out in a new suit, in Peter White's office on the morning of Friday, November 19, and announced to White that he wished to be chairman of Hollinger and asked White to nominate him. White declined and said that the company should not have a chairman, that it was in a transitional phase toward privatization, and that there should be chairmen of meetings only, rotating alphabetically.

Walker smugly stated that he would be elected chairman anyway and left. A series of acrimonious and comical meetings occurred at Walker's office, involving all the directors apart from Peter White. The five were constantly forming and breaking alliances and were unable to agree on a chairman. When they were not in informal session, they were no less cranky and conspiratorial. Our sources kept us well informed of their antics.

On the second full day of fruitless and febrile discussion, Walker went off the walls and distributed a paper threatening to go to the inspector (Ernst & Young, who were looking at related-party transactions and had nothing to do with this sort of issue) and the judge directly, as well as to the Ontario Securities Commission and the SEC (which had no jurisdiction) with the complaint that some remaining directors were not independent of Peter White and me. In his paper, Walker modestly described himself as a "perfect chairman" and "superb consensus-gatherer."

Walker had thrown down the mask the day before and said that privatization would not happen. He revealed that he considered that I was, in effect, a crook, that Ravelston was a corrupt influence, and that this board had a mandate and duty to crush the 78 per cent shareholder and take over the company in whatever direction pleased it. He ignored the fact that was mentioned by several of his colleagues, namely that virtually all the shareholders wanted the company privatized. His judgment of almost everything was warped by his indecent ambitions.

Westwind Capital lined up the Toronto-Dominion Bank and several other large shareholders to commit to or vocally support our privatization offer. We had nearly 40 per cent of the minority in hand before the new board structure was agreed. Walker and Strosberg were starting to look like the East German satellite regime that declared in 1953 that it had "lost confidence in the people."

WE HAD ALSO COME INTO the season of the books and film and television programs about my rise and much-applauded fall. The inevitable Richard Siklos, not the most obnoxious of journalists but no prize winner for quality of research or objectivity either, subtitled his quickie rehash of his earlier *Shades of Black* as *The Rise and Fall of Conrad Black*. From my brief scan of it, it appeared to be a cataract of low gossip and clumsy gropings toward pretended insight.

Jacquie McNish and her co-author, Sinclair Stewart, obsessed with what they took as a morality play in which the corporate governance forces of righteousness prevailed over my chronic wrongdoing, appended to the title of their book, *Wrong Way*, the elaboration *The Fall of Conrad Black*, as if I had managed this feat without ever having risen. I read about ten pages of Siklos and not a word of McNish.

George Toombs, a pedestrian writer, wrote a reasonably fair biography, concluding with a prediction from Donald Trump that I would certainly rise again. He clung to me, rather "creepily," as my daughter put it, more than two years later in Chicago and then rushed out an inelegant hatchet job as a sequel to his initial effort. He gloated that I had bought him a drink in Chicago. Of such trivia are some people's lives made.

Stretching for the metaphysical, *Toronto Life* magazine prominently ran a piece welcoming Barbara and me to Hell. Eddie Greenspan sued and alleged that my Catholic faith made this charge unimaginably abhorrent. In the legal correspondence, he represented me as virtually a holy martyr but extracted an abject apology that, in his version, carried pietistic claims to amusing extremes.

Debbie Melnyk, an engaging and obscure filmmaker, had been following me around with a cameraman for years before the serious problems became publicly visible. Her timely film was telecast in

Britain and Canada. I did not watch it but understand that it was not completely unbalanced and that Melnyk evinced some liking of me.

The celebration of my problems gradually settled down to sporadic outbursts of group media self-reassurance that I really was finished. In general, the press ceased its comparison of Hollinger with Enron or WorldCom and they stopped putting me in the same clause with Dennis Kozlowski of Tyco and other criminal defendants. A mantra of the "disgraced," "fallen," or "ousted" Conrad Black was endlessly repeated. I pointed out in a letter to the *Sunday Telegraph* that when I had been responsible for the contents of that newspaper, it knew the difference between disgraced and defamed.

I enjoyed writing the odd letter for publication. It gave me some satisfaction, however evanescent. When Alexander Chancellor wrote in the *Observer* that I was the greatest embarrassment of the House of Lords, I replied that he had been such an embarrassment to the *Sunday Telegraph* that the editor fired him as editor of that newspaper's magazine after three issues. When Roger Ebert, the well-known, overpaid movie critic at the *Chicago Sun-Times*, purported to agree with the paper's unionized employ-ees threatening to strike, I wrote to that newspaper and the *Tribune*, which eagerly published it, forcing the *Sun-Times* to do the same, that his constant threats to quit his "beloved *Sun-Times*," his $500,000 annual salary and hundreds of thousands of dollars of options, and his website operated at the newspaper's (considerable) expense made his "proletarian posturings" rather implausible. We had a rematch, but it didn't make Ebert appear any more believable.

The mayor of Chicago, Richard Daley, when taxed by a journalist with the embarrassment of a municipal official who had allegedly embezzled funds, referred to David Radler and me as illustrative of how people are surprisingly dishonest. I wrote him a polite but forceful note, which the *Sun-Times* published but which elicited no response from His Honor, whom we had always supported and assisted in any way possible. (After eighty years of the Democrats in power in Chicago and its environs, the system could not and does not fail to be a corrupt regime. Daley, finally unpopular, retired in 2010.)

These were mere pinpricks, of course, in a massive wall of orchestrated press animosity, but I hoped they showed I was still alive and that my (sparsely attended) corporate funeral had not yet taken place.

ON SUNDAY, NOVEMBER 14, 2004, I heard worrisome rumours of an impending SEC action against us. The SEC, contrary to their usual policy of reasonable discretion, leaked accurate summaries of their action to the *Wall Street Journal* and the *Globe and Mail,* which published them November 15 before we received any formal notice of what was afoot. The practice had been for the SEC to reply to the so-called Wells Notice response and then, if the subjects wished, to attempt settlement discussions before charges were laid. An SEC official explained to one of my counsel that this practice was changed in the last year implicitly because of the intense competition to be seen as leading the crusade against corporate licence, greed, or merely, as in my own case, inopportune events. The SEC charges came down on November 15, 2004.

While the sequence was unwelcome, the SEC charges themselves were relatively soft. They wanted us to abandon our appeals to recover the so-called "not properly authorized payments" and demanded an additional $40 million of returned non-competition payments. They had no case for this second provision. They also wanted to ban for life Radler's or my association with a public company and to levy an unspecified fine. (By this time, no one could now pay me enough to be a director of an American public company.) The SEC had discarded 90 per cent of Breeden's Special Committee report, and their spokespersons told my counsel and the press that they would be happy to begin settlement discussions at any time. The claim itself was as modest as we could have hoped in these dismal circumstances and was generally not overplayed by the media.

In an inspired moment, Paul Colucci of Westwind Capital suggested that on that very day we make known our anticipated offer price of $7.25 for the Hollinger Inc. shares, which had been trading at just above $3 a week before our privatization announcement. This was a brilliant method of putting additional momentum behind the privatization move and also of sending the message that we took the SEC in our stride and that it was business as usual. Financial community and press comments were favourable, and the stock rose about a dollar, to $6.90.

We had a public relations success when Hollinger International was required by SEC disclosure rules to acknowledge that Breeden's inquisition had cost $57 million and that they had underestimated its third-quarter cost by $14 million. Even at this revelation, and after a fairly acidulous press release that I had a hand in composing, the institutional shareholders did not rise up. Now the Special Committee was costing more than $1 million a week, and its declared intention was to go on for another two years. Though RICO had been thrown out and the usurpers were unable to deny us our share of the *Telegraph* proceeds, the Tweedy Brownes and Gordon Walkers plodded forward in agreement with Breeden.

IT WAS A GREAT COMFORT to conduct this phase of the battle from my house in Toronto. Barbara and I walked (holding hands, as the *Globe and Mail* breathlessly reported) in the late afternoons along the street my father had created fifty years before when he developed the neighbourhood now known as the Bridle Path. I had carefully assembled and placed twenty thousand books in the libraries and there remained important traces of the original house where I was brought up. The long-serving staff were thoughtful and unobtrusive, and the swimming pool and chapel I had built were great sources of exercise and refreshment of body and spirit.

The chapel, containing my memorabilia of John Henry Cardinal Newman, my friends Cardinal Emmett Carter and Cardinal Paul-Émile Léger, together with some religious artifacts I had collected over thirty years, had a small attached reading room and theological library. It provided a serene end to even the most tumultuous days. This was especially true in the autumn, when I sometimes stayed up so late I could see, often only a few feet away, deer lured up out of the ravine by the delicious apples of our orchard.

I had some comforting sense of fighting for my parents and descendants as well as my wife and myself, and for certain principles. Surrounded with the discreet love and friendship of family, I felt like the home team in a struggle against a numerous and loathsome enemy.

It was heartening when Robert Kent, the assistant U.S. attorney in Chicago, who had carriage of the Hollinger matter, assured attorney Greg Craig, an associate of Brendan Sullivan at Williams & Connolly, that I was not a target of a criminal investigation. Even Eddie Greenspan concluded that a charge of criminal activity was unlikely.

We were convened at the November 30 meeting of the Hollinger International directors to approve implementation of a series of guidelines of the New York Stock Exchange, including enthroning "whistleblowers" and setting up a toll-free number for anonymous telephone complaints about management to the chairman of the Audit Committee, that Lincolnian pillar of corporate disinterestedness, Jim Thompson. It was a regime of squealing, denunciation, and presumption of guilt. There was a scent of Maoism about the proceedings, something of the village committee and their kangaroo self-criticism sessions with a local leader present to report to a regional leader to report to some sub-committee or other of the central committee.

One of the NYSE guidelines required the appointment of a chairman of the non-management directors, who were to meet at least once a year. Thompson and Burt put forward Seitz. I commended them both on their forbearance in promoting the candidacy of one of the co-authors of the Special Committee report, which had denounced Thompson and Burt as grossly negligent and incompetent. Thompson and Burt were like dogs licking the hand of the vivisectionist as he sharpens his knife in his operating room, their tails debouching from between their legs only to wag contraintuitively to appease the author of their impending fate.

Barbara and I voted against Seitz as the new chairman, and so did Richard Perle, disillusioned with his failed dalliance with those trying to destroy him. Barbara added that she did not consider the majority on this board capable of ensuring the honest governance of the company and did not think they should be entrusted with it. That judgment was certainly proved accurate.

It was hard to believe that our fine company, meeting in the same place and with most of the same personalities, could have been reduced by Breeden and those whom he intimidated or suborned to such a degraded mockery of a corporation. As I listened on the telephone to these people dispose of our company, I placed my hopes in privatizing what remained and in so doing salvaging something for the other shareholders and myself.

The privatization of the American company, Hollinger International, was begun in the first week of December 2004 as the investment proposal document was finalized and circulated to possible investors. It had commercial merit, and I was reasonably hopeful it would succeed. Canadian privatization continued to gain strength; American privatization had made a promising start. Though almost every hand had been turned against me, I thought I could finally see a gleam of hope. Such a hope, in such a time, was an invitation to disappointment.

[Chapter Eight]

The thick gloom had lifted and Christmas and New Year's Eve 2004 were far more agreeable occasions than those of the preceding year. Now there was an apparently competent team of counsel and other advisers, a plan of action, visible progress, the rejection of the RICO claim, and a year of implacable endurance to strengthen the soul and temper the steel. Barbara and I even managed modest gifts, accepted almost furtively by her, lest the boot in her sky notice we were having a good moment – something we had judged inappropriate in the hair-shirted, Dickensian bleakness of December 2003.

And although there had been terrible stresses at times in the preceding fourteen months, and indeed on many occasions throughout the twenty-six years since I had taken over Argus Corporation, the structure of assets I had built and enough of the corporate associations in which I had invested such effort had held. Financial ruin had receded as a prospect. It had only been a year before that I had had to borrow money from Nelson Peltz to pay our public relations firm, which was swimming like spawning salmon upstream against a raging torrent of hostile press attention.

Yet I was still strategically on a back foot. The lawyer engaged by Strosberg to advise on honouring the Hollinger Inc. indemnity for legal fees effectively suggested that none of our legal fees could be covered by the indemnity in respect of these accounts. Even the imposter regime at Hollinger International, in all its malice, managed better than this. It was paying half our bills.

Gordon Walker devised other methods for aggravating me. He never ceased to tell the press, especially the *Globe and Mail*, that he was the "new broom," sweeping the corruption of the former regime away. He hired a public relations firm to peddle his nonsense about a "suite of corporate governance reforms," which he had printed up in a self-righteous little pamphlet, at the shareholders' expense.

It was all part of Walker's effort to let everyone know that there would be no privatization, despite the lip service he gave it. His unctuous homilies to the press were exceedingly irritating, but they had the value of helping to lower the noise level. Walker, monotonous and repetitive, was a providential anesthetist.

We had to have independent valuators and Griffiths McBurney & Partners had been retained as a respected merchant bank that would carry weight with the Ontario Securities Commission as valuators of Hollinger Inc. shares. The senior partner, Gene McBurney, a capable and likeable man, despite his supportive stance and comments, soon urged a delay in the valuation. He, too, wanted to await the chimera of quarterly reports of 2004 from Hollinger International, the progress of the inspector, Ernst & Young, and so on.

It was the Bain-Cerberus syndrome all over again. McBurney was showing a level of caution that he ought to have known would push our privatization over the end-of-March deadline. Hollinger International would take its time filing, in part to inflict as much inconvenience on us as possible and in part to enable Breeden to squeeze as much for himself as he could out of his rich feathered bed as special monitor. Ernst & Young simply demanded more and more and more and claimed the need for unlimited time and money.

At this point every possible faction was in feverish and fluid negotiation. Walker was a partisan of pre-emptive concessions to the SEC and Hollinger International. He and Carroll made a Chamberlain-style visit to Thompson and Paris in December that was a fiasco. The Hollinger Inc. lawyer in SEC matters, Nate Eimer, was a compulsive optimist and instinctive author of compromise. He was seeking a voting trust.

We warned Walker that any attempt to settle without full consultation with the controlling shareholder or to institute the infamous executive committee that had been conceived after the Campbell decision and modelled on the Hollinger International Corporate Review Committee would lead to immediate injunctive action. We won those battles.

Hollinger International finally brought out its 2003 annual statement in mid-January 2005 with minimal changes and restatements despite fiendish efforts to detect fraud, causing a good deal of comment that it had hardly been worth waiting for. The interventions of Williams & Connolly and Eddie Greenspan had cleaned up the text by about 20 per cent, but it remained a stated risk factor that I might regain control of the company and disserve the shareholders.

The stock price was a levitation; the Strine-Breeden-Paris-Zachary-Seitz claim of what could be achieved by the Strategic Process had been exposed as very inflated. The initial Wasserstein summary of Hollinger International as being worth from $18 to $24 a share had dwindled by the end of January 2005 down to below $17. Those to whom we sold in June to refinance Hollinger Inc. had taken a loss on their shares. Those who remained would lose everything.

Seeing that there was no chance of getting out their filings in order to be current before May or June 2005, the Hollinger International rump decided on another special dividend of $3 a share to buy them a bit of time with investors getting restless about the stalling of the grand strategic process. Hollinger Inc., which I had been widely advised through the autumn to put into creditor protection, as Peter Atkinson and the Torys law firm and Strosberg had advocated, would as a result of this dividend now have more than US$100 million in the till. The end of its financial crisis had come, or should have.

Barbara and I went to Donald Trump and Melania Knauss's wedding in Palm Beach on January 22, 2005. Trump had been an unfailing and vocal supporter of ours through these difficult times. Former U.S. president Bill Clinton, also a guest, urged me not to give an inch to my legal tormentors. The same message was delivered even more forcefully by Rudy

Giuliani. At times like this, when many so-called friends, some of fifty years or more, had gone missing, such gestures by such well-travelled people were appreciated. Barbara began humming "Little Things Mean a Lot," which was part of her vast repertoire of Hit Parade songs from the 1950s. They did.

I NOW HAD TOO GREAT A PROPORTION of assets in residential property. I did not wish to sell any of my houses; they were fortresses of the life that I had built, and I wished them all to continue into the new and stronger position that would arise from the shambles of my former life. But I did not have an unlimitedly optimistic view of the economy, and I had no banking relationships whatever and needed the cash.

Finally, an offer arrived on our London house. It was a fairly full offer, and at more than £13 million, a heavy profit on what I had invested in it. This should be the end of the personal financial problem. Now I could certainly stay the course to crush out the Walker-Carroll-Kelly insurrection and ride on to the American share takeout and SEC settlement. I didn't want to sell the house, but Barbara had never liked it. The house was in a location she loved (near Kensington Gardens, where she often walked), but it was too large and didn't have a sit-in kitchen, something she apparently liked. She had retreated to living almost solely in her light-filled dressing room and in her top-floor workroom, which overlooked roofs and gardens and was equipped with a refrigerator, microwave, and kettle to keep everyone at bay. The house was hideously expensive to operate and had become symbolic of a life that was over. It was time for a new, but not an inferior, start.

Negotiations over selling the house, always a laborious business under British rules, toed and froed through January and February as we inched tortuously through the minefield Walker and Carroll and their counsel laid on the path to privatization – and as we sparred with the SEC.

Walker had asked Paris for terms of settlement with Hollinger International and Hollinger Inc. to end the cross-litigation between the companies. When settlement terms were made public in February, Paris – true to form and luxuriating in his flush pay packet ($17,000 a day), which aroused protest even from Jereski, responded to Walker that a $175 million

payoff from Inc. to International might do it. Walker showed no recognition of what I had been dealing with from these people; he thought it was
just "two dogs sniffing each other." Part of the metaphor was accurate but
unflattering to canines; Paris was lifting his leg, not advancing his snout
(though he was pretty agile at that also).

Walker and Carroll sought a settlement with the SEC for Hollinger Inc.
Nate Eimer came eagerly to Toronto to sell his settlement in mid-February.
The terms were ostensibly improved to the point that if Hollinger Inc. would
merely give back the so-called improperly authorized non-competition payments received from Hollinger International in 2000 (which it had done
with my money) even if it won the appeal about them in Delaware, the SEC
would ask no penalty and would agree to an overseer. This overseer would
only vote Hollinger Inc.'s Hollinger International shares on certain major
issues, and even then only on instructions from the Hollinger Inc. board.
Apart from that, and from retention of the Special Committee directors, we
could repossess control of Hollinger International without bringing
Breeden down on the company as a special monitor. On this basis we were
prepared to accede.

Less than a week after a perfectly agreeable dinner meeting with
various Canadian and American lawyers in Toronto, the SEC was reserving
to itself the right to impose Breeden as special monitor whenever it chose,
for imprecise reasons. The special monitor would not be confined to con-
serving assets and preserving the status of the Special Committee; he
would be largely controlling, at least negatively, every managerial act. It
was a surrealistic horror watching all these factions jockeying to destroy
companies I had worked thirty-five years to build.

On the privatization front, the Ontario Securities Commission staff,
with admirable flexibility and regard to the shareholders' interest, was now
adjusting to the retreat of valuator Griffiths McBurney. At the same time,
the Walker-Carroll-Kelly axis, having leaked to the newspapers their belief
and determination that "privatization was dead," were startled to discover
that the OSC would grant us the exemptions necessary to provide a litigation
trust for anything material turned up by the Ernst & Young process. Their
entire tactic, of endlessly repeating that the Ernst & Young inspection
would have to be substantially completed before the privatization could

take place, was blown up, and they scrambled from that trench to the rear, to a much less commodious foxhole of trying to perpetuate themselves in a litigation committee that would have an unfettered right to commence litigation on any subject at our expense.

The OSC sensibly concluded that the overarching issue was to give the minority shareholders an exit strategy. No one was impressed with Walker's efforts to pour cold water on the prospect of an offer in one of his garrulous deflationary monologues to the *Wall Street Journal* on February 19. The Ernst & Young inspection generated yet more fees, as it received herniating masses of material but endlessly went whining back to court claiming a requirement for more information. It was always implied that any reticence about the unlimited continuation of their $40,000 per day extravaganza would be represented as a coverup. After Campbell had created this monster, and was pathetically incapable of imposing any bounds on its appetite, we had no choice but to tolerate its existence and to comply.

The capable and congenial Gene McBurney solemnly emphasized his difficulties in completing the valuation. He raised his fee in accordance, while protesting in all directions that he was "not a fee-grabber."

ON FEBRUARY 7 WALKER CONVENED a meeting with various legal and financial advisers but specifically excluded Hollinger Inc.'s counsel Avi Greenspoon, the only person who had been negotiating on the company's behalf with the Ontario Securities Commission.

The meeting predictably produced the result Walker had sought and scripted: privatization within the indicated timelines was impossible. This would ensure that our financing would lapse and the whole plan would crumble.

The next day, I met with Metcalfe and Wakefield, and their privatization committee counsel. They delivered the Walker message, which I rejected. I demanded a new meeting that would include Greenspoon. Bob Metcalfe and the others, who were doing their best to deal with the Walker-Kelly obstructiveness, agreed, and it was scheduled for the next day.

I said that the OSC had accepted that the deal was desirable and that the March 31 date was critical. The noteholders had watched their collateral shrink as special dividends poured out of Hollinger International, reducing the value of the company's shares. The noteholders had agreed to an arrangement that included issuing more of their high-yield notes to a Hollinger Inc. with full-priced Hollinger International shares in its hands, not with shares diminished in value by special dividends from the sale of the company's principal asset. They were understandably unenthused about our method of paying them with money that reduced the value of their collateral and would not grant any extension, as they did not wish to be bought out with the specially dividended money. It was March 31 or never.

That evening, Peter White and I attended a meeting of the Commanderie de Bordeaux, a wine-tasting group that numbered Gordon Walker among its members. I had to duck out of dinner to take the usual medley of calls rearranging what had been agreed upon, and telephoned Gene McBurney to tell him what the real purpose of the previous day's meeting had been, and that the following day's meeting would include Greenspoon. When I returned to the dinner, it had largely broken up, but White had arranged for a triangular talk with Walker, who, mellowed with good wine and the advent of his choreographed burial scene of privatization the day before, was at his most nauseating. With that political reflex for pseudo-collegialization of responsibility, he averred that "the best minds" had determined that privatization would not be possible by March 31.

On February 9, Avi Greenspoon opened the reconstituted meeting with a factual summary of discussions with the OSC. Walker and Kelly said nothing. Their silence was telling. The March 31 target was redesignated as desirable and potentially attainable. A shareholders meeting was tentatively called for March 31.

The infighting and backbiting intensified steadily as the deadline closed in. It was slow, grudging, inching winter warfare. Most of the players were naturally placatory people. At every stage, there was foot-dragging. The Ernst & Young counsel, echoing the Walker spirit, persuaded the directors to seek a court date with Campbell to consider the feasibility of the March 31 deadline.

Walker played his last card. He effectively transformed this court appearance into a request for "guidance" on whether the directors should proceed with the privatization before the inspection had finished. He presented an affidavit, supported by four attachments. These were innocuous, if sharply formulated, emails by me to Hollinger Inc. directors Paul Carroll and himself and Don Vale. In the emails to Walker, I accused him of trying to run out the clock on privatization in order to "perpetuate your sinecure." I also accused him of trying to propagate the theory that I was a notoriously odious character, ineligible because of my turpitude to have any influence on or even knowledge of a company of which I was the controlling shareholder. Kelly cited these emails as evidence of my tendency to bully and threaten directors because I had stated in two of the emails that if the directors "botched" privatization, the shareholders would rise from their "torpor" and hold the directors legally accountable.

Walker's affidavit supported the outrageous demand for a "retention bonus" if the directors remained on the board; a directors' severance if they were removed after privatization; a segregated escrow fund to ensure their welfare and legal costs, and other insulation against the wrath of any shareholder, me in particular. It was a document of stupefying gluttony. As usual, there was wholly inadequate support for the relief they were seeking. The motion was filed on February 25. Walker had collected $97,000 in January 2005 alone, and all of them were at a running rate of more than $1 million a year. I asked our public relations adviser, Jim Badenhausen, to work with this. After a few days, Bloomberg ran with the story and it cracked open, exposing the white knights of the north as money-grubbing ciphers. Walker's affidavit stated that they would all have to restart their "consulting businesses," a confession that none of them had any business. These were the replacements for whom Campbell in his commercial acumen and judicial wisdom had turfed out qualified and blameless directors.

Everything came to a climax on the last weekend before the court hearing, on March 7. The judge had agreed that it was quite in order to begin printing the circular on Saturday evening, March 5. Kelly misled Avi Greenspoon and Steve Halperin about this, causing Avi to impose upon the Ontario Securities Commission to grant a compression of delays and to wring the same concession from all other securities regulators in Canada, including the Yukon. This was nonsense; the judge was happy for us to print on Sunday.

On Friday, February 25, as Walker's motion was filed, I found Paul Carroll in the library of our office looking at old minute books and trying to find backing for the $200 million lawsuit he, Walker, and Kelly claimed they would take on behalf of the Hollinger Inc. shareholders against my associates and me. Like the lowliest of jackals after the sleeker (American) beasts had weakened us with their savage attacks, they came snapping at our heels very late. I resisted, with difficulty, the temptation to eject him from our office.

Peter White and I met with the privatization committee on Friday, March 4. We reached agreement fairly effortlessly on all points, shook hands warmly, and celebrated our community of view. Having been around this track so often, I knew better than to take it altogether seriously. We agreed that we would raise the offer price from $7.25 to $7.60, just above the range GMP Securities, our valuator, had produced. Metcalfe and Wakefield would recommend to the directors that the offer be sent to the shareholders. They would guarantee a majority of directors in favour of doing so, and this would be announced in court on the following Monday. We compromised on an excessive but manageable fund for the litigation committee and to indemnify the directors against lawsuits ($5 million each, outrageous, of course, but sustainable because only we would wish to sue them once the public shareholders had been bought out). As predicted, after they met with counsel and reconvened, the arrangements had started to evolve. We finally agreed, apparently durably, on every material point late in the evening. I sent them a letter incorporating all we had agreed at about ten o'clock. Our informants sent us a fair traffic in copies of the internecine independent directors' emails through the weekend.

ON SATURDAY EVENING, in a piquant intermission, Peter and I went to St. Catharines, Ontario, and I gave an address in a winery to a graduating corporate governance class. It was a pleasant interlude with an interesting and convivial group who warmly received my analysis of the Sarbanes-Oxley Act. Corporate governance had reached a point of self-inflicted absurdity. To say that Sarbanes-Oxley was draconian would be to underestimate Draco's respect for individual liberty. My host crowned an unusually diverting few hours by singing his thanks to me in a five-minute composition of his own devising and bellowing the last verses melodiously as I signed complimentary copies of my Roosevelt book for the guests.

All went well in court on Monday. When Tony Kelly said for the third time that I had held a gun to the head of the independent directors with the March 31 date, Alan Mark replied that that date was agreed by everyone and not imposed.

Alan Mark added that it was nonsense for the directors to ask the court for both a retention bonus and massive severance packages. He pointed out that the directors had awarded themselves $1 million a year, a greater sum than had ever been accorded to any non-executive directors in history in any company, and that they had not bothered to come to the court to authorize it. For once Campbell did the sensible thing and refused to rule in any of it, pointing out that the directors were paying themselves "big bucks" and that they should do their jobs.

It shortly became obvious that Breeden had made a classic mistake, one that Machiavelli, in particular, had warned against: excessive reliance on mercenaries. Walker and Kelly had placed all their trust in the endlessly repeated rosarian mantra that the judge would not allow privatization to proceed before Ernst & Young's mighty fee-generating inspection ended. (An inspection, I now assumed, that could not end before requiring DNA evidence on my exhumed grandparents and interviews with our personnel in Central America.)

The only positive aspect I could see in Walker and his crew was that they certainly had their price and were not shy about naming it. They initially demanded $1.8 million each for quitting as directors. They had been directors for less than a year. We were able to reply rather robustly that they had no moral credibility at all, having been exposed as raping the company for a historic fee. Finally, reluctantly, Peter White and I agreed to $600,000 each. Metcalfe, Vale, and Wakefield at least had earned something significant if they did the necessary to bring privatization through.

When Walker and Carroll hastily packed their saddlebags with their plentiful gains and rode into the sunset, their overloaded steeds belly to the ground and feeling the whip, Breeden was left with no faction to represent him in the endgame in Toronto. The Ontario Securities Commission staff had been unfailingly cordial through months of co-ordinated effort to design an offer that would enjoy their support. And while they had been thorough to a point beyond any normal privatization effort – indeed should not even have been involved in granting permission for it – we had responded to their requests, which, though taxing, were all legitimate and not simply pettifogging.

The ground quickly began displaying unsightly cracks. The OSC staff suggested that we might like to ask for a public hearing into our proposed going-private transaction. Our sources advised us that Breeden had been in Toronto a couple of days before, lobbying the OSC. The enforcement branch of the OSC gave notice of their own intention to call public hearings on whether a raft of copycat SEC-like allegations should be launched against David Radler, Jack Boultbee, Peter Atkinson (despite all his concessions), Hollinger Inc., and me. They gave so short a time for reply that it was obvious they did not want discussion of this between us but just wanted to get it out into the public that they would be holding such a hearing before the determination of our offer.

Another initiative, of which the timing was very suspect, was the revelation by the assistant U.S. attorney in Chicago, Robert Kent, that he was intervening in the discovery process with the SEC to try to withhold one document that the SEC was about to hand over to us under court order. Kent stated that it could compromise a criminal investigation he was conducting into several of my associates and me. This was a tainting gesture, though it had been widely rumoured since the problems arose that such an investigation was in progress. Objectively, if the retention of one document for several months was all Kent wanted and all he would deliver for Breeden after seventeen months of poring over these matters, it wasn't too worrisome. Greg Craig and I wrote up a two-sentence press statement concluding that we'd "welcome any fair-minded investigation.

I WANTED MY ORDEAL AND BARBARA'S, for which I was responsible also, to be seen as a triumph of principle. Such a victory could redeem almost any agony.

As if there were not enough public discussion of my condition, a Florida business publication revealed that my Florida house had been the subject of a lien, for about a quarter of its value, by the Canada Revenue Agency. The world press leapt on this, claiming a "mortgage" had been "slapped" on the house, thus implying imminent seizure. This came at the same time as the cries of joy at my potential criminal status, which Murdoch's London *Times* and *New York Post* happily reported could lead to my imprisonment for twenty-five years. Christopher Browne told the *Guardian* that whether I lived in Palm Beach or the Danbury Correctional Prison was of no interest to him. Nor should it be, but why was this newsworthy? The *Guardian* had also thoughtfully published advice to Barbara on how to get by in poverty, such as by drawing vertical lines on her legs to imply that she could still afford stockings or tights. Nothing was too low for these base mutations of a free press. A talkative spokesperson for Canada Revenue helpfully told Bloomberg that this was a step the agency took when large amounts were owing by people whom the agency thought it might have trouble collecting from.

This was misleading with respect to my case, as well as outrageously indiscreet. I had volunteered this arrangement, transitorily, until something could be set up in Canada. And I was quite satisfied that Canada Revenue would never be adjudged to be entitled to the claim in question (nor was it). I was accustomed to negative publicity, but this was another flood of it.

At the same time, the osc privately assured us at several levels that if we were to ask for a public hearing on the technical question of whether the consolidation we were planning was a trade, they would ensure that the staff would stand fast behind their existing recommendation in favour of our application. If we had refused, they would have invoked the public-interest umbrella criterion and called such a hearing anyway, under less promising auspices than what they were now offering. So, we agreed. The osc hearing was called for March 21 to determine standing to appear and March 23 and 24 for substantive discussion of the issues.

Eddie Greenspan and I wrote out a press release expressing concern about the timing and motives of bringing this forward so quickly and on such a tight schedule to the privatization deadline, although the osc had

had all the material for these matters for seventeen months. We referred to the recent hitherto secret visit of Breeden and warned the OSC against seeming to be a cat's-paw of such an odious figure.

On Saturday evening, March 19, the commission revealed that the staff recommendation, including the enforcement section, was in favour of our application. At least they seemed to be keeping the real public interest, the rights of the minority shareholders, uppermost in mind and we were encouraged.

If the United States is plagued by a strict corporate governance regime that lends itself to the aggressive tactics of the likes of Christopher Browne and Richard Breeden, then flaccid, anti-Darwinian Canada, the victims' paradise, must always have something for everyone. This was the spirit of Campbell's fatuous "win-win" propounded to Jack Boultbee's lawyer as he hung the glorious albatross of the Ernst & Young inspection on us. (Yes, a "win-win" – a win for Ernst and a win for Young.) This seemed to be the spirit of the OSC having the staff so thoroughly vet every detail of the offer and approve it, then as Breeden's influence metastasized, making its gesture against me with these unusual public hearings. I was being whipsawed between the most infelicitous aspects of the systems of both countries.

Terence Corcoran in the *National Post* took up the case on March 22 and warned the OSC not to become a dupe of Breeden. The OSC was notoriously subject to influence from the Toronto financial press, and the *Globe and Mail* could be relied on, as always, to do everything possible to disrupt anything I was seeking to achieve (as it did with the CanWest sale and the peerage). The pressure rose steadily as we headed into the week of the OSC hearings. Jacquie McNish, co-author of her one-sided, school-snitch squeal of a book about these events, moved to protect her version of them through an interview with Breeden.

Breeden garrulously revealed that he had indeed called on the OSC to "lecture" it on the necessity of not allowing the Hollinger Inc. minority shareholders to vote on our offer because it might facilitate my return to Hollinger International. In this interview, as he had in a so-called statement of fact and law filed with the commission by Hollinger International on March 18, Breeden effectively stated that it was the OSC's duty to prevent shareholders from deciding for themselves what they wanted.

McNish followed up with an editorial comment attacking the OSC for even considering allowing our proposal to proceed. The OSC was, I thought, squarely on the horns of a dilemma. Either they would have to prostrate themselves at Breeden's and the SEC's feet and deny the shareholders what they were seeking or they would have to defend the rights of the shareholders and send the Americans packing. We had aligned our interest so closely with that of the minority shareholders, it was going to be very difficult to discomfit me without showering collateral damage on the public shareholders, whose protection was the commission's chief raison d'être.

The main hearings on March 23 and 24 were very comprehensive and fairly conducted. Breeden sketched out clearly in both of his memoranda his fear that I would reassert Hollinger Inc.'s rightful control over Hollinger International, as if this were self-evidently an affront to the indisputable public interest of both countries. There was an almost unquestioned presumption of guilt.

Lawyers supporting the transaction did so effectively, in contrast to the usual bombastic performance by Glassman's lawyer, who was as belligerent as the client but more fluent. It was indicative of the *Globe and Mail*'s difficulty finding respectable opposition to our offer that it reinflated and touted the Vancouver investor-commentator Ken McLaren, who for many years has been seeking recognition from the financial press at almost every controversy, like a child at the back of the class whose hand is in the air eagerly waving at all times. The *Globe and Mail* promoted him as a reliable source of antagonistic comment and used him endlessly as such.

Counsel for Hollinger International and Catalyst (acting for Glassman) followed McLaren and engaged in their customary attempted assassination of me. They had no argument apart from hammering the theme that I was so tainted, corrupt, and dangerous that any means were justified to frustrate me. One of the opposition lawyers referred to me as "Saddam," and claimed that what was afoot was a "titanic struggle between good and evil." I received bulletins as the March 24 session wore on, feeling somewhat numb with the tension of the occasion. I called Eddie Greenspan, who went to the hearing room prepared to speak on my behalf.

Greenspan judged it unnecessary to say anything after hearing Alan Mark's summary and rebuttal. He considered it "stirring and brilliant." Mark gained the "Quote of the Day" in the *Globe and Mail* with "This is a lynch mob persecuting a man who hasn't been found guilty of anything." He pointed out that my associates and I had created value that was being squandered; that Paris's compensation had been described even by Jereski as "grotesque"; and that Breeden had been trying to bully the Commission into crushing the minority shareholders again, as he had persuaded Strine to do a year before.

The OSC staff, though invited by the presiding Commissioner, Ms. Wohlberg-Jenah, to alter their endorsement of the offer, emphatically reaffirmed their decision that it was fair, with the enforcement director as their chief spokesperson. The Easter weekend was a time of great tension as all sides awaited the commission's ruling.

THERE WERE OTHER CONCERNS. I had tried on the two days before Good Friday to close the deal in London for the sale of my house there. This was necessary to provide a reasonable pool of cash, and if the privatization did not go forward, it would be absolutely necessary for financial survival, including, in particular, paying Williams & Connolly's bills. We just missed closing the sale before the Easter long weekend.

More worrisome, Glassman had finally bestirred himself, also on Thursday, March 24, to buy the Toronto-Dominion Bank's shares in Hollinger Inc., a block of about nine hundred thousand shares, at $7. That meant nine hundred thousand fewer votes for privatization if we were allowed to make the offer. As far as we could discern, the other blocks with which we were in touch were solid. But if Glassman, who could muster about $300 million in his Catalyst Fund, went after all the blocks and was not his usual, indecisive self about what he paid, he could be a real threat.

There were only 7.5 million minority shares outstanding. Friendly blocks held about 2.3 million shares. Glassman was now close to 1 million. I believed I had a lead of about 1 million shares among the odd-lot holders, so Glassman would have to pick up more than 1 million shares before 10 a.m. Tuesday. I prepared, if necessary, to raise our offer price and considered methods of bidding for the underlying rights accruing to holders of the Contingent Cash Payment Rights (CCPR) set up by the litigation panel arrangements, as the rights themselves were not transferable. If Glassman

[256]

went far enough above our price to blunder into an obligation to bid for all shares (more than 15 per cent above market price), we would consider selling to him and taking out $200 million.

I believed we had a support strategy that would be adequate and that might again be aided by the Glassman factor. On March 24, he had turned up personally twice at our office. The first time he came to see the head of the Ernst & Young inspection team and was seen off by the receptionist. (He doesn't exactly have the physical presence of J.P. Morgan.) The second time he arrived with five podgy women in tow, who sat in the boardroom transcribing the names of shareholders from the shareholders list. Our informants sent us copies of hilarious emailed bickerings between the independent directors.

The noteholders were not inactive. One of their lawyers telephoned Avi Greenspoon in early March, threatening injunctive action if the special dividends from the *Telegraph* sale were not retained as collateral for their notes. They wanted a 13 per cent yielding, cash-collateralized note and $40 million of notes on the original terms. These people had succumbed to the virus of greed more terminally than anyone except the Walker-led, $100,000-per-month non-executive directors. Ever resourceful, Greenspoon "played the dumb Canadian," a role whose validity, he dryly added, Americans never doubt. He strung it along with the help of Sullivan & Cromwell, and the noteholders more or less folded, illustrating again how fatuous was the position opposite the SEC originally championed by Walker that all would be collateralized: the cash collateral yielding the company 4 per cent and the notes costing it 13 per cent. This was the new-broom rotating chairman.

As light departed Easter Sunday, I finished a brisk neighbourhood walk with Barbara and took a swim, regarding the tattered pink western sky from my swimming pool as I had so often done on Sunday evenings from a nearby prospect in my youth. In those far-off days, I had timorously wondered what another school week would bring. Now I dared, very tentatively, to hope that justice might prevail. The holiday of Resurrection gave way to the long-awaited day of judgment.

MONDAY, MARCH 28, ARRIVED, and I steeled myself to hold any optimism in check, but still I had some excitement that we were about to turn a very advantageous corner. Barbara had retreated upstairs. Her appearances in my library seemed to coincide with bad-news telephone calls, and she had decided she was a hex. I sat like a zombie in front of my computer screen from 8:30 a.m. on, receiving emailed assurances from the OSC that their decision was imminent. The decision was initially announced for 11:00 a.m. When 11:30 a.m. passed and there was still no news, my optimism began to sink.

At 12:29 p.m., it clicked onto my screen. I scrolled to the end to read that the OSC had tersely rejected our application. The feeble rationale harped on the irregularities of the offer and implied that there might be some question of the independence of the directors and valuator. They could not state that they took the allegations Breeden and the SEC had brow-beaten them into making against my associates and me as proved. But the commissioners acted on the theory that they had been proved although I had had no compliance problems with the OSC in my career with public companies of over thirty years. Their own staff had given the green light to our offer, we had agreed to an independently administered litigation fund as a safety net should any irregularities come to light, and 87 per cent of the minority shareholders' votes had come in favouring the privatization, but still the shareholders had been ignored and trashed by the very regulators who styled themselves as their protectors. It was astonishing. I could only suppose that the thrill of actual proximity to the big American former super-regulator Richard Breeden had turned the head of Ontario's public securities protectors, including the robotic Ms. Wolburgh-Jenah, OSC inquiry chairperson.

On the afternoon of this crushing day, I convened a legal teleconference and said that I had to get completely clear of the companies, that we had to remove from Breeden's hand the sword of instant victory he enjoyed by merely reciting my name.

We would have to get rid of Walker and Carroll, who would, by now, be drinking champagne from a fire hose. Otherwise, they would be instantly back, completely in charge at $100,000 per month, and would effortlessly dominate the others to complete the Strosberg playbook by putting Ravelston to the wall and delivering the company to Breeden at a handy payoff for themselves. Ravelston would have to be put into receivership within ten days and administered in its shareholders' interest under court protection, asserting a post-Black right to get rid of Walker and Carroll. I would become a creditor because of my pension rights. Whatever value could be salvaged from my shareholding would be a bonanza to my very diminished expectations.

A little more than two years later, Hollinger Inc. would be worthless – reflecting an astounding performance by the Ontario Securities Commission. Ravelston would be worthless, and Hollinger International would have lost 95 per cent of its March 2005 value, and in another two years it too would be worthless. Judges Strine, Campbell, and Farley,* who is about to reappear, plus Breeden and the OSC, and a few late joiners would wipe out $2 billion of value in the briefly holy name of corporate governance. The only ones to have prospered were Breeden, Paris, Seitz, Walker, Carroll, the lawyers, Ernst & Young, and the receiver. It was for them that officials in Canada and the United States apparently toiled. I still had a good deal to learn about the imperfections of the rule of law in both countries.

I was completely finished as an important businessman, at least for an indefinite period. I would read and write. And something useful might still be possible, if I could survive the ordeal. Barbara and I had a very un-uplifting conversation before she prepared to go to London for the job of sorting and packing up the contents of our home on Cottesmore Gardens, now a mournful monument to a happy and stylish life that had gone forever. Pulling up stakes from the U.K. was wrenching for her. She had been something of a gypsy all her life and had wanted keenly to make a home in the country of her birth. It was the end of a more than twenty-year effort in London. Though Barbara fights it, she is privately a person of faith who in bleak hours falls back on cantorial music and ritual, usually alone in a room out of sight. We held each other before she left: "Whither thou goest, I will go, and where thou lodgest, I will lodge," she said, commenting wryly that the next couple of promises in the text were a step too far.

---

* James Farley was one of Canada's most opinionated and frequently published judges – indeed an older, more voluminous and bombastic, but equally self-preening judge as Leo Strine, complete with the conviction of his riotously amusing wit.

We would surmount this. And yet, Breeden was just as horrifying (if more accomplished) as he had been the day before. He certainly deserved tactical credit for another victory, but our press release referred only to our sadness for the public shareholders, whom we had tried to serve and who had been denied a generous exit strategy twice in thirteen months by unjust judicial and regulatory decisions.

The Ravelston receivership was certainly not entered into because of bankruptcy. It was a prosperous company in assets, strangled of income by the seizure of both Hollingers by Breeden and Strosberg, acting through their respective pawns. Without any income it couldn't possibly make the support payments to Inc. that Maureen Sabia had insisted on. If I put it into receivership myself rather than wait for the event, at least I could choose someone who would look after our interests. The role of a receiver in insolvency proceedings is to sort out claims under court supervision. He or she is sworn to put the interest of the stakeholders first. In Ravelston, the only stakeholders were the shareholders, which in essence meant principally me, so receivership seemed a good way to protect my remaining assets held there – namely my pension and my International and Inc. shares.

I hadn't much time to search for the best receiver – the dominoes were falling all around me – and after speaking to a couple of companies, I took the recommendation of Derrick Tay at Ogilvy Renault, the law firm that had previously been counsel for me and had given me the services of Alan Mark. They recommended RSM Richter and assured us that firm would remember who had hired them and act responsibly. By now that had a hollow ring, but there wasn't much else I could do apart from pray – which I was already doing. Tay's advice, as I suspected, proved completely worthless.

There were still no victims of our misfortune except ourselves, though we would now quickly be joined by all the other shareholders. We knew that the agony would go on, probably for another two or three or more years. I hadn't a hope that any of the Breeden-Paris-Seitz group knew how to manage the remaining newspaper assets. There wasn't a single newspaper person or even manager in any field among them; they seemed uninterested in hiring any senior executive who did know the business, and while the Chicago Group of newspapers was profitable and ought to earn a good sale, it needed clever steering and editorial brushing-up first. I was still defending a noble cause, the right of an honest man to his reputation, though I was still inaccessible to much moral support. I had lost another battle, but not the just war, which had reached a new level of destructive intensity.

[Chapter Nine]

I was reduced to citing Henry Kissinger's gloomy comment at the worst stages of the Cold War: "It is actuarially unlikely that we will lose every round." The situation became instantly desperate. Barbara was at our London home, spending nearly eight weeks of demanding physical and mental work, tearing down the interiors that had taken her several years to complete, sorting books, papers, possessions, and furniture in order to choose what to store, sell, or return to Toronto. Apart from furnishings and art, she was trying to cope with some eight hundred boxes of books to be shipped somewhere. Only the superb organizing of her indefatigable assistant of thirteen years, Mrs. Penny Phillips, could have made this possible. I scrambled to close the sale, because it would now be impossible to recover the $15 million I had advanced Hollinger Inc. to repay the non-competition payments Strine had made me jointly responsible for with the company. The London house would produce enough cash to deal with the urgent payables. More surplus real estate would need to be sold, so we prepared for the next chapter in the ordeal. Our assets in the Hollinger Group were under cease-trade orders, and our other assets were illiquid.

The proceeds from the London sale went to reduce Murray Sinclair's mortgage on my London and Toronto homes from Can$35.4 million to

Can$11.5 million. That mortgage had raised the cash for the payments ordered by Strine to Inc. (and thence to International). I paid Williams & Connolly the very steep sum of US$4.7 million (beyond the US$4 million I had already paid to that law firm). We had left over from that fine house of Barbara's sad and heroic efforts a total of US$103,000. I had thirteen days in which to cobble together the next deal, which would enable me to pay the Canada Revenue Agency $4.2 million and get them off my back for a while and permit me to bring some of the other legal accounts more or less current. I would need some reserve, as I now had practically no income.

Active sources of financial support simply flaked off in the familiar manner. I explored some potential sources in case of dire need. One very wealthy friend of many years said, "Considering where you were a few years ago, it's fantastic you're selling houses to protect yourself." I would have used a different adjective.

Alfred Taubman, whom I had re-elected as a director after he had been convicted of a felony, had publicly defended at the shareholders meeting, and had visited when he was incarcerated, almost wept his gratitude to me. He was at pains to tell me that, although he was a billionaire, his trustees wouldn't let him do anything.

I spoke to a senior financial executive at Brascan, with whom we had done many deals, and where I had been a director for nearly twenty years. He expressed the company's gratitude for what I had done for them in the past, sent a perfectly acceptable term sheet, and handed the matter over to New York affiliates. They phoned me once for information and a second time a couple of days later to announce they weren't interested.

It is a terrible thing to have assets and be partly ostracized and abandoned while staring down the barrel of a complete cash evaporation. I have rarely felt more helpless than when Barbara dropped her own legal bill on my desk and I knew, but did not tell her, that I had no money to pay it with. It had come to this: I was an inadequate provider.

As I negotiated feverishly with a diminishing number of potential mortgagees in Palm Beach, I was running out of money. For a short time, I did not even have the means to pay the severances for the dutiful people who worked for us to the end in our London house. The agile Joan Maida stretched out what payments she could, as everything went to the wire with

D.E. Shaw, a company that includes a high-yield loan unit. They satisfied themselves of the security of the Palm Beach house, coming in after Canada Revenue. Shaw was completely unimpressed by the controversy, which was what enabled them to charge a usurious rate of interest.

The negotiation over details was excruciating. Shaw had an interest rate in the mid- to upper teens depending on the duration of the mortgage, but they rolled up interest, which I correctly calculated would be offset by capital appreciation up to 2008, and they did their best to meet my time-line. In the last week, from May 9 to May 16, I was living on a thin diet: I had little appetite.

Barbara and I were, to all useful intents, alone in the world. We managed. On a couple of occasions, I even balked at Shaw's terms, though I had only the sketchiest of backup plans, and they softened slightly. I put both the Palm Beach house and our New York apartment up for sale. It was a retreat to Toronto, to a house I loved in a city and a country that hadn't been especially congenial as I staggered along the gauntlet of the legal enforcers and regulators and jackal press of both countries (and overseas).

When Barbara returned from London on May 16, I was too engrossed in last-minute details to meet her at the airport as I normally would after being parted so long. About an hour after her arrival at our house, it was confirmed that the funds from Shaw had been wired. Canada Revenue was paid out the next morning and did not complain about a delay of a couple of hours. We had a reprieve.

After these few steps, which relieved acute tension, there was almost exhilaration. Barbara and I had taken on very raw tasks after the privatization disaster. She had unflinchingly liquidated our British life. The house was evacuated room by room as Barbara retreated to our bedroom, where she was accompanied by a large cardboard picture of me that she had used years before when I was unable to attend one of our dinner parties at the last moment. Almost all the contents of that house have been in storage, these six years, awaiting our return.

Her description of going down the front steps of our house for the last time and closing the gate behind her was wrenching. She had been wandering since her early childhood and only her sister and I knew how difficult it was for her to leave London this time. She had thrown herself into a lifestyle she did not seek and lost the secure nest she had been building before I arrived. I felt responsible. But this time, at least, she had full confidence in our love. With the mortgage from Murray Sinclair, I had managed to climb back to a point where Brendan Sullivan of Williams & Connolly, instead of going to war as he had threatened to do in collection of his invoices, was reinstalled as an ally and, so he implied, a deterrent to the enemy. The non-criminal legal work (which was most of it, since the Justice Department was still outwardly inactive) was in the hands of Baker Botts, a fine firm with a more tolerant and restrained view of billing practices. I had got rid of the tax collector for at least a year and had kept us in funds for six months.

The media interpreted Ravelston's receivership as a bankruptcy, though it was public knowledge that the company had $220 million of assets and insignificant liabilities except for the pension plan, whose main participants were the six Ravelston shareholders.

This was the new strategy largely born out of necessity. Let the press, as it did, go cockahoop celebrating my financial demise. We could sell houses we no longer needed, from a life that we no longer led and that now looked less desirable, given the conduct of some of our so-called friends. I had no time to wonder if we would have continued in that society with those "friends" had events not interrupted it, or whether I would have become more discriminating. Our private newspaper companies were making US$30 million per year and would be clear of bank debt in less than three years – although their banking arrangements prevented the removal of any money from them for some time. It was a matter of patching things through until then. The companies, though, were in David Radler's control, which would soon create other problems.

Our friends in Britain had been magnificent with Barbara during her last month there. Peter (Lord) Carrington, Britain's greatest nobleman and ultimate Whig, wrote to Barbara a few days after her return from London, expressing admiration for the "great dignity" with which we had handled our troubles. Elton John came to our London home, at a time of chaos and removals, to take her out to dinner. He brought a little box with a beautiful diamond pavé star from the British jeweller (and loyal friend) Theo Fennell. "You're the star," he said, giving it to her. So was he.

—

THE CASCADE OF UNBIDDEN IRRITATIONS did not abate even for a few days. Two days after I'd paid Canada Revenue, Toronto's chief commercial judge, James Farley, confirmed the eviction of Jack Boultbee, Peter White, and me from 10 Toronto Street. This was the latest indignity and humiliation Walker had devised. I had had my office there for twenty-seven years.

Justice James Farley was a local celebrity and self-styled man of decision, a loud-mouthed hip-shooter in fact, though not as commercially naïve as Campbell. He said that physically separating the Walker faction from the owners of the building and the companies in it would de-escalate tensions. Farley had supported Ravelston's acceptance of U.S. jurisdiction and had made several antagonistic remarks from the bench about "the old guard." And he eventually contended, after he had retired from the bench, that I had been unfairly treated by the Ontario courts. So I had been, but along with Campbell, Farley's judgments had been the most Strine-ish in their gratuitous animosity. At least Campbell, unlike Strine and Farley, did not consider himself a blithe wit.

Then Gordon Walker, Paul Carroll, and Tony Kelly launched a lawsuit claiming I had bilked Hollinger Inc. of more than $500 million. It was a fantastic claim, but in this climate, no attack on me was thought excessive.

The Ernst & Young inspection costs stood at $10 million at this time – no findings, no report, only demands for more money, for prostrate co-operation, and for an ever-expanding mandate. Campbell, for his part, when the inspection he had inflicted on the company was questioned, recoiled and defended the inspector like a child defending a sand castle from an incoming wave. Though I had never laid eyes on either of them, both Campbell and Farley reminded me of Chekhov's prayer that God might protect him "from provincial officials who imagine themselves to be important."

More serious than the antics of these Canadian farm-team bit players in Richard Breeden's assault was the word we received two days after Farley's order. The assistant U.S. attorney in Chicago, Robert Kent, was about to recommend a criminal prosecution. He had invited Hollinger Inc.'s lawyer in to explain why that company should not be a defendant. Walker would have the news and would doubtless ensure the breathless dissemination of it. Kent had obviously subscribed to substantial parts of the Special Committee report.

It was now clear that it had been an act of great good fortune that Barbara had managed to close up the London house on time and that I had, with the help of my friends at Westwind Capital, negotiated with Murray Sinclair a continuing mortgage adequate to permit full payment of the Williams & Connolly legal fees. As it was, Sullivan was in fighting trim, claimed to be heeding the tocsin, and appeared confident of our case. He thought that the chances of avoiding a prosecution were good and those of defeating one were very good. He urged "cautious optimism." In such a foreign and terrifying environment, I continued to put my trust in the indispensable man. I was still unwilling to face the extent to which I would have to rely on myself.

There were always rumours that someone among our executives was co-operating with the U.S. attorney to explain the incomplete documentations. The decisive moment would come when Radler had to choose between "copping" a plea and trying to incriminate me, or deciding to fight it out, protesting his innocence. This is the nexus of the severely flawed American system: plea bargaining in order to pursue the biggest fish, regardless of the facts. On balance, since Radler, I thought, had as far as I then knew a defence of honest error in American Trucker, and I was the principal possible complainant in the Vogt affair, and no one else had committed a crime it seemed unlikely that anyone would perjure himself by trying to implicate me in a crime that had not occurred. But I had a lurking fear, based on Radler's casual attitude to most legal niceties, as well as his role in the Vogt affair, and tendency to lose his nerve under pressure. I thought he might be afraid of conviction in the American Trucker non-competition pay-off which he had ordered (though neither he nor anyone else except Hollinger Inc. had directly profited from it), and of a Canadian perjury charge in the Vogt fraud and perhaps in the *Sun-Times* circulation excesses. He was a pessimist at all times, and more than in the generic Jewish manner. His lawyer, Anton Valukas, a former U.S. attorney in Chicago and protégé of Jim Thompson, had told him that "defendants have a better chance in North Korea than in the U.S." I could hardly believe it, yet also feared that he might be tempted to try to push me under the judicial bus in exchange for a very light sentence for himself and reten-tion of the private community newspaper groups whose acquisition Breeden had attacked.

Valukas had always been a problem. He claimed to be concerned about my "lifestyle" and image and as an ex-prosecutor knew how to amplify such concerns. Early on, he had asked Greg Craig whether I was another Dennis Kozlowski, the eventually jailed head of Tyco, who had received a $17 million apartment from the company; spent millions of the company's money on a party in Sardinia in honour of his wife, including much-publicized ice statues urinating champagne; and had borrowed hundreds of millions of dollars from the company, allegedly on the verbal approval of a deceased director. I don't know if Kozlowski was guilty or not, but he left a great deal hanging out in public relations terms.

Contemplations of this kind enabled me to see how the prosecutors and Breeden had worked to kill the privatization of Inc. I assumed he had told them, as he had everyone apart from me, from October 2003 on, that crimes had been committed. Even the grandstanding hypocrites of the OSC would not scuttle the interests of the public shareholders out of malice or cowardice alone.

I finally faced up to the full gravity of the likelihood that once Breeden was in the frame, a desperate struggle was inevitable. He was determined to exact complete submission and had sufficient knowledge of the official spider web, and had built such a corporate governance brand for himself that he was a far more formidable adversary than he first appeared, in all his ponderousness. All that had happened since he drove off the private equity investors to get undisturbed access to his financial prey, tore up the restructuring agreement, and easily sold Strinc a story to continue gorging himself and destroying our companies and using them as platforms to torment their builders, was inexorable. So was his management of the same tactic again with what he must have regarded (with reason in this case) as the wool-hatted, corn-cobbing yokels of the OSC. The shareholders were doomed, and I would only be rid of him by going through the legal morass until we got to a court of law, and not just another pseudo-legal raising heavenwards of the moist official fingers of bias and psephology.

Once privatization was strangled in its cradle, there was no visible end to the metastasizing litigation. Facing and rebutting criminal charges might be the only way to retrieve my reputation. I had known almost from the start, after he crossed me on the Restructuring Agreement in November 2003, that this was Breeden's fervent ambition, and except for the nonsense about racketeering, he had won every round. He might again find a co-operating judge, this time in Chicago, where any criminal case against me would be heard, by a judge influenced by, and perhaps even named on the advice of, Jim Thompson. But convincing a jury beyond a reasonable doubt that I had committed a crime that did not occur and in circumstances of which I knew nothing, when faced with a barrister of the ferocity and skill of Brendan Sullivan, aided by Eddie Greenspan and Bill Jeffress, would turn out to be, I thought, at least a tougher challenge than poisoning the shallow wells of the media, the cross-border lower courts, and the easily misled regulators. At some point, I prayerfully reasoned, due process would have to intrude on this *ex parte*, bloodless dismemberment.

It would be hellfire and dead cats, but it would be the turning point. We should win, and then the momentum would be broken decisively. Breeden had apparently pushed the Chicago prosecutor into action, but he was gambling almost as much as I was.

I was shaken but not demoralized. The prospect of *United States of America vs. Conrad Black* would have been too horrifying to imagine in my previous life. But as the crisis gradually deepened, one disappointment succeeded another, more people betrayed me and more crowded into the ranks of my enemies, pandering to the basest of the media and one another, it became difficult to be horrified. I would be upholding vital principles, I told myself – honest capitalism and impartial law, both of which had been degraded beyond recognition in this ghastly sequence of outrages.

As I began to accept the likelihood of a criminal trial, I felt like Koestler's Rubashov. The fear of the event had been more torturing than the reality. I would return to Chicago, a city I had romanticized as a younger man because of its writers, architects, lore, and general muscularity, to be wrongfully prosecuted by the U.S. Department of Justice. My decades of love of America would come to this absurd dead end.

In the two years since the Special Committee had been created, it had become necessary to cast this fight as one for principles – a fight that had at least a historical precedent of victory. A rich businessman being unjustly stripped of the proceeds of his work of thirty-five years, his possessions, and reputation is not a sympathetic figure in our society. I was no Dreyfus or Solzhenitsyn. But it inspired me that they both survived terrible persecution. My fate was not going to be physical torture or solitary exile but, incredibly, I was fighting for my freedom, for the right to live out my remaining years with my wife and family. Injustice on the scale I had experienced, even in a society that has abandoned the rack and Devil's Island, is painful beyond measure, particularly when you alone seem to be singled out.

As I was acclimatizing myself to this new test of nerves and fibre, I called Brendan Sullivan, who assured me that the prosecutors were incapable of laying a charge, that they were engaging in a standard tactic to try to shake loose parties ready to cop a plea and inculpate others. He thought they would have a problem cracking David Radler, and that if Radler didn't roll over, they could not charge me. If he did, they would, but they wouldn't win. He thought that the U.S. attorney had not really looked at the evidence and was simply responding to the badgering of Breeden. His firm had recently cross-examined Breeden as an expert witness and judged him lacking.

It soon came to light that Kent's antics were motivated by a concern about the statute of limitations closing out his right of action (only months were left on the five years since the questioned transactions). And that Nate Eimer, Hollinger Inc.'s amiable Chicago counsel, who had presumably been selected as the recipient of the intelligence from the assistant U.S. attorney, because of his excitability, was running around as if his hair were on fire, exclaiming that we were all about to be indicted – as Kent had doubtless intended.

THE ELEGANT LITTLE BUILDING at 10 Toronto Street with its Greek-columned stone façade, which had been built in 1851 and was for many years a post office before Argus Corporation had bought it in 1959 was to be off-limits to me as of May 31, courtesy of Farley's order. There was an order from his like-minded colleague, Campbell, prohibiting removal of documents from the building without the agreement of the inspector and a further order from Farley prohibiting the removal of anything but personal papers. Still, I had to move my office, and remove personal papers. There were a good many boxes that had been returned from England to Greenspan's office (having already been examined), and Joan Maida had had some of them brought over to 10 Toronto Street to see what she ought to move to her new office, which was to be in her home.

My files in the U.K. had all been gone through, copied, and sent off to the SEC before the move. The faithful Rosemary had sent my personal ones (also all gone through in the U.K.) to Greenspan's office while Barbara had sent most of her staggering number of boxes to our home in Toronto, where counsel examined, copied, and sent all relevant material.

By now, all my papers in 10 Toronto Street had been examined for more than a year and photocopied for the SEC, the inspectors, and the Special Committee as well as the new regime. Even annual reports were photo-copied, to the distinct irritation of Joan, who saw this sort of thing as a pure make-work effort for the law firms' billings. She was engaged in a constant battle to keep the voluminous material organized after files were taken out, copied, and dumped back in great piles on her desk or returned in the (dreaded) boxes. By now Joan doubted that there was a telephone message or Post-It that had not been photocopied and numbered. (And deliberately misplaced. Much of my most valued correspondence simply vanished, as part of the services furnished by the Toronto Street usurpers to the prose-cutors. Letters from a great many interesting people (including every prime minister of Canada from Louis St. Laurent to Jean Chrétien, except Ms. Campbell, and even the letters I received on the deaths of my parents in 1976 disappeared.)

Joan sat in an outer office surrounded by filing cabinets. My inner office had been taken over by a law firm that had access to every scrap of paper and computer record and spent their days sifting constantly through all her files, which were never locked.

On May 20, six working days before we would be expelled from a build-ing I technically still owned, I was working at home, hoping to avoid seeing the packing up of my office. Joan asked a security guard to move thirteen boxes to her car. The inspector representative on-site asked that they be moved back. Joan called me. I arrived at the building at about 3:30 p.m. and spoke with the inspector and the acting Hollinger Inc. president, the amiable Don Vale. With their agreement – and Joan's assurance that any commercial papers in the boxes had come in from Greenspan's office and were not in the building at the time of the first court order, and that the rest of the contents was personal and not in contravention of the second court order – I helped my driver, John Hillier, move them from the back door of the building to my car, parked a few feet away, fully aware that I was being filmed by security cameras I had installed, as well as by recently installed ones. I wanted to be filmed so there could be no suggestion of my trying to remove these boxes undetected.

I had no idea that the contents of the boxes, none of which I had selected or was even specifically aware of, could be of interest to any U.S. authority. We had already responded to five SEC subpoenas and sent 124,000 pages of documents, everything their subpoenas covered, more than a year before. It would turn out that there was not one commercially significant document in these thirteen boxes that the SEC did not already possess.

Walker, when the videotape of our removal was shown to him, sent Kelly scampering to court to accuse me of contempt of that court, which had to date avoided no opportunity to humiliate and pre-punish me. Campbell, adhering to his well-established policy, summoned my counsel Alan Mark on the briefest notice. He was abusive to him before the packed press corps. Then in a decision that was to have the worst possible consequences for me, Campbell permitted the playing of the tape, which because of its grainy quality and the poor lighting in the staircase had a shadowy black-and-white look. The court did not see the colour film from different cameras showing the parking lot was full and in blazing sunshine, and that I only handed the boxes to my driver, a distance of two feet. In any case, I was well accustomed to moving much heavier boxes and armfuls of books around my libraries.

With the allegations of Kelly ringing in the reporters' ears, the tape became the definitive proof of a furtive and illegally motivated act in which I had been caught red-handed, rather than the film of a man, in the middle of the afternoon, simply moving his belongings after an eviction order from one known place to another in front of cameras he well knew were there. The watching press went into orbit. Frames from the tape were reprinted and televised throughout the world to inflict the maximum possible public relations damage on me and the media, which in this case, cannot be blamed for believing it.

For a time it was claimed that I had snuck into the building after hours, when it was deserted, and had been caught on cameras of whose existence I was unaware. The idea that I would move large boxes was disparaged as a sign of desperation.

It was a sweet moment for Walker: he was being patted on the head publicly by a Superior Court judge as he continued to collect $100,000 per month from the company for himself and each of his followers. I was expelled from our historic building, for which I had advanced nearly Can$20 million to Hollinger Inc. to prevent it from being seized by Hollinger International. Desiring to be sure I was seen removing the documents, I was rewarded for my guilelessness by being held up to the world as a thief.

There was no possible justification for this pandering by Campbell. That I was being unjustly expelled from a building I owned, where I had had my office for twenty-seven years, to make way for those who represented no one and had been milking the company was not much mentioned. Nor was the fact that what was being removed was not covered by the relevant court order. Some people recoiled at the one-sided presentation of this nonsense. Someone I did not know wrote the *Globe and Mail* that it was little wonder, given that newspaper's coverage of me, that I had chosen to found a competing newspaper.

After Alan Mark called me, immediately after his return from the courthouse on May 25, I went out for a bicycle ride in the park near my home, as I had done thousands of times before. When I moved onto the normally hard-packed earth shoulder to avoid a bump on the paved trail, my front wheel sank into inexplicably marshy ground and stopped abruptly. I was thrown forward and sideways rather heavily. I was covered with mud, the bicycle was bent eerily, but I had only a slightly bruised knee. I walked the unusable tandem home, showered, had a glass of wine on my terrace, and wondered at how unpleasantly bizarre my life could become. I rarely had physical accidents, but this was the second after the fall in Seattle and did not augur well.

Eddie Greenspan took over the contempt case (which was never launched against me). Walker claimed that I was unaware of its existence, and he let it be known that they intended to ask for a jail sentence for me. Greenspan and I both felt that this might be the time, finally, to take the offensive. It was another demeaning and humiliating episode, but I was now inured to these things and took little notice of the endless prattling and nasty caricatures in the press. I knew logically that it could not go on forever. The *New York Times* at least gave me credit for physical stamina in lifting the boxes, and most accounts did refer to Greenspan's assurance that there was no violation of court orders in the removal of personal papers that had not been in the office when the initial order was produced.

I had also been so extensively defamed for so long, I did not fully appreciate the graphic, symbolic damage of this practically irrelevant sideshow.

There were *opéra bouffe* diversions even in these fraught days. Peter White and I were sitting in my office on the afternoon of May 24 when one of the loyal executive assistants informed us that, since one of the directors had phoned in to the meeting then underway in the boardroom between the independent directors and the Ravelston receiver, they could arrange for us to hear the meeting on Peter's speaker phone. We did so.

This was their first meeting with the receiver. I had the pleasure of hearing from Kelly that I would be personally bankrupt within a few weeks. Walker demonstrated his political instincts by accepting the receiver's right to name directors and by renouncing the notion that the directors' previous pay level was justifiable because of the strains of privatization but never intended to be durable. Then came the highlight: an ex-Mountie whom Walker had hired to ensure security (at a prodigious salary) was introduced around. This was the man who would cost $50,000 per month, but this was justified to ensure that no piece of paper that might make a difference, said Walker, "of hundreds of millions of dollars" in their imbecilic lawsuit would not be removed. And this was the man who would prevent them from being bugged.

Of course, while dealing with such imbeciles, bugging was superfluous, not only because we listened to them without recourse to espionage, but also because they were quite predictable. Strosberg, speaking loudly from ignorance, had sold Walker and Kelly the fable that we were heavily indebted to Ravelston and could be seriously inconvenienced if the loan were called. Their disappointment crackled through the telephone when the receiver told them that our indebtedness to Ravelston was non-recourse straw debt, easily cancellable. Their request that the receiver claim a receivership against me personally melted like a snowflake on a warming spring day. The dominoes stopped rolling at Ravelston. The Marx Brothers would have been wittier but no more entertaining.

But they were winning. A few days later, Campbell sustained Walker's decision in throwing Peter White off the Hollinger Inc. board. Campbell had bought the line that we were tainted characters and that our 78 per cent shareholding was a toxic waste area that could not be exercised and whose holder could not even be informed of what was happening in the company. There had been no adjudication of the main issues, no due process, just Campbell following the *Globe and Mail*'s view that I was bad. With the National Hockey League on strike, I seemed to be the *Globe*'s replacement game. *Globe and Mail* reporter Richard Blackwell volunteered to Peter White's lawyer, David Wingfield, that he would like to focus more on the role of Walker and Campbell but that his editors wanted all focus to be on the crucifixion of me.

With immense relief, Barbara and I retired as Hollinger International directors on June 7, 2005. Barbara had been longing to retire since this began but had been urged to stay on in order to keep one oar in should I be turfed before she was. Neither of us wished to participate any longer in the charades of meetings (all decisions were taken at Breeden's Corporate Review Committee) or to legitimize the Paris-Seitz regime. I also assumed that Walker would eventually revoke our status (as Hollinger Inc. still had the right to remove Hollinger International directors by resolution). Never again would the shareholders see the sort of generous offers I had arranged for them with the Barclays and with the privatization process.

An offer came in promptly for our apartment in New York, well above its cost to us and $2 million above an appraisal of just nine months earlier. I did not regret leaving our home in New York as I had London. Manhattan is not a place to sojourn for long if you have no real job – unless you are a genuine New Yorker. We had no job and no reason to be there any longer. If our Florida real estate agent could move out Palm Beach at close to the asking price, I would at least have a war chest adequate to get through any emergency. This would be the definitive end of the financial crisis that had hovered over me for eighteen months and came back with terrifying vengeance after the collapse of the privatization effort.

BRENDAN SULLIVAN AND GREG CRAIG visited the U.S. attorney's office in Chicago in June 2005. It was the main service I got from Sullivan, whose firm I paid more than $8 million in 2004 and 2005. They met with the rather large and unanimated Robert Kent, and his hyperactive, compulsively pugnacious sidekick, Eric Sussman. Sullivan phoned me from the lobby of the federal courthouse in Chicago, which was a milieu I would come to know well, and assured me that "they are a thousand miles from laying a charge." Craig had assured me there was no sign of any grand jury activity, and that if any began, I would receive a suspect letter and then a target letter.

Sullivan made it clear to Kent and Sussman that there was no serious case against me, that any charge would be resisted with extreme strenuousness, and, that to the extent Kent was relying on Breeden's report, the prosecutor would be making a terrible mistake that would bring the Justice Department into disrepute. Kent said that if a discussion of substantive issues seemed appropriate, he would call. Sullivan confimed his view that Kent knew little about the case and that his sabre-rattling with Eimer had just been the usual opening shot.

What concerned us was that, when setting up the meeting, Craig had been told by Kent that the latter would seek a tolling agreement from us that would extend the statute of limitations (five years) on any charges. The statutory end of the period for prosecuting the disputed transactions was close. We had no intention of agreeing to such a thing, but when they met, Kent did not raise it. He did express curiosity about whether I would accept U.S. jurisdiction if charged and whether Williams & Connolly would accept a subpoena for documents on me. This seemed to imply that they were really cranking up to indict soon.

Sullivan's view was that Kent would be insane to do so, as he obviously knew nothing about the case, but that if he did, we should go to the speedy trial provisions and require that the case be brought on in ninety days.

There was at least a very strong feeling with Sullivan, and with Greenspan, that if I were charged, I would win. Under any circumstances, it was a chilling prospect.

I was in such unfamiliar territory that I still stuck to a totem theory that placed confidence in a *deus ex machina* personality, the supreme expert who would deliver me from evil. Sullivan was widely regarded as America's greatest trial lawyer; surely I could trust his judgment, and the U.S. attorney would not wish to tangle with him. That was what I got for the $8 million that Barbara and I had had to scramble like famished wolves to produce: a false sense of confidence.

My early legal strategy failed, but at least it got me through psychologically. The death watch on my financial condition subsided again, but when I left Palm Beach in May 2005, I did not expect to see my house there again.

I prepared yet another partial counter-attack, as part of my fighting a Bataan-like retreat. Eddie Greenspan, with my vociferous encouragement, had determined to try to force Campbell to recuse from our case because of his evident animus, which was clear in every case except the privatization hearings.

An attack on Campbell would, at the least, be like Roosevelt's attack on the Supreme Court in 1937; even if it did not succeed, it might frighten him into more reasonable behaviour. I reviewed Greenspan's draft and removed every use of the adverb "respectfully." Unfortunately, this wasn't pursued either. We kept hoping we would get clear of the Canadian courts. But we would soon have more to fear from Campbell than ever.

The Ravelston receiver, RSM Richter, would be the next unsurprising disappointment. It is well understood that litigants against a company are not stakeholders and I warned Richter that both Inc. and International would try to base their claims as stakeholders on the spurious lawsuits they had taken, which included Ravelston among the defendants. This should be resisted at all costs. They agreed and made firm noises. The key, I pointed out, was for Richter to assert control. Ravelston had 78 per cent of Hollinger Inc. and could use that to remove Walker and his sidekicks.

By now, I didn't actually believe there was a chance of that happening. Bobby Kofman, the Richter partner serving as the Ravelston receiver, came to my home on June 9, 2005, with two of his counsel, and two of ours.

Kofman responded to our exhortation to use his shareholding to force the issues by saying that there was "hair" on Ravelston's 78 per cent control block – "hair" meaning a compromised aspect and specifically the lawsuits.

I pointed out that this was not the case. He was to represent the stakeholders, who did not include the litigants, and the litigants should rejoice at the maximum state of prosperity they could achieve for Ravelston, as it would then be a juicier target for their claims, rubbish though they were. As the Richter group seemed concerned about how their invoices were going to be paid, I thought our strongest card was to appeal to their financial interest. I told them, for about the tenth time, that the only way to get bills paid – and save Ravelston – was to assert themselves at Hollinger Inc. by getting rid of Walker and his gang, then at Hollinger International. Chicago was perfectly able to pay for the receiver, inspector, Special Committee, and so forth. Eventually, we should be able to repossess what was left of the company and rebuild its strength. At the very least, instead of using the company and its resources to attack the people who had built it, we should use it to attack those who were destroying it.

If there had been a chance of getting anything like a fair hearing from any Ontario court I would not have put the company into receivership. As it was, this seemed to be the best way to get rid of Walker and stabilize the company until we could sort out some of the problems.

And so it would have been, if Richter had not scampered down the well-trodden path to the U.S. attorney in Chicago in exchange for a go-ahead to suck every cent of cash out of the company it was there to protect. The only moment of their decisiveness came when, as I counted on, Walker infuriated them and Bobby Kofman and his advisor Max Mendelsohn overcame their penchant for the mousey and consensual. Walker and Carroll had been trying to negotiate a settlement with International, which consisted of giving away Inc.'s super-voting rights in exchange for 5.25 million new single-voting shares, information that we got through our Toronto Street sources and gave to the receiver. The deal blew up. International told Walker they would not deal with him, and that was the end of Walker's fantasy, in which he would become a prominent director of Hollinger International and the trustee of Hollinger Inc.'s International shares, hobnobbing with Henry Kissinger and having lunch with the former governor of Illinois. (A more soporific conversation would be hard to imagine.) Fortunately for posterity, Walker put much of these ambitions in emails, which loyalists sent me.

Walker, Carroll, Metcalfe, and Wakefield were all fired by Richter, more or less publicly, with the acquiescence and tongue-lashing of the perceptive Campbell, who had put them in their jobs in the first place after firing our directors and had tipped his figurative wig to his protegé Walker as the man of the hour. Now they were castigated by the judge, the receiver, and the Glassman group, with loud noises echoing behind them that the shareholders would seek restitution. Up until a few days before, Walker had been babbling on to the press about all that he would accomplish, about his munificences to the shareholders, and about Campbell's protection of him. Campbell's other lapidary comment on one of the other individuals in this case was: "If Mr. Strosberg tells me something, I believe it."

The *coup de grâce* for Walker was a brilliant letter to the *National Post* by Peter White, published July 5. He wrote that he and I had been scraping the bottom of the barrel to find this group of directors, who were not engaged as managers, and that he would not hire any of them "to run a lemonade stand in July." Our intelligence reports from within 10 Toronto Street indicated utter pandemonium, with the ostensible executives running down the halls like frightened schoolchildren. They ordered payroll to prepay their salaries for July, but payroll refused. Walker and Carroll vanished into a greater obscurity than that from which they had been plucked.

Inc. stock sank like a stone. It was evident there was no chance either of privatization or of proper business management. The benefit of Inc.'s existence now was as a well from which accountants, lawyers, and a rotating list of greedy directors could all draw money, paying themselves enormous sums of it for administering the back-breaking task of vacuuming up Inc.'s cash. In spite of the $100 million from the *Telegraph* sale and the $20 million I had lent it, the stock had declined by more than 90 per cent from our offer in less than two years. The Canadian media said almost nothing about this dreadful rape of the public shareholders or about the fact that it was the result of Breeden's unofficial "lecture" to the OSC.

Ezra Levant's *Western Standard* produced a full exposé of the extravagance and incompetence of the Paris and Walker despotisms. The magazine pointed out that I had refinanced Hollinger Inc. twice in 2004, for a total of $236 million, and loaned it $20 million. "His reward for saving the shareholders from bankruptcy was being 'thrown out of the company, evicted from the building and represented to the press of the world as some sort of sneak stealing his own papers out of his own building. . . . The papers were not under any court order and he had a perfect right to remove them. Where's the due process in all this?'" (*Western Standard*, July 11, 2005). This was almost the first journalistic treatment, apart from Mark Steyn, of what was really happening to the Hollinger companies, and was typical of the insight and independent-mindedness of Ezra Levant, who was at this time engaged in a battle with Canada's irresponsible human rights commissions, which he resoundingly and deservedly won.

And more reporting of the true activities of Walker and his group crept into the media after Peter White's letter lifted a rock on them.

I now had no job and no office. I would get to work on writing a book about Richard Nixon, obtain some modest involvement with our continuing interests, and continue to devote myself to enjoying my splendid library. In the familiar precinct of my family home, I was crossing the desert, but I had a compass. I started with intensified Nixon research, not knowing how far it would be possible to go, but it was agreeably diverting work that could be conducted at any time, and painlessly interrupted for legal or other calls.

I read the Special Committee interviews. It was fantastic that we had been stripped of the company, shunned socially, and suffered such massive damage to our reputation on the strength of such puny allegations. Peter Atkinson had been whiny and sanctimonious but alleged no wrongdoing. Instead, he devoted himself to evading his responsibility for the legal work that led to the controversy in the first place and masqueraded as a voice of probity and moderation in a gluttonous atmosphere. Even David Radler, implausibly, attempted a slight bit of this, joking with Breeden about my British title. They did not realize that Breeden could not be appeased that way. Their specious efforts at dumping blame in my lap would be accepted as evidence against me but would not deliver them from the crosshairs.

More alarming was the extent of Radler's delusional and tactical revisionism revealed in the interviews, as will be discussed in the next chapter.

If Brendan Sullivan was right and the Department of Justice would uphold everything for a year, this would merely prolong the Breeden gravy train and build shareholder impatience for a resolution of it. (I overrated the shareholders' sense of self-preservation.) By then, I could buy out the receivership, as some of my assets would ripen, privatize Hollinger Inc., and move on Breeden. He would not be able to pull the same rabbit out of the hat at the Ontario Securities Commission two years in a row.

I HAD A CONTINUING SENSE of relief to be free from the *Telegraph*. Advertising in the London national newspapers had generally collapsed, a very tricky situation for even skilled and experienced newspaper publishers. The Barclays had little idea what to do; their circulation was evaporating and they had no natural instincts as publishers. In firing Dominic Lawson as editor for the *Sunday Telegraph*; replacing him with the pleasant and perky Sarah Sands; retaining Martin Newland; and making Boris Johnson, MP, answerable at the *Spectator* to Andrew Neil, whom David Barclay himself had not spoken of very positively, they assured the continued decline of the group. I regretted that Murdoch might be the beneficiary of it. All the newspapers were losing ground; the British national newspaper industry was in full decline, the *Telegraph* among the most precipitately so. I grieved for the titles I had known, and for what they might have still been, though not for the journalists who had attacked Barbara and me.

A journalist wrote my "living will," flagged on the front page of the weekend *Globe and Mail*. It was an unsuccessful attempt at vivacity of wit. The next week the same newspaper ran a column by Jan Wong, an enthusiastic veteran of China's Cultural Revolution who had confessed to denouncing several people in her zeal. "May God forgive me," she wrote in her autobiography. Whatever God's will in this matter, her little errors in China, which probably cost her victims their lives or liberty, hadn't restrained her. She now devised a scheme to purge Toronto of its dishonest citizens. She left eleven wallets around Toronto, each with a twenty-dollar bill inside and identification showing an Asian family, including a boy in a wheelchair, together with a note and telephone number requesting any finder to call J. Wong. Ten of the wallets were left in public places such as parks and schoolyards. The eleventh was more specific: allegedly thrown over my garden gates and not returned. This was headlined as illustrative of what Ravelston's receivership had done to me. I had had to steal twenty dollars from a handicapped Asian. George Jonas wrote a withering rebuttal with one of his unerringly accurate arrows: "It's easier to take the girl out of the Red Guard than to take the Red Guard out of the girl." (Barbara, ever conscientious to clear me even of such idiocies, spent many hours vainly combing through leaves and debris along the railings and gate at the front of our house.)

Doug Kelly offered me a column in the *National Post* about foreign affairs, and I accepted. I wrote an extensive piece for the *National Interest* on the debacle of the European constitution, which, ever since Giscard d'Estaing unveiled it, I saw as a madly unworkable document, a matrix for utter chaos. Finally, by late June, with criminal action apparently unlikely any time soon and the New York apartment moving toward a sale, I determined that it was time to return to England, not only to show the flag but to actually enjoy friends and spend some weeks with Barbara free of this mad and squalid ethical wasteland. I swept Barbara up like D'artagnan, and we went to Britain and the south of France for a month. The decision was one of my best.

In the past, beginning in July and peaking in August, when all of Europe went into summer holiday mode, we would spend about three weeks in the south of France, often based in Monte Carlo. From there we could rent a car and visit friends who had second homes in France or drive into Italy. Then we would return to Toronto to spend August at our own home. Monte Carlo and August in Toronto were always the happiest times for us. I, briefly, could have the illusion of not working, though in truth too many days were consumed with endless telephone calls to financiers or lawyers. Barbara rarely gave up her column for more than two weeks and got very twitchy if she was not writing it. "The jig is up," she would say in a worried little voice. "The columnist replacing me [for the vacation] is really good." This time, the trip to London and on to Monte Carlo was an almost unqualified success.

We returned to the familiar end-of-season marvellously eclectic gatherings of people in splendid settings. For just a moment, it was as if very little had changed. The warmth was genuine, not just the standard London shrieks of "We must get together," "Longing to talk to you," followed by silence.

We had told only a few close friends we were coming, but on encountering us at one or other place, others seemed enthusiastic in making plans to get together. Peter Carrington and Jacob Rothschild each invited us to dine with them in public places, where the newspapers would certainly hear of it and did. These were delightful occasions; they brought home the isolation of the bunker in Toronto and the solidarity of the British. The conversation was absorbing, the conviviality uncontrived and uncompetitive. After twenty months in the tenebrous thickets of the American legal gulag and the junior-league Canadian juridical survival camp, returning to the London I had known made the endless, vicious defamations in the press and the avalanche of subpoenas all seem a bad and distant dream.

Barbara came alive again, meeting her girlfriends over the most peculiar menus and at odd venues. She and Annabelle Weidenfeld favoured a sidewalk bistro off Knightsbridge that had a direct fronting on the neighbouring hotel's dustbins.

For me there were useful reconciliations with Charles Moore (who said of the *Telegraph*: "You're probably well out of it"); with Boris Johnson, who claimed he would publish a piece of mine; and with Andrew Neil, who revealed how defective Rick Burt had become and how little Burt appreciated his Hollinger depositions. And there was the pleasant London spring season of running into people, from the delightful Barry Humphries (whose alter ego is Dame Edna Everage) and his adorable wife, Lizzie Spender, to the leader of the opposition and my old dining club partner, Michael Howard, at the start of a new Tory leadership race to choose the fifth successor to Margaret Thatcher in the fifteen years since her departure, to the just-retiring prime minister of New South Wales, Bob Carr, head of the Chester A. Arthur Society of Sydney and a very accomplished man, who, since the death of the novelist Morris West, is probably my best friend in Australia.

I took Barbara to dinner at Annabel's (named after Annabel Goldsmith), then still run by Annabel's former husband, Mark Birley, and their son,

Robin. We had had our wedding dinner there in 1992 and Barbara has always loved the club.

Generally we did not refer to our travails except when asked, and then only in the knowing sense that the questioner of course knew the vagaries of the American justice system and the tendency in the United States of litigious fads to get out of control and become plagues. This was rarely a hard sell with the British, as even those who do not resent the United States consider it a half-mad country at the best of times. We made it clear that we would be moving back. I concerted a few points with Rocco Forte about the *Catholic Herald*, which we now owned jointly.

The British are sufficiently worldly, respectful of privacy, and fuzzy about commerce that the appearance of well-being and a level of confidence that is fairly impenetrable without being overegged gets one by. I went round to routine places and resumed acquaintances very affectingly, with the great Doug Hayward, tailor, then suffering from a very rapid case of Parkinson's and now deceased; Roy, my barber at Claridge's; my book dealers, especially Glenn Mitchell at Maggs; and the captains at White's club, Harry's Bar, Mark's, Annabel's, and so on.

At the Brompton Oratory, I met fellow congregants who showed the discreet warmth the British practise so naturally. One of the Oratorians, formerly a *Daily Telegraph* reporter, told me that they celebrated a mass for me every month. My status on many ceremonial invitation lists had depended solely on my position at the *Telegraph*; my status as a distinct personality, like everything else now, depended only on me, and I had discovered through this horrible ordeal that I was not so bad a person to depend on.

In France, we went to Apax founding partner Ronnie Cohen's sixtieth birthday party in Cannes. Barbara had told me how especially kind he and his wife, the successful Israeli-born film producer Sharon Harel-Cohen, daughter of Yossi Harel, captain of the Holocaust survivor ship *Exodus*, had been to her at various times during the past few years when she was alone in London: offering her help with seating in the synagogue to which both Barbara and the Cohens belonged, inviting her to break the fast with them on Yom Kippur, and extending in the warmest way the hand of friendship in moments that had a particular importance to her for both religious and personal reasons.

Barbara was right when she said that no matter how wicked the British press were – and their wickedness could not be equalled anywhere in North America – the staunchness of our British friends could be relied upon. One of the most pleasant evenings was spent at the fine home of Elton John on Mont St. Alban, above Nice. Our relations with Elton and his partner (now spouse), David Furnish of Scarborough (Ontario), as he emphasizes, have always been excellent. They are delightfully talented and witty people and unwaveringly loyal friends. Barbara is a great fan of them both and credits David with changing her views on same-sex marriage. It did not endear her to a number of her readers when she campaigned for its recognition.

We also had a pleasant dinner in Monte Carlo with the financier and philanthropist Ezra Zilkha and Cecile, his wife, of New York. Ezra, a loyal friend, was clearly worn down by the pressures of his wife's illness, and she had the bewigged, reduced, and stoic appearance of someone putting up a gallant fight against a pernicious disease. We spent our last night, August 3, in Nice and had a nostalgic if altogether unsatisfactory evening struggling with gold plastic bathtubs and the exigencies of modern technology, at the Negresco. These brief, happy times spawned the predictable and feeble response by the U.K. tabloids. According to the *Mail* and the *Evening Standard*, I had shown outrageous "chutzpah" in accepting the invitations of old friends to lunch and dinner. It was an interlude that was over too soon.

HORRIBLE THOUGH THE WHOLE Hollinger affair was, as I pointed out to Barbara, it was reassuring to know that we had fought through this ghastly nightmare to this point on our own. What were outmanoeuvring the other factions at Argus Corporation and picking up the *Telegraph* torch from Michael Hartwell compared with a successful defence against the entire thousand-eyed monster of misplaced, perverted American official zeal, aided by the obedient, imitative Canadians? Ours was a triumph in the making, and in London it was not at all a lonely one. This is the only area where Barbara and I differ: she has no understanding of this ringing approach to misfortune. Her natural instinct is to resign herself to the worst possible outcome. In this, she reminded me of a well-known photo I showed her of European Jews during the Second World War being marched along the streets carrying their small bundles of belongings. Behind one such family walked a little girl, her body language summing up utter despair. This was Barbara's posture, pessimistic but never unsupportive of me. She was simply preparing to go all the way down with the ship if necessary.

Despite all the disappointments and the challenges following the involuntary abortion of privatization, this was an infinitely preferable summer to the previous one, when we were awaiting the assault from Breeden's Special Committee and the likely copycat actions of the SEC and OSC. It seemed, misleadingly, that time was starting to heal some wounds.

[CHAPTER TEN]

THE FACT THAT DAVID RADLER'S counsel had withdrawn from the joint defence group indicated that Anton Valukas, his lawyer, thought he could really do something with Radler in Chicago as Queen for a Day – the colloquial term for the procedure of exploring what deal a target might make with the prosecutors. I was disgusted and filled with revulsion that I had spent as long as I had in business with Radler. It was obvious that I could not trust him after the Todd Vogt affair. I should have been more suspicious of his endless grabbing for money and his disparagement of public companies. Once I had seen this, my plan was to let the private newspaper companies he had spun out of Hollinger International ripen and then trade some of my shareholdings in them for Radler's Ravelston shares. I didn't have the means to buy him out earlier without taking on debt I preferred to avoid. This was a mistake. Time had run out on that plan, as on much else.

Radler thought he was the sole architect of our financial success and the only one of us who had any idea how to run a business. He told anyone who would listen that I was the social face of our business while he was the real business brains. His fear, exposed by the ordeal of the legal crisis, for which he was largely responsible as head of the division where they originated, seemed to have produced a bitter and galling response that he smarmily concealed in discussion between us. I still doubted that he could promise the U.S. attorney anything useful and thought he would be back to us eventually, pretending that he had only been exploring alternatives, as Atkinson and Kipnis had. I would have to consider how to partition the private companies, disentangle our interests from his, and end the association.

WHEN WE RETURNED TO TORONTO in August 2005, David Radler's lawyer had just given formal notice of his settlement talks with the U.S. attorney. I still couldn't believe Radler would take the plunge, though I was well familiar with his pessimism, and nervosity. He had shown in 1986 at Dominion Stores (a derelict Argus Corporation supermarket company) that he had no staying power. Even though he had certainly not created the mess there, and had, in fact, helped to resolve it, he scurried out to Vancouver, leaving Peter White and me, on one day's notice, to clean it up. His nerves could not take the pressure.

Having previously disparaged religion and occasionally expressed skepticism (though not in my presence; direct confrontations with me were not his métier) about my conversion to and practice of Roman Catholicism, he had become a Lubavitcher Jew. He had met the late Rabbi Schneerson in Brooklyn, the practising Lubavitcher leader. Radler shooed the press away from his office at times, claiming a prayer meeting was in progress, and told an interviewer that he considered the whole attack on us to be "Go for the Jewish guy." This was an explanation that left my presence inexplicable in the public relations and litigious pogrom he claimed to detect, unless I was included because my wife is Jewish.

We had known each other for thirty-six years. There was no denying Radler's hard work and his success in putting together the hundreds of small newspapers we acquired in both Canada and the United States. We had sat together in Montreal delicatessens the way young men and small businessmen do, dreaming and planning what we could next achieve with our company. Perhaps I did detect the envy and small-mindedness at times that now oozed all over the pages of the Special Committee reports and tried to ease it, but I never suspected it was festering on this scale. I knew he often mocked my vocabulary, speeches, or writing as vanity and affectation, but I took this in stride, and often he professed to be an admirer. We knew little of each other really. I have no idea who any of his close friends are, and in the seventeen years of our marriage, Barbara and I dined with the Radlers as a foursome only once or twice when business found us in the same city. But to chop me up like this for the delectation of criminal prosecutors, to destroy me – could the envy have been so great? And envy of what? He was prominent in the Jewish circles he cared about. He had made himself quite prominent in Vancouver and to some degree in Chicago. He was a wealthy man. His children are high achievers, and his family is close. I wondered if my fears that he really was caught red-handed in crimes were justified (*American Trucker,** Horizon Operations, the Vogt matter, *Sun-Times* circulation), and Valukas scripted him toward a deal with the prosecutors.

His arrangement with the prosecutors would eliminate all complaints about the community newspapers, where he had seen his future, and which Breeden had set out to undo, and would trade a minimization of sentence for inculpation of the rest of us. He would prosper. The opprobrium of being branded a felon and a squealer and perjurer would not have been overly bothersome to him. This was a straight business decision, perhaps. But the David Radler with whom I had worked for most of our thirty-six years of association would not have entertained such a course. With his background as a Chicago U.S. attorney, Valukas would have convinced him of the tactical wisdom of this course. Even allowing for that, a great deal of Radler's testimony to the Special Committee was inexcusably bilious. All Breeden had to do was turn on the spigot and a great sluice of mud and merde poured out.

In his three sessions with the Special Committee, I was referred to sarcastically as "Crossharbour," and every mistake Radler ever made was explained as "Crossharbour strikes again." According to Radler, I was

---

* I had done my part to encourage the sale of *American Trucker* to a KKR (Kravis) company, by sending Henry and Marie-Josée *American Trucker* windbreakers and caps (which, unsurprisingly, I never saw them wearing) and a free subscription to the magazine, which had no editorial content and contained only advertising of used truck cabs.

extravagant; overly interested in Napoleon (a subject I had not referred to five times in my entire acquaintance with him); and a poseur who knew little about business, other than having good connections and some knowledge of deal making. Radler had "built our EBITDA [earnings before interest, taxes, depreciation and amortization – that is, operating profit] to $400 million," he told the Special Committee, as if none of the rest of us had had anything to do with it. He had played a vital role in taking over the *Daily Telegraph* by "encouraging" me to do it, as if any encouragement from him were necessary.

There were also little outbursts of megalomania. Thus his statement, "You'll have a hard time across the street if I am de-balled." Across the street meant the *Sun-Times*, where his departure was greeted with stentorian glee, and where the escalators he had shut down because of their cost were restarted. Even before there were any suggestions of unapproved payments, he was urging Breeden, who, he conceded, now ran the company, not to emasculate him, for the sake of the morale of *Sun-Times* employees. The statement was both false and self-emasculating.

"I know how to handle Hamas," he had grandly stated when explaining to the committee the management aircraft policy relating to the avoidance of terrorist threats. Such insights would doubtless have been gratefully received by the prime minister of Israel and by the Palestinian Authority.

All this material was released to us while I was in Europe, and when I read Radler's comments on my return, it was obvious that he was cranking up to try to lay responsibility for perceived wrongdoing at my door, even though, at that point, the only wrongdoing there could have been was his.

All that was clear apart from that was the inattentiveness of the legal staff, which Mark Kipnis allegedly tried to sidestep by complaining to the Special Committee that a few of the non-compete payments were "silly," though Kipnis later volunteered that he had said nothing of the kind. Atkinson's testimony to the Special Committee was especially feeble, as he glazed over his own responsibilities to assure that all legalities were exactly in place, in inter-corporate transactions and elsewhere. Jack Boultbee, who, though impenetrably enigmatic and monosyllabic, is a man of principle, calmly rebutted every one of Breeden's and his chief attack dog Jonathan Rosenberg's questions.

A good deal more upsetting was the news that my son Jonathan, having located a hard lump on the top of his collarbone, had gone to an emergency room at a Toronto hospital and was told this needed further investigation. When I was advised of this by his mother, I managed to accelerate the timetable. Jonathan went promptly for an MRI in New York. He had Stage Two Hodgkins. This is distinctly treatable but a horrid setback just as he was starting to get his career going. Barbara asked if we had now been spared anything except the proverbial plagues of frogs and locusts. We were both full of admiration for Jonathan's stoicism. He would come through the treatments with flying colours.

AUGUST IN TORONTO IS ALWAYS PLEASANT, whatever the distractions. We enjoyed our property, with the soothing sound of fountains in the walled library garden, and watched the deer and foxes and less graceful wildlife (raccoons, groundhogs, and skunks) from our terrace in the early evening, often with a glass of fine white wine in hand. I was continuing intensive research on Richard Nixon.

The massive and spurious Hollinger International case against us was getting to the point where discoveries were being demanded. The U.S. attorney's office in Chicago had finally revealed in the spring that it was investigating, and it was assumed that if their investigation passed a certain point, they would demand a stay of civil proceedings.

The fact that they had not, and that no suspect or target letter had been received, together with Brendan Sullivan's and Greg Craig's civilized interview with Robert Kent and Eric Sussman in June, had provided some hope that charges were not a foregone conclusion, even eventually. In response to Hollinger International's insolent and belligerent demands for week-long depositions, I told Baker Botts to carpet-bomb the other side with such demands and to emphasize we would be questioning Richard Breeden for at least two weeks. This would smoke out the Justice Department. They would not want us revealing Breeden's shallow allegations if they were planning to prosecute us on his story. I was not prepared to dangle on a string like a hooked trout, awaiting the pleasure of the notoriously aggressive and devious U.S. prosecutors.

However vulnerable my position, I was still ahead of the wolves financially, I still had excellent counsel, and I was, in fact, innocent. I had been horribly defamed but had so far, though by a narrow margin at times, managed an orderly retreat from the extremely overexposed position I had held when the onslaught against me began, in November 2003.

However, the U.S. attorney soon demanded stays in all civil proceedings, which signalled imminent indictments. It also showed they would not bother with the niceties of suspect or target letters and implied they were getting what they thought would be effective evidence incriminating me from Radler. Unfortunately it shook loose my own counsel, as Greg Craig, while appearing in Chicago, told the press that it was not clear his firm would be acting for me in the event of a criminal trial. Brendan Sullivan's evaluation was of my credit, not my case, but I needed strong counsel to make my case.

I made extensive summaries of all the evidence given to the Special Committee and was able to anticipate some of Radler's inculpations. I felt that Radler was going to have to engage in a version that would be vulnerable under cross-examination. All our colleagues would side with me; there would be no corroborative evidence. And Radler, uncertain and inarticulate even when telling the truth, could be easily disembowelled under heavy and skillful questioning.

It turned out that Radler's telephoned wedding anniversary greetings to us in London, on July 21, 2005, were the last contact I would have with him. It was shortly after this that his counsel had told us that they "were no longer pursuing the same objective" we were but were happy to continue in the joint defence agreement otherwise. The suggestion was extraordinary. Their participation in the joint defence group – an arrangement that has lawyers pooling information – had continued for some fifteen months while Radler and his lawyers played footsie with the prosecution. Surely that was a stretch of time that long surpassed the decency guidelines, even of the U.S. Bar. They had doubtlessly been relaying the thoughts of co-defendants' counsel to the prosecutors. I had been bankrolling a data collection system, since one of the major burdens in the case was the hundreds of thousands of documents that were now "evidence," and Radler had been getting a free ride on this. He also had the benefit of knowing some of the exculpatory evidence we had turned up. We expelled his counsel from the group.

On August 18, to put it in Rooseveltese, "The hand that had for so long held the dagger, struck it into the back of its neighbor." Dan Colson and Williams & Connolly both called to say that indictments were about to be handed down by the grand jury in Chicago. Lynda Schuler, Brendan Sullivan's understudy, called back a few minutes later to say that Radler, Mark Kipnis, and Ravelston had been indicted on seven counts of fraud and that Radler would plead guilty to at least one of the charges and would be a cooperating witness.

At the customary press conference at which American prosecutors announce important indictments and try to conclude the first phase of the media pre-trial with a mass conviction and maximum sentence of public prejudice, the U.S. attorney, Patrick Fitzgerald, a notorious headline-seeking zealot, had two charts showing the "scheme." As the *New York Times* wrote, "Lord Black was clearly identified on the top of one chart." On the other chart was only the word "chairman." Fitzgerald said: "I'm not going to say who the chairman was but you can check the public record." Not since Groucho Marx used to ask guests on his quiz show, "Who's buried in Grant's tomb?" has there been a less challenging public guessing game. Fitzgerald continued: "The investing public has the right to expect that officers and directors of publicly traded companies are managing, not stealing the shareholders' money. The insiders at Hollinger made it their job to steal and conceal. This was a systematic fraud on the shareholders."

There was a scheme, but Breeden was the author of it. And to a degree, Fitzgerald, having been convinced by Breeden, was a victim of the real scheme too, as he was now formally throwing the authority of the U.S. Justice Department behind it. Sullivan and Craig had confirmed in their visit to Kent in the spring that the Breeden Report was all that Kent and Sussman knew of the case. Breeden had gone to the highest level of escalation and Fitzgerald had committed to convict on what he must have had some idea was very thin, and in fact, no, evidence. It was unnerving, but I was buoyed by the knowledge that every word and every letter of every word of Fitzgerald's harangue were false. The spectacle of this mindless urge to lynch, to mock justice and due process, recklessly to deploy the power and credibility of the government to a flawed arraignment, and to destroy the innocent (Mark Kipnis is one of the least criminal personalities in the United States), would have been more shocking if I had not already been so well prepared for it. Breeden and I both knew how great was the risk he had just teased and tempted Fitzgerald into taking. And on the day, Radler was the ostensible winner, because he was the criminal and he had scurried out with a six month camping holiday courtesy of her Majesty the Queen in exchange for a story that I did not think could possibly hold under serious cross-examination. Cripsin's day, the day of judgment, was in sight at last.

Kipnis had received no target letter and only sixteen hours' notice of the charges against him. His counsel had flown from New York to Chicago to try to reason with the U.S. attorney's office. My colleagues who had tried to fly under the radar were almost bound to be disappointed. While Kipnis had come in for settlement talks and had done his best to satisfy the prosecutors, he had, unlike Radler, committed no crimes and told no lies. Mark Kipnis was innocent, inoffensive, and utterly honest. He had not received a penny from either the non-competes or the management fees. The sole motivation the prosecution could offer at the trial for his participation in what they called the great "scheme" was the absurd formula that he wanted to be the next Peter Atkinson. I think that, since he had nothing to offer in the conviction of me, Kipnis must have been indicted as punishment for refusing to cooperate, and in the hopes that he could still be terrorized into rolling over.

As mentioned, Atkinson had started sending back his money from the contested non-competition payments even before I was made aware in November 2003 that there was any doubt about the approval of them. While the rest of us were carefully dismembered from all Hollinger associations, he had continued work for Hollinger International for $30,000 per month for about eighteen months, firing the company pilots and aircrews, on Paris's orders. Atkinson negotiated lengthily with Chicago prosecutor Eric Sussman, and Atkinson's counsel, Benito Romano, former U.S. attorney in New York, cold-shouldered Greg Craig. But these gestures had all proved futile.

Atkinson was not prepared to engage in pure invention, though he came close with his self-serving pieties about trying to curb the airplane use and reduce expenses. In fact, he had a mandate from me to produce drastic reductions in aircraft expenses but failed to do anything. Too conscientious not to recognize his own responsibility, too priggish to face up to it altogether, too frightened to fight it out from the start, he was doomed to a sad fate: seeking mercy through contrition, then vindication in court when cornered, and then pity when he declared himself "a broken man" and adopted a policy of total and righteous submission. He snapped like matchwood in the first forty-eight hours of Breeden's takeover.

Atkinson is a proud and honourable lawyer. His life was the judges and senior lawyers in Toronto, where he had earned respect, and he was not going to plead to anything he had not done, or that would compromise his professional standing. He was defeated but proud and fundamentally honest, and in the end preferred to fight than lie. He was not a bad man, but no one could mistake him for a strong man.

The discussions between the prosecutors and Kipnis and Atkinson were dialogues of the deaf. The prosecutors did not understand a mentality that they could not intimidate, regardless of the facts, into pleading guilty and inculpating others, as the plea bargain system requires. And Atkinson and Kipnis could not understand a system uninterested in the truth.

Those talks collapsed, and because the prosecutors did not want to leave me with the option of blaming the alleged wrongdoing on the companies' lawyers (whose negligence had, in fact, been responsible for what Radler's own misconduct had not wrought), they determined to indict them too. It must be emphasized that these lawyers were men of principle in the end. Kipnis, especially, the mouse under the paw of the prosecution cat in Chicago, was a brave man. Jack Boultbee was a star throughout.

IN SEPTEMBER 2009, THE U.S. attorney's office in Chicago released their sentence recommendation on Radler, made two years before to the trial judge. It detailed Radler's very extensive co-operation, beginning in April 2004, a month after the Strine debacle, going through ten all-day meetings, the handing over of reams of documents, while he continued in our defence group for sixteen months, presumably transmitting information to the prosecutor. (There were endless threats from Eddie Greenspan to take this sleazy practice to some authority concerned with barristerial ethics, but, as is almost always the case in the legal fraternity, where in the end almost all lawyers hold hands to protect their guild, nothing came of it.) After his co-operation was confirmed in November 2004, there were "numerous" more meetings, all through our privatization efforts, when he professed to be fully on board with us (which makes Breeden's easy roll-over of the OSC more understandable). After his plea bargain was announced in August 2005, the "numerous" meetings multiplied and continued through and after the trial. The government explained to the judge that it might not have been able to charge me at all without the co-operation of Radler. He apparently held himself out as an expert in all manner of matters of which, in fact, he was completely ignorant, and that were, in any case, innocuous, such as the workings of some private companies of mine. His imagination was clearly in a prolonged state of overdrive as he garrulously babbled on for the delectation of the Torquemadas for whom he had degraded himself, and who had bemusedly enslaved him. He advised on sales and other transactions in Canada to assist the U.S. prosecutors in urging tax liens and assessments on me by Canada Revenue, and purported to identify "attempted stock manipulation" by me, in concert with Brascan Corporation, years before. This was completely false. Some of the annoyances produced by the Canada Revenue Agency and their resolution have been referred to. They provided Sussman with his ammunition in badgering Canada Revenue to charge me, which it would have loved to do (it has audited me dozens of times in the envious Canadian official manner), but unlike American practice, the agency was not prepared to charge in the absence of any evidence.

The usual plea bargain requirement that the dominoes fall upward, from the middle management to the top, was not met, but with two thin lines of saliva curving downward from the corners of their mouths, the rabid prosecutors panted forward, fuelled by the inflammatory vapour of Breeden's lies and what would soon be revealed as Radler's fatuous conjurations of the "silent" scheme.

The prosecutors were noisily thrashing about in all directions, including trying to imply that I had had an extra-marital relationship with Barbara's and my friend, radio and television news and talk-show personality Laura Ingraham. They pursued this even though it was clear from our many emails that that was not the nature of our relationship. They only desisted when she made it clear that she would not cease to object, to her seven million radio listeners, that the pursuit of me was unjust, and would respond vituperatively, as I would, to any effort to propagate this falsehood. That fact that the whole subject was irrelevant to the legal issues was, of course, irrelevant itself; the prosecutors I encountered were perversely, even dementedly nasty. They had dirty, as well as low, minds.

Ravelston was included in the indictment thus paralyzing the controlling shareholder of Hollinger Inc., and Breeden continued to use Hollinger International in what he represented to be the public service of pursuing me. It also assured the prosecutors' complete domination of the receiver.

The game was already clear from their treatment of Walker at Hollinger Inc.: where there was a management, no matter how implausible and self-serving, they traded non-prosecution of the corporation – and the protection of the U.S. government for the ransacking of the company by those who were supposedly managing it – for the complete and servile co-operation of that management with the government's assault on me. Where the management was a receiver or other official, the bargain was similar. The receiver, Richter, could remain in place and rifle Ravelston for whatever it could find, as long as it knuckled under to the U.S. prosecutor and co-operated in any way possible with prosecution battle plans.

Eddie Greenspan would indirectly completely fluster and distract the Chicago prosecutors by giving a tutorial to the Ravelston receiver's counsel on how to avoid the service of the action on Ravelston. As that company had no presence or assets in the United States, it could only be served in that country if it chose to facilitate the prosecution. The American officials were reduced to huffing and puffing and threatening to treat Ravelston like a fugitive from justice. Since Farley, Toronto's chief commercial judge, who had granted the receivership application, had stayed all proceedings against Ravelston, he now had his chance to bat down the Chicago bully boys.

I assumed he would roll over for the American prosecutors, though my absence from a direct involvement made this a more suspenseful issue than it would otherwise have been. One of the Canadian counsel asked the Americans what they were going to do. "Send up the Marines and put Ravelston's corporate seal in prison?"

Predictably, the receiver and its counsel waffled and announced Ravelston would enter a plea of not guilty – a totally unnecessary thing to do – with Farley's permission. They could simply have ignored the whole thing. Ravelston was my private company, holding shares and real estate in Canada. We all assumed (correctly, it turned out) that Richter would change the plea to guilty after the proverbial decent interval as long as they could take everything moveable out of Ravelston for themselves. Ravelston's receiver was supported by Hollinger Inc. and Hollinger International, who presented themselves as stakeholders. However, the only involvement they could claim were spurious lawsuits.

Eddie Greenspan rose splendidly to the occasion in Farley's court on October 3, 2005. He pointed out that Ravelston's receiver's counsel had no capacity to enter a plea and that the U.S. government had no standing to charge Ravelston. It was all very galling. The receiver was pledged to uphold the interest of the Ravelston stakeholders, of which I was the major one, but was appeasing the enemies of the stakeholders and was intimidated by the U.S. prosecutors. The receiver, the controllers of the Hollinger companies, Justices Farley and Campbell, and the Chicago prosecutors were all ostentatious partisans on the same side of this issue.

As I had assumed, Farley threw out Greenspan's motion. He treated Greenspan respectfully, but took his usual free shots at me, referring sarcastically again to the "old guard." He warned that I must not be seen to be dominating the receiver and associated me as closely as possible with Radler by alleging that "Black and Radler had been running Ravelston."

Radler had nothing to do with running Ravelston; he had one-fifth of the shareholding in it that I had. Greenspan went at once to the Court of Appeal with an excellent motion pointing out the many legal errors in Farley's finding. I had seen enough of Toronto's courts to have a strong premonition of the result, and was not surprised when Farley's misjudgment was upheld. The judicial deference system in and around Osgoode Hall seemed to immunize the lower court judges from having most findings of fact overturned. They visited a formidable variety of such unjust judicial divinations upon me, until, difficult years later, the fashion changed and piling on to me was less popular and less fun. It was never after this far from my thoughts that Ravelston need never have reported to the jurisdiction. I assumed that Farley, in his perverse judgment, understood it would penalize us financially, while Richter went happily along to receive their blank cheque from the prosecutors to transfer the whole value of the asset to themselves, from the stakeholders whose interests they were so richly rewarded for protecting.

So my business partner of thirty-six years was a crook and a liar after all. From the start of this horror show, he told me that he would never have dreamt of doing anything illegal and that there had been errors of execution by Boultbee, Kipnis, and Atkinson. Early on, he had claimed to Peter White that after he had completed the negotiations with the buyers of our community newspapers, the financial instructions had come from Jack Boultbee and me. As has been recorded in his lawyer's letter to Paris and Thompson of November 2003, he had claimed that I had "initiated" the payments in respect of the U.S. community newspaper transactions. He had acknowledged to me that what he meant was that I had said that he should be rewarded for such a brilliant disposition of assets. I did say that, and he should have been.

I had in mind, as he knew, a payment from Ravelston, not a non-compete payment, but when he told me non-compete payments had been approved by the Audit Committee for all of us and that nothing from Ravelston was necessary, and when Atkinson assured me that all was in good legal order, I did not intervene from London to have my Toronto office send back the non-compete cheque when it came in. For years afterward, the auditors and Audit Committee confirmed that everything had been done properly. Thus advised by an associate of more than thirty-five years, personal counsel of more than fifteen years, and the company's overpaid accounting watchdogs, I can't imagine anyone acting differently.

If we were successful in a criminal trial, the entire assault on me would collapse. The civil cases would be fallen soufflés and the public and press bias would shift. Nothing could restore the life Barbara and I had lost, nor take back the years Barbara and I, who were no longer young, would have squandered in this desperate defence against American persecution and its Canadian excrescences. But here, at last, was a possible victorious end to the nightmare.

In order to lay in a cash reserve sufficient to deal with the upcoming legal fees, I sold our New York cooperative apartment for a generous capital gain and gross consideration of more than $10 million. The closing kept being rolled back in a manner that made me uneasy. The buyer's lawyer, the ubiquitous Skadden Arps (whose chairman, Ken Bialkin, was and remains a friend and supporter), had written up a title search that presented me as a virtual Al Capone figure and had presumed to contact the ineffable Sussman directly to ensure there was no problem with their clients' acquisition of our unit at 635 Park Avenue.

Once again, and for the second time in four months, the gallant Barbara cleaned out a residence of ours and all the contents were moved to, and generally accommodated in, our Toronto home. The influx of paintings vastly lifted the quality of what was on our walls. She "hated giving up this apartment," which was not large but was comfortable for our purposes, but she did it with pluck and thoroughness. I was still retreating to a defensible perimeter, as the most ominous storm signals yet were being hoisted daily.

The U.S. government was going to indict. My business associate of thirty-six years was not going to snitch and blow his whistle – that would not be possible, since I had not done anything illegal. What he was to swear to, however, was designed to bury me and release him. His lawyer, Valukas, was now seen and reported in ardent whispered debate, rising occasionally into button-holing and shouting, in the corridors of the courthouse, with the prosecutors. And Williams & Connolly, without actually having done anything useful or difficult, or even given correct advice, were still vibrating in public about whether they would really act for me. The legal front was wobbling before a shot of live ammunition had been fired. I was counting on the receding closing in the Park Avenue apartment to keep Brendan Sullivan in the firing line.

Radler finally made and announced his plea bargain in late September, reading his confession to the grand jury, of whose existence Williams & Connolly had been confidently unaware for many months. Radler's statement was as preposterous as could be imagined, even from him. He told the performing bonzes on the grand jury, which the Fifth Amendment to the U.S. Constitution assures us is a solid defence against capricious prosecution, that there had been a "silent" scheme. The scheme had never been discussed, much less written about, as we simply did not tell the Audit Committee about these non-compete agreements I had supposedly told Radler to issue. This monstrous assertion, presented by such an ill-favoured witness, was not going to do it for The People, despite all the prosecution's advantages, when they faced a serious defence, provided I could field competent lawyers.

Radler made his wretched court appearance in Chicago on September 20. He produced nothing useful for his new masters. He had been "tasked" by "Toronto" to get the non-compete payments for Hollinger Inc. and "surmised" that "the chairman" knew about it because only I had the authority to order such a step. In other words, he acknowledged I wasn't on the call, if it occurred at all. This was the best Valukas could do. But so full of blood lust for me were the prosecutors, brainwashed by Breeden (a minimal laundering challenge, as I soon discovered), that they leaked Radler's allegations endlessly to the press, who were at the edges of their chairs after a two-year tease before my indictment.

Hollinger International's lawyer sat at the prosecutors' table in the court. There was no longer even a pretense that it was not a common front against me. My former associate would receive a six-month sentence (twenty-nine months but with a transfer to Canada that would reduce it to six months). But I felt that no jury in the world could convict me on the basis of Radler's evidence.

In the American manner, which bears a startling resemblance to the Stalinist formula of prisoners coming meekly into court and condemning themselves, Radler gave his "allocution," confessing criminality, lies, and cowardice, and apologizing for his contemptible behaviour. This last part was the only accurate part of his presentation, though it is extremely unlikely that he was sincere in stating it.

He was, in fact, pleased that he had escaped the maelstrom, secure, he thought, in his shady swindling of me in the private newspaper company he had siphoned out of Hollinger International (where, again, although he had said we would be equal partners, he had twice as many shares as I did). He was assured of a sentence of six months, in a penal horse farm near Vancouver offering golf therapy, creative theatre arts, and equestrian diversions.

Obviously, the accused in this case was, in fact, a criminal, and he had not been tortured physically, as Stalin's victims were. But the U.S.

prosecution system does seize and immobilize assets, often on the basis of false affidavits and by exploiting laws of questionable constitutionality, designed to combat terrorists or organized crime; deluges a suspect with subpoenas, civil charges from regulators and ambulance-chasers, and relentless harassment from the IRS and SEC; and assures massive defamation. It is a form of mental torture.

Radler, unlike Stalin's targets, did not demand to be executed as soon as possible for his crimes (as an opponent of capital punishment, I would object to such a fate for anyone, but such a demand from him would have been euphonious). The spectacle of this man, who in the thirty-six years of our acquaintance never admitted a mistake other than his harmless clumsiness with gadgets, confessing to criminal dishonesty and cowardice was almost refreshing.

Yet it was also repulsive, not only because it was untrue, like the absurd statement that followed it, but because it demonstrated the dishonesty of a man I had been closely commercially associated with for decades and the power of intimidation of the U.S. prosecutors.

The nature of the U.S. plea bargain system had been repellant to me for many years, and I was, as in so many other related matters, about to receive a bruising practical education in it. It is the exchange of testimony for varied sentences. It generally starts well down in an organization and brings irresistible pressures to bear on people unable to sustain themselves psychologically or defend themselves financially against such an onslaught – until that person promises to inculpate a higher-up.

The process goes through an organization until sometimes scores of intimidated or suborned people are accusing the chosen target. It is an evil and profoundly corrupt process. It is not reconcilable with traditional American notions of the rule of law. Every informed person in the country knows that the criminal justice system is based on officially sanctioned fraud and intimidation, that the courthouses are silent and the courts empty because almost no one can go the distance with the government, and that there are tens of thousands of innocent people in U.S. prisons because of the false confessions and accusations that are extorted. But almost no one says anything about it.

Once Breeden scared off private equity investors, and especially after he crossed me on the November 15, 2003, agreement that unearthed the opinionated, self-gratified hip-shooter Leo Strine, I was in a power dive. I knew the Breeden report would be murderous, and he held up the dividend of any proceeds from the Hollinger International sale of the *Telegraph* (having promised to sell the whole company and failed to do so) until it was very late for me to do anything with Hollinger Inc. The U.S. prosecutors got to the compliant Harvey Strosberg, Gordon Walker, Tony Kelly, and Bobby Kofman very quickly.

My sunset gun was the Hollinger Inc. privatization, but I hoped in vain that the OSC would not destroy the public shareholders and save Breeden's fiefdom. As with the judges and tax collectors in Canada, who wrap themselves in the Maple Leaf at all other opportunities, the national parlour game to get me was too addictive. The proverbial widows and orphans who had invested in Hollinger Inc. could go to the wall.

Radler, skilled at tough talk to defenceless people and at the firing of superfluous employees (a necessary task but one that can be accomplished more humanely and stylishly than was his custom), watched as Ravelston went into receivership and as I was evicted from my own building, and noted my complete humiliation in the videotape affair.

I SUPPOSE I HAD SEEN FROM THE START that it could come to this, even without Radler's defection. It was painfully ironic: I was a qualified U.S. historian; I had been denounced in the parliaments of Canada and the United Kingdom for my pro-U.S. sympathies – and now I was about to be assaulted by the U.S. government. This greatest of all countries was about to try to end the useful career and perhaps even the natural life of one of its most vociferous admirers, in the U.S. prison system, on the strength of baseless allegations.

My former career as a perceived media mogul, a London Fleet Street baron in that formidable tradition, which had been thirty-five years in the making, had been extinguished in a few days. I was realistic about the scale and speed of my reversal. I made no compromise with the objective collapse of my status and the gratuitous cataract of misfortunes that followed. Never had I appreciated so much Napoleon's most brilliant aphorism as he began the retreat from Moscow, that "from the sublime to the ridiculous is a single step." My position had never been sublime, but it quickly became ridiculous.

I was more afraid of the financial wars than of the legal ones. My financial condition was again becoming parlous. I was counting on the proceeds of our New York apartment sale to prevent Brendan Sullivan from deserting a ship from which he seemed to think all the valuable cargo had been removed.

Apart from the legal and financial challenges, which were constant and treacherous, the challenge was now to maintain personal dignity without appearing to be residing in a fantasyland of denial. My new vocation by necessity would be to resist the Goliath of the abusive American prosecution system and accomplices in Canadian middle officialdom and to fight the tendency of the Western media to rush to judgment in a presumption of guilt.

This would be a desperate game of chance. I had no reason to agonize over it, as there was no alternative. I would go to prison for life before I would plead guilty to crimes I had not committed, much less utter a Radlerian allocution and wrongly accuse others.

My Roman Catholicism required me to confess and repent improper conduct, and if I had committed a crime, I would have pleaded guilty and accepted a punishment that would enable me to atone and expiate, to redress society's just grievances against me. I believe in the punishment of crimes. This was something else; it was the punishment of faults, attitudes, and public relations misperceptions, and of misfortune, especially having a crooked associate, but I was the victim, not the author, of crimes – Radler's frauds, the U.S. government's impending false accusations, widespread defamation, and, still to come in a torrent, Radler's and others' falsehoods in the court in Chicago, as eventually even prosecutors would confirm when they turned on their own witnesses. I do not believe in false, extorted, or unspontaneous allocutions, which demean the spirit of confession and repentance and reduce justice to corruptly procured self-humiliation. I regularly scoured my own conscience and was a more frequent confessant and penitent than usual, keeping my moral ramparts strong, but never attenuated by sanctimony.

It was an unsought honour, but it was about to come to me – to try to resist the decay of American justice, the degeneration of the grand jury into a prosecutor's rubber stamp, the hollowing out of due process, and the suspension of the guaranty against uncompensated seizure of property (all in the Fifth Amendment, along with the rights against self-incrimination), and to uphold assurances of prompt justice, access to counsel, an impartial jury, and reasonable bail (in the Sixth and Eighth Amendments). Almost any task, no matter how raw, can be attempted if it has some grandeur, and especially if it is the only way to avoid a terrible fate.

I was very aware that the end might be imprisonment. This was in some respects an ennobling prospect; if I was to be completely humbled, in conventional and bourgeois terms, I hoped to be elevated in moral terms. I could certainly establish that I was innocent, even if an American jury could be cajoled or dragooned by rabid prosecutors into finding me guilty.

Up to a point, the greater the injustice, the more complete the revulsion would be when cant and emotionalism subsided and the degraded system was seen in the light, in its ghastly infirmity.

I had been attempting to privatize my company, retain the *Telegraph* and the Chicago assets, and reorient their brands into the Internet age. It was the only strategy that would have worked, but it collapsed, the companies were destroyed in the name of corporate governance, and the franchises atrophied in incapable hands. It wasn't the exit strategy I had sought, or the successor occupation I would have chosen, but at least I had a mission, full of desperate purpose and some drama. The game was afoot, all could still be won, and victory and defeat both had their attractions: instant vindication or the vindication of aggravated injustice.

And I had already started to envision my strategy for dealing with legal defeat, should it occur: a strategic retreat to another jurisdiction. I could provoke a trial in the U.K. or Canada, on a side issue such as my Canadian libel cases where the Ontario courts have already indicated they might apply the test of whether a court in Canada would return a guilty verdict if seized of the same evidence. Of course, they would not; British or Canadian prosecutors would be disbarred for the routine conduct of American prosecutors, extorting and suborning perjury. I would never relent and I could not be silenced, as long as I remained alive and in funds. This was total war.

—

THE FINANCIAL SQUEEZE WOULD begin again if the Park Avenue sale weren't completed fairly soon. I even entertained an overture from a Russian Canadian for our Toronto house. As usual in these times, it was not so much an offer as a proposal so miserly, it bordered on attempted theft.

I was awaiting the end of the cease-trade order on Barbara's Hollinger International stock, which was dependent on International getting up to date on its quarterly filings. All present and previous officers and directors were under a cease-trade order until that was done. The enemy had dragged out the lawsuit for indemnification of my Williams & Connolly bills until near the end of the year. The endless press barrage and general conventional wisdom that I was about to be indicted complicated matters. Murdoch's *New York Post* opened a column with: "Tick-tock, tick-tock, as the clock ticks toward Conrad Black's imprisonment." Normally one waits for the charge, if not the evidence, or even, in the case of extreme traditionalists, the verdict, but not my former friend Rupert Murdoch's journalists.

Barbara and I went to Washington in late August 2005. The indictments of Radler et al. had caused the Justice Department to stay discovery in the civil proceedings, which spared me the unpleasant choice of testifying or, as was for me inevitable in these circumstances, exercising my Fifth Amendment rights, which is damaging in civil proceedings.

In my more suspicious moments, I wondered whether Breeden had organized the mini-bar inspectors in our hotel. The highlight of the visit was Barbara's and my conversation with Brendan Sullivan. For the first time in my acquaintance with him, he showed some sense of humour, and he revealed with emotional eloquence how much he hated the "evil and repulsive system" we were fighting.

Elton John and David Furnish were in Toronto and came to lunch at our home. It was a generous gesture considering Elton's tight schedule. When Elton came out on our terrace before lunch, his view was of the rolling lawns and hillocks, no flower beds or garden vanities to interfere with the prospect of grass and trees and the ravine. "It's a good thing you have this place, to keep your sanity," he said. This was true.

I managed to get around a bit. Sir Winston Churchill's biographer Sir Martin Gilbert, speaking at a Jewish function, opened with a very warm commendation of my Roosevelt book and of me personally. My social outings were commented on in the press less breathlessly than they had been. I met and quickly became friendly with the brilliant and delightful Richard Bradshaw, who had turned the Canadian Opera Company orchestra into a first-class one and who had built the first opera house in Canada, one hundred and forty years after its founding as an independent country. Richard's sudden death from a coronary two years later at the age of sixty-three was a terrible loss to everyone who knew him and to all of Canada. Barbara took his death very hard, in spite of knowing him relatively briefly. He had, she said, that kind of blazing personality that could bore into your soul in an instant. His being was so intimately tied up in her mind with music, and music in turn was so intimately a part of her being, that she felt it as an amputation.

Writing every other week in the *National Post*, and later every week, and then in Tina Brown's online *Daily Beast* and Bill Buckley's *National Review* as well, was an interesting diversion, and helped me focus on the great world beyond my own travails, including many humorous subjects. Barbara was asked back to *Maclean's* by the new editor and publisher, Ken Whyte. She accepted. Those who had so brutally dismissed her were fired themselves. These were small portents, perhaps, but a start at regaining lost territory, and even a flickering of natural justice. We fought on in sober but stable spirits.

As the impasse over completion of the sale of our New York apartment dragged on, I didn't unpack all the boxes that poured in from there. The Toronto house became very full. Every day at 7:15 a.m. I heard the plaintive beeping of an alarm clock inside one of the packing cases in my dressing room. I finally opened the carton and rummaged through it. It was a little red clock Bill and Pat Buckley had given us for having them as guests on a chartered yacht cruise along the Côte d'Azur in 1996. It had been emitting little squeaks of purposefulness every twelve hours since it was packed up in New York. I resettled it on the vanity of my bathroom.

Brian Mulroney, who was very supportive throughout this ordeal, volunteered to organize a group of wealthy friends who would help me with legal bills by subscribing a second mortgage on our Palm Beach house. I deferred this, though I was grateful, because I hoped to come through the nightmare beholden to no one, having been deserted once before by some from whom I had expected more.

While I was scrambling to find the means to defend myself, Breeden announced he was setting up a hedge fund. This was a man who acknowledged he had not made a success of his own $200 million business in his only foray into commerce. Breeden's hedge fund has, at time of writing, been a failure. He is a plodding stickler, dogged, like a spider killing anything that touches its web. He does not have a personality that can be transported successfully outside exploitation of the inner strings of the official bureaucracy.

I WAS IN WASHINGTON IN OCTOBER, partly for the annual dinner of the Nixon Center, where I had a nice talk with the irrepressible Gordon Liddy, the only one of Nixon's aides who didn't break and run.

I met with an unshakably cheerful Greg Craig, who had assured me constantly that there was no possibility of an interruption of the sale of the New York apartment, which was now my big worry. I had breakfast the next morning with the author and journalist George Will, who could not have been more upbeat and supportive, some other appointments, and was preparing for lunch with another friend when, as *Private Eye* magazine used to write, "the telephone rang."

Craig and John Warden and Ben Stapleton of Sullivan & Cromwell, the firm that had written up the closing in New York, telephoned to tell me that when contracts were exchanged and the cheque handed over at Skadden Arps' offices, two palookas from the FBI rushed in and seized the money, brandishing a warrant issued *ex parte* by a magistrate under what was shortly proved to be a false affidavit, attesting that I had effectively stolen the apartment from Hollinger International. The prosecutors who would have put the FBI agent up to signing the affidavit should certainly have known that the allegations were untrue.

My ten million dollars had been seized by the FBI. The buyer had my apartment, the U.S. government had my money, I had nothing. I had asked repeatedly about the delays before the closing and was assured, with the same chipper confidence with which I had been told that the Barclay transaction was legally unassailable by different lawyers but with indistinguishable self-assurance, that there was no problem. The seizure was under the Civil Assets Forfeiture Reform Act, directed ostensibly against drug traffickers. I was given no notice of anything before the *ex parte* seizure. And it had nothing to do with justice. The FBI affidavit did not mention that I had personally spent $4.6 million on renovating and decorating the apartment, much less that Hollinger International, not I, had been obligated to make those expenditures.

A Tower of Babel of conflicting advice ensued. The lawyers of Sullivan & Cromwell, Williams & Connolly, and even Baker Botts, who were not directly involved, rivalled one another in their war cries of impending victory over this monstrous overreach. Brendan Sullivan himself, who had cost me almost $2 million per brief conversation, called to say that it could be undone.

Craig had thought that there might be some utility in a private talk with the assistant U.S. attorney in Chicago, Eric Sussman, who had orchestrated the seizure with Skadden Arps. The thought horrified me by its naïveté. Sullivan said there was no point having "friendly talks" with U.S. prosecutors, that we should go straight to court alleging a false affidavit, false facts, and false law, all employed for the discreditable and unconstitutional purpose of trying to deny me the means of self-defence. "Prosecutors," he averred, "are like Pavlov's dog."

When I spoke to Sullivan again the following day, though cautious, he thought that "when the government acts this aggressively, it often makes mistakes, and seems to have done so this time. There may be a chance to get a New York court to slap them, hard." Joan Maida had sent them all the supporting materials, showing the millions I had spent on the apartment, and Sullivan instructed his juniors to work through the weekend preparing the papers.

I returned home after dinner on October 11, to find that I had been poleaxed by my enemies again. Despite the fact that there were 380,000 Google entries on asset freezes and forfeitures, it took until that night for the aggregation of Brendan Sullivan, the vacationing Greg Craig (this week in Europe), and the rest of the well-paid Williams & Connolly team to figure out that the Civil Assets Forfeiture Reform Act of five years before ensured that there would be no quick recovery of anything. The freeze was in place, and as soon as we pointed out that their affidavit was fraudulent and the discovery procedure began, our suit would be stayed – delayed – with the other criminal-related civil actions.

The U.S. government was reduced to snooping around like a second-storey man, looking for a balcony door that had been left unlocked, and to mouthing threats in the hope of finding accomplices such as Radler. It put witless FBI agents up to signing false affidavits so rubber-stamp magistrates could conduct *ex parte* asset seizures and defendants could not defend themselves. The constitutional guarantees of due process and against uncompensated seizure and promising access to counsel had become fables, heirlooms of America's past, like the legend of Rip Van Winkle, and George Washington and his cherry tree. In these matters the whole country had gone to sleep. And Sleepy Hollow is terrorized by vicious prosecutors.

Each week in my travails seemed to yield new evidence of the corruption of the system; the plea bargaining–intimidated perjury; the assault on the indemnity for legal costs; the abuse of obstruction of justice; the planted defamations; the threatened invocation of "racketeering" against people who were, as even Leo Strine said of me, anything but racketeers; illegal telephone intercepts (which sweeps revealed, as did bugs on our furniture in New York) – one day the monitor flipped the wrong switch and Barbara and I heard them chatting inconsequentially through their bugging device (which seemed to be concealed in one of her stereo speakers). Normal communication between potential defendants was interdicted. There were fiendish attempts at financial strangulation (asset freezes, fake tax liens, and threats made of unspecific prosecution against mortgagees, such as mine in Palm Beach who was told by the inimitable Sussman that if he renewed my mortgage his company would be prosecuted somehow in the Chicago area). As it arrested the payment side of our apartment sale, the IRS seized $700,000 of refundable tax. Five years later, it was still trying to deny it had the money which at time of writing after threatening to litigate to recover, and after obtained affidavits to prove that they received the money has just been returned to me. No one should invest any credence in the proposition that the U.S. government exhibits many traits of the rule of law that it purports endlessly to be upholding "among ourselves and with all nations." It may do or it may not, and it certainly did not with me.

Rosemary Millar ran my London office from 1989 to 2004. She had a heavy cold at the time my legal problems broke, which shortly became pneumonia, and then was diagnosed as inoperable lung cancer. She paid for expensive treatment at the London Clinic with her Hollinger stock options, but died in 2004, aged only sixty-one. She was a wonderfully capable, dignified, and good-humoured person, and her death is one of the greatest sadnesses of this entire cataract of horrible events.

Joan Maida, my doughty and implacable and very nimble executive assistant in Toronto for twenty years. She is modelling a "Conrad Will Win" T-shirt, which, with other shirts of similar inspiration, were quite successful commercially. She has been invaluable, in good times and bad, and there has been much of both. She and Rosemary Millar got on perfectly, and I am deeply indebted to both of them.

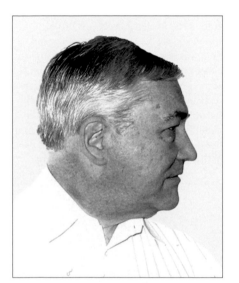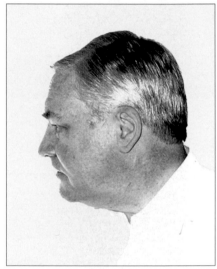

Photographs of me taken at the time I surrendered to custody in March 2008. Though the day of my imprisonment (March 3) began as the worst moment of my life, I soon saw that prison would be survivable, though Spartan, and felt my fortunes, which had plunged so deeply, had begun to recover. So they had.

A sketch of me by a fellow prisoner in the middle of my sentence. There was an immense amount of talent among the prisoners, in all arts and crafts as well as electrical, mechanical, and other trades.

At Coleman Low Security Prison with three inmate friends, Jacques (left), a colourful French Canadian who taught me a rudimentary knowledge of the piano and was a gourmet cook; Francis (centre), an Ecuadorian "exporter" to Russia (both were released while I was in prison); and Jackie, a Colombian in the clothing business. They were memorable characters and I would be happy to see them again.

And there were the grasping lawyers. Most of the private sector counsel, prosecutors, and judges lock arms in a cartel to milk anyone who stumbles into the sticky official bouillabaisse behind the revered facade of the rule of law. They all love the system, they all think they are intellectually more elevated than almost all their clients, they are almost all more interested in being well paid than in the outcome of the case, and they are almost all friendlier with prosecutors and opposing counsel than with their clients. The lawyers had to be fed hundreds of thousands of dollars all the time or they would defect and join the serried ranks of those litigating against me, to collect unearned income. Brendan Sullivan, in the most famous statement of his career, told the Iran-Contra Committee of the U.S. Congress that "the American lawyer is not a potted plant." Perhaps not, but he is watered like one.

Mercifully, there were a few exceptions, such as Sullivan & Cromwell and Eddie Greenspan, and later Andy Frey, Miguel Estrada, and many of our specialist lawyers. And some other lawyers were not exclusively rapacious self-seekers, but many were. Brendan Sullivan himself, whose barristerial talents are not at issue, is not at all a vain man, and he sincerely detests the corruption of the American justice system.

THERE WAS NO RELIEF TO THE terrible loneliness. Barbara and I went out into the world most days, and lived very comfortably in our splendid house in Toronto, yet we had no community of interest with any but a few people, sociable though I was. Others led normal lives, had normal jobs or professions, were not excessively or nastily referred to in the press, and did not fear that any day the police might be at their doors, carrying out search warrants or charging them with heinous crimes of which they were totally innocent.

I had Greenspan school my staff on how to deal with any such intrusion. I had tired of having my files purloined, deliberately misplaced, leaked in spliced excerpts to the press, and destroyed. The terrorist apparat was always with us. It was not, as I often mused, Kafka, Orwell, or Koestler, but it wasn't America the beautiful or Canada the unblemished snow-maiden of the North either.

Every asset realization I made was so long delayed by official obstruction or equal-opportunity, imitative, private sector shilly-shallying that by the time the proceeds arrived, legal bills had grown like steroid-bloated rodents and devoured much of the funds, while the indemnified rebates were denied and had to be litigated endlessly, producing more bills and another round of the cycle. There was minimal due process, only an infernal machine to destroy designated targets and grind them to powder in the gears of the American justice system, while the free press cheered, before anything was adjudicated.

It was all couched in that pompous legalese that would lead the uninitiated to believe that it was an honourable system run by honourable people. In fact, once focused on a target, prosecutors would adapt their interpretations of the facts to produce the desired verdict. The absence of evidence was not indicative of possible innocence but merely of the fiendish ingenuity of the culprit in covering his tracks, and of the superior sleuthing of the prosecutor in continuing to pursue him.

Canada, though less vicious, being a smaller jungle with smaller beasts in it, was not appreciably better. In my experience, the Canadian procedural rules are fairer, the courts are less indulgent of runaway government, fewer judges and legislators are ex-prosecutors, but lawyers were generally not as competent, and the judges were more servile marionettes of the media faddists. As in many other spheres, Canada was a junior league for the colossal engine of injustice Americans know little of as they stand at public events, hands over their hearts, singing their splendid anthems. I wondered how could the country of Franklin and Jefferson, Madison and Lincoln, have come to this?

The Justice Department gleefully announced the New York seizure of my assets, so it was on the Friday late-evening news in Canada when I returned home and in the Saturday morning Canadian and American newspapers. The department intended this to be a show of strength. I thought the reverse. It wasn't so much that the law was an ass, it was that the American state had become a gangster. For almost the first time, I was more disappointed in America than angry, more contemptuous than outraged.

By this time, I had no more faith in the Great Man theory of lawyering than the Great Man in question apparently had in my ability to pay him. Craig had the effrontery to ask me to sign a new retainer agreement before his firm would even appear on my behalf in this New York action. I signed it, but by this time, after a few days, the pep talks of moral and legal invincibility had moderated. It was a familiar pattern: lawyerly bellicosity, new retainer, new invoices, bellicosity gives way to sobriety and staying the course, and then it all fades away like the "lone and level sand" around Shelley's monument to Ozymandias – except for the next Desert Storm of legal invoices.

Craig wrote up a good brief. He recited the omissions in the FBI affidavit and concluded that the government was trying to "take away David's sling-shot just as he is about to meet Goliath." It was a good line, and it was accurate. The government should have known perfectly well that its allegations were rubbish. The prosecutor's sole motive was to strangle me financially just as the government was going to lay its indictment. Sussman cockily took Craig's telephone call and emitted peals of laughter at what he thought to be his surpassing cunning.

Craig happily told me that in the indictment that was about to come, Sussman wanted me to live in my Florida house, presumably to facilitate his further harassments and oppressions (not that the Canadian authorities had been much of a breakwater against them up to this point). Craig, who had been pretty peppy about my chances in a trial, had suddenly become quite sombre and belatedly claimed to realize that the Audit Committee would be frog-marched into court in the same mendacious procession as Radler, and that it would be an "uphill fight." He implied that I should consider Sussman's wish that I move to Palm Beach. I dismissed the suggestion.

The worry about money was haunting me, as my tormentors intended it to do. My homes, all of which had greatly appreciated in value, had been fortresses, as subjects of mortgages and then of sales. Now they were to be turned into a trap, illiquid because of the U.S. government's persecution of me, in response to the antlike movements of Breeden. As Joan Maida said, "People are screaming for money," and I was down to $500,000 in cash, which sounds like a lot but isn't when you have legal bills and houses to maintain and staff to pay, and have great difficulty raising a fair price for any asset. "Money, Money, Money" (from the musical *Cabaret*) was never far from my thoughts.

Months of work and worry and Barbara's evacuation of our home on Park Avenue (during which she sprained her shoulder and developed a tennis elbow from the sorting and packing and unpacking) were snuffed out in a moment with the hippopotamus-walk of the two FBI agents through the closing room. Barbara was now being harassed and threatened by the IRS over her tax arrangements, undertaken on sound professional advice, and unexceptionable at that.

On the Sunday two days after the New York theft, October 9, I was on the upstairs landing of our main staircase, adjusting my sweater before going out for a bicycle ride, when a fine Franck Muller watch Barbara had given me flipped off my wrist, bounced onto the carpet and through the narrow opening between the balusters, and fell fifteen feet to the marble floor below.

To replicate this move, I would have had to get down on my hands and knees and feed it between the spars. It seemed to be the end of a valuable watch that I valued in the way people become sentimentally attached to timepieces. I wondered whether I could do nothing right, no matter how mundane or banal. (The watch was repaired, gratis, by a friendly and thoughtful jeweller.)

In what I am sure he considered a generous and thoughtful gesture, Brendan Sullivan called and said I could give my entire defence to a bright young lawyer. He named Joe Califano's son and said $2 million would do it. (Califano Sr. had been Lyndon Johnson's chief of staff.) Brendan was clearly heading for the tall grass, where so many in this dismal cavalcade had preceded him. His terms now were that if I put up $25 million in advance, he would take the case. If I put up $8 million, I could have Greg Craig. It was like taking the ride up to the observation deck on a high building. You pay on the ground and get on the elevator. Halfway up, the elevator stops, and you can pay again or come back down without having a panoramic view. Out of financial necessity as well as irritation at their behaviour, and at the ravenous practices of American law firms, I took the second of these options and ended relations with Williams & Connolly.

I had paid nearly $9 million for the deterrent and comforting power of Brendan Sullivan. He did not deter, his comfort did not last, and as a parting shot, Williams & Connolly told me that if I did not pay a $400,000 arrears to a data-collection business, for which I had been handsomely billed and on which the other co-defendants, including Radler, had been free-loading, the whole data base would be scrapped. It was very enervating. I retained cordial though distant relations with Brendan and Greg. They are good lawyers but weren't really engaged with me. Greg went on to be White House counsel for President Barack Obama's first year but departed somewhat acrimoniously, and not back to Brendan's firm.

It was a sad Kol Nidre night for Barbara, who, until the FBI stole our money in New York the previous Friday, had been planning to go to London and observe the High Holy days in her synagogue. Instead, she sat with me for a time listening to a recording of the cantor, and I read from her prayer book. I promised that, within my abilities: "Next year in London," where all her friends had been looking forward to seeing her. The previous year she had been at synagogue with Neal Kozodoy, the editor of *Commentary* magazine, in New York. This year she was at home with me on the Days of Awe and Atonement, when she wished to be with her people. American notions of justice denied her even this, and she finished the evening gloomily trying to retrieve records to fend off the IRS witch hunt against her.

Bile continued to ooze and suppurate from some ancient, foul orifices, such as the mouth and pen of Peter C. Newman. The most obnoxious reflections of all, it seemed, were in his autobiography. He managed more than seven hundred pages, in which his principal claim for himself, and the one that was excerpted, was that he had "invented" Barbara and me. He therefore ironically confessed some responsibility for our supposedly wretched and pitiful demise as substantial people. He bought entirely into the "gutsy" Strine line and the imperishable virtue of "Dick" Breeden.

The section about Barbara was the lowest, nastiest, most revolting piece of journalistic sewage I have read. Newman purported to be the all-seeing connoisseur of our bedroom and from his lurid and neurotic imagination explained to readers and then to interviewers that Barbara hooked me with her sexual wiles, which he purported to detail, with a ghoulishly prurient imagination. Further, Barbara had incited me, credulous dupe as I was, to unsustainable extravagance. She had always publicly given Newman credit as the editor who gave her a chance as a columnist at *Maclean's* in 1977 but had no social relationship with him and had no idea that his feelings were so bitter or so twisted. Both her former husband, George Jonas, and I urged her not to read the book, and she has not.

Barbara and I had both long since gone through the wall in terms of being much affected by such comment. But it was hard to believe that matters had sunk to such a point that a supposedly reputable writer could pen such vulgar drivel and that we should have to endure such abuse. Our condition was so strained that there was nothing to do but fight it out and rely on ultimate financial and legal vindication to resolve the public relations disaster – with the assistance of massive libel suits at the appropriate time, when they would not get in the way of more substantive litigation. I did eventually win a partial retraction from Newman, and in 2007 I emerged fully intact from a series of sharp exchanges with him in the *National Post*, where I debunked some of his more notorious statements on subjects having nothing to do with me. Later, when my imprisonment loomed, he delighted every Canadian television program, as he said, "except *Bowling for Dollars*" with speculation that I would be sentenced to fifteen years and would be raped in prison while Barbara would desert me and return to England in search of her fifth husband. This putrefied gossip's preoccupation with such lurid public ruminations was apparently inexhaustible.

It was objectively sad; in addition to his talents, he had also often been a fairly agreeable dinner companion, but had an irrational compulsion to destroy relationships. He had had his moments, including some brilliant moments as a political columnist, author, and editor, but was outrun by events: the name died before the man, and his declining years have been nasty and disturbed.

Another champion of vicious mendacity, and without any redeeming quality or talent or mitigating excuse such as Newman's bilious senescence, was the malodorous English pseudo-biographer Tom Bower. He was a minor pestilence who had festered and pustullated on the edges of journalism and trash books and emerged like the expectant undertaker whenever any prominent financier was under siege. His opening message in a personal email to me was not a surprise, in fact or in tenor. It was an earnest, hearty, old colleagues, jolly-hockey-sticks overture to set the record straight, at the request of unidentified people who felt that he as author and I as subject must be united.

I naturally invited him not to attempt such a pitiful deception. It shortly emerged that he had been put up to this by the Murdoch organization, HarperCollins. I had some friends whom he did not know were particularly friendly with me, ply him with drink (not much of a challenge, apparently), record their conversations, and provide me with the evidence that his book was to be a malicious assault in which he was just going through the motions before smearing everyone related to me.

His violent onslaught on Barbara again amazed me. He accused my father of being a chronic and almost catatonic drunkard, even during his active business career, which was exceedingly successful. I had never made a successful deal, operated an asset effectively, or written competently. This innumerate and venomous gossip claimed that for twenty-five years I had "slithered along Bay Street (Toronto's financial district) on life support." He could not accurately or even grammatically record that Jack and Jill went up the hill, yet he accused me of relying on too many secondary sources in my Roosevelt book. (His life's published work possessed less genuine research than any one of my twenty-five chapters on Roosevelt.)

I assumed that News Corporation had indemnified him or HarperCollins would not have allowed such a contemptible and defamatory volume out under its imprimatur. There were more than one hundred and fifty distinct and major libels in it. And it was so ineptly written and edited, it contained many accidental non-sentences. I wrote a very extensive summary of the libels, and we did sue in Canada for $10 million. Almost all Bower's reviews were negative. The *New York Times* called it "a sad little squeak" of a book and enunciated the rule that writers who write vitriolic attacks on other writers should be able to write as well as their targets, and that Bower had failed that test, in respect of both Barbara and me, and had managed the difficult feat of making us seem boring. The press are almost always a pretty job lot, but Bower is an unrecognizable mutation even of the journalist, much less of the authentic author.

IN MID-NOVEMBER CAME THE centenary dinner of *Maclean's* magazine, which celebrated each ten years of its existence with a brief film on the decade. Barbara was one of the introducers of a decade. She looked even more beautiful than ever. At the dinner, Eddie Greenspan had the pleasure of handing Peter C. Newman a libel notice for calling me a criminal, for which we got a retraction. Three days after the dinner, I was formally accused of being a criminal. Barbara learned this from *Report on Business* TV in her bathroom shortly after getting up. There was no notice to us, though we had expected it any day. Peter Atkinson and the intrepid Jack Boultbee were indicted with me. We would be tried together with Mark Kipnis and Ravelston. "LORD BLACK IS INDICTED" was the headline on the banner of the *Globe and Mail*, with a fine picture of Barbara and me from the *Maclean's* dinner.

So dreadful had the tension been that I was glad to be indicted and come face to face with my mortal enemy, who had been stalking me for two years, stirring up lesser beasts of the jungle to nip and snap at me. Finally, they would have to prove something.

With the disembarkation of Brendan Sullivan and Greg Craig, I now had no lawyer. I tried to engage a number of other American law firms, but they all seemed to have been spooked by fear that my finances were parlous and that the case was even more hopeless than most U.S. criminal defenses. Then I thought of Eddie Greenspan. Of course he was a Canadian lawyer, but I assumed the law was not that different in the United States and that he could recruit a compatible and competent American. Greenspan had been born in Niagara Falls and had told me that he had regretted that his father had not gone a little farther when he emigrated from Europe; then he might have been as famous in the United States as he was in Canada. He had a drawing of Clarence Darrow in his office and revered the bar of Chicago, where his daughter had practised.

I asked him if he was interested. He was. At this point, the relentless Eric Sussman was calling for $60 million bail, and the U.S. attorney, Patrick Fitzgerald, was threatening to extradite us. Obviously, the thought was to keep me in jail until the trial on grounds that I could not make bail and, if I did not surrender voluntarily, to label me a fugitive from justice – thus tripling any sentence I might receive. Craig had made no progress with Sussman, who would have gathered from the press, if not from Craig himself, that Craig and his boss were heading for the exit. Greenspan managed to get bond down to a still record-breaking $20 million, consisting in part of the money seized in New York, and the rest secured on a third mortgage, behind my mortgagee and the oversecured Canada Revenue, on the Palm Beach house.

Exorbitant though the sum was, it did not involve any more cash, which I did not have at this point anyway, after the government's Park Avenue heist. Our houseman in Palm Beach had called Joan Maida and told her that there was $20.67 in the house account there, enough to operate the house for about fifteen minutes. These grand houses were mockeries of our former status; we rattled around in them, I thought, like the Romanovs in the Alexander palace, waiting for the Bolsheviks to take us away and execute us. Yet they now secured direct financing of $20 million, plus bail of $10 million. I believe the extent of bond, which was nearly $40 million as I cleared other encumbrances off Palm Beach and the value of that property went up, was the highest in the history of the United States up to that time.

A few days after the indictment, I went to an annual dinner of the Churchill Society, where Chris Matthews, the U.S. television commentator, gave the address. He generously referred to me, and I received a considerable ovation. There was speculation about not attorning to the jurisdiction, and Greenspan said that I could stonewall the Americans for up to six or seven years, but not longer, if I ignored the jurisdiction.

They would seize my house in Palm Beach, and although their antics in the New York seizure of my apartment sale proceeds had scandalized some, I couldn't do it; non-appearance would be generally interpreted as a confession of my guilt. Besides, though I knew the prosecution had the advantage and was under no illusion about Sussman's rabid aggressivity, I knew the facts. Radler's confession was such bunk, I thought this was the place to give battle, after being struck unforeseeably, like a blindfolded man running a gauntlet, for two years.

Greenspan recruited his daughter's former employer, Eddie Genson, a colourful Chicago criminal lawyer, to be the co-counsel. He was large and overweight, and because of a physical disability moved with the aid of a motorized tricycle and was armed with a silver-handled cane. His bobbing head was covered on all sides and everywhere except his ears, forehead, nose, and just under and beside his eyes with scruffy, reddish-blond hair.

He was a Damon Runyon figure, obfuscatory, stammering, almost incomprehensible in his repetitions and syntax and jangling accent – but clever. He had represented a huge number of thugs and scoundrels and celebrities, and he was a famous figure in the Chicago courthouse.

After the straightlaced playing by the book of Sullivan & Cromwell and high-priced impersonality of Williams & Connolly, I was ready for something altogether different, and in the two Eddies, I certainly had it. For a long time, I thought I had an ideal combination, a pair of streetwise alley cats, one a great traditional barrister and the other a Chicago courthouse roué. Their great advantage in my eyes was that they had never been prosecutors and had never settled a case.

They were both afflicted by the bug of the criminal lawyer, a misplaced reverence for, and amusement by, the hoods and low-lifes they had represented. I doubt if Genson, from his days accompanying his father as a bail bondsman, had ever represented a respectable client. Greenspan had, but they were not his specialty. He was, however, a serious lawyer, who had often appeared before the Supreme Court of Canada.

They proved not to be quite what I had expected, but at least, thanks to Greenspan, I had surmounted the original crisis: I had counsel and a survivable bail arrangement. Sussman tried to prevent my return to Canada after I appeared in Chicago to enter a plea, but Greenspan and his immigration counsel put a stop to that. This was not the first, and far from the last, of Sussman's pestilential interventions with very suggestible, even eagerly complicit, Canadian officials. Addicts and converts to the persecution abounded.

WE APPEARED IN CHICAGO, attended by hundreds of journalists, in late November. The courthouse, a twenty-seven-storey building designed by Ludwig Mies van der Rohe, was a monument to the first Mayor Daley's political influence.

Having so often seen in newsreels and dramatizations accused people mobbed by journalists in front of court houses, I didn't find it such a novel experience. Like many other things, it is surprising how much it resembles the imagination of it. Genson had had no idea of how prominent a case this would be, and performed valorous service for me by clearing a path with his motorized tricycle and threatening to batter intrusive journalists with his silver-tipped cane. The press swarmed, but were not abusive or physically aggressive.

I was surprised by the judge. Amy St. Eve is diminutive and has a mane of well-kempt blonde hair, an intelligent face, bright eyes, and a clever, quick, mobile expression. She wore a U.S. flag pin on her robe (though a couple of times it was almost upside down, like a navy distress signal). She was courteous and rather amiable.

Some of the press called her, generally respectfully, Peppermint Patty, or Mighty Mouse, and she did somewhat fill the latter role when she stood with her hands behind her back and under her robe: a pleasant, pretty, clever mouse. As with Kimba Wood, the New York federal judge who was an Attorney General candidate with Bill Clinton but because of her domestic hiring practices was passed over for the terribly mediocre Janet Reno, Judge St. Eve communicated a scrubbed and groomed pride and authenticity, which indicated that she would be sensible. I was assured, and did not doubt, that compared with the generality of judges in the Dirksen Federal Building, she was a godsend of wisdom and fairness.

Genson entered my not-guilty plea to the many counts of mail and wire fraud, the charge of money laundering, and the inanity that I had obstructed U.S. justice when I removed those thirteen boxes from my office on Toronto Street. There would be superseding indictments for racketeering and tax fraud. I assumed they had delayed charging these because they were afraid I might not appear in the United States if I were aware of them and because Canada would have been reluctant to grant extradition against such a barrage of unfounded allegations.

They need not have entertained any such fear. I would not be a fugitive from justice, and I would not have counted on the Canadian courts for much either. Whatever legal advantage Canada has over the United States resides in the prosecutors and the procedures, including the limits on what is justiciable and what is publishable, and not, from what I had seen, in the judges. St. Eve would prove a better judge than any I had known in Canada since my friend, and eventually Hollinger Inc. director, Charles Dubin, if not my father's friend and mine, Chief Justice Brian Dickson.

We were accused of the American federal offence of not paying taxes owed to a foreign power. The United States was charging me with a Canadian tax offence, as if Canada needed the assistance of a Sussman to collect its taxes. No such charge was ever laid against us in Canada. (The Canadian Justice Department sent two observers to the trial, who concluded there was no case against the defendants.)

The U.S. government, reduced by jurisdictional factors to invoking the mails and wire-links, would lay sixteen charges against me and seek the complete impoverishment of my family and my imprisonment for life. I found it somewhat invigorating, so surrealistically corrupt and dishonest was the process and the conduct of the prosecutors. (The trial was set for sixteen months later, March 2007, and there would be progress hearings every month or two.)

I was unimpressed by Kent and Sussman. Kent was an oaf, tall, slow, and monotonous. He left the case and went into private practice after a few weeks. Sussman had a crewcut top knot, with a pintail swoop to a point at the back, and his head looked like the flight deck of an Essex-class aircraft carrier: top-heavy and rectangular. He had compulsively darting eyes that would stop and then stare, with small pupils amid large, sallow whites, and a triangular nose, like an overly large spinnaker, capable of capsizing the vessel behind it. When he spoke, his wrists and hands moved jerkily, as if they were being manipulated by an amateur ventriloquist. When he stopped speaking, he went to a default countenance that was gape-mouthed, punctuated by his tongue bulging against the inside of his cheek like a lingual erection. He is a hollow-chested man who compensates with heavily padded shoulders and overlong jackets, a retrogression to the 1950s zoot suit. The overall effect was disturbing. He was all nose, mouth, and fake shoulders.

But just as nauseating was the even more mouthy co-prosecutor, a gargoyle. Jeffrey Cramer would soon be strutting in mid-address, shouting and pointing. Sussman and Cramer were a hideous pair.

The third prosecutor, Julie Ruder, had a pleasant face but a grating voice. Her sole manual gesture was putting both thumbs and forefingers together as if describing a recipe to a cooking class. The fourth prosecutor, Edward Siskel, seemed fairly unexceptionable and was completely forgettable, a distinction in such a horrifying quartet. In fact, he was there to familiarize himself with the trial in the event of an appeal.

I encountered Peter Atkinson for the first time in nearly two years as we were being processed, fingerprinted, photographed, and giving urine samples in the "lock-up." We had a cordial chat. The whole ambiance was quite affable; the finger-printer was a very large man who loved camping and hunting trips in Canada and conversed very jovially with Peter and me. Waiting FBI officials were also very agreeable, reminiscing about their time in the Bureau and about FBI directors going back to J. Edgar Hoover. I was prepared to be handcuffed – I was curious about the sensation – but it didn't happen.

The court appearance itself was uneventful. I told the massed and swarming press as I left that the charges were nonsense and that I had been a victim of a smear job, that all the accused were innocent of crimes they would never dream of committing. This was nothing but the truth. I was generally credited with a decorous performance in distasteful circumstances. I told the media that it was like the first day at university registration.

THERE IS A DRAMA IN NOTORIETY that is sanitized, even made wholesome, by being guiltless in fact. Let Breeden and his gullible accomplices in the U.S. attorney's office in Chicago get on with it. My nerves, far from cracking as Radler's had, became serene. I again dispensed with sleeping medicine and awaited events, confident that on Crispin's Day, my innocence and the quality of my counsel would turn the battle. Barbara, family, and friends would help me through, just as sales of a home and some other assets had defeated, by a hand's breadth, at least up to this point, the concerted effort to run me out of cash. In my parish church, the congregation extended their discreet friendship.

The mobs, still snarling with execration, would turn on my tormentors when they failed. I was ready for the fight of and for my life. So Barbara and I even joked about what was coming; what everyone knew was coming and wanted to come; and what, in a way, we, too, wanted to come: judgment, the supreme test, where my enemies would have to prove false charges beyond a reasonable doubt. I conserved what strength I had and awaited the prosecutor, slouching toward us from Chicago, the once "great, brave, heart of America."

[CHAPTER ELEVEN]

IT WAS ANOTHER DIFFICULT Christmas. The 2003 holiday season had been implacably gloomy, but 2004, despite the Breeden report, was upbeat as we charged toward privatization. Now, as of December 15, 2005, the U.S. government was trying to send me to prison for ninety-five years and impoverish me. On Christmas Day, I read the Book of Job. I discovered that while Job had endured more severe oppression than I had, he had been much less patient. I aspired to his deliverance but not to his additional rewards of living one hundred and twenty years and having forty more children.

I now organized what I called "the little boats of Dunkirk" to address the immediate financial crisis and borrowed from Barbara, two of my children, and a few very close friends small amounts of money to pay and thus keep the data company on side. I was told by the company that if their invoices were not paid within days, all outstanding data would be inaccessible to us and could be permanently deleted. Then we would have to try to fight a trial with hundreds of thousands of pages of material available only by hand; it simply could not be done. The pressure for money had driven Barbara to desperate measures. She was trying to sell her jewelry and discovered only gemstones were marketable. The valuable antique pieces she had were not of interest. Her large diamond ring, which became an object of desire for Prosecutor Sussman, was my gift to her on her sixtieth birthday. She knew how upset I would be if I heard what she was doing, and so she kept quiet until it was necessary to get information from me for possible buyers. Being accused of facilitating money laundering was a fear for anyone buying from us because the prosecution had done such a thorough job of tainting us. Barbara was reduced to sitting in odd locations to hand over the stone and its Gemological Institute of America certificate for examination by various oily gem dealers who seemed to take pleasure in telling her how fine it was before rejecting it on moral grounds. Whether this was a negotiating tactic is hard to say. Those with whom I dealt by telephone were among the most repulsive businessmen I have encountered, and I stopped the whole process.

In one of several coincidences that struck me as somewhat providential, on the airplane back from Washington to Toronto on the day of the New York seizure, I encountered Gordon Arnold, a school-friend from fifty years before, whom I had rarely seen since our school days. He was now a neighbour and offered his assistance in any way possible. At the decisive moment, he lent me several hundred thousand dollars against some furniture and works of art. It was a lifesaver in this very difficult time, and he was a true and unsuspected friend.*

When I walked through or around my house, I now found a crowded gallery of mementoes from my early youth, my adult life, and from the residences in London and New York. Even the trees had been familiar to me for more than fifty years. Almost every step, inside or out, brought flickerings, at first premonitory and subconscious, and then precise, of what had been lost or severely compromised: people who had died, friends now lost, pleasant connections gone forever. It was a cavalcade of the departed, great and small, but each person, thing, or revenance was something comfortable or satisfying, and apparently irreplaceable. I was prematurely forced to embrace Dr. Viktor Frankel's famous consolation that "to have been is a form of being, and in a sense, the surest form." I would have to get by for

---

* As I flew from Reagan to Pearson airports, on a flight that offered connections to Trudeau, Lesage, and Stanfield airports – Washington, Toronto, Montreal, Quebec, Halifax – I thought that someone was no longer young who knew the people after whom the airports are named.

the duration of this combat with memories that were beyond re-creation. In our barricaded domesticity, I even set up a little cardboard shelter in the garden room for dazed ladybugs that had been shut in by the elements.

Nostalgia was the constant companion of my thoughts, and melancholia was never far off. I battled to fight off morose impulses, like a retreating army fighting marauders. I retained memberships in all my clubs, in Toronto, London, New York, Montreal, and Palm Beach, but almost never set foot in them. Famous or once-familiar addresses were mute effigies of what life had been. I clung to vestiges of my former life, still struggling to convince myself that some of it could be recovered, that I would find the money to oil the greasy legal system, that justice would ultimately prevail despite its many setbacks. The question of whether I would survive long enough financially to defend myself against false and malicious charges was still unanswered.

HOLLINGER INTERNATIONAL HAD finally come current on its financial reportings, not having fired and sued KPMG as it should have done, because Breeden, who had recommended suing KPMG, had since become the court-appointed monitor of KPMG, and their testimony was thought likely to be useful against us. (In fact, it would be useful *to* us.) He resolved his evident conflict of interest in favour of the larger source of payments to him.

Barbara had exercised her options at Hollinger International and moved to sell her shares in January. The transfer agent, under orders from the company, held up the transaction for almost a week. I got Canadian counsel to threaten the transfer agent, and eventually, just in time, $2.4 million came in from this source. This allowed me to start to pay down Baker Botts, pay the emergency lenders, and start on the Greenspan and Genson retainers.

The light at the end of the financial tunnel was growing brighter – and it was distinctly not an incoming locomotive – when Leo Strine, doubtless pleased at his role in producing the criminal indictment he had effectively solicited nearly two years before and showing no sign of realizing the billions of dollars of shareholders' lost value he had caused, warned Hollinger International that he would not allow them to welsh on their indemnity of former officers' legal fees. The company was happily paying the legal fees of the docile directors, but not of Breeden's foes. Strine, to his credit, balked at this.

My new Delaware lawyers, David Jenkins and Joelle Polesky, replacing the gentlemanly but unsuccessful Jesse Finkelstein, came to see me in Toronto in early February 2006 and soon arranged a deal with Hollinger International's Delaware counsel. Rather than face Strine, with whose equal-opportunity arbitrariness my opponents too were quite familiar, they chose to pay a high percentage of my past and current legal bills. This was another big step forward, as it wiped away most of the arrears to Baker Botts and further assisted me with my new lawyers.

These were stop-gaps, but they kept body and soul together. I really cracked the financial problem when I recruited Stan Freedman, an able commercial lawyer, to become so obstreperous as a minority shareholder in Horizon Operations, one of the private newspaper companies, that we effectively obliged Radler to buy us out. Radler had recruited new investors, so this now became possible for him. He was happy enough, I'm sure, to see the back of me.

The formal defection of Radler prompted us to consider what deal he had made. His sentence was twenty-nine months and non-objection to a treaty transfer, which, in practice, meant a six month, minimum security confinement in Canada, and he appeared to have saved the private newspaper companies, which were his intended corporate destination anyway. This assumedly meant that the Canadians had passed on their threat to charge him with perjury when he testified in Kelowna (BC) that he and I were equal shareholding partners in Horizon Operations, where Todd Vogt (innocently, as he later assured me) fronted a third 25 per cent block of stock that was in fact, Radler's. Atkinson had scratched this out of public filings when we were squaring my position with foreign ownership rules governing newspapers in Canada, after I had ceased to be a Canadian citizen following my fracas with Chrétien.

Vogt, when contacted, would not appear as a witness in Chicago, though he was very embittered by how Radler had treated him, having formerly been virtually one of the family, and was severely embarrassed, he said, opposite his own in-laws, when Radler had tried to pretend in court that Vogt really was a serious Horizon shareholder while also being associated with his father-in-law in the competing local newspaper. The fact that he did not wish to testify did not mean that we did not have plenty of room to undermine Radler as a witness when the time came. He had not aroused Atkinson's and my fullest suspicions when his chicanery first came to light in 2002 because Radler always went to ground an observed complete silence whenever anything embarrassing to him occurred. There was no shortage of these things: the failure of most of his private ventures on behalf of the small venture capital business he ran with Peter White and me as silent partners. There were the motels, jewellery stores, oil and gas wells, or at least sites drilled in the hope of finding some accessible energy reserves.

He showed the same furtiveness about the endless losses at the *Jerusalem Post*. He overpaid for the newspaper, left me to justify to shareholders the US$17 million he had paid, and held himself out to the world's Jewish community as a champion of Israel. He was addicted to his status as an international notable in the Jewish community and too egotistically vulnerable to admit that his formula of endless cost-cutting would not eliminate the loss at the *Post*. He had put our Israeli partner in the printing of the *Yellow Pages* in that country on the board of Hollinger International. He didn't tell us that our partner ditched us and took the profitable printing business elsewhere.

He compounded our problems by sponsoring an editorial policy that was too hawkish for all but the most ardent Zionists. Under Radler, the *Post* adopted a Jabotinskyan posture of pursuing a greater Israel; the inconvenient Arab populations that happened to be there would be induced to emigrate by unspecified means. It was an editorial and financial embarrassment, but it conformed to the Radler method: tough talk regardless of its cost and futility. He was a sort of misguided, kitsch John Wayne with both employees and readers.

I had a reasonably conservative definition of Israel's security interests, but Radler's ideas, imparted to him by tough-talking Israeli charlatans of a greater Israel, were too much for me, and Radler put some strain on my relations with sensible Israelis such as Teddy Kollek, Jerusalem's brilliant fourteen-term mayor.

To accommodate the nasty gnome from Chicago, the Canada Revenue Agency had issued an absurd assessment, just as the OSC had laid ridiculous charges, to show Canada had not lost interest in, or even become a farm team in, the great championship round of what some of my friends now called the game of Let's Kill Conrad. As in so many other competitions, Canada emulated the worst and not the best of America, and here earned a good second prize in the Lottario of persecution.

I relied on the cockiness and belligerency of Sussman to drive Atkinson and Kipnis and their counsel more closely into our arms and hoped that their presence would dampen any tendency by the jury to single me out for the punishment of the formerly rich and famous. It was a tenuous strategy, dictated more by necessity than by choice – there was hardly a menu of valid options. After a brief holiday in the now famous house in Palm Beach (an aerial photograph of it appeared in the *New York Times*), wondering again as I left whether I would ever see it again, we returned to Toronto and to the campaign for a buyout by Radler from more of the private news-paper operations.

The initial payment for Horizon Operations (Canada) under the shareholders' agreement for Horizon Canada enabled me to remove all the Canada Revenue liens and appeal their entire assessment after I had paid it. Within a year, having done their obeisance to the shrieking Sussman, Canada Revenue remitted to me three-quarters of what I had paid, with interest, and acknowledged that it had not been owed. The Horizon payment left us a couple of million extra, which, coupled with Strine's indemnity, enabled me to deal with the lawyers more effectively. As the Canada Revenue money came back and more of the community newspaper sale proceeds came in, cash piled up in amounts I had not known for some time, and, once again I wondered at the strange turns in these struggles. Acute cash penury was transformed in a few months to a comfortable state and the defrayal by indemnity of most of my legal bills. This latter munificence at the behest of the inevitable Vice Chancellor Strine, who on his forays on the lecture circuit took to referring to me almost as Montgomery had described Rommel, saying I was "a great presence in [his] court," as if to take some grandeur for himself in his scandalous ruling.

The removal of the tax lien on the Palm Beach house provoked Sussman to a bizarre exercise of frustrated aggression. Despite all the illegal telephone intercepts and pseudo-knowing tips from Radler (whom I never told anything about my investments and interests), and his incitements to belligerency of Canada Revenue, Sussman had no idea what my resources were. I had moved so cautiously to liquidate assets gradually and at reasonable values, that my durability galled him.

He had assumed that after his seizure of the proceeds of the New York co-operative apartment sale, I had no money and would be passing the begging bowl among my wealthy friends. Since Sussman was leading Radler by a chain, trussed, bound, and gagged, he could have stopped the Horizon buyout, but either Radler's pride prevented him from mentioning it until it had happened or Sussman was already on to his next wheeze.

At Alberta Newspapers, the acquisition of which had not been a related-party transaction (Hollinger International had had no involvement), Radler had also brought in new investors to facilitate paying all the restitutions he had made himself liable for. I generated an offer for the entire group that was entirely reasonable, and this forced Radler to bring his new partners into line and meet the offer. In order to satisfy his concerns about foreign ownership, I had sold shares to Barbara at the formula price and in an arrangement entirely designed by the company lawyer, an obtuse minion of Radler's. Now that arm's-length, enterprise-value prices were being invoked, there was a real profit for Barbara. This had the double effect of producing cash and enriching Barbara, who was practically insusceptible to the rapine of the U.S. attorney and his Canadian accomplices. It was a win double, in sporting parlance, and Sussman was not much of a sport.

Sussman reacted to my defeat of his financial strangulation plan like an angry U-boat admiral dismayed that wartime Britain was feasting on tropical fruit. He began a new offensive based on the canard that since obviously I wasn't broke, I must have lied in my obligatory financial statement filed with the court and underestimated my net worth. In furtherance of this argument, Sussman, a bold but reckless tactician, ordered Radler to repay the shareholders' loans at Horizon Publications (U.S.), a company that Breeden had called a scam by Radler and me but that had been passed as part of the Radler plea bargain so that after he had delivered my head on a plate and had his correctional golfing holiday, Radler could live prosperously ever after, screaming at the advertising sales-people in such centres of urban vitality as Punxsutawney, Pennsylvania, and Medicine Hat, Alberta. What Sussman was doing was a gamble: he was releasing money to me deliberately to further his argument in court that I had lied about my net worth. Two years later, which justified Radler's soft sentence, praised him for keeping the prosecution abreast of all payments I received from the private newspaper companies. This helped Sussman allege that I had misrepresented the value of my assets, and assisted him in asking the Canada Revenue Agency to challenge my tax returns.

This generated $6 million for me, which, in one of our last conversations, Radler had told me would not be shaken loose for a long time, if ever. Sussman rushed to the judge to accuse me of perjury, released inflammatory filings to the press, and demanded that U.S. marshals be empowered to sell my Palm Beach house, that my bond be revoked, and that I be taken into custody at once. So began a four-month struggle that was a trial within the trial. The $6 million was put into escrow.

The world press was incited to new flurries of enthusiasm at the speed and proportions of my descent; the British press especially, which normally sniped at the vagaries of the U.S. justice system, became almost bestially aroused at the prospect of my being imprisoned without even the irritating formality of a trial. If I could be imprisoned *sine die* without trial, this would be a miraculous consummation, and the British press bandied it about as a live possibility for several weeks. The implication was that this would not indicate any absence of due process, merely a confirmation of my infamous crimes.

It would be unjust to underestimate the loyalists and the steadily growing group of supporters who saw at least part of the sham that was being perpetrated. Many friends – Elton John and David Furnish, Barry Humphries (Dame Edna), Lizzie Spender, Joan Collins and Percy Gibson, Martin Feldstein, author David Pryce-Jones and his wife Clarissa, historian Andrew Roberts, Anna Wintour and Shelby Bryan, and others – honoured us by coming out of their way to see us. William Buckley, George Will, Donald Trump, Seth Lipsky, Laura Ingraham, Rush Limbaugh, Ann Coulter, and more were publicly supportive. Philanthropist Lee

Annenberg, financier Roger Hertog, *New Criterion* editor Roger Kimball, *Commentary* editor Neal Kozodoy, Brian Mulroney, writer Norman Podhoretz, international financier Ezra Zilkha, and many others were unwavering. Old friends rallied, from my early days, and virtually all my relatives. Many of these people I had not seen for decades, and I did not even know the current country of residence of many others. While there were many disappointing desertions, we never felt ourselves outcasts. The loneliness arose from the fact that though we had our supporters, social contact became difficult. Friends didn't want to talk about our travails, yet ignoring them completely was difficult for everyone, as they were so pre-occupying. The legal front either oppressed conversation or was the unmentioned 900-pound gorilla in the room. There was also a steady shift in the nature of friendly acquaintances. An increasing, and eventually very large, number of people from many countries who were complete strangers to me, including a large number of Americans, recognized the unfairness of the plea bargain system and many of the legal precedings, and the catastrophe of my successors' management, came forward in droves, every week. I developed some close cyber-friendships with these far-off supporters.

WHEN SUSSMAN BEGAN HIS CAMPAIGN to have a forced sale of my Florida house and have me imprisoned for perjury because of the financial statement I had signed, it was hard to believe that a U.S. court would take such nonsense seriously.

Sussman poured it on: our Black Family Foundation's contribution to the Canadian Opera Company was an act of fraud by me to deprive litigants and creditors. The contribution came from my father's estate. Next, he put it about that Jack Boultbee was posting $10-million bond, when, in fact, Boultbee was posting $1.5 million. Sussman had already had his try at intimidating my mortgagee in Palm Beach not to renew my mortgage (though he also declined to call it) and then claimed that I was in default, and thus in violation of bail terms. Sussman endlessly accused me of sham transactions in transferring money to my wife, when the fact was that Radler had asked for these transfers to meet the foreign owner-ship of media restrictions in Canada and that Radler's counsel had arranged all of it, including the sale to my wife, according to the formula that applied to all shareholders, as a matter of contract law.

Yet my own counsel fumbled meekly through these monthly scheduling meetings and Judge St. Eve felt her way very cautiously between the conflicting views. Finally, I prevailed on Eddie Genson and his colleague, Marc Martin, to produce a filing that detailed the assistant U.S. attorney's many outrages. When our gloves-off rejoinder, imaginatively entitled "Basta," came in, Judge St. Eve found resolution, and rejected Sussman's demand for a revocation of bond. She released $5 million of the $6 million of shareholder advances at Horizon U.S. that Sussman had instructed Radler to pay to advance Sussman's case for bond revocation and immediate imprisonment of me, by claiming I had deliberately undervalued these assets. She added a further $1 million to bail, bringing it to $21 million. She emphasized that she was not seeking the sale of my Palm Beach house.

My $21 million bail was secured now by more than $30 million, as Canada Revenue had departed Palm Beach (and other targets of mine for their abusive, Sussman-inspired liens and attachments). Another US$5 million from this unsuspected source, on the judge's order, illustrated again the mercurial nature of my financial fortunes; four months before, I had been gasping for every cent. Now, Barbara and I had many millions in the bank. Between that and Strine's enforcement of the legal costs indemnity, I could have afforded Brendan Sullivan after all, as I had unsuccessfully assured him would be the case.

IN APRIL 2006, I WAS READY TO START writing about Nixon. For two years I had been devouring books and documents about him, and my researchers, Adam Daifallah, a very intelligent young man who had helped me with FDR, and Edward Saatchi, son of British friends, were about to start work, with the blessing of the Nixon Library and Center, in the vast Nixon archives. I set myself the ambitious goal of writing three thousand words per day. It was an antidote to the legal travails. Instead of waiting for lawyers to telephone, I just wrote from the research material and interrupted myself as necessary to take calls from counsel and others.

I met my writing goals and had audaciously calculated that I could finish a draft of a four-hundred-thousand-word life of Nixon by mid-autumn and did so. My editor, the brilliant and delightful Bill Whitworth, former editor of *The Atlantic* magazine, and I spent two months editing it and started into production. Publishers in Canada, the United Kingdom, and the United States all came forward nicely, and I received five times the advance I had had for FDR. I was now a known quantity, and the universal opinion on first reading was that this was a book of equivalent quality to my Roosevelt, and about a hotter button (though less distinguished) president. I must credit the ubiquitous Toronto-based entertainment lawyer Michael Levine for much of that; he is the personification of the conflict of interest, but also of the honest resolution of it, and of the related-party transaction that works for everyone. I wish that I had had the assistance of such a person in corporate matters.

It was a good time to be a Canadian. Barbara thought I was waving the Maple Leaf around a bit exuberantly in my newspaper columns on Canadian affairs, but I was both sincere and accurate. I concluded that a few interviews and three speeches – one to Moses Znaimer's Idea City, one to the Empire Club of Toronto, and one to the World Presidents and Young Presidents – could be useful. They were well received. Even Eddie Greenspan, who had counselled silence, as lawyers normally do to clients, acknowledged that I had been correct. Miraculously, we even began to win a few motions in the courthouse in Toronto.

As my book on Nixon steadily advanced, it was inevitable that gratuitous comparisons, involving psychological liberties, would be made between my subject and me. In fact, there was little comparison, and not only because of the huge disparity in our positions and newsworthiness.

In my case, I could not give the authorities enough, was never reluctant for the whole story to be told, and wanted everything laid out. It was the prosecutors who were trying to suppress evidence of the looting of our companies by our successors, and to introduce the ravings of Strine and Breeden. I'm not a bit like Richard Nixon, though in most respects he was an admirable person with whom comparisons would be flattering.

EVENTUALLY, THE RAVELSTON RECEIVER changed the company's plea to guilty and promised to pay a fine of $7 million to the United States, money

CONRAD BLACK

that by now the company did not have. There was also an open-ended claim for restitution. It was completely irresponsible, and despite a brilliant argument by Peter Howard on our behalf in the commercial court, the atmosphere had not sufficiently evolved, there or on appeal, to prevent the judge from approving this insane scheme. The steamroller of the American prosecutors rolled on. At least I could afford to wait until my day in court.

Succeeding Walker, Carroll, and Kelly at Hollinger Inc., Wesley Voorheis's regime carried to new depths the pursuit of the creators of the company's wealth, which they had entirely dissipated by mid-2007, as the share price evaporated and the company for which we had bid $7.60 per share in 2005 sought insolvency protection. In exchange for Hollinger Inc. not being indicted, Voorheis pledged every possible assistance against me. On this one point, at least, he was as good as his word and he outperformed even Walker and Strosberg.

At this point, the American prosecutors had sixteen charges against me. They had thrown all the spaghetti at the wall, and the general practice was that some would stick. If the jury clung to a sensible notion of a reasonable doubt, we should win – as long as Greenspan proved as good a barrister in his U.S. debut as he had been for nearly forty years in Canada. That was to prove a larger imponderable than I had foreseen.

The prosecutors withdrew their claim against me for receiving the CanWest non-competition payments (though they still claimed I had fraudulently included Atkinson and Boultbee in them). They also withdrew the charge of not paying taxes in Canada, to enable, Sussman explained with his usual veracity, the Canadian taxing authorities to proceed against me. He knew perfectly well that Canada Revenue was returning most of the money it had wrongfully assessed.

Sussman – stung by the sharp defeat he suffered after he had prepared the world for my imprisonment without trial, and hyperactive – advanced swiftly from another direction. Voorheis devised a lawsuit that held that my associates and I, twelve years before, had stripped Hollinger Inc. The allegation was that we had enriched Hollinger International, where our equity interest was 24 per cent, at the expense of Hollinger Inc., where we were 65 per cent shareholders. The transactions all produced huge gains for the Hollinger Inc. shareholders and were approved by outside advisers and independent directors in both companies. It was the most inane lawsuit that had yet surfaced in this mad sequence of almost totalitarian fantasies.

Voorheis told Sussman that, based on this lawsuit, he might be able to find a judge willing to impose a total worldwide-asset freeze on me *ex parte*, a secret hearing at which I would have no representation, as in the New York apartment-sale freeze (it makes the prosecutor's task considerably easier when the judges just seize the defendant's ability to defend himself and tell him afterwards). He did just that. The most abysmally predictable of the mindless Osgoode Hall meddlers, the inevitable Colin Campbell, produced reasons for an asset freeze on my wife and me without notice to us that were so outrageously unfair that none of my counsel could believe at first that it wasn't a send-up.

In a special Voorheis touch, the service of the "Mareva" injunction, which had been obtained two weeks before, was effected at 6 p.m. on August 25, just before the arrival of my dinner guests for my sixty-second birthday and in front of my children. At the front door, a woman with a video camera taped the serving of the order to our baffled houseman, who had been told on the speaker phone from the gate that some boxes from Eddie Greenspan's office were being delivered.

A Mareva injunction tightly controls the access of an individual to his or her own money, ostensibly from fear that the person might move it to another jurisdiction and flee righteous creditors. By including Barbara, the claimant and the court were giving credence to the Sussman claim that the Chicago court had rejected as false – that I had improperly transferred assets to her. It also lent a completely unwarranted legitimacy to the unutterably fatuous Voorheis action.

This was an almost unbelievable development. I was convinced that even in this degenerated jurisdiction, this was going too far. Despite the implications of it, I was determined not to mention it to my birthday guests, though it was hard to put it out of mind. We had a pleasant birthday dinner. I did not mention the latest and most hideous manifestation of the evil of the American prosecutors, the complicity of my usurpatory successors, and the witless credulity of the Toronto bench.

Greenspan was on holiday in Venice. I worked with Earl Cherniak, and with David Roebuck and Peter Howard, all distinguished lawyers. Roebuck, cautious though he was, said that the Mareva conditions, which would have forced the sale of both my homes, could be beaten back.

Voorheis's lawyers wrote at once to the mortgagee of my Toronto house, Murray Sinclair of Quest, forbidding him to accept a mortgage payment. (Glassman had already tried to buy the mortgage from Murray, who explained that "that is not how we do business." Thank God for a few honest men.) It had come to this new low tide in my affairs. Greenspan returned; I had summarized the statements in Voorheis's supporting affidavit, and a group of my counsel, among the most distinguished barristers in the country, called on the chief justice of the court and suggested that in light of Campbell's evident bias, he should recuse. They were referred to Campbell himself, who declined but admitted curiosity about why such a request could possibly be made of him. Greenspan walked him through the shortcomings of Voorheis's affidavit. We did not want a court case on the subject at this point, as it might not be possible to keep Campbell's mad Red Queen reasons for granting an *ex-parte* Mareva injunction out of the court record in Chicago.

Both Campbell's reasons for granting it and Voorheis's reasons for getting it were so inflammatory they could have seriously affected my trial. Voorheis had to acknowledge that there were a few inexactitudes in his affidavit. Campbell urged compromise. Hollinger Inc. retreated to a point that permitted all existing normal expenses. In addition, as usual in legal matters, any payments to the professional legal class were permitted. The clannish solidarity in the matter of getting all bills paid is a tighter bond at the bar and bench than any other professional association I have known.

The revised agreement effectively released Barbara from any onerous requirements. The remaining financial restraints on both of us were very irritating but could be managed. An impartial monitor was agreed and installed. Once again, the Americans, as Machiavelli had warned of mercenaries, had found their (Canadian) collaborators almost useless and completely self-interested. I could trace the jack-knife arc of Sussman's disappointment from the tenor of press inquiries that he had eagerly generated and then vainly tried to control.

There was a sad aspect that still perplexes me. Barbara was furious: she did not want to sign the revised agreement. Her inclusion in any sort of monitoring was so unwarranted that she was prepared to go to court and fight. "Let them send me to jail," she said. Unfortunately, I knew that when she hit on a theme, she would follow it anywhere. She had no independent lawyer in Toronto at that point and so was dragged into this settlement without representation. "I'm trying to get my mouth to say yes," she replied when my lawyers urged her to sign the settlement for my sake. I shared the view of counsel that we should take this deal now, to keep these bizarre allegations out of the Chicago case. Barbara went along with well-founded reluctance. In Vancouver, the judge turned down the request for a Mareva injunction against Radler, based on exactly the same claims, writing that "the evidence tendered in this case, including significant portions of the Voorheis affidavit, was objectionable on many bases. In many places in that affidavit, it is difficult to extract 'facts' from opinion, 'opinion' from 'hearsay' and 'hearsay' from 'invective' and 'argument.' In fact, I would describe a large portion of that affidavit as argument dressed up as evidence. . . ." But in Toronto, Barbara, who had not a single criminal or civil charge against her, had to sign an agreement obligating her to follow tight reporting requirements. As Voorheis kept touting the fiction of "litigation assets," i.e., against us, he appointed as trustee a contemporary of Justice Campbell, retired Justice Jack Ground. This boil will have to be lanced and will be, shortly after this book is published.

The three usurper regimes at both Hollingers and Ravelston steadily devised new ways to annoy me. Richter claimed that Argus Corporation owned the three paintings of me by Andy Warhol, apart from the one I had given to an art museum in Vancouver. The actual papers were ambiguous, but in fact I owned them, as I had paid Andy for them. It was just another method to curry favour with the puppet-master in Chicago and try to generate demeaning publicity. We finally agreed to leave them where they were, one in my home, one in storage in London, and one in the office in Toronto, and I posted an insurance bond, through the courtesy of Duncan Jackman, Hal and Maruja's capable and gracious son, who was now in charge of the Jackman group's extensive operations. Though the temporary break I had had with his father naturally never came up, I was pleased to retain a relationship with the next generation of that talented family.

This issue would arise again, as Richter desperately tried to extract the last cent from Ravelston and Argus. We eventually arranged that I would have an opportunity to buy two of the paintings at auction, and one at the auction price without auction. As I, in fact, owned them, it was inexpressibly irritating to have to pay for them twice, but I was not prepared to put the matters before another Toronto kangaroo court for the delectation of the press.

AT EACH NEW STATION IN THE long, tortuous assault by the U.S. government and its quislings, there would be the very irksome racket of media helicopters. As our home is only about two miles from a hospital, we were accustomed to the noise of distant helicopters transporting emergency cases. The photographers were a different sound, closer, noisier, and aggravatingly persistent. Aerial photographs of both my homes were constantly in the press, as Sussman fulminated and erupted in his ambition to pitch me out of them. He later confessed that his chief ambitions were to force the sale of the Palm Beach house and to seize Barbara's diamond ring. This was the infernal and psychotically aggressive mentality that was opposing us, in the name of American justice. (He failed in both ambitions.)

In the spring, summer, and early autumn months, I enjoyed spending mornings working in the walled garden between my library and my chapel, with fountains on each side. There I altered completed Nixon chapters before sending them to editors or made notes for a *National Post* column, or read the daily newspapers. And in the late afternoon, I enjoyed the same activity on our terrace, watching the chipmunks and squirrels and bigger game including foxes and deer. This was the view from our drawing room terrace that Elton John had instantly recognized as "necessary for [your] sanity." At such occasions, half-hour, low-altitude circlings of the house by helicopters with large cameras protruding in pods from their fronts incited musings about a loaded, over-the-shoulder, ground-to-air missile launcher.

SUSSMAN'S ACTIONS WERE BOTH fanatical and vulgar. In dealings with my New York lawyer over Sussman's seizure from me of the proceeds of the New York co-op sale, Sussman continuously referred to parts of "Black's conspiracy to defraud the shareholders." In part, he had taken the bait from

Breeden. In part, he had torqued up his frenetic natural aggressivity and focused it on whoever happened to be in his sights. Thus any exculpatory evidence was, as he put it several times, "a hand-job for Conrad" or a "self-serving letter." The absence of evidence merely meant it had been removed. Even when his case seemed to disintegrate, there was not a faint possibility that the targeted people might be innocent.

It is a problem for all prosecutors to distinguish between their important duty to punish crime and protect society from criminals and the prior step of coming to reasonable opinions about whom to target. Since the subjects of prosecutor wrath are deemed by prosecutors to be offenders who have wronged society, there is a very swift leap from the presumption of innocence to the extermination of the possibility of innocence in the mind and hearing of the prosecutor. The cart surges in front of the horse, and instead of defending society against people who had been proved, or who he had good reason to believe, to be bad, by focusing on people presumed to be innocent, Sussman was instantly making them guilty.

Because I had agreed with Malcolm Muggeridge's view that almost anyone, in certain circumstances, could be guilty of crimes, and because I had seen enough of police and prosecutors to know how unreliable their judgment was, my attitude and behaviour to people I knew who came under this sort of scrutiny and accusation did not change. I had not foreseen the sadistic, bourgeois pose of offended decency that many would adopt toward me. This was why the posturing of seedy journalists, suddenly made over as Victorian dowagers, bandying about censorious descriptions of totally innocent people was especially odious. Being removed from Christmas card lists was particularly irritating. An abrupt end to most Canadian and American (but not British) invitations, the one place where it was practically impossible for us to attend such occasions, created a sense of eeriness.

As a former chairman of the cardinal's dinner in Toronto, a gathering of about twenty-five hundred people at the Convention Centre, I generally attended this gathering. In November 2006, when introduced along with many other former chairmen, I received a prolonged ovation. It was a moving moment. People I knew by sight but had not conversed with in my parish church wished me success with that Canadian understatement and even shyness that is such a pleasing contrast to the hale and bluff back-slapping of some other nationalities, including the most proximate one (as even Ernest Hemingway, briefly a Toronto resident in the early 1920s, observed).

There were particular individual disappointments. Not just financiers I had dealt with, but a frequently consulted doctor who had been something of a friend, whom I had supported through financial adversity, and who had stayed at our home in London; an eminent clergyman also withdrew. They became insufferably indiscreet and unacceptably testy. These relationships just fell away. It was disorienting, but they were eventually replaced by happier successors.

One of the most grinding clichés of the time was that we would "find out who are friends were." More of a revelation was who our enemies were, and the crossover between them was substantial and sometimes piercingly disappointing. Yet there were heartening moments and many, in all countries, remained not only solid, but rallied in contrarian manner.

In addition to winding up the Nixon project and going through the editing, and my writing in the *National Post*, I was composing case summaries for counsel. We now had the FBI–U.S. attorney interviews with scores of people. I wrote a seventy-two-page dissection of the contradictory remarks and testimony of Breeden, Thompson, Kravis, Burt, Healy, and Kissinger, as well as an outline of a response to all the counts.

I eventually discovered that these interviews were rarely written up accurately by the government and the interviewees were not shown the summaries. With that said, as all interviewees had their own counsel present, those who wrote up the interviews couldn't engage in wholesale fabrication. He recorded that Kissinger said that he believed I was guilty as charged of every allegation.

This included a large number of charges that were later dropped or thrown out by the jurors. Kissinger supposedly added that this would not affect our friendship, but that our friendship made my crimes more painful. I can hardly believe that Kissinger thought I was a racketeer and money-launderer, and I would certainly rank his credibility above that of the FBI. But the formula is familiar. Henry professed agreement with the apparently winning side and imperishable goodwill to the other side. This technique may work in the Middle East and Indochina, where treachery and violence are everywhere, but it is not an appropriate way to treat a "best friend in the world" and "indispensable pillar of my life." Five years later we rehashed these unhappy times. It was a cultural difference. Henry did what came naturally, and as he was advised by the doubtless dessicatedly cautious Paul Saunders.

This work on the prosecution interviews and my wind-up of the Nixon book gave me some considered perspectives on my tortuous relationship with Henry Kissinger. Friendship is fine, but Richard Nixon warned me that Henry Kissinger is not reliable in a crisis. He does possess admirable physical courage, as when he proceeded to chair a conference session after being up all night when he lost the sight of his right eye due to a thrombosis.

Henry owed me benign neutrality at least. I never asked for his help or for him to become involved at all. I sought only the heavily qualified prestige of his abstention. He withheld even that. I admire him. I greatly enjoyed my relations with him. It was an honour to be his friend, as he idiosyncratically defined friendship.

And it did bother him to abandon me. He told several people, including some that he would not have imagined would communicate with me, that he regretted the strain on our friendship.

Henry Kissinger deserted me by rote, by intuitive recourse to his formula, seeking the strategic position between principle and expediency even in this small matter, as a cat reflexively stalks a bird. There was no animosity in his sudden desertion, and he meant me no harm, any more than a cat dislikes animals it tries to kill. The Kissingers, though still sending amicable gestures, were among those who could not bring themselves to send us a Christmas card after 2003. Voting for Breeden's outrageous putsch at every stage when he could have abstained, or even, with an updraft of bravery, dissented, was deeply offensive. His conciliatory messages in the latter stages of these events seemed to me to express a breezy idea that it had all been unpleasant but now we could be friends again.

Henry had never really understood the cultural difference between Metternichian compromise and Reaganian focused strength, or between a ramshackle empire preserved by manoeuvre and autocratic chicanery, and a mighty republic with the strength to assert itself, but with the conscience to require that it be in a presentable cause. He and Nixon worked well together because both were devious and the fragility of Nixon's political position required him to do a great deal by stealth. Henry came through Watergate apparently unscathed, but he never came back to government. He prided himself on the prestige he retained, but after 1977, they were barren years. Reagan didn't trust him ("He wasn't loyal to Dick," he told me in 1989), and neither did George Bush Sr. His regime of endless conferences with other ex-office holders was no substitute for the real thing.

One of his biographers said, with some reason, that Henry was "a combination of Beelzebub and Woody Allen." Kissinger's actions take nothing from his public career or his private standing, but I had taken his professions of friendship seriously, and reciprocated them. I must blame myself for not recognizing the nature of the beast. But abandonment by Henry Kissinger in the greatest crisis of my life, after decades of friendship, wreathed in superlative testimonials, following many years of my prior admiration of him, though it has had little practical consequence, was a terrible wound that I feared would never heal. In this, as will be recounted in the appropriate place in this narrative, I am grateful to report that I was mistaken.

I WROTE FURTHER MONOGRAPHS on various parts of the case, as well as my fifty-page refutation of Tom Bower's and others' libels. I was a veritable torrent of composition from late morning to early morning, with only the twilight interruptions to watch the sunset from the terrace, and not even those once the mercury descended and daylight time was over.

The immense, outsized United States has many faces. For four decades I was a vocal defender of most of them. It was now my strange misfortune to encounter, at point-blank range, the ugliest and nastiest American face of all, that of its legal system. Among these were Richard Breeden and Patrick Fitzgerald. The experience has been so repugnant that it could not fail to reduce my confidence in the country that I had admired above all others, for all my conscient life.

Fitzgerald had held the press conferences in our case and had wildly exaggerated any possible negative construction of the facts; there was no evidence that he knew the case well or that any of the prosecutors had done more than take Breeden's report and launch the usual trial opener of two years of press assassination, witness intimidation, and financial strangulation. Now that the trial was nearing, even the elements of the media that had so diligently personed the shovels in my interment had, if only to build drama, to acknowledge that it was going to be a main event after all. A main event cannot have a foregone conclusion. At this long undreamt-of extremity, the odds seemed to be narrowing.

[CHAPTER TWELVE]

TO A QUESTION OF WHETHER I might want to escape jurisdiction, as Fitzgerald had suggested, I told the media outside the court house after a status hearing: "The U.S. Marines could not stop me from appearing." I knew the trial would be difficult, but I knew that the charges were so unfounded that as long as Peter Atkinson and Mark Kipnis did not break and join the finger-pointing ranks of the plea bargainers, this would be the place to expose the fraudulence of the case against me. Forcing the enemy to prove the guilt of the innocent beyond a reasonable doubt had been my strategy, and it had to be seen through to the end, despite the procedural stacked deck in favour of the prosecution, who, I discovered, would address the jury last, unlike the practice in other advanced countries I knew.

There were times when I worried about the preparation and general agility of Eddie Greenspan. I had taken the measure of Eddie Genson as a crafty lawyer in essentially low-life cases, and a man who certainly knew the local people and tricks. I had bought into the Greenspan view that big firms were cynical, indifferent, and overpriced or even exploitive, and that ex-prosecutors could not be trusted. Like George Jonas, I had urged Greenspan to make himself aware of American procedure. We, and Barbara, feared that U.S. procedure could be invoked against him to offset his well-established competence as a trial lawyer. Barbara tried hard to persuade him to go to Chicago to observe a trial; she offered to pay for an American trial lawyer of his choice to come to Toronto and take him through a moot court of procedure to familiarize himself with differences in courtroom practice. He said he would think about it and never took up either offer.

I believed that Greenspan saw this as the crowning opportunity of his career. He would now become a famous lawyer in the United States. He had a maximally publicized case, a decisively winning case on the facts; the co-defendants, contrary to the predictions of Genson, had held. This should be the occasion for a star turn. All anticipated it, and the Toronto press carried Greenspan's reputation ahead of him to Chicago like the Infant of Prague.

I never received much response from him to the lengthy summaries of the case I wrote for him. Greenspan claimed that he would be fine with U.S. procedure because he had read all ten volumes of Wigmore (the leading American proceduralist). I assumed and had reason to believe that he had examined whatever problems might arise, to immunize himself as a cross-examiner to the harassments of the prosecutors. If their performance with me up to now had been any guide, they would certainly nip at Greenspan's heels if they could.

There was also a factor of stamina. Greenspan had had open heart surgery in August 2005. His diabetes was a problem, and I was always concerned at how ponderous his movements were. I urged him repeatedly to act as chief counsel, but he almost never spoke in our seven status hearings with Judge St. Eve. Genson carried the ball right up to trial. The conference table in Greenspan's office was covered with files for the cross-examination of Radler; there were six hundred of them, indexed and sequential. He was preparing a destruction of the government's star witness that appeared to be worthy of the cause. (He was very proud of his intended opening question: "Mr. Radler, have you ever lied to Mr. Black?" The question, notionally excellent, would never be asked.)

I worried that Greenspan wasn't really on top of the case and might not have the physical and mental energy to carry such a heavy burden. I asked him if he was sure he could do it; it was now an academic question unless he invoked a medical reason to withdraw. It would be very late to bring in anyone else in such a complicated case, and the judge would not allow a change on any but medical grounds. There was not much to be done unless Greenspan confirmed that he needed reinforcement; we might then have been able to introduce another counsel to join the fray with the improbable pair of Eddies.

In a moving exchange motivated by my concerns, I tried to have this out with him, at his office on a Saturday about a month before the trial began. Eddie Greenspan took from his pocket something he had written down and had typed up, from when he visited the Cabinet War Rooms in London some months before: "My whole life had been a preparation for this hour and this trial."

On invitation I identified it as Winston Churchill's comment on returning from Buckingham Palace on May 10, 1940, after being invested, in desperate circumstances as the German blitzkrieg broke in the West, as prime minister by King George VI and accorded practically unlimited powers as head of a national unity government. Greenspan told me in the most emphatic terms that the particular wording of Churchill's statement applied to him and this case. In the circumstances, I was happy and relieved to believe him, and assumed that he was preparing himself for such a trial.

There was nothing for it but to go with the team I had, heavily reinforced as it was by bright younger personnel from Baker Botts and by Greenspan's dedicated and capable articling student, Chris O'Connor.

As 2006 ebbed away, I prepared for what would be the supreme crisis of my life. I had stabilized the financial and public relations war, I thought, especially in Canada. I wrote an extensive comment on the case for *Tatler* in the United Kingdom, as I distrusted all the London national newspapers. Everyone conceded that a Big Battle was looming, and the media had to take note of my repeated references to the charges as unfounded and at the failure of the government to roll any of the accused after Radler took his dive.

Genson claimed to be confident, but I had learned the wisdom of a British friend who had had serious legal problems, that the lawyers could never be believed in anything they said. Certainly, it was obvious that Genson was an inveterate old journeyman and I wasn't much inclined to take him literally. Barbara had taken an instant dislike to him on his one visit to our Toronto home. She sat silently listening to him answering my questions. "He hasn't the slightest idea what this case is about," she said afterwards, conceding that he had a charming wife. After that meeting, she lapsed into complete pessimism. From prior observation younger lawyers tended to be more forthright but insufficiently experienced for their opinions to be accorded great credence. Experienced lawyers regarded the client as a bloody nuisance, and it was true that almost nothing they said could be believed. The more they expressed a desire for instructions, the less likely they were to carry them out. I hoped that, given the relations I had had with Greenspan, this truism might not apply to him.

I wasn't especially impressed with the entourages of the two Eddies, except for Chris O'Connor and the young Baker Botts people and Carolyn Gurland in Genson's office. She seemed to know the documents well and was a lively personality, and an attractive youngish woman. Jane Kelly, who had worked with Greenspan for many years and did a lot of legal research, was likeable and jolly but a trifle unserious.

Terry Gillespie, Genson's partner, had a good reputation and was available. Marc Martin, another semi-associate of Genson and a successful counsel to many of Chicago's Mafia figures, and a friendly acquaintance of the judge, was a motions and procedural expert, and a good meat-and-potatoes lawyer but a bland barrister and a defeatist. He thought all Chicago jurors were overawed by the presence in the case of the U.S. government.

It was all coming down to the two Eddies. If they could do it, we would win, because we were innocent and seemed to have a fair judge. The prosecution was completely overconfident; Sussman would have been constitutionally incapable of any other attitude. He would have been cocksure when in his diapers. Right up to the trial they were scrabbling unsuccessfully after my tax records (which would not have yielded them anything of interest).

THE LAWYERS OF THE CO-DEFENDANTS were a mixed bag. Gustave Newman for Jack Boultbee was a legend, with more than fifty years of trial experience. He had won the Bank of Credit and Commerce International (BCCI) case for Roger Altman, who was implicated by prosecutors in the $10 billion bank failure. A broad New York accent and a display of silver facial hair gave him an Old Testament appearance and rich cadences of a bygone New York. He sometimes quoted 1920s New York governor and presidential candidate Al Smith, a vintage character but no longer well known, especially in Chicago. His co-counsel, Pat Tuite, was originally a Chicago lawyer who now conducted a practice of sorts in Florida. He was a charming man, and though he had once been a prosecutor, briefly, he was now, like Greenspan and Genson, steeped in the lore of the demi-monde of hoods and thugs, and was addicted to anecdotes about colourful clients who had been unalloyed criminals.

This was one of the problems of these cases. The lawyers were either ex-prosecutors – who had no objection to the prosecution except they wanted to make more money and would generally be prone to cut a deal with the prosecutors – or lifelong defence counsel who were generally unaccustomed to having respectable clients and tended not to know much about real commerce.

Atkinson's lawyers were Benito Romano, a former U.S. attorney in New York, and Michael Schacter, who had been one of Martha Stewart's prosecutors but who now wished to make a name for himself as a defence counsel. To date, in discovery that was recorded on videotape in Toronto, he had mainly been noteworthy for making completely unnecessary distinctions between non-compete and bonus payments in a way that could be exploited by the prosecutors.

Another former prosecutor, Ron Safer, who seemed and proved to be very capable, was acting for Mark Kipnis. All the other counsel for the defence were constantly asking for severance from us and were already claiming mistrials before the real trial began. Their repetitive note was the irritating scramble for sideline status in the government's witch hunt for me. They had the moral courage not to plead guilty to crimes of which they were innocent, but not the strategic sense to see that trying to throw up petty distinctions between their and my legal positions would just play into the prosecution's hands. I feared that only our counsel knew that the only way to win the case was a take-no-prisoners frontal attack on the government and its witnesses.

Apart from Radler, the prosecutors would frog-march through the entire Audit Committee, who would state in unison that they knew nothing of the contested payments. They would also have to bring in Paul Healy, to try to make the case on the New York apartment. Only I was involved in the charges about taking the airplane to Bora Bora, and the dinner that fell on Barbara's sixtieth birthday, and the supposed obstruction of justice with the removal of the boxes from my Toronto office, and RICO. Jack Boultbee was charged with me in the New York apartment. Everything was set up to encourage the others to try to distance themselves from me, and I had no confidence that the other counsel would resist the temptation to try to fly under the government radar. The trial would pivot, I thought, on the ability of the Eddies to destroy the government's main witnesses. Nothing else would exonerate anybody from anything.

I FINISHED THE NIXON TEXT, and after final editing it went to the printers in February for a March launch. It would receive admiring reviews in Canada and Britain as well as the United States, and most reviewers generously acknowledged that it was a considerable feat given the other concerns I had had while writing it.

Friends gave me several parting dinners and an avalanche of messages arrived, many accompanied by prayers and uplifting poems. There was a Conrad Black Fan Club website and a sequence of supportive T-shirts: "Conrad Will Win," "Go Conrad," "Free Conrad," and so forth. These gestures were comforting after the endless bad weather since the clouds originally burst in November 2003.

In my last column, for a time, in the *National Post*, I wrote of my long-standing admiration of Chicago as, among other attainments, the bar of Abraham Lincoln and Clarence Darrow. I mentioned that Barbara had bought a Hungarian Pulli, an adorable puppy to accompany two aging and amiable dogs of the same breed, but that he would not have grown unrecognizably when I returned. (She named it George-Black after my father.) I wrote that those who had buried me and covered the surrounding ground with garlic and crucifixes would be disappointed to discover that I was, as I had never ceased to claim, innocent, but that I bore no hostility to those who had opposed me, except for a few outright crooks whom I did not need to name.

In a touching demonstration of solidarity, as well as an addition of great insight to our inner circle, my daughter, Alana, retired from her apprentice job in a fashion clothing store and came with us to Chicago, enlisting for the duration of the case.

I had an early foretaste of the absurdity of the advice I might receive. Through the generosity of the chairman of Four Seasons Hotels, Isadore Sharp, we got a comfortable apartment-suite in the Ritz-Carlton Hotel at a reasonable rate. The views of Chicago were magnificent on our high floor. The suite had no special grandeur, but a room each for Barbara and me to work and a galley kitchen. Greenspan was very concerned that the media would bribe a housekeeper to take pictures of it and that the name of the hotel would antagonize the jurors. I had the lease signed by a society of supporters that I had formed, to cushion any public relations problem. None arose.

Greenspan's own proposed hotel, the Palmer House, was not a success. The famous El (elevated railway) came clattering past his window at a distance of about forty feet every few minutes, and as he put it, the room was darker when he opened the curtains than when they were closed. His party checked out after one night, greeting him in the lobby with their packed luggage. They moved to a Renaissance Hotel that answered its phone with "your urban sanctuary."

Genson had had the insane idea that Barbara – and Alana, whom he had not met – should not come to court. They were to sit dutifully in the hotel watching soap operas and playing gin rummy, for months, awaiting the return of the client each day. I literally prayed that my counsel would be the font of more promising ideas when we finally, imminently, came to grips with my mortal enemy, in what we all kept referring to as a court of law, though little law seemed to have intruded into the prosecution.

IT WAS IN A SPIRIT OF GRIM BUT hopeful determination that Barbara, Alana, and I flew to Chicago on March 13, 2007, on the charter I usually use. (Commercial air travel to the United States was practically impossible, because of the unpredictable number of hours required to penetrate the security system once my name popped up in the computers.) We arrived on a premature spring day and settled quickly into the Ritz-Carlton. The hotel personnel, throughout our stay, could not have been more agreeable. The next day began the four months of Judge St. Eve's dawn patrols, requiring everyone to be present at hours ranging from 8:45 a.m. to 9:15 a.m. Generally Fridays were off, but not always. They would be intense sessions.

The court setup did not resemble any American TV series apart from the fact that the jury sat in a box in two rows to the judge's left. However, about three feet away at a table directly in front of the jury and facing it head-on were the four prosecutors, who would grin and smirk at the jurors and make exaggerated gestures in response to defence lawyers and witnesses. This was, to say the least, irritating. The next table, immediately in front of the judge, was our defence table. I sat at the far end on the right side, again from the judge's perspective. The next table had the Boultbee team at the front of the room and the Atkinson team at the farther end. At the last table, sitting with their backs to the wall, were Mark Kipnis and his counsel. I supposed my position as chief defendant, with the honour of fourteen unfounded criminal charges against me (three had not been proceeded with), gave me the central position directly beneath the great seal of the United States of America over the judge's well-coiffed head. The gallery held about eighty spectators, and there was an overflow room upstairs, served by a single, fixed camera, which was focused solely on one of the technicians who put documents up on projection screens. The marshals, who were friendly and genial, regularly banished and admonished journalists for one offence or another.

On the morning of March 14, there began the rather depressing procedure of empanelling a jury. I was ready for an unprepossessing sample of the great American public. I was underprepared for such a procession of mainly monosyllabic and listless people. For three days, they filed through, usually in groups of eight. We had their questionnaires, which gave their occupations, areas of residence, educational backgrounds, and family history, and explored whether they had prejudices that might be tweaked in the case: nationality (none had any notion that Canadians were different in any degree from Americans), economic status, social position, and so forth. Something of their thinking and articulation could be divined from their handwriting and choice of words. Some had an unpretentious dignity and candour, and some were fairly educated.

They gave their preferred reading, favourite television programs, and hobbies. Apart from the choices of one man who claimed regularly to read the *New York Times* and *The New Yorker*, and appeared to be likely to suffer extreme lip strain if he tried to read more than one paragraph of either, most were low-brow magazines, soap operas, bowling, bingo, gardening, and attending to dogs. There did not appear to be as many as half of them who had ever read a book, played a game of chess, or watched a serious newscast.

The judge wanted twelve jurors and six alternates. I had been conditioned to expect some leftish and podgy housewives, reactionary postal or local government workers, and some utter cretins. These groups were out in numerical strength. Some astonishingly inappropriate people answered the call: a gigantic, moustachioed woman who acknowledged that all accused people were guilty; an advanced technician who admitted to the same views, and tenaciously clung to them, presumably to avoid spending three months or more as a juror; a corporate activist who believed all shareholders were victims and all executives were dishonest; and a thick slug of what would in another time and place be called the *lumpenproletariat*. The judge had her own idiosyncrasies. Anyone, she said, who had already booked a ticket for their summer holidays (this was early March) was excused from jury duty – no evidence of ticket required. This news got out pretty fast, and anyone that had anything approaching a genuine occupation or interests solemnly informed the court that, regrettably, their June and July were otherwise occupied.

The jurors, from beginning to end, seemed determined to dress down as much as possible. Blue jeans were the uniform for almost all. Men never, once, wore jackets, much less a tie, and only a couple of the finalist women ever wore a dress or skirt. I had been conditioned by black-and-white films, more recent television, and even news coverage of other trials to imagine that these people would dress up a little for the judge and the media of several countries. It seemed to me they were more concerned to show how unimpressed they were with the whole process. So was I, but not, I suspect, for the same reasons.

The procedure for selection allowed both sides a number of rejections without any reasons given, and there was room to challenge jurors for stated causes. Odd moments occurred. When several of the potential jurors answered "no" to the question "could you be fair," the judge argued passionately with them, conveying her confidence that they could. "Different tax treatment for rich and poor people is wrong," said one, echoing a theme that emerged. "You will hear about people receiving sums of millions of dollars," the judge would say. "Can you put that aside when judging the case?" Eventually, most of the advocates of wealth redistribution would self-righteously proclaim their fairness and on to the list they came. The judge asked Genson, as apparent senior counsel to the chief defendant, if he sought a greater number that could be rejected as jury candidates without explanation, and Genson, in a way that I was to become familiar with and always made me very uneasy, quickly said no. Michael Schacter leapt to his feet and said that he did want more, and the judge immediately agreed. I asked Genson what had motivated him, and he nonchalantly replied, "I thought she'd reject it. I blew it." I asked why he didn't ask anyway, what was the downside? "I said, I blew it." He was to shoot from the hip and blow it a distressing number of times.

Greenspan said that Barbara and Alana should not attend the jury-choosing session of clients, counsel, and advisers, but he moved so slowly that the agile ladies preceded him into the selection room and sat down, and by the time Eddie shambled in, he had forgotten his nonsensical prohibition. He and Genson slumped into chairs and dozed off, leaving it to Marc Martin and me to represent our side in the entertaining but undignified session that ensued.

The defence counsel and the defendants were allocated one of the neighbouring, unoccupied courtrooms (they were nearly always unoccupied, as almost no one can afford to go all the way to trial in federal court), and jury selection began from the list of eligibles we now had. All the defendants had their own jury consultants. I never had the impression that any of them actually knew what he was talking about. More knowledgeable, perhaps, but no more reassuring was Mark Kipnis's counsel, Ron Safer. He did not fire me with confidence in the pursuit of a condign verdict when he stood on a chair and declaimed, with the confidence of an ex-prosecutor, that: "We have to get rid of any juror with any intelligence." With this group of candidates, that did not seem an insurmountable challenge, but it was not encouraging.

The few people who appeared to be well disposed would certainly be opposed by the government, and they were. One prospective juror had read and liked my book on Roosevelt, but was disqualified (not for that but because Marc Martin had represented someone accused of murdering one of the candidate juror's relatives). We accepted a few howling opponents, as we thought, as alternates, on the theory that they would never make it onto the jury. One such person had to withdraw after a few weeks, for health reasons, news that we all received with relief, and then she gave an interview to one of the Canadian reporters and said that she was well disposed to the defendants.

The most visibly memorable of the jurors was the woman with long curly blonde hair, a formidable cleavage, full-figured to overflowing, who blew impressive pink bubbles of chewing gum, which, as Mark Steyn would write, hovered over the prosecution table threateningly, like First World War Zeppelins. Shortly after this description by Mark, the bubble-blowing stopped, presumably at the behest of the judge.

Two of those selected seemed to be narcoleptics and slumbered through most of the entire trial. The dozier of the two (they became known as Dozey and Dopey) looked fully awake and ramrod straight only on the last day of the trial, when she was startled to such an unprecedented state by what Mark Steyn considered the mind-altering monotony of Sussman's final statement. To be fair, this woman had written three times on her questionnaire that she did not want to serve. No one could say that we had not been warned.

As the trial progressed, their simplicity and determined lack of style caused me to admire some of the women jurors. They did, for the most part, seem like decent people, and they were all very reliable and prompt attenders. Some had made their way in the world with a lack of presumption and edge that did legitimize idealized versions of the virtues of a juror, as espoused by Chesterton and others. On balance, I preferred jurors to judges after all I had endured from the bench in the U.S. and Canada.

Lacklustre though they were as a group, I managed, as I always had, to attribute superficially indiscernible strengths of mind and character to the American public, even this little echelon of it, and persuaded myself that they might be up to the task that was now theirs. After these years of waiting, it was oddly reassuring to look on these unexceptional people and reflect that they would decide if my family and I would be impoverished and whether I would spend the rest, or any, of my life in prison for offences I did not commit.

On the day when the jurors were approved, as I was leaving the courthouse, a journalist with a London East End (Cockney) accent, said: "A jury of your peers, Lord Black?" My reply, that "Any citizen of this great country is my peer" was not facetious.

THE TRIAL BEGAN ON MARCH 20. There were hundreds of accredited media, and they swarmed us at every opportunity. Alana immediately became the star of the entire proceedings, by her beauty, carriage, and poise. She said at all times that she would not speak with the press, and reinforced this when a particularly bumptious reporter pushed in beside her at an evening social gathering and suggested they go on a shopping expedition together. Alana smiled pleasantly at everyone, but apart from Mark Steyn and Theresa Tedesco of the *National Post*, and a couple of others, she didn't care for the journalists, in varying degrees, as if judging the different venomous potentialities of poisonous snakes.

The opening statement confirmed the Stalinesque flavour of the prosecution. Prosecutor Jeff Cramer, in all his primeval brutishness, strode about the court, pointing at the defendants and naming us individually, and likened us in his opening sentences to bank robbers and street thugs and burglars. We had stolen $60 million from the unsuspecting people who had put our stock away "for the retirement or college fund." We did not wear masks, use guns, or resort to violence, he acknowledged, but we were morally indistinguishable from those who did.

Cramer's children were present, excused from school to sit in the front row and hear their father liken innocent men to hardened and violent criminals. Mark Kipnis's very gracious mother and other members of his family were there, along with Barbara and Alana, who each managed almost every day of the trial.

My son Jonathan came in two stretches, and James came near the end. Big and strong young men, they resisted urgings from the defence team to seduce female jurors or at least rough up a few journalists. As a group, they were a fine-looking family, and a great source of pride. Jack Boultbee's wonderfully outspoken wife, Sharon, and their witty son, Michael, and briefly Jack's daughter, Leslie, also came in mid-trial. Alana's and Barbara's messages, handed up to me, were usually insightful and sometimes uproariously amusing.

Barbara was understandably appalled at Cramer's excesses. I found them reassuring, as he obviously had no idea how vulnerable the government's case would prove, and he and Sussman should finally discover that aggression is not an adequate substitute for the law and the facts.

Genson followed Cramer. The consensus was that he was fairly effective. At my insistence, and over Greenspan's protests, he put in that there had been theft in our company, but that I had been the victim rather than the author of it. The whole company had been stolen from me. Greenspan had opposed this because he did not want to get sidetracked by the narrative of corporate factionalism and internecine strife in which this trial was just one of the more dramatic rounds. He thought it tactically better to seek a reasonable doubt on the exact charges. The opening statement is the single place to give jurors the overall picture and set up the scene for what is about to unravel before them in confusing bits and pieces. I wanted my lawyers to explain very briefly just how this battle between shareholders over-selling the company had roller-coasted into a criminal trial. It was not to be. Both Genson and Greenspan were afraid of confusing the jury with the facts of the case. But they were unafraid of leaving the jury with no context for what they were hearing. I felt that the smoke-and-fire theory was likely to prevail to some degree if the jurors did not understand that this was part of a corporate factional war. What, after all, was the reason I was thrown out of the company apart from the prosecution's contention that I was a racketeer and thief? They were given none. Genson said in his opening that the prosecutors were tools of a faction, but I could never get either of them to explain even a hint of the real story beyond that. I was dragging two great wet blankets behind me. It was immensely frustrating, but at least we had hinted at the full story in the opening.

Genson gave a strenuous and detailed refutation of most of Cramer's points. He found it necessary to deprecate me as self-important and "arrogant." I could take that, but not his unimaginative and inaccurate claim that I had a "snotty attitude." His vocabulary was inadequate to furnish him the right words; I have my faults but that is not among them. (Nor was I paying him generously to insult me in front of the court and the media.) His desire to soften the impact of some emails the government would produce and represent as, to say the least, high-handed was understandable. But I thought there were better ways of challenging the contention that I was an unpleasant or overbearing personality. To start with, none of the prosecution witnesses who knew me would have made any such claim. The only one who was asked was the doorman at our office building, who said "Oh yes, he is always very courteous." Genson's stammering, mispronunciations, confusing word-substitutions, and syntax that would have made Casey Stengel seem like Thomas Hardy, all horrified me, but he made his points, and was humorous, comprehensive, and clearly appeared to be well liked by the jury. Both his joviality and his infirmity, which he had gallantly overcome through a long career, would have endeared him to the jurors at least at the start of the trial.

Genson had a technique that was a little like a vaudeville act, and his specialty was confusing jurors through obfuscation, ingratiation, and muddying the waters. I was concerned about whether such a shtick would hold up through a long trial, and I was rightly confident that Genson had no other method. This was a case that required precision to extract the facts from a vast mass of contending charges and defences.

Generally, Genson was commended on a good start. We had given notice that there would be an argument. Gustave Newman, the legendary New York barrister who had just celebrated his eightieth birthday and had barely recovered from a bout of pneumonia, followed, and impressed the court with a powerful address that presaged the great attack on Radler that was to come. "Would you buy a used car from this man?" was part of his theme. His tall, slender, white-bearded, well-accoutered appearance and powerful voice, as well as his almost Old World courtesy ("Pardon my back," he would say when he turned to produce an exhibit), made a strong impression. Benito Romano followed for Peter Atkinson, and was quiet, diminutive, undemonstrative, and made no impression. This was carrying the co-defendants' attempts to fly below the radar to a newly reduced altitude: Romano mounted what was almost a stealth defence. Apart from asserting his client's innocence, he gave little indication of what line he would follow to establish that.

The defence opening arguments closed with Ron Safer's very powerful presentation for Mark Kipnis. He waved about "Mark's anti-fraud pen" as he marched to and fro, as if holding up a battle standard, and repeated the mantra: "Mark did the best he could with the information he had." Safer spoke with great emotion in a very Chicago accent, and moved around the room almost majestically, unlike Cramer, with his irritating cobralike lurches. Safer, on this and future days, almost held the court spellbound at times. He hinted still at his desire to separate from the others, especially me, as the principal recipient of the amounts at issue. But at least he went to some length to debunk the prosecution generally.

Sun-Times Media Group (stmg), as Hollinger International was now called, had just announced a further cash settlement with Radler, who repaid his CanWest non-competition payment, which was not even alleged to have been illegal. Radler had also committed the private companies he had created from former Hollinger properties, without serious consultation with any of the other shareholders, to repay sums to stmg. Much of this repayment was simply monies owed from the original sale, but much of it was involuntarily paid by other shareholders, to clean up Radler's own liabilities to stmg and the sec. This was all dressed up as a massive financial coup for stmg, to distract from or disguise the more than $100 million net cost of the Special Committee process and the 90 per cent decline in the stock price.

The government, buoyed by this loudly proclaimed bit of financial flim-flam, called Gordon Paris as their first witness. He was to explain the corruption he found and repaired but was destabilized as a witness within a few minutes by one of Genson's better tricks. In the guise of conducting a voir dire, approaching the witness to go over a document with him as part of an objection, early in Sussman's examination, Genson wobbled up and, hovering and nodding over Paris at a range of one foot and malapropistically interrogating him, was understandably unnerving, especially given what Paris was selling and he wasn't fast on his feet at the best of times.

Paris scored no points at all, and Sussman abruptly handed the witness to the defence. Greenspan cross-examined. The intention was to use Paris's cross-examination to start laying out the enormous amounts of money made and spent by the usurpatory regime, who were completely without newspaper experience. We wanted to expose their low motivation, greed, and incompetence.

It was obvious early on that Greenspan's unfamiliarity with American procedure was going to be a problem. Sussman stood straight up from his chair like an emerging champagne cork on every question, his rectangular head and large nose suddenly appearing right beside Greenspan, very distractingly, putting his objection. Greenspan appeared to have no idea how to deal with the objections technically, and no idea whether they were well founded or not. Sussman was like a hyena nipping at the legs of a lumbering beast, and unfortunately, to some extent, Greenspan played his part of the role. He privately blamed Genson for not warning him about American procedure, and Genson seemed to me consolable that the much-announced star Canadian barrister was encountering such difficulties.

At that, Greenspan elicited from Paris the fact that he was paid $17,045 per day in 2003 and $15,805.17 per day in 2005 (there was a legal reason for not getting into figures for 2004), but the impact of these revelations was diluted by the blizzard of objections, most of which were sustained after several sidebars and voir dires. Here we encountered the problem of admissibility of evidence subsequent to the contentious events. Sussman came marching forward, holding the Breeden report over his head, jauntily assuming that he could get it into evidence. Defence counsels' well-prepared storm of objections prevented this, as we prevented admission of the joint agreement the former Audit Committee members had signed with the SEC to avoid prosecution (almost as complete, if not as voluminous, a fantasy as the Breeden report). We also excluded Strine's infamous judgment and later the effort to call evidence from the Ravelston receiver and the stated reasoning of the more antagonistic Canadian judges.

This was a win, but it had mixed consequences for us. A strong motivation for the determination of Breeden & Co. was their need to get me convicted on at least some of the charges in order to save themselves from my libel suits in respect of the Special Committee report and the annual report (Form 10K) of $1 billion each, launched in Canada, where, contrary to practice in the United States, the civil tort of defamation is a serious threat. Those suits would be lethal were I acquitted. Our other suits and counter-suits were also in the billions, to be able to weigh it in judging the motives of my accusers.

The concern about giving the prosecution any opening to introduce Breeden's report, Strine's remarks, and the reasoning (if such it could be called) of the more antagonistic Canadian judges, especially Campbell, prevented my lawyers from exposing the full perfidy of the usurpers who followed us and lined their pockets while destroying the shareholders' interest. We could not demonstrate how they had used the companies the defendants had built to destroy the defendants. The prosecution initially was going to lead with a line of reasoning that would have allowed us to ask Paris and other witnesses for the prosecution a number of deadly motive-revealing questions. But on seeing where it would go, the prosecutors decided to pitch that approach in one of the sidebars. On looking over the transcripts of those sidebars, it seemed to me that had my lawyers shown more mental agility or at least argued with more clarity, we could have introduced a number of questions leading to motivation without stirring up the ashes of the Breeden report. But that is Monday-morning quarterbacking. We won, on balance, in this exchange, but it left us with a truncated argument.

Eddie Greenspan's debut had not been auspicious, and there were audible concerns at the defence tables, though in their desire to pretend they were in a different company, if not on a different planet, from me, the other counsel gave Paris almost a pass. He had not been a successful witness, but my star lawyer was obviously vulnerable to the prosecution's hyena attacks. It was curious to see Gordon Paris again. I had grown accustomed to his swagger at Breeden's side. At the trial he was diffident, inarticulate, and had no presence at all, not even the upbeat cheerfulness he had had when I first knew him, as a bond salesman for the Toronto-Dominion Bank.

After Paris's ineffective opening, the prosecution brought on a sequence of buyers of Hollinger International assets, all primed to say that they had not requested and did not care about non-compete agreements from individual Hollinger executives. None of them mentioned me, other than saying that they had heard of me, but that we had had no contact of any kind. All the negotiating was with Radler and Mark Kipnis. The principal lawyer in two of the biggest deals, Jim Henson, a courtly southerner, made it clear that he found Radler vulgar and abrasive.

The buyers were a pretty phlegmatic group. Mike Reed of Community Newspaper Holdings Inc., who had paid out more than $500 million to us and was subsequently dismissed from his job, in large part, no doubt, because he was taken over the barrel by Radler, was dismantled quite effectively by Genson. While Reed said he did not want the executives' non-compete agreements, and started out rather jokily responding to Genson, he acknowledged that in the non-competition clause, by asking for "affiliates" as well as the vendor company, he meant the executives and corporate affiliates of the vendor company. (In the midst of the trial, the *Chicago Tribune* changed hands, along with its television and radio and cable properties; the *Los Angeles Times*, the *Baltimore Sun*, and *Newsday* [Long Island]; the Fort Lauderdale, Hartford, and other newspapers; extensive real estate, and the Chicago Cubs, for $311 million, plus a special dividend and a large participation by the Employees' Share Ownership Plan, though the buyer assured the press that he would dismiss a large number of the employees. This illustrated the tremendous payoffs Radler had negotiated in the sale of these community newspapers. The newspaper industry had gone into steep decline; we had started into and out of the business at good times, and Radler, however objectionable they found his personality, had dealt very cleverly with these provincial buyers.)

Gus Newman and Ron Safer further extracted that Reed had signed an agreement stating that the non-competition clauses were required conditions of sale. He wanly said that he did so because it didn't cost him anything, but Safer eventually produced the fact that the funder of the deal, the Alabama state pension fund, had required these clauses as a condition of advancing the money to make the acquisitions. Reed, though well-rehearsed, had not scored for the prosecution.

The representative from Forum, owner of the leading newspaper in North Dakota, was a straightforward but cautious Midwesterner, even refusing to let it be known if the company had borrowed money to pay us $14 million for the newspaper in Jamestown, North Dakota. He, too, was clearly taken for quite a sleigh ride by Radler, but at least he had held his job. He, too, claimed that they had not cared about competition from individual executives but could not adequately explain why he wanted the inclusion of "affiliates" in the language of the agreement. He, too, was routed on cross-examination, as he acknowledged that Radler had bought, just after the non-competition agreements expired, a newspaper in a neighbouring county to Jamestown.

Radler had made huge gains for our shareholders with these deals at the very brink of the great newspaper decline. The buyers had not done their due diligence properly and had no idea that the senior executives of Hollinger International – key players in creating and then maintaining these properties – were in fact employees not of International but of the ultimate parent company, Ravelston. Since a subsidiary could not bind its parent, the "affiliates" reference in the non-competes did not achieve what they had hoped. Radler had certainly not disguised these arrangements, which were publicly disclosed. Having been carefully prepared by the prosecutors, and angry at having been clearly foxed by Radler into overpaying, they all repeated their lines, but they all disintegrated under serious cross-examination. Genson and Safer, and to some degree Newman, accomplished this. Atkinson, who was not mentioned, continued to fly just above the treetops, sharing with his counsel the fantasy stratum that this would liberate him from suspicion.

The best of the community newspaper buyers was David Paxton, an alumnus of Oxford University from Paducah, Kentucky. He answered all questions in a forthright manner and acknowledged that there could have been some utility to the non-competition payments to executives after all. The buyers had not made the case the government promised, and Newman, in particular, had made the point that whatever the buyers now claimed had been their wishes eight years before, they had signed binding and enforceable contracts containing a precise wording about the contested payments, and their verbal revisitation of the deals after government tutorials could not trump signed written contracts that had been publicly disclosed and discussed for years without any comment from them. The non-compete payments in each case had been stated to be "conditions of closing." This was a promising start for the defence.

GUS NEWMAN, ALWAYS A GENTLEMAN, committed an astounding breach of professional etiquette by approaching me, another attorney's client, and expressing his concern about whether Greenspan, for whom he said he had great respect, could carry the weight placed on him in the trial. I answered noncommittally but made hopeful sounds. Barbara had been watching the manoeuvrings and facial grimaces of the other defendants' counsel whenever Greenspan was on his feet and thought that Newman was simply reflecting the concerns of all the other lawyers. I had the same concerns, but I didn't think it was for Newman to raise it with me, and suggested he raise it with Eddie directly. He did so, at a stormy Easter weekend luncheon that offended Greenspan and raised his paranoiac instincts but did not advance the cause of his adaptation to American courtroom rules.

Greenspan told me that the reason for Newman's criticism was concern that Mrs. Newman was unwell. She may have been, but she appeared pretty chipper in her many appearances at the trial. And I think the reason for Newman's concern about Greenspan was that Greenspan's ponderousness and vulnerability to Sussman's harassments warranted concern.

At the end of the parade of buyers, we had made the point that noncompetition payments were normal and regular in the newspaper industry, frequently paid to individuals, and that these buyers wanted comprehensive guaranties against competition from the companies and people who were the vendors in these cases for good commercial reasons. It had gone quite well, and some journalists who had been at Delaware and presumed that such payments were a scam were now of another mind.

The government thought it could make its financial case, and especially the allegation about misusing corporate funds, with the infamous trip to Bora Bora, with Fred Creasey. I was pretty confident that they would find him a disappointing witness. As always with government witnesses throughout this long trial, they performed quite persuasively as long as they were repeating back the catechism they had been taught to answer prosecution questions.

I knew that Creasey was a man of collapsible nerves. He had fainted to the floor of his office when informed that the SEC wanted to interview him, though he was not suspected of wrongdoing, and had never returned to work, being mentally unfit for more than three years. Though easily frightened and a pessimist, he was diligent, honest, and would not lie under oath. Mark Steyn and others thought that he exuded an air of natural believability when under direct examination and felt he was a strong prosecution witness. I assured them that he would be just as believable answering our questions and would be completely useless to the government and that this would be clear after an hour's defence questioning, because the charge was unfounded, and Fred would tell the truth.

Creasey had recorded that our trip to Bora Bora in 2001 had cost the company $565,000 because he divided the entire cost of the aircraft operation, including salaries, the charter, and hangar rental by the proportion of the year that was taken up by the trip. Of course this was nonsense, since the fixed costs were inevitable and would have been incurred if the airplane had not moved one inch in its hangar.

Greenspan took the cross-examination, and I thought he performed well. Creasey retreated at speed from all the overexposed positions to which the government had led him. Yes, I could have chartered a comparable plane for a quarter as much. Yes, I paid half the cost, as he had calculated it, which was more than twice the variable costs, which were what were normally charged. Yes, I had been assessed a taxable benefit for much more than industry practice would have indicated. Yes, the company made $125,000 transporting me. I thought Greenspan did particularly well with the exchange that ended: "I'm sorry. I thought that when you said that you were an expert in corporate finance, you meant that you were an expert in corporate finance." Creasey: "Not necessarily." Greenspan concluded with one of the more memorable lines of the trial: "You provided Mr. Black with the most expensive airplane trip in the history of manned flight."

In their redirect examination, Julie Ruder introduced a new tactic, which was to become tiresomely familiar. "Where in this document do you find any reference to . . . ?" Anything could be inserted here, from supposedly unauthorized non-competition payments to the remotest and feeblest parts of the prosecution's case. Since she was asking non sequiturs, the answer always had to be "nowhere." A long sequence of these questions, which I told some members of the press would eventually include references to my participation in the assassination of Abraham Lincoln, as well as my habitual severance and boiling of little boys' heads, would give way to a further series of: "If you had known of . . ." and all the earlier horrors were repeated, more or less in order, "would that have altered your judgment of" whatever. It was the shabbiest, most sophomoric device I had heard in decades, and visibly made little impact on the jury, whose members were not electrified by Creasey at any point.

Mark Steyn changed his tune and agreed with Theresa Tedesco's overly harsh view that far from being a threat to the defence, Creasey was an Elmer Fudd figure. Mark added that Hollinger should have gone more quickly out of the newspaper business and into aircraft chartering, an immensely remunerative form of commerce on this occasion. Fred Creasey left as he had come, a beetle-browed, beleaguered but good man who had achieved negative yardage for the prosecution because he did not lie under oath and was never snide or malicious.

The first week in April produced good press responses to the Creasey appearance, and a pleasant diversion when the eighty-one-year-old Dominick Dunne, an acquaintance of Barbara's from the 1970s, came to town and Barbara, Alana, and I had dinner with him. Alana continued to be the great star of the trial. Her lovely appearance, beguiling manner, attentiveness, charm, and complete lack of interest in the press conquered almost everyone.

AFTER THE UNSUCCESSFUL Easter luncheon between Greenspan and Gus Newman, I spoke to Genson and Martin about Greenspan's problem with American procedure, I thought that he did well with Creasey. Genson clearly wanted the cross-examination of Radler, but Greenspan had earned that. It was agreed that Genson's partner, Terry Gillespie, would give Greenspan a crash course on procedure.

I had a cathartic meeting with Greenspan in our little lunch room in late afternoon. I asked him very calmly to "raise my comfort level about your ability to master U.S. procedure." He flared up and threw all the toys out of the baby carriage and announced he would return to Toronto at once. Barbara, when I told her, thought this was a golden opportunity not to be missed, felt there were better American lawyers at our table that were not being used, and had to be restrained from paying for a private flight to take him home that day. I ignored both her and Greenspan's suggestions and urged him to compose himself and just give me more confidence that we were turning the corner on his adaptation to this court.

Because Greenspan had been the most famous lawyer in Canada for many years, it was both touching and worrisome to see the sudden erosion of his prestige. I was now quite accustomed to the sudden collapse of a prominent individual; seldom had a prominent person's status and reputation been destroyed more quickly than mine. But I had at least carried myself with outward dignity toward everyone, even the diminished number of confidants and did not impute animosity, much less conspiracy, almost indiscriminately.

Eddie Greenspan's methods were far too ponderous for the rapid cadence of American trials. Generally, objections are just ignored by defence lawyers, who proceed whether the judge sustains or overrules. Greenspan had been accustomed to the Canadian method of arguing over each objection, which completely broke his rhythm.

Sussman, overconfident as always, referred to Greenspan as "an old water buffalo" and said to Jane Kelly that I would be convicted in the minds of the jury before Radler even took the stand. That was not how it worked out.

The next phase of the trial consisted of very lengthy videotapes of Torys lawyer Darren Sukonick and a former partner of that firm, Beth DeMerchant. Videotape depositions consist of a fixed camera on the face of the deposee, who appears in limbo being questioned by a disenthralled voice from an invisible source. When you are watching a large screen with the close-up of a sombre Canadian accountant or lawyer such as Beth DeMerchant talking for five or six hours straight, it becomes almost humorous in its monotony. A silent hum of boredom descends over the courtroom. After about three hours of videotape, the deposee could have said she was a terrorist from Sri Lanka and no one would have noticed. The judge seemed to use much of the time to get papers on her desk cleaned up and fiddle with the two computers on her desk. At least, unlike various jurors and counsel, she didn't doze off. The tapes had been taken in Toronto in February, and edited by joint agreement. It was never clear to me what the government thought it would achieve with this. Both lawyers expressed confidence in the integrity of Atkinson, their contact person in our company. (Sukonick and DeMerchant were later investigated by the Law Society. I was never overly impressed with their imagination, and some of their advice was incorrect, but I don't think they were unethical or negligent. The singling out of them, as well as the Law Society's rather banal allegations, seems to me to be shabby and tokenistic placation of opinion by the Toronto legal establishment, at the expense of two relatively defenseless scapegoats.)

The issue was whether we had tried to withhold disclosure of the CanWest non-competition payments. Torys had advised us that we need not disclose them, so we didn't. The U.S. firm Cravath, Swaine & Moore, through Bud Rogers and Paul Saunders, the next two witnesses, advised us that we must, so we did, four days after receiving their definitive advice. This was not much of a case for a coverup. Rogers and Saunders both greeted me cordially. They confirmed both the advice they had given and our quick follow-through on it. Saunders had acted for me in the Hanna Mining affair in 1982, and we had remained in occasional contact since. He was an ascetic, austere, painfully fit, and thin man with an inflexible formality, like a retired Marine colonel. His cordiality to me now was carefully calibrated, in the subtle manner of the chief professional servants of the New York financial establishment, and was conditional, curt, and even tentative. He was a cold-blooded follower of the tide of events, a sand shark serving larger and fiercer fish. If I had had any need of a barometer of my status, he could have provided it.

It emerged clearly from all the lawyers that we had faithfully tried to follow exactly the disclosure regulations, irrespective of our own perceived convenience. A month into the trial, most of the press had backed off a long way and acknowledged that it was a much less clear-cut case than had been represented in government and Breeden-sponsored leaks and allegations. My former editor at the *Globe and Mail's Report on Business* magazine, Margaret Wente, who was strangely nasty in her written references to Barbara and me, though cheerful when we actually met, wrote that while she hoped that I would go to prison, she now doubted that I would. Given her animus, her premonitions made her a hopeful weather vane. The prosecutors had not laid a hand on us. None of the community newspaper buyers had ever had any exchange with me, and I was not mentioned by the Torys and Cravath lawyers. And we had clearly won the arguments about the legitimacy of the non-competition payments and the response to legal advice.

While the lawyers appeared by video, I launched a side offensive in Toronto, and Peter White published a letter I had received from loyalists in the former Hollinger International exposing Voorheis's desperate effort to sell Hollinger Inc.'s super-voting rights to STMG (again, the former Hollinger International). Stan Freedman represented us at the annual meeting of Hollinger Inc. and posed a series of questions to Voorheis, which he completely failed to answer, particularly why he had fiercely opposed the Hollinger Inc. privatization two years before and there was now a 95 per cent deterioration of share value.

Voorheis had also made erroneous representations about imminent realizations on litigation to Richter (the Ravelston receiver), which re-elected him despite his failure and his self-overpayment, as Richter too was overpaying itself to strip the carcass of what it was sworn to protect, and Richter too was a puppet of the prosecutor. The vandals had to protect one another: it was a brotherhood. Sussman wanted Voorheis in place because of his ability to aggravate me and destroy what little was left of the value of Hollinger Inc. assets. We at least attracted press attention to the stunning collapse of Hollinger Inc. since we had been betrayed by the Ontario Securities Commission on the instructions of Breeden in March 2005. The only hope for salvaging anything for the shareholders or bondholders of any of the former group was in our complete acquittal, and swift reassertion of control and sweeping out of the parasites.

The prosecution's next try was with the auditors, and they brought in Marilyn Stitt (of KPMG), a solid professional who would not spin her testimony. The direct examination was brief, designed to incite the inference that the auditors had been misled by the management, though this was never asked or stated. It was insinuated from very bowdlerized extracts from the auditor's professional handbook that implied it was virtually up to the management to audit itself.

The defence counsel quickly wrung from her (with no reluctance or evasion from the witness) the extensive sections of the handbook that required auditors to do a great many things that gave the jurors a clear idea of the scope of an audit. More valuable, she confirmed to Genson that when she and other KPMG people had visited the Hollinger International Audit Committee on February 25, 2002, it had been confirmed by Jim Thompson and Marie-Josée Kravis to the satisfaction of the auditors that the contested payments that had started this landslide of events had been approved. Genson and other defence counsel walked Stitt through her notes of her and her colleague Pat Ryan's meeting with the Audit Committee.

Pat had explicitly stated, as Stitt's notes of the meeting revealed, that KPMG wanted the Audit Committee's confirmation that it had approved the (later) contentious non-competition payments. Thompson nodded and Kravis remained silent. Richard Burt was not at the meeting. The auditors concluded that they had their confirmation. Marilyn Stitt assured the Hollinger Inc. Audit Committee of this the next month.

The fact that the prosecutors had ignored this key meeting completely, and had tried to misrepresent the nature of the auditors' obligation to the client, did not resonate well in the court. Again the press took a step back, almost unanimously, from their preconceptions of the guilt of the accused. Marilyn Stitt would not lie to please the government and answered a long series of questions from defence counsel clearly and truthfully, and very helpfully to the defence. The government case had been set back by the cameo appearance of the auditor.

After nearly six weeks of trial, the government had not begun to make a case, and I had scarcely been mentioned, apart from the foolishness about Bora Bora. Despite the implicit claims of the co-defendants to be mere bystanders in a dispute between the U.S. government and Radler and me, they had all been heavily involved with the buyers of the community newspapers, or with the lawyers on disclosure matters, or with the auditors. I had not. Cramer started out comparing us to bank robbers and street thugs. At this point, I appeared to be detached (as I was) from controversial matters, and Mark Kipnis, Peter Atkinson, and Jack Boultbee appeared to have been preoccupied with serving the letter of all laws and regulations (which they were).

Sussman in particular, impossibly thin-skinned, and egocentric, was stung by press criticism, including repeated disparagements from the *Chicago Tribune* and local television and radio stations, and he reacted peevishly to many of the journalists. The British press had come for the opening, would be back for Radler and for the end, but never really followed the case. The *Daily Express* representative, a woman with a piercing East End accent, offered Mark Steyn £1,000 if he would take Alana out and pry loose secrets from her. If Mark were so inclined, and if Alana were susceptible to such overtures, Mark might have taken the initiative on his own account and published them himself.

Even the *Sun-Times* had become almost impartial after hearing the prosecution's weak early efforts at incrimination. Among the more publicized moments in our press relations were Barbara's descriptions to Alana of two journalists trying to eavesdrop on them as "vermin" and of another nosy journalist, when speaking to Alana and me in the elevator leaving the courthouse, as "a slut." She was using the word as a general derogative in the way that "whore" is sometimes used. In both cases the journalists were going beyond commendable enterprise, and though Barbara's comments were intemperate, they were, I am afraid, *le mot juste*. They were widely quoted.

[Chapter Thirteen]

Finally the prosecutors would have to try to put on a case. The Audit Committee would be next. These would be the respectable, unassailable truth-sayers, giving the Radler line from under the impeccable carapace of their careers and reputations. It was hardly a secret that all the defence counsel were going to attack Radler violently. The prosecution hope was that their bullets would bounce off the Audit Committee, lending credence in advance to the carefully crafted testimony of the chief cooperating witness. This, too, is not how it worked out, as we knew that the allegedly secret payments had been reviewed by the audit committee many times.

Richard Burt, whom I had known for many years, and with whom I had often been socially friendly, came first. He was elegantly dressed but seemed to have aged by twenty years since I had seen him last. His face was haggard and his complexion rough. He had been undersecretary of state for Europe and Canada, ambassador to Germany, and chief arms control negotiator. Since he left government, where his service was well-regarded, he had not shouldered such responsibility, and worked for a time for a Saudi group, in which capacity he pestered me unmercifully to buy very questionable assets. That was his notion of the fiduciary duties of a director, a concept in which he now wrapped himself as if in a winding sheet. He had brought Breeden in as Special Committee counsel, and I assumed that he made a sweetheart deal for the Audit Committee as he did so. Of course, Breeden castigated the Audit Committee in his report.

Burt announced that his present occupation was that he was a member of Henry A. Kissinger and Associates. Henry had told me many times that Burt was mediocre, with little aptitude for geopolitics. Henry told me four years later that Burt had never been an associate of his, only of someone with whom he had shared office expenses and other overheads. Rick Burt was just name-dropping, and Henry Kissinger was astounded to learn that Burt had claimed to be an associate of his. Burt would join the other Audit Committee members in the incriminating line they had subscribed to in exchange for non-prosecution by the SEC, and Kissinger would give Burt a needed job, though I doubt if it paid enough to cover his alimony.

It must be said that Rick Burt put on a pretty good show. He was not present at the Audit Committee meeting that had satisfied the auditors that they had approved the contentious payments, and beyond that, the many attestations he had signed or given in teleconferences of approval of the contested payments were just oversights. "I don't remember" recurred quite frequently, but with the quiet confidence of a former ambassador.

Because Burt had alleged to the Special Committee that Peter Atkinson had broken down and in his testimony to the Audit Committee had admitted a fraudulent scheme of doling out non-competition payments to ourselves, Benito Romano had asked to go first for the defence. He did so, although there was no such allegation in Burt's evidence at trial. Benito brought out the vital fact that all the Audit Committee members had signed a statement for the SEC and had achieved a promise of non-prosecution. He was careful not to claim an exact quid pro quo, but this was his chief contribution to the trial. When I had urged my own counsel to do this, Genson had insisted that this deal with the Audit Committee could not be introduced at all, or the Strine-Breeden-like document written up by the prosecutors for the SEC and pushed in front of and signed by the Audit Committee members would come into evidence. In fact, the non-prosecution agreement was revealed, but the joint statement was not. This was one advantage of having several groups of defence counsel. At least one of them was usually right. This information grievously damaged the Audit Committee's credibility, even before a third of their evidence came in.

Most of the cross-examination of Burt was ineffectual apart from that. Gus Newman came next and was too jocular with Burt and too deferential to him as a former ambassador. On the second day, April 26, Newman started to make serious inroads on Burt, but then asked him about the February 2002 Audit Committee meeting. When Burt pointed out that he had not been at the meeting as was recorded in its minutes, Newman, inexplicably for such an experienced barrister, became evidently flustered and said, "Heads will roll in my brain trust."

He should have said that he was aware of that but presumably Burt had received a description of what had occurred at the meeting; anything but appear completely nonplussed as he did. He then wasted the court's time with a long irrelevancy about a non-compete deal Burt had approved at the Weirton Steel Company (a single, obsolete mill), of which he had once been the chairman. Newman's cross-examination fizzled.

Newman's sudden erosion, coupled with all the concerns we had about Greenspan's serviceability, and Genson's evident infirmities, though rather flamboyantly borne, highlighted the trouble with the disparate energy levels of the prosecution and defence tables. The four prosecutors were young, obnoxious, and prone to tactical blunders rooted in Sussman's endless schemes and Cramer's belligerency and the innate weakness of their case, but they had the energy of comparative youth, a fervent belief in their case, and the self-confidence that the usual success of the government's steamrolling techniques gave them. If one devious tactic didn't work, they knew another one could be improvised, always with impunity opposite the judge.

At one point Greenspan had laid out two large boards (called "demonstratives") in front of the jury. He had secured the assistance of Chris O'Connor in setting them up on tripods, but unfortunately they barricaded Chris into the far corner of the courtroom, where he had to remain for ninety minutes until there was a break and he could decently extricate himself. The jury found this rather amusing.

Genson rose to the occasion and tore into Burt, and recovered the situation quite well for the defence, asking him about each individual occasion when he had seen the non-competition payments referred to (Chris O'Connor had discovered the number of 10K drafts* that contained these references that had been circulated, so that each member of the Audit Committee had seen the paragraphs on the payments eleven times). Genson also brought up a due diligence teleconference† that Burt had attended by telephone, in December 2002, in which the same payments were declared by Thompson to have been approved. Burt waffled and didn't recall. He didn't lose his composure, though he lost his verbal swagger, and Genson exposed his memory, if not his veracity, to be deficient many times. Nothing was made of Burt's brain tumour and operation, as that would arouse sympathy and give cover for his amazingly selective amnesia, though I believed the tumour had contributed to his peculiar mental state. He seemed as unbothered when inaccuracies were revealed as he was when he uttered them.

I encountered Rick Burt as he was leaving and I was entering the washroom. When the door was opened and we came face to face at a range of barely two feet, I groaned, he sighed, and we passed by. That, I hope and assume, is the last contact there will ever be between us, the unforeseeable end of a friendship of twenty-five years.

As a witness, he credited me with "an intimidating vocabulary" and other attributes of intelligence but threw in completely with the abominable falsehood that I was part of a scheme to defraud the shareholders and directors in favour of my associates and me. On his character, Kissinger had been right.

All was now in readiness for the appearance of my old and formerly somewhat close friend Marie-Josée Kravis. Greenspan had Pat Tuite start, because he wanted him to establish the basic facts. The suspense about whether Greenspan was up to the task of being chief cross-examiner was about to be addressed.

—

---

* The 10k is the financial and related material in the annual report.
† Due diligence is the research an underwriter and its counsel do to ensure accuracy before guaranteeing a prospectus and marketing the issue.

M-J, TOO, SEEMED AGED SINCE I had last seen her, three years before. She appeared to be embalmed, so white and taut was her face, though that might have been the result of having a bad allergy and flu that day. She was well dressed and walked and spoke confidently. Her rather high hair appeared to be set with magic glue, and her wax-works face was not well served by dollops of red lipstick like Ann Hathaway's in *The Devil Wears Prada*. It had been a grand progression from convent girl in Duplessis's old French Canada to liberated career woman admirably ahead of her time in Quebec in openly leading a relaxed personal life, to cohabitant with one of Trudeau's ministers, to wife of the all-purpose-energetic conductor of the Montreal Symphony Orchestra, to the highest socio-economic stratum of New York. I had known her socially through most of this time and she had managed each stage with admirable sang-froid and panache.

When she raised her hand for the oath ending "So help you God" intoned by the judge, it reminded me of the picture she had once shown me of her at her First Communion. What unexpected and contrary currents had carried us along, and where might they take us yet?

The direct examination led her, in the manner that was now familiar, through a very labyrinthine course around awkward facts and events and obligatory admissions, but, like a good mystery hunt, to the objective: the witness knew nothing about the money we had supposedly taken for ourselves.

Pat Tuite started and was worrisomely deferential. I asked him at the break what he was doing and he said, "The jury likes her." (The usual pallid excuse for defence counsel not doing their jobs properly.) I said that it was his task to disabuse the jurors of that. Tuite's soft methods did entrap her several times in the dense 10Ks, where she claimed to have read things adjacent to the related-party section that detailed the matters she claimed not to have read. In his gentle way, Pat had made inroads and attracted the curiosity of the jury, which was not an effortless intellectual accomplishment.

They closed out Friday, April 27. She would be back on Monday, to face Greenspan. This was the time for him to show his mettle. Monday, April 30, opened with a more determined M-J striding to the witness box. I assumed that her husband's public relations apparatus had got her the quite good puff-piece in the *New York Times* on the weekend, and where she had been demure on Friday, she came back in black and with spikier shoes, a slightly dominatrix look. Her face was less stiff and the overall effect was good. She rebutted Tuite quite effectively and his strategy of undermining her popularity in folksy increments made no progress on this second day. She won the first round. If we were going to derail the prosecution strategy of using the Audit Committee as respectable beaters for Radler's tales, it had to be now.

Greenspan stepped to the questioning podium and, as was his custom, gave no greeting or introduction, in the falsely folksy American manner, paid no deference to her status as an economist or as president of the Museum of Modern Art, and started into a trenchant series of questions. She fought scrappily, challenged, and sometimes tried to speak over him, but he bore down on the real questions. She claimed not to remember being on one teleconference where she was recorded as present and where the contested payments were confirmed as having been approved. Then she answered that she could not speak of what she did not remember. Greenspan pounced on this with the agility of a cougar and went through a long series of confirmations of the payments that she had signed or attended, where the Audit Committee approved, and claimed now to have read but did not now remember. "We can't count on your memory for anything." If she had read the 10Ks, how had she missed, etc?

He went through version after version of the approval of these payments. He even wrung from her that she had read the first 104 pages of the 2002 10K very carefully, by establishing that she had read a selected paragraph that stopped on that page. This happened to be the very paragraph before the exposition of the disputed payments. This was not credible. Even less credible was the fact that, as she emphatically restated that she had read everything up to that point, she somehow missed the original reference to the same payments, in an identical paragraph, forty pages before.

What particularly incensed me about her performance was that she fell in enthusiastically with the government's position on the perquisites of the Hollinger executives with enthusiasm and determination. These were not areas that involved the SEC, and a refusal to comply with these trumped-up charges would not have inconvenienced her husband's business. (I assumed the SEC had threatened KKR, as well as the defendants as individuals.) She had caused the Audit Committee to adopt the position that Radler and I should always travel on the company planes for security reasons, as she was aware of the security threats we had had, from extremist Irish and Muslims. We received threats almost every week. Now she was conscripted, with no knowledge of the facts, and after the matter had been demolished by Greenspan cross-examining Creasey, to object to my flight to Bora Bora. When Greenspan asked to confirm that there had not been a policy permitting or prohibiting personal use of the airplane, she replied: "That's not correct. There was the law." He said, "I'm sorry. There was what?" "The law." "The law is policy?" "I would hope so." He pointed out that she had moved the requirement that senior management use the company's plane for security reasons, and her attempt to masquerade as a sheriff petered out in a debate about when the IRA had blasted our old office buildings in London. It was a very irritating rodomontade.

Even more outrageous was her pompous disparagement of the December 4, 2000, dinner that was billed as a birthday dinner for Barbara, as illegitimate for any corporate participation in the cost. I had consulted her about what arias should be sung by the person from the Metropolitan Opera that I engaged. She knew perfectly well that it had begun as a corporate dinner, and was approved in the minutes of the previous directors' meeting as such, and she was aware from attending the last phase of it that it was certainly a corporate occasion. The commercial role played by Barbara's conversation with Donald Trump, whom she sat next to and had never met before (an unusual placement for a supposed birthday party), was also referred to subsequently, and Kravis knew about it.

In becoming so sanctimonious about routine corporate expenses, and in trying to incriminate an old friend whom she should have known to be innocent and, indeed, morally incapable of crimes, and who had done her many favours in days when she was less exalted, she was betraying the professed ethos of the big business, big philanthropy culture where she had coquettishly bluffed, conferenced, and made her way to the summit. Her perseverance was commendable, and I had been happy for her, despite her recently acquired and unbecoming *du haut en bas* self-importance. At her new socio-economic echelon, inculpating former close colleagues and social friends was unseemly.

The jurors, unworldly in these matters though they were, were not inexperienced and recognized moonshine when they heard it, and saw at least that her testimony was not believable. So did the press, and they pierced the lingering prosecution bias of much of the media to arraign my formerly good and glamorous friend for incompetence and lack of credibility. She was guilty of both; worse, and bitterly surprising, she was contemptible.

Romano again brought out the non-prosecution deal with the SEC, which tore the rug out from under whatever was left of the credibility of the former Audit Committee. Kravis walked upright and ostensibly shameless from the courtroom. She had walked brazenly away from many embarrassments before, but she did not have the dominating air she had affected on her second day. She had the slightly wan air of the naughty convent girl who has endured Mother Superior's wrath, the rosary, even the hairbrush.

The New York Times revealed that she had returned to New York in time to be the hostess at one of the MOMA evenings, which I was thankful I was no longer asked to contribute $25,000 to attend. Being spared the rigours of the New York society charity circuit was one of the few dividends of my present thralldom. Press reaction to her performance under Greenspan's questioning was uniformly disrespectful.

A final thought on the Kravises: a few weeks later, Marie-Josée expressed the hope to a mutual friend that I be acquitted. That may be how it works in the heady echelon where she now lives and reigns, but it won't do. Albrecht has his Laurentian Rhine-Maiden, and Marie-Josée has the magic (cushion-diamond) ring and the gold, but she was speaking for the record under oath, before a federal judge, a jury, and the press of the Western world, on matters of high principle and public policy interest.

She chose the path of the low and mindless Park Avenue gossip. I had thought better of her as an *aventurière* who had hit the jackpot and had raised herself up.

I had admired her and rejoiced for her success, and success it was: she is a good wife and chatelaine and carried off her relaunch in New York with tremendous aplomb before the most skeptical audience in the world, including many "friends" to whom Barbara and I strenuously championed her and who now coo about her French *savoir faire*.

I had watched as Marie-Josée left the Bilderberg conference I invited her to near Athens, in 1993, when she got into a taxi with Henry Kravis, whose acquaintance she had recently made. She was wearing a short pink mini-suit, to start, I surmised, a new life. Most of what followed was foreseeable and, for me, who liked her, heart-warming. She was moving off a rough road onto a great boulevard.

Unfortunately, her success had affected her sense of decency. If she would go before the press of the world and under oath to incriminate me in matters that had nothing to do with her or the SEC, nothing was beneath her. I didn't expect the truth from many witnesses, and would have been astonished to hear it in these circumstances. I did expect a closer approximation of it from her.

She would have lost nothing and gained much if she had stuck to the "story" she told the SEC but not looked down her nose at an air trip that it was now public knowledge I had overpaid the company for, and a dinner that she knew to be a largely corporate event, which she had helped plan.

The wanton climber is morally clothed with some rules of the road. Once arrived at her destination, in that one sense, Marie-Josée was naked; there was no haute couture or expensive lingerie to disguise her performance. The spectacle of her testimony was ugly.

NOW THAT THE TRIAL HAD REACHED the Audit Committee, the stakes were greater, the theatre was higher quality, and the possibilities were intriguing.

The press leapt at the appearance of Eddie Greenspan in the role that he had been touted to fill. He was an instant hero, and left Eddie Genson feeling quite disconsolate. Fortunes shifted quickly, and where there had been some thought of importing Terry Gillespie to cross-examine Radler, Greenspan was now the leader of the defence counsel. I had a reprieve from my fears about the competence of my counsel, even if my daughter and wife did not. If Greenspan could thrash the nimble M-J Kravis to a pulp, as he had, I knew he would not have much problem with the ponderous Thompson, who was in the muck of the Audit Committee's lapses more than Burt and Kravis.

He had been the well-paid committee chairman, and anyone who had seen his rather inept performance as a member of the 9/11 committee would know what a mismatch there would be between Thompson's amnesia and Greenspan's questions.

Sussman gave Thompson a very breezy, flippant, direct examination and then tendered him to the defence. Greenspan tore him limb from limb. He dragged him like an un-housetrained dog to the sight of his many incontinences and asked him how he could claim to be unaware of the payments. Thompson acknowledged, as every director of a public company knows, that the first item to be read in any 10K or financial statement is the related-party section. When asked if he had read the eleven versions of the 10Ks he had signed and the offering memorandum and the proxy circular that he had signed and approved that contained approvals of the contested payments, he said, "I skimmed" them.

Greenspan instantly saw the potential for that. "Skimmed?" This started a long series of questions brilliantly played by Greenspan. He established that Thompson made $80,000 a year for two days work for Hollinger International and that he spent as much of the company's money travelling with his wife to one of our corporate dinners in London as the company paid for its part of the December 4, 2000, dinner I was charged with embezzling. Thompson blundered headlong into one baited trap after another for about four hours. It was a thoroughly enjoyable performance. Greenspan concluded with a mortally damaging question: "I suggest to you that you and the other Audit Committee members knew all about these payments, that you approved them all, and that when criticism arose, you all conveniently forgot. No more questions." Greenspan left his podium while Thompson spluttered his unconvincing demurral.

Everyone in the courtroom knew that they had all given inaccurate and misleading testimony and only the protection of distinctly uncomfortable U.S. attorney Patrick Fitzgerald, who favoured us with one of his visits to the courtroom, prevented them from suffering for it.

Safer took a line at some distance to the position of the other defendants, as Kipnis had been a salaried officer and had received no non-compete payments, but he did a great deal more harm to Thompson's credibility than to the co-defendants when he wrung from Thompson the fact that his committee had approved more than $216 million of payments over seven years to the senior management (not an unreasonable figure given the number of people involved and the performance of the company), without once asking for a single page of documentation. Safer ripped into Thompson with great histrionic emotion and scored very heavily for his client, an evidently decent man who was following Radler's orders and had not profited at all from the contested payments. Safer presented a very large demonstrative exhibit (a panel about twelve feet long and four feet high), detailing the many Audit Committee approvals of the disputed payments.

Where he had arrived as the former U.S. attorney and four-term governor, much deferred to, Thompson left as a joke, discredited and unconvincing. For weeks after, weather girls on Chicago television and traffic reporters in helicopters spoke of "skimming clouds" or "skimming over" an expressway. The truth-sayers who were to pave the way for Radler, and respectabilize and render credible his orchestrated story, had failed completely. They had been torn to pieces, and were revealed as, in Mark Steyn's words, "Olympic-scale synchronized skimmers." They accustomed the jury to the relentless exposé of the frailty that comprised the prosecution's case. I suggested to counsel that they say that these witnesses are indistinguishable from bank robbers and street thugs. As usual, my advice was too bold for the lawyers. There were three of them (on the Audit Committee); they had eleven draft 10Ks, which each had two prominent references to the contested payments, plus proxy circulars and the due diligence teleconference and visits from KPMG. There were more than seventy-five sightings of these approved payments by Audit Committee members. The government case was a shambles, and knives were noisily being sharpened for their long-awaited star witness.

There were temperamental problems with both Greenspan and Genson, as well as physical ones. They frequently slumbered in the afternoons, facing the jury, not a very dynamic or purposeful image to project to those who would decide if I would spend the rest, or any, of my life in prison. Greenspan would awaken occasionally, like a crocodile whose nostrils have been tickled by a ripple on the water, and advise me to sit differently, that my posture was too erect for the jury, and then doze off again. (Mark Steyn called them "the dream team.") It was very disconcerting.

Any new development tended to panic them. On several occasions they rushed into our little luncheon room and announced we had to demand a mistrial. I asked why, since there was no chance of obtaining one; wasn't there a tactical response? Usually there was. When it was suggested that my "Musings" – which I had written periodically for the Ravelston partners and which tended to be intricate, and florid at times, but were always respectful of the shareholders and certainly never came anywhere near anything unethical – could be brought into evidence, Greenspan immediately said that in that case I would have to testify. This was nonsense. I didn't think he had read any of the Musings anyway, and I said we would have no problem explaining them.

The issue of my testifying was something Greenspan and I had always thought was an ace up our sleeve. The prosecution had so oversold the idea that I was a snob and a brigand that I would be like an owl to crows. I knew the facts and had already memorized a great deal of the material. We put it about that I was desperate to testify and that Greenspan was horrified at the prospect.

Neither was the case. I could have seen off the prosecutors, but we were not sure how jury-friendly it would have seemed. Under U.S. rules, if I had testified, the prosecutors could have questioned me on many subjects they were not otherwise allowed to touch. Under U.S. rules of procedure, the prosecution can designate a wide range of subjects it reserves the right to raise if a defendant consents to testify on his own behalf. I could have fielded any admissible question, but my testifying would have prolonged the trial, made it much more complicated, and put us more on the defensive. It would have vastly raised my status as an accused above the other defendants, among whom I was trying to obscure myself, as much as they were trying to pretend this had nothing to do with them. We were doing very well pummelling government witnesses.

The government was promising to play the audio tapes of the 2002 and 2003 shareholders meetings, and I was confident that I would come through them well. In the end, we felt we got most of the benefit of my testifying through those audio tapes, with none of the downside that could have arisen from the Picador antics of Sussman and Cramer. I would have enjoyed slapping them around, but I might not have won friends on the jury doing so.

I had written hundreds of pages of explanations covering every allegedly inconvenient statement I had ever said or written, covered by condensed summaries. I rarely had the impression that either of my principal lawyers read much of it, other than when something was directly related to a cross-examination of theirs, though the junior counsel certainly did. Chief counsel were expected to be cool, unflappable, and physically and intellectually vigorous. Mine were not always encouraging in these respects.

On Monday, May 7, Sussman brought on a snoozer from KPMG, whose testimony was not relevant to anything, and then my former New York secretary Jan Ackerhielm, who was innocuous but irritatingly allied to the enemy. A pleasant, loquacious woman, she had been the secretary to Democratic Party chairman Larry O'Brien.

Then, at long last, David Radler emerged. He was hunched, very tanned, and trying to put a positive face on the shameful tale he had to tell, after ratcheting up his version of events to clear the hurdle set by the prosecutors. He seemed fairly cheerful, and at times witty, and less odious than defence counsel had prepared the jurors to expect. He had a bright-orange tie. No family members accompanied him. After all that we had been through together, and after such a build-up of anticipation, his appearance, though dramatic, was an anti-climax; it was hard to believe, even as it unfolded, in his first days as a witness, that any such preposterous scene was really happening.

The Rat bit on the second day. It had been a scheme to defraud the shareholders. He had picked it up a notch since his grand jury testimony, when he had claimed a silent conspiracy. Then he had simply not reported these payments to the Audit Committee and no one spoke of it. They augmented his grand jury statement by saying that there had been two or possibly three telephone calls, the last possibly involving Boultbee as well as, or instead of, me. This was where and how he received his orders to cheat the company out of $30 million in now claimed, undeserved, unapproved non-competition payments to individuals and to Hollinger Inc.

It need hardly be stated that no such conversations ever took place. The snitch, the whistleblower, one of the exalted figures in contemporary American commerce, is a familiar and generally despised figure, in schools and families, now revered only by the prosecutors and emasculators of the

U.S. executive class. But Radler was operating on a different plane. He told a story that would bring me down and thus hold Breeden harmless from the consequences of his misconduct. Like dog trainers, Sussman and his interrogators kept raising the bar and told Radler he would have to incriminate me convincingly if he wanted a deal, to alleviate the punishment of his own crimes. Thus appeared in Radler's sworn testimony the "two or three" telephone calls.

To inculpate me and equally totally innocent colleagues as collateral damage, to satisfy Breeden's and Fitzgerald's rabid lust for the big fish, and Breeden's fear of my Canadian libel suits, and to secure an almost painless reprieve from his own crimes and the enjoyment of his newspaper acquisitions, Radler told his version and swore under oath to its authenticity. To Radler, it was a shabby but comprehensible business proposition. But it was despicable for the chief law enforcement officials of one of the country's greatest cities, and the U.S. Department of Justice itself, to be full, knowing accomplices.

On the afternoon of May 8, as court was adjourned, I wrote a summary of the many errors and falsehoods in Radler's testimony. He had implied, echoing the Audit Committee, that there was no geographic division in our company and that we were both immersed in all the operations of the company. This was a complete fiction; the East-West division had existed since he moved to British Columbia in 1972. (Israel, which he ran, and Australia, which Dan Colson and I ran, were exceptions to the rule.) He tried to involve me in *American Trucker* and now claimed that his fax to all of us that the buyers in Paxton and Forum wanted non-competition agreements from us was a joke. Radler had the effrontery to wave at my son Jonathan (to whom, I must say, he had always been very kind), who joined us for the week, in the corridor, and who resisted the temptation to give a digitally coarse, or any, response.

Radler claimed that we could not show these Paxton and Forum payments to the Audit Committee. In fact, as they represented a small percentage on a book profit of $562 million on the community newspaper sales, and a real profit of about $1 billion (because accumulated profits from the assets had retired their acquisition cost), there would have been no difficulty with them, if they had been requested, which previous testimony at the trial confirmed, through the buyers' wish for non-competition from "affiliates" of the vendor company. Otherwise, the Audit Committee would not have reconfirmed the contested payments at least fifteen times.

As has been mentioned, when Radler had told me of his sales of the community newspapers, which I had proposed, I told him that his success would have to be rewarded. I spoke to Boultbee about giving Radler a $1-million note from Ravelston, to be cashed when this would be practical. He had called back a few days later and said that there was no need for that, as recent buyers had requested and the Audit Committee had approved additional non-competition payments. And the executive committee (with only Richard Perle voting, as Radler and I were interested parties) approved the Forum and Paxton payments and was ratified by the whole board after what the adopted minutes of the meeting called accurately "extensive discussion."

After Israel Asper had requested non-competition payments from me, Radler had become intoxicated with them, especially their tax-free character in Canada, and devised them where he could, but failed to get an orthodox approval for some of them. The rest of us accepted his word that they had been specifically approved and requested, as the CanWest ones were, in a deal I had made and supervised, and we kept seeking routine confirmation from the Audit Committee of what we believed they had done. They gave that confirmation many times, and were confirmed in that by the auditors. This was the most fantastic fable of a silent conspiracy I have heard of; Gus Newman was correct when he said in his opening remarks that Soldier Field or one of the other Chicago stadiums would be necessary to hold all the conspirators, including dozens of lawyers and auditors.

Sussman had a weak conclusion with Radler on the morning of May 9, and it was Greenspan's turn. This was the moment we had all been awaiting for sixteen months; it was Crispin's Day.

Greenspan had an odd start. He demanded, for more than ten minutes in a tone of biblical wrath, to know if "God" had been mentioned in the oath Radler took in Kelowna claiming falsely to be an equal shareholder to me in Horizon. Radler replied with excessive deference in contrast to Greenspan's pugnacity.

Greenspan: You were sworn before a Canadian court to tell the truth, so help you God in a trial that was conducted on January 25th, 2002, in the case of Winkler versus Lower Mainland Publishing Ltd. Correct?

Radler: That's correct, yes.

Greenspan: You swore at the trial to tell the truth, correct?

Radler: Yes, I did.

Greenspan: And you swore to God to tell the truth, right?

Radler: I swore to tell the truth. I don't remember the actual, the actual –

Greenspan: You swore on a Bible, you swore with a Bible in your hand. Correct?

Radler: I don't recollect the Bible but I will accept that it's possible.

Greenspan: Canadian courts are no different than American courts, right? On that, at least on that point, when you swear to tell the truth.

This unfortunately was another procedural difference of which Greenspan was unaware. U.S. courts don't require a Bible.

Radler: I swore to tell the truth.

Greenspan: And you swore to God that you would tell the truth "so help you God" correct?

Radler: You can . . . do you have the transcript of what I did swear?

Greenspan: Yes, I have the transcript, which summarized that you were duly sworn. And duly sworn I am going to suggest to you, you well know that you took the Bible in your hand to tell the truth, so help you God.

Radler: I was only in court once – twice in my life, sir.

Greenspan: I don't know . . .

Radler: So I do not . . .

Greenspan: Are you having difficulty with my question?

Radler: I just want to see the basis on which you said it. You said I swore with my hand on a Bible. Show me the basis.

The Rat was chasing the Cat.

> Greenspan: Well, I'm going to suggest – did you swear with a Bible
>   in your hand here?
> Radler: No I didn't.
> Greenspan: You didn't swear with anything in your hand?
> Radler: That's correct.
> Greenspan: OK. I see. So the testimony you are giving is not sworn
>   testimony?
> Radler: It is sworn testimony, yes.
> Greenspan: It is sworn testimony. How?
> Radler: I swore to tell the truth.
> Greenspan: With no Bible?
> Radler: With no Bible.
> Greenspan: And you swore to tell the truth in British Columbia
>   with no Bible?

So it went.

On and on and on. Greenspan was revealing that he had not paid attention when Radler had been duly sworn in front of him just two days earlier. His repetitive and unproductive questioning was minimizing the valid point that Radler had not told the truth in that earlier court case. Greenspan's next move was to become infuriated with Radler when he fumbled with pages shown to him. At one point, more or less predictably, Barbara passed me a note suggesting that I interrupt proceedings and tell the court that there was a medical emergency that required Greenspan to withdraw. This would have been the most catastrophic course imaginable, and I ignored it, but it did betray the flaring nervosity in our camp, which I shared.

Greenspan had serious points he wanted to make, but his delivery and courtroom manner seemed out of synch with his material. He began with fury and had nowhere to build when he got to the heart of the matter. Radler quickly saw that Greenspan was having difficulty and began to enjoy himself. Over at the defence tables, the mood was grim. Safer held his head in his hands and only looked up to mouth the words: "They hate him, hate him," referring to the jury's feelings about Greenspan. The impossible was happening in front of us. Greenspan was turning Radler into a sympathetic witness.

Greenspan gradually strengthened, and was counselled by other lawyers at the break and came back fairly well. He scored heavily, again and again eliciting that Radler had lied. He pounded through many instances of his lying, and followed the sixteen meetings with the Special Committee and the U.S. attorney, tracing the evolution of Radler's story until he eventually claimed that he had been instructed by me to conduct a criminal conspiracy against the shareholders. Endless admissions of lies as he scaled the heights of accusation necessary to secure his undisturbed control of the Horizon newspapers and the penitential golfing holiday in British Columbia wore down Radler's jauntiness. There was no jokey or respectable way of admitting to such a dismal sequence of lies and thefts. Radler himself had none of the contrition of the wrongdoer confessing to a conspiracy he was part of in order to atone for his crimes and oblige others to do the same.

He made a mechanical admission that he had lied and what he did was wrong, but said that Boultbee and I had told him to do it and that Atkinson was in it up to his eyeballs too. He did perform the commendable service of trying to excuse Mark Kipnis. He said that Kipnis had not been given a $150,000 bonus because of his role in the controversial payments, but because he had been terribly overworked, especially in the CanWest matter, and had saved the company $750,000 in legal fees. This, apart from stating his name, acknowledging that he was a liar, and defending the payments from American Publishing, were practically Radler's only truthful utterances in his many days of testimony.

I occasionally reflected, as the Radler showdown wore through the May days, what a strange relationship we had had. We had both believed in the newspaper business and determined to expand as quickly as possible, having seen the profits that could be made from the *Sherbrooke Record*, which had been completely derelict when we had bought it in 1969.

He married and moved to Prince Rupert, British Columbia, when we bought the newspaper there, and then to Vancouver. And in 1974, I moved to Toronto. We spoke on the telephone about once or twice a week, depending on business factors, and each of us took responsibility for expanding his "division." When the opportunity to take over Argus Corporation came up in 1978, I became more preoccupied with other things and he broadened into other, not very successful ventures, such as a group of B.C. motels that were chiefly maintained in business by the government of Canada, which housed welfare cases in them, and a jewellery store in San Diego that never made money.

David Radler told me that he had always filed his tax return with an obvious error in it, so that the tax inspector would think he had caught any liberties in the return when he discovered that. Similarly, it was part of his personality that he seemed to think that in admitting he couldn't send a fax or an email, he was making up for the millions and millions we lost on the *Jerusalem Post*, the eighteen-month delay in starting up the new printing plant in Chicago, and his other blunders.

Once the Internet arrived, David Radler pretended it wasn't happening. He claimed total vindication when the dot-com bubble burst, and he was opposed to spending anything on promotion of the *Sun-Times*, or any Internet aspect to it. He was a poor publisher in Chicago, intimidated by a large unionized property, a large strange city, and the pre-eminence of the *Tribune*. He was never interested in editorial matters, other than laudations of Israel, and his answer to everything was to cut costs. He caused terrible ill will to arise against us in the Chicago properties, largely because of his propensity for mad, counter-productive economies such as shutting down the escalators.

Despite management errors, we did get the *Sun-Times* off ancient letterpress machinery that produced a visually terrible product. And we did buy many of the surrounding community newspapers to give the *Sun-Times* a solid framework of supportive local titles. Because Radler was so capricious, overbearing, and insensible of elemental personnel relations, there was no esprit in the company at all in Chicago.

After I went to London in 1989, I saw Radler only at occasional board meetings in Toronto or New York. The prosecution had tried to make the case that we were intimates and that our families holidayed together. Greenspan quickly elicited the fact that the one time we had holidayed as couples (with my first wife, but a few months before we were married) was in 1978 and that it was, as Greenspan put it, "so memorable, it has not been repeated in 29 years since." In fact, though his wife was pleasant and had a good sense of humour, the only basis on which I ever enjoyed him after we left Sherbrooke was hearing his recitations of amusing business experiences over the telephone.

It was naturally a very strange experience listening to his false incrimination of me but also seeing his squinty, evasive eyes. As he was brought through the court by the government handlers, or from the elevators to the holding room, he appeared an outcast, even to himself. Hunched, furtive, with darting, fearful eyes, he looked like a man bound for the gallows, worn down as much by a knowledge of his own wretchedness as by the impending punishment.

Now despised, perhaps even despising himself, a derisory shadow of the former strutting, orders-barking executive, as exhausted of wisecracks as of integrity, unattended by any family or friend or even a lawyer of his own (apart from one day), David Radler was too distasteful to be pitiful, too diminished to remind anyone of his days of consequence, too banal to arouse any interest at all.

I had always known there were compatibility problems with him, but I had never until now realized the scale of them. When I saw him leave the courtroom for the last time, as if in a trance: twitchy, timorous, and bowed from the battering meted out to him, abetted by the prosecutors' obvious indifference to him personally, unlike other government witnesses, whom they cosseted with feigned respect, I hoped and expected that I would not see him again. His was a strange and affecting tale. He had been an upwardly mobile Duddy Kravitz, but was gradually transformed by the thinning air and rising pressures of the spheres he rose to, not toward self-confidence and serenity, but rather misshapen by envy and insecurity that drove him to treachery and cowardice. The fearful deserve sympathy. But in this case, it must be deeply mitigated by David Radler's dishonesty. Yet it is very sad.

There would be some drama yet, before the curtain came down on him in these proceedings. The next day, May 10, was the anniversary of Winston Churchill's installation as prime minister and his utterance of the words Eddie Greenspan had carried in his pocket: "My whole life has been a preparation for this hour and this trial." On this day, inexplicably, Greenspan simply collapsed, and was terribly ineffective. He was ponderous, repetitive, disorganized, and excruciating. It was mortally embarrassing. More and more frequent and urgent messages came up from Barbara, Alana, and Jonathan, two rows behind me. Fortunately, it was only a half-day, and court would adjourn until Monday, May 14.

Greenspan continued to expose Radler as a liar, but with no novelty and in a terribly slow and laborious way that almost incited sympathy for the witness. Finally, when he put, for what must have been the fiftieth time, the question "And that was a lie?" Safer, of all people, objected: "Asked and answered." "Sustained," said the judge at once. It was a crushing insult to a lawyer of Greenspan's stature, for a defence co-counsel to humiliate him before the whole court and the media. He looked quizzical, and had no apparent notion of what a slow-motion taxation he was putting on the court and everyone in it.

IT WAS A FUNCTION OF HIS DIABETES and medicine and eating habits, which his daughter Juliana and document lawyer Jane Kelly were supposed to oversee. If everything wasn't in balance, Eddie would run down like a clock, and become slower and more tedious. It was a cruel fate for such a good lawyer, but it was an unkind destiny for the client, too, especially at such a crucial moment in this trial and in my life. I could hardly believe that I was now to deal with another unbidden crisis. As Gus Newman said to me, my counsel had to tear Radler down and, as he put it, "expose him as a scum-bag."

There was a new crisis in our camp, as we considered what to do with Greenspan. May 10 had been a disaster. Court would resume on Monday, May 14. Earl Cherniak, a distinguished Toronto barrister who was acting for me on many of the civil matters I was involved in in Canada, and his associate, Lisa Munro, came to Chicago to test me as a witness, in case I decided to testify. For three days I had Earl doing a pretty fair simulation of Sussman, though much more intelligent and, when he worked at it, almost as obnoxious. All thought we were winning our case, and had established much more than a reasonable doubt on every count. Any fair reading of the transcript and examination of the exhibits confirms that we did.

Earl's preparations were useful. While Greenspan was in the room, I couldn't resist giving outrageous answers, but after he left, I toned down my responses and got through the questions fairly painlessly. When the time came, though I was well-prepared, all the defendants and their counsel thought such an appearance unnecessary by any of us.

One of the problems Greenspan had, which had not been anticipated for so legendarily quick-witted a person, was that though all of his questions to each witness were written out for him as in a script, between Sussman's interruptions and Radler's diversions, he tended to lose his way. Radler had developed the technique of claiming to be unable to answer questions without seeing the document referred to, and Greenspan fell into the habit of showing it to him. I asked why this indulgence was given to Radler; why not oblige him to answer? Greenspan thought that it was better to allow him to read what he had written or said in order to force him to reconcile it with contrary statements or facts rather than merely saying that he didn't recall. He was probably right, but it made for a very grinding cross-examination. Sussman and Cramer were likely pleased with this tactic, which cushioned the impact on the jury of the credibility problems of the witness.

When Greenspan did not get the answer he was anticipating, it tended to throw him off, and he moved on to the next question on his list, even if it was made a non-sequitur by the unexpected answer. It created the impression of a disjointed, somewhat feckless, cross-examination. He had done a good deal of damage to Radler initially but had been so repetitive and ineffectual on the tenth that none of us was confident that the jury, as several of its members descended toward the arms of Morpheus, grasped the implications for the prosecution's case of the enormity of Radler's falsehoods.

Over the weekend, the tactic emerged from lawyers meetings, as I was being tortured by Earl with his super-Sussman simulation, of dealing rapidly with five separate themes with Radler on Monday. George Jonas, by telephone, and Earl and I went over things carefully with Eddie Greenspan. I attended the strategy conference, which was an unusual event and not particularly welcomed by the lawyers, who tended to regard the client as an annoying object, as opposed to an animate subject, who caused their effort to be exerted and their invoices to be generated and paid. I had a heart-to-heart talk with Eddie, and checked Eddie's sleep and diet matters with Jane Kelly. It seemed like what we were planning was a sensible change of pace that the enemy would not anticipate. When I called on the evening of May 13 to give him a final word of encouragement, he was so tired, he was almost incomprehensible but assured me he was about to retire for the night.

MONDAY, MAY 14, WAS A SMASHING success. Greenspan was alert and crisp, and Radler and his masters had no idea how to deal with what we threw at them. Greenspan had caught Radler saying on his first day of cross-examination that he had read the Special Committee reports, and on his second day that he had not. He could not explain the contrary transcript extracts when they were placed in front of him. Eddie walked him through the Horizon swindle, where he had pledged to be a passive, minority shareholder, and controlled the company; where he had pledged that our shareholdings were equal and lied under oath in court in Canada about it. There was a series of other inconsistencies that were quickly raised and that Radler could not answer. He floundered and waffled and clearly disgusted the jury. The prosecutors, who delighted in mimicry and juvenile facial gestures to the jury, looked very wan and drained and studied the tabletop like chastened schoolchildren rather than the faces of the female jurors.

The climax was when Radler claimed not to have had any idea that being transferred to Canada would reduce his sentence to six months. Greenspan was well prepared for that and recited extracts from the relevant texts, described the facilities he would go to, with theatre and golf and horse-riding therapy. Greenspan eventually revealed that Radler had retained one of the foremost parole counsel in Canada three years before, and demanded to know what lawyer had advised him to give the false answer he did in court in Kelowna on the Horizon issue. It was a rout, Radler was smeared over the floor and walls, and it was the Greenspan of olden time. Regrettably, the court refused to allow us to call him back as a witness to plumb the depths of the Canadian perjury and treaty transfer issues.

The Canadian media at the court, which had touted Greenspan to their skeptical British and American colleagues as the trial began, and had seemed to be justified after his demolition of Kravis and Thompson, had been scandalized by the disaster of May 10. The *Toronto Star* wrote that

Greenspan was washed up and had always been overrated and that I should put him on the first plane home to Canada. After May 14, however, everyone conceded that he was the leading figure of the courtroom. The *CTV National News* opened with five minutes on his demolition of Radler. On May 10, the *Toronto Star* reporter (Jennifer Wells) had predicted life imprisonment for me. On May 14, CTV's correspondent (Steve Skurka) predicted victory for the defence.

Gus Newman followed Greenspan and was at his best. All the defence counsel had the same interest in the destruction of Radler, and there was no difference in this respect between the interests of any of us. Ron Safer wound up the cross-examinations on May 17 with one of the trial's spectacular moments and histrionically tore the Rat to pieces yet again. He dwelt upon the relations between Radler and Thompson, pulverizing two already dying birds with the same stone. He referred to Radler's letter to Thompson and Paris in November 2003, in which he stated that Thompson's committee had approved the contested non-competition payments. This gave the lie to all Radler's assertions that there had been a scheme to steal money. "You wouldn't write a letter to Governor Thompson stating that he had done something you knew he had not done, would you?" Radler wobbled badly again.

When Safer got to the December 2002 teleconference, when the counsel for the lenders asked about Audit Committee approval of the non-competition payments, he asked Radler: "Were you panicked?" Radler thought not. (If the payments were furtive and unapproved, the questions to Thompson and Kravis would have blown up Radler's "scheme.") "Weren't you afraid that your entire scheme was about to be exposed?" Radler again wobbled very implausibly. The judge frequently told Radler to answer counsels' questions.

Safer had great forensic talents and always had a voice and countenance that burned with emotional sincerity. He moved all around the front of the room and always had his own exhibits and evidentiary documents in perfect order and at his fingertips. None of the prosecutors, or even the judge, won an exchange of repartee with him, as he always was quick but earnest, and had the knack of scoring his points without ever seeming condescending or belligerent. Over all, he was the most impressive barrister in the court. But my counsel did the most damage to the witnesses we had to destroy, and no other team had the will to destroy them.

Mark Steyn's splendid summary of Radler's testimony, in his blog of May 17, was:

> Mr. Radler told the truth to the U.S. Attorney's office when he said he lied to the SEC about telling the truth to the Special Committee about whether he'd lied to the Audit Committee about telling the truth about the non-competes.
>
> As to whether he lied to the court in Chicago by claiming to have told the truth to the court in British Columbia about whether he'd lied to Conrad Black by not telling him the truth about Todd Vogt, he was in fact telling the truth when he said the lie he told had been approved by his lawyer, whom he had no reason to believe was lying.
>
> On the matter of whether he lied to the court this week about claiming to have told the truth last week about not having reviewed the transcripts of earlier lies from 2003 to 2005, he was telling the truth when he said he would need to review the transcripts of last week's lies before he could ascertain whether he was telling the truth about the transcripts of his previous lies.
>
> On the question "Are you lying now, yes or no," Mr. Radler said yes, he would be lying if he were to claim to be telling the truth, but no, he told the truth when he said he was a liar. Also, both of the above, as he was not familiar with counsel's use of the word "or" but had been advised it was a breach of attorney-client privilege, and neither of the above, as he would need to review transcripts of what he had said 30 seconds earlier as he had no rec-ollection of whether he was telling the truth or lying at the time he began speaking this sentence.; which is a longer sentence than he'll be serving at that British Columbia country club.

It was to this farce, draped in infamy, that my associate of thirty-eight years had descended, and to which he had reduced our companies. As if in a trance, Radler was led away from the court by his handlers to await gentle imprisonment, a publicly admitted liar, thief, perjurer, squealer, and cheat. Everyone who witnessed it shared the resulting distaste, apart from the prosecutors, who got a good deal less from the witness than they had been sold by Radler's counsel, when he procured his client's golfing holiday and prosperity ever after with his doubtfully acquired assets.

If it had been possible for Sussman to offer Atkinson and Kipnis acquittals, I suspect they would have been prepared to impute something unworthy, though not illegal, to me, but not, I think, total inventions. Fortunately, the rules did not allow Sussman and his co-sorcerers to make such an offer. The best they showed Kipnis, late in the trial, was three years in prison. So, finally, by the bungling of the prosecutors, which was all that tempered their zeal, and by the integrity of the other accused, we cobbled together a logically unanswerable case of innocence.

Whether it would be so decided depended on the susceptibilities of a jury that was yet, in that distinctive elbows-and-shoulders, swaggering, blue-collar Chicago manner, apparently oblivious of its limitations. The jurors were flattered by the endless attentions of the judge, peppy and bright, but for all the world, she too was apparently unaware of the decadence of the system that generated this degradation of due process in which she served with such pert agility.

[CHAPTER FOURTEEN]

THE GOVERNMENT FOLLOWED the burnt-out wreck of their star witness with Jonathan Rosenberg of O'Melveny & Myers, the associate counsel, and, with Richard Breeden, co-author of the infamous Special Committee report. His firm had made about $50 million on this case, and he had a bigger vested interest than almost anyone in guilty verdicts. He followed much of the proceedings from the overflow room upstairs, so intimately entwined with the prosecution were the *Sun-Times* acting management and Breeden's Special Committee. Rosenberg was brought in as if he were an impartial expert witness. We had arranged with the judge that Rosenberg would not comment on my non-appearance at the Special Committee and that we would not cross-examine him if he did not mention me at all in his testimony.

Rosenberg did imply high corporate wrongdoing, and at the lunch break both Eddies were flapping like Ibsen's Wild Duck, swearing motions for mistrial and so forth, their and other counsels' usual placebos. In fact, they negotiated a strong instruction from Judge St. Eve that none of this applied to me. It was one of her better moments at the trial, as she had refused to admit as evidence that I had declined to appear at the Special

Committee at the time I went to the SEC in December 2003, and she rather eloquently emphasized my "absolute right to remain silent."

Rosenberg managed to avoid being torn to pieces like the government witnesses who came in with official rods on their backs (testimony in exchange for immunity or a plea bargain), but he didn't seem to accomplish much, either, once it was established that he was a party profoundly in interest. I thought it a disgrace that not one of the counsel asked how much his firm had made from their relationship with the Sun-Times Media Group, but the legal brotherhood held firm and avoided so indelicate a subject as fees in spite of my pleading. In the corridor, Barbara and I passed Rosenberg, the caricature of a self-important former prosecutor, and Barbara managed to get to the word "shit" in her sentence as we came abreast of him, and she directed that word at him.

After the break, Sussman demanded a sidebar and excitedly told the judge that "Mrs. Black uttered a derogatory word to Mr. Rosenberg in the corridor." (I saw an instant transcript of these sidebars, meetings with counsel on the far side of the judge's bench away from the jury, and inaudible to the court, on the monitor.) The judge asked what Sussman expected her to do about that. No coherent reply followed. Sussman was also running to the judge with some frequency about my having told the press no jury in the world would convict anybody of anything on the basis of Radler's testimony, and my having told the *Guardian*, in an interview about *Nixon*, that the prosecution case "is hanging around their necks like a toilet seat." (The *Guardian* had published excerpts of the Nixon book, and part of my deal with them was that I would give them an interview.) The judge asked Greenspan to ask me to be a little more restrained. Sussman could not take the needle for an instant, and it became a sport for many of the press and some of the defence group to send him up the wall.

The government case dwindled after this. They brought in my former groupie, Hollinger International's vice-president for investor relations, Paul Healy, on May 21 as their closer. His little porcine face was so puffy it made his spectacles seem smaller, like those of a Stalin apparatchik, a little Breeden of the future, perhaps. Cramer in his opening remarks had said that Healy, on my instructions, had "dummied up and lied" when he certified that I was paying a fair price at $3 million for the unit on Park Avenue. He appeared with an immunity from prosecution, and filled the transcript with a false revival of the apartment allegation. We established that the company had had a contractual obligation to renovate, decorate, and furnish the unit and that I had volunteered to pay it myself after Healy claimed he was hearing some shareholders' complaints about the unit.

We also established that I had paid $4.635 million to this end, that I had the right to remain in the unit as long as I was an officer of Hollinger International, and that I could block any sale of it, which obviously lessened its market value to the company. In fact, the company had only a partial interest, especially as the building did not allow corporate owners above the ground floor, and I was the trustee for its interest. Sussman at one point tried to establish that we were obscuring the "substantial reimbursement" for the $4.635 million it was the obligation of the company to pay (as the FBI agent who signed the false affidavit which secured the seizure of my sale proceeds must have known). Under intense objections from Genson, Sussman was forced to admit that the substantial reimbursement for my $4,635,000 was $2,200. Never in the whole four-month trial was the brazenness of the prosecution more vividly revealed. It was one of Genson's finest hours. The judge did not comment, but Barbara and Alana and I agreed when we returned to our hotel that we would have been in despair if my credibility had suffered such a blow before the jury. This largely demolished the apartment issue, and Healy remained as the witness for the playing of the audio tapes of the 2002 and 2003 annual shareholders meetings. Healy had never been at a loss for hymns of praise, and a number of utterly obsequious emails he sent to me were compared with elements of his testimony and remarks to the FBI.

Healy appeared pretty much as he was: a maladjusted, scheming courtier, alternately fawning and snarling at the hand that fed him for so long. He was reduced to complaining that he had only made $10,000 per week even while he was clearly disloyal to the management. Mark Steyn recorded how he had flipped suddenly in late 2003 from my being his "favourite name-drop" to my instant, new status as a satanic figure, as he ingratiated his way into the entourage of Breeden, for whom he later worked, one of Breeden's lesser acts of subornation.

The battle with activist shareholders had first surfaced at the 2002 annual meeting of shareholders and climaxed the following year. We couldn't see that the prosecution gained anything by playing the audio tapes of the meetings in court. I answered all questions knowledgeably and courteously (the Ruffo intervention where he called me a "thief" and I invited him to leave was excised). Healy had called my performance "brilliant," and confirmed that in his testimony, and we felt that we did have much of the benefit of my testifying without any of the disadvantages.

On May 24, Barbara and I returned to Toronto. Whenever I return to that house, I am instantly reminded of how much I have missed it. As it turned out, I would not be back for a long time. This was becoming a dreary pattern – of leaving a home not knowing when I would see it again, or not knowing that I would never see it again, as in both London and New York. We went back to Chicago on May 28, with Joan Maida and her sister and lawyer. She was preparing to rebut the obstruction charge, over the removal of the boxes. The government case was almost over.

On May 29 came the painful episode of watching the video film of 10 Toronto Street. This building had symbolized a part of my birthright since 1959, when I had first visited it. It had become a symbol of the Canadian establishment, the classic, columned, graceful former Bank of Canada stone building in the shadow of taller buildings, and I had had my office there from 1978 to 2005. Being ejected from it at the request of Gordon Walker by Justice James Farley was one of the many immense humiliations I had suffered in this horrible debacle. I was almost impervious to anything, but the film of the building was upsetting.

The infamous affair of the boxes was represented as the "corrupt removal" of material, contrary to a court order, and to impede the progress of a grand jury, SEC, or criminal proceeding in the United States. I had hoped that Greenspan would take on this count and George Jonas had begged him to as well. Though the charge was absurd, the penalties for conviction on this count could be very serious, and Greenspan knew the facts well, having already prepared the defence against any Canadian proceeding. (There was none.) The judge instructed the jury that no

Canadian proceeding was relevant to this issue. But Sussman routinely implied and endlessly repeated that I had violated a Canadian court order, and despite my repeated interventions with Eddie Genson, this was not contradicted effectively. There had been no Canadian proceedings on this subject, and the endless implicit references to such proceedings by Sussman and Ruder, and instructions by Judge St. Eve to ignore such proceedings, incited the inference that I had already been found wanting in the local jurisdiction.

All that was relevant to a conviction on this charge was my knowledge of any official proceedings in America and a corresponding intent to impede any investigation by removing documents. As my office had been open for months to one and all, with inspectors and lawyers rifling through all the files, photocopying and seizing masses of material, neither Joan Maida nor I could imagine that after all these months any document pertaining to events at least three years earlier would still be virgin material. I had stopped going to the office on any regular basis for some time: the swarms of intruders were too irritating. Anything I had wished to remove I could have taken out in a briefcase or my pockets at any time.

Two pleasant security guards who spoke well of me personally were marched in to report the obvious, that they had seen me moving boxes. The film, some from new cameras, some from cameras I had had installed myself, supposedly made their case. A letter was faxed to Jennifer Owens (one of our Baker Botts Washington lawyers) on the day before the removal of the boxes, indicating renewed interest by the SEC in documents in that office. I knew nothing of that, as Jennifer and others would testify. Various documents were produced from the thirteen boxes of apparent significance to the case, and there were a number of agreed stipulations of fact on various subjects, including that I had handed over 124,000 pages of documents in response to five SEC subpoenas long before this incident.

This was another area where it proved impossible to introduce evidence of the sleazy practice of the government. Sussman had threatened Don Vale with drastic consequences if he appeared as a defense witness, to attest that I had had his approval, as acting president of the company, to remove the boxes. Don later explained this to the judge in a letter, but it had no impact on the verdict. Sussman also threatened Joan Maida, but Genson refused to adduce this in evidence. Prosecutors and the FBI tried intensively to intimidate our driver in New York, Gus Pedernura, with threats against his tax status and his visa to enter and remain in the U.S. (from his native Argentina). Intimidation of witnesses are routine, and apparently insusceptible to response. The FBI effort to muscle Gus was presaged by Healy's drunken telephone call to him late one Sunday night in December 2003, during which Healy hiccupped uncontrollably as he laid out his threats and blandishments. It had come to this: Healy as trail-blazer for the FBI in the bribery and intimidation of honest people, unsuspected at any point of anything improper, lest they tell the truth about the chosen target.

The government finally rested on May 30. It seemed to all of us that they had not made their case anywhere beyond, or even near, the elimination of a reasonable doubt. Their witnesses who had attempted to incriminate anyone had all been torn down and exposed as liars.

WE WOULD HAVE TO CALL SOME witnesses for our own counts – the New York apartment, Bora Bora, the dinner supposedly for Barbara, and the nonsense with the boxes. Beyond that, there would be some specialty and expert witnesses. We were quite optimistic. The defence kicked off with Jennifer Owens and Alex Bourelly of Baker Botts, who effectively extinguished any idea that I knew the SEC had any interest in my documents, beyond my full compliance with their five earlier subpoenas. Laurent Weisel, an able young lawyer at Sullivan & Cromwell, originally from Montreal, testified to the same effect a few days later.

Joan Maida came next and was plucky and ingenuous, proud of sending out "Conrad Will Win" T-shirts. Genson brought her through fairly well, and then Cramer set upon her, bullying and engaging in a good deal of gratuitous sarcasm. Unfortunately Joan had not been prepared by our lawyers with any thoroughness. Rattled, she gave some regrettable answers, never admitting wrongdoing, but in places defensive or argumentative. The truth would have served me well but wanting to avoid traps, she froze. She had no idea what I was doing on the film when I pointed at the camera. And she seemed to acknowledge that it was improper to remove the boxes. The jury was laughing at her. At one point she agreed that the watercooler gossip was that criminal charges would probably be laid against me. Genson failed to assault the relevance of such evidence.

Being a shy person, Joan had not wanted to testify; the notion of standing up in court terrified her, and she did it only to help me. She was literally shaking in the corridor before going into the courtroom. Her sense of honour was outraged that I was being blamed for some low and cowardly act of hiding documents, which she knew to be false. Genson had sent her into battle with insufficient preparation. The problems with Joan's testimony appeared to please Greenspan in some perverse way, as he had warned against calling her but had declined to give any assistance when she arrived in Chicago.

I found his rather smug comments about her uncalled for, given some of his own performances, including the immediately succeeding one in which he managed to make *Maclean's* magazine publisher and former *National Post* editor Ken Whyte seem dull. It was an unnerving day, made more so by my attempt to take a walk at lunchtime, when I was pursued by a number of appalling photographers, terribly overweight, faceless louts whose cameras substitute for and obscure their features, unspeaking, always retreating before you after they have run after you. There is something primitive and barely animate about them, and in swarms they are like a great mass of Jurassic rodents, grunting and heaving.

There had been an absurd scene over my venerable and colourful houseman in Toronto, Werner Jankowski, who loyally appeared in Chicago twice and was ready to be a witness that, as far as he knew, I had not looked at the boxes when they were in our house. I warned Greenspan and Genson that he couldn't possibly claim to have watched them all the time, particularly after he left the house for his 8 p.m. bedtime, and that because of his endearing Germanic accent the whole affair would become a Colonel Klinck farce. Barbara stalked out of our claustrophobic little lunchroom after saying what an insane idea it was, and Genson drove his electric tricycle around in circles, remonstrating with me. I ignored it, apart from saying that if he had a grievance with my wife he could take it up with her and that antics like this were not professional. He always cooled down quickly, and graciously called me to apologize later. I thanked him and said that there was no need for that. I thought we had a won case, but my counsel continued to worry me.

I had arranged for Donald Trump to come to the trial to debunk the birthday dinner issue and he was much anticipated. This, too, dissolved into farce. I couldn't reach Greenspan for advice. I wrote a letter to Trump inviting him to the trial some days before and faxed a copy to my lawyers. In the usual, insufferably amateurish ways to which these fire-wagon single serious partners were addicted, he and Genson only looked at it at the last minute and decided that my letter could be harmful. Their subpoena of Donald was withdrawn. It would have been less irritating if I had not again been given the distinct impression that my hypersensitive counsel were rather pleased to assert themselves over the client.

No one should imagine that the rapine of American lawyers is different in character from that of Canadian lawyers. Some genuinely care for the client more than others, and Greenspan was better than most in this regard. But lawyers are unaccustomed to the real world; they are friendly with prosecutors. Unless they commit heinous crimes, they never get a bad press, and their world is a circumscribed one where the client is a miscreant who has bumbled into the web of the legal system and what happens to him, as long as the lawyer is paid, is more or less beside the point. All the Robert Redford, Gregory Peck, John Travolta, and Tom Cruise dramas about conscientious lawyers going broke for a cause or a client are bilge.

As the trial progressed, I read a number of apposite books, including about the parliamentary trial of Warren Hastings, and I reread Franz Kafka's *The Trial* for the first time since I was an undergraduate. Kafka's summary of the lawyers in his otherworldly ordeal was familiar: "The same old exhortations would begin again, the same references to the progress of the petition, to the more gracious mood of this or that official, while not forgetting the numerous difficulties that stood in the way – in short, the same stale platitudes would be brought out again either to delude him (the client) with vague false hopes or to torment him with equally vague menaces." I had thought Kafka a novelist all these years. But if history repeats itself as farce, fiction returns as journalism. By the time I left Chicago, I thought Kafka clairvoyant.

Justice in the United States (and Canada) is like fishing. The system casts a net and occasionally drags in a big fish for a show trial to enhance the career of a prosecutor and give a placebo to the grumpy masses upset at the uneven distribution of wealth in American society. In our case, as in Hemingway's ultimate masterpiece, *The Old Man and the Sea*, there was nothing left after the sharks had finished, when the catch was brought to shore. The sharks, Breeden, Rosenberg, Voorheis, even Walker, and the others had eaten the great Hollinger fish to the bone.

It is a terrible thing to feel so alone when facing the greatest crisis of your life, especially against such formidable opponents as the U.S. government and much of the international media. My wife and daughter, sometimes my sons, were all there and all were magnificent. They all thought my lawyers incompetent and unreliable. They were a little severe, but there was not much I could do about it now anyway. We were almost down to closing arguments.

We got into specialist witnesses through the week of June 4. Genson had a very good specialist on New York real estate, who completely surpassed the catechetical witness Sussman had produced. Atkinson had an excellent Chinese-Canadian tax law professor who explained how non-competition payments work in Canada. She was very plausible and helpful, and rather ingenuous. Ron Safer produced Pat Ryan, the long-time KPMG customer's man, a charming James Garner lookalike as a hostile witness, to lay bare the dishonesty of the Audit Committee. Pat was cool and definitive. He and Marilyn Stitt had the assurance they sought when they met the Audit Committee in February 2002. They had not been misled by the management; they had been assured by the Audit Committee that the contested payments were approved and appropriate and that the disclosures were correct. Safer also had a very impressive professional witness, a forensic accountant calling himself Mr. Funk, who was amiably unshakable under Cramer's heavy-handed efforts to rattle him. His scrutiny of four hundred thousand pages of documents revealed a conclusion "inconsistent with fraud."

On Monday, June 11, John O'Sullivan, former editorial page editor of the *London Daily Telegraph* and *Times*, the *New York Post*, and *National Post*, and Bill Buckley's successor as editor of the *National Review*, took the stand and was extremely effective about the supposedly criminal birthday dinner for Barbara. The defence rested the following day; Sussman brought in a couple of expert witnesses on arcane subjects, and very suitably, the last of them, on an issue concerning Kipnis, was torn to pieces by Ron Safer in less than three minutes. "You don't know, do you?" Bumbling answer is followed by: "That wasn't my question. You don't know, do you?" "No." "No further questions of this witness," as Ron walked away, flipping his clipboard and somehow managing to show respect for the judge, neutrality to the witness, and contempt for the prosecutor.

CLOSING ARGUMENTS BEGAN on June 18 with Julie Ruder, who went on all day. She was by far the most effective of the prosecutors. Faced with evidence from the government's own witnesses that the so-called undisclosed payments had been disclosed time and time again, she now abandoned her witnesses one by one.

> You heard a lot of testimony from Darryl Sukonick, who is a very young lawyer at Torys. He was in his fifth year of practice. . . . And this non-compete was far from the only thing he was doing. I mean, he was telling you about seventeen-hour days. Paper flying everywhere. . . .
>
> The audit committee did fail the shareholders. They did. They should have read things word for word, sentence by sentence, paragraph by paragraph. . . .
>
> Mr. Radler told lies too. There's no question about it. He lied to the special committee and he lied to the auditors and he lied to the government.

All the exculpatory evidence her own witnesses gave, she told the court, was misleading. The fact that there was so much evidence exonerating us was evidence of the cleverness of the crime. She had developed a new sort of evidentiary analysis, a psycho-forensic approach that could conveniently be used to justify the charges. In essence, she told the jury to disregard all the witnesses and look for the "why" in actions that were perfectly legal. Ruder said:

> You have heard every penny is disclosed. Anyone in the world with a computer could log on to sec.gov and see exactly how much

money Peter Atkinson got. That's not what this case is about. It's not about the fact that money was paid to Mr. Atkinson. It's not about dollar amounts, it's about the why. Why was that money paid to Mr. Atkinson. It says here that it was a condition to the transaction. That's not true. And listen, if defence counsel wants to parse out the [contract] language and say "Well, it was technically a condition of the transaction because there was in the contract on page whatever a little subsection that says 'Conditions of Closing,'" well, that's part of the cover story too. That's the paper trail that they left behind to be able to argue something like this.

In other words, disregard all the evidence and convict these foreigners because that's what your government expects of you. As she stamped like an angry elephant all over her own witnesses, she also hammered the theme that the defendants were getting too much money, maybe not illegally, but too much. "Those management fees that International had been paying, that was a lot of money – we're not claiming there's anything illegal about the management fees. What we're saying is that they are really really high. And the shareholders were also saying they're really really high." This wound into a patchwork quilt of selective examples of my extravagance in particular and my "unbelievable pay day." Every string of envy and prejudice was being tugged as Ruder implied that I needed to steal to buy expensive items. This was just a dodge for not looking at the evidence, ignoring the witnesses, and deciding against the defendants because they were more educated and wealthier than the jurors; it was never put so crudely, but that was the only argument left to the government, and all that remained of Breeden's infamous half-billion dollar kleptocracy. To paraphrase Mr. Shapiro, of his co-counsel Johnnie Cochrane at the O.J. Simpson trial, Ruder "not only played the social and financial prejudice card; she dealt it off the bottom of the deck." The removal of the boxes was "truly startling." (It's hard to move offices without moving boxes, unless you carry out twenty-seven years of files loose-leaf.)

My mind wandered until I heard "It was dirty, ladies and gentlemen. It was dirty" and thought for an evanescent moment the spirit of confession might have seized this unlikely convert to straightforward rules of evidence.

But she was speaking of an innocuous and unexceptionable act by the defendants. It was inexorable; she stood imposingly before the jury, like a battleship delivering broadside, raised her dinning voice, held up her two thumbs and forefingers touching and forming circles, as if portraying in digital zeros the credence that deserved to be attached to the prosecution's case, and shrieked her ending. My wife and daughter both thought she was effective with the jury. I couldn't believe them. We were watching the faces of the jurors as this monstrous charade was enacted and we all read something different.

The following day, June 19, Eddie Greenspan opened for the defence. The view that the jury did not like his tactics at times had been made clear to him by both our team and others. "I want you to know," Greenspan told the jury, "that if at any time in this trial I have pressed a point too hard, if I have been too tough or aggressive, it is only because, I assure you, of my anxiety to make certain that no stone is left unturned to show you the innocence of Conrad Black . . . so do not hold that against Mr. Black."

There had been a good deal of collaboration in his remarks, especially by George Jonas. But the continued effort to have Greenspan tackle the obstruction of justice issue was to no avail, as was the attempt to get both counsel organized to tackle properly the counts in detail, although Greenspan was considerably more organized than Genson. Not only did the prosecution have the final word of the trial, contrary to the practice in other sophisticated jurisdictions – they also took more time. Ruder spoke for almost an entire day. Her remarks were outrageous, but they were rehearsed, precise, and thematically organized. Greenspan spoke for only an hour and a half with a good fifteen minutes of that devoted to praising a clearly skeptical jury.

Oratorically, it was his best performance of the trial, and his observations on the credibility of Radler and the naked attempt to prejudice the jury through envy of the rich were elegant and to the point. Greenspan failed to blow up the thesis that Ruder had placed in the minds of the jury, that somehow all evidence should be ignored because the guilty act was something she surmised but couldn't possibly prove – that we had all lied in order to get naïve buyers to give us non-compete payments that were really due to the company. She was saying, essentially, forget about the contracts the buyers signed – they didn't mean them. Forget about disclosure of all payments – it was just a cover story. Forget about the huge profits the company made for shareholders and focus on something I can't possibly prove – namely, that this rich man Conrad Black, who uses long words and historical references in his memos that are intended to mock the shareholders and ordinary people like you and me, organized a scheme to gull everyone: that the huge numbers of accountants, lawyers, buyers, shareholders who approved what was placed in front of them and reassured the defendants that everything was in order were wrong to have done so. It was a desperate gamble to try to evade the weight of evidence that had built up in our favour. For Ruder and her fellow prosecutors, there was no longer any downside in counting on the jealousy and ignorance of most of the jurors, because no alternative remained.

Nor did Eddie give the jurors sufficient context, as I had so often begged, for all these events that started with a battle between shareholders and a corporate struggle that had ended in a pyrrhic victory for the activists. Eddie read his concluding remarks. There was no suggestion of improvisation, nor of a mnemonic feat. But it was one of the most eloquent periods in the trial. He was vigorous, unargumentative, uninterrupted, and in good voice, and his contents were strong as far as they went, which was not far enough by half.

Eddie Genson followed. He started fairly well but drifted as the day went on. I later read his text, which was clear and very good, and compared it with the transcript. As the day wore on, they diverged more and more sharply. Genson has some cognitive disability that causes him to stutter, repeat, foul up, and mispronounce words, and misrecollect nouns or groups of initials. He never once in the trial sorted out CNHI 1 from the non-existent CCN 1 or some such, and was constantly attributing to me a receiver, as if I were bankrupt, instead of a monitor, who supposedly wishes to help conserve my means (as I do).

I can only conclude that he is so accustomed to guilty clients that he sees his mission as the creation of confusion, to incite doubt in the minds of the jurors. This was not at all what we needed at this point. What we needed was what we partly got from Greenspan – a declarative statement not only to incite a reasonable doubt, but to lay out the whole narrative of how the company had been hijacked as I was executing an orderly exit strategy from the newspaper business, and had been destroyed by the sponsors of the prosecution case.

Ungrammatical polemics were what we got instead. Genson had his moments and scored a lot of points, but it was not a great success. Trying to sum up the Bora Bora plane charge, he ran into heavy turbulence:

> Genson: Conrad wound up getting the most expensive airflight to Bora Bora in history. He paid half a million dollars for something that wasn't worth a third of that. And if they billed his variable costs or commercial costs – and then had to pay income tax on top of it. And Ms. Stitt, Ms. Stitt told us in that March 13, '03 – in that March 13,03 submission that Ravelston and Inc. paid variable costs. That's what she said in the submission. And, Dan, what is the – what is the – what is that, trip what? Do you know?
>
> Mr. D'Angelo: Which one, Eddie?
>
> Genson: Trip 1 – the audit committee meeting for '03. I wanted to get – I want the jury to see that. I just misplaced it. I have it right here. I'm sorry. Black International Audit 35 and I'd like you to look at page 2, paragraph 1. All right. Now let me talk just briefly before I get into the apartment – well, let me talk briefly about the airplane, one other thing . . .

Finally, his years and infirmities caught up with him, and he asked for a deferral to the next day. This was granted by the judge, who was generally quite indulgent of the counsel, and conducted the case with exquisite courtesy throughout.

The next day, June 20, Genson finished relatively strongly, though he underargued and botched the box affair, but I could not imagine anyone taking it seriously anyway. Pat Tuite and Gus Newman alternated for Jack Boultbee and were strong. Both my sons were in court this week and, with Barbara and Alana, made a great physical and moral statement of solidarity, which was a matter of pride as well as gratitude. Never did I understand so well Freud's statement that "My children are my joy and my riches."

Then Michael Schacter concluded very powerfully for Peter Atkinson on Monday, June 25, and was followed by a tremendous tour de force by Ron Safer for Mark Kipnis. He tore the entire government case to pieces, one last time. The defence could not have had a better closer. The government had no case, and Safer pointed this out in ringing, apparently emotional, terms. He gave the likely motive for Radler having rolled over: that he was caught in the *American Trucker* payment and cut his sentence by pledging to destroy others.

Sussman, the stuffing having been knocked out of his case for a week by better and more persuasive lawyers than he, summed up on June 26 and 27. It was another wobbly and inane catalogue of false facts and erroneous suppositions. Why did Mark Kipnis do all this though he gained nothing from the non-compete payments himself? "Perhaps he wanted to be the next Peter Atkinson." I could not believe anyone could subscribe to such rubbish. Like a clumsy sheepdog, Sussman careened around, trying to keep Atkinson and Kipnis in the group headed both to shearing and to slaughter.

What would prove to be the most contentious element of the instructions resulted from the government proceeding simultaneously on fraud allegations and the ill-defined offence of "a scheme or artifice to deprive another of the intangible right to honest services." This statute had been devised to deal with abuse of public office (where bribes were taken but there was no direct harm to the public interest), but like so many other U.S. statutes, such as RICO, it had been warped into a catchment for miscellaneous complaints. The sponsor, Senator and future Vice President Joe Biden, who jammed it through in a twenty-three-word amendment on the eve of the Christmas holiday in 1989, called it a "temporary fix," yet it was still on the books twenty years later. In his soporific wind-up, Sussman put up two demonstratives – single-word signs for HONESTY and INTEGRITY, as if he were leading kindergarten students out of the world of monosyllables. This was the signal that the prosecutors knew that their entire fraud case had collapsed and that the phantom offence of honest services was all they had, apart from the boxes.

Finally, it ended. The judge read the fifty-six pages of instructions to the jury, clearly enough but with no special emphasis on reasonable doubt and with a great deal of emphasis on fiduciary responsibility, to open the door for an honest services guilty finding. The different U.S. judicial circuits were divided on its interpretation, but Judge St. Eve, following the precedent in her circuit (the seventh), instructed the jurors that they were free to convict on honest services even if there was no economic harm to the company, nor any evidence of intent to harm. Breach of fiduciary duty, corrupt intent, and materiality were required. After Radler testified that the American Publishing payments were redirected management fees, this became very important. Defence counsel did not ask for a verdict form, which, in the event of conviction, would require statutory specificity on the grounds. Research had shown that such a form increased the likelihood of a guilty verdict. They relied (mistakenly) on the right to require a poll of the jurors if any guilty verdicts were returned. Thus, on three of the counts, jurors could find any of the defendants guilty without specifying which was the offense, and different jurors could find the defendants guilty of the same charge for different reasons.

UNSURPRISINGLY, THE LEGAL PROFESSION formally congratulated itself on what had just taken place. The judge made her little speech: "I want to tell the lawyers in here what a pleasure it is to preside over a case and be the judge on a case with such highly skilled lawyers across the board. The professionalism that you have brought into the courtroom, as well as your legal skills, are appreciated and it is a pleasure to be the judge on such a case." The marshals' mouths moved in synch with her words. They were clearly familiar with the homily.

Pat Tuite, author of the remark to Barbara and me that a trial is entertainment for everyone except the defendants, rose to take a bow for the cast: "And we want to express our pleasure to you for making this such a pleasant experience. I think I speak for all sides, Judge."

Eric Sussman caught the bouquet and returned it: "You do."

Tuite took the encore: "And we'd be glad to appear before you in any other case."

Judge St. Eve responded: "See you back here."

A last moment of shared jollity from Gus Newman: "I don't know if she'll admit me again!" General laughter all round. Rarely had I found the legal cartel so nauseating in its misplaced self-praise and conviviality. Safer and Greenspan, to their credit, abstained. Then the court rose on the afternoon of June 27.

I went back to the hotel for a nap, pleasantly interrupted by Julie Nixon Eisenhower, calling to thank me for my book about her father. Her last words to me were: "Justice will prevail!"

Alana turned twenty-five on June 28 and we had a rather successful party for her, with the Boultbees, and Genson's flamboyant driver, who had got us to court on time every day for more than three months, and some of the younger lawyers. It started with dinner at an excellent French restaurant near our hotel and moved on to a racy nightclub. I walked back to the hotel, but the owner of the nightclub, a professed admirer of mine, had me escorted by the formidable young Carl Davis, the tenth-ranking heavyweight prizefighter in the world.

There wasn't a great deal of social life in Chicago for us, and Barbara, especially, didn't feel much like socializing. I had gone out to dinner most nights during the trial, often with Mark Steyn, but there were few people left in Chicago with whom I had that kind of a relationship. But during the trial, as has been mentioned, friends came a great distance to have dinner with us. It was a great comfort having the Jonases on the same floor of our hotel for a good part of the trial, until nearly the last day. This included Maya Jonas's lovely seeing-eye black Labrador, the cheese-eating Daisy. It was almost like home, dropping in for a nightcap, and relieved the severity of the trial regime.

Tiny ceremonies of continuity throughout had reminded Barbara and me of what normal life was like: every morning she had put cereal in my bowl, though I often did not eat it until I returned after five o'clock. She bought a folding shopping cart and would walk weekly to do grocery shopping at the Treasure Island Food Mart. Even in such a modest gesture there reposed the hope and the conviction that we would again live like normal people and not constant targets of misguided prosecutors and all the avaricious litigants and malicious journalists who surged at and besieged us. I kept repeating, "The night will end," but it often required prodigies of faith to believe it.

I walked almost every night along the splendid Oak Street Beach north of my hotel, and was always greeted by many anonymous well-wishers. The general tenor of press comment in Canada had turned quite positively, faced with the evident poverty of the government's case. The Chicago media – where we had initially feared a mugging, especially from the *Sun-Times*, whose management was quaking in their shoes in contemplation not only of our acquittal but of the shambles they had made of the fine assets we left them – were fair. (Although Mark Steyn was fired mid-trial by the *Sun-Times*, for being too favourable to me, that paper played it fairly straight coming through to the end of the case.)

We all thought we had won the case, or rather I thought we all thought we had won the case; Alana subsequently told me she thought we would lose something, and Barbara, faithful to her profound rabbinical pessimism, later told me she thought we would lose on three or more of the counts. Once she saw Cramer in his opening, careening around the court room, raving about bank robbers, "I knew we hadn't a chance." (I had thought his performance so over the top and off the wall, it would backfire.) The hostility of both of them to Genson and especially Greenspan was very high. I spent a great deal of time trying to preserve civility in our camp. I did not want the press getting hold of internecine problems, though Mark Steyn, a surpassingly alert reporter, apart from his other talents, had a pretty good insight into what was happening.

Alana felt that Genson was courteous and oddly likeable, and that he was out of his depth but had done his best and worked very hard. Alana and Barbara both felt that Greenspan was a disappointment.

Up to a point, I shared their view. Greenspan had been very supportive in the early stages as the world I knew was crumbling, in 2003, and graciously came to Chicago to sit with me at the SEC as I invoked the Fifth Amendment in December of that year. He was invaluable when Williams & Connolly flaked off in 2005. He had underestimated the impact of health problems on his physical and intellectual stamina in a long U.S. trial. He was casual about his health and on one night fell into a diabetic stupor onboard a chartered plane in Toronto after having been with his daughter on her birthday at a big occasion in Toronto. He was cross-examining the next day and the plane had to be held late at night while my driver careened around trying to find a convenience store that had the food to overcome his condition. He had not done enough to prepare himself for

U.S. courtroom procedure, and left us for a time as laughing stocks at the defence and prosecution tables.

He rendered great service in tearing down Kravis and Thompson, when other defence counsel were still pussy-footing about trying to pretend that I was the only person on trial. Those witnesses and their testimony were carried out and burned, and their ashes flushed into Chicago's miraculous sewer system (like everything else in that muscular city, like the pectorals of a boastful teenager, the biggest and best water purification system in the world).

He did well with Creasey, and adequately with most of the others, but courted disaster with Radler before finishing well. His presumption that he could just slide into U.S. procedure like a duck entering a pond was mad. He was often plodding and obtuse, and unnecessarily antagonized the jury. He rarely asserted himself as chief counsel, never grasped the larger canvass the case required, to make comprehensible to the jury how this shareholders' dispute escalated as it did and became a Breeden power-grab. He was immoveable in clinging to establishing reasonable doubt about the allegations, even after it was clear to George Jonas, Marc Martin, Ron Safer, and others that we had won that argument on fraud but not necessarily on honest services. He ignored my theory that we would have to explain in outline how, mistakenly and for discreditable motives, it came to be a criminal case at all, other than with Radler alone. It was terribly exhausting and frustrating to remonstrate with counsel all the time. The only way to get anywhere was to side with one of them on one of the many issues being disputed between them and extract a concession in return for tipping the scales. It was a daily return to freshman model parliament. Greenspan seemed as concerned with his own public image as with the case, as if the first did not depend on the second. He had promised a Churchillian performance, and did not come close to delivering one.

Greenspan would tell the *Globe and Mail* in an interview published on October 3, 2009, that he regarded his performance in our trial as a victory, taking some credit and vindication in the progress of my counsel who succeeded him, and implying that I had been responsible for strategic errors, a bit rich given that he would ignore almost all my suggestions (and having already falsely blamed my wife for intruding in the case in a *National Post* interview).

He had been an able lawyer, a genuine friend, and a true believer in the right of all to representation. The deterioration of such a man is objectively sad, and is made more so by the inelegance of his acts of denial and displacement of responsibility for his own shortcomings and aggressive paranoia. And it is aggravated by the fetid atmosphere of toadyism in his entourage of worshipful followers. Withal, he assisted me vitally in time of dire need, played a vital role in severely damaging the prosecution case, and was often a very entertaining sidekick. His time is passing; I wish him well.

Greenspan had selected Genson, a man whom I liked but who was devoted altogether to creating some doubt. He was quite effective when he caught Sussman in his many errors and sat, spread-legged in his chair, and crowed, "Objection, Judge!" (Because of his condition, the judge did not expect him to stand.) But when he had to make serious and coherent argument, he became the victim of what Dr. Johnson called the "disingenuousness of years" and incomprehensibility sometimes resulted. George Jonas perfectly described the chipper smile of satisfaction that he struck up when convinced that he had confused his interlocutor, without, as he thought, making it obvious that that is what he had done. George thought him "an obfuscatory shyster." Toward the end of the trial, I rarely knew what line Genson was going to take, what witness was being called, and how they were being prepared – if at all. Had he accepted some of the help on hand from the younger lawyers and discussed with me his closing remarks, he might not have had what he (accurately) described in court as his "4.30 p.m. nervous breakdown."

There was a melancholia about them. They both barricaded themselves from their own clients and colleagues, Greenspan by vanishing at various times during the trial and refusing to communicate; Genson by refusing to reveal his strategy to the client or colleagues, as if we were all opponents in a game of whist. Both, along with the eighty-year-old Gus Newman, were obviously near the end of their serious careers, and Greenspan had so failed to forge any relationships, he was lonely in his hotel. (He had had to move hotels because, he claimed, Jane Kelly had failed to renew their status at "the urban sanctuary," and this contributed to the end of a fifteen-year professional relationship between them. Jane was, however, shortly after appointed a judge, which, from what I have seen, will raise the standards of fairness of the Toronto bench.) Greenspan had to import his daughter from Toronto to go to movies with him in the evening. "No one wants to hang out with him," as one of the younger lawyers put it.

A TENSE TIME ENSUED, as all waited upon the doubtful jurors. There were a couple of calls to hear jurors' questions, necessitating running the gauntlet of the assorted media. Finally, the judge realized there was no point in subjecting us to that, and there was silence from the court for many days.

The jury was deliberating on sixteen separate counts, including the three in which withholding honest services was the alternate charge in the fraud counts. The first count was the allegation against all the defendants of mail fraud because of a group of non-compete payments couriered from Chicago to Toronto. There was no possible doubt that such payments were routine in the industry, approved by the Audit Committee, and repeatedly publicly disclosed and discussed. The auditors and outside counsel were satisfied with all aspects of them, and the buyers, whatever their revisionism eight years later, after bullying from the Justice Department, wanted them and signed that they were conditions of closing. This was a straight attempt, retroactively, to criminalize normal and unexceptionable conduct, and to trump signed and disclosed contracts with extorted, *ex post facto*, oral testimony. The evidence revealed that as buyers we ourselves had paid obscure vendors non-compete amounts dozens of times, often a larger share of the purchase price than the payments objected to in this case. The implications of this attempt at criminal retroactivity were very serious for American business; if the prosecutors could do this, no businessperson was safe from having actions reinterpreted and charged as criminal, years after they were made public.

Counts 2, 3, and 4 were mail and wire fraud charges against Mark Kipnis only, and concerned documents he sent related to various community newspaper sales. Mark had not profited a cent from the payments involved, and had only done what Radler, as chief operating officer, had asked him to do. Everyone in the court knew Mark Kipnis was innocent, and even Radler said so. These counts were just an effort to bludgeon him into a plea bargain. The prosecutors, in their blood lust for me, were, as is their unvarying tactic, knowingly trying to obtain testimony against the chief defendant by intimidation of a relatively vulnerable and obviously unoffending co-defendant.

Count 5 was a mail fraud charge concerning the non-compete payment to David Radler of $4.3 million, in the sale of some small American newspapers to Community Newspaper Holdings Inc. (CNHI). The contract in question was binding, fully executed, approved by the Audit Committee, and disclosed publicly and in SEC filings. This was an assault on contract law. As Mark Steyn wrote: "To allow that a freely signed contract can be overridden by oral testimony from one party almost a decade after the event would be deeply damaging to the integrity of American business."

Counts 6 and 7 were mail fraud charges against all of us about the non-compete agreements with American Publishing. This was a division of Hollinger International and was relatively inactive at the time the payments were made. Breeden, the Special Committee, and the prosecutors all represented the payments as the defendants paying themselves not to compete with themselves. In fact, the non-compete agreements only came into effect after each of us left the Hollinger group, and were still in force at the time of the trial, and applied to all affiliated properties, including those in Chicago. This did not prevent the prosecutors from histrionically claiming that we paid ourselves generously not to compete with the *Mammoth Lake* (Washington) *Times*, a total canard, as they ought to have known. More important, David Radler had said, from the start, all the way through, and at the trial that these were unallocated management fees that he alone redesignated as non-compete payments, and did not testify that I even knew of this redesignation. They were approved as management fees and reapproved as non-compete payments, and did not cost the company a cent, given that the management fees were not in dispute. There was no evidence, ever, none, of any wrongdoing related to these counts.

Counts 8 and 9 concerned the CanWest transaction, which the government had originally charged against Radler and me, but withdrew in respect of us before the trial. They retained the claim that I had fraudulently included Atkinson and Boultbee as non-compete recipients. The prosecutors didn't call anyone from CanWest, knowing that they would support the defence, as our evidence showed. These were the most substantial amounts Peter Atkinson and Jack Boultbee received, and the related charges were necessary to enable the government to represent them as sizeable profiteers in this great scheme to steal millions. These were among the shabbiest counts of all (wire fraud over a fax and mail fraud over a FedEx package). The government admitted that CanWest was an untouchable deal, that non-competes are standard in the newspaper business, and that the big recipients were unassailable, and they could not produce anything to contradict defence evidence that the payments to Atkinson and Boultbee reflected the wishes of the buyers.

Counts 10, 11, and 12 were against Jack Boultbee and me, and concerned the so-called "perks" – the trip to Bora Bora, the dinner on Barbara's birthday, and the acquisition by me of the apartment in New York. These allegations were all riddled with holes by the time they went to the jury. Creasey and Healy when cross-examined, and John O'Sullivan under direct examination, had pretty thoroughly discredited them. The company made a good deal more from me than the variable costs on the airplane for the trip to Polynesia and back. The dinner was obviously a business occasion, and immaterial, and if it were a benefit to anyone, it would be Barbara (although she did not, in fact, enjoy it). I paid a third of it personally, to cover any non-business aspect, though told by Radler and others that that was unnecessary. The evidence had clearly shown that the company had defaulted on its obligation to renovate and furnish and decorate the apartment, that Healy had claimed to have researched it and attested to the fairness of the price, that the company had had only a partial interest, and that I had spent a total of $7.6 million on the apartment, counting renovations. These counts were wire fraud because of supposedly incomplete disclosure in the proxies (annual meeting voting forms sent out with the annual report), of the relevant years, based on the theory that I had benefited by more than $50,000 on each of the three events, and because I had supposedly wired a fraudulent amount when I sent my payment for the apartment to the company.

Count 13 was for obstruction of justice against me alone, for the removal of the thirteen boxes from my old office in Toronto on May 20, 2005. To convict, the jury had to conclude that I had "corruptly removed" documents for the purpose of impairing a U.S. proceeding, either the grand jury, the SEC, or the criminal case. I had Gordon Walker and Justice Campbell to thank for handing this fatuous charge to Sussman. Our witnesses had shown that I had no idea the SEC wanted anything more, after I had fully complied with five of its subpoenas and produced 124,000 pages of documents. It occurred a month before Brendan Sullivan told me they were a "thousand miles away" from laying a charge. It was clear from the evidence that I had had no knowledge of the contents of the boxes, nor anything to do with selecting their contents. There was no evidence that the boxes contained anything relevant to the case that the SEC did not already have, or that I had altered or even examined any of the boxes in the few days I had them. (I had not.) The judge emphasized that no Canadian proceeding was relevant to this case, but Sussman kept repeating that I had violated a Canadian court order. I did not and have never been accused of doing so. The government was caught red-handed, lying that I had furtively entered the building after hours in the dark and removed the boxes when the building was deserted. The colour film the government introduced (which Kelly had not shown to Justice Campbell in Toronto) showed that it was a bright afternoon, that I had arrived at 3:30 p.m., and that the parking lot was full of cars.

It was at least discernible in the evidence, though not as clearly as it should have been that I had cleared it with the acting president of the company, Don Vale, before I touched the boxes. Vale would happily have testified to this if Sussman had not threatened unspecified action against him if he even entered the United States. It could also have been found in the evidence that I could easily have destroyed or removed in a briefcase any documents in my office. There was absolutely no evidence to support this fantastic charge. Apart from being a deliberate and malicious fiction, it was, as Mark Steyn wrote, a "most shameless jurisdictional overreach."

Count 14 charged me only, with violation of the Racketeer Influenced and Corrupt Organizations Act. This was a statute passed as part of legislation against organized crime in 1970, and it alleged that our company had been a criminal enterprise since 1998.

This charge had been thrown out in the civil case and was so outrageous I had trouble taking it seriously too. Julie Ruder had explained chummily to the court that racketeering "isn't Al Capone and organized crime. It's nothing like that, okay? . . . Racketeering is a group of people working towards a common purpose and they do that through a pattern of criminal activity and the group of people we're talking about here is Mr. Black, Boultbee, Atkinson, Kipnis and Ravelston." She did not explain why only one of the group, I, was charged with racketeering. Mark Steyn pointed out that Al Capone was a gangster convicted of tax evasion, and I was accused of being a gangster for licitly trying to reduce my taxes in a foreign country.

Counts 15 and 16 were tax fraud charges against all of us except Atkinson, for filing a false corporate income tax return in 1999, and against all four of us for doing so in 2000. The charges were based on the theory that we knew the non-compete payments were fraudulent. Even if the non-compete payments had been something else, they were still tax-deductible and we had not deprived the Internal Revenue Service of a cent. The idea that any of us had falsified a tax return was absurd.

The prosecutors had claimed as one of the instances of fraud that I had conspired to evade Canadian taxes with false non-compete payments. The Canada Revenue Agency has never claimed that, and the separate count making this charge was dropped early on, as even Sussman realized that it wasn't his place to usurp the position of the Canadian tax collector. The earlier charge of money-laundering was dropped in mid-trial, as even Sussman acknowledged (surprisingly, as the same could be said equally of the rest of the courts).

None of the counts, against any of the defendants, had the slightest merit, and if the jury took the judge's caution to have proof beyond "a reasonable doubt" seriously, justice would be done. The prosecution had only raised a reasonable doubt of the probity of our conduct in one or two counts, and the defence had laid the doubt to rest. It was clear to much of the press and most qualified legal observers that this should never have been a criminal case and that there was no believable evidence at all of misconduct by any of the defendants – no victims (apart from ourselves), no crime, except by Radler, nothing.

THE VAST PRESS CONTINGENT was like a pack of scavengers, hunting for scraps of news. Unfounded rumours swept like forest fires through their ragged ranks and were played in the British press as semi-authoritative hunches. On one sudden call to court, as we were changing units within our hotel and my socks had been packed, I went to court with my bare feet in my shoes, like many others there, men and women. This became a great news story. As I pushed through the cameramen toward the revolving door, a British photographer shouted an obscenity at me just as I entered the door. I gave him "the bird" in Trudeau manner, and this became a *cause célèbre*. One commentator proclaimed that as this was undoubtedly directed at the jury and the entire U.S. justice system, I was doomed. It was really one of the better-aimed barbs of the trial, possibly along with my references to the *Toronto Star* to Sussman and Cramer as Nazis.*

On that day, July 10, the jury reported that they were unable to reach a verdict on one or more counts. We urged, through Safer, as agreed defence spokesperson, that they report what they had, but the judge sent them back to try to resolve matters. On July 11, we remained downtown all day, expecting the call at any moment. Nothing happened, and then silence on July 12. Greenspan had arranged press interviews for me, and I had written post-trial pieces for the *Globe and Mail* and the *National Post*, anticipating the end of the long nightmare.

I wasn't sleeping well. Barbara and I were both drained. I had a special telephone beside the bed. Only Genson's office knew the number, and that was to be used only to call us to court. It rang at 10:00 a.m., July 13. Genson's genial assistant, Nicki, said, "We have a verdict." By a considerable feat of logistics, Barbara and Alana and I arrived at court at 10:25 a.m. A few minutes later the judge entered, then the jury. In that quaint way that still preserves the solemnity of the day, all rose for them. The jury had not dressed up for the occasion. The foreman, whom we identified from his questionnaire as a supervisor in the Chicago Department of Streets and Sanitation, as well as the owner of an insurance appraisal business with his wife and a real

---

* I early developed the habit of replying only to questions put to me in French; initially to assist the French over the British (whose journalists never spoke a word of French despite their communautaire enthusiasm), and to favour the French Canadians, who would feel themselves in a very foreign city in Chicago, where almost every Western language except French is widely spoken. When asked why I did this, I explained to the French that I was a zealous European and to the French Canadians that I was demonstrating my love of minorities, "shareholding and otherwise."

estate broker, seemed to us commercially knowledgeable, a member of the junior grade of the Daley political machine, and unlikely to be an unusually puritanical person. Rumours abounded that he was going to produce some guilty verdicts in exchange for Fitzgerald's getting off the mayor's back, and some preferments for himself. After the trial, someone known to one of our allies engaged the jury foreman as a valuator, took him out for a few drinks, and elicited his confirmation that the fix was in from City Hall. St. Eve determined that the source was not sufficiently believable to take it further. The source perhaps was not, but the allegation was.

The foreman gave the judge the verdict sheets. She started with me as principal defendant. "*United States of America vs. Conrad Black.* First count: Guilty." I sighed and braced myself for a sand-bag job. It didn't happen. I won nine of the counts and lost four. All the rubbish about racketeering, looting, personal extravagance at the expense of the shareholders, Breeden's and Rosenberg's "$500 million kleptocracy" – all this had gone over the side. I went down on two counts to do with the so-called non-transaction with American Publishing (counts 6 and 7), which Radler had said throughout and right through the trial was the redesignation of unallocated management fees.

Creasey had testified that he had not thought these were management fees, but acknowledged that he was "confused." The jury had obviously not taken this on board. I lost on the one count of supplemental payments on Forum and Paxton (count 1), but not the initial non-competition payments, and, incredibly, I was convicted of obstruction of justice on the asinine box affair (count 13). On Forum and Paxton, the only evidence was Radler's (false and uncorroborated) claim that I had asked if there were any non-compete payments to come from those deals, and that when he phoned back with a proposed division of the $600,000 he claimed was available and had been approved by the Audit Committee, I agreed with him. Even if his testimony had been truthful, it wasn't incriminating.

Because we won all the counts related to real transactions, and all the prosecution's drivel about a "scheme" had been rejected by the jury, it was clear that honest services was the problem, and in most U.S. circuits we would have been acquitted. The others were convicted on the same counts I was, except for obstruction.

The jury implicitly declared that Burt, Kravis, Thompson, Radler, and Healy had failed to tell the truth. The main non-competes were deemed to have been approved by the Audit Committee, and the Park Avenue apartment, Bora Bora, and birthday dinner as well as the IRS and SEC filings and racketeering counts were also thrown out.

Judge St. Eve had them well rehearsed. They all stood promptly and said, "Yes," apparently understanding that that meant they were convinced beyond a reasonable doubt that we were all guilty of crimes and must go to prison. The jurors actually looked slightly impressive, standing up like synchronized pistons proclaiming their adherence to the verdicts.

There was no evidence of wrongdoing in respect of any of the counts that yielded convictions. It all came down to St. Eve's instruction on honest services. The jurors appeared to have been distracted by the endless false allegations that I had violated a Canadian court order. (Later, one of the narcoleptics revealed in an interview that she had woken up for the tape's screening. "You could see him doing wrong right there on the film," she was quoted as saying. Another told the press that even though she thought I might not have intended to do wrong, I had.) It was clear that some jurors didn't think there was proof beyond a reasonable doubt and that the jury had ignored the judge's instruction to avoid trade-offs. One of the jurors who had ignored the judge's instruction to avoid media coverage of the case, had come frothing into the jury room one day saying that the media thought they were incapable of reaching a decision, so they must reach one. The three women who had been defending us agreed to convict on four counts, and the militant majority agreed to acquit on the rest, and they went on their summer holidays. In this system, and given the ferocity and force of our tormentors, we could have done worse.

I felt that given the four-year assault on me, I had almost won the financial battle; Barbara was prosperous and unassailable, and the much-touted attack on her never occurred; and I had defeated the effort to send me to prison for life. Whatever happened on appeal, the absolute worst prediction was about five years served, and sentencing counsel assured me that we could do a lot better than that. Though I tended to discount anything optimistic from any lawyer, indeed almost anything of any tenor from counsel, there was a ring of plausibility to this.

Sussman again asked that my bail be revoked and that I be imprisoned at once. There were eight marshals at the door of the court, ready to take us all into custody, but the others were all released under existing arrangements, and Boultbee returned at once to Canada. Judge St. Eve declined to imprison me but said I must remain in the Chicago area, and scheduled a further hearing for July 19.

The initial reaction of Fitzgerald and his underlings was not one of great celebration. Needless to say, Greenspan proclaimed to me a great victory and said he would tell the press that it was a "devastating defeat for the government," by which he meant a glorious victory for him. Since he knew nothing about the U.S. appeal process and his client was facing a prison sentence, I suggested that he not strain credulity to that extent. He and I agreed a statement expressing satisfaction that we had got rid of the allegations of racketeering, looting, and personal extravagance at the shareholders' expense, and that the "$500 million kleptocracy" was down to $2.9 million of payments, which had, in fact, been approved and disclosed, and that we would appeal the convictions. Barbara, Alana, and I left through the back of the building, avoiding most of the press, and left Greenspan in his happy role of talking to the press, who were out in jubilating numbers.

My sober reaction was disappointment, but if the jury was prepared to convict even Kipnis, it implies that they were determined to give something to the government, and even better counsel might not have achieved complete victory for us. Safer had been brilliant, and Kipnis had not profited from the contested payments and was defended by Radler, but he had lost as badly as Boultbee and Atkinson, while I had won three-quarters of the charges the government started with, and 90 per cent in terms of potential financial downside.

Once again, Providence had rescued me from the abyss, but left me still in the coils of severe adversity. My enemies would not impoverish my family or imprison me for life, and we still had a chance at acquittal, or at least a reduction to a Martha Stewart-gotcha offence. I thought I had defeated the attempt to brand me as an outright crook who had robbed the company of huge sums of money. I wasn't especially afraid of prison, but there was no gainsaying that time out of my life spent there would be horribly inconvenient. After four years, it was possible to wonder when the war would end. Even if I stayed out on bail, it was no better than a fifty-fifty chance to win the appeal on all counts, and that might defer matters for up to another eighteen months.

I was not giving up on the appeal to the trial judge, much less the appeal judges, and sentencing counsel was hopeful we could get the sentence down to the point where the judge had to grant an appeal bond. I took Alex Bourelly's advice and met with lawyers from Mayer Brown et al., a famous appellate firm. They looked like the quality of counsel I could not afford at the start of the trial, after Sussman seized the proceeds of the New York sale, which he would now have to relinquish.

I also spoke to Alan Dershowitz, and met with him a few days later when he came to Chicago. I retained Marc Martin, who has a good record on appeal, and provided continuity, a Chicago presence, and procedural expertise. I was pedalling away from the Eddies. Mark Steyn produced a fierce diatribe against them in *Maclean's*, highlighting their lifting of $2.2 million from me just as the trial was ending, to pad their retainers. It was the end of Greenspan's mystique, other than in the eyes of his worshipful claque. I took no pleasure in this, but his evident depression at the first bad press of his life amplified my awareness of his vulnerable ego.

An avalanche of messages came in, several hundred, all but two of them generously supportive. I laboured through the days following the verdict to reply to them all and to take the many telephone calls. The press in Canada was mixed; in the United States it was factual, except for a reversion to extreme antagonism in the *Sun-Times* and an uncharacteristically inane editorial in the *Wall Street Journal* (now a Murdoch newspaper). The British media were as abominable as could be imagined, though they continued to run favourable reviews of my Nixon book. It was now time for silent manoeuvring and skirmishing. The argument for injustice could be made by discerning observers. I declined all contact with the press, other than on the subject of my Nixon book.

On July 19, I went to see the probation officer, Sheila Lally, a very pleasant and thoughtful woman, and had a good talk with her. She allegedly carried some weight with the judge. Barbara and Alana also spoke to her, and Jeffrey Steinback (sentencing counsel) told me, which I do not doubt, that they were both very persuasive.

That afternoon, Greenspan, with the aid of David Roebuck, tried to explain to the judge the civil law of Canada. For either Barbara or me to provide more bail might be deemed a breach of the Confidential Settlement Agreement (which Greenspan kept calling the "Confidential Security Agreement" until the judge corrected him), which emerged after the Mareva fiasco in September 2006. Roebuck, never an expeditious speaker, taxed the patience and the comprehension of the court with a very circumlocutory explanation, and he and Greenspan, bowing to the judge in the Canadian manner, seemed at times almost like a slapstick routine. She again rejected Sussman's request for revocation of bail, and told me I could go to Palm Beach, but not to Canada. She professed to be concerned that if I went to Canada, I would fight extradition. "He's not a flight risk," she was fond of saying, "Mr. Black is a fight risk." This appeared to be based on a case she had had in her time as a prosecutor when some wily Canadian had left her jurisdiction for Canada and had been very difficult to extradite for one of her trials. I did not believe she thought that I would fight extradition, as it would be insane. They had not rebutted at all Sussman's repeated allegations of my untrustworthiness. Greenspan pronounced it "a good day," meaning, I assumed that since he had done much of the talking, it must be a good day. It wasn't. A new hearing was scheduled for August 1.

It was starting to seem like the summer of 2006, where the judge just kept punting forward Sussman's demands for revocation of bond and the forced sale of the Palm Beach house. The summer was slipping by. Almost everyone we knew had left Chicago, and we remained in our very comfortable hotel, but after more than four months, it was time to go.

BACK TO COURT ON AUGUST 1, the crush of reporters, the judge, Greenspan, this time with George Glezos* and Stephen Green in tow from Toronto, civil and immigration counsel. (Every step involved more lawyers.) Voorheis on this day finally packed the *Sun-Times* board with Hollinger Inc. nominees, which he should have done as soon as he displaced Walker and Carroll. He put Hollinger Inc. into creditor protection,

---

* George Glezos, a good lawyer and a delightful man, died of a coronary a few weeks later. He was fifty-three and apparently very fit. He had a bad lottery ticket and is much missed.

which made it too late to do anything with Hollinger International. And he sent to Chicago a Rent-an-Affiant, claiming he had reason to believe that I had stashed 40 million Euros in Gibraltar. George Jonas knew and had employed Voorheis's affiant, an erratic and absurd Israeli named Aviv who had been branded "a liar" by a serious U.S. court and had offered the theory that a rogue unit of the CIA had blown up the Pan American 747 over Lockerbie, Scotland, in 1989, killing hundreds of Americans. (He had hatched this imaginative theory on behalf of the insurers of the aircraft. It didn't fly well either.) His affidavit was a complete invention, and Greenspan opened with a very thorough demolition of Aviv. So much so that Sussman didn't touch it; this one was too rank even for him, and the judge and most of the press ignored it. This was the customary response to unambiguous successes of ours: silence, as if it had not really happened.

Eddie Greenspan was better organized than on July 19 and answered the judge's questions fairly crisply. They had chased up the Mareva monitor on holiday in Israel, and Greenspan could confirm that an attempted variance of the settlement could be construed as a breach, so neither Barbara nor I could add to the bail if we wanted to, because of the settlement. (No one had imagined that more bond than the $38 million already posted would be requested. Sussman's position was that civil claimants were going to take all my money anyway, so there was no disincentive to fleeing. His impudence was inexhaustible.)

The judge stuck to her nonsensical point that she wanted more bail. Greenspan gave an impassioned and rather eloquent speech about my right and desire to go home. Genson stirred himself and also made an impassioned statement that I was indeed a fighter, but that I would fight through the normal channels. They both did their best. Sussman didn't have to say anything. The judge was not buying it.

Even though it came into evidence that the Canadians would admit me without a passport, she clung to her fear that I would return to Canada and then fight extradition. I had thought her quite a fair trial judge, but this was rank discrimination. How she imagined that borrowing more bail from rich friends, since I couldn't provide it myself under the Mareva agreement, would reduce the chances of my jumping bail, I didn't understand either.

She seemed to have made the Manichaean leap from comparative fairness to part of the prosecution because of the findings, as if it were a rigorously condign process, the operation of which required the defendant to accept entirely a guilty verdict, no matter how passionately he had fought it and was still pleading his innocence, and no matter that he had debunked ninety per cent of the case. There was also a chance that she was just making an example, after months of press attention, of the consequences to my conspicuous lack of regard for the prosecution.

I REFUSED TO ASK ANYONE for money and I refused to consider more bail. I would go to Palm Beach. This I did on August 8, as Barbara flew to Toronto. It was not the end we had wished for our sojourn in Chicago. Barbara was welcomed back by Canada Immigration, by a woman who claimed to have been an admirer of ours for twenty-five years, and said that the U.S. treatment of me had been an outrage. Barbara wept at being kindly treated by a government official. She tried to pay duty at Canada Customs, but the inspector would not hear of it and said that the U.S. treatment of me had been disgraceful and waved her through.

HOT AND HUMID THOUGH Florida was, I was glad to return to our home in Palm Beach. It had been much publicized, but it was still ours, and had gone straight up in value throughout the persecution of us. It was time to regroup, yet again, in this long and horrible war.

Palm Beach proved a perfect place to rest. The long trial had been so enervating, I sometimes slept for more than ten hours a day. I worked on this narrative and contributed to motions and filings in the afternoon and evenings, and slept most of the morning. The evenings and nights, from my eastern terrace, overlooking the ocean, were very refreshing, with a warm, slightly salted breeze coming in off the water.

Alana came for a time. There was no shortage of well-wishers, by telephone and in person. Friends came from as far away as Britain and Italy and stayed with us. Barbara came from Canada after about two weeks and I had a good time with my neighbours, Ann Coulter and Rush Limbaugh, flamboyant champions of the political right. I had an amusing little spoof for Canadian television with humorist Rick Mercer, about waxing maple leaves when unable to enjoy the autumn within Canada. Seth Lipsky organized an uproarious dinner at the Breakers Hotel with some journalistic friends, including Mark Steyn, Ken Whyte, Taki, Bob Tyrrell (the *American Spectator*), and Roger Kimball (the *New Criterion*).

The eminent novelist and good friend Margaret Atwood assisted in setting up a Long Pen signing of my Nixon book from my southern home. Sitting in my library in Palm Beach in front of a camera, I was able to write a note on screen and have it exactly reproduced in the customer's book in one of Heather Reisman's Indigo bookstores in Toronto and later at Waterstone's in London. My friend the historian Andrew Roberts, who with his wife had stayed with us in Palm Beach a few weeks before, moderated a press session at Waterstone's. Here and in subsequent radio and television interviews with the BBC, I chided the British media for "bourgeois priggishness" and explained what rubbish the few remaining counts were. I reminded them of their usual relentless criticism of the U.S. justice system. When asked my opinion of Judge St. Eve, I replied that judges do the judging, not the defendants. All these events had the effect of psychologically loosening the impact of St. Eve's unnecessarily restrictive bail terms.

The countless irritations incited by our discomfort did not abate. My dear friends at the Canadian Imperial Bank of Commerce noticed in the newspapers that there was some restraint on my spending and abruptly determined to pass none of my cheques, or Barbara's. This was a breach of their banking covenant and of the Bank Act. The information on which they acted had been in the public domain for more than a year, since the Mareva nonsense began. We demanded that Hollinger Inc. give CIBC the necessary assurances. Instead, it tried to renegotiate the Confidential Settlement Agreement. Campbell was now so overwhelmed by the controversies he had helped to precipitate and infect that he refused to judge anything, and his answer was to tell the parties to try to settle any issue. He had gone from a gavel-happy judge of poor judgment to a timorous judge reticent to judge. It was a marginal improvement. Finally, as Hollinger Inc. was besieged for demands that it be plunged from creditor protection into bankruptcy, and there was pressure on it to reduce legal bills, a passable settlement was agreed.

The nonsense with the Warhol silkscreen portraits of me arose again, and I secured funds for a bond, enabling me to buy the Warhol in my house and bid on the other two, of which the receiver, now desperate to find more money in Ravelston to appropriate, had the most inflated notions of value. In fact, I owned them, but the paperwork was almost non-existent and ambiguous, and I remained unwilling to entrust this issue to the Toronto courts. It was very annoying, but I was accustomed to this sort of harassment. I declined to chase the first one in New York, but determined to press for the second one, which Barbara bought at Christie's in London in February, and to return to a quartet by having the silkscreens copied – not a great challenge.

For no given reason the insurer of my homes and their contents, abruptly defected. I was a toxic waste area. My legal condition had no bearing on such matters and it was high-quality business. Working with my agent (the daughter, as it turned out, of a man I had gone to high school with), I found other insurers. Having registered my grievance with Hal Jackman's public comments about Barbara and me in 2003, I would be remiss if I did not emphasize the very benign role his son and their corporate group played in both the Warhol and insurance questions.

I learned from the press that the U.K. Conservative Party no longer considered me a Conservative peer. Departing that oft-defeated party was no great sacrifice, but learning of it in this way, and not being given the opportunity to await appeal, explain my side of things, or to withdraw voluntarily, was gratuitously insulting. I received a somewhat condescending letter from the chief whip eventually, to which I replied with approximately equal condescension.

Even Cardinal Leger's charity sent me a letter purporting to require my retirement as a director, which was in fact an honorary position. I was threatened with being expelled by three-quarters of the members at the annual meeting in May 2008. I replied, in acidulous terms, with a handwritten riposte on their faxed letter to me that, given my past services (raising and contributing large sums of money) and the excellent prospects of my appeal, I would await the annual meeting. I eventually agreed, when they made a more diplomatic approach, not to stand for re-election. I had not attended one of their meetings in thirty years.

I responded to a request for funds from a friend for a conference at Laval University, and was advised that the university could not accept a contribution from our foundation. I was invited to send a non-charitable contribution but naturally declined. Toronto's venerable York Club, where I used to debate with Walter Gordon over his sponge cake and where my picture is on the wall for having given their annual Hungerford Address, sent me an annoying letter stating that I was suspended awaiting appeal, by unanimous vote of the directors. I gave the letter to Eddie Greenspan, whom John Turner and John Fraser and I had sponsored as a member of the York Club some years before. The club retrenched somewhat, and there was a good deal of toing and froing, but we sorted it all out eventually.

The tax-collecting authorities of Canada and the United States started up again, claiming to find unpaid taxes and wishing endlessly to converse with my counsel. Plodding, repetitive, and greedy, these people didn't change much from one decade and country to another. After all I had been through, I wasn't much concerned, and had little doubt we would see them off, once again. The IRS also intensified a spurious and systematic harassment of Barbara. I suspected that few of the people scoring off me in the press over these points had had to put up with more than the odd angry word or memo, and lacked the imagination to guess what Barbara and I were enduring.

THE WEEKS DRIFTED BY IN PALM BEACH as agreeably as they could. We had offered a solution to the Hollinger Inc. bondholders, who were now under water by 50 per cent on the cost of their investment. The fools did not wish to deal with us. Hollinger Inc. was, in fact, bankrupt, and Voorheis, now exposed, was reduced to claiming that the future of the company reposed in "litigation assets." These were unfounded lawsuits against ex-directors, banks, the former management, launched by people who had milked and destroyed the company at great profit to themselves. This was the effect of the Campbell-Farley-OSC axis: the elimination of $250 million of the shareholders' money, about half of it mine.

The bondholders shortly had the pleasure of seeing their position under water by 85 per cent, then 95 per cent, then 100 per cent, as the *Sun-Times* stock that secured it descended beneath $1. It had been at $22 after

Strine's infamous misjudgment in February 2004. Tweedy Browne bailed out, having lost their investors about $70 million, and helped indispensably (as Kissinger would say) to destroy the companies and the interests of all. This was the supreme coruscation in these matters of the corporate governance movement.

The surreal injustice and absurdity of it all continued to escalate. A 10 per cent shareholder of *Sun-Times* finally revolted and demanded the removal of Seitz as chairman and the complete departure of Paris, so horrible had his management performance been. The latest wrinkle was that Paris had invested $59 million in Canadian real estate–backed investments that had not met their redemption obligations. A loss of $42 million was booked. Paris had been fleeced by Canadian real estate financiers and piled into foreign sub-prime mortgages, just before they evaporated. This was an odd inspiration for a newspaper company, but a typical initiative of the Paris-Seitz-Breeden executive suite, effortlessly losing almost ten times what we had been falsely convicted of receiving improperly. There was some justice in this, but not for the suffering shareholders.

The myth continued to circulate that I could have got rid of the whole problem by paying a few million dollars at the end of 2003 and only my stubborn pride had prevented a settlement early on. This canard was propagated by Henry Kissinger and his New York social entourage of bearers, beaters, and trumpeters, to reinforce Henry's inevitable self-image as a peacemaker frustrated by my inflexibility. I had done my best to settle with the institutional shareholders. Breeden was a mortal assailant even before he physically appeared. It was obvious from Breeden's violation of the Restructuring Agreement and his refusal to deal seriously in January 2004 that this was always a vendetta, and the easy, early avoidance theory was one of the many self-serving myths confected for this case.

Henry's approach reminded me of his exhortations to Nixon in 1969 to 1971 to be fierce with North Vietnam and North Korea, while assuring his liberal journalistic and social friends that he, Henry, was all that was preventing the madman president from blowing up the world. To adapt Churchill, it is in small as in great matters that statesmen fail to distinguish themselves.

As the fourth anniversary of the start of the nightmare approached, my $250 million of value in Ravelston had evaporated. The companies had been almost completely destroyed. America's greatest, most prestigious, and most reliable source of general support in the international media, The Telegraph plc, was now in the hands of owners who were far from pro-American (the Barclays were influenced in part by Strine's gross misjudgment). The corporate governance zealots had been exposed as the cynical or naïve but money-grubbing frauds I had always claimed they were. This was the fruit of the U.S. government's four-year assault on honest men, at the behest of Breeden. Still, three-quarters of the allegations against the management had been rejected, and we retained a substantial possibility of complete official vindication. It was a war of attrition, and as Mort Zuckerman had said to me when early on we met on Madison Avenue, "It's the last man standing." Shortly after the trial, Candice Bergen, a very intelligent and generous-minded person, in addition to her better known talents and attractions, told Barbara what I took to be the view of her husband, the very able Marshal Rose, and the sophisticated circle of his business friends, who included my former director, Leslie Wexner: "What a time you're having! Conrad will probably win, but at what cost!" Indeed.

THE JUDGE REJECTED THE defendants' motions to overturn the convictions or declare mistrials, other than an acquittal of Kipnis on one count. Her reasoning, as Ruder was fond of saying, was "ridikalus" and disappointing: the fact that I hired a law firm that had a sizeable criminal practice demonstrated that I knew of the grand jury investigation of me, and confirmed the obstruction charge in the judge's mind. How could an apparently serious judge write such bunk? We awaited her judgment on forfeiture (where Sussman had reduced his claim from $80 million to a still phantasmic $18 million); the sentences; and the continuation of bail, before taking the survivors among the government's farrago of false charges to the Circuit Court of Appeal.

Sheila Lally submitted a favourable probation report, and I rounded up about a hundred letters of support from people in every conceivable walk of life. Many were very generous and moving. Barbara's, Alana's, Jonathan's, Brian Stewart's were among those that were particularly exquisite.

It was a little like reading my own obituary and being pleasantly surprised. Many former employees, people I had helped at various stages of their careers, as well as prominent people in many fields and from many countries, wrote embarrassingly generous requests to the judge for clemency. Carolyn Gurland performed prodigies in writing up materials for the judge and probation office, and by her fine sense of humour was a delight to deal with as well. I received up to fifty letters or emails of support a day as the sentencing date, December 10, approached. These ghastly afflictions are not without their rewards.

WE ATTENDED UPON THE judge yet again. The huge press contingent was relatively respectful: little jostling and no audible coarseness or abrasive questions on the way in or out (unlike the occasion early in the trial when Barbara had almost been knocked cold by a boom microphone). I sat between Jeffrey and Carolyn, majestic and well exercised as she entered the ninth month of her pregnancy. The Eddies, looking a bit out of place, were opposite; there was no shortage of people in the room who thought that if Greenspan and Genson had been up to the task, there would have been no sentencing. I shook hands with each of them on the way in and out, but there was no conversation between us.

Gene Fox from Cardinal Capital, a small institutional investor and former obsequious supporter of mine, rambled on in a hastily misconceived victim statement blaming me for the collapse of the company starting long after I had left. Sussman asked twenty years – a likely life sentence, as might be asked for murderers and rapists – and $27 million of fines and forfeitures.

He grumbled about lack of "remorse," as if the limited perspective and incoherent judgment of the jurors on a quarter of the counts must cause me at once to do a U-turn, acknowledge my guilt, and renounce everything I had said on the subject for the last four years. I was delighted that he was particularly miffed that I had publicly called the prosecutors "Nazis" and complained vociferously about my recent BBC interviews. Most of the media and even some of my counsel had expressed confidence (though not to me personally) that my remarks would cost me years in prison. I was to surface only occasionally, like the orange-suited defendants shunted into court in handcuffs to be momentarily represented by blasé legal-aid public defendants.

Jeffrey Steinback, a chronic optimist, thought he could get the announced sentence under three years; I thought a bit more. Barbara and Alana thought a little more negatively. Jeffrey rebutted the complaints about the interviews and produced a rather awful mangle of Portia's speech on mercy from *The Merchant of Venice*. The judge invited me to comment.

I had planned to speak at length about the nonsense of the convictions and the whole lethal assault of the U.S. government and its accomplices, but Jeffrey and Carolyn persuaded me that this wasn't the place for that, and that Judge St. Eve could raise the sentence if I did so. They understood there would be no statement of remorse, even if making such a statement was the only way to spare me the fate Sussman had been seeking. I had no notes and spoke from memory in an even voice. After all I had been through, I did not find addressing the court and the media in the slightest unnerving, and spoke for less than five minutes.

I referred to arguments and filings made on my behalf, especially Marc Martin's Basta filing from July 2006, which detailed Sussman's false accusations to the court, and Carolyn Gurland's letter to the judge of two days before, debunking the madly delusional *Sun-Times* victim statement. The fact that we were appealing the remaining counts "speaks for itself." I later said that I would have "no difficulty at all rebutting the most recent statements of the prosecutor, and of Mr. Fox." I offered to explain my public comments on the prosecutors, but St. Eve shook her locks unthreateningly to confirm that that was not necessary. Thus, as she doubtless foresaw, she spared the court and media what would have been a calmly delivered but pyrotechnic summary of the prosecution's more outlandish infelicities.

"We have the verdicts we have and we can't retry the case here . . . I do wish to express my very profound regret and deep sadness" (the press strained audibly to hear) "at the severe hardship inflicted upon all of the shareholders, including a great many employees, by the evaporation of $1.85 billion of shareholder value under my successors." (And the press sank back, denied the Sussmaniacal "remorse.") This not only laid the lash where it belonged, but emphasized that I had no apology to make for my own conduct. I denied that I had ever uttered a disrespectful word about the judge, court, jury, or process (a slight liberty with the facts) but declined to withdraw or modify my reflections on the prosecutors. I made the point that the stock price had remained between $18 and $22 for a year after I retired, and was then under $1, largely because my successors ignored my advice as a continuing director, to avoid many of the catastrophic errors they plunged into like beasts into well-set traps.

I concluded: "It only remains for me to thank Your Honor for the unfailing courtesy and efficiency with which you have conducted this trial. Prior to arriving under your jurisdiction, I was the subject of an almost universal presumption of guilt, including the theory that I violated a Canadian court order, which I did not and have never been accused of doing. This presumption of guilt applied to all counts and prevailed in almost every court, both of law, and of public opinion." I thanked her and she thanked me.

She rather mechanically read assertions that I had been convicted of serious offences, and implicitly acknowledged that I had had an impressive career (and added with a smile that I would not need vocational training). I was not particularly tense, as the probation report was favourable and the judge was very deferential to Sheila Lally in court, and I was satisfied we had a strong appeal, and that I was putting the worries generated by the Eddies behind me. I did not see this as the end of the line, whatever her sentence.

She expressed no objection at all to my comments on the prosecution. Her disdain for Sussman was fairly well known, as was the fact that Sussman was desperately and unsuccessfully seeking a legal position in the private sector. (He did eventually find one. So did Cramer, two years later.) That very day a Supreme Court judgment had confirmed her ability to vary sentencing guidelines; but while this ruling was referred to in court, she chose not to follow Sheila Lally's advice to go below the guidelines and took the low end of them, clearly thinking she was being merciful. She acknowledged that I was appealing the sentence, imposed a sentence of seventy-eight months, recommended minimum security, and again ignored Sussman's request for immediate imprisonment. She gave the maximum time to self-surrender (twelve weeks) and imposed a fine of just $125,000. Even more important, the judge threw out the request for forfeiture based on the claim that the government had proved that I was guilty of the acquitted acts under a civil standard of proof. Judge St. Eve's assertion that they had not even met a civil standard of proof was the victorious end of the financial struggle and effectively sank most of the civil suits against me.

We felt that the letters, Carolyn's written arguments, and Sheila's recommendations made a useful difference and Mayer Brown had set no store by any of it. Andy Schapiro of that firm had said that we should just send a pro forma response to the the Probation Office, and that the officer would "not have the intelligence to understand anything we wrote anyway, and no one would pay any attention to it." My evaluation of Ms. Lally was that she was a serious and credible person who would be listened to by the judge and was favourably disposed and should not be treated cavalierly.

The long-standing pattern was retained: taking custodial and financial matters together, we had won about four-fifths of what was in dispute with the prosecutors. The six years and six months would really, in practice, and after accessing certain programs, be about four years, in fairly manageable conditions. This was a long way from the "conspiracy so immense"* that gave rise to the demands for life imprisonment with hardened criminals and sodomites and complete impoverishment. And the battle continued; we would seek continuation of bail, and I had already engaged appellate counsel in whom I tentatively had confidence, despite their advice virtually to ignore the probation officers.

Two days later, a month-old Greenspan interview with the *National Post* was disembargoed, as the revisionist campaign heated up; he attacked Genson as an incompetent, and blamed Barbara for "insinuating" herself into the case. He had no criticism of Alana, Jonathan, or me. I declined to reply. It was objectively sad and that chapter was over.

THE NEXT TWELVE WEEKS IN Palm Beach became steadily more Damoclean, as the self-surrender date approached. Judge St. Eve, true to her new persona as a virtual bailiff cleaving like a limpet to the fiction that the process had produced condign verdicts, declined bond pending appeal. We applied to the Circuit Court of Appeals. Bill Buckley and I exchanged

---

* Senator Joseph R. McCarthy's attack on General George C. Marshall, U.S. Senate, June 14, 1951.

comments in published columns in the *New York Sun* and *National Post* about my case. (See appendices.) He came to Fort Lauderdale for a month, and we had dinner twice in Palm Beach. He was approaching death, was almost looking forward to it. Pat, his devoted and riotously witty Canadian wife of more than fifty years, had died in 2007. I was, he thought, reasonably prepared for what I was fairly convinced was coming next (though not quite as sanguine about it as he was about what he was facing). The coils were tightening and the fanatical determination of the U.S. justice system, as manipulated by Breeden, to send me to prison, was coming to pass. There would be nothing for it but to prove that theirs was a hollow and fleeting victory; that I was unintimidated, unjustly confined, and undaunted by the vast machinery of incarceration, humiliation, and stigmatization that had assaulted me. And I would continue to pursue victory: appeals, and if necessary, evocation of the whole sordid proceeding to the judgment of an unbiased foreign jurisdiction.*

Barbara and I went to Fort Lauderdale to have lunch with Bill Buckley the day before he returned north. It was an exquisite occasion, but we all knew it was goodbye. He was a great man and a dear friend, and he died about three weeks later, February 27, and I was just finishing a remembrance of him for the *National Post* when Andy Frey of Mayer Brown telephoned to confirm that the Circuit Court had refused bail. I was to report to prison four days later.

---

* This was my plan, referred to earlier, of taking some attempt in Canada or Britain to remove me from a club or some other association, as the opportunity to go to court to apply the test of whether any guilty verdicts would have been returned on the same evidence in that other jurisdiction. Of course, none would have been in Canada or Britain, where prosecutors would not be allowed to offer the inducements Fitzgerald and his entourage had to some of the witnesses.

[CHAPTER FIFTEEN]

ON MONDAY, MARCH 3, Barbara and I got up wordlessly. We had held each other during the night. Barbara walked her puppy in the garden to the pleasure of the press who were on the other side of the road waiting for my departure. The puppy was too young to understand his routine anywhere but on the little strip of grass that had become familiar to him – and now to the press. This tiny, white, lamblike puppy: I wondered if he would remember me.*

---

* He grew quickly to be a large, much-loved dog, but died, very sadly, less than two years later, while I was still incarcerated. Barbara was inconsolable, and bearing this loss alone was another rod at a terrible time. There are many casualties even in a non-shooting war, but fortunately, they were not all on our side. Barbara's dog outlived, by a few weeks, Bruce Wasserstein, sixty-one, of Lazard, whose passing was observed with commendations of his deal-making talents and general craftiness, though not panegyrics to his ethics or suavity; and poor Christopher Browne, who died pitifully at sixty-three, a hopeless alcoholic, in Palm Beach, a town he had professed to despise. His obituaries referred exclusively to his role in my travails, now generally hinting that it had not worked out quite as he had hoped, and to the fact that his predecessors in his company had done some early work for Warren Buffett. His uprising against me was his only hurrah, apart from a few cultural munificences and his conviviality in the gay community of the Hamptons. He was an intelligent and, at his best, moderately entertaining man. It was obvious to me that he was seriously maladjusted, but while I cannot claim to be crestfallen that he is dead, I do regret what must have been a much steeper and more tortured decline than I ever imagined or would have wished.

I looked at the sparkling-blue, foam-capped Atlantic crashing onto our beach from our drawing room for a couple of minutes and then the stately progress of yachts and criss-crossing of small boats in the placid Intracoastal Waterway out our loggia windows for a little longer. The recollection of these perspectives would be a source of serenity in the sober, contemplative times to come.

We drove away in a rented SUV that had windows largely impenetrable to cameras. The trip was uneventful after we got clear of the photographers outside our gate at Palm Beach, who pressed their cameras against the windows. They were only doing their jobs, but to what awful tastes they pandered.

Barbara and I held hands during the ride and spoke little. There wasn't much left to say. The scrubby topography of the Florida interior, with its endless commercial signs, strip malls, and one-storey buildings, provided little visual diversion. The only phone call was to the tireless Carolyn Gurland, who was already hard at work on the menu of strategies we had developed for mitigating my stay in the prison I was now approaching. The long struggle against my accusers could have gone much worse, but it had gone badly. Therefore, it must continue.

My thoughts were that this was the worst the enemy could do, that it had loomed darkly in my thoughts for four and a half years, and that if I could endure it, the end of the ordeal would finally be in sight. My imprisonment should also slake the blood thirst of my more vociferous enemies. The sated prosecutocracy and its cheerleaders would move on to other prosecutions of real or imagined crimes. I was determined, above all things, whatever indignities might occur that I would not give way to self-pity, affected hauteur, or anger, much less despair.

To the chroniclers, I had had a crushing reversal. I had. It was all that and more. Having hoped so much and proclaimed so forthrightly that I would be vindicated, I had lost more than I could ever have imagined. That is what made it also a huge challenge and opportunity. To rise above what I was about to face after years of calumny, persecution, and heavy collateral financial damage would at least temper in my mind the unjust and fleeting victory my opponents had achieved. I was sustained, on that and future days, by the solidarity of the growing army of my supporters; thousands of messages of goodwill arrived in the last days before I passed through the prison gate. I would keep faith with those who had maintained or developed faith in me, and especially with those who had loved me, living and dead, above all with my magnificent wife and family.

Nor was my faith shaken. I had realized from the beginning that it was a severe challenge, but the facts that my mental and physical health and my marriage and family had borne it showed I was not God-forsaken. As Pope John Paul II told Emmett Cardinal Carter about the cardinal's stroke, to bear such a burden was a divine gift, a demonstration of God's confidence in the afflicted, and a subject of rejoicing. Like the cardinal, I found the flourish about rejoicing a rather stiff challenge. I had long believed the Jesuit formulation that resistance to tyranny is obedience to God (though I frequently disagreed with the definitions of tyranny targeted by members of the Society of Jesus). In any analysis, there was no practical alternative to fighting it out, and there was never a thought of any other course.

John Hillier delivered us to the long-imagined destination after a three-hour drive, right on time. There had apparently been a media attempt to follow us and attempts to televise us, as in the flight of O.J. Simpson, as if there were any suspense about our destination, but it wasn't very successful, and we weren't aware of it.

My first views of my new address were not reassuring: relatively modern buildings, watchtowers in the adjoining higher security facilities, a generous use of barbed wire. Quite a large press delegation was at the gate but was kept back and got no view of us as we entered the complex. I learned later that the recreation area had been closed, to prevent the press from photographing inmates at leisure, and that an atmosphere of some anticipation had been generated.

The Coleman Federal Correctional Complex has two penitentiaries (often referred to as the "thunder domes" or "gun clubs"): a medium-security facility, a women's camp, and the low-security facility to which I was assigned. With a total of about eight thousand inmates, it is the largest correctional complex in the vast U.S. federal prison system. Though the architecture is red-brick, low-rise, and relatively unforbidding, it possesses the monolithic, dehumanizing arrogance of banal official buildings of all times and governments.

The indifferent visage of the buildings is studiously replicated by many of the personnel. Barbara and I entered the reception centre; I waited for someone to speak. We were ignored. Barbara, thinking I had been struck dumb, said, "My husband, Conrad Black, is here to self-surrender." We sat for a few minutes in the waiting room, and then a beefy correctional officer, unarmed but heavy-laden with gadgetry, surged into the room and pointed at me with well-rehearsed purposefulness. I answered a few questions and handed over $2,500 in cash for my commissary account and a little paper carrier bag from a pharmacy with sleeping pills, cholesterol-reducers, and lip balm, which was confiscated. They gave Barbara the lip balm and told us to say goodbye. A kiss, a searching look, a very few words, and I walked forward, not turning back to wave lest I be reproved in front of her and add to the distress of us both. She departed.

The process of accustoming arrivals to their absence of rights was, as I had assumed, begun at once. I was handcuffed, in accord with the inexplicable American official compulsion, for no reason, to manacle as many people as possible as often and publicly as possible, in this case for the challenging one-hundred-foot walk to the induction centre (after I had voluntarily come two hundred miles), and delivered over to another uniformed official, a large, black, bald man who evidently considered himself endlessly intimidating and riotously witty. I removed all my clothes and satisfied my captor that nothing was concealed in my mouth, underarms, behind my scrotum, or in the approaches to my rectum. (I would receive a great many medical and security anal inspections over the next couple of weeks, and was slightly mystified at the extent of official curiosity about that generally unremitting aperture.) A brief medical consultation and a few words of elemental guidance followed, and, dressed in painter pants, a T-shirt, and blue canvas shoes, with some bedding in my hand, I debouched into the compound and was pointed toward my unit (B-1). The blithe wit who had conducted the body search with such exuberance told me that if I departed the correct paths, I would be "shot." Withal, the official greeting was quite civilized, and my first glimpse of the regime was of a tolerably good-natured group. (The man who had inducted and handcuffed me soon proved quite convivial.)

That evening I began a prison diary, which for security reasons I wrote in French, with many abbreviations, words spelled backward, and argot. It would not have taken a skilled cryptographer five minutes to decode it, and there was nothing of much interest in it anyway, but it assisted me in a slight Chateau d'If fantasy, easing those first days. I wrote: "I proceeded a bit reticently toward my unit, and was accosted by some very affable residents, who seemed like typecasters' simulations of the charming rogue: easy, toothy smiles, relaxed and jovial conversation, an oddly warm welcome to a total, though apparently much-publicized, stranger." I was well received by everyone, residents and personnel, and some of my neighbours in my unit generously provided me with necessities. It soon emerged that I was in a completely black-market environment. Initially, most of the people that I met were relatively presentable, white-collar offenders (or at least people convicted of white-collar offences). On my first night, I was summoned to the lieutenants' office and greeted with the words: "Black, I don't consider you to be different to anyone else, and you won't be treated differently." I responded that I was not different to anyone else, and what earthly reason possessed him to imagine that I wanted to be treated differently, "which I do not"? We quickly crossed that drawbridge together and I was urged, in an almost avuncular manner, to "antiquate" to the community. I resisted the temptation to lure the lieutenant further into the tenebrous thickets of polysyllabalism, divined that he was urging me to "acclimate," and promised to do my best, but added that I "don't expect to grow old here." A round of knowing nods ensued and I departed the citadel of local authority. I would shortly learn what an intensely and credulously gossipy place I had arrived in: my arrival had been endlessly discussed. I was greeted as something of a celebrity, as well as one of the few who had fought the government with what was perceived to be relative success, as everyone seemed to realize that I had won 85 per cent of my case and was pursuing a serious appeal.

It was not a great challenge to be a refreshing surprise to those who had been expecting me to be an aloof hoity-toit. I always find almost anyone somewhat interesting, and many of my new co-residents actually were rather interesting, albeit often in a Damon Runyon way of hoods and scoundrels. The top of the pecking order appeared to be the few authentic Mafiosi. They were elegant, extremely courteous, even courtly, and had a sardonic sense of humour. On my first night, one of them approached and said that mutual friends had said to look out for me, that I was not to be "bothered" and wouldn't be. If I caught "a cold, we will find out from whom" and "that we have a lot in common." I surmised that he meant the comradeship of persecution by the U.S. government. He replied, "Yes, but more than that, we are industrialists."

The interior of the residential units had laundry and microwave rooms, a games room (chess, cards, board games), three television rooms, and a residential area of about sixty feet by one hundred and fifty feet, divided into four rows of fifteen to twenty two- or three-man cubicles, divided by painted, concrete block walls about five feet, six inches high. It was to one of these that my snug defence perimeter, which a few years before had linked continents, had shrunk, as I plotted the next phase of my struggle to save or recover my interests and reputation. I was now in the belly of the beast. After most of the lights went out, at 10:30 p.m. (it was possible to read by night-light for as long as desired), only red overhead lights provided any illumination. In this eerie light someone of my height could see the constant movement of quasi-sleeping men in the upper bunks, an unearthly Dante purgatorial scene. Many of the Hispanic inmates, finding the air conditioning cool, wore long underwear as outerwear in the evenings and wandered unselfconsciously about like giant bunny rabbits and slept with the covers over their heads like pre-natal caterpillars. It would be in this bizarre ambiance that I would listen to Barack Obama's election victory speech in November. I had to stand up to get clear reception on my hand-held radio and earphones. On this one night, almost all the African Americans were also awake and listening on their earphones, in their upper berths, in the roseate gloom. I thought of Henry Ward Beecher's famous eulogy of Abraham Lincoln. America had come full circle from the despair of the recent slaves following the murder of the Great Emancipator: after 143 years, the stifled sobs of the liberated black man, in the dark, had given way to the quiet and deserved celebration, also in the dark, of his imprisoned descendants.

My accommodation reminded me of boarding schools. (Not an unpleasant memory, as I had somewhat enjoyed them: people relied on their personalities. Nothing on the outside, such as family prominence, much mattered.)

—

THERE WAS A LUMPY, NARROW BED with a thin pillow, one metal locker, and two other occupants in bunk beds in a ten-foot by eight-foot cubicle. There were demeaningly precise rules governing almost everything. Yet there was almost unlimited access to emails, five hours of telephoning per month, full access to newspapers, periodicals, television, and radio, and visitors up to five days a week for up to six hours a day, but not more than nine days a month. I would soon learn that the six hours were sharply reduced on many occasions by the often lengthy waits visitors had to endure and by the habit of ending visiting hours early. The personnel at what was called, with unintentionally pious overtones, the visitation centre oversearched and harassed visitors and were themselves searched by other correctional officers in a futile effort to reduce smuggling. In my cubicle with me were two extremely pleasant and unobtrusive Hispanics, including one who had paddled from Cuba to Key West on the detached roof of an ice-cream cart. He assured me that he preferred an unjust sentence in an American prison to "freedom" in the Castroite paradise. Their English was limited, but we got on quite amicably. I did not sleep badly on this first night, after the strain and apprehension of the last few days. This was the grim fate that had been hanging over me for almost five years. On first sight, it was not as grim as I had expected.

Relief almost became serenity on discovering that the worst the enemy could do would be quite survivable. There had been much speculation in the Canadian media that I would be sexually assaulted, beaten up, blackmailed, and made to clean latrines (preferably, no doubt, with my tongue and bare hands). I quickly found that these fates were rare in this place and that I was not in the categories of people to whom any of them occurred. There was no violence, except in occasional scuffles that were easy to avoid, and sometimes toward child molesters. Homosexual activity was not apparently widespread and was by consent only. The rudest jobs were correctly the best paid and were sought by those who needed the money. I resumed my column in the *National Post* and often the *New York Sun*, and when the *Sun* closed, in the online *Daily Beast* of Tina Brown, and then the *National Review*. This was made possible by email access and agreement with the unit manager. After a lapse of only two weeks (to a heartening volume of comment), I felt I was in touch with the outside world again and made it clear to visitors that this life, though no country club, was not onerous. The media sought information from sundry inmates by letter and email, and soon discovered and published that I was tutoring high-school-leaving students in English, giving lectures on U.S. history that were well attended, and getting on with inmates and guards in a perfectly normal way. My experience in more complex, if perhaps less unsavoury, milieus taught me to be polite to everyone, reveal nothing to anybody, outwardly respect the authorities, and give no hint of self-importance nor self-consciousness at the temporary loss of status. I regarded my confinement, though not voluntarily assumed, as like St. Thomas More's hair shirt, an abrasive but bearable reminder of my imperfections. It was also reassuring to confirm that I could equably forego all luxury and revert to a less sumptuous life than I had had since my expulsion from my last boarding school forty-eight years before, almost to the day (for insubordination).

I was fortunate that the inmate to whom I was handed over in my unit was a street-wise, corn-fed Southern boy of integrity and intelligence, whom I could always rely on for solidarity, guidance, and companionship. We agreed that, when we could, I would accompany him to a NASCAR race and that he would come with me to an opera. He was of the other Florida I did not much know: beer, air-boating, and hunting everything from bullfrogs to alligators, panthers, and bears. These authentic Floridians are a far distance from the condominium towers of Miami and the movie-set estates of Palm Beach, only ninety minutes or so away from them, and no less estimable a part of what FDR used to call "the great voice of America."

After the genuine Mafiosi, the leading figures in the compound seemed to be real executives, prominent drug dealers, artful swindlers, lawyers who had strayed from the rules of the profession, such as they are in the United States, before descending into overzealous telemarketers, common or garden fraudsters, routine drug dealers, petty larcenists, and, finally, child molesters. There were many original characters, some by virtue of the elaborate impostures they made for themselves, aggregating grand theft auto up to Professor Moriarty–like criminal fiendishness in the telling. In the valley of the designated wrongdoers, next to those who have the money and the muscle, the most flamboyant are the kings. I sat down at lunch one day, in the noisy dining hall, opposite someone I had seen before but did not really know and asked him why he was here. "I steal airplanes." When one of the men in my cubicle had to go to court to testify and was away a few weeks, a pleasant Puerto Rican moved in. I asked him his occupation: "I rob banks," he replied with a touch of self-importance. I met other bank robbers, including one proud scion of a family of bank robbers, whose matriarch, his aunt, had robbed scores of rural banks, from the Carolinas to Florida, and had always arrived and fled on horseback. Another neighbour in the unit was proud of having sold, on cold calls, an astounding number of DVD-dispensing machines at "prime locations" that were in fact at rural road crossings or in the most remote or undesirable places. Outrageous though it is, in its apostasy from the world of affected, bourgeois respectability, it was almost refreshing.

I was automatically enrolled in a crash course in the parlance, mores, and folkways of the carceral state. One of the first people I encountered was a former armaments dealer who had, he claimed, roamed the world of mercenaries and irregular warfare. In these circumstances, it mattered little whether the talents of raconteurs were devoted to truthful accounts or fables, as feats of the imagination are also worthy achievements, and some of my fellow residents were Jules Vernes of autobiographical embellishment. The armaments dealer claimed that he wore an SS officer's spruce black uniform at home, that he had been arrested by a flying squad of thirty FBI agents at his home, and that of all his experiences in selling, testing, buying, and evaluating weapons from side arms to battle tanks and ground-to-air missiles (all for freelance operations all over the world), his greatest satisfaction was in firing rocket-propelled grenades at cows in Cambodia. His descriptions of the cows blowing up reminded me of Mussolini's son's description of the joys of bombing defenceless Abyssinians in the Duce's invasion of Ethiopia in 1935.

Because of the fussing about my arrival, some of my new neighbours surmised that with their brains and my presumed money, much could be done. I had been fielding this sort of pitch for more than forty years and generally replied with suggestions that instead we try my ideas and my interlocutors' money. One of the early candidates in this crowded field started out explaining to me his relationship with a U.S. senator but was exposed as an FBI plant and shortly shipped out after being threatened with grievous bodily harm. He was also under suspicion of impregnating one of the (female) correctional officers.

Another early acquaintance, who had apparently damaged his mind with his drug habit, answered almost any conversational gambit either by describing his subterranean marijuana-growing facility or by holding forth on the anthropological insights of the animated cartoon television series *The Simpsons*. This inmate had a wisp of a goatee, like Ho Chi Minh, and had such large-bore ear piercings, he occasionally suspended padlocks from each ear, creating a very bizarre effect.

The child molesters (chomos, they are called) were a peculiar group. Some hobbled about with canes or walkers from the beatings they had received from some other prisoners because of their perceived moral degeneracy, or to provide themselves with weapons of defence against such attacks. One, with the massive spectacles provided by the Bureau of Prisons (BOP), but otherwise slight and with a shaved head, had been sentenced for performing circumcisions on underage girls. He always took a cup with him to the bathroom because he had modified his own urinary tract by self-administered surgery and required the cup to avoid unsanitary spillages at the urinals.

There was an informal group of chomo-bashers (literally). One of the most colourful was a central Floridian, always friendly to me, at whose home police had allegedly discovered a severed human hand. He told me that the hand was planted by the police, in their unfailing incompetence, ten feet beyond his property line, and that he had self-righteously demanded that his neighbour be interrogated and chastened for besmirching the reputation of the neighbourhood. He was a physically formidable man with a delightful sense of humour but was accustomed to beating or shooting those he disliked. He was banished to the isolation accommodation (Special Housing Unit, or SHU, pronounced "shoe") for threatening an alleged chomo who was blocking the door to my room, but he returned to the unit after three months in the SHU and shouted, on re-entering our unit, "Fuck the chomos." For my part, I found the alleged chomos that I met quite pleasant and sometimes rather intelligent. It was impossible to know whether they were really guilty of anything. Some had answered email enticements from middle-aged policemen claiming to be young girls. Some had huge collections of lewd photographs. I am not convinced that these are facts that justify imprisonment. If they were guilty of physical abuse of defenseless people, their offences were disgusting and the fate of their victims was pitiful; but I also sympathized for the maladjustment that would have driven them to such acts. If they were not guilty, they were fellow victims of the corrupt prosecutocracy. In either case, it was not ultimately my place to judge them.

MANY OF MY NEW ACQUAINTANCES assuaged the inborn anxieties of imprisonment by professing to believe that they were immensely wealthy, or that a legislated or litigated liberation was imminent, or in intense religious practice or obsessive physical exercise. Some would periodically announce that they had just scored another epochal financial coup, and that their already large net worth had grown by billions. Invariably, these captains of industry and finance were represented by the public defender, and they usually did not have the resources to buy anything at the commissary and were relying precariously on the regime for soap and deodorant.

Rumours were launched with conviction every week that legislation to shorten sentences had passed through the Congress and was about to be signed by the president. Carolyn Gurland was monitoring this front for me, and I was able to hose down febrile expectations of early release as diplomatically as possible. The fiancée of an inmate telephoned Barbara to say that I would be home soon of just-adopted legislation. Barbara's great joy was dashed by going to the BOP website, and discovering that no such law had been passed. A large number of inmates were very heavily medicated and were essentially incomprehensible zombies, shuffling aimlessly about. One very presentable and well-spoken Cuban was paying a contact in Seoul to journey to North Korea to discover something that could be traded to the CIA in exchange for a shortened sentence. He eventually left our facility after an anonymous report was made to the regime that his life was in danger for selling participations in this scam. Another inmate in our unit, a pleasant expert in cooking pizzas (there were six microwaves in the unit) who eventually fell to fisticuffs with a competing pizza supplier, wrote a six-hundred-page (unpublished) book, explaining that General Patton and Field Marshal Montgomery had successfully won the battle for Sicily in 1943 because the Mafia had thrown grenades into German artillery bunkers.

There were several Vietnam War veterans, quite nonchalant about having killed a good number of North Vietnamese and Viet Cong. Their fairly reliable accounts of conditions there were quite interesting and squared with what I had learned when I visited Vietnam in 1970. There was an expatriate French-Canadian film financier and marketer of self-cleaning toilets. He hosted a select gourmet luncheon every Saturday, and was one of the leading music teachers in the compound. His astute mastery of the official tides and currents, shoals and opportunities, created by the shambling operation of the system reminded me almost every day of how the French Canadians have effectively governed Canada for most of its history without having more than 30 per cent of its people.

Partly to satisfy a frustrated childhood ambition, partly to please my dear Barbara, and to make what I could of this captivity, I took piano lessons from him. The sessions were a triple win, as we spoke French, brushing up our practice, and reminisced about old times in Quebec. He often mimicked Duplessis, and I responded with my imitation of Cardinal Léger,* both distinctive speakers. He gave me his well-thought-out theory of music, and I determinedly inched ahead with the piano. In a particularly entertaining version of a familiar pattern, he explained how (unknown to him at the time, he said) some of his investors in his self-cleaning toilet business had randomly telephoned people in the United States, telling them that they had won the Quebec Lottery, and that their net winnings would be sent as soon as they sent the caller their windfall income tax assessments. In his florid French-Canadian patois, it sounded like Rocket Richard reciting a translation of Mark Twain's "The Royal Nonesuch." They "raised" millions of dollars in this way.

The telemarketers and newsletter circulators were among the most entertaining and engaging of all the sharpers in the compound, full of amusing stories, fast talk, and entertaining cynicism. Various of the financial scammers were still inveterately hustling, undeterred by former reverses

---

* Maurice L. Duplessis was premier of Quebec, 1936–1939 and 1944–1959, and the leading political personality in Quebec for thirty years. He was the subject of my first book, *Render Unto Caesar*. Paul-Émile Cardinal Léger was archbishop of Montreal 1950–1967, and I was the vice president of his charity for some years.

or current impecuniousness. Like kindred creatures tightly confined in zoological experiments, they acted out the roles they knew and hustled each other with the most fantastic propositions. It was interesting to see them compulsively peddling and promoting their moose pastures and Ponzi schemes in all directions. Eventually, several of them explained to me the addictive pleasure of swindling people, and confounding the hypocrisy of the system that claimed to protect the weak but really only served the incumbents. I understood their dislike of some officialdom but have always found exploitation of the defenceless or unwary to be repulsive.

My other effort at self-improvement beside the piano was weight loss and exercise. I became concerned by spiking blood pressure, especially when I contemplated the outrages inflicted on me in the name of justice, and put myself in the hands of our unit's wellness experts, a perfectionist former U.S. Marine and a former telemarketing muscle-builder. I lost thirty-five pounds over a couple of months of their program and daily work on a rowing machine (in the air-conditioned leisure centre) and what was called "resistance training," but which I likened to the Death March in Bataan, put me in the best shape I have been in for decades. Barbara and I made a pact that we would do the necessary so that when I left here, we would both be in better physical condition than when I came in.

Another colourful figure had been convicted of conspiring to murder a wealthy Chicago society doyenne (and disposing of her remains in a blast furnace of the Inland Steel Company). He was one of eight or ten inmates who wanted me to help him publish his story. And there was an eminent businessman, university regent, and political organizer shafted by the absurd McCain-Feingold Campaign Financing Act. I had had some hope for McCain's campaign, having met him quite often over the years. I even predicted early on in the *New York Sun* that he would win and make the eighty-five-year-old Henry Kissinger secretary of state. But I lost all hope for his candidacy in the week when he started by quoting Herbert Hoover about the soundness of the economy, spent Tuesday excoriating greed, Wednesday demanding regulatory mummification of the financial industry, Thursday calling for the firing of Chris Cox as chairman of the SEC (and replacement by the Spitzeresque New York Attorney General and later Governor Andrew Cuomo, who would have been an appalling choice), and on Friday "suspended" his campaign to return to Washington to fight for the emergency financial rescue bill by failing to say anything at the bi-partisan White House strategy session, or to persuade his Republican colleagues in the Congress to support their president's and presidential candidate's bill.

One of the peppier of the younger inmates, almost a mascot to the grizzled old-timers in our unit, performed in the Coleman Idol musical competition, and presented a spirited rap piece that ended: "Fuck the BOP." The lieutenant present apparently imagined that this might not be a widely shared sentiment, and asked the cheering audience if he should send the vocalist to the SHU. He apparently hoped for a "Give us Barabbas" response, but the crowd supported the performer, who was banished anyway. He was an ingenuously, spontaneously mischievous young man, whom it was hard not to like. He was imprisoned for burning down part of his school, an impulse for which I had some sympathy.

I became fairly friendly with some of the prominent African-American inmates. The leaders of that group were large drug dealers, legendary figures in their milieus. The older ones were like the stars of the old Negro Baseball Leagues, honoured pioneers, and the younger ones were more like rappers. Perhaps the most formidable was an old gentleman in a wheelchair, universally known as "Mr. Bobby." He told one of the bright, presentable, younger black inmates: "I know your mother, boy. You're lucky I'm not your father, or maybe I am." Despite his infirmity, he asserted himself, on one occasion chasing a white inmate out of the television room for changing the channel away from one of Mr. Bobby's favourite programs. He was wheeled by one of his acolytes while brandishing his cane like a Dickensian school master. He died in captivity a few months later.

I was honoured to be invited to address Black History Month, the first white inmate to do so. In deference to the older members of the audience, who remembered the days of outright segregation, I said it was not my place to tell them of their history, but that I had a few thoughts on some white statesmen who had advanced the cause of the African-Americans. I spoke of five or six of the presidents, concluding with the quote from Lincoln's Second Inaugural: of "every drop of blood drawn with the lash" being repaid "by the sword." An unconditional commitment from America's greatest leader.

The compound had a rich religious life. The Nation of Islam had, as in the days of Elijah Muhammad and Malcolm X, the fittest, most well-turned-out, and courteous lay officers. The most alluring circumstances of any of the religious groups were those of the self-proclaimed Native Americans. There were probably only a very few real American Indians on the compound. But as they took off all Wednesday to sit in the so-called "sweat-lodge," smoking (and there was a good deal of speculation about what they really were smoking), playing cards and board games, beating their tom-toms, and telling ribald stories, the ranks of the religious Indians increased, and inmates with head bandanas from which immense feathers protruded were the compound's most numerous beneficiaries of the grace of conversion. Dietary factors also seemed to play a role in the movement between denominations, depending on menu fluctuations. One inmate entered and departed the compound group of approved Jews five times in one year, after consulting the BOP monthly menu.

Coleman Low's principal clergyman, the chief chaplain, was a beefy, guitar-strumming white southern Baptist who was essentially a cop, visibly carrying handcuffs, the universal American icon of authority, and helpfully patting down inmates exiting the dining hall to see if they had stolen inventory from the massive black-market operation in the kitchen. His handcuffs were even sometimes in evidence when he gave his Sunday service. He used his position to harass Jews and Roman Catholics, and even prevented our priest from showing his own DVD of *It's a Wonderful Life* with James Stewart as Christmas entertainment at which people of all faiths, and none, were welcome. In fact, he was an overbearing loudmouth, lacking any semblance of spirituality or even concern for others. He was singularly disagreeable and unecclesiastical.

Our Roman Catholic group had a kindly Vietnamese pastor when I arrived, followed by a scholarly but not altogether comprehensible Nigerian. The Nigerian improved his homiletic delivery and by October was scourging the regime as corrupt and degraded, and urged us not to yield. It was a refreshing recurrence of the traditional role of the Church as a conscientious monitor of secular affairs, especially the omnipotent state. There was a bit of the Mindszenty and Wyszyński in him, and he regularly reviled politicians and politics as "the most hopeless thing in the world." He was the victim of the Baptist film censor, and gave another stirring address, drawing on his experience as a veteran of the Nigerian army during the Biafran War. He sometimes opened his remarks: "You are in no one's bondage while you are here."

Since I respect sensible religious opinion and am a religious person, I found the profusion, at the beginning and end of each day, of inmates kneeling in their cubicles in prayer, reading their Bibles, or pressing their foreheads to the floor and inclining to the East quite reassuring. The African and Latin Americans were generally quite practising, even fervent. I had a natural bond with my fellow worshippers, as I always attended Roman Catholic services, where I was regularly a lector, often read from the Bible a kind British stranger sent me, and believed that if it were feasible, we all should spend a good deal of time on our knees before a Godly effigy, trying to comprehend the sacred, potentially noble, and comically absurd qualities of life. (It seemed to me from when I first read him that Santayana was correct when he wrote that life was "admirable in its essence, tragic in its destination, and amusing in its experience.") In that narrow channel where people are unaffectedly and even gracefully religious, without being ostentatious or distracting, there is room for swift, tacit empathy. Less agreeable is the frequently overheard hazardous admonition of one religiously impassioned friend to another that "God has said" and so on. And altogether jarring can be the antics of outspoken Christians claiming to find Revelation even in the most mundane acts.

I was astounded when I first visited the library to find whole rooms of jailhouse lawyers toiling on their own and "clients'" cases. They ranged from reasonably informed and clever drafters of motions to outright frauds bilking blacks and Hispanics not fluent in English with nonsensical petitions to the Supreme Court of the United States, handwritten on lined paper. Religion and legalism intertwined in certain nostrums for reducing sentences, which were devised and shopped around by some of the inmates, both professional scoundrels and some relatively earnest amateur lawyers. Some of these ideas were embraced and preached with a fervour worthy of the Godly zealot. Somewhere in the bowels of the U.S. prison system, the idea arose and began lurching about that the Universal Code of Commerce forbade imprisonment in the United States because the federal government was unconstitutionally borrowing against the lives of the people of the country after Roosevelt largely abandoned the gold standard in 1933 and that the country had supposedly gone bankrupt. It is a slightly more intricate argument than this but just as preposterous, but the law library is full of people beavering away like Nibelungen, preparing petitions on this point.

One such believer, a slight, sixtyish man with a full white beard and mane that made Santa Claus look like Hank Paulson, packed himself up, prepared a full copy of his extensive petition, and arrived at the receiving and departing centre (R&D) early one proud morning and told the rather torpid officials there to call him a taxi and be quick about it. He gave them a copy of his legal claims and said that if he wasn't released at once, he would add these correctional officers to the warden and others as defendants to his lawsuit. He was sent to Miami for psychiatric examination and, at writing, has not been heard from since.

ON MY SECOND DAY, A DISTILLERY was uncovered in the space above the artificial lighting in one of the unit bathrooms. These discoveries recur fairly often. Almost anything can be had, including liquor, hard drugs, and cellphones. It is an unnatural milieu in that it is like a cat-and-mouse game where the ostensible mice are often smarter than the cats. The correlation of forces is with the regime, so it is unwise to mock or defy it too brazenly, again like a shabby but not totalitarian despotism. The applause of the insubordinate is an insufficient incentive for the risk involved in affronting the system. I was careful from the start to avoid unpleasantness with anyone. Most of the correctional officers, unit and case managers and counsellors, and even some of the lieutenants I met were reasonable people. But there were some conspicuous exceptions, and the system itself was moribund, punitive, and largely ineffectual. Even as a semi-detached observer, I was sorry to see the lives of recuperable men reduced to such narrow parameters. As with the decrepit dictatorships of bygone Eastern Europe and Latin America, issuing pompous pronunciamentos but only stirring itself to any energy when perceiving some threat to its incumbency, the more mundane and farcical the function and official, the more pretentious the recourse to the symbolism of the state. Notices about use of the recreation yard were apt to be emblazoned with the great seal of the United States. Posted warnings against suicidal temptations were on paper with faintly printed American flags streaming over the whole page. It has been my honour to receive correspondence from every U.S. president from Lyndon Johnson to George W. Bush, the last four while in office, and I have extensive examples of many previous U.S. presidents' correspondence. The insignia of their great office was, in every case, very discreetly deployed. The BOP's style reminded me of the eagle-, Minuteman-, and flag-festooned Spirit of America Car Wash near Midway Airport in Chicago.

When my unit counsellor, a generally fair and intelligent man, decided that because I had not left the unit by eight o'clock one morning, I should work with the orderlies, I expressed delight at the prospect and thoroughly cleaned the shower stall that I normally use. It was such an occasion, he had other officials from our and the next unit in to watch "a millionaire cleaning a shower stall." I did so with some feigned gusto and when asked at the end by one of the little knot of officials if I had enjoyed it, I replied that domestic work was "morally uplifting."

A spectacular farce occurred when I noted on the callout list that is posted each night that I was to pack out to leave the facility the next day. I ascertained from available espionage that it was for a court appearance in New York. This could only be my civil case against Sotheby's Realty for its collusion in the improper seizure of the proceeds of the sale of the New York apartment on the basis of the false FBI affidavit. We already had a court authorization for me to give evidence in the legal section of the Coleman visitors' centre, by video. After a somewhat frantic call to Barbara, counsel was mobilized and all seemed to be resolved. The following morning I was awakened early by one of the palookas from R&D and told to get up. I assured him that I wasn't going anywhere, which my unit counsellor kindly confirmed, and I went back to sleep. When I awakened, my name was being incanted on the compound public address system to report to Receiving and Departing (R&D), and I did so, to, I assumed, recover what I had packed the previous day for the trip to New York that I would not be making. I was ordered to come in, strip naked in the little voyeurs' paradise where I had arrived, contribute my clothes back to the taxpayers, and put on the orange jumpsuit of the higher security convict. I was shackled, hands, waist, and feet, and put in a holding room with others about to enjoy "diesel therapy:" being shunted in this demeaning state all around the country in buses and BOP aircraft. Casual efforts I made to explain that this was a mistake were greeted with torrents of threats and epithets. At one point, it was appropriate to say: "I recognize a fellow officer," and I had the pleasure of telling the more officious of them that I was a colonel in a historic guards regiment. It bought a slight moderation in their demeanour. I didn't want to muddy the waters by adding that I was really an honorary colonel. The lieutenants masqueraded as an ersatz elite guard, and reminded me of nothing so much as Hemingway's description in A *Farewell to Arms* of Italian officers shooting their soldiers who retreated after the Battle of Caporetto: they "looked very military in the early morning" as they executed survivors of a battle they themselves had managed to avoid. After about fifteen minutes with my fellow transportees, as I considered whom to recruit to replace the lawyer responsible for this fiasco, I was asked with distinctly more courtesy than earlier in the morning to leave the holding room, and the previous process was reversed. The judge's order had been received and had registered with the custodians. The officials offered no apology and I neither gloated nor reproached, but I was quite undeservedly feted throughout the compound for facing down the regime. Delegations of total strangers came by my room to congratulate me. I was not about to provoke the authorities by claiming that I had merited any such distinction. Nor had I.

In theory, everyone works at this facility, but like most other aspects of this Ruritanian dictatorship, things are not what they seem. The real jobs, which pay tolerably well, are working in the Unicor furniture factory, or as an orderly doing the more challenging cleaning work. In fact, it is a Potemkin village, where most of the jobs don't really exist, and most of those that do require a maximum of five minutes a day. One friend's "job" was to write out on a blackboard in the recreation area an inspirational quote for the day, which he took from a book of famous quotations. I suspected him of testing the borders of philistinism in some of this by presenting gradually more outrageous or banal comments and improbably attributing them to famous people: a stirring martial tocsin from Mae West, complicated metaphysical deductions from Yogi Berra, Chauncey Gardener and Forrest Gump statements from Caesar, Napoleon, Lincoln, and Bismarck. (I must confess to a slight role of complicity by incitement.) Other friends spent two minutes a day emptying recycling bins.

Occasionally the regime would flex its muscles and demand the presence of all registered yard maintenance people at the little hut in the middle of the compound, which squats contentedly under an aluminum flagstaff. The Stars and Stripes were lowered, in a pretentious little ceremony where a few inmates were dragooned into a clumsy simulation of a Marine colour party, at sunset and when a BOP official was killed in the performance of his job anywhere in the country. The death of an inmate passed unnoticed. On these occasions when the nominal ground staff was mustered, the public address announcer called repeatedly for up to half an hour, rousing them, as in the immortal Peter Sellers–Terry Thomas send-up of 1950s British labour and industry, *I'm All Right Jack*, from their beds, card games, showers, and leisure activities. Eventually, the stentorian summoning produced an astoundingly numerous host of ostensible compound maintenance workers, milling dazedly around the little hut. After a lengthy and chaotic roll call, the demobilized pseudo-workers repaired to their previous pastimes with the countenances of perplexed sheep. The regime, having noisily asserted itself, lapsed back into an inertia as comatose as that of most of its charges.

I was advised that if I did not arrange a job for myself, the regime would produce one, and it might be unimaginably absurd or tedious. Because of the books I had written about Franklin D. Roosevelt and Richard Nixon, I was known to some of the library and education community, and recommended for a job as an English tutor for high-school-leaving candidates, in the vocational training department.

This proved to be a turn of luck. There was initial skepticism that there was any need for a tutor, but I was given a desk and a comfortable chair and those entering the vocational training pavilion could see me at a distance, at the end of a room about a hundred feet deep. It was a little like a scene from *The Great Dictators*, as I watched people approach for half a minute before they reached me. Like anything in such a climate, it grew from a desk and chair to three tutors, a group of desks and filing cabinets, and a steady stream of students. Our success rate at helping people graduate from secondary school was high. The number of matriculants more than doubled because of the tutors, and we had the pleasure of helping some people seriously in need of it.

At first there would be a few people straggling back and I would help them with essay writing, sentence structure, and spelling. I would start with light conversation to put them at their ease and to get a preliminary idea of how much of a challenge it was going to be. It quickly became obvious to me that even after desegregation the education of African Americans had largely been a mockery designed in many parts of the country to keep the blacks in ignorance and subordinacy. I had always disliked teachers, except for a few very good and stimulating ones I remembered with gratitude and admiration. But with this experience, I saw the joys and frustrations of teaching. Many of those entrusted to me started out surly and skeptical, but after a bit of jocularity and clear evidence that I was not part of the custodial apparat, but a victim of it also, things loosened up; we both made an effort and all my candidates graduated, though some required two or even three tries at the examinations. It was often important to make the point that we owed it to ourselves to make the most of the sojourn. I represented high-school graduation as opening up a possibility to develop a solid legally unassailable income, through higher education or a skilled trade, an alternative to drug-related law-breaking, which led straight back to prison with one denunciation, inevitable in that activity. I had some motivational success, and it was very fulfilling helping them to get a foot on the Up escalator. Because of the pride of successful students and their families, and the generous applause I received, the graduating ceremonies were among the more moving occasions I have attended.

THE EXCITEMENT OF MY STUDENTS when they learned that they had graduated was affecting, and I shared in it. One of them – a twenty-nine-year-old African American with gold teeth and a shaved head who had the equivalent of perhaps a grade five education and had six children with five women, none with the antiquarian benefit of wedlock – turned up religiously every day and worked his heart out. The day he learned that he had matriculated, he risked being banished to the SHU by entering my unit, finding me at the computer, and embracing me. Rarely have I been so happy for anyone, or so happy to have been helpful to anyone.

The essays I received from students were sometimes unexpectedly memorable. A three-hundred-and-fifty-pound man writing about his favourite sport explained in graphic detail his love of contact, especially of the variety that broke other people's bones, which he described vividly. A lusty young southern lad wrote of his favourite and least favourite cities. He had been short-changed by call girls in New Orleans, which left him so disgruntled that he welcomed Hurricane Katrina because New Orleans "needed a good washing down." But he had been so splendidly served in the Korean bath houses of New York that he revered the Big Apple as the "world center of creative perversion." He seemed to be qualified to express such an opinion.

One of my fellow tutors, who often worked at the front of the vocational training area, had the habit of screening out the most idiosyncratically sluggish learners and wandering back to the area I shared with my other tutoring colleague, a very pleasant and conscientious former U.S. Navy nuclear submarine torpedoman and graduate of the Navy's nuclear propulsion course. The screener always wore a hangdog look of grief as he approached, as if his best friend had just died, to explain that he had to inflict "Will" or "Alphonse" on us. One of them believed verbs were just nouns with "to" in front of them and was not certain that General Washington had been correct "to revolution." Another thought that any effort to persuade him to learn anything was a government conspiracy to dominate him, as he explained through narcotics-blackened teeth. Yet another was so sex obsessed that to hold his attention for more than a couple of minutes, it was necessary to resort to the most innovatively salacious, foul-mouthed language that had crossed my lips since I left Australia.

Our efforts to help our assignees took place against a backdrop of the culinary arts instructor holding forth in a loud voice about every subject under the sun on the other side of a seven-foot partition, including, within earshot of the female supervisors, the inadvisability of allowing restaurant waiters to "scratch their balls" in the presence of paying customers. If we rose above a whisper he appeared like a rotund Prometheus at the door of his enclosure, complaining of distractions to his "important" work, vastly outdistancing our efforts to help people graduate from high school and become eligible for university. It was impossible not to overhear his stentorian pontificating about the French Revolution, the history of restaurants, and the eating habits of U.S. presidents, or conducting hour-long lamentations about the theft of a minuscule container of garlic powder. He was a very agreeable man, and was an able self-promoter. For giving his part-time cooking course, he was apparently paid more than the wages of two correctional officers annually. (He made wickedly good cookies.)

It was impossible not to hear some strange things at times. On one occasion, I was picking away at the emails when someone on the telephone, about twenty feet away, bellowed into the receiver: "I didn't kill the motherfucker, but he deserved it! Don't make me break out of this prison and come and give you a whuppin.'" Street-level dialect is a cultural and acoustic challenge, but it has its rewards.

One of the country bands that specialized in old-time Hank Williams, Merle Haggard songs reached an affecting state of vocal drama with prison songs: "Mama Tried" and "My daddy warned me, but I didn't listen!" There weren't many genuine *cris de coeur* in this place.

One of many comical diversions of my life at Coleman arose from the libel suit launched by the owner of the *London Daily Express*, Richard Desmond, against the calumnious Tom Bower. Desmond sued over Bower's claim, in his malicious novel allegedly about Barbara and me, that I had taken Desmond over the barrel in my lawsuit against him in 2003, referred to in Chapter 3. I sent him a supportive email and in his scatter-gun enthusiasm, Desmond flew from London to Orlando and bustled to the Coleman facility to concert with me, despite warnings from Barbara and Joan that gaining entry required certain formalities. I managed to get approval for him for the following day, but he returned to London, rebuffed by the impenetrable pettifogging of the BOP. He had nothing to show for his whirlwind excursion (but perhaps the obligatory Mickey Mouse cap from Disney World given to most Orlando visitors). Unfortunately, Bower won the case, but it was a pleasant, glancing reacquaintance with Desmond who is nothing if not an entertaining character.

My schedule was not too uncivilized. On weekdays I normally got up at about 7:15 a.m., had some granola and tea in bed, washed, dressed, went to my tutoring functions, ate lunch about 10:30 in the dining hall with my colleagues, worked on emails for about two hours, returned to work from 1 p.m.

to 3 p.m., worked on emails and read the just-delivered mail and newspapers, took a nap from 4 p.m. to 6 p.m., rowed 5,000 metres on a machine in the leisure centre, practised the piano for an hour, socialized over Colombian coffee until recall at 8:30 p.m., spent the evening reading, writing, and phoning (mainly Barbara), showered and so on just before midnight, and read in bed and did the *USA Today* or *National Post* crossword puzzle until between 1 a.m. and 2 a.m. I usually had visitors on Monday and Friday, and on the weekends slept until 10 a.m. and spent the days as I pleased. There was always a heavy correspondence and columns to write and a lot of reading to do. Our Roman Catholic weekly service was on Sunday at the civilized hour of 12:30 p.m., and I was often a lector. The only television program I regularly watched was *Damages* with Glenn Close, on Monday nights. It was a fairly predictable but also productive routine, and it beat breaking stones.

I sometimes stopped in my thoughts and reflected on what brought me to this singular way station, as when one of the senior officers, a sociopath who prorupted noisily around his little domain, started raving at me for taking too long to answer a recall to the units at night. (One of his early brainwaves was to remove an air-changer from the leisure centre because it might be used by inmates to launch a projectile at the captain's and lieutenants' office. The idea is not entirely without merit, but there are easier ways to accomplish it.) I stared at him quizzically, as I often did here, but generally I just soldiered on, making of it what I could, serene yet that "The night will end."

ROUGHLY ONE-FIFTH OF THE people in the Coleman low-security facility, discounting a good deal of fabulism, are, like myself, not guilty of anything. Approximately an equal number love it here, and if the gates were opened and the fences taken down, they would remain behind and cling to the sparse furniture like tree-huggers. They would be skidrow alcoholics or drug addicts on the outside, and at Coleman they have a roof over their heads, three meals a day, free medical care (of indifferent quality but better than they would receive on the outside), and companionship, and they watch television and play cards all day and have cheap access to email.

The population of U.S. mental asylums has declined since 1975 from 600,000 to 50,000, so these unfortunates are treated as criminals. Their contingent at this facility are much in evidence, shuffling about in an almost comatose state. Most of the remaining inmates are guilty of some genuine offence but at least half have received draconian sentences. And many of the offenses, including almost anything to do with marijuana, are nonsense.

The inmates who are grateful, resigned, or medicated into insensibility rush, or even run, to the dining hall and generally walk with a spring in their step (apart from those who are too sedated) that I have never observed in the confined members of any other species (a discouraging contrast to the hauteur of caged lions and tigers and the majestic indifference of confined bears and elephants). They adjust to close horizons; most have no interest in the outside except perhaps for some sports matches and bets, and juvenile, violent, and vulgar videos and films. They make appointments to see each other, shake hands whenever they meet a friend or acquaintance, even if it is just ten minutes since they had last met and shaken hands on parting. This is the result of living in a shrunken world, circumscribed by fences, endless instructions delivered by an ear-rattling public address system, or an even more acoustically irritating correctional officer screaming banalities at point-blank range. There is an eerie movement of people; men one has become quite friendly with are suddenly gone. There may be a letter or two after, but they vanish into the vast, seething underclass of America, remembered but unlikely to be encountered again.

There is not one that left without my good wishes, but many will be back in a system that thrives on its recidivism rate and has every economic incentive to maintain it. The United States is alone among advanced countries in seeking an ever larger prison system, the longest possible retention of all incarcerated people, and the maximum possible likelihood of their return to custody. It makes only a token effort, entrusted in practice to the teaching inmates such as me, to assist the prison population in relaunching their lives. It is an evil system that awaits the millions of unwary, improvident, and felonious, after they have been crowded through the debased gauntlet of American justice, which in practice, as prosecutors win an implausible (and almost totalitarian) 95 per cent of their cases, is less a due process than a demonstration of the force of gravity by the operation of a trapdoor when an accused is frog-marched onto it.

I had thought that the U.S. custodial system discouraged and despised the squealer, the snitch. But with the suffocating pervasiveness of the plea bargain, the prisons are full of people who have borne false witness, and of their victims, and of those who have been severely oversentenced to make an example of them. Like the whistleblower in the workplace, the squealer-plea bargainer has become the key figure in the contemporary American courthouse, the Minuteman of the new American Millennium. The Coleman Low facility, like many others around the country, is full of people who constitute a brimming information pool for the FBI centre at the complex, which endlessly dangles reduced sentences before convicts in exchange for incriminating testimony about others, whether accurate or not. Its informants honeycomb the inmate population, scouring for plausible scraps of damaging information or possible fabrications that might transpose some of their sentence on to someone else (a reduction in their sentence for a conviction or augmented sentence for someone else). The cancer of the plea bargain has spread through the prison system and jaundiced or otherwise afflicted everything within. Before and after the trial, it is a regime of unrelieved subornation. The prison is a seething mass of informers and fabricators, in what must be almost the greatest possible affront to the constitutional (Fifth Amendment) guaranty of due process. This atmosphere didn't particularly affect me, as I am innocent and no one else here could plausibly claim to know anything about my case. But this cynical bartering of human souls – prisoner betraying prisoner – contributes to the systematic degradation of all inmates despite the human qualities of a reasonable number of the people here, both personnel and residents.

Arriving visitors are harassed, sometimes in an almost sadistic manner. When an old friend from Palm Beach in his seventies, now wheelchair-confined, arrived with his wife, he was sent to the WalMart store twenty miles away to change his trousers, which were not an admissible colour. When he returned, his wife was not admitted because she did not have the photo identification that they required, though she did have other photo identification. My friend's driver could not push his wheelchair to the visitors' centre because he was not an approved visitor, and the helpful correctional officers declined to push it, ostensibly because of legal concerns, even when the visitor offered to write out and sign a legal waiver right there. So my friend, who did not have the strength in his hands to turn the wheels, turned the chair around and pushed it slowly and painfully backward with his feet, until other arriving visitors took charge and pushed him the hundred feet or so to where I was waiting. He exited in the same way.

My wife, who visited nearly one hundred times, and my daughter, suffered through various inanities about their clothing. The rules change arbitrarily, different colours are prohibited, and knowing visitors bring several alternatives stashed in their automobiles. Dashes to the carpark to change to accommodate the latest official sartorial whim are, apparently, a feature of the front entrance.

There are problems with the medical facilities. An inmate of nearly six years, a Spanish citizen with a cardiological condition, who had fifteen stents and had undergone four bypass operations at the taxpayers' expense, was spuriously denied a treaty transfer to Spain, which had requested his return and promised the surgery he urgently needs. Another resident, a very pleasant former reserve player for the Detroit Tigers, was told to shape up and "be a man" for a year as he reported blood in his stools and assured the medical officers he did not have hemorrhoids. He was eventually moved, a year late, and probably too late, to a medical facility to treat his rectal cancer. There are many such cases. One of the regulars at our tutors' table, a delightful former Havana roué and anti-Castro CIA operative, had various problems of eyes, teeth, legs, and back and spent much of his time with us brushing up his English by writing protest forms, railing against various medical personnel, frequently commenting on what he alleged to be their deviant foibles, and latterly always headed: "For the Love of God!" He wasn't well served, but protesting his mistreatment undoubtedly assured his survival to release and return to his home and yacht (and real doctors) in Puerto Rico. I helped him with his protest forms, devising elaborate word-ings that would express his contempt for the regime without transgressing permissible standards of impolity. We confused the authorities by writing an ironic message of commendation for every four or five complaints. It was more mouse and cat, but quite amusing, and better for my friend's medical condition than all the regime's ministrations.

Although many individual BOP employees are pleasant, or at least civilized, many senior people of the regime and some of their subalterns in the ranks are specialists in swaggering, shouting, belittling; in adolescent, verbally challenged emulations of a John Wayne figure. It is all part of the process designed to break the morale and destroy the lives of anyone who becomes ensnared in the U.S. criminal legal system, despite the tired and inconsequential pieties about rehabilitation. (I shall comment in the postlude on the gap between the espoused aims and the facts in what are called re-entry programs.) Much of such efforts as there are in that direction, apart from some of the high school teaching, tutoring, and technical training, are just exercises in hypocrisy designed to maintain the fiction of rehabilitative ambitions.

The bureaucracy is impenetrable. A friend asked why he would not benefit from regulatory changes about reduction of sentences for extended halfway house or home confinement. He received back, by post, despite the short distance between him and the responding official's workplace, the information that he wouldn't receive a reply because he had not returned a four-page version of the official three-page form, but that the regime would generously consider his request if he did produce the non-existent four-page form within ten days of its December 3 mailing of the response. Unfortunately, the form only covered its two-hundred-foot route of delivery after three weeks and arrived on December 24, 2008. Sagas of this sort recur almost every day to one acquaintance or another in this relatively gentle and bumbling gulag. It took me four months of negotiation to give two of my Roosevelt books to the library.

Staggering amounts of inventory leave the kitchen in unauthorized ways, and plausible rumours are that a good deal of stock marches determinedly out the back of the commissary also. After thirty seconds in the dining hall, it was a bath of nostalgia for my 1960s and 1970s visits to Hungary, Czechoslovakia, Portugal, Cuba, and the markets of West Africa, the Middle East, and Vietnam. The dining hall was an anthill of people haggling over contraband, a scarcely concealed bazaar, determining the destination of mountains of the taxpayers' inexplicably shrinking food inventory. It also reminded me of my piping days in the supermarket business at Dominion Stores, when the customers stole $10 million of product annually and the overachieving employees stole $30 million while their union leaders whined of their exploitation. (The employees' self-help surpassed the annual net profit to the shareholders.) A year into my sentence, security at Coleman was tightened up a good deal, and inventory shrinkages became less conspicuous, if not much reduced in volume.

The residential units are beehives of ingenuity: distillers, opticians, carpenters, metal-workers, reconstructors of mattresses, modifiers of prison pillows, talented chefs, purveyors of authentic Colombian coffee, launderers, pressers, seamsters, radio technicians, cleaners, and the jurisconsults all abound, clever and nimble and highly motivated, as long as it is all outside the ambit of the official command economy, and they are adequately compensated for their efforts (usually in postage stamps, which is the local currency). The regime soaks its captives at the commissary and overcharges for use of the telephones. Of course the brighter official lights know generally what is afoot. The counsellors have a small army of informants, sycophants, and favourites, a microcosm of American society's lionization of the denunciator.

There are regularly arrests and prosecutions of correctional officers for smuggling and related offences. They only make about $40,000 to $60,000 per year and many are eager to add to their incomes. Almost $1,000 can be made from just one smuggled carton of cigarettes. Hannah Arendt famously wrote of the banality of evil; the U.S. justice system, even in this relatively up-market house of detention, and at every preceding stage, reveals and enforces the evil of banality.

From when I arrived on March 3, 2008, my ambitions were fixed on the court of appeals in Chicago. The fact that it had agreed to hear the appeal expeditiously, and the general reputation of the Seventh Circuit, and the juridical tradition of higher court Chicago judges, the famous law schools in that city, and the fame of the former chief judge Richard Posner, who seemed likely to hear the case as he had sat on the appeal bond panel, seemed good auguries. Peter Atkinson and Jack Boultbee had been granted bail though I was not, and the court had expressed interest in the honest services question through the eminent (despite the fact that he went to high school in Buffalo with our avaricious former employee at the *Jerusalem Post*, Wolf Blitzer of CNN) Chief Judge Frank

Easterbrook's written reasons for granting the appeal. Almost the whole case in U.S. appeal proceedings is in written pleadings, and ours were very well formulated and, it seemed to me, unanswerable. The contemptible poverty of what the prosecutors had put over on the uncomprehending jurors and their elfin champion on the bench was laid bare. This, I had long before learned, didn't guarantee anything. But, with unquenchable hopefulness, I thought the most renowned judge on the highest court in such a great and famous jurisdiction might rise at least to simple reason, a task that had intimidated and eluded Strine, Manning, Farley, Campbell, the trans-border securities regulators, and at times even Judge St. Eve. I had strong hopes that I would only be a few more weeks at Coleman as Barbara flew to Chicago and she and Carolyn Gurland attended the hearing on June 6, 2008.

The precise honest services points again were that Judge St. Eve had allowed the jurors to convict either on a money fraud or the withholding of honest services, which need not have required any cost to the company nor an intent to harm the company, without specifying which was the basis of conviction. What was required was some disloyal or unfiduciary act that, while not harmfully intended nor costing anything, could still be construed as materially harmful in an intangible way. Such a vague and arbitrary trip-wire for conviction was clearly an invitation to injustice. The Supreme Court had struck down such a law before, in 1989, and an almost identical one replaced it. Thousands of people had been convicted on this argument. Because all the counts alleging a scheme to defraud were rejected by the jury, it seemed clear that honest services was the problem, and this was the exclusive burden of Ruder and Sussman's summations. St. Eve's instruction went as far as it could to accommodate a conviction, though she claimed only to be following the precedent in her Circuit (the Seventh). It was contrary to the position taken by most other circuits of the United States, where we would have won all the counts. The further complexity of a special verdict form that would require the jury, if there were convictions where alternate charges were made, to specify the grounds of conviction, caused. The government's contention that we had lost any right to challenge on this point after we had declined it (because counsel believed, on the basis of research, that requesting one would increase the likelihood of conviction, and that we could poll the jurors later if there were a need, which the judge denied when we asked for it). In this case, there was no evidence of a fraud – money theft – and the cooperating witness specifically denied it, and honest services was a very tenuous proposition. In most other circuits, we would already have won on all counts, including obstruction, if I had a counsel with the stamina to argue it cogently.

I called on Carolyn's cellphone as soon as I thought the supposedly forty-minute hearing would be over. She and Barbara disabused me at once of any thought that justice would finally raise its comely head at this point. Applicants do not know the identity of the three judges until the day of the hearing. Easterbrook, who had expressed interest in the honest services question, was not among them, but Posner was. Posner had a female judge, new to the court and virtually silent, on his left. The second judge, on his right, seemed intelligent but barely asked a question while Posner ran the court, leaning back and swivelling in his chair with apparent boredom or irritation when the defence pleadings were attempted.

He had not read the defendants' brief, was almost completely ignorant of the facts of the case, and was gratuitously hostile throughout. The hearing was slightly more than an hour. My counsel, Andy Frey, led off for the defence, a well-regarded former deputy solicitor general for sixteen years. The audio was available on the court's website and I quickly received the transcript. In my reading of the proceedings, Posner reminded me of newsreels of Hitler's favourite judge, "Raving" Roland Freisler, who "tried" the July 20, 1944, plotters, shouting at the shambling defendants for the benefit of the cameras, and his Führer. When I felt sufficiently medicated against nausea and headaches to listen to the audio of the hearing, I was reminded of Armando Valladares's description of his Castroite judge reading a comic book and joking before sentencing him, on no evidence, to thirty years in prison.

Andy Frey was ineffectual against such a belligerent judge. In his ten-minute opening segment, he was interrupted twenty-four times by Posner, twenty-one times after less than two sentences. It is impossible to make an argument under these circumstances, but I was disappointed that Frey wasn't more assertive to make a better record, as a couple of the other defence counsel were. He did make the point that in forty-five years of practice, he had never seen as weak a case as the government's on the obstruction count. Posner affected not to understand how Radler could have redesignated a management fee as a non-compete payment and then devised a non-compete agreement that was real.

He either deliberately missed or did not understand how we could argue that the money was voted as a management fee and was then changed into a non-competition fee by the devising of a suitable non-competition basis for it and the retroactive confirmation of those arrangements. Posner kept tediously repeating that the payments in question had to be one type of fee or the other. He professed to be unable to grasp how they could be legitimately re-designated from a management fee to a non-compete fee, but declined to allow counsel to explain it. "You're arguing with me," he said. "It's time to move on to the next case." He did not wish to be confused by the facts, and was not. He deliberately missed the point that since the money had been voted to us by the Audit Committee and the directors, it could not have been a deprivation of the company. He refused to understand that it had nowhere been made clear where any honest services had been withheld, and how the trial judge could have instructed the jury that they could find us guilty on this charge even where no harm to the company was done or intended.

In the nonsense about removing the boxes, he was reduced, in the absence of any evidence, to a snide, smirking comment about a timing "coincidence." So the rot in the U.S. justice system had corroded even this high level. There was no chance of a positive outcome here, so I emailed a response to a query from the *Globe and Mail* that it was obvious that Posner had not read the defence filings, and merely was "part of the prosecution," that his performance was "scandalous," but that the fight would go on. Frey was candid in affirming the negative prospects, but other counsel, loyal to the legal cartel, heaped praise on Frey and predicted a favourable outcome, as if it were a real judicial process. By this time, I knew better. Later on, many senior lawyers confirmed that Posner was the nightmare of the Seventh Circuit. He was known for his neglect and lack of thoroughness in his work on the bench, which played a secondary role to his writing and lectures. Though acknowledged as an extremely clever man and very knowledgeable about the law, his very high opinion of himself seemed to have blinded him to any shame he might have been expected to have about flippant and negligent decisions. The consensus was that, feet up, he flipped through a brief, came to a hasty opinion, and would not be moved by anything as clearly intellectually subordinate to his whims and biases as some lawyer merely equipped with the law and the facts. I was already lamentably familiar with the type.

Posner fancies himself an intellectual, and an economist. I cited his book on Justice Holmes – a respectable but far from exciting study, in my Roosevelt book. After the enormity in his courtroom, I looked into his oeuvre a little more closely. On his website, he highlighted his writing back to undergraduate essays. My study was facilitated, and even summarized, by a quickie he rushed out in May 2009 about the economic setback, called *A Failure of Capitalism: The Crisis of '08 and the Descent into Depression*. This was an exercise in alarmism and pedantry. Of course there was no descent into depression, and once the Federal Reserve started distributing money with steam shovels and fire hoses, there wasn't going to be any. Posner, in a surge of imagination, made four points: the profit motive sometimes leads businesses to bad decisions; the country may need more financial regulation; and the government regulators failed the country. And his book on the causes of the recession concluded with a call for a commission to determine the causes. My offer to review this piercing glimpse into the obvious for the *Wall Street Journal* (properly, in the circumstances) was declined. It would have been my pleasure to give Posner a crisp review. He has all the signs of a judge too much deferred to through decades of drinking his own bathwater.

Frey held out no hope except possibly on obstruction (the boxes). Barbara bravely came to see me the next day, though she returned late from Chicago to Palm Beach and only had forty-five minutes of sleep the night before visiting me. We prepared ourselves for having to serve much of the sentence, and planned yet another defence strategy after a further orderly retreat. Contingency arrangements were already in place. The other (hobnailed) jack-boot fell on June 25 with what I described in my notes as a "cowardly, cavalier, and perversely stupid" judgment by Posner. It was riddled with factual errors and seasoned with painful Strinish attempts at witticisms. At least Strine's strivings toward wit were spontaneous verbal sallies. Posner couldn't master that incline, even with weeks of laborious composition.

Yet we managed to recover most of the case, despite an uneven barristerial performance, a prejudicial instruction from the judge, and some serious frailties of perception on the jury. After this dismal cataract, I should not have been surprised by Posner's infamy, but I was. I thought we would win something. Again, Barbara came the next day, again at huge inconvenience for what on Thursday can only be a short visit ending at noon, and again after little sleep. We would counter-attack on all fronts: try to continue the appeal to the Supreme Court; prepare a treaty transfer application for Britain; pursue the essentially political process of a commutation request of the president; ask for confirmation of my status, as recommended by the judge and the probation officer, as not a security risk, making me eligible for further reductions of the sentence; launch a new series of constitutional attacks based on clear recent precedents for violation of my Sixth Amendment right to counsel with the false cash seizure in New York, which chased off Brendan Sullivan; and assault the outrageous Mareva (Barbara's assignment, presaging my own attack on it) – all while awaiting, with some justified hopefulness according to the congressmen involved, legislated sentence reductions. I replaced the very gentlemanly and altogether admirable Andy Frey with the more aggressive Miguel Estrada for the application to the Supreme Court. (I had Barbara's tireless research to thank for this, as it proved to be a fortuitous change.)

Oddly, the U.S. government doesn't necessarily win a war of attrition against a resourceful individual. As we have seen, it practically always imprisons its target, who has no useful constitutional rights in fact, except entitlement to some sort of counsel in a public show trial. Prosecutors do anything they want including holding inflammatory press conferences, before and along with indictments; defendants are spuriously accused of tampering with witnesses or violating bail arrangements and are harassed by arbitrary asset seizures as part of the effort to deny them counsel, in distracting pre-trial skirmishes.* The media amplify defamatory leaks from the prosecution, and the trial and appellate judges I encountered and read, with rare exceptions such as federal District Judge Lewis Kaplan in

---

* The public defenders are usually just Judas goats, paid by the court, intimidated by the prosecutors, part of the charade of preservation of the constitutional rights to due process and advice of counsel and paid by the numbers of people they supposedly represent, not the results they achieve.

Manhattan, appear more often than not to be wise-cracking toadies of the Justice Department, concerned for headlines and often promotion to a higher public trough, which in the current political atmosphere can only be attained by draconian severity.

BUT AFTER WINNING SOME of their cases, the persecutors and the attendant media, having consigned their victims, they imagine, to the dustbin of the "disgraced," and so on, move on to new victims, and the confined innocent, if he retains the determination and the means, can pick away at the weaknesses of the false case that has been made against him.

The endless much-savoured references to me as "disgraced" caused me to rummage through the Bible the kindly British stranger sent me to find an apposite quote. Like so much else, it came in Isaiah: 50: 6–8. "I have set my face like flint knowing that I shall not be put to shame. Who will prove me wrong?"

AT THE END OF 2008, Richard Breeden, Gordon Paris, and Raymond Seitz announced their retirement from the former Hollinger International and the disbandment of the Special Committee. The vulture funds moved to sweep out the other directors and the pseudo-"management" installed by Breeden. There have been more improbable resurrections than Sun-Times Media Group, though perhaps not without widespread religious adherences as a consequence. The vandalized hulk of STMG was sold out of bankruptcy to fly-by-night financial buyers in late 2009, in another vintage Chicago court stitch-up. I pipelined in advice to the stakeholders many times on how to salvage something for themselves, but like so many others in this tawdry farce, they allowed their sense of self-preservation to atrophy at the mere Medusan presence of Richard Breeden.

On inauguration eve, January 19, George W. Bush rejected fifty-eight hundred commutation applications and left the other twenty-two hundred, including mine, to his successor. We had a magnificently written and sponsored application, and put it into the president's hands via both a close family member and his own counsel. But the outgoing president, whose career had been saved by Richard Breeden's whitewash of his insider sale of Harkin Energy Company stock during his father's term, said he didn't approve of people using highly paid lawyers to make such applications, and rode unlamented into the sunset. (I found the monthly requests for contributions to the George W. Bush Library, exactly addressed to me in prison, and warmly machine-signed "George," though they were obviously computerized, indicative of a man who incited the dispatch of shoes at his head, when visiting Iraq.)

I KNEW THE HOLY GRAIL of justice was out there somewhere, beyond the barbed wire and the comedians in Receiving and Departing. And in May 2009, finally, unmistakably, came the apparition of justice. Breeden, Healy, and the former Hollinger International directors who had published and circulated the Special Committee report and 10Ks had tried to eliminate my libel suits. They claimed in court in Toronto that I was just jurisdiction-shopping to sue in Canada, and that the action should be brought in the United States, where intent to defame has to be proved for the plaintiff to succeed, an almost impossible burden. And they claimed that since some guilty verdicts had been returned, I had no reputation to protect anyway, and so my action was unfounded.

The traditions of Canada as a country of the rule of law, which had partly prompted me to graduate in law in Quebec forty years before, almost miraculously reappeared like a phoenix (or even the well-travelled but infrequent flyer, the Archangel Gabriel, who allegedly appeared to Christ, and six hundred years later to Muhammad). Superior Court Justice Edward Belobaba threw out the change-of-jurisdiction request very declaratively, adding that I appeared to have well-founded grounds of action, without at all prejudging them, and that the misdeeds alleged by the defendants vastly exceeded the convictions of the plaintiff. Then, showing again that when fortune returns, it often comes in a flood, as it had fled, Judge Belobaba added: "Juries, including American juries, are fallible." He implied that the standard of whether a Canadian court would return any guilty verdicts on the same evidence (it would not) could be applied. This had long been my reserve position, in case nothing further could be achieved in the U.S. justice system. I could arrange, in effect, for that system to be, itself, tried in Canada, Britain, or the European Court of Justice.

At last, now I could be sure of my ability to put Breeden, Thompson, Seitz, Paris, Healy, and the others in the witness box without immunities or a right to remain silent (as I promised Seitz and Thompson would happen when they deposed me as chairman of Hollinger International five years before) and under the full penalties of perjury. It was and is a delicious prospect.

Two weeks later came an even greater seismic change. The Supreme Court of the United States, which consents to hear only 1 or 2 per cent of the applications it receives, but reverses 70 per cent of the verdicts it does review, agreed to hear our appeal. This was a headline news story throughout the Western world. The enemy dug in again, blinking in the unaccustomed daylight, as the rock was lifted away. St. Eve gave Jack Boultbee bail, and he went home to Victoria. Peter Atkinson was treaty-transferred to Canada and released.

The Supreme Court, through its erratic Chicago representative, Justice John Paul Stevens, took the position that bail was beneath its dignity and denied my application. The mask was thrown down; Breeden and Fitzgerald had never cared about the others, except technically. It was my honour to be the sole real subject of their cause. Our informants told us that Judge St. Eve was outraged that the Supreme Court would review her jury instruction that the jurors could convict in the absence of a fraud, or of harm, or evidence of intent to harm, the company. She dug in her Nike-clad, nimble little feet and rejected my bail application without a hearing, I suspect out of fear of the tatters the very able and motivated Miguel Estrada* would make of her instructions, rulings, and sentence before the international media. She and the private sector's own Eric Sussman acknowledged the possibility that the fraud counts would be struck down, and clung like drowning people to the flimsy life preserver that what would then happen to the obstruction charge was "speculation," as St. Eve put it. (So had been that small part of the prosecution case that had not been simply false.)

Our sources also reported (well-founded) consternation in the U.S. attorney's office in Chicago, and in Breeden's suddenly jittery camp.

---

* Judge St. Eve jogged many days at noon. Miguel Estrada had been filibustered six times by the Democrats when nominated to the U.S. Circuit Court of Appeals for Washington, D.C., by President George W. Bush. He believes strongly in the rights of defendants, and proved a magnificently thorough counsel.

Prominent members of the financial media rediscovered our coordinates. Strong amicus curiae briefs supporting us came in from the U.S. Chamber of Commerce and the Criminal Defense Trial Lawyers' Association. Words of encouragement and congratulation flooded my email terminal and mail box, from most U.S. states, all Canadian provinces, and many countries.

After nearly six dire years, finally, the enemy, which had no more ammunition to fire at me, would have to account for itself in serious courts of law, and not just in echo chambers for frenzied prosecutors, the Chicago political machine, and the media tricoteuses, none of whom have any more interest in justice than a tomcat has in a marriage license. The mills of justice are proverbially slow, but they would finally test Breeden and his accomplices. Of course, the outcome was not a foregone conclusion, but the prospect of a fair hearing was a novelty of inexpressible consolation. I felt, of the judiciary, and soon of the media too, of both countries, in Schiller's famous phrase: "Late you come, but still you come."

The Honest Services Statute, appropriately from a draftsman (Joe Biden), who plagiarized a political theme from one of Britain's most forgettable political leaders (Neil Kinnock), was a menace to all American business. This was now a landmark case that would sort out differences between the U.S. circuits and subject aspects of the U.S. justice system to intense scrutiny. My father used to quote Browning's "It is a long lane that knows no turning." I was still in captivity, but my tormentors were doing a fearful tap dance, and the banshees of pharisaical bigotry were finally silent (as surveys confirmed a seismic shift in Canadian public opinion).

It all began, finally, majestically, to turn. The *Washington Post, Wall Street Journal* (television year-end roundup), *National Law Review, Fortune*, even the *Guardian*, and many individual writers and bloggers called for or predicted my vindication. Long silent former friends mysteriously reappeared in my email queue.

The heavily attended hearing at the Supreme Court of the United States on December 8, 2009, could not have gone better. Miguel Estrada and David Debold wrote a brilliant brief, and Miguel's court performance matched it. The justices, from right to left, challenged the assistant solicitor general representing the Justice Department and expressed concern, and even contempt, for the Honest Services Statute. Justice Stephen

Breyer (the only one of them I had actually met) said the statute could convict 140 million of the U.S. workforce of 150 million people. Chief Justice John Roberts said that it was impossible for a reasonable person to read the statute and judge if his own conduct was legal. Justice Antonin Scalia said it wasn't the place or task of the Supreme Court to rewrite defective statutes for the Congress.

Suddenly, the odds and the omens, and not merely the law and the facts, were with us. There was now room for great hope and cautious optimism. Whatever might happen, I had never felt so strongly how great is the reward for being true to oneself.

ALL THIS RAISES THE QUESTION of why, apart from desperately missing my beloved Barbara, I was not completely miserable as a prisoner, as long as it didn't go on indefinitely, and I knew it would not. As I had been unjustly accused and convicted, I had the somewhat bracing status of a relatively comfortable martyrdom. No one who has not experienced such an injustice can easily appreciate how repulsive it is, but the enormity of it is morally empowering without being a lifetaking or life-threatening sacrifice. It had deprived me of many pleasures and liberties but reaffirmed my self-confidence that I have not lost the ability to live simply, to socialize easily with, to say the least, a very disparate group, and even to accept an unnatural subordinacy. When the crisis burst and fortune fled, I did not know what I could endure. It has been, in the abstract, a fearful but broadening experience. I will emerge stronger and certainly wiser, and with the actuarial right to look forward to a golden afterburner to my life and career.

It has been an education. People from my socio-economic background may suspect what goes on in the dark, vast, unwashed underside of life, which throbs and heaves just out of sight to the inhabitants of Norman Rockwell's and Bill Buckley's Americas. But suspecting how the justice system works, and how it interacts with everything that shares its corrosion, does not prepare someone at all adequately for going through it from the wrong end. Nor does it prepare someone to endure the sudden, completely unwarranted inversion of fortune, and unbidden plunge from one of the powerful to one of the designated pariahs, and to see how strong still is the moralistic, disgracing whiplash of this deeply corrupt process.

No one conscripted me to go into business in the United States, and I knew when I did that there were some wild and woolly aspects of the country's justice system. But it is becoming a prosecutocracy and a carceral state where what has happened to me could happen to anyone, and often does. In a democratic country, the people are always right, and if the American people are happy with their justice system, their will is sovereign. Once clear of it, it will be no concern of mine. But the majority of Americans have no idea how far their justice system has putrefied. When the victims of official injustice and their families and supporters, tens of millions of people (as there are an astounding 47 million Americans with a criminal record, most of the offenses relatively minor) become so numerous and aroused that every congressman receives fifty messages a week from them and there are, as there will be, extreme actions by people whose lives prosecutors and judges have broken unjustly, change will be possible. That is democracy too, but as long as these problems are not addressed, the human and moral damage to American society will become steadily more severe.

My admiration of the United States is well known – notorious, in fact – and it continues yet, in some ways, despite being so prodigiously unrequited. I do not take America's persecution of me personally; indeed, the impersonality makes it even more irritating. While my admiration of aspects of America perseveres, my affair with that country has ended. It won't be revived but is remembered fondly. I am not Captain Dreyfus or Dr. Mudd, but I have a legitimate grievance, and I have been reassured to find that I am happy enough to be who I am. Whatever the sophistries of the law and the vagaries of the bench, I have committed no crimes. This is already widely recognized.

The foregoing is accurate and indisputable in all material respects. By surviving it all, physically, morally, and financially, despite everything and against all odds and disappointments, I win.

Inmate 18330-424
Cubicle 30, Unit B-1,
Coleman Low Security Prison,
Federal Correctional Complex,
Coleman, Florida
May 15, 2010

Epilogue

"Comes now the United States of America" as professional jargon couches a government legal initiative, and a large swath of the legal, commercial, and media communities waited for the Supreme Court of the United States to bring down its decision before the court term ended at the close of July 2010. Ours was one of several prominent cases that would affect the lives of many, and was featured with gun control and intellectual property cases as the most closely watched and carefully awaited.

The Court announced its decisions on its website at 10:00 a.m. Eastern Time, each Monday (and later Thursdays as well), scrolling through the judgments, and finishing by 10:30 a.m. I called Barbara at 10:35 on such mornings, but there was nothing for several weeks. On June 26, she took the call after half a ring, and said in a very calm voice: "Miguel [Estrada] is evaluating this; the Court has vacated all counts unanimously, but has sent them back to Posner to determine if they are the subject of harmless error. They were pretty hard on Posner in the opinion, which was written by Justice Ginsburg." The Honest Services Statute was rewritten to require a bribe or kickback for conviction, which, the high court mentioned, was not applicable in our case. Justice Ginsburg decried "the infirmity of invented law" and the "anomalous" nature of Posner's findings; pretty severe strictures between eminent judges. But it seemed to us perversely American that, having administered such a battering to Posner, that he would have a cranium like the skin of a golf ball, it invited him to determine the gravity of his own errors.

It was a decisive turn and a great victory. The Honest Services Statute had been struck from the hands of the prosecutors and thousands of cases had been reopened. Our informants shortly confirmed that the prosecutorial community was none too pleased with Posner for having fumbled them out of this very efficient method, which almost all had happily abused for decades, of taking down their targeted opponents. Fitzgerald had been propelled by Breeden to go after me for life imprisonment and complete impoverishment, and was now disarmed and humbled.

The press was very extensive and unambiguously generous. I gave a press statement to Theresa Tedesco of the *National Post* that was widely taken up: "The decision of the Supreme Court of the United States is very gratifying. It has been a very long struggle and a difficult time. Our camp is very hopeful but naturally cautious about what will come next." It was no time for triumphalism, both because indignities would be out of place, and because the process of Posner reviewing his own errors would naturally be unpredictable.

True to form, as the sort of Comical Ali (Saddam Husssein's notoriously mendacious press officer, constantly announcing great Iraqi victories against the U.S. and its allies) of the prosecution committee that he had departed two years before, Eric Sussman claimed a victory and said that "the Justice Department dodged a bullet today." His interviewer, finally, was incredulous. He said I had a "five percent chance of a reduced sentence," and almost no chance of bail. Posner's initial pass at the case had been such a monstrosity of bigoted ignorance and he was such a notorious egomaniac that we did not think he would grant bail, but felt we must ask for it, to show we had faith in our case. We did not see how he could salvage the fraud counts, no matter how redoubled his desire to do so.

Congratulations flooded in from around the world: thousands of messages, and astoundingly supportive press comments. As fortune had fled totally, so it returned in a flood. In a mighty back-flip by Rupert Murdoch, for such an editorial could not have been written without his authority, the

Wall Street Journal ran a lead opinion piece entitled "Conrad Black's Revenge," and apologized prominently and unequivocally for not having realized earlier the righteousness of my cause. They then ran a signed piece by my friend Seth Lipsky, former editor of the *New York Sun*, that was entirely laudatory. There were many similar comments, with George Jonas and Jonathan Kay in the *National Post* among the most gratefully appreciated.

Wonderful moment though it was, we were not clear of it all yet. My fellow residents at Coleman Low were heart-warming, even heart-rending, in their solidarity. Complete strangers arrived in droves to wish me well, and all those hundreds whom I did know were unanimous in treating my success as their own. I was invited to prayer meetings in my honour. It was deeply affecting, and inexpressibly reassuring that decency survives, even against such odds, in such battered souls, and in such an unremitting place.

Counsel thought we had won the frauds, meaning the complete collapse of the entire Breeden allegations and the swift counter-advance of my civil and libel suits. Obstruction was still a problem and if Posner was determined to give the government something, he could give them that.

I spent several weeks replying to emails, writing articles that I had previously agreed to, and concerting strategy with various counsel. Then in a new, unforeseen bombshell on Monday, July 19, I called Barbara as usual at 11:00 p.m. and she said: "Have you heard?" "I haven't heard anything worth remembering." "You have bail." Without trying to puzzle out what this might mean in terms of Posner's thinking, it was an immense relief and an event impossible to think of negatively. I offered Miguel the thought that Posner was just creating the appearance of liberality in order to cover his next outrage. Miguel thought he might have the impulse, but that he would not try it after a pasting from the Supreme Court and with the entire legal community and much of the media watching.

Judge St. Eve approved the bail terms on the morning of July 21. My dear friend Roger Hertog flew to Chicago and pledged $2 million, which I was able to guaranty without violating Mareva requirements so he was neither out of pocket nor at risk; it was an immensely gracious gesture from an extremely distinguished and valued friend in all seasons.

I shortly became the subject of respectfully formulated messages over the compound public address system, which had been the source of so much ear-splitting annoyance, almost ceaselessly from 6:00 a.m. to 9:00 p.m. every day for twenty-eight months. My alien status was waived, as I was informed by my unit manager, who said that it would require me to be taken to solitary confinement. I replied that "Not one cent of bail will be pledged to send me over to the Special Housing Unit." Off it came, as I spoke. Barbara was in Toronto, but managed to get a chartered plane to fly her to Palm Beach that night, so we could celebrate our eighteenth wedding anniversary.

She arranged for a car to collect me. The driver was besieged by the media at the gate, waiting to enter, as she watched on television. Over a hundred of my friends had asked to accompany me to the gate, but I was rushed out while the compound was generally shut down, and only one friend was able to bring back the cart on which my books and other belongings were piled up. I took just one piece of government property: the shirt bequeathed by the former don of a New York underworld family. When I declared it to an amiable correctional officer who processed me, he said he did not wish to incur the rancour of both of us, and on I went.

There were cordial farewells with as many as ten officials but I exchanged no words with the dour lieutenant present. The compound counsel had arranged for my departure via a padlocked gate, avoiding the press, and with remarkable swiftness and lack of ceremony, jovial waves and salutations, I passed back through the gates and had a very pleasant three-hour drive to my fiercely disputed home in Palm Beach. I called Barbara and Joan and Miguel, watched the nondescript Florida scenery and townscapes as we passed, and reflected on the unevenness of my blessings.

Our devoted and talented houseman, Domenico, who had previously worked for the Wrightsmans; and the Bruces, and the Annenbergs in the U.S. embassy in London, greeted me as I arrived in my track suit, past a knot of cameramen indistinguishable from those that had filmed my departure. We had a glass of wine, as I had so often dreamt of doing, overlooking the ocean. We reminisced a bit, and then he withdrew, and I breathed free in the sunny, salted breeze, and the absence of any noise except the sea.

Barbara arrived about midnight. It was one of the very most exquisite moments I have known; her constancy, resolve, and affection, and my gratitude for her is beyond words, and we were finally able to go beyond words to express them.

We returned to Chicago the next day, and to St. Eve's court the following day. Again, St. Eve would not hear of allowing me to return to Canada. It was utter nonsense, of course, because the Canadians would admit me again without a passport, and no one would extradite me back to the U.S. after this turn of events. However, it was irrelevant because I would in no circumstances consider being a fugitive from justice. The U.S. must either release me unconvicted or compound its injustices, even if that meant St. Eve, as she clearly wished, sending me back, however briefly, to prison. Withal, it was a much more relaxed appearance, opposite the judge and the press, than previous occasions. I greeted some of the marshals cordially, and even some of the journalists, then Barbara and I departed for New York.

After two weeks in holiday mode, and many agreeable reunions, particularly with, as Barbara calls them, the cubs (Jonathan, Alana, and James), we returned to Palm Beach. There were no tropical storms, the weather was warm but not insufferable, and we had the most spontaneous and carefree days in many years with Barbara's delightful Kuvaszok, splendid large, eccentric white Hungarian livestock-guardian (but not shepherding) dogs. There were thousands of emails for reply, this manuscript to get into shape, friends to receive, medical and dental work to be done, and generally, a world to rediscover.

The Ontario Court of Appeal threw out the Breeden group's (from Kissinger all the way down to Healy) suddenly urgent effort to resist the inexorable approach of my libel suits. The exchange of briefs on the Circuit Court re-hearing, and the supplementary briefs, were the now traditional mismatch. The government's feeble efforts to keep the Breeden demonology alive were now a pathetic wail to Posner to stick to his guns, without a mention of the 9-0 immolation from the U.S. Supreme Court.

The fact that the government had no argument left did not mean that justice would finally, unambiguously be done. That had never been the nature of these proceedings. In the terrible early defeats, I had yet salvaged enough to fight on and now all 17 counts had been abandoned, rejected by the jurors, or unanimously vacated by the Supreme Court, the evil spirit of injustice flourished yet. I told many prison friends as I left that I expected to be back, (though for less than my current full sentence), and was too wary of the wickedness and official advantages of my enemies to be free of that concern. Posner reviewing Posner's own errors was a most unpromising forum.

Barbara and I, despite Miguel's view that Posner couldn't just ignore the Supreme Court opinion, continued to think that, contrary to our expectations, he had granted bail in order to incite, and then brutally extinguish, false hopes of an early end to the persecution. He could have rejected bail and left me in prison, as I and most observers expected, but that would have accelerated the end of my punishment. Letting me out of prison to live a half-life seemed a way to extend it, and with a touch of sadistic destruction that would please this, as he acknowledged himself (to Larissa MacFarquhar in the *New Yorker*), "callous and cruel" man. He and his co-panellists could take as long as they wanted to issue their opinion.

I had done a slight bit of research on Posner, and recalled Milton Friedman telling me once that he was "a serious intelligence." I suppose he was, once. In the famous sketch in the *New Yorker* in 2001, Posner was portrayed as having "a limp hand . . . eyes pale as a fish . . . the distant, omniscient, ectoplasmic air of the butler in the haunted house." Posner on Posner: "If someone is obviously guilty, why do you have to have all this rigmarole?" So he doesn't; he just assumes guilt and reasons backwards. "I am cold, furtive, callous, snobbish, selfish, and playful, but with a streak of cruelty. . . . I'm like an imperfectly house-broken pet," he explained to the interviewer with evident pride. I could see why Fitzgerald and Ruder were so cocky (in separate conversations with Miguel Estrada), that he would protect something of their false and vacated convictions, but I was at a complete loss for a theological explanation why, after all this, my fate was in the hands of such a mutation of the bench. Elsewhere in the same article, Posner acknowledged that he was neurotic because his cat, Dinah, preferred Mrs. Posner to him, not a difficult conclusion to imagine, cats being legendarily intelligent.

Posner proclaims himself a Nietzschean, and despised his parents in the infirmity of their eighties. When Larissa MacFarquhar asked him what he felt when his parents died, "he looked puzzled, as though the question didn't make sense to him. 'I don't have any feeling about it,' he said." He had not wanted doctors to prolong the lives of his debilitated parents. "I'd like to choose my own time of exit." I was tempted by unchristian thoughts.

He became famous for emphasizing the economic consequences of laws and urging these as criteria in determining their application. He professes to believe that he has not been elevated to the U.S. Supreme Court because he favours the legalization of marijuana. But his proposal to deal with child adoption by public auction, and his sociopathic personality, are generally thought to have more to do with it. However and why ever, I was stuck with him, a dreary, unreasoning pustule of animus, infesting my path on the way to the judicial summit of America, and on the way back down.

Miguel and David Debold again overwhelmed the government in written arguments for the Circuit Court rehearing, and atomized the four vacated counts all over again. The government again had recourse to lies and evasions, pretended that Fitzgerald's scheme had survived the trial, that I had snuck documents out of my office, and pretended that the APC payments were not with money that had already been voted to us, and that the Forum and Paxton payments had not been voted by the Executive Committee and ratified by the directors.

They remained on autocue at the Circuit Court rehearing in October, as they had been for the last five years, as if their case had not been shot to pieces again and again. Posner was almost as argumentative, querulous, and overbearing and obnoxious as he had been with poor Andy Frey in 2008, but Estrada wasn't having it and insisted on his right to complete a few consecutive sentences. It seemed to us, hearing the audio of the arguments, that while Posner would like to retain all four counts, he was going to have to let the APC counts go, but that obstruction was likely to remain and the Forum-Paxton count was a toss-up, not because the slightest credence could still be attached to either, but that Posner probably possessed the conceit to claim some colour of right to retain them. On the law and the facts, as always, we had won easily, but we were dealing with a judge who seemed determined to send me back to prison for as long as possible, and whose ego would accommodate almost any decision that gave effect to that wish.

Miguel Estrada knew a lot of people in and around the Seventh Circuit and heard a lot, and so did some other contacts. In the aftermath of the hearing, we thought that the other two panelists would be less sanguine about being rebuked by the Supreme Court than Posner was, and that they would probably help to resist Posner's desire to reimpose all four vacated counts. This was what happened. On December 17, Posner produced another false and shameful judgment, allowing the APC counts to fall, but fabricating, ignoring and distorting evidence to keep the Paxton-Forum and obstruction counts.

He accomplished this end by interpreting Radler's jokily worded advice to the rest of us that the buyers (Forum-Paxton), wanted non-compete agreements as an admission that they did not; by ignoring that the payments had been ratified and approved, and by ignoring the fact that the defendants had absolutely nothing to do with the arrangements. On obstruction, all the relevant facts were ignored, such as that I knew nothing of the contents or of any continuing SEC interest in my files, had not been accused of violating a Canadian document retention order, had spoken with the interim president of the company before acting, made sure that the removals were recorded by the security cameras so there could be no thought of trying to avoid them, and could have taken anything I wanted out at any time in brief cases or coat pockets for weeks before and after without any review or incident.

For good measure, Posner urged the trial judge to ignore, for sentencing purposes, the fall of the APC counts, and to send me back to prison for the entire original sentence. This was what Barbara and I had suspected was his game all along, but we all doubted that St. Eve was going to buy into anything so Draconian and dishonest. We were, however, quite certain that she would send me back to prison and it became a matter of trying to hold that to the lightest possible renewed sentence, and setting matters up as well as possible before I surrendered to custody. Though we were prepared for this setback, Barbara and I were still very disappointed.

Miguel Estrada's statement on December 17 on our behalf promised a further appeal to the Supreme Court, and said that "Posner's opinion for the panel did not accurately reflect the facts, misapplied the test for harmless error review, is inconsistent with the Sixth Amendment and did not remotely respond adequately to the Supreme Court's instructions. Instead, the panel recounted the government's spin on its supposed evidence, trivialized the strong defence case, and all but ignored the jury's rejection of any proof of a real crime with the sweeping acquittals on most of the counts in the original case." The charge of fraud alone had led to acquittals. The only convictions had Honest Services attached to them. That statute had gone, but Posner had in effect still managed to impale me on it. We asked for an en banc hearing, the whole Circuit Court sure that Posner would not be rebuked by his colleagues, and were not surprised when he even denied the right of a reply (after we had filed it). The profligate jurist was approving his own judicial expense account.

We had no practical expectation that the Supreme Court would take the case back again. It had no interest in the equity of lower court decisions, and had rewritten the Honest Services Statute to assure uniformity of interpretation throughout the country. But it only chose to be insulted by being flipped the bird by a lower court if it actually wanted to notice it. Miguel and David crafted a clever and brilliantly worded demolition of Posner's reasoning and the tatters of the government's case, hanging it constitutionally on Posner's violation of the Sixth Amendment by usurping the role of the jury for himself and denying trial by jury to me, with the subtext of trying to incite what must have been a temptation by the high court to wallop this impudent and much-talking judge about his glabrous head once and for all.

The confidence of the prosecutors that I would be sent back to prison made them complacent about asking revocation of bail, as they subscribed to the Posner timetable of stretching out my time roasting on the spit for as long as possible, preferably, though they would never publicly say so, until the undertakers removed me from the prison medical facility.

A considerable race ensued to get as many things cleared up as possible and to do everything we could to eliminate or at least minimize the remaining sentence. Since the retention of any felony count would make me persona non grata in the United States, (a country that was in any case, patria non grata with me), there was no longer any argument for retaining the Palm Beach house. If I were still the owner when the Supreme Court declined to hear our appeal again, the value of it would again crash as the bottom-feeders would be out in their former numbers, avarice, and abrasiveness. After delicate negotiation with a number of people, a sale was negotiated for $25 million, not a miraculous price, but not a risible one either, and the entire contents were evacuated hastily to Toronto. The utmost discretion was maintained, with unmarked small trucks and larger vans only coming in at night, and on completion of conditions the proceeds were wired out of the country at once, to avoid any replication of the outrage that stalked and befell the New York transaction, though the circumstances now, with no prospect of further criminal proceedings, would make any such intervention much more difficult and this time we would be prepared for it.

It was time to complete the drastic deconstruction of our former lives, but now with a clear timetable, a practical certainty of financial survival, and in a planned and not desperately reactive way. At least, unlike in London and New York, I was present to help Barbara pack up the house. I had come to Palm Beach from Cuba in 1969, and was influenced by the legacy of my former senior partner, Bud McDougald, the long-serving president of the Everglades Club, and had seen Palm Beach, through the decades, as a fine monument to the appetites and attainments of American capitalism. After the economic debacle of 2008 and the humbling and collapse of Wall Street, I no longer had much respect for American capitalism, and did not feel that Barbara had been very generously supported by many of the people we knew in Palm Beach, when she was alone there. We left on April 26, and I do not expect to return. Barbara's splendid dogs preceded us in a van to Toronto (heavy-coated Hungarian kuvaszok, they intensely disliked the heat). I flew to New York and checked into the Mark Hotel, and remained for over four months.

Now the libel suits from 2004 based on the accusations in the Special Committee report, commissioned by Breeden and signed by most of the directors, were reaching the point of depositions. I couldn't wait to get everyone, especially Breeden, under aggressive questioning. This process was held up now only by the last fling of the libel defendants, before the Supreme Court of Canada, that I had no right or standing to sue in Canada and was merely jurisdiction-shopping, a fatuous argument that had been dismissed by the Superior and Appeal Courts in Toronto, settlement discussions now increased to ramming speed. (I was the only person in history, for a few months, to be simultaneously before the Supreme Courts of Canada and the United States.) Despite the efforts of the other side to dismiss our action as frivolous, my constant response that in that case, let us resolve the other actions that were at issue, and try the libel case, quickly brought them back to what I had always predicted: their absolute inability to face intense questioning on the allegations in the infamous Breeden Report and the shameful derelictions and financial disaster of their own administration of the assets whose control they usurped and milked for $300 million for themselves while vaporizing $2 billion of the savings of the average shareholder whose interests they were supposedly promoting.

They wobbled and jerked the line, but it was a very unconvincing negotiation. In the end, they conceded a $6-million cash payment to me in respect of the libel action, a significant part coming from their own pockets, as well as $6 million more, almost all to me, in respect of the original phony Breeden action of January 2004, the Interpleader action on division of insurance money, and the feeble effort to take back some of my indemnified legal payments. It was a rich and savoury victory.

In New York, I finally enjoyed talking face-to-face with the friends who had helped me through these very trying times, with their emails, visits, and supportive blogging and writing on my case. Among these were Roger Hertog, Seth Lipsky, the Podhoretzes, Roger Kimball, The National Review people and other writers and business people with whom I shared an enduring spirit of comradeship, whom I admired, and to whom I was grateful.

A pleasant and unexpected dividend was a very direct and rather affecting peace overture from Henry Kissinger. He invited me to dinner at his home and we went over it all, briefly and, of course, unrancorously. I told him that I thought he was largely responsible for the myth that I could have settled matters easily at the outset, a fraud of Breeden's, and that because Breeden had the upper hand, he had rather uncritically accepted Breeden's version of why our discussions had broken down in 2004. I didn't blame him for not wanting to become involved and never asked him to, but I thought he owed me a better hearing, and at least benign neutrality. I understood how threatening Breeden could be, and how cautious the advice of Saunders would certainly be, and I knew from many years of observation and discussion with Richard Nixon and others that Henry's technique in such matters was to go to a neutral corner and stay clear of the fracas, and see what could be put together later.

I volunteered that it was not my place to remonstrate with a man of his stature at his age on a modus operandi that had obviously served him well in great and world-historic matters, whatever my disappointment in this small case. And I volunteered that I did not believe the claim of the FBI that he had said that he believed me guilty as charged, because I had learned how unreliable the assertions of agents of that Bureau were apt to be. My only litmus test at this point, I told Henry Kissinger, was that if he actually believed that I had committed crimes, we would not be able to repair our relations. If he did not, and could tell me that, privately and without any request by me for a hint of explanation, much less apology; I suggested we put it all behind us and not speak of it again. This is what happened. He telephoned Barbara a few days later, who was astounded to hear from him, and had more difficulty than I did in getting over our differences. He and I soon settled back into the frequent telephone and dinner conversations of historic and international affairs of olden times.

For the rest of social New York, the habitués of the boxes at the Metropolitan Opera House and the most exalted socioeconomic echelons of the Style section of the Sunday *New York Times*, I met, quite cordially, in passing with many of them. There were many smiles and kisses, a few small dinners, and I was glad to see them again, but it was over. Our lack of interest is mutual, and, I think, not spiteful or antagonistic. One grows apart. I was glad to have seen them up close, and a few remain good friends, but they and I have moved on in different directions. In one case, I unguardedly got off my chest a few reflections on America that were, in the abstract, excessive, though not inaccurate, and I apologized for them. My apology was accepted, but the relationship was strained. It was the last occasion where the prolonged process of disengaging from the United States, a country I had so admired, and by which I had been so disappointed and offended, was painful. I would like to return to New York some day, and friends are already considering how to facilitate that. I will miss it, as anyone would.

In all that has happened, these are not great sorrows, just the gentle melancholy of autumn, as one prepares for another season in another place. There are only a few of these prominent New Yorkers whom I remember with any hostility, and I have been grateful to find that time heals most wounds. These will not linger long, and some brilliant friendships remain. As we prepared for the resentencing hearing in Chicago, the U.S. Probation Office produced a very supportive report that clearly raised the question of whether I had ever really been guilty of anything and strongly recommended release for time served. My friends in Coleman had provided a herneating mass of supportive letters and emails and even the correctional personnel had spoken positively. The prosecution is accustomed to the Probation Office parroting its position and was so startled by this turn of events that it extracted two affidavits from Coleman personnel, one a vocational training person and the other a unit manager, that retailed false tittle-tattle, and in one case contradicted what the affiant had said to the Probation officer. We challenged this and demanded subpoenas for these people and the relevant correspondence, and the prosecutors sped backwards like alarmed canaries, claiming that they were not trying to contradict what the inmates and personnel had said in my favour. I now knew the prosecutors and their techniques so well that I was not surprised by their small-minded attack even on my life as a prisoner, with incredible affidavits, one contradicting a signed statement from the affiant, and by their cowardly retreat when buried under a tidal wave of contradictions from the Probation Office and the inmates. Nor was I surprised that when reviewing the dubious affidavits the judge said she didn't believe them, without rebuking the government.

Barbara and I returned to Chicago on June 23 for the final hearing in Judge St. Eve's courtroom the next day. Given that this was the end, I considered my remarks carefully and delivered them directly to the judge at a range of about fifteen feet, from memory, in a firm and fluent, but not bombastic, voice. They are in the Appendix and were widely reprinted and commented on; essentially I repeated that I was not guilty, that the government's case had been entirely destroyed and had only been revived at all by an unrigorous and far from disinterested act of casuistry by a perverse judge. The prosecutors' disappointment in the shattering of their case was understandable, but I was not the rightful subject of their vindictive sentiments. I expatiated somewhat philosophically and gave a glimpse, without indiscretion or, I trust, any lapse of taste, of my religious and psychological assimilation of these unbidden events. The judge listened very attentively as I spoke for about twenty-five minutes.

She had made her decision, and it was not, as I had assumed, possible for her to abandon the pretense that I had actually been convicted of something, however, as I put it in my remarks to the court, "tortuous the process and threadbare the evidentiary basis of the convictions now are." Though counsel (Miguel, David, and Carolyn) thought the chances of release for time served were about 50-50, Barbara and I did not think St. Eve capable of such a complete implicit abandonment of the prosecution, and it had been her practice up to this point to play it down the middle between Scylla and Charybdis and give something to both sides. I assumed that she was under some importunity, even if it were merely telepathic, from Posner and Fitzgerald to send me back to prison and try partially to validate the entire shabby process that had preceded this climax.

She had already prepared the ground in her earlier remarks by adding the enhancement of sophisticated planning to the remaining fraud count, although the evidence (uncorroborated and in fact fictitious) only was that I had telephoned Radler and asked if there would be a non-competition payment in respect of the Forum and Paxton transactions, which if true, would not have been improper, much less sophisticated planning for a crime. This enabled her then while rejecting quite emphatically the government's attempted dismissal of my good conduct while in prison still to have enough enhancement points to send me back. She declared that I was "a better person" as a result of having been sent to prison. I took this as a somewhat self-serving comment by her, auto-felicitation for having sent me there in the first place. But I believe that it is true, and that the experience of being a prisoner conferred on me some generally welcome, increased humility and a broader appreciation of the lot of disadvantaged people. Certainly, without understanding why I had been convicted and imprisoned at all, as I had not committed a crime, I tried, as a principle of my religious beliefs, to extract something useful from the experience.

Judge St. Eve thanked me for my comments and reduced the sentence from 78 to 42 months, which after the good time reduction and crediting my 29 months already served, was a sentence of an additional seven months and three weeks. Unfortunately, Barbara thought that she was sentencing me to another 42 months, which she could have done, though it would have been very severe, and she fainted, falling sideways on the front bench of the court. I heard the commotion, but assumed that it was reporters rushing out to file that I would be returning to prison. Barbara was revived by people near her and helped from the room to the cramped holding room where we had eaten our lunch during the trial. When I arrived, some very pleasant and professional members of the Chicago Fire Department were just completing their observations that she had not suffered a coronary but only a fainting spell, due to momentary bradycardia. The judge also ordered, finally, the return to me of the $5.5 million plus interest still owing from the seizure of the proceeds of the condominium sale in New York six years before. We returned to the hotel and the next day to New York.

The judge robotically pretended that there were incontestable convictions in the case and declared that "I scratch my head that you did this," although by now nothing could be clearer than that I had not done it. But, as with the father of the narrator in *Brideshead Revisited*, fixated on little fictions, the charade had to be seen out to the end. And as if relieved to be at the end, the judge stood to say "The court wishes you well, Mr. Black," and then sped from the room. I don't think she believed any of it at the weary end of the long case (any more than the programmed government witnesses had), but was committed to the script, and some of counsel thought she might still imagine I was guilty of something. There was a brief, concerted media attempt to pretend Barbara was medically in extremis, but, as with so much else, we overcame that.

Of course, though a disappointment, after so many, it was not a surprise and there finally was an end in sight, and my financial resources, from one source and another, were accumulating. There would be the vexatious nonsense in Campbell's Posnerian, Red Queen court to deal with and a few other legal harassments and opportunities (including the delectable prospect of the libel suit against Bower), but after the tempests of the last eight years, these would not be too challenging. I was pushing forward with a number of business relaunch projects, and also another book, that I had long researched and began writing just before the end of 2010. This was my strategic history of the United States, almost certainly the last serious historical writing effort I will commit to this country. I will finish a draft of it before returning to custody although the bibliography will probably have to be furnished later by Internet, as most of my sources were shipped back to Toronto. The idea for the book arose from my lectures on U.S. history to rather sophisticated audiences of lawyers and former political activists in prison.

This is no place for a synopsis of it, but it starts with the genius of the colonial leaders, especially Benjamin Franklin, encouraging the British to evict the French from North America, and then persuading the French in helping to evict the British from America, and goes in fairly clear stages up to the end of the Cold War. It is a great story of a great nation, now in decline, but not necessarily or even probably irreversibly so, and fortunate, at least, that its decline coincides with the Spenglerian collapse of Western Europe, Russia, and Japan; while China and India, the fashionable coming powers, each has nearly 900 million peasants living as they did 3,000 years ago.

Even at this late stage, the imperishable animosity of frustrated officialdom abides. A security provision has been invoked to prevent me completing my sentence at Coleman Prison, because I might supposedly be a physical threat to the two correctional managers there who gave false affidavits against me. In that now so outworn Canadian branch-plant reflex, there have been challenges to my suitability as one of their honorees, because of this American pseudo-legal charade. It is often hard to believe that these cowardly ambushes will ever end.

As I conceded in Chapter Five, I had had both the commendable and sinful versions of pride at the onset of these events, have tried to retain the first, and have almost scourgingly confessed and repented the second. In the jungle of large competing beasts where I have been, what happens generally reflects the correlation of forces and sagacity of the combatants and is usually what should happen by laws of that world. I had an haughty spirit, though some of it was optimism and inexperience. I fell, and perhaps my downfall was partially deserved. But the heavy punishment I have received for crimes I did not commit was not deserved, though the chastisement has been educational. Soon it will be on to pastures new, and this terrible American midnight will swiftly fade away. I'm still here, and in all respects I still care about, I will be back, soon.

New York, New York, July 31, 2011

The End

AFTER A GREAT SURGE OF INTERVIEWS with the international media, including some peppy pre-taped television sessions, I packed up what little I had left in the United States and checked out of the Mark Hotel after four months. Our Toronto driver was easily able to put our last American belongings into a minivan Barbara had bought to convey her splendid dogs around, and with the usual intense grilling from Canada Customs and Immigration at Niagara Falls, he completed my unvexed Dunkirk departure from America (except for my own person).

This was the only time since I bought my first house in Palm Beach in 1980 that I had no property or assets at all in the United States, apart from a few shareholdings. It had been a relatively orderly withdrawal, and while it was a sad end to what had at times been an ambitious, or at least fond, reconnaissance in the United States, after all I had been put to, I was relieved and happy to have evacuated as much as I had from a country I no longer, on balance, liked. I regarded the United States with disappointment, and with fear of its sadistic leviathan of a justice system, and with a complicated combination of dislike, resentment, and affection for the America I had once known.

There were touching partings, and a birthday dinner. There were many friends, but the affair with that country was over and I will never feel at home in it again, though I assume I will return eventually. Time heals most wounds.

Barbara and I flew to Miami on September 5. On the plane and on my last night before what I publicly called my victory lap began, I wrote my review of Mark Steyn's pungent book on the decline of America, for Roger Kimball's *New Criterion*. Barbara had arranged for the driver that had usually brought her to visit me in Coleman, to take us from the hotel to the prison in Miami. I telephoned the British consul in Orlando, Dean Churm, just before departing the hotel, to arrange Barbara's collection of my new passport. He had been heroically cooperative at every stage. Barbara sat with me for forty-five minutes, most of it in boiling heat outside the front door, as they would not admit us. We were subjected to the presumptuous lethargy of the Bureau of Prisons receiving a new consignment of the unfortunates to their vast, inept indifference. Barbara was finally sent away. I watched her car disappear; even after all these years and sadnesses, and although this really was the last lap, it was one of the more piercingly poignant moments in this entire narrative.

I had done what I could, including launching this book to good reviews and brisk sales, against the well-intended advice of many, including counsel, as likely to be seen as a rude digital gesture to the U.S. justice system at an untimely moment. But that was exactly how I wished it to be seen; when in revolt (albeit compliantly) against an evil, such gestures are the only weapons and must be used at the most telling, not the most convenient, times. I had also put everything on as unworrisome a financial footing as possible. And now it was one more turn of the dehumanizing rote of American punishment, in this case of a non-offender, but one unit of the inmate commodity of its hopeless and gargantuan prison industry.

After being locked for a time in an isolation cell, I was submitted to the fetishistic search: standing completely naked for ten minutes before examination of my "private area" (behind the scrotum), and bent over for further exploration. Official curiosity about my contours *au naturel* was never more than perfunctory. My preparatory experiences at Coleman, and distant recollections of boarding school, made it fairly humdrum, and my unclothed presence has never been sufficiently noteworthy to incur embarrassment or incite much enthusiasm in any company.

I was processed by a rather jovial Haitian and assured that Miami FCI was the five-star hotel of federal prisons and was conducted to my quarters. Unlike at Coleman, it was not judged necessary to handcuff me for this arduous promenade of a few hundred feet. The initial impression of it is of a junior college built around a lake with gulls, coots, and a few feral cats about. But Receiving and Departing gave directly into the unit to which I had been assigned. I was conducted into a large, two-storey cellblock, crowded and noisy, like a penitentiary. My destination and new home was a cell with a heavy metal door, bars on the window which commanded a panoramic view of a crabgrass greensward six feet wide and three feet deep, in the gentle shade of a high concrete wall. Barely perceptible above was what Oscar Wilde famously called "the little tent of blue prisoners call the sky."

We were locked in the cells in a noisy ceremony of authoritarian loudhailing and clanking keys and bellowed instructions, for counts, and from 9:40 p.m. to 5:30 a.m. There were three metal bunks, vertically stacked, with paper-thin mattresses and pillows, a sink and toilet, and about twenty square feet of free floor space.

This seemed a distinct step backwards, even from Coleman, and far from the BOP's most swank accommodation. I learned that it had been a medium-security prison and when redesignated as a low, the BOP did not apparently spend a cent on the conversion, or even use the artisanal talents of the inmates for that purpose. The name and timetable were changed but the physical circumstances were not.

In the cell with me were a Boston chef and part-time land developer, and a roustabout journeyman Maine labourer and drug dealer. Both were quite interesting in different ways. The chef was a rather cultured man and a great culinary talent, and we quickly made arrangements for a sharp gastronomic uptick from what was on offer in the dining hall. African-American inmates controlled the kitchen and inventory shrinkages were prodigious. Our suppliers arrived, almost every day, bearing whole stocks of bananas, loaves of bread, and remarkable quantities and varieties of meat, butter, cheese, and vegetables. They ordered the food for the compound, including the so-called correctional personnel, and graciously added the requests of their more reliable customers. The methods of acquisition and delivery of contraband sometimes went to astounding and amusing lengths of ingenuity, but it would be indiscreet and potentially harmful to friends left behind to relate them. Having nothing to read on the first night, I took out *A Tale of Two Cities* from the library and reread it.

A brief visit to the dining hall was sufficient to deter me from returning, other than for Thanksgiving and Christmas, just to show the flag, and the annual dinner for the practising Roman Catholic community. On that first night, the food was challenging even to my relatively tolerant palate. But more of a problem was the unrelievedly correctional ambiance: ill-favoured BOP guards plying between tables shouting a countdown for swallowing our dinners. One, with huge hands but thick, short arms, appeared to be at an earlier stage of evolution. The ensemble of the fare and the authoritarianism were unconducive to the appetite.

There were no facilities at Miami for taking forward my very tentative studies of the piano at Coleman, nor an air-conditioned room for exercising, and outdoor exercising in the steam-washed lint-air of the Florida summer was out of the question, unless I obliged my oppressors and succumbed to suicidal impulses. I took to walking around the lake for two hours every evening, but was waylaid by seekers of financial advice (which usually transmogrified within a couple of laps into requests for tangible assistance). I soon tore a meniscus in my knee, diagnosed through email by my doctor, having been driven by my customary hypochondria to think it might be phlebitis. Exercise then became rather sketchy for some months.

While I found being locked in disconcerting, and it made me almost claustrophobic, it had its advantages: relative quiet and the ability to leave the light on to any hour. All of us stayed up late. The chef was, he told me, bisexual, and had been convicted of downloading child pornography. In fact the porn included photos of himself as a child being abused and molested as a youth. This was not disputed at trial and he authorized me to write this. This is a fabricated offense – the downloading of pornographic material which is disgusting to most people, but which the accused did not create or distribute and from which he has not profited. This offense began as political pandering to the hysteria about pedophiles, but like so much of American criminal justice, it quickly got completely out of control. Far more people than the legislators or jailers had imagined were dragged from their private delectation of these perverted salacities, and not sent for treatment, but put on the U.S. justice conveyer to prison. There, their alleged maladjustments are exacerbated by verbal and sometimes physical abuse throughout their draconian sentences, followed by lifetime supervised release, a nightmarish overlordship, as a part of systematic stigmatization. Certainly, my friend the chef had never been and would never be a threat to anyone.

He was an urbane and delightful companion throughout our time at such close quarters, without an awkward or inopportune moment. The other occupant of the cell was a roughly-cut drifter, who had frequently lived without a fixed, or even any, address, eating berries or the recoveries from garbage cans (dumpster-diving), and on one memorably described occasion, a seal that he killed with a rock. We often played chess in the evenings. He was an erratic player: clever combinations but frequent blunders, and the annoying prison tendency to play with his mouth as much as with the pieces, with irritating attempts at verbal gamesmanship. I generally won, but he had his moments.

He had become quite prosperous in the marijuana business, but then lived ostentatiously, was denounced, as almost all such people are, and was, with his common-law wife and nephew, thrown into prison. His children were removed from the care of their mother's parents when their grandfather, in a drunken stupor, fell on top of one of them. It was an atavistic socioeconomic echelon I was aware of but had not much known at such close quarters. He was an engaging, and in his earthy way, a memorable character.

Unlike the chef, he was rather complicated to live with; he frequently suffered, which meant that we suffered from, his bouts of prolonged and extreme flatulence, which were a serious olfactory challenge in such a small and indifferently ventilated enclosure. The BOP officially disapproved of three-man cells as illegally over-crowded, but in this facility, never seemed to get rid of them entirely other than just before regional inspections. The former marijuana dealer's nights were so sterterous, it was often impossible to sleep through his snoring, and his manner of arising (early to get insulin for his diabetes) was startling, even after it became familiar. We were unlocked at 5:30. He opened the door to the already noisy unit at around 6, and in ill-fitting underwear and night-shirt, peered myopically at the distant clock with his facial and cranial hair jutting and thrusting wildly in all directions, like a cave monster from one of the Grimms' more disturbing fairy tales.

One day I returned to find the cell reeking like a methane factory, and he soon moved out to an under-occupied cell. The regime then played one of its silly games, by moving a new arrival into our cell, despite a policy that opposed such over-crowding and the close proximity of under-occupied cells. We transitioned them out quite quickly, usually with their own emphatic agreement, but it was an irritating little flourish of caprice from the custodians. A new cultural or behavioral misfit was dropped among us every few days for over a month, toward the end of my sentence.

Because my case had been highly publicized, and it was so rare for anyone to be released early in his sentence by a unanimous verdict of the Supreme Court, I was something of a celebrity when I arrived. There were some veterans from Coleman also, and my columns from the *National Review Online* and the *Huffington Post,* and even my books, had readers around the compound. A few of my U.S. political commentaries were even appreciated by some of the education personnel.

I adopted my Coleman policy of being courteous with everyone, which is generally my practice in all milieus, and of being revealing with no one. I did nothing to affront the regime and stayed almost completely clear of it. No one bothered me, though the routine operation of the system and the grating foibles of some of the correctional officers assured constant minor abrasions and reminders of the prisoner's status as an outcast at the bottom of society, with, effectively, no rights at all, except subsistence, and even that eroded by degradation, mindless regimentation, poor food, and sometimes endlessly deferred medical attention. This is particularly bad in the American system, where so many inmates are innocent or mentally incompetent, and almost all are grossly over-sentenced. (A special category is the substantial number of inmates who were paid by prominent drug-related convicts to drive trucks or boats laden with drugs to prearranged busts, to gain sentence reductions for the drug-lords for identifying other felons; promotions and good publicity for the corrupt arresting officials, and a life of subsequent comparative ease for the fall-guys after a few years in a low-security facility. Everyone is happy and it is consistent with the integrity of the rest of the system.)

I tried hard to get a job in Education, and even in the chaplain's office. But Education was convinced it already had ideal personnel (although it was in fact in shambles and soon had to import the pleasant lady I worked for in Coleman to clean it up). The whey-faced, effeminate Baptist chaplains were as bigotedly anti-Roman Catholic as the ogre at Coleman (and the Jewish chaplain that replaced them was not much better). I had signed on for a one-afternoon-a-week yard job, when one of a colourful pair of Argentinian banker brothers, former partners of the Royal Bank of Canada in Nassau, prevailed on one of the education officials to engage me as an advisor on organizing history courses.

In practice, this meant sitting in the library reading room from 12:30 to 3:00 on weekday afternoons when I did not have a visitor, and being available, usually for very pleasant historical discussions with the supervisors, who were historically literate, and could not have been more considerate. I spent the rest of my time reading the newspapers and high-brow magazines I received, to inform the three columns a week I wrote, and whispering with people who sought me out for an infinite number of conversational ends. I generally slept most mornings, again, when there weren't visitors, and sent emails in the late afternoons, and went outside between 7:00 and 8:30, usually in the company of some interesting fellow prisoners. I read and wrote in the evenings after my chess-playing cell-mate moved out. As my last act of the day, with my earphones in for the excellent Miami Public Radio classical music station, I did the *National Post* or *USA Today* crossword puzzle in bed by my night-lights, half-propped on my double-stuffed pillow, as there was insufficient room between the bunks to sit up. Compound merchants provided me with extra pillows, including for the wafer-thin mattress, but the bedding was always uncomfortable and it was impossible to sleep uninterruptedly for more than forty-five minutes.

I made steady progress with the columns, which apparently on good weeks grew to a combined weekly readership of about four million, and I received a huge volume of readers' letters, via Joan Maida. All messages, including a large number from readers of my books, were answered, though, with limited access to the email machines, it was a challenge, and

Joan and I sometimes had recourse to generic messages. But the traffic was very inspiriting and with the writing, enabled me, in large measure, to live psychologically outside the prison. (When responses were very heavy, Joan, whose son is a rock star, would write: "You've gone platinum.")

As the *Huffington Post* (which I had never read) was intrinsically less serious than the *National Review* or *National Post,* and Arianna Huffington herself, whom I had first met through Andy Warhol in 1981, was more of a promoter than a steady editorial voice, I sometimes used the HuffPost for what was called in Victorian times, "mere controversy." The only defense I had against enemies, as well as my only psychological escape from my confinement, was my pen.

The first of the three *Vanity Fair* profiles I had had, and by far the nastiest, had been from Duff McDonald as the original Hollinger story broke in 2003. He was a journeyman writer now with *Fortune* on a shared Time-Warner–CNN website. He hadn't really followed my case, but returned to it and called me a "thief," proudly recording that he had written a "vicious" piece about me in VF. I worked into a HuffPost piece a reference to McDonald as a flaccid writer with "the personality of a turbot and the professional ethics of a baboon," and sued him for libel in Canada as well. The word "thief" was retracted, my modest legal costs were paid; and McDonald pseudo-jauntily emailed me that he enjoyed being compared to a turbot.

Almost all the time I had been a home-owner in Palm Beach, I had detested the utterly moronic local newspapers, which had been relentless and often gratuitously hostile throughout my legal travails. They imputed to me some views of Palm Beach that slightly spooked some of my so-called Palm Beach friends (of the variety that made Barbara feel lonely during her time alone there). It gave me the opportunity to pen a slightly florid physical and sociological portrait of the town, and throw in a violent side-kick at the local press as so unutterably vapid that a foretaste of them might, I wrote, have caused Gutenberg to do a rethink before inventing the printing press.

Time Magazine, in one of its fatuous, under-researched, puff-piece cover stories, praised the U.S. attorney in New York, and in their story about bringing down corporate wrongdoers referred inaccurately in two places to me. *Time* acknowledged that I had dismembered the initial case but still kept me in the castigated ranks of the rightful targets of prosecutorial wrath.

The biggest blow was reserved for the biggest target and most destructive enemy. Rupert Murdoch had terminated twenty-five years of our cordial coexistence when my legal problems broke in 2003 and ordered the most malicious possible demolition of me throughout his media group (as was later revealed in the British press inquiry and in *New York Times* interviews of former *New York Post* writers). He responded very disingenuously to my initial message to him (the last ever sent for me by dear Rosemary Millar in London), and did the same with overtures on my behalf from Henry Kissinger, Seth Lipsky, and others.

His newspaper operations in Britain finally received unintimidated scrutiny for the first time after it came to light in 2011 that some of his journalists had been routinely hacking the telephones, not only of the Royal Family and other swells, but also of, it seemed for a long time, an adolescent kidnap victim who was subsequently murdered. The British establishment had shamelessly kissed Murdoch's under-carriage like the colonel in the film *The Bridge on the River Kwai* for forty years. It had tacitly hoped and expected that Murdoch would win the price war he unleashed against the *Telegraph*. Almost to a man and woman, they had constantly fulfilled George Bernard Shaw's description of the British *haut bourgeois* reflex to lick the boots (not to mention other places) of those more powerful than themselves, as they ground down those beneath.

All the time I had known Rupert he had sniggered with well-earned satisfaction at how he had cowed the British upper classes. He has thought all his conscient life that they lorded it over his father and over Australians generally. The standard London toff sophistry was "I thoroughly disapprove of Rupert but I quite like him." I told the eminent source of this particular formulation that he recognized Murdoch for the sleazy and vicious Anglophobe that he was, but that Murdoch was such an influential media owner in Britain that my lordly friend would follow the familiar British practice of appeasement. I received the customary constricted glare of the British upper classman caught in po-faced pusillanimity: with their usual admirable talents at improvisation, he professed to find me impertinent.

All Britain was suddenly outraged by the wickedness of News Corporation, which had reduced successive British prime ministers to doting courtiers, as revelations of the company's outrages were confessed and babbled forth. A tidal wave of sanctimonious claptrap broke over the arrogant facade of Murdoch's company. He tried his usual tired wheezes at defusing embarrassments: he had known nothing of it (that would be aberrant of course, he micro-managed all the principal titles in important policy matters, as we knew from watching them closely, sometimes working with him, and from the many former *Times* people we had employed).

At the first Parliamentary hearing, he arrived shored up on each upper-arm by minders, and drifted through the hearing like a semi-animated waxen dummy, almost a criminal accused feigning senility. He was only one remove from deposed Egyptian president Hosni Mubarak, who appeared at his trial on a stretcher with his sunglasses still on and tubes protruding from his nose.

Rupert went through his whole hackneyed repertoire. He purported to close the offending *News of the World*, Britain's largest-selling newspaper, quite spuriously, since after what he took to be the decent interval, he launched the *Sunday Sun*, which was all the *News of the World* had been anyway. He called upon the families of the hacking victims, making pre-emptive financial settlements and claiming to be enduring the greatest humiliation of his life. He also said he set great store by an investigation by his independent directors: my former colleague Andrew Knight, an avaricious Vietnamese lawyer (Vin Den) who once sought to represent me in immigration matters, and former U.S. prosecutor and New York schools chancellor Joel Klein. Representing this obsequious trio as possessing any moral authority opposite Murdoch was a Brobdingnagian canard.

The highlight of the initial Parliamentary hearing was when a Canadian anarchist, Johnny Marbles, threw a pie at Murdoch, and his agile young wife, Wendy, intercepted it and propelled it back into Marbles' face. Scotland Yard did its usual methodical job and kept rounding up Murdoch acolytes. They don't bully the entourage of a target into logorrheic outpourings of choreographed inculpatory perjury as American prosecutors do, but they elicited some good back-biting. Now that nasty head prefect was receiving a good caning in front of the whole school, the former followers and new boys were cheering. Ironically, they confirmed much of what Rupert had always said about the hypocrisy of the British upper bourgeoisie and nobility.

I wrote as much in the *Financial Times* in August 2011, and described Murdoch in Clarendon's famous summary of Cromwell as "a great bad man." I again credited him with being history's greatest media proprietor, and required myself to give Murdoch the benefit of the legal doubt. The affiliated publication, *The Economist*, which has been generally hostile to me throughout my legal problems and had an astonishing esteem for Breeden until that became an embarrassing misconception, generously wrote that I had uttered *le mot juste* on the subject. (In that irritating, naïve, and priggish British manner, it couldn't resist adding that I was between stints in prison, as if, in America, that condition automatically denotes wrongdoing.)

News Corp.'s outstanding bid for the public shares of Sky Television had to be abandoned (I wrote that it should be allowed to proceed – those shareholders who wanted the offer shouldn't have been punished for Murdoch's thuggishness). James Murdoch virtually scuttled out of England. And the *New York Times* led fierce agitation for prosecution in the U.S. under the egregiously extra-territorial Foreign Corrupt Practices Act. There were questions about industrial espionage arising from the years earlier complaints of New Jersey website operator Floorgraphics, with whom News Corp. had settled a lawsuit for $29 million, and then bought the complainant company for an undisclosed sum, damping down the controversy.

If Murdoch could firewall it in England, he wouldn't suffer much inconvenience personally, and his company was flourishing. If American prosecutors could find some way to sink their teeth into it, Murdoch was finished; they would tear his company to pieces, and at nearly eighty-one, he would not physically survive such an assault. In our own relations, he exacted his revenge for my relatively positive FT piece by banning Andrew Roberts' favourable reference to this book in his Christmas book recommendations in the *Wall Street Journal*; and presented a rogues' gallery in the WSJ of "Corporate Criminals," in which my picture appeared next to Bernard Madoff's, and I was tagged with my original sentence, as if the Supreme Court vacation of the counts (on which the *Journal* had so graciously congratulated me), had not occurred.

As I explained to Barbara, vulnerability to skyrocketing blood pressure required me to take the gloves off with Murdoch this time. Even I had been gentle with him, despite all his outrages, and, it must be admitted, because for most of the time since 2003, he was too invulnerable and my condition was too parlous for any worthwhile countering. I replied to this shameful misrepresentation in the *Journal* in the *Huffington Post*, assured that it would be published in all editions and that there would be many knock-on postings to other sites. The column is in the Appendix, and it makes the point that bold and brilliant media owner though Murdoch is, he is a psychopathic hypocrite and a terminal cynic who cares for no one, exhibits dangerous sadistic instincts, such as his continued assault on me long after I had ceased to be a competitor of his, double-crossed almost every political benefactor he ever had except Ronald Reagan, and had overseen an empire that conducted a lawless assault on the integrity of the media and public tastes wherever and as long as he had been in the industry. (The *Wall Street Journal* is the only quality product he has not debased.) To the best of my knowledge, no News Corporation media outlets have referred to me since.

He returned to Westminster for the Leveson Inquiry on April 25 and 26, 2012, and was much more robust than at his first go-round. He lay about him, disparaging John Major, Gordon Brown, Andrew Neil, and others, and accusing his former corporate lawyer of lying. It was a vivid, though not overly credible performance, but one or two contradictory emails, and many had already turned up, could cause him severe problems, since his disclaimers of any knowledge of the conduct objected to could not be believed by anyone with the least acquaintance with his company's operations.

Murdoch will limp through his problems. But it is a heavy blow, especially as I well know how neurotically sensitive he is to any public criticism (he used to phone me from all over the world to complain about puckish asides even in the *Spectator*). This was why he could never accept that we had won the price war, and had confected the myth that the pressure of that war had driven me to rob from my company to maintain my supposedly extravagant lifestyle (which was one of grinding poverty compared to his).

The other enemies who had improvidently appeared or abruptly turned their coats in this squalid cataract of venality and treachery had not all prospered either. The pitiful fate of Christopher Browne has been mentioned.

Breeden's career as a hedge fund manager, like his pretense to being Mr. Corporate Governance, had collapsed. He and the decayed servitors Seitz and Burt, who descended into an obscurity more sombre than would have awaited them if they had not been dragooned by Breeden into becoming useful idiots in his infamies, also had to pay my large libel award. Two weeks before I was released from prison, on April 18, the Supreme Court of Canada unanimously upheld my right to sue Breeden and the others for libel in Canada. We already had an enforceable agreement, but this reinforced it and required the other side to pay my legal costs. After all this, it was pleasing to win a clean sweep of the justices in the highest courts of the U.S. and Canada, and send the bill for the Canadian action to my erstwhile tormentors. (I believe no one else has ever succeeded before both Supreme Courts unanimously, but I've been more litigious and litigated against than most.)

The lesser ranks of apprenticed commercial treason, the Parises and Healeys, don't merit revisitation. Fitzgerald has a black eye. There isn't much I can do about Kravis or Posner except lay out the facts for those who are interested. Strine's throbbing little ego propels him along and he turned up in Toronto to give his Mr. Peepers-as-bantam rooster shtick, and a follow-up interview with the ultimate corporate governance lickspittle, the *Globe and Mail*'s Jacquie McNish. I "warned Canada" about Strine in the *National Post*, citing the $2 billion of shareholder value that he had flippantly vaporized in our case. At dinner on that visit, Strine criticized my libel action and was, for once, silent, when informed of its success. I concluded my column with the comment that he should have bells on his head like medieval lepers to warn the unsuspecting of his approach. In my very last days in captivity, we launched the long-prepared offensive against the saprophytes who had destroyed our Canadian companies and pretended to be emissaries of the stakeholders. It is the reckoning at last; their peaceful, greedy blood-sucking is over. As my father used to say quoting Browning, "It's a long lane that knows no turning."

As at Coleman, there were many pleasant and interesting people among my fellow prisoners in Miami, although the majority were small cogs in the eddies of the drug business, alleged child-pornography downloaders, another Damon Runyan assortment of scoundrels, and not a few other outright innocents (in criminal terms). In such company, humour is precious. Among the outrageous rogues and fraudsters, one who stood out and was even humorously diverting, was the self-righteous scammer who bills himself as a serious investor and actually just printed counterfeit corporate bond certificates of non-existent municipal utilities in his basement and he and his wife sold them until the rightful thing happened and they were both sent to prison (where he continues to try to part commercial fools among the inmates from what little money they have left). More sad is the rather cultivated art thief, who can't help himself, doesn't really mind prison, knows he belongs there, and compulsively steals food from the kitchen and gives it away. If released, he will soon be sent back. Everyone has a story, most of them false, but most of them worth a listen, if only just as a yarn. An eminent and very educated former Caribbean drug lord near the patient end of a 30-year sentence (brought down because he refused to return a cent or squeal on anyone) was a very rewarding conversationalist. So was another man of the same former occupation, apprehended when he bought two submarines from the Italian government to facilitate his maritime importing business. The best apparently true story was from the man whose legal problems began when the Food and Drug Administration thought his refrigerated storage business had rats in it. A 300-pound African American female agent was deployed to sit on a folding chair in front of what was thought to be the rats' access to a space between the walls. The agent dozed off, a giant Norwegian freezer rat emerged, 15 inches long plus a one-foot tail, rose to its hind legs, cheeped noisily, awaking the agent who leapt from her chair, concussed herself on an overhead pipe, fell down unconscious, soiled herself, and caused my friend to be charged with negligently causing a sanitary hazard and putting a federal agent at risk. He had other legal problems, but this was an inauspicious start.

The personnel of the regime were, on balance, a little less overbearing than those at Coleman, though there were the inevitably belligerent and stupid officers, such as a chubby, stentorian guard who liked to tell us we had no rights. A group of my discontented fellow residents, before I arrived, dumped some excrement in the air conditioning duct of his little official festering place. It took him an inordinate time to notice the deterioration in air quality, and he was known thereafter to the Hispanics as "Cacita," "the little shit," a fair description in all respects and in any language (though I must say that my last dealings with him were quite civilized).

This time round, there was no novelty nor any suspense about the end of it. I would leave May 4 (the official departure date was May 5, but that was a Saturday and that section of the BOP does not work on weekends, so I got a final small edge in my long and unequal tussle with the Bureau).

In my last three months, I gave a weekly Tuesday evening class in American history to an intelligent group of volunteers, frequently using my strategic history book (my next book now being edited), as my main source. These weren't the education assistance challenges with high school drop-outs I had had at Coleman; the feedback and debate were more stimulating, but there wasn't the tremendous satisfaction of helping give very disadvantaged people a place on the up-escalator they had never believed existed.

I used every available visiting day, and reluctantly had to decline offers of visits, including from Britain and Australia. One particularly appreciated visitor, even more for the affecting trouble he went to than because of his great eminence, was Henry Kissinger, who arranged to give a speech, pro bono, in Miami, to have an occasion to visit me. His chosen day was not one for visits to this facility. That was never a problem at Coleman, which a couple of times kindly accommodated the British consul in Orlando, Dean Churm. At Miami, the warden, whom I never met, convened his leadership group, my informants told me, deliberated lengthily on this challenging question, and solemnly declined Dr. Kissinger.

He came anyway, on a regular day, chartering a plane to come from Nassau, and we had a delightful conversation. Some other very busy people did me the honour of a visit, despite all the BOP's vexations, including Mark Steyn, Ann Coulter, and Brian Mulroney. The visits were a marvelous escape to the world, family, and to friends and a free future, though I often found the departures sad, especially Barbara's.

The highlight of each week, apart from visits, was a private film showing that a considerate and enlightened member of the education personnel put on for a couple of friends and me of historic DVDs, including fascinating studies of aspects of the Third Reich. As with the films my fellow tutors and I could watch at Coleman on Saturday afternoons, they were a few hours when it was possible to imagine I was leading a normal life.

The final days seemed to accelerate and were eased along by some interesting commercial possibilities that arose. Barbara and I could scarcely believe that it was finally ending. There was intricate planning for this book, in the U.S. and the UK., and for the next book; for the legal counter-offensives, including a final assault on the remaining convictions, and on the pestiferous remnant of our legal assailants in Canada; a huge range of financial scenarios and a vast horizon of possible future writing. I had a lengthy and somewhat emotional farewell in my unit on the evening of May 3, and after an ingenious decoy motorcade sped downtown followed by the press, American Immigration officials Diaz and Carrera (who have asked to be named) conducted me to the plane chartered for the occasion. (It had all been agreed with both for governments months before and I was mystified by the press controversy in Canada.) I left Miami for Toronto, with Barbara, come to bring me back, as she had brought me. I looked down on America as I departed it, and watched what was long the closest to a land of my dreams fade away with relief, but with sorrow. Almost all my thoughts and efforts now were devoted to resuming the offensive. There remained little need, after nine purgatorial years, to parry or duck slings and arrows any more.

I had returned to my home in Toronto after many vicissitudes and from the farthest corners of the earth, spanning sixty years, but never so thankfully, nor after such a long or wrenching absence, as in the golden sunset of May 4, 2012, after five full years in or on the edges of the American Gulag.

I watched the sunset with its unearthly dying hues of pink and yellow, as I had from the same place with every gradation of fear and hope and pleasure and sadness since often unhappy, far-off days. I wandered through my house, stuffed now with the evacuated instances of life in other decades, countries, and occupations. It was gratifying to see my libraries almost exactly as I had left them, to see that faithful people had drawn the curtains every morning and evening and dusted my tens of thousands of books, every volume placed in a particular order by me, all through these five Babylonian years. Dozens of cartons of papers cluttered many rooms, after having been ransacked for years by prosecution lawyers and the parasites of endless litigation.

And I returned to my chapel, and surrounded by the documentary and iconic stages of my gradual adherence to Rome, I gave a silent, prosaic but heartfelt Te Deum in thanks for the sacred gift of life, delivered at last from evil and from squalor. I was thankful above all for my marriage, for my family, friends, and for the privilege of being able to fight for my life in a good cause, and even for enemies it is so easy and just to despise.

In the final twilight of this unimaginable day, which began in a foreign, tropical prison cell with the ear-shattering pre-dawn wailings of an ostensibly female African-American correctional officer, I stood before my very large likeness of the almost sainted Newman. I recalled silently reciting, in the same place, at the worst of this long cycle, his lamentation that "blessings of friendship...came to my great joy (and) went to my great sorrow." Now I thought of his timely admonition "in our height of hope ever to be sober, and in our depth of desolation never to despair." Mine was now, at last, a life restored.

Postlude: Reflections on the American Justice System

THERE IS UNDOUBTEDLY A VERY LARGE number of capable and completely honest lawyers in the United States, and of courageous and incorruptible prosecutors and judges. The country has a storied and often distinguished judicial tradition, and the guaranties of individual liberty and due process have inspired and helped positively to reform the world, and have been defended and promoted, under provocation, by the steadily mightier and generally victorious armed forces of the United States, incurring, when the Civil War is included, the highest and noblest sacrifice of more than 1 million Americans in mortal combat.

A serious examination of the U.S. legal and justice systems would be a massive undertaking, and apart from undisputed statistics, my experiences of it are all that I can write about with authority. Such an undertaking is desperately needed. The statistics cited and basic comparative research indicate that in liberalizing the world, the U.S. has steadily undermined its own tradition of respect for individual liberty. As this narrative illustrates, in the shadow of "Freedom's Holy Light," terrible abuses and hypocrisies are commonplace in the justice and custodial systems of the land that most noisily and relentlessly celebrates its illumination.

One of the great ironies of modern times is that the United States is the author and champion of triumphant democracy, but is not now a very well-functioning democracy itself. From the end of the American Revolution in 1783 to the end of World War II in 1945, democracy in the world had progressed very little, other than in the sense that the populations of almost all countries had increased. The British Isles, America, Switzerland, and the Netherlands and parts of Scandinavia were the only democratic jurisdictions in 1783. And they remained so, with the additions of the British Dominions which had been settled in the meantime, and the expectations of France once a republic was restored, in 1945.

But when the American strategic leadership concluded that the Cold War was a battle for survival with a deadly rival, and billed it as a fight to the finish between Godless communism and the free world, the pro-democratic pressures generated by the United States became irresistible even though the free world included such doubtful adherents as Franco, Salazar, Chiang Kai-Shek, the Shah, Syngman Rhee, and the bemedalled juntas and Generalissimos of Latin America. The Free World gradually became overwhelmingly, relatively free, and came to include the largest emancipated colonies, especially India, and almost all of formerly Soviet-dominated Europe, almost all of Latin America, and many of the great states of East Asia, including Japan, Indonesia, South Korea, Malaysia, Taiwan, and Thailand. Many of these new democracies have innovated brilliantly, such as Germany's entrusting to independent investigative commissions the question of whether there are grounds to prosecute, as opposed to what has become the mockery of the U.S. grand jury system.

The end of the Cold War was the greatest, most bloodless strategic victory in the history of the nation-state, as the Soviet Union imploded, China became a capitalist though authoritarian state, and international communism collapsed, without a shot being fired between the great protagonists.

Unfortunately, as that has happened, the United States ceased to attract huge numbers of very talented and motivated people fleeing oppression, as fewer people in fewer countries are being oppressed, and the choice of destinations for those who are has become so much larger. And the United States's own institutions have largely calcified. Now at least twenty countries have a superior education system to the U.S., at least twenty a superior health care system, at least twenty a superior justice system.

The American justice system has become a gigantic legal cartel, where there are too many laws, and the legal profession is a terrible taxation on the country. The U.S. is a terribly over-lawyered country (having about half the lawyers in the world, over a million) where legal bills routinely consume $1 trillion a year, almost as much as the GDP of India. Most judges are ex-prosecutors, and so are a very large number of legislators. The criminal justice system has become a prosecutocracy where more than 90 per cent of indictments are successful. The country has become a carceral state detaining an obscene number of its own citizens, and a vastly disproportionate number of the world's prisoners, often in conditions that are shocking, especially in such a rich and generous-minded country, so proud of its humanitarian traditions.

An astounding 47 million Americans have a criminal record, albeit most of them are for minor offences long ago, but about 750,000 people are sent to prison in the U.S. every year and the country has six to twelve times as many incarcerated people per capita as other wealthy and sophisticated democracies: Australia, Canada, France, Germany, Japan, and the United Kingdom.

THE PLEA BARGAIN

THE AMERICAN CRIMINAL JUSTICE SYSTEM is based on the plea bargain, which is hideously abused, and it could not possibly be otherwise. Prosecutors single someone out and threaten all sorts of acquaintances or colleagues of the target with prosecution if they do not "cooperate," which in practice means producing inculpatory evidence against the target, with negligible concern for its veracity, and an immunity against prosecution for suborned or extorted perjury.

In our case, the prosecutors negotiated the evidence with their main witnesses, and knew perfectly well how they were "preparing" the testimony of witnesses. As the reader has seen in this narrative, and most readers would have observed the same pattern elsewhere, all the important government witnesses in our trial were press-ganged into pre-agreed, catechetical evidence, which was torn to pieces and debunked by defense counsel. They did this in exchange for immunities from prosecution on charges that would have been spurious (except for Radler), but dangerous in this system; and in the case of the one person who actually had committed crimes, a very soft sentence in consideration for his confession and denunciation of former colleagues he surely knew to be innocent.

It is terrifying to see how the prosecutors can, as they did with Burt, Kravis, and Thompson in our case, intimidate prominent and successful people who in other contexts would have some moral authority and no absence of goodwill to me. And it was very disturbing to see what a bully-boy like Sussman thought nothing of threatening to do to my mortgagee in Palm Beach if he renewed the mortgage and denied Sussman his false claim to St. Eve that I was in default of my bail conditions. This was the basis of his demand that accordingly, my house should be seized, bond rescinded, and I should be sent to prison at once, without the annoying formality of a trial — with no critical comment whatever from the world media. It was disturbing to see his threat of prosecution of the acting president of Hollinger Inc. (Don Vale), if he so much as entered the U.S. to testify that I had pre-cleared removal of the famous boxes with him. These outrages are routine and mention of them brought no response even from a relatively fair-minded judge, as St. Eve was.

The plea bargain is nakedly the exchange of altered testimony for varied sentences. It generally starts well down in an organization and brings irresistible pressures to bear on people unable to sustain themselves psychologically or defend themselves financially against such an onslaught — until that person promises to inculpate a targeted higher-up.

The process goes through an organization until sometimes scores of intimidated or suborned people are accusing the chosen target. It is an evil and profoundly corrupt process, and is not reconcilable with American notions of law. Every informed person in the country knows that the criminal justice system is based on officially sanctioned fraud and intimidation, and that the federal court houses are silent and the courts are empty because almost no one can go the distance with the government, and that there are tens or hundreds of thousands of innocent people in

U.S. prisons because of the false confessions and accusations they are forced to make. Everyone who knows anything about comparative law knows that prosecutors in Britain and Canada, to name only the other jurisdictions I know well, and which have their judicial failings too, would be disbarred for the imposition of what are routine plea bargains in the United States. But almost no one says anything about it.

I was the real target in our case, because of my comparative prominence, and to get at me, it was necessary to allege a scheme and take down some close associates with me. We were all innocent, all benefited from the destruction by our counsel of the government's rehearsed and mendacious witnesses, but because of one of a number of catch-all statutes that make conviction almost inevitable, we were all convicted and all but one of us were sent to prison.

The Prosecution Advantage

It is terribly important that I make the point that I was not especially singled out for this assault. This is the routine modus operandi of the U.S. prosecution service. It does what it wants and persecutes whomever it wishes for as long as it likes.

As the Chief Justice of the United States said at our Supreme Court hearing, whoever a prosecutor takes against is a criminal, and under the statute that convicted us, anyone could be so designated, charged, convicted, and imprisoned. The Chief Justice made the point that even an intelligent member of the public would not know when he was committing a crime under the honest services provision, and one of the other justices said that a derogation from honest services could probably be alleged against 90 per cent of the U.S. workforce, at any time, or about 140 million people.

In my own experience, it will be recalled that I did not benefit from the constitutional guaranties of the grand jury as assurance against capricious prosecution; the ban on seizure of property without just compensation; the guaranties of due process, access to counsel (of choice), an impartial jury, prompt justice, and reasonable bail. A statute that should have been completely inapplicable was invoked, ex parte, to seize my assets. Illegal telephone intercepts had informed prosecutors I had earmarked for the retainer of my counsel of choice, who was thus denied to me. And the affidavit that was used to justify the seizure is one that the jury judged to be, and the prosecutors should have known to be, false. Again, there was no sanction for this from an indulgent court presided over by an ex-prosecutor, any more than for the endless inaccuracies the prosecutors inflicted on the court.

The government rehearses its witnesses, whom the defendants cannot interview, intimidates them with threats, and shelters their extorted testimony with guaranties of immunity, but any contact from the defense is deemed to be witness-tampering and obstruction of justice.

To establish federal jurisdiction in cases like mine, charges are ridiculous interstate technicalities like wire fraud. Charges come in large bunches, as jurors are normally reluctant to give their government nothing at the end of a long trial.

Notice is given very late of documentation to be used; false accounts of prosecution interviews are handed over, which cannot be shown to interviewees; and the prosecution speaks last before the case goes to the jury, which generally has to rely on its memory of the proceedings, no matter how long and complicated the trial. The prosecutors routinely indict amid a media extravaganza that would be considered grossly prejudicial and grounds for a mistrial in any other legally civilized country. I was accused of money laundering and, inter alia, racketeering, and the preposterous concept of civil racketeering. The law of the United States is not only an ass; it is an ass spavined beyond recognition. It pains me to seem ungrateful to the Supreme Court for overturning the abusive measure that was used against us; but I can't help wondering where that court, amid the vast media and professional cult of its composition and the philosophies of its members, has been while the Bill of Rights has been put to the shredder for decades.

The court unanimously gutted and rewrote the statute that sent my co-defendants and me to prison for more than two years, but it had struck down the statute more than twenty years before, and it had been instantly replaced and continued to be used to send the innocent to prison for decades until we brought it back to the high court.

The importance of the Supreme Court among the equal branches of the federal government has risen because of the moral abdication of the

Congress and President. The other branches could not face the issue of abortion, or of the illegal immigration of approximately 15 million people, or of acute income disparity, or of health care for the country's 45 million uninsured. But they and especially the Congress have been responsible, instead of addressing these and other urgent public policy concerns, for an assault on civil liberties vastly beyond anything ever entertained by the government of King George III, against whose heavy-handedness about two-thirds of Americans revolted in a seven-year war of independence.

As legislators and presidents have copped out, the executive branch's prosecution arm has become an enforcement elite, holding hands with ex-prosecutors in the Congress and the judiciary, and progressively terrorizing more and more people, including senior members of the Congress and Administration. They are a state within a state, which, in 2007 and 2008, destroyed the career of a five-term senator, by recourse to fraudulent evidence, and of the former chief of staff of the vice president, on a charge by the special prosecutor (the inevitable Patrick Fitzgerald) who was soundly thrashed in the media. Prosecutors are not now checked or balanced.

And beyond that, although this is not a political science treatise, Congress is now mainly composed of rotton boroughs controlled by particular interests. It has become a vast and sleazy earmark-trading, log-rolling, and back-scratching operation that all polls indicate disgusts the great majority of Americans. The core of the American system, identified with the unexampled rise of the country and the ideals that give the Americans their sense of exceptionalism and is much of what they have fought for in their many wars, is the concept of individual rights, due process, and equality before the law. This has putrefied. American criminal justice is a conveyer belt to imprisonment or the place of execution, festooned with a few trimmings and a bit of window dressing of a just society of the rule of law.

Prosecutions in the United States have become steadily more numerous and are almost always at least partially successful, and the political class, from left to right, claims success against crime through righteous severity. The public scream for blood; judges are named or elected on the basis of their propensity to aid the prosecutors and become, with few exceptions, the Zeitgeist in robes.

In our case, settling, or "cooperating," as it was euphemistically called (it should have been called co-conspiring), was a win double for almost all involved. Lawyers and consultants and often their clients, while helping the U.S. government assault me, could enrich themselves splendidly by leeching onto Hollinger. In my wildest nightmares, I had never believed that so many people of relatively serious mien could so easily be tainted and bent. But very few missed an opportunity to vacuum up the money. In this case, "following the money" would create a stampede in which many would be trampled underfoot by the surge of mindless seekers of their own enrichment. Courts support and are part of the legal cartel, and piled costs onto our companies until they were bankrupt, and the devil take the public shareholders in whose name all their infamies were executed. It was disgusting.

When the recession came in 2008, many large U.S. firms paid promising graduates $100,000 or more per year not to sign with any other firm, so confident were they that the fat days would soon return. (They did.) Various American and Canadian lawyers advised me to sell all my assets pre-emptively, to be able to pay the legal bills for as long as possible.

When a defendant in the U.S. concludes that his defence was deficient, and files an action after the trial to emphasize a relevant point that was overlooked and could perhaps have affected the outcome of the trial, the cartel rallies and the prosecutors argue the outstanding qualities and unsurpassable legal expertise of the defence counsel whom they have defeated. It is the litmus test of the solidarity of the profession, and never fails. In the end, the law is a medieval guild and the clients are the material the guild works with, like shoemakers' leather, and usually with almost as much impersonality.

The victims of the uneven grinding of the U.S. justice system are not a political constituency. The United States has 5 per cent of the world's population and 25 per cent of the world's imprisoned people (about the same numbers as apply to its GDP); it has nearly five times the population of the United Kingdom and yet, at 2.45 million, nearly forty times as many imprisoned people. The masses of America are not as free as they think, and again, America does have almost half the world's lawyers.

CANADA AND THE UNITED KINGDOM

CANADA IS A SMALLER JUNGLE than the U.S. with smaller beasts in it; the lawyers are generally not as competent as the Americans, and the Canadian judges are more servile marionettes of the media faddists. But the rules and practices are fairer and the results less savage than in the United States. The Hollinger Inc. cooperation agreement, which Walker, Strosberg, and Kelly negotiated with Sussman, showed the ease with which Canada slides into its branch-plant status with the United States even in the adoption of its sleaziest practices. The agreement spared the company prosecution (for which there was no conceivable cause), ostensibly in exchange for information. In fact, Sussman instructed the "management," which happily purloined, destroyed, and mislaid my documents, seized personal property of mine, and did everything inhumanly possible to defame and aggravate me. This process culminated under Walker in the obstruction nonsense, and under Voorheis in the Mareva outrage, both blessed and sanctioned by Canada's very own Richard Posner *toute proportion gardée*, Colin Campbell.

Despite these and many other failings, the hand-holding in Canada between the prosecutors, judges, and legislators, is not as intimate or cynical as in the U.S. Not so many judges are ex-prosecutors and crime has not been so shabbily politicized. There has not been the same drive in Canada as in the U.S. to end penal reform, and turn the convicted into a permanent wretched band of outcasts inaccessible to social utility or respectability. The Trudeau era defined more socialistic public policy as a raison d'être of Canada vis-à-vis the United States, albeit largely as a blind for buying Quebec's adherence to federalism through colossal largesse disguised as uniform social programs. This has helped Canada avoid the barbarity, demagogy, and primitiveness that have afflicted American justice. So has the abolition of the death penalty, which has achieved a morbid, fetishistic status in the minds of many great Americans, including the forty-third president, who seemed to find rejecting commutation requests from the denizens of death row one of the great pleasures of being governor of Texas.

It is very worrisome to see the Harper government trying systematically to import American severities of longer sentences, reduced efforts at rehabilitation, more prosecutions, and the extreme discouragement of continued contact with family and friends (not even a handshake with a visitor—I lived from week to week on the permitted arriving and departing hug and kiss with Barbara). I will do what I can to oppose this. Margaret Atwood and I have gone joint account in buying a cow from the "historic herd" adjacent to the Kingston penitentiary, which is being dispersed to expand the prison, to admit the anticipated droves of people convicted of habitually unreported crimes. Kafka, Orwell, and Koestler never tried this one, and we are referring to Canada, not the gulags of Euro-totalitarianism.

As in many other spheres, Canada is a junior league for the colossal engine of injustice Americans know little of as they stand at public events, hands over their hearts, bellowing out their splendid anthems, apparently never wondering how the legal system of Madison, Jefferson, and Lincoln permutated into this giant cesspool of officious legal hypocrisy.

My one parallel experience with British counsel was with a libel firm, where the partner I was in touch with inadvertently sent me an email intended for one of his colleagues, suggesting that they could demand £500,000 to start and wouldn't have to do much. I found British solicitors pusillanimous, pettifogging, and grossly overpaid when I lived there, and I would always be prepared to fear the worst of them.

I think their judges are better than in Canada and the U.S., less hypnotized by the media and more fluent, of tongue and pen, and their barristers are often impressive. Again, I had occasion to deal with many of the most prominent when I was at the *Daily Telegraph.*

The Custodial System

THE CRIMINAL JUSTICE SYSTEM IS as much devoted to the creation of an untouchable caste of the wretched, tainted with conviction, in a sort of Roman imperial lottery, as it is with condign justice and the gathering of as many people as possible into a normal diverse, law-abiding polity. The regular visits of the director of the Bureau of Prisons to Congressional subcommittees, which I read with avid astonishment when I was one of his guests, are an exercise in Orwellian newspeak. Po-faced Congressmen listen credulously as the director describes an elfin workshop of happy inmates singing "hi ho" as they proceed inexorably toward rehabilitation. The whole system is a tenebrous and deadly thicket, designed to ensnare, benumb, and break all those who blunder into it, whether by misdirection, victimization, or genuinely criminal or sociopathic behaviour. As one who rushed home early from school to watch Army—McCarthy hearings on television in 1953, I felt it grimly nostalgic to read the director of the BOP's bucolic fables before the legislators to whom he is ostensibly responsible.

BOP Director Harley Lappin told a sub-committee of the House Committee on Appropriations on March 10, 2009, that "the mission of the BOP," apart from protecting society by confining offenders, is "to provide inmates with a range of work and other self-improvement programs that will help them adopt a crime-free lifestyle upon their return to the community. As our mission indicates, the post-release success of offenders is as important to public safety as inmates' secure incarceration." He assured the Congressmen that there was a "plethora of inmate programs, including work, education, vocational training, substance abuse treatment, observance of faith and religion, psychological services and counseling, Release Preparation," etc.

I was in one of the BOP's premier, deluxe prisons. Only one or two of the teachers actually educated anyone (though they and the educational administrators did genuinely care about advancing the student inmates). The tutor-inmates did the teaching, though we were compelled to attest otherwise. The vocational courses were of the most superficial nature and did not qualify anyone to go forth and earn more than the minimum wage, thus reducing competition for the unionized building and maintenance trades that control those occupations. Almost all the release preparation was done by inmates such as me giving advice for job resumes and career choices at variance from the pap uttered by the BOP, which effectively advised its charges to bag groceries and not think that they could be making one hundred times as much dealing drugs.

There was no manual available to inmates to move on to higher education by correspondence, so I bought one myself, walked dozens of students through it, and in a number of cases helped arrange the financing for going into university by correspondence, in the absence of any official encouragement.

There are wellness facilities, but it may surprise Director Lappin to find that religion is not a BOP program. At that, the BOP chaplain, as was mentioned in Chapter 15, was a specialist in divining whether inmates had taken a piece of bread from the dining hall and in discriminating against all but his sect of white Baptists. He helped banish our priest when he declined to apprehend those removing food from the dining hall, saying "I don't work for the BOP, I work for the Pope." He tried to bar me in consecutive years from attending the annual Roman Catholic luncheon on Ascension Day.

I have nothing but compliments for what I have seen of the U.S. probation service, in Chicago and Palm Beach, but the post-release rules are designed to maximize the likelihood of a return to custody. If I, for example, went to dinner in the home of a friend where there was a licensed gun, whether an antique, or a hunting rifle, in the basement or attic and without ammunition, I would be liable, while bonded, to be sent back to prison. Charlatans like Congressman Danny Davis called his act expanding availability of extended halfway house accommodation and home confinement "historic, landmark" legislation. I assisted many inmates in trying to take advantage of this opening, always to get back the stone-faced response that such a reduction of prison time would be "against policy."

Almost all the "jobs" at the facility apart from cleaning the washrooms and mowing the lawns, making furniture, and educating inmates, and some kitchen duties were the most absurd make-work, involving five minutes a day, if that. And the anti-substance abuse program was a series of self-confessions and denigrations interspersed with puerile sing-songs. Three-quarters of the participants were there to reduce their sentences. The educational, psychological, and most of the rehabilitative staff tried to encourage the inmates, but many of the correctional officers were devoted altogether to aggravating, provoking and belittling us. Gentle and thoughtful officers are often reprimanded or demoted for their civility.

The great majority of convicts return older but no less vulnerable to those temptations that ensnared them, justly or otherwise, than when they first arrived. (I have even urged former drug dealers to become bail bondsmen – they can take from the same huge pot of drug money, have a good income, and be legally employed in a growth industry.)

More than 90 per cent of the country's residential mental patients have just been tossed into the prison system. Each prisoner costs directly about $40,000 annually to detain, and the total annual cost of the country's prisons is about $250 billion. Imprisonment has become a discreditable substitute for racial segregation, chunks of the welfare system, treatment of mental illness, and amelioration of the effects of drugs on American society.

Unlike other advanced countries, all U.S. prison systems (in all jurisdictions) are bent on retaining as many prisoners as possible for as long as possible, and to maximizing the prospects of repeat offenses. Like other businesses, the prison industry seeks endless expansion. Former public-sector prison executives join private-sector prison companies and work their connections assiduously, like retired generals and admirals in defence industries. The political intitiatives of the correctional officers' unions are very sharply focused and effective.

The correctional officers are poorly paid and smuggling is widespread. There is endless investigation, shuffling of personnel, and charges of financial and not infrequently, sexual, indiscretion. Graduates of the higher security facilities adjacent to our low security prison tell me those places have higher levels of violence (and therefore more respectful correctional officers), and have stabler populations. Almost anything is available there: a menu of alcoholic drinks for in-cell service, cellphones, etc. There is obviously substantial inventory shrinkage out the back of the commissary as well as through the kitchen, and the BOP personnel can lay it all off on the inmates. And it would be counterintuitive, ahistorical, and astounding if there were not massive kickbacks on arm's length purchasing. The whole ambiance of the BOP is corrupt, and the inmates are not the chief source of it. From all accounts, the states and counties, more strapped for funds, are worse.

In California, the number of prison employees multiplied from 1977 to 1998 by six, and of prisoners by eight, to 160,000, more than the combination of France, Germany, the United Kingdom, and the Netherlands, which together had more than seven times as many people (and in each case a lower crime rate). Since then the number of California's prison employees rose from one-fourteenth of the state's employees to one-third, and the prison budget has exceeded the state's university budget for many years.

Other advanced countries concentrate on constructively training and releasing non-violent offenders as quickly as possible. Senator Jim Webb of Virginia, in his essay "Criminal Injustice," makes the point that as the countries mentioned above have from one-sixth to one-twelfth the number of incarcerated people as the U.S. per capita, either Americans are more naturally addicted to criminal behaviour than other countries, which is nonsense, or the other countries are indifferent to crime, which is also nonsense, or the U.S. overcharges and oversentences, which is obviously true.

Up to the 1970s, the United States was a reasonably liberal country in custodial matters; it had about as many imprisoned people per capita as Australia, Canada, France, Germany, Japan, and the United Kingdom; had a prison system that gave some attention to rehabilitation; and had an active prison reform movement.

The U.S. media, both in information and entertainment, have for decades hyped the problem of violent crime out of all proportion to its real importance. This was almost the only way for local news programs to attract viewers. Whatever is the principal local crime of the day leads the news, even if it is the brazen and frightening theft of a five-cent cigar. CNN's Nancy Grace has never to the best of my knowledge tackled any crime other than kidnapping, rape, and murder. She always presumes guilt and sometimes seems to demand the execution of suspects before they have been charged. Her voice resonates in my thoughts as, speaking about some untried individual, whose guilt is a matter entirely of television speculation, she inquires yet again in her mellifluous southern accent of another prosecutor: "John, can you tell me why this man/woman/child/sheepdog has been allowed to roam the streets without being put on a register/picked up for questioning/jailed/flogged/put to death/drawn-and-quartered years ago?"

Trial by media is taken for granted in a society whose prosecutors, unlike those of any other civilized country, give inflammatory press conferences asserting indisputable guilt long before any juridical assessment. Virtually all politicians went berserk hammering crime as an issue, starting in the sixties. Liberals like Nelson Rockefeller and Robert Kennedy and Bill Clinton were as oppressive and demagogic as centrists like Richard Nixon and conservatives such as Ronald Reagan and George W. Bush. Absurdly repressive laws tumbled forth; mandatory minimums, the three-strike rule, truth in sentencing (which eliminated parole), and the artificially inflated mystique of the death penalty as a macabre ritual of moral and social purification. Then Texas Governor George W. Bush took to publicly mocking death-row petitioners when they asked for commutation.

The consequence of these developments was that designated crimes received draconian sentences, with no discretion to the judges to alter them. A third conviction, no matter how trivial or far apart the convictions were, is now grossly overpenalized, and no federal sentence can be reduced by more than 15 per cent. Despite all the fear-mongering about violent crime, for the first time since Prohibition, there are more Americans imprisoned for non-violent than for violent crimes. Only 4 per cent of three-strike prisoners in Los Angeles were convicted of violent crimes. In the whole country, less than 15 per cent of prisoners are repeat violent offenders.

Prison reform collided with the feminist movement, which claimed that violence against women was out of control and was tacitly sanctioned by a large part of male America. The bloody riots in Attica and San Quentin prisons in the early 1970s caused the conflation in the public mind of prison reform with black radicalism and the blood-curdling ambitions of black extremists including Bobby Seale, Eldridge Cleaver, Angela Davis, and H. Rap Brown, and brought down a heavy backlash on all accused and confined people. The crime rate declined because the twenty years of Reagan, Bush Sr., and Clinton were basically full-employment, inflation-free decades of huge job creation (an astonishing 47 million net new private-sector jobs), and because police techniques were improved and numbers of police increased throughout the country; and perhaps most importantly, the population aged, losing some of its taste for the exertions of crime as it did so. The politicians sold the public the bunk that they were responsible for bringing down crime by conducting a war on crime and a war on drugs based on more arrests, high conviction rates, more imprisoned people, and longer sentences.

Since the 1970s, the public has happily approved countless state referenda authorizing bond issues for building new prisons. When this cut into welfare and education budgets, and the public in many states voted down the special prison-building bond issues, the state governments gave long-term lease-backs to private-sector companies that built the prisons and guaranteed them a high occupancy level and rental payments whether the facilities were full or not. This saddled the states with an effective average interest rate of 37 per cent, but excused the politicians from an insupportable referendum or the dread appearance of being soft on crime.

Tens of thousands of shareholders of Wackenhut and Corrections Corporation of America and other publicly traded prison companies demanded more and more prisons and prisoners and steadily harsher sentences. The prison companies hire former prison and security officials as executives and directors, including former directors of the FBI and CIA. The correctional officers are militantly organized, and their unions are rivaled only by the National Rifle Association as the most effective political lobbying organization in the country in election campaigns over the past thirty years. They and the politically potent police unions lead the political agitation against any sentencing reform and in favour of longer sentences and more prisons.

Whenever (and however) a prison correctional officer dies in the line of duty, it is treated in all prison facilities as a re-enactment of the perils of the flag at Mount Suribachi (Iwo Jima), though prisoner violence against guards is now quite rare. Deaths of prisoners are officially ignored. There is a deliberate, implicit effort within the system to present all convicted people as indistinguishable from killers and rapists; we are all miscreants outside the law. Overflow prisoners of state systems are shipped out from one state to another and often housed in abominable conditions. The nation's county jails, bulging with nearly a million prisoners, are just dustbins of gangs and miscellaneous alleged law-breakers, huddled in appalling conditions amid shockingly high levels of violence.

Once someone is in the web of the accusatory system, all the spiders swarm and tangle and sting the dazed newcomer. And once in the custodial system, the dehumanization is almost relentless but usually trivial: the caprices and discourtesies and inanities of a system that is mindless though largely in the hands of decent, limited people. And the orchestrated public attitude has been one of Salem-like ostracism. This will subside, as the frailties of the system become better known and the absurd numbers of potentially stigmatized people exceed society's powers of misplaced righteous ostracism. None of this is to whitewash the misdeeds of a great many convicted people. But for such an advanced and brilliantly innovative country, it is an amazingly clumsy, unjust, and corrupt desecration of the nation's ideals and squandering of its human resources.

The prison industry has become a gigantic Frankenstein monster, feeding on public ignorance and paranoia, political corruption and cowardice, and with the rails greased by the endless media blurring of the line between the suspected and the convicted, and the entertainment industry's portrayal of uniformly heroic police, prosecutors, and judges, and monochromatically horrible and psychotic criminals. In an earlier time, the media lionized defence lawyers such as Perry Mason as much as civilized police officers such as Joe Friday in *Dragnet*.

I am a fierce defender of private and even public property, but their theft or misappropriation is not morally equivalent to the physical battery of a person. What is required is to rewrite the laws, impose the rule of law on the conduct of prosecutors, and revive the Fifth, Sixth, and Eighth Amendment guaranties of due process, no arbitrary and uncompensated property seizure, a serious grand jury assurance against capricious or vexatious prosecution, access to counsel, an impartial jury, prompt justice, and reasonable bail. This will require profound procedural changes, an end to the plea bargain in its present grotesquely deviant form, and rousing the Supreme Court from its star-gazing self-absorption and rubbing its collective, exalted nose in the Bill of Rights, which it has complacently allowed the prosecution to smother and perforate for decades, as softly and thoroughly as moths.

Treatment of Minorities

The cruelly unintended consequences of the great society programs of President Johnson were to break up low-income families. Men were financially incentivized to drift around impregnating as many women as possible, an activity that was generally seen as a tribal rite of masculine virility and feminine fertility anyway, and so, culturally commendable, as indeed it is when done responsibly. The randomly seed-scattering fathers return on "Father's Day" when the monthly welfare cheques arrive, and the golden youth conferred upon the nation in the flowering of this ethos is generally advised, I learned from interviewing many scores of exemplars of it (and not all of them non-whites), to be a chip off the old block: proliferate and rip off the (white) system. When the utility companies threaten to cancel the electricity, cut off the telephone, and repossess the appliances, Mama needs some drug sales to keep the home fires burning, and Daddy, the proverbial "motherfucker," is nowhere to be found.

The country's incarceration policy has the benefit to the government of removing almost a million unemployed African Americans and at least half a million ethnically diverse correctional officers from the unemployment statistics. Treating white-collar crime like violent crime appeases the left and slightly balances the racial numbers in the prison system. The percentage of African Americans in the prison system is more than three times that in the entire population, and there are three times more African Americans in prison than in higher education. I was caught in this in part because of the refusal of the U.S. legislators to deal with the issue of the ballooning unequal distribution of wealth. I cannot be described as a socialist in anyone's wildest imagination, but I feel there should in a decent society be limits to such disparities.

It is a scandal that there are 30 million or 40 million poor people in such a rich country, and as hard-pressed as the U.S. now is by international competition, it should not, as a strategic as well as a moral issue, be squandering so much labour in social inequities and in a hideously expensive, unjust, and ineffectual correctional policy. Until late 2008, there were hundreds of billionaires in the country, and millions of millionaires. Instead of a serious public policy debate about how to lift the socio-economic floor, this disparity has led to a totemistic assault on a few prominent people who misstep into the cross-hairs of the system: Leona Helmsley, Michael Milken, Martha Stewart, Alfred Taubman, and perhaps even me.

This shabby tokenism is the best American official policy has been able to do to address income disparities. The symbolic indictment of a few wealthy people, like sentencing the swindler Bernard Madoff to an imbecilic 150 years of prison, is just a placebo, a rabble-pleasing gesture.

Amy Bach, in her very scholarly analysis of the U.S. criminal justice system, *Ordinary Injustice: How America Holds Court*, recounts how legal aid lawyers bid for the government business, and the lowest bid takes, and how underfunded they are and how they have almost no time for individual clients. They are paid and evaluated by the court and always deferential to the prosecutors. They settle almost all cases because they are paid by the number of cases they address, not by the results or quality of service. Scores of my students and other acquaintances told me of the sequence: all assets are seized as ill-gotten gains, microcosmic outrages compared to the illegal seizure of my Park Avenue proceeds. The public defender is imposed, counsels the necessity of pleading and then purports to have negotiated a relatively light arrangement. Once in court, the prosecutor asks for much more than has been agreed, after the guilty plea has been entered.

The judge is a rubber stamp for the prosecution service, and the public defender, when interrogated by his client, shrugs and says the prosecutor broke his word. The entire system is a mockery; the public defender is a Judas goat restraining the fiscal burdens of sending 750,000 more unfortunates off to prison each year (more than three times the entire prison populations of France, Germany, Japan, and the U.K. combined, which have 110 per cent of the U.S. population), by persuading the untouchables not to exercise their fictional, though constitutionally guarantied rights. I saw them every day in St. Eve's court; the wretched refuse from the municipal corrections centre in their orange jumpsuits, heavily shackled, being treated as mere freight by their slovenly, undemonstrative, court-appointed "defenders."

The notion of one's day in court is threadbare enough for those who can afford proper counsel. It is a complete fraud for the tens of millions who cannot. Ms. Bach estimates, after very professional and thorough research, that the 47 million convicted felons in the U.S. includes very many relatively minor offences such as disorderly conduct and impaired driving. But it is 15 per cent of the population, and tens of millions of these people were put away for a significant time.

Two of my fellow tutors and I had the privilege of reviewing films for possible educational reuse, at screenings on Saturday afternoons, and one of them was Henry Fonda's performance in *Gideon's Trumpet*, about a poor white man who secured, through a hand-written petition to the U.S. Supreme Court in 1963, the right of all Americans to have criminal counsel if they are unable to afford it themselves.

The film ends with a fine comment from then Attorney General Robert Kennedy, after eminent lawyer (and future Supreme Court Justice) Abe Fortas won the argument for Gideon. And the implication is that this was a great legal breakthrough. As has been described, the real result of this gallant effort is the colossal and contemptible scam of the U.S. public defender system. These sociologically deeply rooted, economically related problems will require more than reform.

MORE THAN 5 MILLION African Americans have been disenfranchised because of their legal records, and we are now getting back to the level of black disenfranchisement that prevailed prior to President Lyndon Johnson's Civil and Voting Rights Acts of 1965. The per capita number of blacks to whites in prison is nine times greater. Nearly half of American black males between twenty and twenty-nine are under some form of criminal justice supervision. In practice, where it is decided whether indicted offenders will be streamed through federal or state courts to prison, the African Americans are almost invariably fed in overwhelming numbers to the harsher federal system. No one audible seems to take it amiss, including most black leaders, among them the president and the attorney general.

THE WAR ON DRUGS

CRACK COCAINE DEALING WAS UNTIL RECENTLY treated up to one hundred times more severely than powdered cocaine. Because crack is heavily used by African Americans, this law is, in effect, another racial discriminatory measure designed to create an immense racial imbalance in the makeup of the prison population, as it has. These inequalities are becoming steadily more extreme along racial and economic lines. After slavery, what Lincoln called "the bondsman's 250 years of unrequited toil," and a century of demeaning and often brutal segregation, which Lyndon Johnson called "a century of 'Nigra, Nigra, Nigra,'" despite all the progress and thirty months of an African-American president (who attracted the votes of ninety-nine per cent of African Americans) and

Attorney General, but who have only just reduced the disparity. The disparity between crack and powder cocaine offenses went from 100 to 1 to 18 to 1, which is still outrageous. Drug laws are being used to extend the history of the unequal treatment of blacks in America into a fifth century.

The American black problem is showing a satanic tenacity and ingenuity. And it must be said that this is due to the failings of the whites. There is too much black victimhood and no shortage of black racism, and there has been great progress, but the legacy of slavery is fiendishly persistent. And the even larger Latin population fares little better.

It is indicative of official American arrogance at its most inflated and obtuse that instead of suppressing drug appetites among its dilettantish bourgeois youth and degraded underclass, or using its immense military strength to secure its borders without strangling legitimate commerce and tourism, it has purported to require other countries to eliminate supply. This is a potentially terminal hubris. The United States has reduced Mexico to a state of virtual civil war and escalated the wars in Colombia and Afghanistan, claiming to fight drugs at their source, rather than in domestic U.S. demand.

The drug war has been a perfect illustration of the strength of supply-side economics, as the price has come generally down through greater supply, improved product quality, and rising demand, despite the imprisonment of more than one million small fry which are easily replaced by the drug trade kingpins. The War on Drugs has cost $1 trillion, and within America has almost nothing to do with violence. Drugs are involved in one-third of property crimes, but only 5 per cent of violent crimes. People growing a thousand marijuana plants get mandatory life sentences. Now that the methamphetamine drugs can be concocted by amateurs without importing or growing anything, alternative policy options will *finally* have to be considered. But all the current administration's senior appointments in drug enforcement discourage any optimism that more enlightened policies await.

The Congress declined money requested by the Clinton administration for more methadone treatment, though it is fifteen times more effective than imprisonment for reducing drug use, and hugely less expensive. The War on Drugs has been a complete failure, except for the beneficiaries of the proliferating prosecution, prison industries, and the principal drug suppliers and traffickers themselves.

Marijuana is the largest cash crop in California, and 42 per cent of Americans use it at some point in their lives. Prohibition was a howling success compared with this, and Al Capone and other great liquor profiteers of that era were pacifistic Sunday school teachers compared with the leading Mexican and Colombian drug lords.

Manipulating the System

WHAT WAS UNUSUAL ABOUT OUR CASE was not the brutality of the U.S. prosecutors and their trans-border accomplices, or of the legal and judicial personnel they infected for their purposes. It was that instead of settling on the target themselves, they allowed Richard Breeden to do the targeting for them, and he was on a mission and thought the battle won when he set the cross-border legal and regulatory apparatus on our backs. No one made any allowance for the fact that we were not guilty; that it would not be possible to seize or strangle my ability to pay for a legal defence from assets situated outside the United States; that Radler's crimes had not been concerted with the rest of us; or that we would have counsel able (Miguel Estrada and David Debold) to raise the constitutionality of the government's habitual procedure and evoke the issue to the country's highest court, far from the fetid, ward-heeling political bazaar of the Chicago Federal Courthouse, made no less sinister by the Little Red Riding Hood demeanor of St. Eve and the sterterous and insolent biases of Posner.

It followed the normal pattern for several years, as more and more people were cajoled or dragooned into the swelling lynch mob, gorging themselves on the hundreds of millions of dollars that erupted from the Hollinger piñata when they had ruptured it. As has been recounted, Strosberg, who didn't need any instruction from the Americans about how to stuff himself like an Alsatian goose (financially and otherwise), paid himself more than $1 million for four months of unsuccessful legal work, approved mechanically by his local Windsor Law Society. Walker, after nine months at $100,000 a month for non-executive meddling and diddling, took another $600,000, which he brazenly demanded from Peter White in face-to-face straightforward negotiation for his vote for approving the privatization for which the shareholders had been clamouring, after having feverishly tried to sabotage it for many months. Richter, the Ravelston receiver, having insanely responded to the U.S. charges, eagerly accepted the yoke of Sussman's despotism like the others, milked Ravelston for $8 million, pledged $7 million to the U.S. government and unspecified restitution (of which the United States will never see a brass farthing), promised questionable evidence that was ultimately not admitted, and even deprived the small-income pensioners of a large chunk of their accumulated pensions, which I hope to make good from my own resources when I dispose of the accursed idiocy of the Mareva. Voorheis drained Hollinger Inc. of more than $5 million as he drove it toward and into bankruptcy, and was re-elected by Richter on Sussman's orders a few months before the rich company we had left was capsized into the bankruptcy they had so wantonly engineered, against all their and their legal sponsors' promises at the time of their engagement, not to mention their duty to the stakeholders, and the spun sugar candy of the Law Society's ethical standards.

Of course this was just an hors d'oeuvre compared to the orgy of wickedness in America. O'Melveny & Myers mined the Breeden lode in Hollinger International for more than $150 million, had the effrontery to bring in one of their partners as an expert witness in our trial, then po-facedly piggybacked on our appeal to the Supreme Court, where they represented Geoffrey Skilling and gave him, as they had at trial, a half-hearted argument, to avoid too great a solidarity with us, in defence of the fact that they had raped Hollinger for five times as much as they were able to wring from the writhing financial corpse of the former Enron boss.

Having championed honest services against us, when receiving $150 million for acting for the Hollinger International Special Committee, O'Melveny's didn't raise it at the Supreme Court, though honest services was the only reason they got to that court, following us. Finally, since the petition from Skilling had been accepted on the honest service issue, the bench asked the O'Melveny partner who was arguing the case about that statute, and received a rather underwhelming response. When we won,

O'Melveny launched a public relations blitz claiming credit for it. This is not entirely atypical of the ethics of the profession that is responsible for keeping the rule of law alive and prosperous and respected in America.

In the zeal of its agents to crucify me, the U.S. government brought financial sorrow to scores of thousands of homes in all parts of the United States and Canada. It showed no concern for those whose innocence was never in question, and is the principal author of their loss of $2 billion. But even as the continental official scorched-earth policy destroyed the small shareholders' interest, I had partially rebuilt my means from the large gains on the value of my homes, and, ironically, from the gains generated by ruthless Radlerian management of the private newspaper companies that had been accumulated fraudulently by him but approved of as untainted in the deal the prosecutors made in exchange for his inculpatory perjury against my co-defendants and me.

Of course I had lost my biggest asset with the ruination of the Hollinger companies, but not so much that I could not pay to fight my way through the case and to restore my financial and moral position when the war was over, provided some public curiosity persisted about my side of the case, and my liberty and other non-Hollinger resources substantially survived the trial. They did. Punishment before trial was never contemplated by America's founding fathers.

When I adjusted from my precipitate downfall from my previous position and accepted the inevitability of criminal prosecution and the possibility of imprisonment after Strine and the OSC stopped my efforts to salvage something for all the shareholders, I discovered my new, involuntary midlife vocation. If I could resist the tyranny and corruption of the U.S. prosecution service, I might be able to show, regrettably, but more persuasively if unjustly imprisoned, that the plea bargain system has become, in Brendan Sullivan's phrase, "evil and repulsive." The almost universal practice of exchanging false testimony against targeted victims for relative leniency will rot the judicial soul of America.

While I was at it, I could get in a pretty good shot at the short-comings of the corporate governance movement. Chris Browne, who had held a continuous press conference celebrating his great victory over me for eighteen months, revealed in occasional grumpy interviews later that he was just as hostile to Breeden and Paris. He had precipitated a disaster for his investors (a loss of more than $150 million from its highest price and $70 million on his cost) and other Hollinger international investors. A war of attrition affects all combatants, not just the party initially attacked.

The great newspapers and renowned commentators, even those most sympathetic to me, said nothing publicly about the rot of the system, though some, including Bill Buckley and George Will, spoke out publicly for me personally. Mark Steyn, Robert Tyrrel (*The American Spectator*), Roger Kimball (*The New Criterion*), and Seth Lipsky (*New York Sun*) were exceptions and warned darkly of where the plea bargain system could lead.

America has witnessed, almost silently, the triumph in its justice system of persecution abetted by denunciation. The Constitution has guaranteed rights that, if exercised, would overload the system, as defendants normally just give up after being treated to the pre-trial antics of prosecutors. And as has been described, most defence lawyers aren't really barristers; they get a slight reduction in sentence by sparing the prosecutors the tedious formality of a trial. The U.S. justice system had many fewer plea bargains and more integrity fifty years ago, apart from in racial matters, and the trend is dangerous for every person in the country.

The executive community of America has been cowed. It may have been unbecoming for J.P. Morgan to say, "The public be damned!" publicly, but so is the mousy, insincere, and platitudinous do-goodism of almost all of America's current leading financiers. The notion of a day in court in matters involving the federal government is illusory, and in criminal matters is, as has been extensively described, a farce, a national rodomontade, in fact. Justice is blind, but not in the sense intended. The law that rules is not the law that is written, much less celebrated, and there are obviously scores of thousands of innocent people in American prisons, and hundreds of thousands of grossly oversentenced convicts.

They are not yet numerous or respectable enough to constitute a strong political constituency, but they will be. The impoverished simply are ground up mechanically by the system, and don't even try to fight it because they don't have the means. The middle-class small business owners and professionals fight according to their means, but almost all are ruined, imprisoned, disgraced, and personally broken. Even the wealthy victims –

Michael Milken, Alfred Taubman, Martha Stewart – go quietly off to prison, like children to be thrashed at the woodshed, and return chastised but say nothing of the system that assaulted them. Whatever might happen, I resolved that the same would not be said of me.

It is not the least irony of contemporary American affairs that as the United States has successfully and bloodlessly crushed the Communist illusion of a command economy, it has delivered its justice system, the moral centre of any democracy, to a command requirement for more and more convicts to fill the prisons that the unjust laws, the stacked deck of criminal procedure, the biased judges, the stifling ambiance of prosecute and convict and elect, the bloodthirsty media, and the sucker deals with rapacious private prison companies, prison industry suppliers, and the Luddite prison workers unions, and the rights-blind police associations, produce and require. The law, an occupation I almost pursued, is a very necessary but much-debased profession. The putrefaction of the U.S. justice system is rampant and, I repeat, is a mortal threat to the integrity, institutional soul, and historic purpose of America.

In the piping days of my great affair with America, I thought it a rough-and-tumble legal system that might have the upside of motivating and sharpening the American elites and workforce. Perhaps it was, once. Now it is just the noisome slough of moral carrion, ruined lives, and broken faith. It inspires not Olympian competition or the splendour of a great jungle beast, but rather disillusionment, misery, and ultimately, revolt.

Altruistic or meliorist instincts cannot be relied upon to achieve much politically in the United States. Fundamental change is accomplished by the forces of the economic and political market, harnessed or guided by talented and often benignly devious leaders, such as Lincoln slipping emancipation into the suppression of the rebels; FDR redefining neutrality as undeclared war; Martin Luther King holding the reins of the militant blacks while conquering the consciences of the moderate whites; LBJ with civil rights ("the idea whose time has come"); Reagan ending the Cold War by raising the poker ante with defensive weapons, the Maginot Line that worked politically (if not, altogether, militarily).

There is plenty of opportunity to discuss all these subjects here with knowledgeable people. Bill Buckley and George Shultz, and even

Richard Posner, were right; the War on Drugs is a fraud and a failure and should be abandoned.

Always in its history when the United States had to have outstanding leadership, it has emerged: Washington, Lincoln, Franklin D. Roosevelt. It needs it now, and not only for the reasons detailed here. In announcing their result of the Constitutional Convention in 1789, Benjamin Franklin said, "A republic, if you can keep it." The country has faced greater threats since then than it is facing now, but the Constitution has not.

In the end, the United States is always governed from fairly close to the centre. The prison industry is more threatening than the defence industry that President Eisenhower warned the country about in 1961, which at least promoted sophisticated technology, protected national security, and didn't shred the Constitution and tyrannize the people. It will be exposed and tamed. The excesses of the media, endlessly inciting paranoia about crime and the supposedly cowardly mollycoddling of criminals by the politicians, allowing the wrongful and unconscionably prolonged imprisonment of millions of people, all under the tired and fetid mantra of "law and order" — all this will abate or be corrected eventually, as witch-hunting, slavery, industrial feudalism, Prohibition, isolationism, segregation, McCarthyism, and the violent domestic left did or were.

I can forgive America for wrongly imprisoning me and victimizing my shareholders. I now know that the lowest echelons of American society are in some ways more endearing than the highest, an unsuspected insight. I still love the country, though I do not now especially like it. And if, as I hope, I have been able to contribute anything to overcoming this terrible erosion of the justice system, it is my honour.

The treatment of the accused, as Thoreau, among other prominent American intellectuals, wrote, is one of the greatest criteria of the civility, integrity, and moral strength by which societies are themselves judged. When the unanswerable mass of sensible American opinion recognizes this, the United States will no longer fail that test, but much more sorrow and anguish will have been needlessly brought upon the land.

I will return to prison, finish my sentence, and leave the country for the great world beyond as soon as possible.

APPENDIX A: HOLLINGER, INC.

My successors violated six of eight clauses of the Restructuring Proposal.

November 15, 2003

Restructuring Proposal

1. Hollinger International Inc. (the "Company") will immediately give notice of intent to terminate the Ravelston Management Agreement effective June 1, 2004.

2. The Company and Ravelston will negotiate a new Management Fee applicable to the period January 1, 2004 through June 1, 2004. The new Fee will be reduced from the 2003 Fee in respect of, among other things, the personnel and other changes contemplated by this Restructuring Proposal. The Company may elect to prepay all or a portion of the Management Fee for the period January 1 to June 1, 2004, provided that the Company receives appropriate security ensuring repayment of such prepaid amounts in the event the services related to such Fee are not provided.

3. The investigation presently being conducted by the Special Committee will continue and will not be affected by the restructuring described herein.

4. As used in this Restructuring Proposal, the term "Payments" shall mean the aggregate US$16,550,000 paid to Hollinger Inc. ("HLG"), the aggregate US$7,197,500 paid to each of Messrs. Black and Radler, and the aggregate US$602,500 paid to each of Messrs. Atkinson and Boultbee from 1999 to 2001. The payments were not properly authorized on behalf of the Company. The Payments received by HLG and Messrs. Black, Radler, Atkinson and Boultbee will be repaid to the Company by each such recipient in full, with interest calculated from the date of receipt of the payment to the date of repayment at the applicable Federal rate of interest in effect on the date of the receipt of the Payment. Each of Messrs. Black, Radler, Atkinson and Boultbee will make an initial, partial repayment on or before December 31, 2003 in an amount of not less than ten percent (10%) of the total amount of the Payments received by each of them, plus interest. The balance will be evidenced by a promissory note and will be repaid on or before the earlier of a Liquidity Event (as defined below) or June 1, 2004. The Special Committee and the Audit Committee will entertain proposals from HLG with respect to the schedule of repayment by HLG of the Payments it has received, provided that repayment in full is received on or before the earlier of a Liquidity Event and June 1, 2004. As used herein, the term "Liquidity Event" means (i) in the case of HLG, the consummation by the Company of a transaction (or series of related transactions) that result in HLG realizing net proceeds of at least US$50,000,000; (ii) in the case of Messrs. Black and Radler, the consummation by the Company of a transaction (or series of related transactions) that result in either of them realizing net proceeds of at least US$5,000,000; and (iii) in the case of Messrs. Atkinson and Boultbee, the consummation by the Company of a transaction (or series of related transactions) that result in either of them realizing net proceeds of at least US$400,000.

5.   Appropriate disclosure will be made by the Company to correct prior public
        disclosures by the Company that were incomplete or inaccurate. Such corrective
        disclosure will be subject to comment by Lord Black and the Audit and Special
        Committees, but will be subject to final approval solely by the Audit and Special
        Committees.

6.   The full Board of Directors will engage Lazard as financial advisor to pursue a
        range of alternative strategic transactions ("Strategic Process"). The Chairman of
        the Company will devote his principal time and energy to pursuing the Strategic
        Process with the advice and consent of the Executive Committee and overall
        control by the Board. Lazard will be directed to give regular reports of progress
        and developments in the Strategic Process to Lord Black and Gordon Paris; in
        addition, Lazard will be directed to give periodic reports to the Company's
        Executive Committee or upon request of the Executive Committee.

7.   During the pendency of the Strategic Process, in his capacity as the majority
        stockholder of HLG, Lord Black will not support a transaction involving
        ownership interests in HLG if such transaction would negatively affect the
        Company's ability to consummate a transaction resulting from the Strategic
        Process unless the HLG transaction is necessary to enable HLG to avoid a
        material default or involvency. In any such event, Lord Black shall give the
        Company as much advance notice as reasonably possible of any such proposed
        HLG transaction.

8.   The following changes will be implemented:

        A.   F. David Radler will resign in writing all positions he holds with
                the Company or its affiliates or subsidiaries, including his positions
                as an officer and director of the Company, and as the Publisher of
                the Chicago Sun-Times, effective immediately.

        B.   Jack Boultbee will resign in writing as an officer of the Company,
                effective immediately.

        C.   Peter Atkinson will resign in writing as director of the Company,
                effective immediately. Atkinson's continued involvement with the
                Company will be directed at assisting with the Strategic Process
                and assisting the Special Committee.

        D.   Mark Kipnis will resign in writing as an officer and employee of
                the Company.

        E.   Lord Black will retire in writing as the CEO of the Company, but
                will retain the position of Chairman to pursue the Strategic
                Process. He will continue as Chairman of the Telegraph Group.

        F.   Gordon Paris will be appointed as interim President and CEO of
                the Company. Paris will maintain his existing role as a Managing

Director at Berenson & Company. In his capacity as interim President and CEO, Paris will have the authority to hire or retain such resources as he reasonably believes necessary to support his role as interim President and CEO.

G. Daniel Colson will be appointed Chief Operating Officer of the Company.

H. The Executive Committee of the Company will be reconstituted to include the following persons:

    1. Raymond Seitz, Chair

    2. Lord Black

    3. Richard Burt

    4. Graham Savage

    5. Governor James R. Thompson

I. The interim CEO and the Chairman will jointly develop a proposal to the Board regarding the appropriate policy for ownership, lease and use of corporate aircraft, which shall be restricted solely to business purposes.

Accepted and agreed:

_____
James R. Thompson
Chairman
Audit Committee

_____
GordonParis
Chairman
Special Committee

_____
Lord Black

Press Holdings International Limited
Le Montaigne
7 Avenue de Grande Bretagne
98000 Monaco
(Correspondence address)
Tel: + 377 93 15 94 93
Fax: + 377 93 30 20 13

<u>BY FAX AND OVERNIGHT MAIL</u>

January 18, 2004

Board of Directors
Hollinger International Inc
401 North Wabash Avenue
Suite 740
Chicago
Illinois 60611

Dear Sirs:

We wish to take this opportunity to inform the Board of Directors (the "Board") of Hollinger International Inc ("Hollinger International") that Press Holdings International Limited ("PHI") has signed an agreement today with The Ravelston Corporation Limited and The Lord Black of Crossharbour, which provides for PHI to make a tender offer for all outstanding common and preferred shares of Hollinger Inc. The tender offer will be fully financed at the time of commencement. Upon completion of the tender offer and second-step acquisition of any shares not tendered, Hollinger Inc will become a privately-owned company.

We are convinced that PHI's acquisition of Hollinger Inc is in the best interests of Hollinger International and its stockholders. We would like to meet with the Board at the earliest possible time, to discuss in detail the benefits to Hollinger International and its stockholders that we believe would result from the transaction and the role we envision for the Board in the process. Aidan Barclay is prepared to meet with you in person, or, if you prefer, to speak by telephone.

Press Holdings International Limited

PHI is the sister company of Press Holdings Limited, itself the holding company for a media group which owns and operates the following newspapers in the UK: The Scotsman Publications, which includes "The Scotsman", "Edinburgh Evenings News", "Scotland on Sunday" and, separately, "The Business" newspaper which is printed and sold throughout the UK and Europe.

Registered office: 22 Grenville Street, St Helier, Jersey, Channel Islands

PHI and Press Holdings Limited are both ultimately controlled by Sir David and Sir Frederick Barclay. Aidan Barclay is the Chairman and Chief Executive of Press Holdings Limited.

Privately-owned business activities of Sir David and Sir Frederick Barclay include newspapers (detailed above); hotels – The Ritz, London, and the Mirabeau, Monte Carlo as well as UK retail businesses – Littlewoods Stores, Littlewoods mail order catalogues, Index Catalogue shops and Shop Direct mail order catalogues, and business operations in Japan, Sweden and Ireland. These businesses have combined annual gross revenues of over US$7 billion.

Benefits to Hollinger International and its Stockholders

After careful study and consideration, we are confident the acquisition of Hollinger Inc by PHI will provide immediate and long-term benefits to the stockholders of Hollinger International for a variety of reasons, including:

a) Lord Black's controlling interest in Hollinger International and his associates' and affiliated companies' relationship with Hollinger International and its subsidiaries have brought (and most likely will continue to bring) significant media controversy to Hollinger International. We believe this continued media controversy is significantly harming the public image and stock price of Hollinger International and undermining its credibility in the financial markets. As part of the acquisition, the negative media attention should cease.

b) The purchase of Hollinger Inc by Press Holdings International Limited which is part of a financially strong and well-managed organisation with extensive experience in owning and operating a broad range of industries, including UK newspapers, we believe will have a substantial benefit on the stock price of Hollinger International as it will bring credibility to the company and enable it to renegotiate its financial borrowings on improved terms.

We have carefully considered the potential impact that the acquisition could have on the financial position and liquidity of Hollinger International and its subsidiaries and, in particular, the impact of a change of control on Hollinger International's and its subsidiaries' debt instruments. We are prepared to work constructively with the Board and its senior management to ensure that Hollinger International will continue to have

Registered office: 22 Grenville Street, St Helier, Jersey, Channel Islands sufficient financing in place after the acquisition to enable Hollinger International to continue to operate and grow its businesses.

Our intentions are well meaning and constructive and we have no wish to interfere with the review that Lazard LLC has been instructed to undertake at the direction of the Board as well as the Special Committee work that is currently being undertaken. We should mention that we have had a longstanding business relationship with Lazards spanning some 20 years.

After completion of the acquisition, we will arrange the payment to Hollinger International of amounts acknowledged by Hollinger Inc to be owed to Hollinger International, subject to confirmation that these amounts are due.

We would be prepared to explore the possibilities, with the approval of the Board, of commercial opportunities that exist to increase shareholder value for all Hollinger International stockholders. In particular these would include substantial synergies between the existing Hollinger publications and ours in the UK.

We have established a level of trust and confidence in our ongoing negotiations with Lord Black to ensure a timely and successful transaction for all parties involved. We believe that our acquisition of Hollinger Inc is the only viable alternative that brings to a positive conclusion the existing relationships among Lord Black and his associates and affiliated companies, on the one hand, and Hollinger Inc and Hollinger International and their respective subsidiaries, on the other hand. In addition, our acquisition of Hollinger Inc removes the uncertainty in the financial markets regarding the financial health and viability of Hollinger International.

It is clear to us that our acquisition of Hollinger Inc is the best way to start the process of improving stockholder value at Hollinger International.

We look forward to hearing from you at your earliest convenience, so that we can begin discussing how to realise the benefits of our acquisition of Hollinger Inc for all parties involved.

Yours faithfully

Sir David Barclay
On behalf of Press Holdings International Limited

January 18, 2004

Dear Members of the Hollinger International Board of Directors:

I am writing to you today about three major developments regarding issues facing the Board:

- First, my legal counsel has determined that documents not available to us in November clearly show that certain disputed non-compete payments were in fact known to and approved or ratified by the independent directors of Hollinger International, including Audit Committee Chairman James Thompson. And, as a result of these discoveries, I am not obligated to and do not feel it is appropriate to return these non-compete payments to the company. The entire sequence of events based on the premise that these were "unauthorized payments" has been invalid. I am of the view that this Board was misled.

- Second, the restructuring proposal that I agreed to on November 15 is invalid since I relied upon the false claims that these non-compete payments were unapproved in agreeing to the proposal, and since the Special Committee has breached that agreement in any event by breaching most of its provisions.

- Third, Ravelston and Argus have accepted an offer from Press Holdings International Ltd. for their shares of Hollinger Inc. They have done so as the two-week standstill with respect to selling shares of Hollinger Inc., having been egregiously violated by the Special and Audit Committees in their improper collusion, expired today. I believe that this agreement will not only provide substantial value to all Hollinger Inc. shareholders, but also will allow the media properties of Hollinger International to move forward unhindered by recent controversy and uncertainty.

Let me expand on these points. As you know, in November, I agreed to the Restructuring Proposal made by Special Committee Chairman Gordon Paris and Audit Committee Chairman James Thompson based on their representation to me of certain facts. Specifically, Mr. Paris and Mr. Thompson told me that after months of joint investigation by their committees, they had concluded that $32.15 million in non-compete payments paid to Hollinger Inc. and certain executives of Hollinger International were not authorized by either the Audit Committee or the full Board.

Mr. Paris and Mr. Thompson provided no documentation to support their conclusions and offered me just three days to accept their proposal. Nonetheless, I assumed that they were acting in good faith, since our legal officers could not contradict them, and I had nothing to do with generating the payments myself. I accepted their factual findings, and I ultimately accepted the agreement reached on November 15.

Since that time, however, my legal counsel has identified documents not known to us in November. Those documents clearly indicate that the factual basis on which we accepted that agreement – specifically, that the non-compete payments were not approved – is inaccurate. These documents include, among others:

- Notes of a conversation that Mr. Thompson had with legal counsel at Shearman & Sterling and others regarding due diligence on several transactions that included the disputed non-compete payments. Handwritten notes include the answer "CONFIRMED – APPROVALS OBTAINED AND ITEMS DISCLOSED" as the response to a question for Mr. Thompson regarding Audit Committee approval of the transactions' terms, including the non-compete payments.

- Minutes of the February 25, 2002 Hollinger International Joint Audit Committee and Compensation Committee Meeting indicating unanimous approval of financials previously distributed to the Audit Committee with notes that said:

  > "In connection with the sales of United States newspaper properties in 2000 . . . the Company, Lord Black and three senior executives entered into non-competition agreements with the purchasers . . . for aggregate consideration paid in 2001 of $0.6 million. These amounts were in addition to the aggregate consideration paid in respect to these non-competition agreements in 2000 of $15.0 million. Such amounts were paid to Lord Black and the three senior executives."

- Minutes from March 12, 2002 indicating that senior partners at KPMG, which served as auditors for both Hollinger Inc. and Hollinger International, confirmed to the Audit Committee of Hollinger Inc. that having attended the February 25 meeting "all such payments had been approved by an independent committee of the Board of Hollinger International and the Auditors had reviewed the relevant Minutes of the independent committee and were satisfied."

These are among numerous documents indicating knowledge and approval or ratification of non-compete payments by independent directors. Not only were these documents unavailable to me when I agreed to the November 15 restructuring proposal, they were initially withheld from my legal counsel when we subsequently requested relevant documents from the company.

In addition to making misrepresentation to me, the Special Committee also repudiated the restructuring agreement almost from the moment it was signed – for example:

- Although the agreement explicitly referenced my continuing involvement in the strategic process being pursued by Lazard, the company subsequently informed the media that I would not be involved in the process and Lazard informed potential investors in the process, including the Barclays with whom we agreed to a transaction, not to communicate with me.

- The Special Committee also prevented Hollinger International from paying management fees to Ravelston Corporation Limited that the restructuring agreement explicitly committed International to continue paying through year-end 2003.

Even after discovering the new information regarding approval of the non-compete payments, I engaged in good faith discussions with the Special Committee and the Audit Committee in an attempt to address these various matters. They, however, have refused to explain the misrepresentations made to me in November or to justify their breach of the restructuring agreement.

While we continued these discussions, we agreed to refrain from selling Hollinger shares for a period of two weeks. That agreement expired today, and Argus and Ravelston have accepted an offer to sell their shares in Hollinger Inc. to Press Holdings International Ltd. This sale to a highly respected strategic buyer will not only provide substantial value to shareholders of Hollinger Inc., but will benefit Hollinger International by reducing distractions and eliminating financial uncertainty from its media properties.

Prior to agreeing to the transaction, on January 13, 2004, I offered the Chairman and Counsel of the Special Committee, Gordon Paris and Richard Breeden, the right to match, with a purchase through preferred shares, any bona fide offer for control of Hollinger Inc., and we suggested that Goldman Sachs or Morgan Stanley stand as arbiters of equivalent value. Mr. Paris and Mr. Breeden, however, declined that offer and terminated discussions without explanation.

The Special Committee subsequently launched a series of steps, including filing litigation yesterday that clearly can only be seen as a desperate attempt to prevent me from completing a transaction for Hollinger Inc. and divert attention from misrepresentations they had made about the non-compete payments in November. Neither of those efforts will be successful.

It is astonishing that the Special Committee, after conducting a joint investigation with the Audit Committee, would seek to undo a series of transactions going back five years, including transactions that were admittedly approved by the members of the Audit Committee who never once claimed that they received insufficient or inadequate information regarding the transactions or offered a word of dissent. In addition, these transactions were reviewed by the company's independent auditors, who deemed them properly approved and disclosed. You will note that their recent legal claim demands repayment of dividends paid to Hollinger Inc., but not those paid to other shareholders, and repayment of all the renumeration received by David Radler and myself during a period when we greatly increased the value of the company. It is a spurious complaint.

Further, I do not accept the validity of the Executive Committee's purported removal of me as Chairman of the Board, nor most of its other recent initiatives, which clearly were undertaken because the authors of these steps lack confidence in their ability to win a vote of the whole Board.

As you know, I originally proposed the creation of the Special Committee and have offered my full cooperation with the Committee's investigation. I want to be absolutely clear: I fully support a thorough, fair and complete airing of the facts relating to all of the questions that have been raised.

Sincerely,

Lord Black

APPENDIX B: COLUMNS,
MARCH 2007 – MARCH 2008

These are columns published in the National Post. *The first when I departed Toronto for Chicago at the outset of the trial in March, 2007; the second, a response to William F. Buckley's article about me in the National Review, and to Henry Kissinger's interview about our case with the FBI; and the third on surrendering to federal prison to begin serving what was then, with probable reductions, a sentence of five years and eight months, a substantial reduction, at least, on the life sentence the prosecutors were seeking. It has been very gratifying to have had a complete reconciliation with Bill Buckley in the last few months before he died, and with Henry Kissinger while I have been in New York between April and September 2011, as described in Chapter 15 and in the Epilogue. It has been my honour to have such good and eminent friends. My assertion of faith in the American justice system at the end of the last item of Appendix B is a complete falsehood. I never had any faith in it and I think it is largely corrupt, intellectually and otherwise, from the law schools to the steps of the Supreme Court, but as I was in the appellate process as the only early exit from an unjust prison sentence, I felt obliged to a gesture to tactical submission. I do believe, fervently, in the preceding quote from Thoreau, and am about to return to prison and practice it.*

I Am Not Afraid
March 10, 2007

This is the last of these columns I shall write before I have to defend myself against the unfounded charges that have stalked and shadowed me these several years. The trial of the facts that approaches has been amply publicized, but I hope I may be permitted a few reflections now.

When the life that I had worked more than 30 years to build, as a serious, reasonably respected newspaper publisher, was suddenly assaulted with extreme violence on every side more than three years ago, my wife and I returned to Canada, seeking a legally and financially defensible perimeter.

Apart from those who knew us well, there were cries of joy that I might be a corporate wrongdoer, and an almost Times Square New Year's countdown to my anticipated conviction.

Other than receiving news of a well-advanced terminal illness, an experience of which we have unfortunately had some experience in our family, I can hardly imagine a more startling change of life and prospect, since I had done nothing illegal. The principle of the presumption of innocence was largely ignored by the press and regulators.

Friends offered financial assistance, as my income suddenly almost dried up, yet my expenses, especially related to self-defence, multiplied. I managed to refinance myself, but was no less grateful for their offers. A legal team was assembled.

It was always obvious that the lies agreed upon by parties in interest with the complicity of parts of the press would likely become a criminal prosecution. Our companies, which had been built almost from nothing into billions of dollars of tangible value (not creatively accounted vapour), were, in the manner of these times and jurisdictions, transformed into platforms from which we were tormented.

As the largest shareholder, I was made to pay for my own persecution. The immobilizations or seizures of assets, defamatory leaks to the press, and neverending harassments, continued, year after year (precious years at this stage in life). Eventually, I was, and am, posting bond of almost US$40-million, which is some kind of a record high. But I was able to stabilize finances, return to writing (with great thanks to the editors of this newspaper); the novelty of our discomfort abated, and life and the war of attrition ground on. Finally, our enemies would have to prove the innocent guilty, not just to the malicious and the envious, but in a court of justice.

There was great irony, whose piquancy was never lost on me, that I, who have been denounced in the Parliaments of the U.K. and Canada for excessive pro-Americanism, should be so savagely attacked by the U.S. prosecution system. Frustratingly, I could not seriously reply to the wild allegations, shovelled out by the usurper regimes in our companies or in garish prosecution press conferences, about our claimed excesses, as counsel urged that all response must be held for trial. Such is the unevenness of the system. I had to rely on the innate decency of most people to wait until the other side was heard and require that a presumption of guilt had at least to be substantiated.

From there it was a fairly short step to the Big Battle, which required even those elements of the media that had danced on Barbara's and my supposed graves like Transylvanians heaping garlic on the resting place of Count Dracula to acknowledge my resuscitation. Big Battles cannot be conducted with corpses. As I know the facts and believe in the fairness of 12 randomly selected Americans, I am confident of the outcome.

It has been a splendid time to be in Canada. A united Conservative party, for which I and many others fought, has produced a federal two-party system for the first time in a hundred years in Canada. The huge economic growth of China and India has enabled Canada to keep its generous social benefits and reduce taxes to a point where the brain drain to the U.S. should now dry up. Richard Bradshaw and Jack Diamond, who are from far countries, have built a fine national opera house where the performances are of outstanding quality. The percentage of Canada's GDP that is exports to the U.S. has declined from 44% to about 35%. Quebec separatism, a spectre that hobbled the country for decades, has died. Canada has become one of the 10 or 12 most important countries of the 192 in the world. Those of us brought up to believe that Canada's foreign policy was to tug at the trouser-leg of the Americans and British must realize that it is unnecessary and undignified to continue do so.

For the first time in decades, not having a large executive job, I have been able to appreciate and comment on national affairs. I left this country when the courts upheld the right of the then-prime minister (Jean Chretien) to create a sub-category of one in a foreign country (the U.K.), ineligible to receive an honour in that country for services deemed to have been performed in that country, because Chretien did not approve of coverage (in this newspaper) of his government's financial conduct (coverage that has since been vindicated). I said I would be back (though I anticipated a less controversial return). I was also, for commercial reasons, departing the newspaper business, (but had not foreseen such a perturbed exit strategy). The years have been full of surprises.

Barbara and I go now to try these issues at the bar of Abraham Lincoln and Clarence Darrow, in the city that I have long regarded as the great, brave heart of America. We have survived the "shock and awe" campaign of intimidation, defamation and asset seizures. We built a great company that our accusers have destroyed to their own profit, as they have been sumptuously paid to obliterate over a billion dollars of shareholder market value. We acted lawfully and are not afraid.

Despite its legal vagaries, the United States remains the indispensable country of Western civilization of the last century, a society of laws in a largely lawless world, and a country overwhelmingly composed of decent people.

I have no bitterness to those who have opposed me in this country, apart from a few outright thieves, who know who they are. To my wife, children, family (including my ex-wife), friends, in this and other countries, colleagues, fellow parishioners, and the thousands of e-mail and postal correspondents who have inspirited me through these challenges, my gratitude is beyond my ability to express here.

In Toronto, we are cat and dog owners, and Barbara has just received a little Hungarian puli from Alberta, an adorable but dignified little proof to its older companions that life goes on. We will be back before it is much bigger.

I will write here when I can; justice will prevail, and Barbara and I will celebrate with our friends, never more easily identified than in these challenging days. When nightmares pass, all things are possible. I have never been happier to be Canadian.

A Reply to Two Friends
December 15, 2007

For two years, I have avoided mention in this column of my legal travails, and only vary that this week, in matters already on the public record, at the request of the commissioning editor. Throughout these five challenging years, most people whom Barbara and I really considered to be friends, have behaved as friends.

My late father, who died more than 30 years ago, and was a very intelligent, if somewhat eccentric man, in his later years, admired William F. Buckley and Henry Kissinger more than any other living Americans. It was a particular honour, later, to have had those men as friends for more than 20 years now. They have both referred to our relations in those terms publicly many times, and Dr. Kissinger did so under oath early in these baneful proceedings. I am often asked about my current relations with them, in particular.

Bill Buckley sent the judge in our case an extremely generous and unjustifiably flattering letter about me. Given his great prestige and celebrity, it was surely useful. He also published a piece about me last Wednesday, which I saw on the National Review Web site. He confirmed that he was a friend, and that all our mutual friends were "close to unanimity of opinion that Conrad Black has nobly enhanced the human cause"; embarrassingly high praise.

However, he also wrote that he had been asked by one of my lawyers to write to the judge for me, and that this was a "painful commission _ It seemed to this friend, as to quite a few others, that he [i.e. I] probably was guilty on at least one of the charges." He helpfully advised his readers that the convictions are "not quite the same thing as" what Lee Harvey Oswald did to John F. Kennedy; that I had presented an alternative defence of innocence and, even if not innocent, that what I did wasn't illegal; and that he had had to restrain himself from writing to the judge about the law and facts of the case.

For no evident reason, he also gave his bowdlerized version of why I am not, at the moment, a Canadian citizen, and concluded that "the tragedy is now complete in the matter of Conrad Black. Only he had the courage and the sweep to throw it all away. Leaving, for his friends, just terrible sadness that it should end like this."

One of the most professional journalists who covered the trial in Chicago wrote asking me if, since "WFB _ obviously thinks the jury got it right, do you feel you are being tossed under the bus by your friend?"

No, I do not, though I am disappointed. The facts are that I asked a mutual friend to ask WFB if he would prefer not to be asked to write a character reference for me to the judge. I wanted to make it easy for him to decline. He replied that he would like to do so, and so I asked him, explaining that if, on reflection, he would rather not, I would perfectly understand. He insisted that he did wish to write the judge, and asked for guidelines, which one of my counsel sent him, asking him to avoid all discussion of the case itself. He claimed to find it a pleasing "commission." My counsel have never hinted at an alternative defence; my defence is and always has been: Not Guilty.

More perplexing is his assertion that my "friends," including Bill himself, thought I was probably at least partially guilty as charged. Well-disposed people who think that are likely not to be familiar with the facts and the current state of U.S. criminal procedure. Friends don't usually act like that.

Bill Buckley's late, wonderful, Canadian wife, Pat, concluded our last exchange by proclaiming that it was obvious that I was innocent. Bill Buckley and I share many philosophical and religious views. He knows my admiration for the United States. And he cannot be unaware of the gradual redefinition in recent decades of the Fifth, Sixth and Eighth Amendment guarantees of due process, the grand jury as insurance against capricious prosecution, the prohibition against seizure of property without just compensation, speedy justice, access to counsel of choice and reasonable bail.

He, of all people, knows, and has written countless times, that some principles transcend the convenience of those trying to defend them. He referred on Wednesday (as have some less eminent commentators) to my "raw impiety" for criticizing the prosecutors

To question the antics of some U.S. prosecutors is not impiety. I would not expect most observers to recognize that I am fighting not just for my life and liberty, but also for the benefit of certain constitutionally guaranteed rights essential to the rule of law. I did expect that from Bill Buckley, a conscientious, loyal and intellectually fearless friend.

Knowing Henry Kissinger as well as I do, I suspected that he would behave as Richard Nixon told me he generally did when a colleague came under pressure: privately declare solidarity with both sides and separate himself, so that neither side would confuse him with the other side, until it became clear which side had won. He promised more, and I hoped for more, but Henry Kissinger is an 84-year old fugitive from Nazi pogroms, and has made his way famously in the world by endlessly recalibrating the balance of power and correlation of forces in all situations.

The correlation of forces between the U.S. government and me has obviously been generally unpromising, and Henry has less natural affinity for the principles involved here than Bill Buckley does. His statements, publicly and to the FBI, that I am probably guilty of something but that he "never deserts a friend," are not heroic or even accurate, but on past form, not altogether a surprise either.

William Buckley wrote on Wednesday that I had claimed from the start that the charges against me "sought to vest in judicial infamy that which is in the nature of things blameless." Those "contending otherwise were obtuse and vindictive, and should be put away somewhere to prevent the toxification of the Common Law and the resources of reason on Earth." This is an endearing exaggeration. But the underlying points of my resistance are not a suitable subject of mockery from one of America's greatest champions of individual liberty.

They are both great men, in their different ways, and their friendship, no matter how idiosyncratic, would be a matter of pride to anyone, as it is to me. I am sure that they will eventually see that it is not necessary to dissemble about our relations and that I have not thrown "it all away." If our appeal is unsuccessful, they can share their "terrible sadness" with their country and aspects of its justice system.

For such men and for the sake of happy days gone by, that could yet return, I offer the other cheek, but not unilateral verbal disarmament. They need only survive and retain their faculties a while longer, to see that my present embattled condition is not, as Bill wrote, "the end." I wish that for them, and all other good things.

Unjustly Incarcerated
March 3, 2008

The legal case involving me began as a factional dispute between groups of shareholders of Chicago-based Hollinger International. Some wanted the company broken up or sold for a quick gain. Others, including the largest institutional shareholder, Southeastern Asset Management, agreed with management. We had produced nearly $2-billion of capital gains for the shareholders in sales of U.S. community and Canadian newspapers. We foresaw the problems of the newspaper industry and were conducting an orderly withdrawal from it.

To prevail, the dissident shareholders had to remove the controlling shareholder. To destabilize my position, they began giving hostile interviews to competing publications, and attempted to depress the share price. In the commercial atmosphere after Enron and other accounting fraud cases where billions were lost and tens of thousands of people thrown into unemployment, the most effective way to force out an incumbent management was to attack their integrity. The dissidents asked for a special committee, and I agreed at once. I believed any fair-minded investigation would lay any ethical considerations to rest. That has been my response to all serious examinations of our conduct, including the trial and the pending appeal from the remaining counts.

The special committee seized control of the company when they represented that there had been $30-million of unauthorized payments to executives and to the parent company. I was horrified at the thought that any such thing could happen in a company where I was the chief executive, and retired as executive chairman. I felt that the buck stopped with me and that it was the honourable thing to do. I was prepared to do almost anything that was legal and ethical to help the company through these problems. Eighty per cent of those payments were found by the jurors to be legal and by the trial judge to be valid even by civil law standards. And 95% of what is left has already been judged by the Court of Appeal to raise "substantial questions." All were legal and appropriate and I am confident that they will be judged to have been so.

The special committee counsel, Richard Breeden, and the new CEO, Gordon Paris, asked me to remain as non-executive chairman. Mr. Breeden assured the directors, and then said publicly, that there was no evidence of wrongdoing by me. No evidence to contradict this view has arisen since, except what was given in testimony in exchange for a plea bargain and immunities from prosecution. The jurors disbelieved almost all of that evidence as extorted perjury in the routine operation of the U.S. plea bargain system.

We reached a restructuring agreement on Nov. 15, 2003, to determine our future roles in the company. Within a few weeks, the special committee had violated six of the eight clauses in the agreement and had generated a great deal of fantastically hostile publicity for us. A presumption of guilt arose, and remains, though it has been diluted.

I offered Mr. Breeden and Mr. Paris a number of proposals, including the sale of the parent, Hollinger Inc., to Hollinger International for preferred shares, and a first refusal on any bona fide offer for control of the parent company.

Mr. Breeden and Mr. Paris replied by representing to the SEC that I was threatening the special committee, which I was not, and falsely admitting to wrongdoing and entering into a costly consent decree; launching a lawsuit against the former management, and removing me as chairman.

I then contracted to sell Toronto-based Hollinger Inc. for $8.44 per share for all shareholders. The same buyers filed an SEC form 13D stating that they had expressed a willingness to bid $18 per share for every Hollinger International share. The Hollinger International shares have since descended from $18 to 94¢, almost a 95% decline. And the Hollinger Inc. shares, for which we bid again less than three years ago at $7.60 for each minority share, are now worthless, a 100% decline in value. Our successors have made every conceivable business blunder and have eliminated $1.85-billion of shareholder value.

They have, however, taken good care of themselves. Mr. Breeden has pocketed about $25-million, plus $750,000 in each of the last two years for his completely redundant status as special monitor. Mr. Paris, who had no management experience, nor any knowledge of the newspaper business, made $13-million in three years, $17,000 a day, to deprive tens of thousands of shareholders of many hundreds of millions of dollars. The special committee law firm, O'Melveny and Myers, has probably made about $100-million on this account. The local Canadian plunderers of Hollinger Inc. have performed to scale.

The next escalation of this factional struggle was the special committee report, in the late summer of 2004, which was foreordained to be a massive smear job designed to generate criminal charges. It was, and it did. We were accused of conducting a "$500-million corporate kleptocracy." Almost all of that has already been determined to have been legal.

The special committee report promised "greater prosperity and profits" at Hollinger International, and a recovery of $1-billion. The recoveries have been much less than the $200-million-plus the special committee and endless litigation has cost the company, while its capitalization has withered from $2-billion to $70-million.

I believe that I have endured the most comprehensive international defamation I can recall in over four decades of close acquaintance with the media, and the special committee report was the tidal crest of it. I naturally sued the authors of the report for a very large amount, in Canada, where the civil tort of defamation is much less restrained than it is in the United States. Avoidance of facing those lawsuits is doubtless one of the reasons for the tenacity of the persecutors, who would be at risk in the event of full acquittals.

Our offer to privatize Hollinger Inc. in early 2005 was supported by the staff of the Ontario Securities Commission, and by 87% of the minority shareholders who voted. But Mr. Breeden, as he happily told a Toronto newspaper, "lectured" the commissioners that they had to kill the offer because of our moral unsuitability. Even if there had been any truth to this, it was irrelevant to the offer, as privatizing Hollinger Inc. would not reduce the ability of the U.S. Justice Department to charge us if it wished. This was the death-knell for another $250-million of shareholder value, and a spectacular disservice by the OSC.

Just before most of the charges were laid in this case, in October, 2005, these prosecutors seized the proceeds of the sale of our co-operative unit in New York, on the basis of an affidavit from an FBI agent, who signed that he was fully aware of the laws against perjury. The affidavit omitted any reference to the facts that the company had been obligated to pay for the renovation and decoration of the unit, and that I had done so, at a personal cost of more than $4.6-million.

The seizure was conducted ex parte, with no notice and no due process, under the Civil Assets Forfeiture Reform Act.

The jurors determined that that affidavit was mistaken (i.e. false). When we pointed out its deficiencies in our legal motion, the prosecutors laid the charges in this case, stayed other proceedings and froze almost $10-million owed to me. The action achieved its objective: Brendan V. Sullivan of Williams & Connally, one of America's most respected trial lawyers, who was my chief counsel, was unable to take this case, because I was unable to provide him, for a time, after the New York seizure, with the retainer he required.

In the climate created by these charges and the press reaction to them, I was unable to raise cash for the retainer any prominent U.S. lawyer would require for a trial of several months, without time-consuming liquidation of assets.

The assistant U.S. attorney attempted to intimidate my mortgagee in Palm Beach by telling him that if the mortgage was renewed, he would prosecute his company in Chicago, for unspecified offences to be named later, and then told this court that I was in default on the mortgage and in breach of the bail terms. We won that skirmish.

I was advised that no British or Canadian court would have extradited me after my money was seized in New York ex parte, on the basis of a false affidavit. But I never considered fleeing for a moment. I am not interested in staying away from lawful authority. I seek justice where it is available. And I still believe it is available in the United States. I would never flee any serious jurisdiction.

As my counsel said in closing remarks at trial, the U.S. government became a tool in what was and remains a factional struggle within what were formerly the splendid companies that the defendants in this case, and others, built. The U.S. government and the sponsors of the indictments, and their acolytes in Canada, have destroyed these companies. The Hollinger earth is scorched, the shareholders wiped out, many of the employees laid off, but the factional war continues to the Circuit Court of Appeal in Chicago.

There was no evidence to support two of the remaining convictions, and the only evidence, from the chief cooperating witness, was exculpatory. For the third count, the evidence was an uncorroborated allegation of a non-incriminating telephone conversation, which did not, in fact, take place.

On obstruction of justice, it was in evidence that I completely complied with all document requests, that the boxes being moved as I vacated my office of 27 years contained nothing relevant to the case the SEC did not already possess. I had no knowledge of any further curiosity of theirs, nothing to do with selecting the contents of the boxes and knew nothing about their contents, and did not look at the boxes on the weekend they were in my home. I have never been accused of violating a Canadian court order, and did not do so, and ensured that I was recorded by security cameras I had had installed to assure that there could be no suggestion of my doing anything underhanded. We have a Toronto court to thank for the massive and misleading exposure that the grainy security film that caused me to appear furtive, has caused. We have the same court to thank for a number of other unjust decisions.

This was what the prosecution described as a "unique, brazen, calculated, manipulative and complex" scheme, having initially called us all the moral equivalent of bank robbers, who had stolen $60-million in "money grabs." The prosecution is at least correct in calling it a "unique" scheme. So, I suppose, are all schemes that don't exist.

It is a terrible thing to be falsely accused, and wrongly convicted, even of a fraction of the original charges, and unjustly incarcerated. For persisting in seeking the recognition of my innocence of these charges, I have been portrayed as defiant, or at least in denial. I defy and deny unjust charges, not the practical difficulties I have faced for the last four years and am facing now.

I would qualify in political terms, as a reasonable member of the law and order section of the public. And as a conscientious and religious matter, I believe in the confession and repentance of misconduct, as well as in the punishment of crimes. If I had committed any of the offences charged, I would have pleaded guilty and asked for a sentence that would enable me to atone for my crime and assuage my guilt and shame.

Some of the jurors, in post-trial comments, by e-mail and on television, where there can be no question of a journalist misunderstanding what was said, confirmed that there remained a reasonable doubt, but that a compromise was reached on acquittals and convictions, contrary to the judge's instruction.

One of the jurors stated that it should have been a civil case. So it would have been if the special committee report had not sold it to the prosecutors as a criminal case. And it would not be much of a civil case either. This is the criminalization of what was and remains a civil factional corporate dispute.

My faith in the United States has inspired me to persevere, despite what I believe has been the prosecution's insufficient respect for the Fifth, Sixth, and Eighth Amendment guarantees of due process, of the grand jury as an assurance against capricious prosecution, of no seizure of assets without just compensation, of speedy justice, access to counsel and reasonable bail. I have been besieged by various agencies of the U.S. government for more than four years, and I know of only one higher bond in U.S. history than the $38-million I have been posting.

Thoreau wrote: "Under a government which imprisons unjustly, the true place for a just man is also in prison." These charges, and the actions leading up to them, have been unjust. Most of them have already been found to be unjust. I cherish my liberty as all people do, but I am unafraid. I have faith in American justice.

Appendix C

It was with this extremely generous and gracious message that my very long and warm relationship with Henry Kissinger really resumed. I understood that he had been misinformed and explained that I was not the author of these problems. He volunteered that he had never thought I had committed crimes and with that we agreed to put it all behind us and never speak of it again. Unknown to me, he wrote generously on my behalf to Judge St. Eve in 2007. He is one of the most brilliant and witty individuals I have met, and has certainly earned his status as a world historic figure.

February 17, 2011

Dear Conrad:

A mutual friend sent me your Valentine to Barbara. I was deeply moved. What has happened is a tragedy, and I hope it will find a definitive conclusion soon.

On the strong advice of counsel, I could not make the statement suggested by your counsel. And it also seems to me wrong to deal with the resumption of friendship as a legal arrangement.

Because the wounds are not entirely on one side, we should deal with the future and leave the assessment of what has happened to a personal conversation. Your major grievance against me seems to be that, after months of hesitation, I voted with a unanimous board to accept a report written by people you had appointed. While neither of us can change the past, we can at least share the wish that this entire chapter in our lives had never occurred. For my part, I will never forget how you stood by me when I lost an eye and in its aftermath. I admire your courage and tenacity. Despite the bitterness that has developed, I have done what I could do to make clear my commitment to you. I wrote a private letter to the sentencing judge outside the legal process to make clear my views about your human qualities. I also offered to intercede with President Bush (with whom I had developed a personal friendship), but your counsel rejected the suggestion.

I will be prepared to state, at any point, what I never doubted: that you are an extraordinary person; of fundamental decency; an important contributor to the thinking of our time; a sterling defender of freedom. And at one time a valued and trusted friend. This feeling will remain no matter what storms are ahead of us.

You are going through an ordeal at the limits of human endurance. It is a pity for both our lives that this situation has arisen. But whatever happens, remember I consider you an important part of my life and of the future of free peoples.

Sincerely,

Henry A. Kissinger

Appendix D: Statement to the Court, June 24, 2011

The statement to the court on June 24, delivered directly to the judge, eye-to-eye at close range, from memory and improvisation, was heartfelt and exact, and will stand as my last word on the subject. When I am at liberty in a few months, I propose not to speak or write of this protracted unpleasantness again.

On the occasion corresponding to this four years ago, the fact that the counts that had survived the trial were under appeal spoke for itself, and I didn't think it appropriate to say much more. As we are now back, one last time, in your court, at the weary end of this very long and fiercely contested proceeding, there are a few things that I think should be said.

The prosecutors have never ceased to accuse me of being defiant of the law, of disrespecting the courts, and of being an antagonistic critic of the American justice system. Nothing could be further from the truth. I have obeyed every order of this and other courts, every requirement of the United States Probation Office, in this and other cities, and while I was its guest, every rule and regulation of the BOP, no matter how authoritarian. I have been and remain completely and unwaveringly submissive to legal authority, yours in particular.

What I have done is exercise my absolute right to legal self-defence, a right guaranteed to everyone who is drawn into the court system of this and every other civilized country. All my adult life I have been a member of the moderate section of what is commonly called the law and order community, and I shall remain in it, whatever sentence you impose on me today. I always keep a firewall between my own travails and my perception of public policy issues; otherwise I would retain no credibility as a commentator.

Your Honour, many years ago when I was a student and licensee in law in Quebec, I read a large number of cases from British and French courts, including the principle established by the eminent British jurist,

Lord Denning, that "Parties coming to court must be prepared to practise what they are asking the court to approve." The prosecutors have never ceased in this case to advocate respect for the law, and to accuse me of lacking it.

But since that is an unfounded complaint, the real source of their irritation must be that as chief defendant, I have led the destruction of most of their case, and have successfully protested my innocence of charges of which I have, in fact, been found not to have been guilty. I understand their disconcertion that of the 17 counts they originally threatened or actually launched against me, all were either not proceeded with, abandoned, rejected by the jurors or vacated by a unanimous Supreme Court of the United States. But the problem is not my lawlessness; it is the weakness of their case. I have done nothing but uphold and respect the rule of law and the system of justice, in which my faith has never flagged.

This entire prosecution, and a number of civil suits as well, were based on the report of the Special Committee of the board of Hollinger International, directed by its counsel, Richard Breeden, and published in September 2004. That report accused me of having led a "$500-million corporate kleptocracy." The non-competition payments almost entirely legitimized in this case were described as "thefts." And the authors of the report promised to lead the company back to unheard of levels of profitability. They did but not in the direction indicated. I launched the largest libel suit in Canadian history against Breeden and the others responsible for writing and publishing this infamous report.

My libel suit, and several other lawsuits around this case, are being settled, including a sizeable payment to me on the libel claim. This is the ultimate collapse of the Breeden Special Committee report, whatever other interpretation the defendants in the case may, consistent with their notions of accuracy throughout these proceedings, seek to place on it.

The authors of the report were not prepared to defend it where they would not have an immunity for perjury as most of the government witnesses did here. Nor were they prepared to defend their self-directed largesse of $300-million, as they drove the company into bankruptcy, taking down $2-billion of shareholder value with it.

Over 80 per cent of that value belonged to ordinary people throughout the U.S. and Canada, the type of people Mr. Cramer spoke about at the opening of the trial when he likened us to masked and violent bank robbers who stole depositors' money at gunpoint, because we had supposedly rifled the shareholders' family college funds. And Breeden's original action of January 2004, containing the false charge that I had threatened the Special Committee, repeated just last month by the government in its presentence filings on May 27, has also been abandoned.

Mark Twain famously said that "A lie gets halfway round the world before the truth gets its trousers on." It is very late in this case, Your Honour, but the truth has almost caught up with the original allegations.

I have at times expressed concern about the ethics of some of the prosecutors in this case, Your Honour, but never of the role of prosecutors, or of the necessity to convict criminals and protect society. But I must emphasize that I consider that the prosecutors, too, are victims. If they had not believed Breeden's lies, now effectively abandoned in the face of my libel suit, the U.S. Attorney would surely not have launched such a fantastic assault on us.

And I can assure the assistant U.S. attorney that I did not say on Canadian television that I was like the person checking his own expense account. I said that for the appellate panel that had been excoriated by Madame Justice Ginsburg on behalf of a unanimous Supreme Court, when assigned the task of assessing the gravity of its own errors, to resurrect these two counts after a gymnastic distortion, suppression and fabrication of evidence, was like someone reviewing his own expense account.

Your Honour, these are, in any case, very threadbare counts. Is it really conceivable to you that if I were inexplicably seized with the ambition to embezzle $285,000, I would have it ratified by a committee and then, after what the minutes of the meeting described as "extensive discussion," by the whole board? I would have to have been mad.

And obstruction: It is clear from the evidence that I had nothing to do with selecting or packing the contents of the boxes, had no knowledge of any SEC interest in them after complying with five of its subpoenas, and after being assured by Mrs. Maida that it did not violate the Canadian document retention order, and checking with the acting president of the company, whose letter you have, I helped to carry out the boxes under the gaze of security cameras that I had installed. When these boxes arrived here, they were very full, so if I had taken anything out of them, why would I not have put them at any time over many weeks in my pockets or a brief case? Your Honour, again, to remove documents improperly in this way, I would have had to be barking, raving mad, and insanity is almost the only failing of which the prosecutors have not accused me.

I would like to express here my gratitude to you, Your Honour, for sending me to a prison with email access, where I was able to stay in touch with supporters and with readers of my newspaper and magazine columns. And I must also express my gratitude to the originally small but distinguished and often intellectually brave group of friends, but also of total strangers, who never believed I was guilty, when that was a less fashionable position than it has become. Their numbers grew to be an army that now includes many people in every American state and Canadian province, and region of the United Kingdom, and people in many other countries.

And my gratitude to the many friends I made, inmates and correctional personnel, at the Coleman Low Security Prison, whom I shall not forget, is beyond my ability to express today.

I am of the tradition that tends not to speak publicly of personal matters, but Your Honour, I hope it is acceptable to you if I vary that practice slightly, and briefly, in concluding, today. As you would know, or could surmise from many letters that have been sent to you qualified to comment, and as is mentioned in the presentencing submissions, I believe in the confession and repentance of misconduct and in the punishment of crime. I don't believe in false or opportunistic confessions.

It is not the case, as has been endlessly alleged by the prosecutors, that I have no remorse. I regret that my skepticism about corporate governance zealotry, though it was objectively correct and has been demonstrated to have been so in the destruction of these companies, became so identified with the companies themselves that the shareholders all suffered from it.

I regret that I was too trusting of the honesty of one associate and the thoroughness of some others, and the buck has stopped with me. I repent those and other tactical errors and mistakes of attitude, Your Honour, and

I do not resent paying for those errors, because it is right, and in any case inevitable, that people should pay for their mistakes.

I concluded many years ago in my brief stint as a candidate psychoanalyst that it is practically impossible to repress conscientious remorse. And I concluded some years later in reading some of the works of the recently beatified Cardinal Newman, that our consciences are a divine impulse speaking within us, as Newman wrote, "powerful, peremptory and definitive." My conscience functions like that of other people, and I respond to it, if not precisely as my accusers would wish. But they are prosecutors, not custodians of the consciences of those whom they accuse.

Your Honour, please do not doubt that even though I don't much speak of it, my family and I have suffered deeply from the onslaught of these eight years. I agree with the late pope who said "Life is cruciform." All people suffer. It is a stern message, but need not be a grim one. We rarely know why we suffer, and only those who have faith even believe there is a reason. No one can plausibly explain in moral terms a natural disaster, or a personal tragedy. I see life as a privilege and almost all challenges as opportunities, and have always tried to take success like a gentleman, and disappointment like a man.

Whatever the reason my family and I have had to endure this ordeal, for our purposes today, in these personal questions, I only ask that you take into account the messages you have received about collateral medical problems in my family. I do not worry about myself, and I will not speak further in open court of the worries I do have for my family. But I most earnestly request, Your Honour, as someone who has shown and expressed family sensibilities several times in this case, that they too be taken into account in your sentence.

And I believe that even if a reasonable person still concludes that I am guilty of these two surviving, resurrected, counts, tortuously arrived at and threadbare though their evidentiary basis now is, that the same reasonable person would conclude that I have been adequately punished. I only ask you to recall the criterion you eloquently invoked near the end of the trial that the justice system not be brought into disrepute by an unjust sentence.

I conclude by quoting parts of a famous poem by Kipling, with which I'm sure many in the court are familiar, and which I had known too, but not as well as I knew it after it was sent to me by well-wishers from every continent except Antarctica. And to the extent I was able, I tried to keep in mind throughout these difficult years, what Kipling wrote, which was, in part and as memory serves:

> If you can keep your head while all about you are losing theirs and blaming it on you, If you can trust your own counsel though all men doubt you, but make allowance for their doubting too, If you wait but are not tired of waiting, Are lied about, but don't deal in lies, If some men hate you but you don't stoop to hating; And don't look too good or talk too wise; If you can talk but don't make words your master, Can think but don't make thoughts your aim, If you can meet with triumph and disaster, But treat both those imposters just the same.

And I address this directly to the prosecutors and some of the media:

> If you can bear to hear the truths you've spoken, Twisted by knaves to make a trap for fools, And see the work you gave your life to broken, And stoop to fix it up with worn-out tools.
> If you can make a pile of all your winnings, And risk it on a turn of pitch and toss, And lose and start again at your beginning, And never say a word about your loss.

And Kipling goes on to say that the reader will then be a man. Your Honour, when I first appeared in your court six years ago and you asked me my age, it was sixty-one. If I'm not a man now, I never will be.

I never ask for mercy and seek no one's sympathy. I would never, as was once needlessly feared in this court, be a fugitive from justice in this country, only a seeker of it. It is now too late to ask for justice. But with undimmed respect for this country, this court, and if I may say so, for you personally, I do ask you now to avoid injustice, which it is now in your gift alone to do. I apologize for the length of my remarks, and thank you, for hearing me out, Your Honour.

Appendix E

The Real Rupert Murdoch
October 21, 2011

On Oct. 14, the *Wall Street Journal,* in reporting on the main sentence in the Galleon insider information case, ran a series of five photographs of what were described as "corporate criminals" with their sentences attached, from Bernard Madoff (150 years), down even unto me at six and a half years. On July 18, 2010, the same newspaper ran an extensive lead editorial, headlined "Conrad Black's Revenge," in which it recorded that the four surviving counts against me (of an original 17) had been unanimously vacated by the Supreme Court, the principal prosecuting statute (the much abused concept of Honest Services), had been struck down and rewritten, and the *Journal* graciously apologized to me for having underestimated the merits of my defense. The high court excoriated the panel of the Seventh Circuit of the Circuit Court of Appeal from which I petitioned for, among other transgressions, the "infirmity of invented law." My cameo appearance in the *Journal*'s rogues' gallery on Friday pretended that the original sentence had never been assailed or reduced.

In the perverse American manner, the Supreme Court remanded the vacated counts back to the appellate court to assess the gravity of its own errors. This self-interested process produced a spurious but unsurprising resurrection of one fraud count and a finding of obstruction of justice. The fraud count involved a payment to me of $285,000. That it was undisputed in the evidence had been approved by the executive committee and board of directors of the company, and the obstruction was simply nonsense, and was not pursued in the local jurisdiction (Canada) as a violation of a document retention order, and it had no monetary significance. It was accurately described by a former deputy solicitor general of the United States at the Seventh Circuit, as "in 45 years of practice the feeblest case of obstruction of justice I have seen."

It was these legal fictions, maliciously retrieved to plaster a fig-leaf of plausibility on a misconceived and failed prosecution (that originally sought my imprisonment for life and fines and restitution of $140 million), on the destruction of which the *Journal* had so generously congratulated me 15 months before, that were invoked to put me in the company of Mr. Madoff and the others.

I have written elsewhere of my protracted legal travails and the remaining entrails of them will be dealt with satisfactorily in the appropriate courts (largely, fortunately, out of this country). What is noteworthy in this dishonest donkey kick from the *Wall Street Journal* is what it tells us about the controlling shareholder of that newspaper, the now, to return a frequently proffered favor he served on me, thoroughly "disgraced" and in his own admission, "humbled," Rupert Murdoch.

As I have often written before, he is probably the greatest media-owner in history, and his achievements in becoming the tabloid leader in London, in cracking the egregious Luddite print unions there, in breaking the triopoly of American television networks, promoting vertical integration with television outlets and film production, and his pioneering breakthroughs in satellite television worldwide, are Napoleonic in boldness of concept and skill of execution. And no one has been more vocal or consistent than I in saluting them.

I competed with Murdoch, successfully and quite cordially, in Britain for 15 years when we had the *Telegraph* newspapers, and for a time in

Australia. Our relations and those of our wives were always quite convivial. I never joined the chorus of those who objected to his newspaper cover-price cutting in London; as a capitalist I thought he had every right to cut prices if he wished. And I publicly supported him when he almost went bankrupt 20 years ago, denouncing his critics as motivated by envy.

I was naturally disappointed when, as my own legal problems arose eight years ago, his vast media organization swung into vitriolic defamatory mode, endlessly accusing me of crimes years before any were alleged. When revelations of his own sleazy behavior came to light in the hacking scandals in England, it also came out, confirming what I had heard from my own sources, and which I would have known from my knowledge of how his company is run, that Murdoch had personally intervened to make reporting on my problems nastier (despite having assured me in writing that he would try to prevent excesses). My Madoffization last week almost certainly has the same exalted source.

In earlier times, whenever there had been anything even slightly unfavorable about him in any of our publications, he had called me to object, or had his British managing director call my co-chief executive at the *Telegraph*. Even as he was stoking up the media lynch mob against me, he told his latest biographer, Michael Wolff, as he told others, of his high regard for me as a publisher, as if his febrile libels and fabrications were the coincidental, spontaneous antics of autonomous underlings.

Now Murdoch's company has been stripped naked as the lawless hypocritical organization it has long been; its employees think nothing of trolling for the private conversations of the British royal family, bribing the police, meddling in criminal investigations, tampering with the cell phone of a kidnap victim, and engaging in wholesale industrial espionage.

For decades, Murdoch's publications have smeared, lied, double-crossed his political benefactors, including Jimmy Carter, Margaret Thatcher, John Major, a long sequence of Australian leaders, and the democratic forces of Hong Kong.

When the extent of his companies' skullduggery finally oozed out, sluggish and filthy, including the details of the British government's dotage on him, this summer, Murdoch's old possum routine didn't play as convincingly as it had in its many previous auditions, when he purported to be contrite over the shortcomings of errant employees. Bumbling into a parliamentary hearing in London, supported on each arm like a centenarian semi-cadaver, mumbling about humility, trying to represent News Corporation's board as independent when it is public corporate America's most docile board of directors and is composed entirely of hacks, retainers, and ex-employees; scrambling and whimpering and paying millions to victims of his outrages; putting his name on a *Journal* op-ed piece about education last Saturday; it's all of a piece and none of it resonates anymore. In bygone days, he somehow carried off sprawling in a black costume on a bed in a glossy and ruminating about being an "ambassador to Joe Six Pack," a champion of the little guy, and a spiritual person contemplating the consolations of Catholicism. At its most improbable, it was a passably imaginative imposture.

My admiration for his boldness and acumen and our previous 25 years of more than civil relations make it unpleasant, despite his unspeakable assault on me, to have to conclude that he is, I believe, a psychopath. Behind his nondescript personality lurks a repressed, destructive malice. He has proved to be, in some measure, a proprietor of a criminal organization. This, apart from weaknesses of leadership, was always the greatest vulnerability of post-Reagan America's conservatism: its reliance on a man who would put anyone over the side and hoist any colors when the wind changed. Now that the great defamer is a tottering, cowardly supplicant and a prime candidate for criminal prosecution on at least two continents, no one should count on his continued support for more than 24 hours at a time.

For my part, I am already suing his company in Canada for the most artlessly libelous book since The Protocols of the Elders of Zion, by the defamer Tom Bower. In the extreme winter of his days, Rupert Murdoch's failing hands have dropped the mask; he is a malignant force and it would be a good thing for the world to be done with him.

INDEX

Note: The abbreviation CB in subheadings refers to Conrad Black. The lowercase letter *n* following a page number indicates a footnote.

9/11, 71, 94

Ackerhielm, Jan, 385
Afghanistan war, 73, 518
Agnelli, Gianni, 40, 61, 62, 67
Agnelli, Susanna, 62
Aitken, Jonathan, 65
Alberta Newspapers, 331
Ambrozic, Aloysius M. (Cardinal), 58
American Publishing, 41, 97, 130, 390, 414, 420
American Trucker, 267, 289, 289*n*, 386
Amiel, Barbara: after trial, 431, 432; asset freeze ordered by Campbell, 337, 338-39; buys shares from CB, 331, 334; and CB's appeals, 470-71, 474-75, 482; and CB's bail and sentencing, 429-30, 484, 487, 489, 494-96; and CB's criminal charges, 299-300; and CB's criminal trial, 323, 347, 352, 355, 357-58, 365, 367-68, 372, 389, 393, 400-401, 405, 407, 410, 412, 415-16, 424, 427, 436; and CB's imprisonment, 444-45, 454, 459, 464, 468, 480; and CB's legal bills, 277; on CB's reaction to restructuring demands, 143; and CB's sentencing, 438; as director of Hollinger, 126, 140, 142, 144-45, 160, 161-62, 164, 183, 227, 229, 235, 240, 275; dismissed from *Telegraph*, 127, 197; false reports about, in press, 59, 148-49, 150, 156, 215-16, 215*n*, 236, 253, 315-16, 317; final days before CB's imprison-ment, 441, 442-43, 445; finances, 325-26; friendships, 59, 133, 244-45, 283, 307, 381, 415, 436, 493; homes with CB, 57-59, 188, 245, 262-63, 264-65, 270-71, 300, 313-14; as hostess, 59, 106, 152, 153, 202, 379; included in International lawsuit, 197; IRS harassment, 314, 315; Jewish faith, 30, 51, 53, 288, 315; legal bills, 263; legal unassailability, 426; letter of support for CB, 436; life with CB, 59-60, 94, 147, 152, 157, 164, 212, 239, 242, 259, 264, 291, 311, 335; at *Maclean's*, 200, 307, 318; marriage to CB, 18, 57, 119; Newman's writings about, 315-16; newspaper expertise, 24*n*, 33; pets, 351, 442, 442*n*, 486, 491; purchases Warhol of CB, 433; researches Strine, 185-86; reunited with CB, 485-86; and sale of Inc. to Barclays, 179-80; and sale of Palm Beach house, 491; social life, 59, 65, 105, 196-97; stock in International, 306, 327; and stresses of CB's struggles, 171, 176, 224, 252-53, 258, 259, 282, 285-86, 495-96; travels with CB, 20, 22, 26, 27, 30-31, 85, 89-92, 110, 282-85, 289, 306; unease with royals, 69; view of Genson, 348-49; work for Murdoch, 23-24; writings, 52, 171
Anderson, Bruce, 44
Andreas, Dwayne, 40, 61, 63, 126, 200
Annenberg, Lee, 333
Annenberg, Walter, 103
Arafat, Yasser, 54, 55
Ardell, Bill, 28
Arens, Moshe, 61
Argus Corporation: approves sale of Inc., 178, 180; CB and brother take control

of, 6-7; CB's holdings, 111; CB's restructuring of, 7-8; debt, 39; dependence on dividends, 32; privatization, 18; and Warhol paintings of CB, 339-40

Arnold, Gordon, 326

Asper, Israel, 84-86, 87, 93, 96, 387

Asper, Leonard, 93

Aspinall, John, 65, 66, 132

Associated Newspapers, 135, 151, 169

Astor, Brooke, 70-71

Astor, Vincent, 70

Atkinson, Peter: assures CB that accounts are in order, 120; bail granted, 470; in Breeden's report, 213, 280; character and personality, 143, 280, 295; convictions, 425, 427; criminal charges against, 294-95, 318, 323, 346, 420-21, 423; criminal trial, 330, 350, 353, 359, 369, 371, 374, 398, 407, 408-9, 413; as director of Hollinger, 126, 160, 162; lack of suspicion about Radler, 329; looks into Vogt affair, 328; and non-competition agreements, 96, 122, 133; OSC hearings, 252; Radler's testimony on, 390; resignation, 176; response to Special Committee demands, 137, 138, 139, 140-41, 294; on Sabia, 160; and sale of Hollinger's U.S. papers, 83; Special Committee's demand to oust as director, 136; suggests Savage for Special Committee, 128; targeted by Breeden, 180; testimony to Special Committee, 280, 290; transferred to Canada and released, 478; visits BNS with CB, 102

Atwood, Margaret, 432

Audit Committee, Hollinger International: accusations in Breeden Report, 218-19; accusations in Breeden's report, 213; approves Hollinger management fees, 40, 97, 371; approves non-competition payments, 134, 171, 299; approves sells of

U.S. papers, 97, 123-24; asks CB about non-competition payments, 133-34; assures CB that accounts are in order, 120; Breeden's control over, 140; composition, 114-15; members questioned during criminal trial, 350-51, 373-83

Aufhauser, David, 195

Australian Financial Review, 16

Australian newspapers, 16, 42, 386

Aviv (Israeli), 430

Axel Springer, 169

Bacall, Lauren, 25

Badenhausen, Jim, 249

Bain & Company, 120, 121

Baker Botts (law firm): and CB's criminal trial, 348, 349; handles non-criminal legal work, 265, 291, 309; payments to, 327-28; retained by CB, 225

Baldwin, Stanley, 11

Bank of America, 89, 95, 103n

Bank of Nova Scotia (BNS), 95-96, 102-3, 103n

Bank One, 95-96, 103n

Barak, Ehud, 55

Barclay brothers: buy *Telegraph* from International, 191, 210; interest in *Telegraph*, 169, 185, 204, 205; lack of success with *Telegraph*, 281; negotiations to buy Inc., 171, 173, 175, 177-79, 182, 183, 193-94; own Telegraph plc, 436; and suit to prevent purchase of Inc., 184-85, 189, 190, 191, 192

Barclay, David, 169, 171, 177, 189, 194, 281

Barclay, Frederick, 169

Barford, Ralph M., 98

Bar-Illan, David, 54, 73

Bassett, Douglas, 160-62

Bass, Mercedes, 157

Bass, Sid, 157

Belobaba, Edward, 477

Benedict XVI, 48

Bergen, Candice, 157, 436
Berg, Morton, 226
Bernard, Daniel, 51-52
Berry, Adrian, 9
Berry, Michael (Lord Hartwell), 8-9, 285
Berry, Nicholas, 9
Bialkin, Ken, 300
Biden, Joe, 413, 479
Bilderberg conferences, 110, 129, 200-201
Birley, Mark, 283
Birley, Robin, 284
Black, Alana: and CB's bail and sentenc-
    ing, 428; and CB's freedom, 486; and
    CB's sentencing, 438; at CB's sixtieth
    birthday, 226; journalist's attempt to
    pry secrets from, 372; letter of support
    for CB, 436; star of the trial, 357, 367;
    supports CB during trial, 351-52, 355,
    357-58, 393, 401, 407, 410, 412, 416,
    427; twenty-fifth birthday, 415; visits
    CB in Palm Beach, 431; visits CB in
    prison, 468
Black, Conrad: citizenship, 77, 79-80,
    158; columns, 537-49; directorships,
    126, 165-66, 433, 453n; education, 4-5,
    158; faith, 118-19, 304, 444, 456-57;
    financial struggles, 164-65, 167-70, 207,
    304, 306, 311-12, 313, 325-26, 328;
    freedom, 485-86; health, 454; holidays,
    30-31, 85, 89-92, 282-85, 330; marriage
    to Barbara, 18, 57, 152; newspaper
    columns, 282, 307, 342, 351, 448;
    peerage, 76-80, 94, 433; relationship
    with shareholders, 66-67n; sixtieth
    birthday, 225; titles, 2, 58
Black, Conrad, as book author:
    Duplessis book, 5, 453n; FDR book
    promotions, 150, 155, 156, 157; FDR
    book reviews, 149, 150, 307; FDR
    books donated to Coleman library,
    469; FDR book writing and publica-
    tion, 3, 116-17, 121, 461; impugned in
    Breeden report, 214-15; Nixon book
    promotion, 432; Nixon book reviews,
400, 428; Nixon book writing and
    publication, 280, 334-35, 340, 342,
    343, 351, 461; U.S. history, 496-97
Black, Conrad, as Hollinger chairman:
    diminishing authority, 116, 121; firing,
    179; management fees, 38, 40, 97,
    111-12
Black, Conrad, as magazine publisher:
    Saturday Night, 34; *Spectator*,
    25-26, 39
Black, Conrad, as newspaper publisher:
    buys out brother, 18; in Canada, 16-17,
    27-37; combining quality and prof-
    itability, 17-18; early years, 4-5; in
    England, 8, 9-10, 14-15, 42; and expan-
    sion of company, 16-17; internationally,
    39-40; price war with Murdoch,
    20-24; relationship with staff, 12, 15,
    17-18, 24-25, 45; removed as chairman
    of *Telegraph*, 199
Black, Conrad, imprisonment: lifestyle,
    1-2, 443, 445-48, 480-81, 495, 499-505,
    511-513; piano lessons, 453; work, as
    English tutor, 461-63
Black, Conrad, legal battles: acquittals,
    convictions, bail, and sentencing, 2,
    425-28, 429-31, 437-41, 483, 484-86,
    494-96; appeals, 428, 440-41, 470-75,
    478-80, 482-84, 488-90; asset freeze,
    337-39; criminal charges against,
    269-70, 293-94, 318, 321-22, 323, 351,
    419-23; criminal trial, 384-85, 393-94,
    400, 402-4; deposition before Strine,
    187, 189-90, 192; eviction from 10
    Toronto Street, 266, 270-73, 402;
    Glassman's oppression action, 221;
    libel settlement, 491-92; OSC hear-
    ings, 252; and prosecutors' manipula-
    tion of system, 519-21; statement to
    court (June 2011), 550-56; sued by
    Desmond, 104; sued by SEC, 190,
    220, 223-24, 238; sues *Daily Express*
    for libel, 104; suit against Newman,
    316; suit against Sotheby's Realty,

459; suit by Voorheis, 336-38; suits against Breedon, Seitz, Savage, Paris, and Healy, 220, 477-78, 486; Walker–Carroll–Kelly suit claiming bilking from Inc., 266

Black, Conrad, public and media image: after CB steps down as Hollinger CEO, 148, 149, 150-53, 158, 169; after criminal trial, 428; after Ginsburg ruling, 483-84; after release of Breeden's report, 215-16, 236-37; before and during criminal trial, 340-42; in Britain, 10, 158; in Canada, after sale of papers, 86; in Canada, in early 1980s, 7-8; in Canada, over CB's citizenship, 79-80, 158; during Iraq war debates, 73; of homes and lifestyle, 59-60, 156; in United States, 158

Black Family Foundation, 333

Black, James: and CB's freedom, 486; at CB's sixtieth birthday, 226; supports CB during trial, 357, 407, 412

Black, Jonathan: and CB's freedom, 486; at CB's sixtieth birthday, 226; health, 291; letter of support for CB, 436; supports CB during trial, 357, 386, 393, 407, 412

Black, Monte, 6-7, 18, 117, 132

Blackwell, Richard, 275

Blair, Tony, 19, 40, 46, 76-77

Blatchford, Christie, 93

Block, Dennis, 130, 193, 219

Bloomberg, Michael, 157

Boies, David, 125, 134-35, 142-43, 164

Boies, Schiller & Flexner, 142

Boultbee, Jack: assures CB that accounts are in order, 120; bail granted, 470, 478; cautions White about Chant shares, 227; convictions, 425, 427; criminal charges against, 295, 318, 351, 419-21, 423; criminal trial, 349, 353, 372, 412; as director of Hollinger, 160, 164; evicted from 10 Toronto Street, 266; family support during trial, 357-58; friendship with CB, 415; handling of Hollinger accounting, 104; and International debt, 220; knowledge of CB's finances, 204; and non-competition agreements, 96, 122, 133, 387; OSC hearings, 252; posts bond, 333; Radler's testimony on, 390; removed from Hollinger board, 235; response to Special Committee demands, 139, 140, 146; Special Committee's demand to oust as officer, 136; struggles to save Inc. after U.S. restructuring, 163, 194; suggested to step down as director, 227, 229; testimony to Special Committee, 290

Boultbee, Leslie, 358

Boultbee, Michael, 357

Boultbee, Sharon, 357

Bourelly, Alex, 404, 428

Bower, Tom, 316-17, 344, 464

Bradford Publications (U.S.), 84

Bradshaw, Richard, 307

Braff, David, 164, 172

Brascan, 166

Breeden, Richard: attends July 2003 directors meeting by telephone, 124; CB's libel suit against, 220, 361-62, 477-78, 486; CB warned about, 115, 129; character and personality, 135-36, 159-60, 195, 260, 270; and charges against Ravelston, 297; as counsel to Special Committee, 115-16, 125, 154, 187, 290, 374; and criminal charges against CB, 268, 344; dealings with OSC, 185, 254-55, 258, 279, 371; earnings from Hollinger, 191, 231, 233, 243, 259; errs in reliance on subordinates, 251; false allegations against CB and others, 293-94, 296, 302-3; hedge fund, 308; and Inc.'s privatization attempts, 252, 254, 268; intent, power, and tactics, 164-65, 167, 169, 171-72, 174, 180-81, 185, 192-94, 221, 260, 483; keeps Lazard process closed, 232; and lawsuit against Inc., 183; limits Strategic Process just to British assets, 198; lip service to Inc., 174; as monitor for Special Committee, 191-92, 246; not well remembered by previous colleagues, 115, 225; and Ravelston receivership, 260; reaction to Barclay deal, 182; refuses settlement talks, 199; relationship with Cerberus, 202-3, 206; reneges on Restructuring Agreement, 162-63, 193, 435; repayment and restructuring demands, 135-37, 138, 140, 141; Restructuring Agreement negotiations, 141-46; retirement from Hollinger, 476; role in Hollinger bankruptcies, 260, 435, 436; sale of *Telegraph* to Barclays, 191, 208n, 208-9, 211; Special Committee report, 213-15, 217-19, 221, 361-62, 399; Special Committee timeline, 134; as special monitor at WorldCom, 202-3; suit to prevent Barclay deal, 188-90, 198; takes control of International, 177-78, 180-81, 246; targets CB, 193, 195, 207, 280, 301, 361, 435, 441, 478-79; testimony to FBI, 342; view of corporate governance, 186

Bremner, Rory, 12

Breyer, Stephen, 479-80

Brinkley, David, 61

Britain *see* United Kingdom

Browne, Christopher: agitation about management payments, 99-100, 112-13, 218; on CB's Palm Beach home, 253; death, 442n; final conversation with CB, 114; friendship with Healy, 156; and negative reports about CB and Hollinger, 108-9, 110; urges sale of Hollinger, 109

Brown, Tina, 157, 307, 448

Bryan, Shelby, 332

Brzezinski, Zbigniew, 61

Buckley, Pat, 131, 307, 441

Buckley, Tommy, 3, 188

Buckley, William: at FDR book launch, 157; holiday with CB and Amiel, 131, 307; on Hollinger advisory board, 61; loyalty to CB, 332, 440-41; runs *National Review*, 307

Buffett, Warren, 99, 442n

Burnham (Lord), 10

Burt, Richard: accusations in Breeden report, 219, 240; on Audit Committee, 114; brings in Breeden, 128; cautioned about Breeden, 219; CB's last encounter with, 376; character and personality, 193, 283; deposition before Strine, 187; as director of Hollinger, 127; expresses interest in settlement talks, 199; follows Breeden's lead, 192, 219, 240; on Hollinger advisory board, 61; and NYSE guidelines, 240; and Restructuring Agreement negotiations, 139, 144, 146; testimony at criminal trial, 373-76, 426; testimony to FBI, 342

Bush, Barbara, 103

Bush family, 40

Bush, George H.W., 344

Bush, George W., 47, 71, 459, 476-77, 478n

Buthelezi (Zulu chief), 3, 67

Califano, Joe, 314

Campbell, Colin: animus toward CB, 277; castigates Walker et al., 279; and CB's removal of boxes from 10 Toronto Street, 270-71, 272-73, 422; character and personality, 221, 233-34; and Confidential Settlement Agreement, 432; ejects White from Inc. board, 275; freezes CB's and Amiel's assets, 337, 338; hears of money transfer to Chant estate, 228; and Inc.'s privatization attempts, 248, 251; orders CB, Amiel, Boultbee, and Radler off board of Inc., 229, 235, 249; role in destroying Inc., 221, 247, 259, 266, 434

Camrose (Lord), 10

Canada: CB's advocacy and love for, 5-6, 78-80; incarcerations, 500; justice system, 312, 321-22, 406-7, 506-7; media ownership rules, 82; protocols surrounding U.K. peerages for Canadians, 76-77
Canada Revenue Agency, 253, 263-64, 296, 330, 336, 423
Canadian Imperial Bank of Commerce (CIBC): CB's directorship with, 165-66; cuts off CB's credit, 432; directors dine at Black's, 106; failure to refinance CanWest, 87-88; finances Asper, 86
CanWest: buys Hollinger papers, 84-86, 96; CB's directorship, 166; Hollinger payment to, 121; non-competition payments, 336, 369, 420-21; owns part of *National Post*, 92-93; Radler's testimony on, 390; refinancing, 87-88
Caracciolo, Carlo, 26
Cardinal Capital, 437
Caroline, Hereditary Princess of Monaco, 69
Carr, Bob, 283
Carrington, Peter (Lord): on CB's understanding of England, 10; as director of Hollinger, 225; friendship with CB, 265, 283; on Hollinger advisory board, 61; meets Kissinger, 132; military service, 63; sponsors CB for peerage, 94
Carroll, Don, 229
Carroll, Paul: against privatization, 245-46, 249; character and personality, 224, 251-52; as director of Hollinger, 224; earnings from Hollinger, 259; fired by Richter, 279; lawsuit against CB regarding Inc. payments, 250, 266; need to oust, 258; wants to settle with SEC, 243, 246
Carter, Gerald Emmett (Cardinal), 48, 58, 61, 117-18, 239
Carter, Jimmy, 20

Catalyst Fund, 221, 233, 255-56
Cates, Stanley, 111, 113
Cazenoves company, 23, 67
Cebrián, Juan Luis, 26
Cerberus, 202-3, 204, 205-7
Chambers, Ray, 126
Chancellor, Alexander, 237
Chant, Dixon, 227, 229
Charles, Prince of Wales, 42
Cherniak, Earl, 337, 393, 394
Chicago Sun-Times: circulation "scandal", 203-4, 289; falling income in early 2000s, 87; head office for International's community paper division, 84; reports on CB, 215, 416, 428; stocks fall, 434-35; strike threats, 238; under Radler, 290, 391
Chile, 56
Cho, Maya, 173, 226
Chrétien, Jean: complaints about *National Post*, 75-76, 77, 78, 94; opposes CB's peerage, 77-79; public opinion, 79; relationship with CB, 76, 271; sued by CB, 78
Churchill, Winston, 10, 11
Clarke, Kenneth, 211
Cliff, Ron, 30
Clinton, Bill, 244
Clinton, Hillary, 20
Cockwell, Jack, 102
Cohen, Ronnie, 284
Coleman Federal Correctional Complex, Florida: appearance, 444-45; CB leaves, 485; CB's lifestyle in, 1-2, 445-49, 453-54, 459-60, 464-65; inmates, 446, 449-52, 453-54, 455, 465-66, 494; medical facilities, 468; personnel, 445, 459-61, 465, 469, 494; religious life, 455-58; underground economy, 469-70; visitors, 467-68; work for inmates, 460-62
Collins, Joan, 157, 332
Colson, Dan: added to lawsuit, 197; and Australian papers, 16, 386; on

circulation practices at *Chicago Sun-Times*, 203; and criminal charges against CB, 293; as director of Hollinger, 126, 140, 145, 183-84; does not buckle to Breeden, 164; fired, 196; Hollinger refinancing negotiations, 103; management of *Telegraph*, 24-25, 199, 209; sells Hollinger's French-Canadian papers, 88; sensitivity to value of *Telegraph*, 109

Colucci, Paul, 238

Community Newspaper Holdings Inc., 363

Conacher, Lionel, 207

Conservative Party, Britain, 10, 12, 211, 433

Constantine II, 69

Cooke, Joe, 24

Cooperman, Lee, 100, 112

Corcoran, Terence, 150, 254

Corporate Review Committee (CRC), Hollinger, 183

Coulter, Ann, 333, 431

Craig, Greg: as attorney for CB, 240, 252, 268, 276; billings, 312-13, 314-15; CB ends relationship with, 315, 318-19; and CB's criminal prosecution, 291, 292-93, 294; and sale of CB's New York apartment, 308-9

Cramer, Jeffrey: character and personality, 322, 375, 424; opening statement at CB's trial, 357, 358, 372, 400; questions Funk at trial, 407; questions Maida at trial, 404-5

Cravath, Swaine & Moore, 96, 369

Creasey, Fred: and non-competition payments, 122; on Sabia, 160; stress of restructuring, 176-77; testimony at criminal trial, 365-67, 379, 417, 421, 425

Crown Trust Company, 84

Dacre, Paul, 25

Daifallah, Adam, 334

Daily Beast (online), 307, 448

Daily News (Prince Rupert, B.C.), 16

Daily Telegraph (London): Argus shares in, 18; Barclays' interest in, 169, 185, 204-5; Barclay's lack of success with, 281; Barclays' purchase of, 191, 204; as bastion of British Conservative Party, 10; CB acquires control of, 8, 9-10; CB's chairmanship of, 3; CB's relief to be free of, 281; criticisms of Major government, 14-15; employees' reaction to Hollinger restructuring, 151-52; endorses Hurd, 12; and EU, 47; falling income in early 2000s, 87; foreign policy debates, 44-46; and Israel–Palestine conflicts, 54, 55; price competition with other papers, 20-24, 26-27, 41-42; privatization, 23; removes CB as chairman, 199; reports on CB, 3; reports on Hollinger restructuring, 151; sale of, and shareholder votes, 199, 204-5, 206, 208; success in late 1980s/early 1990s, 16; under Hartwell, 9; value, 109

Daley, Richard, 238

Dalrymple, William, 53

D'Angelo, Dan, 412

Davies Ward Phillips & Vineberg, 162

Davis, Carl, 415

Debold, David, 479, 488, 490

Deedes, Bill, 10

de la Renta, Annette, 70, 157

de la Renta, Oscar, 157

Delors, Jacques, 49

DeMerchant, Beth, 368-69

Denton, Herbert, 109, 112

Dershowitz, Alan, 194-95, 428

D.E. Shaw, 264

Desmarais, André, 27-28

Desmarais, Paul, 27-28, 30, 40

Desmond, Richard, 104, 151, 211, 464

Despont, Thierry, 58

Diana, Princess of Wales, 68

Diller, Barry, 157

Domenico (houseman), 485

Dominion Stores, 7, 288

Domtar, 7
Döpfner, Mathias, 169
Doull, Matthew, 130
Dunne, Dominick, 367
Duplessis, Maurice L., 5, 453, 453n
Dutoit, Charles, 128

Easterbrook, Frank, 470-71, 472
Eastern Townships Advertiser, 5, 39
Eaton, Fred, 14, 160-62
Ebbers, Bernie, 202
Ebert, Roger, 238
Eimer, Nate, 195, 244, 246, 270, 276
Eisenhower, Julie Nixon, 103, 415
Elizabeth II, 68, 69, 77, 161
Elizabeth, The Queen Mother, 68, 69
England *see* United Kingdom
English, David, 25
Enright, Michael, 155
Ernst & Young: billings, 221, 243, 246,
    248, 251, 259, 266; investigation of
    Inc., 221, 235, 243, 248, 251, 254
Ertegun, Ahmet, 157
Ertegun, Mica, 157
Estrada, Miguel, 311, 475, 478-79, 478n,
    482, 484-85, 487, 488-90
Etherington, Bill, 165-66
European Union (EU): difficulties of
    union, 46-48; U.K. avoids, 48-49, 76;
    view of Israel, 51

Fairfax (Australian newspaper company),
    16, 18, 42
Farley, James: character and personality,
    259n, 266; evicts CB and others from
    10 Toronto Street, 266, 402; and pro-
    ceedings against Ravelston, 297-99;
    prohibits removals from 10 Toronto
    Street, 271; role in destroying Inc.,
    259, 434
Feldstein, Martin, 61, 332
Fell, Tony, 167
Fennell, Theo, 265
Financial Post, 94

Finkelstein, Jesse: advice in specialist
    Delaware questions, 164; advice to
    CB on Barclay deal, 177, 182; and
    CB's deposition before Strine, 190;
    and CB's responses to Special
    Committee, 133-34, 139-40, 143;
    replaced by Jenkins and Polesky, 328;
    retained by CB, 124-25; on Strine, 185
Fitzgerald, Patrick: attends criminal trial,
    382; brings criminal charges against
    CB, 293-94, 344; humbled, 483; not
    happy with trial results, 427; suggests
    CB might try to escape jurisdiction,
    346; threatens extradition, 318
Flumenbaum, Martin, 199, 207
Fogler Rubinoff, 232
Ford, Gerald, 103
Forstman, Teddy, 121
Forsyth, Freddie, 151
Forte, Rocco, 284
Forum, 363, 386, 387, 425
Fox, Gene, 437-38
Francoeur, Jacques, 88-89
Fraser, John, 434
Freedman, Stan, 328, 370
Freisler, Roland, 472
Frey, Andy, 311, 441, 472, 474-75, 488
Frost, David, 41
Frum, David, 150
Fulford, Robert, 155
Funk (forensic accountant), 407
Furnish, David, 285, 306, 332

Gadhafi, Muammar, 44, 62
Gates, Bill, 99
Genson, Eddie: awaits verdict, 424;
    and CB's bail hearing, 430; on CB's
    co-defendants, 347; at CB's sentenc-
    ing, 437, 438; character and personal-
    ity, 319-20, 346, 348-49, 375; closing
    remarks at trial, 411-12; defends CB
    against criminal charges, 320, 374,
    403, 404, 405, 407, 410; effectiveness
    at trial, 416, 418; files listing of

Sussman's lies, 334; and Greenspan's lack of U.S. experience, 361, 367, 381; jury selection, 355; opening statement at trial, 358-59; plans for Alana and Amiel, 352; questions Burt at trial, 375-76; questions buyers at trial, 363-64; questions Healy at trial, 401; questions Maida at trial, 404-5; questions Paris at trial, 360; questions Stitt at trial, 371; retained by CB, 319-20, 327; and Rosenberg's testimony, 399; in scheduling meetings, 347

Gibson, Percy, 332
Gilbert, Martin, 306
Gillespie, Terry, 349, 367
Gingrich, Newt, 61
Ginsburg, Ruth Bader, 482
Giscard d'Estaing, Valéry, 61, 63, 64
Giuliani, Rudy, 244-45
Glass, Charlie, 53
Glassman, Newton: action to remove all Ravelston directors, 228; buys TD shares in Inc., 256; and Chant transfer, 228; objects to refinancing of Inc., 197; oppression action, 221, 223, 234, 255; solicits new directors, 230-31; tries to buy CB's Toronto house mortgage, 338; view of independent directors, 207, 208n
Glezos, George, 429, 429n
GMP Securities, 250
Godfrey, Paul, 82
Godsoe, Peter, 102
Goldsmith, Annabel, 67, 283
Goldsmith, James, 40, 61-62, 64-67, 134
Goldsmith, Manos, 66
Gordon, Walter, 434
Gotlieb, Allan, 60-62, 68, 160-62
Goyer, Jean-Pierre, 128
Gramm, Phil, 48
Grasso, Dick, 165
Greenspan, Alan, 201
Greenspan, Eddie: accompanies CB to SEC hearing, 172, 416; advice to CB

on counsel, 164, 195; arranges press interviews, 424; on Breeden, 164-65, 185; and CB's bail hearing, 429-30; at CB's sentencing, 437; character and personality, 311, 383-84, 418-19; and charges against Ravelston, 297-98; cleans up 2003 International statement, 244; closing arguments at trial, 410-11; concern about CB's Chicago apartment, 352; considers criminal charges unlikely, 240, 277; considers forcing Campbell off CB case, 277; counsels silence, 335; defends CB against criminal charges, 269, 318, 319-20, 400, 402-3, 405, 415; effectiveness at trial, 416-19, 428; fights freeze on CB's and Amiel's assets, 338; friendship with CB, 176, 349, 416; gets CB's bail reduced, 319; gives libel notice to Newman, 318; handles potential contempt case for CB, 274; handles York Club incident, 434; health, 347, 393, 394, 416; and Inc.'s privatization attempts, 253-54, 255; interview with *National Post*, 440; jury selection, 355; lack of U.S. experience, 346-48, 361, 362, 365, 367-68, 375, 376, 388, 417; and Maida's testimony, 405; and opening statement at trial, 358; performance in United States, 336; and possibility of CB's testimony, 384; questions Creasey at trial, 366, 379, 417; questions Kravis at trial, 377-79, 417; questions Paris at trial, 360-61; questions Radler at trial, 387-89, 391, 393-95, 417; questions Thompson at trial, 381-82, 417; questions Whyte at trial, 405; on Radler's sleazy practices, 295-96; reaction to trial results, 427; retainer, 327; and Rosenberg's testimony, 399; strategy sessions for Glassman case, 222; on Strine, 195; sues *Toronto Life*, 236; *Telegraph* hearing before Strine, 208;

tutors CB's staff on dealing with intrusions, 311

Greenspan, Juliana, 368, 393

Greenspoon, Avi, 234, 247, 248, 249, 257

Green, Stephen, 429

Griffiths McBurney & Partners, 243, 246

Griffiths, Sally, 199-200

Groia, Joseph, 160

Gross, David, 54

Ground, Jack, 339

Gurland, Carolyn, 349, 437-40, 443, 452, 471

Hague, William, 76

Halberstadt, Victor, 200

Halperin, Steve, 249

Hanson, James (Lord), 40, 134

Harel-Cohen, Sharon, 284

Harmsworth, Vere (Lord Rothermere), 25, 45

HarperCollins, 317

Harper, Stephen, 40

Harriman, Pamela, 62

Hartwell (Lord), 8-9, 285

Hastings, Max: anti-Major sentiment, 13; character and personality, 24-25, 44; as editorial writer, 15; on EU disputes, 49; influenced by Hurd, 12; on Irish Question, 45-46; marriage to Jewish woman, 56; reaction to Hollinger restructuring, 151; relationship with Moore, 13; resigns from Telegraph, 24

Hawkins, Mason, 110, 112, 113, 116

Hayward, Doug, 284

Healy, Paul: CB's libel suit against, 220, 477-78; character and personality, 401-2; as director of Telegraph, 199; lack of knowledge of CB's finances, 205, 207; leaks false stories about CB, 156-57; testimony at trial, 351, 400-402, 421, 426; testimony to FBI, 342; threats against Pedemura, 404; turns against CB, 107-8, 109

Heath, Edward, 11, 73

Henson, Jim, 362-63

Hertog, Roger, 333, 484, 492

Herzog, Chaim, 61, 63

Heseltine, Michael, 11-12, 26, 211

Hillier, John, 272, 444

Hogg, Sarah, 12

Hollinger Digital, 130

Hollinger Inc. (Canada): advisory board, 60-62, 67-68; Argus shares in, 7, 18; attempted sale to Barclays, 169, 171-72, 173, 177, 178-80, 182; backed by Ravelston, 105-6; balance of debt with acquisitions, 37-41; collapse, 370-71, 434-35; and corporate governance, 97-98; debt, debt reductions, and refinancing, 87, 89, 92, 94, 98, 103-5, 110, 121, 135; Glassman's oppression action against, 221; management fees, 110-11; media reports of financial pressures, 108; mining ventures, 60, 124n, 369; non-competition agreements, 83, 96-97, 110, 160, 174, 246; OSC hearings, 252; ownership in daily newspapers in Canada, 32; privatization attempts, 120, 203, 220, 229, 231-35, 238, 245-50, 253-56, 303; receivership, 221, 259, 429-30, 433; relationship to International, 6-7n, 95, 104; response to International's lawsuit, 184; and Restructuring Agreement, 142, 144, 145, 162-63, 174-75, 526-36; restructuring demands, 160-62; sale of papers, 82-86; sale of secondary assets, 88; seeks insolvency protection, 336; Series III liquidity warning, 107; shares in Southam, 27, 30, 82; Special Committee demands, 135-38, 139; Special Committee review, 121-22, 136-37; structure, 111; struggle for survival after Breeden report, 220, 231-32; struggle for survival after U.S. restructuring, 160-63, 165, 169, 171, 173-75, 194-95, 196, 197-98, 202, 206; sued by

International, 177, 178-79, 183;
Voorheis's atttempts to sell super-
voting rights, 370
Hollinger International (U.S.): *see also*
Sun-Times Media Group (STMG)
2002 annual meeting, 99-100; accepts
terms regarding Inc., 232; attempts to
break up, 3-4; catches up its financial
reportings, 327; challenges Inc.'s right
to sell to Barclays, 184-85; cost of
Breeden's inquisition, 238-39; creation,
41, 130; debt, debt reductions, and
refinancing, 95, 98, 103-4, 105, 220;
demands for depositions, 291; failure of
Strategic Process, 244; management
fees, 40, 97, 105-6; non-competition
agreements, 83, 96, 122-24, 246;
offered first refusal on Inc., 175, 177;
privatization attempts, 120, 203, 206,
220, 240-41; profits affected by newspaper price war, 21-22; reaction to
Barclay deal, 182-84; receivership,
259; refuses to deal with Walker, 278;
relationship to Inc., 6-7*n*, 95, 104,
254-55; reneges on Restructuring
Agreement, 162-63, 184; required to
pay legal fees, 327-28; Restructuring
Agreement/Strategic Process negotiations, 141-46, 174-75; retains *Telegraph*
and some U.S. papers, 86; sale of
papers, 81, 88, 123; sale of secondary
assets, 88, 92; sale of *Telegraph*,
209; shares decline in mid 2000s,
248; shares sold to SEAM, 110-11;
Special Committee demands,
135-38; Special Committee review,
121-22; stocks rise after Strine judgment, 194; Strategic Process, 191,
198, 220; structure, 111; sues Inc., 177,
178-79, 183
Home, Sir Alec-Douglas, 11
Honest Services Statute, 479
Horizon Operations (Canada), 84, 289,
328, 330

Horizon Publications (U.S.), 84, 331, 334
Howard, John, 16
Howard, Michael, 211, 283
Howard, Peter, 336, 337
Howe, Geoffrey, 11
Humphries, Barry, 283, 332
Hunkin, John, 166
Hurd, Douglas, 12, 49
Hussein, Saddam, 72

Icahn, Carl, 100
Independent (London), 26
Ingersoll, Bret, 203
Ingraham, Laura, 296-97, 332
Internet, 29, 38-39, 391
Iran, 72
Iraq war, 72-73
Ireland, 45-46
Irish Republican Army, 46
Irvine, Derry, 57, 94
Israel: CB's views, 50-51; history, 54-55;
peace process, 53-54; views on CB, 73

Jackman, Duncan, 339
Jackman, Henry (Hal) N.R., 40, 150,
339, 433
Jackman, Maruja, 340
Jankowski, Werner, 405
Jeffress, William, 225, 269
Jeffries & Company, 109, 220
Jenkins, David, 328
Jereski, Laura: agitation about manage-
ment payments, 99, 112, 113, 218, 245,
256; negative reports about CB to
media, 108, 233; reports to Special
Committee, 127
Jerusalem Post: board, 39-40; contract to
print *Golden Pages*, 127, 329;
Hollinger's ownership, 2, 53; losses
under Radler, 329, 391; and Oslo
Accord, 53-54
Jerusalem Report, 53
Joffe, Joseph, 61
John, Elton, 265, 285, 306, 332, 340

Johnson, Boris: character and personality, 26; political career, 26, 51, 65; reaction to Hollinger restructuring, 151; reconciliation with CB, 283; as *Spectator* editor, 26, 53, 281
Johnson, Frank, 26
Johnson, Lyndon, 459
Jonas, George: and CB's criminal trial, 346, 368, 394, 410, 417, 418; friendship with CB and Amiel, 173, 176, 226, 316; rebuttal to journalist's charge of CB's thievery, 282; on Supreme Court decision on Posner's hearing, 484; on U.S. and Canadian judges, 230; and Voorheis's false affidavit, 430
Jonas, Maya, 415
Jordan, Vernon, 200
Joseph, Greg, 231
Journal Pioneer (Summerside, P.E.I.), 16

Kaplan, Igor, 125
Kaplan, Lewis, 475
Kay, Jonathan, 484
Keating, Paul, 16, 20
Kelly, Doug, 282
Kelly, Jane, 349, 368, 393, 394, 418-19, 422
Kelly, Tony: accuses CB of contempt of court, 272, 274; character and personality, 250; comments on Hollinger/CB debt, 230; delays Inc. privatization, 246, 248, 249, 251; lawsuit against CB regarding Inc. payments, 266; prosecutors get to, 303; replaces Strosberg, 231; venom against CB, 274
Kenny, Mary, 216
Kent, Robert: assures Craig that CB is not target of criminal investigation, 240; conducts criminal investigation into CB and others, 252; and criminal charges against CB, 276-77, 291, 322; recommends criminal prosecution, 266-67; reliance on Breeden report, 267, 276, 293
Kimball, Roger, 333, 432, 492

Kinnock, Neil, 13-14, 479
Kipnis, Mark: acquited on one count, 436; assures CB that accounts are in order, 120; character and personality, 294; convictions, 425, 427; criminal charges against, 293, 294-95, 318, 346, 419-20, 423; criminal trial, 330, 350, 353, 360, 371, 382-83, 398, 413; family support during trial, 357; jury selection, 355; and non-competition agreements, 122, 133; Radler's testimony on, 390; response to Special Committee demands, 138, 139, 140; and sell of Hollinger's U.S. papers, 83, 362; Special Committee's demand to oust as officer, 136; testimony to Special Committee, 290
Kirkland, Lane, 63
Kissinger, Henry: abandons CB, 141, 145, 184, 343, 435; advises CB on Breeden's attempt to block Inc., 173-74; on Burt, 374, 376; character and personality, 130, 131-33; deposition before Strine, 187, 189; as director of Hollinger, 111, 126, 129-30, 137, 225; friendship with Aspinall, 66, 132; friendship with CB, 3, 94, 129-30, 133, 157, 173, 218, 343-44, 492-93; interview, 536, 540-42; learns about Breeden, 115; letter to CB, 549; as member of Hollinger advisory board, 61; and Pinochet's detention, 57; renown, 192; retains Saunder, 124; Saunders' view, 143; society life, 70; testimony to FBI, 342-43; visits CB, 588; votes for lawsuit against Inc., 183-84
Kissinger, Nancy: attends CB's induction into House of Lords, 94; friendship with CB and Amiel, 94, 157, 173; travels with Henry, 132
Knight, Andrew, 25, 64
Koch, Ed, 157
Kofman, Bobby, 277-78, 303
Kohl, Helmut, 49-50, 73

Kollek, Teddy, 55, 329

Kozodoy, Neal, 196, 315, 333

KPMG: Breeden as special monitor of, 171; Breeden's criticism of, 138, 327; as International auditor, 84, 171, 327, 371, 383, 407; questioned at criminal trial, 327, 371, 385, 407

Kravis, Henry: company, 115, 289n; friendship with CB, 150; prominence, 115, 128

Kravis, Marie-Josée: accusations in Breeden report, 219; and *American Trucker*, 289n; approves non-competition payments, 371; on Audit Committee, 115; character and personality, 128, 380-81; as director of Hollinger, 225; on Hollinger advisory board, 61; resigns from Hollinger, 115-16, 127; support of CB, 150, 157; testimony at criminal trial, 376-80, 381, 417, 426; testimony to FBI, 342; warns CB about Breeden, 115, 129, 193

Lally, Sheila, 428, 436, 439-40

Lamont, Norman, 14

Langone, Ken, 165

Lawson, Dominic, 25, 151, 281

Lazard: Barclays' promise to support process, 183; discusses Hollinger's future with CB, 110; engaged for Strategic Process, 136, 142, 144, 169, 175; negotiates *Telegraph* deal, 205; and refinancing of Hollinger, 121

Leblanc, Roméo, 76

Le Droit (Ottawa), 16

Léger, Paul-Émile (Cardinal), 118, 239, 453, 453n

Le Soleil (Quebec City), 16

Levant, Ezra, 280

Levine, Michael, 335

Levy, Yehuda, 54

Liberal Party of Canada, 75, 79

Liddy, Gordon, 308

Limbaugh, Rush, 332, 431

Lipsky, Seth, 332, 432, 484, 492

Livanos, George, 157

Livingstone, Ken, 26, 65

London Daily Express, 104

London, England: CB's home in, 3-4, 57-58, 188, 211, 245, 256, 259, 262-63; society life, 69

Maclean's, 200, 307, 318

Madoff, Bernard, 178, 515

M.A. Hanna Company, 124n, 369

Maida, Joan: and CB's criminal trial, 402-3, 404-5; and CB's freedom, 485; and CB's imprisonment, 464; manages Toronto office, 263, 271-72, 309, 313, 319; receives emails about New York office doings, 204-5; and removal of boxes from 10 Toronto Street, 271-72, 402, 404

Major, John, 12, 13-15, 20

Mark, Alan, 233-34, 251, 255, 260, 272-73

Marshall, George C., 440n

Martin, Marc: expertise, 349, 428, 438; and Greenspan's ineffectiveness, 417; jury selection, 355-56, 367; scheduling meetings, 334

Martin, Paul, 40

Massey Ferguson, 7, 9n

Matthews, Chris, 319

Maxwell, Robert, 8, 20

Mayer Brown, 428, 440

Mayhew, David, 23

McBurney, Gene, 243, 247, 248

McCain, John, 454-55

McCarthy, Joseph R., 440n

McDonough, Jim, 135, 138, 139, 145, 163

McDougald, John A. (Bud), 6n, 491

McLaren, Ken, 255

McNish, Jacquie, 236, 254

Meitar, Shmuel, 127

Melbourne Age (Australia), 16

Melnyk, Debbie, 236

Mercer, Rick, 432

Merrill Lynch, 135
Metcalfe, Robert, 228, 234, 247, 250, 251, 279
Miami Federal Correctional Institution, 499-505, 511-513
Millar, Rosemary, 146, 175-76, 188, 226, 271
Mills, Elinor, 152-53, 153n
Mills, Russell, 31
Mitchell, Glenn, 284
Montgomery, David, 26
Monty, Jean, 37
Moore, Charles: becomes editor of *Daily Telegraph*, 25; becomes editor of *Sunday Telegraph*, 13; as editorial writer, 15; and EU disputes, 49, 50; introduces Mills to CB, 153; on Irish Question, 45-46; on Jewish people, 56; reaction to Hollinger restructuring, 151; reconciliation with CB, 283; relationship with Hastings, 13
Morgenthau, Robert, 157
Morris, Roger, 149
Mulroney, Brian, 40, 194, 199, 307, 333
Munk, Peter, 40
Munro, Lisa, 393
Murdoch, Anna, 26, 41
Murdoch, Rupert: agrees to support Portillo to replace Major, 14; beneficiary of *Telegraph* decline, 281; fires Montgomery, 26; as great media proprietor, 18-19; papers' reporting of Hollinger finances, 108, 113; papers' reporting on CB, 148-49, 306, 483-84; political influence, 45; price war with London papers, 20-24, 26-27, 41-42
Murray, John, 44

National Post: CB's column, 282, 307, 342, 351, 448; CB sells, 93-94; CB's relationships with editors, 15; Chrétien's complaints about, 75-76, 77, 78; founded, 34-37; half sold to CanWest, 85, 86; reports on CB, 215
National Review, 307, 448

Neil, Andrew, 283
Neporent, Mark, 203, 206
Netto, David, 70
New Atlantic Initiative Conference, Prague, 30
Newland, Martin, 197, 281
Newman, Gustave: character and personality, 393; closing arguments at trial, 412; closing remarks to judge, 414; concern about Greenspan, 364-65, 367; effectiveness at trial, 418; experience, 349-50; opening statement at trial, 359, 387; questions Burt at trial, 375; questions buyers at trial, 363-64; questions Radler at trial, 396; on Radler, 393
Newman, Peter C., 315-16, 318
New York (city): CB's home in, 59, 264, 275, 282, 300, 304, 306-10, 312, 313-14, 401; September 11 terror attacks, 71, 94; society life, 69-70, 125
New York Stock Exchange, 24
New York Sun, 448
Nicki (Genson's assistant), 424
Nixon Eisenhower, Julie, 103, 415
Nixon, Richard, 47, 343-44
Northern Ireland, 45-46

Obama, Barack, 315, 447
O'Connor, Chris, 348, 349, 375-76
Oddie, William, 151
Ogilvy Renault, 260
O'Melveny & Myers, 186, 399
Ontario Securities Commission (OSC): charges against CB, 330; does not intervene to protect Inc. shareholders, 185, 303; and Inc.'s privatization attempts, 246-48, 249, 252, 253-56; rejects privatization offer, 258; role in Inc.'s receivership, 221, 259, 371, 434; sets conditions for Inc. sales, 195-96
O'Reilly, Tony, 151
Oslo Accords, 53-54
O'Sullivan, John, 35, 407, 421

Ottawa Citizen, 31
Owens, Jennifer, 403, 404

Packer, Kerry, 16, 40
Palestine, 53-55
Palm Beach: CB's home in, 58, 107, 156, 169, 194-95, 253, 263-64, 319, 330, 331-32, 333-34; final days there before prison, 431, 440-41, 442-43; sale of CB's home, 490-91
Paris, Gordon: asks CB about non-competition payments, 133, 134; assumes CB will default payment, 207; on Audit Committee, 115; CB's libel suit against, 220, 477-78; and Cerberus deal, 206; as chairman of International, 180, 183, 196; character and personality, 193; and corporate airplanes, 156, 294; cuts off CB's company expenses, 164-65; as director of Hollinger, 127; does not endorse Breeden's "statement of principles", 189; earnings from Hollinger, 191, 245, 256, 259, 361; extravagance and incompetence, 280; joins Special Committee, 113, 114, 127, 129, 191; lip service to Inc., 174; offers terms of settlement between Inc. and International, 245-46; on price of International shares, 185; Radler's false testimony to, 299; relationship with Radler, 396; repayment and restructuring demands, 134-35, 136, 138, 142, 146, 174, 175; retirement from Hollinger, 476; role in Hollinger bankruptcies, 280, 435; sale of *Telegraph* to Barclays, 191; and Strategic Process, 144, 156, 163-64, 169; and suit to prevent Barclay deal, 190; suit to prevent Barclay deal, 198; testimony at criminal trial, 360-61, 362; vouches for accounts, 217*n*
Paul, Weiss (law firm), 186

Paxton, David, 364, 386, 387, 425
Pedemura, Gus, 404
Péladeau, Pierre, 89
Pelletier, Jean, 77
Peltz, Nelson: character and personality, 100, 170; congratulates CB on Inc. shares sale, 198; lends money to CB, 170, 242; offers to finance CB, 207; views on Inc.'s ability to be sold, 171, 178
Perle, Richard: abandons CB, 141; cautioned about Breeden, 219; as chairman of Hollinger Digital, 130; character and personality, 130-31; as director of Hollinger, 126, 129, 136, 140, 183, 387; friendship with CB, 129, 219; on Hollinger advisory board, 61, 193; renown, 192; response to Breeden, 180; and Restructuring Agreement, 144, 145, 184; suggests that Cerberus finance Inc., 202
Philip, Duke of Edinburgh, 42, 69
Phillips, Melanie, 151
Phillips, Penny, 262
Phillips, W. Eric, 6*n*
Pinochet, Augusto, 56-57
Pipes, Richard, 200
Podhoretz family, 157, 492
Podhoretz, Norman, 218, 333
Polesky, Joelle, 328
Portillo, Michael, 14, 92
Posner, Richard, 470, 472-75, 482-83, 484, 486-90
Powell, Charles, 11
Powell, Colin, 103
Powell, Enoch, 3, 73
Power Corporation, 27, 29, 30, 82, 88
Progressive Conservative Party of Canada, 75
Pryce-Jones, Clarissa, 332
Pryce-Jones, David, 332

Quayle, Dan, 202, 203
Quebec, 4-6, 33

Quebecor, 82
Quest Capital Corp., 207-8, 338

Racketeer Influenced and Corrupt
    Organizations Act (RICO), 183, 197,
    230, 422-23
Radler, David: Boultbee's concerns
    about, 146; buys more newspapers, 16;
    buys out CB on private newspapers,
    330-32; and CB's criminal prosecu-
    tion, 270; and CB's sale to Amiel, 334;
    character and personality, 267-68,
    287-89, 329, 390-92; and *Chicago
    Sun-Times* circulation, 204; company
    travel, 379; criminal charges against,
    293; as director of Hollinger, 126, 160;
    failure of private ventures, 329; false
    reports about, 156-57; false testimony,
    287-90, 292, 294, 300-302, 303, 304,
    319; financial misdoings, 127, 237, 299,
    314; Greenspan's preparation to
    examine, 347; handling of assets, 193;
    hears nothing about Chant shares,
    227; hires Healy, 107; Hollinger
    refinancing negotiations, 103; last
    contact with CB, 292; in Newman's
    opening statement, 359; no asset
    freeze, 339; and non-competition
    agreements, 83, 96, 122, 133, 489; no
    say in running Ravelston, 298; OSC
    hearings, 252; plea bargain and testi-
    mony, 295-96, 300-302, 303, 328;
    relationship with CB, 5, 390-92;
    removed from Hollinger board,
    235; repays CB's loans to Horizon
    Publications, 331-32; response to CB
    about payments to executives, 138-39;
    response to Special Committee
    questions and demands, 137, 138-39,
    140-41, 145; retains counsel, 124,
    396; runs newspaper companies,
    84, 265; sells Hollinger's Canadian
    papers, 84; sells Hollinger's U.S.
    papers, 81-83, 84, 122, 362-64; settle-
    ment with STMG, 360; Special
    Committee's demand to oust, 136;
    successes, 288; suggested to step down
    as director, 227, 229; suggests Amiel
    for *Evening Standard* vice-presidency,
    24*n*; talks to banks about Hollinger,
    95-96; targeted by Breeden, 180, 219;
    testimony at criminal trial, 385-90,
    394-98, 408, 410, 413, 414, 417, 419-20,
    425, 426; testimony to Special
    Committee, 280-81, 289-90; Vogt
    affair, 84, 267, 289, 328-29
Rainer, Madeleine, 205
Ratzinger, Joseph, 48
Ravelston Corporation: approves sale of
    Inc., 178, 180; backs Inc., 105-6; CB
    and Radler employed by, 83; CB's
    holdings, 111, 220; Chant's shares, 227,
    229; criminal charges against, 293,
    297-99, 318; employer of senior
    executives at International, 364;
    Glassman's oppression action against,
    221; International stops payments to,
    162-63, 202; non-competition agree-
    ments, 83, 96; receivership, 258-60,
    265, 274-75, 277-79, 335-36, 340, 433,
    436; Restructuring Agreement negoti-
    ations, 144, 160; and Special
    Committee review, 136, 138; struc-
    ture, 6, 6*n*; struggles after Hollinger
    (U.S.) restructuring, 163; Walker's
    and Strosberg's battles against, 230
Read, Piers Paul, 53
Reagan, Nancy, 103
Reagan, Ronald, 19, 39, 47, 200, 344
Reed, Mike, 363
Rees-Mogg, William (Lord), 151
Reichmann family, 40
Reisman, Heather, 155, 432
Rendell, Ed, 103
Reynolds, Neil, 31
Roberts, Andrew, 332, 432
Roberts, John, 480
Robinson, Linda, 163

Rockefeller, Margaretta, 157
Roebuck, David, 231-32, 337-38, 429
Rogers, Bud, 369
Rogers, Ted, 82
Rohmer, Richard, 177, 207, 208n, 222, 223, 225
Romano, Benito, 294, 350, 359, 374
Rose, Charlie, 70
Rose, Marshal, 436
Rosenberg, Jonathan, 215, 231, 290, 399-400
Rothermere, Jonathan, 135, 137, 169
Rothermore (Lord): Vere Harmsworth, 25, 45
Rothschild, Evelyn de, 40
Rothschild, Jacob (Lord), 40, 61, 283
Roy (barber), 284
Royal Bank, 167, 167n
RSM Richter, 260, 277-79, 297-98, 339-40, 370
Rubin, Robert, 157, 201
Ruder, Julie: and CB's removal of boxes from 10 Toronto Street, 403; character and personality, 322; closing arguments at trial, 408-11; explanation of RICO to jury, 422-23; questions Creasey at trial, 366
Ruffo (shareholder), 100, 402
Ryan, Pat, 371

Saatchi, Edward, 334
Sabia, Maureen, 160-62, 194, 260
Safer, Ron: acts for Kipnis, 350, 424; closing arguments at trial, 413; effectiveness at trial, 417, 427; experience, 396, 414-15; and Greenspan's lack of U.S. experience, 389, 393; jury selection, 355; opening statement at trial, 360; questions buyers at trial, 363-64; questions expert witness at trial, 408; questions Radler at trial, 396-97; questions Ryan at trial, 407; questions Thompson at trial, 383
Sands, Sarah, 281

Saturday Night (magazine), 34, 60
Saunders, Paul: advises CB on Breeden's attempt to block Inc., 173-74; advises CB on disclosure of non-competition payments, 369; friendship with CB, 124, 143; recommends Finkelstein, 132; represents CB in M.A. *Hanna* case, 132, 369; represents Kissinger, 143, 189, 343; on Strine judgment, 193
Savage, Graham: CB's libel suit against, 220, 477-78; elected to Special Committee, 114, 128, 192; restructuring demands, 139, 146; vulnerability to CB's libel suits, 175
Scalia, Antonin, 480
Schacter, Michael, 350, 355, 413
Schapiro, Andy, 440
Schneerson, Menachem Mendel, 288
Schröder, Gerhard, 50
Schuler, Lynda, 293
Schwartzman, Steve, 120
Securities and Exchange Commission (SEC): Breeden's chairmanship, 115; charges CB with civil infractions, 190, 220, 223-24, 238; and corporate governance, 67n; and criminal investigation into CB, 252; gets statement from Audit Committee, 374; and H. Kravis's company, 379; Hollinger's filings of non-competition payments, 124, 136; receives papers from CB, 271; and Restructuring Agreement, 145-46, 178; stirs up OSC to slow Inc. sales, 195; subpoenas, 158, 172, 272, 404, 422; takes Audit and Special Committees seriously, 140; told that Special Committee was under threat, 177-78, 179; wants International sold, 220
Seitz, Raymond: calls for dismissal of all, 137; CB's libel suit against, 220, 477-78; character and personality, 159, 192; as co-author of Breeden report, 240; earnings from Hollinger, 192, 259; elected to Special Committee,

114, 129, 192; on EU disputes, 49; follows Breeden's lead, 192; moves to fire CB as chairman, 179; payments from Hollinger, 192; removed as chairman of International, 435; and Restructuring Agreement negotiations, 144, 146; restructuring demands, 139; retirement from Hollinger, 476; review of FDR book, 150; and Special Committee's review of CB's emails, 116; suit to prevent Barclay deal, 190, 198; as U.S. ambassador to England, 161; vulnerability to CB's libel suits, 175

Sharp, Isadore, 352

Sherbrooke Daily Record: CB's purchase of, 5

Shultz, George, 103

Sieghart, Mary Ann, 216

Sifton, Michael, 88

Siklos, Richard, 236

Silvers, Bob, 157

Simon, Bill, 126

Simple, Peter, 216

Sinclair, Murray, 207, 262, 265, 338

Siskel, Edward, 323

Skadden Arps, 185, 189, 300, 308-9

Skurka, Steve, 396

Sotheby's, 166

Sotheby's Realty, 459

Southam: CB buys shares in, 17-18; changes under CB, 31-32, Chrétien's complaints about, 76; founds *National Post*, 34-37; Hollinger–Power Corporation shares, 27, 30; Hollinger shares in, 16-17, 82, 97; poor management, 18, 21, 27-30; privatization, 32

Southeastern Asset Management (SEAM): buys shares in Hollinger, 96, 110-12, 114, 116; seeks super-voting shares, 110, 114; warned about impending Restructuring, 146

Special Committee, Hollinger International: asks CB about non-competition payments, 133-34; auditing process, 120-21; Breeden report, 213-15, 217, 361-62; Breeden's control over, 140; Browne nominates self to, 113; claim of threat, 177-78, 179; continued for years after needed, 191; cost to International, 191, 239; created, 112, 114, 128-29; disbanded, 476; Radler's answers to, 289-90; testimony to, 280-81, 290; usurps CB's ability to act as real CEO, 193

Spectator (magazine), 25-26, 39, 53

Spector, Arlen, 103

Spellman, Francis J. (Cardinal), 71

Spender, Lizzie, 283, 332

Stapleton, Ben, 164, 171, 226n, 308

Steinback, Jeffrey, 428, 437, 438

Stephens, Bret, 73

Sterling Newspapers, 83, 84-85

St. Eve, Amy: and CB's appeal and sentencing, 471, 489, 494-96; on CB's right to remain silent, 400; character and personality, 321-22, 432; declines to immediately imprison CB, 427; grants bail to Boultbee, 478; grants bail to CB, 484; instructions to jury, 403, 413-14, 422, 424, 426; judgments on forfeiture, bail, and sentences, 436-40; on jury foreman's possible "fix", 425; jury selection, 354-55; noontime jogging, 478n; refuses to allow CB to return to Canada, 486; rejects bail for CB, 429-31, 478; requires early morning sessions, 352-53; in scheduling meetings, 334, 347

Stevens, John Paul, 478

Stewart, Brian, 226, 226n, 436

Stewart, Martha, 149

Stewart, Sinclair, 236

Stewart, Tina, 226

Steyn, Mark: attempt of other paper to bribe, 372; covers criminal trial, 357, 383, 402, 416, 420, 422-23; on Creasey, 366-67; fired from *Sun-Times*, 416;

friendship with CB, 415, 432; on Greenspan and Genson, 428; on Radler's testimony, 397; on Sussman's final statement, 356; writes about what was really happening at Hollinger, 280

Stitt, Marilyn, 370, 407, 412

St. Laurent, Louis, 271

Strauss, Robert, 61, 126

Straw, Jack, 77

Strine, Leo: background, 186, 187; on CB's character, 310; character, 186, 191, 210; dismisses CB's lack of counsel in Restructuring Agreement, 143; emphasis on independent directors, 199, 207, 222-23; hears suit to prevent Barclay deal, 188-91; and Inc.'s loans to CB, 194; indemnifies CB's legal bills, 330, 334; influence on Barclays, 436; and injunction against *Telegraph* sale, 205-6, 208; judgment not permitted at criminal trial, 361-62; misgivings about Breeden, 208*n*, 211; offers opinions on subjects not his, 198-99; on possibility of CB's transferring assets, 195; requires adherence to Strategic Process, 232; requires CB to make payments to International, 201-2, 204, 206-7, 262-63; requires Hollinger International shares sold, 211-12, 220; requires International to pay legal fees, 327-28; role in Hollinger bankruptcies, 259; urges arbitration of financial disagreements, 199, 208; urges compromises, 199, 208, 231

Strosberg, Harvey: brought in as counsel to independent directors, 208, 222; on CB's indebtedness to Ravelston, 274-75; character and personality, 222, 250; dismissed, 225, 231; learns of Chant transfer, 227; and Ravelston receivership, 260; strives to eject CB and others from directorships, 229, 230; targets CB, 223, 236; U.S. prosecutors get to, 303

Sukonick, Darren, 368-69, 408

Sullivan & Cromwell: advice to CB on Barclay deal, 177, 182; engaged by CB, 163-64; exception to rule of lawyer rapaciousness, 311; informs Breeden of Inc. sale, 180; and sale of CB's New York apartment, 309; strait-laced, 320; unaware of Breeden's intent and power, 144, 164

Sullivan, Brendan: billings, 276, 304, 311, 314-15; CB ends relations with, 314, 475; and CB's criminal prosecution, 267, 269, 270, 291, 292, 293; and CB's financial problems, 265; character and personality, 195; and Kent, 276-77; lack of good advice for CB, 300, 422; retained by CB, 195, 225; on role of money in case, 168; and sale of CB's New York apartment, 309; on U.S. legal system, 306, 311

Sunday Telegraph (London), 12, 13-14, 44, 281

Sun-Times Media Group (STMG): *see also* Hollinger International (U.S.)cash settlement with Radler, 360; Hollinger name-change to, 7*n*; sold out of bankruptcy, 476

Sussman, Eric: and Amiel's diamond ring, 326, 340; asks for CB's bail to be revoked, 427, 429; badgers Canada Revenue to charge CB, 296, 332; and CB's removal of boxes from 10 Toronto Street, 403, 422; and CB's sentencing, 437-38, 439; character and personality, 276, 322, 330, 334, 340-41, 349, 424; closing argument at trial, 413-14; considers Supreme Court verdict a victory, 483; and criminal charges against CB, 318-19; efforts to crush CB financially, 331-32, 340; expert witnesses at trial, 407-8; forfeiture claim, 436; on Greenspan, 368;

interview with Sullivan and Craig, 291; negotiations with Atkinson, 294; objections during trial, 361; on potential for fraud counts to be struck down, 478; questions KPMG employee at trial, 385; questions Paris at trial, 360; questions Radler at trial, 386, 387; questions Thompson at trial, 382; reliance on Breeden report, 293; and sale of CB's New York apartment, 300, 309; sidebars to St. Eve, 400; St. Eve's disdain for, 439; stung by press criticism, 371; tries to force sale of Palm Beach house, 331, 332, 333, 340; unscrupulous tactics, 310, 313, 319, 320, 336-37, 375, 403-4, 418; and Voorheis, 370

Sutherland, Peter, 201

Sydney Morning Herald (Australia), 16

Taubman, Alfred, 126, 178-79, 263
Taubman, Judith, 153
Tay, Derrick, 260
Taylor, E.P., 6n
Taylor, Martin, 200
Tedesco, Theresa, 357, 367, 483
Telegraph plc, The, 8-10, 9n, 64, 196, 210, 436
Thatcher, Carol, 25, 44
Thatcher, Margaret: anti-German attitudes, 50; eulogizes Goldsmith, 67; friendship with CB, 3, 11, 12, 39-40; as member of Hollinger advisory board, 61; Murdoch's desertion of, 20; offended by Hastings, 25, 44; party view of, 11; sponsors CB's pecrage, 94
Theodoracopulos, Taki, 53, 65, 151, 432
Thompson, Jim: at 2003 annual meeting, 111, 112; accusations in Breeden report, 219; on Audit Committee, 114; and CB's firing, 179; and CB's struggle to save Inc., 163; character and personality, 192; deposition before Strine, 187; as director of Hollinger,

127; earnings from Hollinger, 382; expresses interest in settlement talks, 199; and firing of Colson, 196; follows Breeden's lead, 192, 219, 240; grounds corporate aircraft, 156; lip service to Inc., 174; and non-competition payments, 133, 134, 174, 370; and NYSE guidelines, 240; Radler's false testimony to, 299; relationship with Radler, 396; repayment and restructuring demands, 134-35, 138, 142; Restructuring Agreement negotiations, 145, 146, 162; testimony at criminal trial, 382-83, 417, 426; testimony to FBI, 342

Thomson Corporation, 36, 37, 82, 123
Thomson, Ken, 69
Thomson, Roy, 17
Toombs, George, 236
Toronto, 58, 239, 262, 264, 307, 311, 402
Toronto-Dominion Bank (TD), 95-96, 102, 103n, 104, 235
Torstar, 16
Tory & Tory (law firm), 76, 96, 107, 369
Tory, John, 82
Triarc, 170
Trilateral Commission, 201
Trump, Donald, 105, 114, 126, 236, 244, 332, 379, 406
Trump, Melania, 114, 244
Tuite, Pat, 350, 376, 377-78, 412, 414
Turner, John, 434
Tweedy Browne: complaints about management fees, 106; complaints about non-competition payments, 97; concerns about Hollinger shares, 99; files 13D as hostile shareholder, 110, 113; pulls out of Inc., 435
Tyrrell, Bob, 432

Unimédia, 88
United Kingdom: anti-Semitism, 52-53; CB leaves, 212; and EU, 76; Iraq war debates, 72, 73; Irish Question, 45-46;

justice system, 507; offers peerage to CB, 76-78; relationship with United States, 80; U.S. efforts to coerce into EU, 48-49; view of Israel and Jews, 50-51, 55-56

United Nations Security Council, 72

United States: 9/11 terror attacks, 71, 94; Afghanistan war, 73, 518; and CB's legal issues, 80; CB's newspapers in, 41; CB's views, 6, 50-51, 71, 303, 481, 524; as democracy, 499; education system, 500; and EU, 47; financial degeneration, 2; health care system, 500; incarcerations, 500, 505; International Commerce Commission, 48; Iraq war, 72-73; judicial tradition, 498-99; justice system and minorities, 514-17; justice system and plea bargains, 302, 466-67, 500-502; justice system and prosecutorial power, 302, 311-12, 321-22, 475-76, 481, 502-5; justice system and public defenders, 475n; justice system costs, 500; justice system "is like fishing", 406-7; justice system manipulations, 519-22; justice system putrefaction, 481, 523; justice system undermines individual liberty, 498; mental institutions, 465-66; prison system, 465-67, 469, 470, 500, 507-14, 524; reaction to Southam privatization, 32; recidivism rates, 466; relationship with United Kingdom, 80; war on drugs, 517-19

Vale, Don, 225, 228, 249, 251, 272, 403-4, 422

Valukas, Anton, 267-68, 287, 289, 300, 301

Vogt affair, 84, 267, 289, 328-29

Vogt, Todd, 84, 328

Volcker, Paul, 61

von Fürstenberg, Diane, 157

Voorheis, Wesley: attempts to sell Inc.'s super-voting rights, 370; false affidavit that CB had money in Gibraltar, 429-30; as Inc. director, 434; role in injunction against CB and Amiel freezing assets, 336-38, 339

Wachovia Bank, 102-3, 104, 105, 220

Wakefield, Alan, 228, 234, 250, 251, 279

Walker, Gordon: accuses CB of contempt of court, 272-74; Breeden's treatment of, 297; character and personality, 221, 243; and criminal prosecution of CB, 266-67; delays privatization of Inc., 243, 245-50, 251; as director of Hollinger, 177, 208, 208n, 223; earnings from Hollinger, 259, 273; extravagance and incompetence, 280; fired by Richter, 279; has CB and others evicted from 10 Toronto Street, 266, 402, 421-22; on Inc.'s privatization committee, 234; lawsuit against CB regarding Inc. payments, 266; need to oust, 258; and Ravelston receivership, 278; seeks chairmanship of Inc., 235; self-promotion to media, 243; severance payment, 251; solicits new directors, 230-31; suggests that CB and others cease directorships, 227, 229, 230; and terms of sale for Inc., 232; U.S. prosecutors get to, 303; venom against CB, 274

Walters, Barbara, 70, 157

Warden, John: accompanies CB to SEC hearing, 172, 188, 189; advises CB on Breeden's attempt to block Inc., 173-74; engaged by CB, 164; excellence as lawyer, 225n; prepared to testify before Strine, 188-89; prepares terms for sale of Inc., 232; recruits Joseph, 231; and sale of CB's New York apartment, 308; as securities counsel for CB, 225-26; talks to SEC, 195; *Telegraph* hearing before Strine, 208

Warden, Robert, 203

Warhol, Andy, 339

Wasserstein, Bruce: advice on Strategic Process, 142; death, 442n; discusses Hollinger's future with CB, 110; instructed to ask Barclays for higher price for International shares, 185; learns of tactics to prevent investment in Inc., 178; and refinancing of Hollinger, 121

Weidenfeld, Annabelle, 157, 283

Weidenfeld, George (Lord), 49, 61, 116, 126, 157

Weisel, Laurent, 404

Wells, Jennifer, 396

Wente, Margaret, 369

West, Morris, 283

Weston, Galen, 166

Westwind Capital Partners, 207, 220, 236, 238

Wexner, Leslie, 126, 436

White, Peter: assists with Hollinger management, 177, 288; attends winery address with CB, 250-51; declines to sponsor Walker as chairman, 235; ejected from Inc. board, 275; evicted from 10 Toronto Street, 266; exonerated by Campbell, 234; explores Delaware bonding procedures, 222; exposes Voorheis, 370; and Inc. privatization, 248, 250; letter to *National Post* about Walker et al., 279; listens to meeting of directors and Ravelston receiver, 274; negotiates Walker's and Kelly's severance, 251; payment to Chant estate, 227, 229; purchases newspaper with CB, 5; Radler's false claims to, 299; recruits Wakefield and Metcalfe, 228; sells paper to CB, 4-5, 39; Walker's suggestion to dismiss, 230

Whitworth, Bill, 335

Whyte, Ken: asks Amiel back to *Maclean's*, 307; editorials on Chrétien, 75; friendship with CB, 226, 432; helps CB found *Post*, 34-36; spending on *Post*, 93; support of CB, 150; testimony at criminal trial, 405

Whyte, Tina, 226

Will, George, 61, 200, 308, 332

William, Prince, 68

Williams & Connolly: billings, 256, 263, 265, 276, 306; CB ends relations with, 314; clean up 2003 International statement, 244; and criminal prosecution against CB, 276, 293; impersonality, 320; lack of correct advice, 301; retained by CB, 195; and sale of CB's New York apartment, 309; *Telegraph* hearing before Strine, 208

Wilson, A.N., 53

Wilson, David, 102

Wingfield, David, 275

Wintour, Anna, 332

Wintour, Charles, 21

Wohlberg-Jenah, Susan, 256, 258

Wolfensohn, Jim, 157

Wong, Jan, 281-82

World Economic Forum, Davos (1995), 26, 38

Worsthorne, Peregrine, 11-12, 44-45

Wrightsman, Jayne, 70, 71, 157

www.canada.com, 86

Wyatt, Woodrow (Lord), 14-15

York Club, Toronto, 434

Young, David (Lord), 92

Zachary, Louis, 142, 178

Zilkha, Cecile, 285

Zilkha, Ezra, 285, 333

Znaimer, Moses, 335

Zuckerman, Mort, 436